Lecture Notes in Computer Science 8144

Commenced Publication in 1973
Founding and Former Series Editors:
Gerhard Goos, Juris Hartmanis, and Jan van Leeuwen

Lindsay Groves   Jing Sun (Eds.)

Formal Methods and Software Engineering

15th International Conference
on Formal Engineering Methods, ICFEM 2013
Queenstown, New Zealand, October 29 – November 1, 2013
Proceedings

 Springer

Volume Editors

Lindsay Groves
Victoria University of Wellington
School of Engineering and Computer Science
P.O. Box 600
Wellington 6140, New Zealand
E-mail: lindsay@ecs.vuw.ac.nz

Jing Sun
The University of Auckland
Department of Computer Science
Private Bag 92019
Auckland 1142, New Zealand
E-mail: j.sun@cs.auckland.ac.nz

ISSN 0302-9743   e-ISSN 1611-3349
ISBN 978-3-642-41201-1   e-ISBN 978-3-642-41202-8
DOI 10.1007/978-3-642-41202-8
Springer Heidelberg New York Dordrecht London

Library of Congress Control Number: 2013948611

CR Subject Classification (1998): D.2.4, D.2, D.3, F.3, F.4.1, C.2, C.2.4

LNCS Sublibrary: SL 2 – Programming and Software Engineering

Typesetting: Camera-ready by author, data conversion by Scientific Publishing Services, Chennai, India

Printed on acid-free paper

Springer is part of Springer Science+Business Media (www.springer.com)

Preface

This volume contains the papers presented at the 15th International Conference on Formal Engineering Methods (ICFEM 2013) held during 29 October–1 November 2013 in Queenstown, New Zealand.

Since 1997, ICFEM has served as an international forum for researchers and practitioners who have been dedicated to applying formal methods to practical computer systems. This year, we received 88 full paper submissions from 38 different countries. Each paper went through a thorough review process by at least 3 Program Committee members. After extensive discussions, the Committee decided to accept 28 papers, giving the acceptance rate of 31.8%. The proceedings also include the abstracts from 2 keynote speakers.

ICFEM 2013 is organized and sponsored by The University of Auckland. It is the first time that the conference has been held in New Zealand. We acknowledge the financial support received from the Department of Computer Science at The University of Auckland, the Image & Pervasive Access Lab (IPAL) – a French-Singaporean joint research laboratory at National University of Singapore, and the School of Engineering and Computer Science at Victoria University of Wellington. We owe our thanks to the Organizing Committee for their hard work in making ICFEM 2013 a successful event, especially to Sarah Henderson for her technical support to the conference web site.

We are grateful to the Program Committee members and additional reviewers for their support and expertise in completing high quality reviews on time, and most importantly, to all the authors for their contributions to the conference. Finally, we would like to thank the EasyChair conference system, which indeed made the whole process much easier to manage.

July 2013

Lindsay Groves
Jing Sun

Organization

Program Committee

Bernhard K. Aichernig	Graz University of Technology, Austria
Yamine Ait Ameur	LISI/ENSMA, France
Keijiro Araki	Kyushu University, Japan
Farhad Arbab	CWI and Leiden University, The Netherlands
Richard Banach	University of Manchester, UK
Nikolaj Bjorner	Microsoft Research, USA
Jonathan Bowen	London South Bank University and Chairman of Museophile Limited, UK
Michael Butler	University of Southampton, UK
Andrew Butterfield	Trinity College Dublin, Ireland
Wei-Ngan Chin	National University of Singapore, Singapore
Jim Davies	University of Oxford, UK
Jin-Song Dong	National University of Singapore, Singapore
Zhenhua Duan	Xidian University, China
Colin Fidge	Queensland University of Technology, Australia
John Fitzgerald	Newcastle University, UK
Joaquim Gabarro	Universitat Politecnica de Catalunya, Spain
Stefania Gnesi	ISTI-CNR, Italy
Radu Grosu	Stony Brook University, USA
Lindsay Groves	Victoria University of Wellington, New Zealand
Ian J. Hayes	University of Queensland, Australia
Mike Hinchey	Lero - the Irish Software Engineering Research Centre, Ireland
Peter Gorm Larsen	Aarhus School of Engineering, Denmark
Michael Leuschel	University of Düsseldorf, Germany
Xuandong Li	Nanjing University, China
Yuan-Fang Li	Monash University, Australia
Shang-Wei Lin	National University of Singapore, Singapore
Shaoying Liu	Hosei University, Japan
Yang Liu	Nanyang Technological University, Singapore
Zhiming Liu	United Nations University - International Institute for Software Technology, China
Tiziana Margaria	University of Potsdam, Germany
Hong Mei	Peking University, China
Huaikou Miao	Shanghai University, China

Peter Müller   ETH Zurich, Switzerland
Shin Nakajima   National Institute of Informatics, Japan
Sebastian Nanz   ETH Zurich, Switzerland
Jose Oliveira   Universidade do Minho, Portugal
Jun Pang   University of Luxembourg, Luxembourg
Shengchao Qin   Teesside University, UK
Zongyan Qiu   Peking University, China
Steve Reeves   University of Waikato, New Zealand
Alexander Romanovsky   Newcastle University, UK
Wuwei Shen   Western Michigan University, USA
Marjan Sirjani   Reykjavik University, Iceland
Graeme Smith   University of Queensland, Australia
Jing Sun   The University of Auckland, New Zealand
Jun Sun   Singapore University of Technology and Design,
                                Singapore
Kenji Taguchi   AIST, Japan
Tetsuo Tamai   Hosei University, Japan
Yih-Kuen Tsay   National Taiwan University, China
T.H. Tse   The University of Hong Kong, China
Viktor Vafeiadis   MPI-SWS, Germany
Farn Wang   National Taiwan University, China
Hai H. Wang   University of Aston, UK
Jim Woodcock   University of York, UK
Wang Yi   Uppsala University, Sweden
Jian Zhang   Chinese Academy of Sciences, China
Hong Zhu   Oxford Brookes University, UK
Huibiao Zhu   East China Normal University, China

Additional Reviewers

Arlt, Stephan   Ferrara, Pietro
Bartocci, Ezio   Gao, Honghao
Bendisposto, Jens   Geeraerts, Gilles
Breuer, Peter   He, Guanhua
Bu, Lei   Huang, Yanhong
Carmona, Josep   Iliasov, Alexei
Chen, Liqian   Isobe, Yoshinao
Chen, Yu-Fang   Jafari, Ali
Chen, Zhenbang   Jiao, Li
Ciancia, Vincenzo   Jiao, Wenpin
Costea, Andreea   Khakpour, Narges
Da Cruz, Daniela   Kitamura, Takashi
Dobrikov, Ivo   Kleijn, Jetty
Fantechi, Alessandro   Kong, Weiqiang

Kromodimoeljo, Sentot
Kusakabe, Shigeru
Le, Duy Khanh
Li, Jun
Li, Qin
Lin, Hsin-Hung
Liu, Shuang
Liu, Xuanzhe
Lorber, Florian
Ma, Feifei
Macedo, Hugo
Markovski, Jasen
Omori, Yoichi
Payne, Richard
Pierce, Ken
Rossi, Matteo
Rutten, Eric
Sabouri, Hamideh
Satpathy, Manoranjan
Schäf, Martin
Serrano, Yamilet
Shi, Ling
Snook, Colin
Song, Songzheng

Steffen, Bernhard
Stewart, Alan
Stigge, Martin
Stolz, Volker
Tan, Tian Huat
Thai, Trinh Minh
Trung, Ta Quang
Tsai, Ming-Hsien
Wang, Yasha
Wijs, Anton
Winter, Kirsten
Wu, Xi
Xiong, Yingfei
Yang, Hongli
Yeganefard, Sanaz
Yu, Fang
Zhang, Chenyi
Zhang, Wei
Zhao, Hengjun
Zhao, Jianhua
Zhao, Yongxin
Zheng, Manchun
Zhu, Huiquan
Zhu, Longfei

Keynotes
(Abstracts)

Lattices of Information for Security:
Deterministic, Demonic, Probabilistic

Carroll C. Morgan*

School of Computer Science and Engineering
University of New South Wales
carrollm@cse.unsw.edu.au

Abstract. Security-oriented analyses of information flow can be in terms of channels (entropy leakage), or in terms of programs (noninterference); and for each we can consider deterministic, demonic or probabilistic instances. We discuss all $2 \times 3 = 6$ cases from a common point of view, seeking a uniform approach to a partial order of information. In some cases this is a lattice (as is already known); and in some cases it seems not to be (novel).

* I am grateful for the support of the Australian Research Council via DP120101413.

Analysis of Continuous Dynamical Systems via Statistical Model Checking

P.S. Thiagarajan

School of Computing, National University of Singapore,
thiagu@comp.nus.edu.sg

Abstract. Systems with real-valued variables that evolve continuously w.r.t. time arise in many settings including cyber-physical systems and biochemical networks. The dynamics of these variables will be typically specified in terms of differential equations. An important verification task is to determine whether the global behavior of the system has the required (reachability) properties. The number of the the real-valued variables can be large and their dynamics can be non-linear. For instance, in models of biochemical networks ordinary differential equations are typically used to specify the dynamics. Further, there can be multiple modes of behavior where each mode is governed by a different system of differential equations. Hence the behavior of such systems can seldom be analyzed effectively let alone efficiently.

To get around this we advocate statistical model checking as an *approximate* but scalable analysis technique in these settings. The basic idea is to assume a probability distribution over the initial states of the system. This in turn -under suitable continuity assumptions- induces a distribution over the trajectories generated by the initial states. Hence one can construct a statistical model checking procedure to verify bounded LTL specifications using a simple sequential hypothesis testing method. We demonstrate the applicability of this approach using a number of large biopathways models.

Table of Contents

Timed Systems

Concurrency

SysML/MDD

Verification

Application

Static Analysis

Lattices of Information for Security: Deterministic, Demonic, Probabilistic

Carroll C. Morgan*

School of Computer Science and Engineering
University of New South Wales
carrollm@cse.unsw.edu.au

Abstract. Security-oriented analyses of information flow can be in terms of channels (entropy leakage), or in terms of programs (noninterference); and for each we can consider deterministic, demonic or probabilistic instances. We discuss all $2{\times}3 = 6$ cases from a common point of view, seeking a uniform approach to a partial order of information. In some cases this is a lattice (as is already known); and in some cases it seems not to be (novel).

Keywords: security, information theory, program refinement, information channels, lattice of information.

1 Introduction

Security in Computer Science concerns the computer-mediated flow of private information to adversaries who should not have access to it.

One popular view addresses programs directly, classifying their variables as either high- and low security: the high variables h (for *hidden*) are private, and the adversary tries to deduce the high variables' values, based on his observation of the public, low variables v (visible) and the program's source code. For security we want high variables not to *interfere* with low variables [2].

A second popular view addresses communication channels that take (hidden) inputs h and produce (visible) outputs v, in which case the adversary tries to deduce the inputs from the outputs. Here we want the input *entropy* not to decrease *a posteriori* as a result of observing the output and knowing the channel's functionality [9]. [1]

We note that a "good" (i.e. secure) program *conceals* its hidden data as much as possible, whereas classically a good channel should *reveal* its hidden data as much as possible. Thus, for us, secure channels will be "bad" channels. [2] In spite of that, the theory turns out to be the same modulo the opposing points of view.

---

[*] I am grateful for the support of the Australian Research Council via DP120101413.
[1] The adjectives "visible" and "hidden" avoid taking sides between programs (high/low) and channels (input/output), since they apply equally well to both.
[2] This is not the only place where terminological reversals occur.

L. Groves and J. Sun (Eds.): ICFEM 2013, LNCS 8144, pp. 1–3, 2013.

This contribution is about that theory, presented in three levels of increasing complexity: deterministic programs and channels, nondeterministic programs and channels and probabilistic programs and channels.

2   The Deterministic Case

2.1   The *Secures* Order for Programs

Here a program is a function from initial values of h,v to final values of v. A program S is said to be *secured by* a program I just when every attack, of a certain type, can succeed against I only if it can succeed against S.

These attacks concern how much can be discovered about h by observing v, and have to be formulated so that the induced securing order is *compositional*, i.e. that if I secures S then $\mathcal{C}(I)$ secures $\mathcal{C}(S)$ for any context $\mathcal{C}$.

An example of a secures order for programs is refinement of ignorance [8].

2.2   The *Secures* Order for Channels

Here a channel takes its inputs h to outputs v, and a channel I secures a channel S if I's leakage is no more than S's, where *leakage* is how much less entropy (either Shannon- [9] or some other [3, Sec. 3.1]) you ascribe to the input once you have seen the output. The order should satisfy the *data-processing inequality*, that it is preserved by cascading.

An example of a secures order for channels is the *converse*[3] of composition refinement [1].

2.3   The Lattice of Information

Landauer and Redmond [4] showed that if the connection between h: $\mathcal{H}$ and v: $\mathcal{V}$ is captured as a mathematical function $f: \mathcal{H} \rightarrow \mathcal{V}$, the equivalence relation induced by f on the hidden values, its *kernel*, contains the essential information both for comparing programs and comparing channels [10,5]. These equivalences have a partial order which is in fact a lattice: the *Lattice of Information*.

3   The Nondeterministic Case

Here we admit *demonic* choice, and the visible v: $\mathcal{V}$ is *related* to the hidden h: $\mathcal{H}$ rather than being a function of it. The equivalence relation (§2.3), instead of inducing a partition on $\mathcal{H}$, becomes a more general structure: still of type $\mathbb{P}^2\mathcal{H}$ but one where the subsets can overlap. In spite of that, an analogous procedure can be followed to produce a lattice of information on those sets of subsets.

---

[3] You were warned: refining a program secures it; refining a channel insecures it.

4 The Probabilistic Case

Here we admit *probabilistic* choice (instead of demonic-), and visible v: $\mathcal{V}$ is produced from a *distribution* determined by hidden h: $\mathcal{H}$ [1]. The sets of subsets $\mathbb{P}^2\mathcal{H}$ (§2.3) become distributions of distributions, "hyperdistributions" [6], and again a partial order can be defined that captures relative information release.

This time, however, we don't seem to have a lattice nor even a *CPO*. For completion of the order we require proper measures. Is that a bug, or a feature?

References

1. Alvim, M., Chatzikokolakis, K., Palamidessi, C., Smith, G.: Measuring information leakage using generalized gain functions. In: Proc. 25th IEEE CSF, pp. 265–279 (2012)
2. Goguen, J., Meseguer, J.: Unwinding and inference control. In: Proc. IEEE Symp. on Security and Privacy, pp. 75–86. IEEE Computer Society (1984)
3. Köpf, B., Basin, D.: An information-theoretic model for adaptive side-channel attacks. In: Proceedings of the 14th ACM Conference on Computer and Communications Security, CCS 2007, pp. 286–296. ACM, New York (2007), http://doi.acm.org/10.1145/1315245.1315282
4. Landauer, J., Redmond, T.: A lattice of information. In: Gray, J.W. (ed.) Proc. CSFW 1993. IEEE Computer Society Press (1993)
5. Malacaria, P.: Algebraic foundations for information theoretical, probabilistic and guessability measures of information flow. CoRR, vol. abs/1101.3453 (2011)
6. McIver, A., Meinicke, L., Morgan, C.: Compositional closure for Bayes Risk in probabilistic noninterference. In: Abramsky, S., Gavoille, C., Kirchner, C., Meyer auf der Heide, F., Spirakis, P.G. (eds.) ICALP 2010. LNCS, vol. 6199, pp. 223–235. Springer, Heidelberg (2010), Full version available at [7]
7. McIver, A., Meinicke, L., Morgan, C.: Compositional closure for Bayes Risk in probabilistic noninterference (2011), http://arxiv.org/pdf/1007.1054v1.pdf, extended version of [6]
8. Morgan, C.: *The Shadow Knows:* Refinement of Ignorance in sequential programs. In: Uustalu, T. (ed.) MPC 2006. LNCS, vol. 4014, pp. 359–378. Springer, Heidelberg (2006)
9. Shannon, C.: A mathematical theory of communication. Bell System Technical Journal 27, 379–423, 623–656 (1948)
10. Yasuoka, H., Terauchi, T.: Quantitative information flow — verification hardness and possibilities. In: Proc. 23rd IEEE CSF Symp., pp. 15–27 (2010)

Algebraic Laws for Process Subtyping

José Dihego[1,2], Pedro Antonino[1], and Augusto Sampaio[1]

[1] Centro de Informática, Universidade Federal de Pernambuco, Recife-PE, Brazil
{jdso,prga2,acas}@cin.ufpe.br
[2] IFBA, Feira de Santana-BA, Brazil
{jose.dihego}@ifba.edu.br

Abstract. This work presents a conservative extension of *OhCircus*, a concurrent specification language, which integrates CSP, Z, object-orientation and embeds a refinement calculus. This extension supports the definition of process inheritance, where control flow, operations and state components are eligible for reuse. We present the extended *OhCircus* grammar and, based on Hoare and He's Unifying Theories of Programming, we give the formal semantics of process inheritance and its supporting constructs. The main contribution of this work is a set of sound algebraic laws for process inheritance. The proposed laws are exercised in the development of a case study.

Keywords: Behavioural Subtyping, *OhCircus*, UTP, Algebraic Laws.

1 Introduction

Several formalisms offer support for modelling behavioural and data aspects of a system. For instance, CSP-OZ [9], CSP-B [19], Mosca (VDM+CCS) [21] and *Circus* [15] are some contributions in this direction. Particularly, *Circus* is a combination of Z [20] and CSP [10], which includes constructions in the style of Morgan's refinement calculus [13]. With the intention to also handle object orientation, the *OhCircus* [6] language has been proposed as a conservative extension of *Circus*.

Circus has a refinement calculus that embodies a comprehensive set of laws [5,15,18]. These laws are also valid for *OhCircus*. Nevertheless, although there is a notion of process inheritance in *OhCircus*, the current calculus does not include any laws for dealing with process inheritance. The laws developed in Section 4 aim to contribute to a more comprehensive set of algebraic laws for *OhCircus*, taking into account this relevant language feature.

Class inheritance, in the object-orientated paradigm, is a well-established concept [12]; several works, based on the substitutability principle, have developed theories that recognize suitable inheritance notions between classes [1,12]. On the other hand, the semantics of process inheritance is not consolidated. Some of the most well known works [9,14,22] have used the failures behavioural model of CSP to define a process inheritance relation.

Process inheritance, as originally defined for *OhCircus*, has a practical disadvantage: there is no way of explicitly referencing the inherited elements in

L. Groves and J. Sun (Eds.): ICFEM 2013, LNCS 8144, pp. 4–19, 2013.

the subprocesses; as a consequence, there is no support for taking advantage of redefinitions, which are strongly connected with the concept of inheritance. As our first contribution, we develop an extended syntax for *OhCircus*, which allows reuse of all the process elements, but still keeping processes as encapsulated units concerning their use in process compositions. Typing rules are developed to validate programs considering the new syntax, and a formal semantics is given in the Unifying Theories of Programming (UTP) [11]. The second major contribution of this work is the proposal of sound laws to support the stepwise introduction or elimination of process inheritance and process elements in the presence of this feature. We have also mechanised these rules based on the Eclipse Modelling Framework and on the Xtext and the ATL integrated tools. The overall approach is illustrated through the development of a case study.

In the next section we briefly introduce *OhCircus* through an example, already considering the extended grammar we propose. The semantics for process inheritance is presented in Section 3. A selection of the proposed laws is given in Section 4; the laws are exercised in a case study in Section 5. Finally, in Section 6, we present our conclusions and future work.

2   Process Inheritance with Code Reuse

We have extended the syntax of *OhCircus* in two central ways: the creation of a new access level to allow visibility of process elements (state and schema operation) by subprocesses (like the protected mechanism in Java) and the addition of a new clause to define Z schemas [20], very similar to the Z schema inclusion feature, with the aim of allowing schema redefinitions.

As originally designed, a process, both in *Circus* and *OhCircus*, is a black box with interaction points through channels that exhibit a behaviour defined by its main action. Actually, in a subprocess specification, all the definitions of the superprocess (state components, actions, and auxiliary definitions) are in scope; this has been motivated by the fact that the main action of the subprocess is implicitly composed in parallel with the main action of the superprocess. On the other hand, there is no notation for explicitly referencing the inherited elements for supporting code reuse, for instance, in operation redefinitions. The effort of introducing inheritance with this process structure is prohibitive because the benefits of code reuse cannot be reached and the introduction of a type hierarchy, by itself, is not enough to justify inheritance, from a practical perspective.

The syntax for the proposed extensions is presented in Figure 1, where the three central elements of our strategy are underlined. A process is a sequence of paragraphs, possibly including a state defined in the form of a Z schema (formed of variable declarations and a predicate), followed by a main action that captures the active behaviour of the process. A process paragraph (PParagraph) includes Z schemas (typically defining operations) and auxiliary actions used by the main action; a paragraph is allowed to refer to one or more Z schemas defined in the process itself or inherited from its superprocesses, in any level of inheritance.

OhProcessDefinition ::= **process** N $\widehat{=}$ [**extends** N] Process

Process   ::= **begin**
                            PParagraph*
                            [**state** N Schema-Exp | Constraint]
                            PParagraph*
                            • Action
                            end
                        | ...

PParagraph   ::= SchemaText | N $\widehat{=}$ Action
                        | [PQualifier] N SchemaText

SchemaText   ::= ((Ξ | Δ) N)$^+$ [Declaration$^+$] [**super**.N$^+$] [Predicate]

Schema-Exp   ::= ([PQualifier] Declaration)*

PQualifier   ::= **protected**

N   ::= *identifier*

Fig. 1. *OhCircus* extended syntax

A process might extend only one process; multiple inheritance is not allowed, mainly due to the possible duplication and ambiguity that arise from this feature.

A Z schema can be defined using an explicitly access modifier, **protected**, or, if no modifier is used, the default level (inherited but not directly referenced by subprocesses) is adopted. Only Z schemas in the protected level are eligible for use in a **super** clause. The overriding of protected schemas is also supported and it allows a subprocess to redefine a protected schema introduced in or inherited by the closest superprocess up in the inheritance tree.

Similarly to schemas it is allowed to define an access level for each state component. It generates some restrictions in the subprocess state component declaration. This new syntax and its restrictions are exemplified in the sequel.

2.1 An Example

We model the standard concept of an abstract unbounded buffer considering the extensions we propose to *OhCircus* (see Figure 2). The relevant channels are *start*, *input* and *output*. The first one is a signal for the buffer initialization, and the other two communicate inputs and outputs, respectively. We introduce the process *Buffer* that implements the buffer concept in *OhCircus*. The singleton state component of the *Buffer* process is a sequence of natural numbers, which is used to implement the behaviour of a queue. It is initialized by the *Init* schema.

The behaviour of the buffer is to input and output on different channels, according to a FIFO policy. Whenever it is empty, it cannot refuse to input and, whenever it is non-empty, it cannot refuse to output. The schema *Add* receives and adds an element to the buffer, by storing it in the end of the sequence representing the queue. The schema *Remove* retrieves and removes an element from the buffer (the head of the sequence). The behaviour of the *Buffer* process is given by a main action in the style of CSP, but may also reference the process

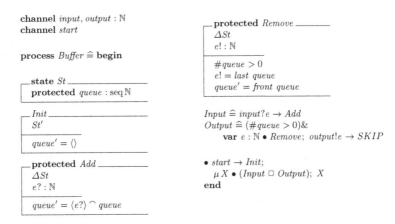

Fig. 2. *Buffer* specification in (extended) *OhCircus*

paragraphs. The process *Buffer*, after engaging in an event communicated by the *start* channel, executes its initializer *Init*. The operator ';' stands for sequential composition, and indicates that if and only if *start* → *Init* finishes successfully the process behaves like $\mu X \bullet (A)$; X, a recursive process that behaves like A and if A terminates successfully it behaves again like A, and so on. In our example, A stands for an external choice of input and output actions (*Input* □ *Output*). The *Input* action receives an input value through the channel *input* and then behaves like the *Add* operation; this establishes a binding between the variable e in the input communication and the homonymous input variable in the schema *Add*. In the case of the *Output* action, a local variable is introduced to create a binding with the corresponding variable in the *Remove* schema. Then its value is communicated through the *output* channel.

We provide specialisation of this abstract unbounded buffer, *BufferImp* (see Figure 3). It has a flexible capacity that duplicates whenever it is full. It is possible to query the ratio size/capacity. Furthermore, it provides double addition capability.

The schema *Add* in *BufferImp* uses the **super** clause to reuse the original behaviour of the *Add* operation of *Buffer*, plus duplicating the buffer length whenever it is full. The schema *Add2* adds two elements to the buffer by sequential executions of the *Add* operation. The operation *FactorCapacity* gives the ratio between the buffer's size and length. In Z, Ξ is used to indicate that the state is unchanged by the operation, whereas Δ indicates the possibility of state modification. The main action, after initializing the buffer initial length, recursively offers the behaviour *Input2* □ *Fac*. The local action *Input2* receives two elements through the channel *input2*, adding them to the buffer by behaving as *Add2*. The action *Fac* uses the Z schema *FactorCapacity* to inform the ratio size/length.

The semantics of process inheritance is given by the parallel composition of the main action of the subprocess with that of its immediate superprocess.

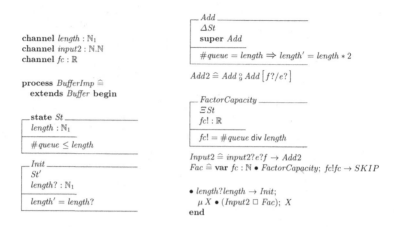

Fig. 3. *BufferImp*: a subprocess of *Buffer*

The formal details are the subject of the next section. In our example, the semantics of *BufferImp* is given by the parallel composition of its main action with the *Buffer* main action. The schema *Add* is redefined in *BufferImp* and, by dynamic binding, the redefined version is the one considered when the main action of *BufferImp* is executed. Although relatively simple, this example already illustrates one of our contributions: the extension of *OhCircus* to allow operation redefinition and reuse in process inheritance.

3   Semantics

Three models to define the behaviour of a CSP process are formally established in [10,17]: traces, failures and failures-divergences. A trace $s \in traces(P)$ of a process P is a finite sequence of symbols recording the events in which it has engaged up to some moment in time. Another model to describe the process behaviour is based on failures. A failure $f \in failures(P)$ is a pair (s, X) meaning that after the trace $s \in traces(P)$, P refuses all events in X. Finally, failures-divergences extend the failures model with the addition of the process divergences. A divergence of a process is defined as a trace after which the process behaves like *Chaos*, the most nondeterministic CSP process.

Perhaps the most well-established notion of process inheritance is that defined in [22], in which a process Q is a subprocess of P if the following refinement holds in the failures model: $P \sqsubseteq (Q \setminus (\alpha Q - \alpha P))$, where αP is the alphabet of a process P (set of events in which the process can engage), $S_1 - S_2$ stands for set subtraction, and $P \setminus S$ for a process that behaves as P but hiding the events in the set S. Considering the failures semantics, the previous refinement holds if and only if $failures (Q.act \setminus (\alpha Q.act - \alpha P.act)) \subseteq failures(P.act)$. This notion of inheritance from [22] is the same adopted in *OhCircus*. This is reflected in the obligation that a subprocess main action (its behaviour) must refine, in the failures semantics, the main action (hiding the new events) of its superprocess. In this way the substitutability principle is satisfied. We have actually formally verified this refinement for *Buffer* and *BufferImp* presented in the previous section, as can be found in [8].

A complete account of the *Circus* denotational semantics based on Hoare and He's Unifying Theories of Programming [11] is presented in [15]. As *OhCircus* is a conservative extension of *Circus* we can use the semantics defined in [15] as a basis to formalise the process inheritance notion. So if two processes P and Q have, respectively, $P.act$ and $Q.act$ as their main actions, Q **extends** $P \Leftrightarrow P.act \sqsubseteq_F Q.act \setminus (\alpha Q - \alpha P)$. Here we adopt the same model as that of [22], and consider only failres (not divergences). The reason is that we use hiding in our formulation, and this can introduce divergences, which, in general, makes the failures-divergences refinement fail to hold.

3.1   Semantics of Inheritance

We define a semantics for process inheritance, from which we prove algebraic laws that deal with this feature. Particularly, we define a mapping from processes with inheritance into regular processes, whose semantics is completely defined in [15]. Therefore, it is possible to formally prove the soundness of the proposed set of laws. We give a UTP semantics for a new parallel operator, which turned out to be necessary in the definition of inheritance, as well as for the **super** clause and the **protected** mechanism. Consider the processes *Super* and *Sub* below:

process *Super*	**process** *Sub* $\hat{=}$ **extends** *Super*
state $st \hat{=} st_1 \wedge st_2$	**state** st
pps_1	pps
pps_2	• act
• act	**end**
end	

In the above definition of *Super* we assume that the state st can be split into state schemas st_1 and st_2; these are assumed to be qualified with protected and default visibility mechanisms, respectively. The same visibility considerations are assumed for the schemas $Super.pps_1$ and $Super.pps_2$. In the process given below, $Super.pps_2{}^{ref}$ is obtained from $Super.pps_2$ by eliminating the paragraphs redefined in $Sub.pps$. Then, given the above considerations, the meaning of *Sub* is defined as:

$$Sub \hat{=} \begin{pmatrix} \textbf{begin state} \ \hat{=} \ Super.st \wedge Sub.st \\ \quad Super.pps_{1 \wedge \; \Xi \; Sub.st} \\ \quad Super.pps_2{}^{ref} {}_{\wedge \; \Xi \; Sub.st} \\ \quad Sub.pps \\ \quad \bullet \ Super.act [\![Super.st \mid Super.st \wedge \ Sub.st]\!] Sub.act \\ \textbf{end} \end{pmatrix}$$

In the context of *Sub*, paragraphs in *Super.pps* do not modify the state elements in *Sub.st*. The Z schema expression $\Xi Sub.st$ captures this state preservation. The effect of $Super.pps_{1 \wedge \; \Xi \; Sub.st}$ is to ensure that no paragraph in

Super.pps$_1$ modifies state elements in *Sub.st*; the same is true of paragraphs in *Super.pps*$_2$^{ref}. Although all components of *Super* are in the scope of *Sub*, only its protected components can be directly accessed by the original declared elements of *Sub*; as already explained, those with the default qualification cannot be accessed by *Sub*. Because *Super.act* can refer to any schema in *Super.pps*$_1$ or in *Super.pps*$_2$, and these to any state in *Super.st*, we need to bring all protected and default elements from *Super* to *Sub*.

Concerning the main action in the semantics of *Sub*, it is given by the parallel composition of the main action of *Sub* with that of *Super*, but we need to impose a protocol concerning access to the shared state elements. This required the definition of a new parallel operator for *OhCircus*, as further explained in the sequel.

3.2   A New Parallel Operator

As originally proposed for *Circus* (and *OhCircus*), the notation for parallel composition of actions A_1 and A_2, synchronising on the channels in the set *cs* is given by $A_1 [\![ns_1 \,|\, cs \,|\, ns_2]\!] A_2$, such that the final state of the variables in ns_1 is given by A_1 and those variables in ns_2 by A_2, with the restriction $ns_1 \cap ns_2 = \emptyset$. It avoids conflicts about what action will determine the final value of a possible shared variable. With this operator, it is not possible to capture the semantics of process inheritance concerning the behaviour of the action in the subprocess. This becomes evident from the main action of *Sub*, *Super.act* $[\![Super.st \,|\, Super.st \,\wedge\, Sub.st]\!] Sub.act$ presented above. The restriction that the two sets (ns_1 and ns_2) must be disjoint can be relaxed if we consider that the changes made in a state component by a schema *sc* in a subprocess cannot contradict the changes made by *sc* in its superprocess, since the former refines the latter; it follows the same principle described in [12]. Also, note that, in the semantics of process inheritance, we do not need the synchronization set *cs*, as there is no channel to be shared by a sub and a super process. So our extension is based on a simpler form of parallelism that is actually an interleaving.

Before giving the semantics of the new parallel operator, we introduce some basic notions of the UTP. There are four pairs of observational variables used to define the behaviour of a reactive program in the UTP: the boolean variable *okay* indicates whether the system has been properly started in a stable state; *okay'* means subsequent stabilisation in an observable state; *tr* records the events in which a program has engaged at some moment (*tr'* records such events at a later moment); the boolean variable *wait* distinguishes the intermediate observations of waiting states from final observations on termination; in a stable intermediate state, *wait'* has true as its value (a false value for *wait'* indicates that the program has reached a final state); all the events that may be refused by a process before the program has started are elements of *ref*, and possibly refused events at a later moment are referred by *ref'*. In addition to these observational variables, *v* and *v'* stand, respectively, for the initial and intermediate or final values of all program variables.

$$M_{|||} \ \widehat{=} \ tr' - tr \in (1.tr - tr \ ||| \ 2.tr - tr)$$
$$\wedge \begin{pmatrix} \begin{pmatrix} (1.wait \vee 2.wait) \wedge \\ ref' \subseteq (1.ref \cup 2.ref) \end{pmatrix} \\ \vartriangleleft wait' \vartriangleright \\ \neg \ 1.wait \wedge \neg \ 2.wait \wedge MSt \end{pmatrix}$$

$$MSt \ \widehat{=} \ \forall v \bullet (v \in ns_1 \wedge v \notin ns_2$$
$$\Rightarrow v' = 1.v)$$
$$\wedge (v \in ns_2 \wedge v \notin ns_1 \Rightarrow v' = 2.v)$$
$$\wedge (v \in ns1 \cap ns2 \Rightarrow v' = 1.v = 2.v)$$
$$\wedge (v \notin ns1 \cup ns2 \Rightarrow v' = v)$$
$$Ui(\{v'_1, \ldots, v'_n\}) = i.v'_1 = v_1 \wedge \ldots$$
$$\wedge \ i.v'_n = v_n$$

Fig. 4. The semantics of our new parallel operator

The formal semantics of the new parallel operator is presented in Figure 4. The merge function $M_{|||}$ is responsible for merging the traces of two actions, and the final values of state components (MSt), local variables and also those of the remaining UTP observational variables; $|||$ takes of two traces and gives a set containing all the possible combinations of them. In $M_{|||}$ the sequence of traces generated by the execution of A_1 and A_2, $(tr' - tr)$ must be a sequence generated by the interleave composition of the traces of A_1 and A_2. The interleaving terminates only if both actions do so. So if $wait'$ is true it is because one of the actions has not finished, $1.wait \vee 2.wait$, and the refusals is contained or equals to the refusals of A_1 and A_2 together. Otherwise if $wait'$ is false it means that both actions has terminated $\neg \ 1.wait \wedge \neg \ 2.wait$ and the state components and local variables have changed according to the predicate generated by MSt. To avoid name conflicts in the predicate we use a renaming function Ui that prefixes with i the variables in these actions.

This predicate says that each variable in v is changed by A_1 if it belongs uniquely to ns_1, by A_2 if it belongs uniquely to ns_2. If $v \in ns1 \cap ns2$, A_1 and A_2 must agree in the final value of v.

4   Laws

This section presents a small selection of a comprehensive set of algebraic laws for *OhCircus*, particularly addressing specifications with a process hierarchy. The complete set of laws can be found in [8], together with their proofs; these laws range from simple transformations to introduce/eliminate state elements or paragraphs, to more elaborate laws that capture moving elements between super and subprocesses, some of which are presented in this paper. Each law is presented in the form $pds_1 =_{pds} pds_2$, meaning that the set of process declarations pds_1 has the same semantics as the set of process declarations pds_2 in the context of process declarations pds. When a law is valid for any context, we omit the parameter pds. A law may also have a **provided** clause that contains the premises that must be satisfied before its application. As an algebraic law has always two directions of application, we must define the premises for each direction.

Law 1 (process elimination)

$pds \ pd_1 = pds$
where
$pd_1 = $ **process** $P \mathrel{\widehat{=}}$ [**extends** Q] **begin** $\bullet$ *Skip* **end**
provided
$(\leftrightarrow)$ ¬ $occurs(P, pds)$
$(\leftarrow)$ $occurs(Q, pds)$

A process that has its main action as *Skip* (and is not referenced by other processes) does not affect the meaning of a program in *OhCircus*, even if it extends an existing process. We use the notation $occurs(R, pds)$ to represent the fact that the process R is used (as superprocess or in a process composition) by at least one process in *pds*. For a left to right application of this law, the first proviso guarantees that the process P is not used in *pds*. For a right to left application, the first proviso ensures that the process declared in pd_1 has a fresh name in *pds*, whereas the second proviso guarantees that Q must have been previously declared, so that it can be used as a valid superprocess of P. The double arrow in the provided clause means that the condition applies in both directions; otherwise the condition applies only in the direction pointed by the arrow.

Law 2 (super elimination)

This law (see Figure 5) removes the **super** clause from a schema. To remove **super** sc from a schema sc in R, it is necessary that there exists a protected schema sc, in a superprocess of R, as made explicit in the figure. This superprocess must be the closest process to R in its hierarchy. If $P.sc$ has the **super** clause, this is first resolved; as a process hierarchy is a finite structure, it is always possible to find a schema without **super**. The symbol $\oslash$ stands for the Z notation Ξ or Δ. This law is a direct consequence of the semantics of **super** and has no side condition.

Law 3 (splitting a schema among processes)

If part of the behaviour of a schema in a superprocess (including a subset of the state components, related declarations and a predicate) are relevant only for one of its subprocesses, we can introduce a redefinition of this schema in the subprocess and move this part of the original schema to the subprocess as a redefinition of a schema in the superprocess with the remaining part of the original schema.

The state components of P (see Figure 6) are partitioned in two sets st_1 and st_2. $P.sc$, on the right-hand side, changes only st_1, but st_2 is left undefined. $R.sc$ includes $P.sc$ and explicitly constrains the values of the st_2 components according to the predicate $pred_2$; this requires that the state components in this set have the protected access level. Finally there must be no redefinitions of $P.sc$ except in the subprocesses of R.

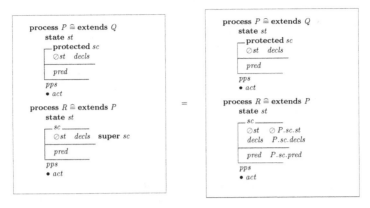

Fig. 5. super elimination

provided

($\leftrightarrow$) $\forall S \in pds \mid S \leq P \wedge \neg (S \leq R) \bullet \neg occurs(st_2, S.pps) \wedge \neg occurs(st_2, S.act) \wedge$
$\neg impact(st_1, st_2)$
($\rightarrow$) $PL(st_2) \wedge N(sc) \notin N(R.pps)$

Fig. 6. splitting a schema among processes

In the provided clause in Figure 6, the function N defines the set of process names of a set of process declarations. We overload the function *occurs* in *occurs*(*sc*, *R.act*), *occurs*(*sc*, *R.pps*) and *occurs*(*sc*, *R.sc*). The former represents the fact that the schema *sc* is used in *R.act*; the second, the fact that *sc* is used in *R.pps*; the latter the fact that *sc* is referenced via the **super** clause in *R.sc*. $PL(sc)$ represents the fact that *sc* is a protected schema, and $impact(st_1, st_2)$ is true iff the value of a state component st_1 is affected by the value of st_2.

Law 4 (move action to subprocess)

If the main action of a process P (see Figure 7) can be written as a parallel composition of two actions act_1 and act_2, that access exclusively st_1 and st_2, respectively, we can move one of these actions (in this case, act_2) to a subprocess of P, say R. The state components in st_2 must be protected, so it is possible to refer to them in the R's main action. This law changes the behavior of P, so it cannot be extended by any process in *pds* except for R and its subprocesses

$$
\boxed{
\begin{array}{l}
\textbf{process } P \,\widehat{=}\, \textbf{extends } Q \\
\quad \textbf{state } st_1 \wedge st_2 \\
\quad pps \\
\quad \bullet\, act_1[\![st_1 \mid st_2]\!]act_2 \\
\textbf{end} \\[4pt]
\textbf{process } R \,\widehat{=}\, \textbf{extends } P \\
\quad \textbf{state } st \\
\quad pps \\
\quad \bullet\, act \\
\end{array}
}
\;=_{pds}\;
\boxed{
\begin{array}{l}
\textbf{process } P \,\widehat{=}\, \textbf{extends } Q \\
\quad \textbf{state } st_1 \wedge st_2 \\
\quad pps \\
\quad \bullet\, act_1 \\
\textbf{end} \\[4pt]
\textbf{process } R \,\widehat{=}\, \textbf{extends } P \\
\quad \textbf{state } st \\
\quad pps \\
\quad \bullet\, act[\![st \mid st_2]\!]act_2 \\
\end{array}
}
$$

provided
$(\leftrightarrow) \forall S \mid S \in pds \wedge S \neq R \bullet \neg\, occurs(P, S)$
$(\rightarrow) PL(st_2)$

Fig. 7. move action to subprocess

$$
\boxed{
\begin{array}{l}
\textbf{process } P \,\widehat{=}\, \textbf{extends } Q \\
\quad \textbf{state } st_1 \wedge st_2 \\
\quad pps \\
\quad \bullet\, act \\
\textbf{end} \\[4pt]
\textbf{process } R \,\widehat{=}\, \textbf{extends } P \\
\quad \textbf{state } st \\
\quad pps \\
\quad \bullet\, act \\
\end{array}
}
\;=_{pds}\;
\boxed{
\begin{array}{l}
\textbf{process } P \,\widehat{=}\, \textbf{extends } Q \\
\quad \textbf{state } st_1 \\
\quad pps \\
\quad \bullet\, act \\
\textbf{end} \\[4pt]
\textbf{process } R \,\widehat{=}\, \textbf{extends } P \\
\quad \textbf{state } st \wedge st_2 \\
\quad pps \\
\quad \bullet\, act \\
\end{array}
}
$$

provided
$(\leftrightarrow) st_2$ is **protected**
$(\rightarrow)\ \forall S \mid S \le P \wedge \neg\,(S \le R) \bullet \neg\, occurs(st_2, S.pps) \wedge \neg\, occurs(st_2, S.act)$
$(\leftarrow)\ \forall S \mid S \le P \wedge \neg\,(S \le R) \bullet st_2 \notin PS(S.st)$

Fig. 8. move state component to subproces

(indirectly). Finally, P cannot be used by any process declared in pds, except via inheritance as already mentioned.

Law 5 (move state component to subproces)
A state component st_2 (see Figure 8) of a process P can be moved to one of its subprocesses, say R, if st_2 is not used by P neither by its subprocesses, except those that are also subprocesses of R, including itself. For these, the state component st_2 will be inherited from R instead of P, and no restriction must be applied to them. It must be clear that st_2 is unique through the P process hierarchy. The provisos consider $P.st_2$ as a protected element. The function PS yields, from a set of state components, those in the protected level.

Law 6 (move a protected schema to subprocess)
To move a schema sc (see Figure 9) from P to R, where $R < P$, it is necessary, if sc is protected, that it is not being used by P, neither by its subprocesses, except for those that are also subprocesses of R. Note that we can apply this law, even if a subprocess of P (except for R) has a redefinition of sc.

To move a protected schema $R.sc$ to P, where $R < P$, we must guarantee that neither P nor its subprocesses, except for those that are also subprocesses of R, have a schema named sc.

```
process P ≙ extends Q                    process P ≙ extends Q
    state st                                 state st
    protected sc                             pps
    pps                                      • act
    • act                                end
end                        =ₚds
                                         process R ≙ extends P
process R ≙ extends P                         state st
    state st                                 protected sc
    pps                                      pps
    • act                                    • act
```

provided
$(\leftrightarrow)\ \forall S\ |\ S < P \wedge \neg (S < R) \bullet \neg\ occurs(sc, S.pps) \wedge \neg\ occurs(sc, S.act)$

Fig. 9. move a protected schema to subprocess

Law 7 (subprocess extraction)

In the initial specification of a system it is common to model processes with a very specific behaviour that hides a generic behaviour specialized in face of a particular situation. We propose a law (see Figure 10) that extracts from a process this generic behaviour as a superprocess specializing it with a subprocess. This promotes code reuse and favors a better conceptual representation of the system. The set $R.pps_2'$ in R stands for the schemas in $P.pps_2$ affected by the law, and the set $P.pps_2''$ stands for the updated set $P.pps_2$.

Particularly, it can be proved (see Figure 10) from laws 1, 4, 3, 6, 2 and 5 (*LHS* stands for the left hand side of the law). First Law 1 is applied creating the process P'; It is easy to observe that P' is equivalent to P. In the next step we apply a double renaming $[P, R/P', P]$ (which clearly preserves the behaviour, since the semantics of P is preserved) followed by Law 4, which moves some elements from R to P. Law 3 is then applied for each schema in $R.pps_2$; the set $R.pps_2'$ stands for the schemas in $R.pps_2$ affected by the law and $P.pps_2''$ for those created in P; as part of this transformation, Laws 6 and 2 are needed when there are protected schemas involved, but we omit these details for conciseness. Finally, Law 5 is applied to move of the unused state components of R to P.

An important issue is a notion of completeness for the proposed set of laws, particulary with respect to inheritance. Our measure for the completeness of the proposed laws is whether their exhaustive application is capable to remove all subprocesses from the target specification. Broadly, by exhaustively applying Law 7, from right to left, we are able to completely remove process inheritance from the specification. In practice, however, it is more common to apply the laws in the opposite direction, since the purpose in design evolution is to introduce (rather than eliminating) inheritance.

5 Case Study

Consider the process *Buffer* as defined in Figure 11. Our intention is to transform this design into a more reusable one, as presented in Section 2.1 (see Figures 2 and 3). The process *Buffer* (in Figure 11) encompasses two abstractions: an

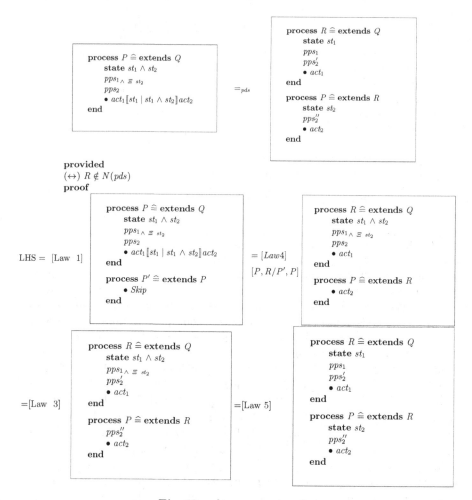

Fig. 10. subprocess extraction

abstract unbounded buffer with no concerns about memory space, and a more concrete specialisation that deals with practical memory limitations and offers more functionalities: memory size monitoring and double buffer addition.

Separating these concerns increases reuse and maintainability, and the nature of the design is more faithfully reflected. To achieve these benefits Law 7 (subprocess extraction) can be applied generating the two processes shown in Section 2.1. A key point, before applying the law, is the adaptation of the specification of *BufferImp* to exactly match the left-hand side of Law 7.

Figure 12 shows part of the adaptations we need to perform to apply this law. As a first step, the schemas *Add* and *Remove* are signed as **protected**. Then, the process state is represented as a conjunction of St_1 and St_2; the initialization schema and main action are split accordingly. These transformations are justified by laws of actions, which are not our focus here but can be found in [5]. With

channel $input, input2, output$: $\mathbb{N}$
channel $length$: $\mathbb{N}_1$
channel fc : $\mathbb{R}$
channel $start$

process $Buffer \mathrel{\widehat{=}}$ begin

__ state St _____
$queue$: $\mathrm{seq}\,\mathbb{N}$
$length$: $\mathbb{N}_1$
_____
$\#queue \leq length$

__ Init _____
St'
$length?$: $\mathbb{N}_1$
_____
$queue' = \langle\rangle$
$length' = length?$

__ Add _____
ΔSt
$e?$: $\mathbb{N}$
_____
$queue' = \langle e?\rangle \frown queue$
$\#queue = length \Rightarrow$
$\quad length' = length * 2$

__ Remove _____
ΔSt
$e!$: $\mathbb{N}$
_____
$\#queue > 0$
$e! = last\ queue$
$queue' = front\ queue$

$Add2 \mathrel{\widehat{=}} Add \mathbin{\S} Add\left[f?/e?\right]$

__ FactorCapacity _____
ΞSt
$fc!$: $\mathbb{R}$
_____
$fc! = \#queue\ \mathrm{div}\ length$

$Input \mathrel{\widehat{=}} input?e \rightarrow Add$
$Output \mathrel{\widehat{=}} (\#queue > 0)\&$
$\qquad$ var e : $\mathbb{N} \bullet Remove;\ output!e \rightarrow SKIP$

$Input2 \mathrel{\widehat{=}} input2?e?f \rightarrow Add2$
$Fac \mathrel{\widehat{=}}$ var fc : $\mathbb{N} \bullet FactorCapacity;\ fc!fc \rightarrow SKIP$

$\bullet\ start \rightarrow length?length \rightarrow Init;$
$\quad \mu X \bullet (Input \mathbin{\Box} Output \mathbin{\Box} Input2 \mathbin{\Box} Fac);\ X$
end

Fig. 11. *Buffer* without inheritance

these transformations we can apply Law 7. As explained in the previous section, it embodies several small transformations, resulting in the design in Section 2.1.

6   Conclusions

In this work we proposed a set of sound algebraic laws for *OhCircus*, with focus on process inheritance. As far as we are aware, this is an original contribution, as it seems to be the first systematic characterization of a comprehensive set of laws for process inheritance in the context of rich data types and access control for state and behaviour components. With this goal in mind we started by defining a notion of process inheritance in *OhCircus*. Extending the model of process inheritance [22] for CSP, based on the failures model [10], we defined the semantics for process inheritance in *OhCircus*.

The original design of *OhCircus* makes process components invisible even for its subprocesses, which prevents code reuse. This motivated us to extend the syntax and the semantics of *OhCircus* through the creation of a new access level to signalise the superprocess elements that will be visible to its subprocesses. This also required the definition of typing rules [8] for the new constructs, but we were able to achieve a conservative extension of *OhCircus* [5,15,18], despite the fact that we needed to introduce a new parallel operator, and its UTP semantics, to be able to define the meaning of process inheritance.

We illustrated our overall strategy in a case study where we apply some of the proposed laws. In [8] we address soundness in detail. We have also developed a tool to support our strategy based on the Eclipse Modelling Framework (EMF),

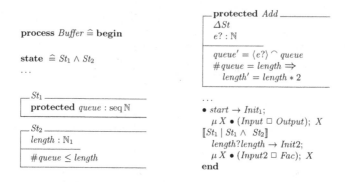

Fig. 12. *Buffer* adaptations

which was chosen mostly because of the facility for integrating the variety of tools needed, which is archived by the use of a default metamodel, Ecore, across most of EMF technologies. Among EMF tools, we used Xtext for describing the *OhCircus* language, and ATL (Atlas Transformation Language) to encode the algebraic laws and to carry out the mechanised application of the laws. These have not been addressed here for space limitations.

Several works have addressed notions of behavioural subtyping [7,12,16,22] [1,2,3,4]. In [1,12] a subtype relation is defined in terms of invariants over a state, in addition to pre/post conditions and constraint rules over methods. The other cited works define a subtype relation based on models like failures and failures-divergences proposed for CSP, relating refinement with inheritance [22].

In [12] a subtype is allowed add new methods, provided there exists a function that maps these new methods as a combination of the supertype methods; this is not allowed in [22]. Here we allow, in a subtype, new methods like in [12] and even new state components, method overriding, reducing non-determinism, and methods that change both inherited and declared attributes.

Previous works have proposed refinements and algebraic laws for *Circus* [5,18] and these are consequently applicable to *OhCircus*. In [18] the meaning of refinement of processes and their actions are defined based on forward simulation. It also provides an iterative development strategy, involving the application of simulation, action and, most importantly, process refinement. In this context, our work complements [18] with a formal notion of process inheritance and the associated laws.

The mechanization of the formal semantics of *Circus* given in the UTP is provided in [15]. The extension of this work for *OhCircus*, in the form proposed here, is our next immediate goal.

References

1. America, P.: Designing an Object-Oriented Programming Language with Behavioural Subtyping. In: de Bakker, J.W., Rozenberg, G., de Roever, W.-P. (eds.) REX 1990. LNCS, vol. 489, pp. 60–90. Springer, Heidelberg (1991)

2. Balzarotti, C., Cindio, F., Pomello, L.: Observation equivalences for the semantics of inheritance. In: Proceedings of the IFIP TC6/WG6, FMOODS 1999, Deventer, The Netherlands. Kluwer, B.V. (1999)
3. Bowman, H., Briscoe-Smith, C., Derrick, J., Strulo, B.: On Behavioural Subtyping in LOTOS (1996)
4. Bowman, H., Derrick, J.: A Junction between State Based and Behavioural Specification (Invited Talk), Deventer, The Netherlands, pp. 213–239. Kluwer, B.V. (1999)
5. Cavalcanti, A.L.C., Sampaio, A., Woodcock, J.C.P.: A Refinement Strategy for *Circus*. Formal Aspects of Computing 15(2-3), 146–181 (2003)
6. Cavalcanti, A.L.C., Sampaio, A., Woodcock, J.C.P.: Unifying Classes and Processes. Software and System Modelling 4(3), 277–296 (2005)
7. Cusack, E.: Refinement, conformance and inheritance. Formal Aspects of Computing 3, 129–141 (1991), doi:10.1007/BF01898400
8. Dihego, J., Antonino, P., Sampaio, A.: Algebraic Laws for Process Subtyping - Extended Version. Technical report (2011), http://www.cin.ufpe.br/~jdso/technicalReports/TR015.pdf
9. Fischer, C.: CSP-OZ: A combination of Object-Z and CSP. In: Proceedings of the IFIP, FMOODS 1997, London, UK. Chapman & Hall (1997)
10. Hoare, C.A.R.: Communicating Sequential Processes, vol. 21, pp. 666–677. ACM, New York (1978)
11. Hoare, C.A.R., He, J.: Unifying theories of programming, vol. 14. Prentice Hall (1998)
12. Liskov, B.H., Wing, J.M.: A behavioral notion of subtyping. ACM Trans. Program. Lang. Syst. 16(6), 1811–1841 (1994)
13. Morgan, C.: Programming from specifications. Prentice-Hall, Inc., Upper Saddle River (1990)
14. Olderog, E.-R., Wehrheim, H.: Specification and (property) inheritance in CSP-OZ. Sci. Comput. Program. 55(1-3), 227–257 (2005)
15. Oliveira, M.V.M., Cavalcanti, A.L.C., Woodcock, J.C.P.: A UTP Semantics for *Circus*. Formal Aspects of Computing 21(1), 3–32 (2007)
16. Puntigam, F.: Types for Active Objects Based on Trace Semantics. In: Proceedings of the FMOODS 1996, pp. 4–19. Chapman and Hall (1996)
17. Roscoe, A.W., Hoare, C.A.R., Bird, R.: The Theory and Practice of Concurrency. Prentice Hall PTR, Upper Saddle River (1997)
18. Sampaio, A., Woodcock, J.C.P., Cavalcanti, A.L.C.: Refinement in *Circus*. In: Eriksson, L.-H., Lindsay, P.A. (eds.) FME 2002. LNCS, vol. 2391, pp. 451–470. Springer, Heidelberg (2002)
19. Schneider, S., Treharne, H.: Communicating B Machines. In: Bert, D., Bowen, J.P., Henson, M.C., Robinson, K. (eds.) ZB 2002. LNCS, vol. 2272, pp. 416–435. Springer, Heidelberg (2002)
20. Spivey, J.M.: The Z notation: A reference manual. Prentice-Hall, Inc., Upper Saddle River (1989)
21. Toetenel, H., van Katwijk, J.: Stepwise development of model-oriented real-time specifications from action/event models. In: Vytopil, J. (ed.) FTRTFT 1992. LNCS, vol. 571, pp. 547–570. Springer, Heidelberg (1991)
22. Wehrheim, H.: Behavioral Subtyping Relations for Active Objects. Form. Methods Syst. Des. 23(2), 143–170 (2003)

Boundness Issues in CCSL Specifications

Frédéric Mallet[1,*] and Jean-Viven Millo[2]

[1] Univ. Nice Sophia Antipolis, I3S, INRIA, CNRS, F-06900, France
[2] INRIA Sophia Antipolis Méditerranée, I3S, INRIA, CNRS, F-06900, France
Frederic.Mallet@unice.fr

Abstract. The UML Profile for Modeling and Analysis of Real-Time and Embedded systems promises a general modeling framework to design and analyze systems. Lots of works have been published on the modeling capabilities offered by MARTE, much less on verification techniques supported. The Clock Constraint Specification Language (CCSL), first introduced as a companion language for MARTE, was devised to offer a formal support to conduct causal and temporal analyses on MARTE models.

This work introduces formally a state-based semantics for CCSL operators and then focuses on the analysis capabilities of MARTE/CCSL and more particularly on boundness issues.

The approach is illustrated on one simple example where the architecture plays an important role. We describe a process where the logical description of the application is progressively refined to take into account the candidate execution platforms through allocation.

Keywords: Logical Time, Architecture-driven analysis, UML MARTE, Reachability analysis.

1 Introduction

The UML Profile for Modeling and Analysis of Real-Time and Embedded systems [1] (MARTE), adopted in November 2009, has introduced a *Time model* [2] that extends the informal *Simple Time* of The Unified Modeling Language (UML 2.x). This time model is general enough to support different forms of time (discrete or dense, chronometric or logical). Its so-called *clocks* allow enforcing as well as observing the occurrences of events and the behavior of annotated UML elements. The time model comes with a companion language called the *Clock Constraint Specification Language* (CCSL) [3] and defined in an annex of the MARTE specification. Initially devised as a simple language for expressing constraints between clocks of a MARTE model, CCSL has evolved and has been developed independently of the UML. CCSL is now equipped with a formal semantics [3] and is supported by a software environment (TimeSquare [4][1]) that allows for the specification, solving, and visualization of clock constraints.

---

* This work has been partially funded by ARTEMIS Grant $N°269362$ – Project PRESTO - http://www.presto-embedded.eu
[1] http://timesquare.inria.fr

L. Groves and J. Sun (Eds.): ICFEM 2013, LNCS 8144, pp. 20–35, 2013.

MARTE promises a general modeling framework to design and analyze systems. Lots of works have been published on the modeling capabilities offered by MARTE, much less on verification techniques supported. While the initial semantics of CCSL is described as a set of rewriting rules [3], this paper proposes as a first contribution a state-based semantics for each of the kernel CCSL operators. The global semantics emerging of the parallel composition of CCSL constraints then becomes the synchronized product of the automaton of each individual constraint. Since automaton for some CCSL operators can be infinite, this requires specific attention to compute the synchronized product. The second contribution is an algorithm that builds the synchronized product. The algorithm terminates when the set of states reachable through the synchronized product is finite. The third contribution is a discussion on a sufficient condition to guarantee that the synchronized product is actually finite.

Section 2 proposes a state-based semantics for CCSL. Section 3 discusses boundness issues on CCSL specifications. Section 4 illustrates the use of CCSL for architecture-driven analysis. It shows how abstract representations of the application and the architecture are built and how the two models are mapped through an allocation process. Section 5 makes a comparison with related works.

2   A State-Based Semantics for CCSL Operators

This section starts with a brief introduction to CCSL and then gives a formal definition of CCSL operators in terms of labeled transition systems. Some of the CCSL operators require an infinite number of states.

2.1   The Clock Constraint Specification Language

The Clock Constraint Specification Language (CCSL) has been developed to elaborate and reason on the logical time model [2] of MARTE. A technical report [3] describes the syntax and the semantics of a kernel set of CCSL constraints.

The notion of multiform logical time has first been used in the theory of Synchronous languages [5] and its polychronous extensions [6]. The use of tagged systems to capture and compare models of computations was advocated by [7]. CCSL provides a concrete syntax to make the polychronous clocks become first-class citizens of UML-like models.

A *clock* c is a totally ordered set of *instants*, $\mathcal{I}_c$. In the following, i and j are instants. A *time structure* is a set of clocks $\mathcal{C}$ and a set of relations on instants $\mathcal{I} = \bigcup_{c \in \mathcal{C}} \mathcal{I}_c$. CCSL considers two kinds of relations: *causal* and *temporal* ones. The basic causal relation is causality/*dependency*, a binary relation on $\mathcal{I}$: $\preccurlyeq \subset \mathcal{I} \times \mathcal{I}$. $i \preccurlyeq j$ means i causes j or j depends on i. $\preccurlyeq$ is a pre-order on $\mathcal{I}$, i.e., it is reflexive and transitive. The basic temporal relations are *precedence* ($\prec$), *coincidence* ($\equiv$), and *exclusion* ($\#$), three binary relations on $\mathcal{I}$. For any pair of instants $(i, j) \in \mathcal{I} \times \mathcal{I}$ in a time structure, $i \prec j$ means that the only acceptable execution traces are those where i occurs strictly before j (i precedes j). $\prec$ is transitive and asymmetric (reflexive and antisymmetric). $i \equiv j$ imposes instants

i and j to be coincident, *i.e.*, they must occur at the same execution step, both of them or none of them. $\equiv$ is an equivalence relation, *i.e.*, it is reflexive, symmetric and transitive. $i \# j$ forbids the coincidence of the two instants, *i.e.*, they cannot occur at the same execution step. $\#$ is irreflexive and symmetric. A consistency rule is enforced between causal and temporal relations. $i \preccurlyeq j$ can be refined either as $i \prec j$ or $i \equiv j$, but j can never precede i.

In this paper, we consider discrete sets of instants only, so that the instants of a clock can be indexed by natural numbers. For a clock $c \in \mathcal{C}$, and for any $k \in \mathbb{N}^\star$, $c[k]$ denotes the kth instant of c.

2.2   CCSL Clocks and Relations

Definition 1 (Labeled Transition System). *A* Labeled Transition System *[8] over a set A of actions is defined as a tuple $\mathcal{A} = \langle S, T, s0, \alpha, \beta, \lambda \rangle$ where*

- *S is a set of* states,
- *T is a set of* transitions,
- *$s0 \in S$ is the initial state,*
- *$\alpha, \beta : T \to S$ denote respectively the* source state *and the* target state *of a transition,*
- *$\lambda : T \to A$ denotes the action responsible for a transition,*
- *the mappings $\langle \alpha, \lambda, \beta \rangle : T \to S \times A \times S$ are one-to-one so that T is a subset of $S \times A \times S$.*

In the context of CCSL, the actions are clocks. For each CCSL **clock** c, we build the Labeled Transition System $Clock_c = \langle S, T, \alpha, \beta, \lambda \rangle$ over $A_c = \{c, \epsilon\}$ such that

- $S = \{s\}$, $T = \{t, e\}$, $s0 = s$,
- $\alpha(t) = \alpha(e) = \beta(t) = \beta(e) = s$,
- $\lambda(t) = c$ and $\lambda(e) = \epsilon$.

The ϵ action allows for doing nothing. This is to allow composition with other LTSs. $Clock_a$ is given in Figure 1.a as an illustration.[2]

Definition 2 (Synchronization constraint). *Given n sets of actions $A_1, \ldots, A_n$, a synchronization constraint is a subset I of $A_1 \times \ldots \times A_n$.*

Definition 3 (Synchronized product). *If, for $i = 1, \ldots, n$, $\mathcal{A}_i = \langle S_i, T_i, s0_i, \alpha_i, \beta_i, \lambda_i \rangle$ is a labeled transition system over A_i, and if $I \subseteq A_1 \times \ldots \times A_n$ is a synchronization constraint, the synchronized product [8] of $\mathcal{A}_i$ with respect to I is the labeled transition system $\langle S, T, s0, \alpha, \beta, \lambda \rangle$ over the set I defined by*

- $S = S_1 \times \ldots \times S_n$, $s0 = s0_1 \times \ldots \times s0_n$,
- $T = \{\langle t_1, \ldots, t_n \rangle \in T_1 \times \ldots \times T_n | \langle \lambda_1(t_1), \ldots, \lambda_n(t_n) \rangle \in I\}$,
- $\alpha(\langle t_1, \ldots, t_n \rangle) = \langle \alpha_1(t_1), \ldots, \alpha_n(t_n) \rangle$,

---

[2] The ϵ transitions are not shown to simplify the drawings. In all the presented LTSs, it is always possible to do nothing by remaining in the same state.

- $\beta(\langle t_1, \ldots, t_n \rangle) = \langle \beta_1(t_1), \ldots, \beta_n(t_n) \rangle$,
- $\lambda(\langle t_1, \ldots, t_n \rangle) = \langle \lambda_1(t_1), \ldots, \lambda_n(t_n) \rangle$.

Synchronization constraints allow for capturing the semantics of CCSL polychronous operators. In this section, we focus on CCSL (binary) relations.

Relation 4 (Coincidence). *Given two clocks c1 and c2, coincidence c1* $\boxed{=}$ *c2 is the synchronized product of $Clock_{c1}$ and $Clock_{c2}$ with respect to the synchronization constraint $I = \{\langle c1, c2 \rangle, \langle \epsilon, \epsilon \rangle\}$ (Fig. 1.b).*

Relation 5 (Subclocking). CCSL *subclock (c1* $\boxed{\subset}$ *c2) is the synchronized product of $Clock_{c1}$ and $Clock_{c2}$ with respect to the synchronization constraint $I = \{\langle c1, c2 \rangle, \langle \epsilon, c2 \rangle, \langle \epsilon, \epsilon \rangle\}$ (Fig. 1.c).*

Relation 6 (Exclusion). *Figure 1.d illustrates* CCSL *excludes (c1* $\boxed{\#}$ *c2) defined as the synchronized product of $Clock_{c1}$ and $Clock_{c2}$ with respect to the synchronization constraint $I = \{\langle c1, \epsilon \rangle, \langle \epsilon, c2 \rangle, \langle \epsilon, \epsilon \rangle\}$.*

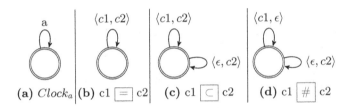

(a) $Clock_a$ | (b) c1 $\boxed{=}$ c2 | (c) c1 $\boxed{\subset}$ c2 | (d) c1 $\boxed{\#}$ c2

Fig. 1. Primitive CCSL relations as Labeled Transition Systems

2.3   CCSL Bounded Expressions

In CCSL, expressions allow for the creation of new clocks based on existing ones. Expressions can also be represented as labeled transition systems. Union and intersection are two simple examples of CCSL expressions.

Expression 7 (Union). $u \triangleq c1 + c2$ *(u is the* union *of c1 and c2) is represented by the synchronized product of $Clock_{c1}$, $Clock_{c2}$ and $Clock_u$ with respect to the synchronization constraint $I = \{\langle c1, c2, u \rangle, \langle c1, \epsilon, u \rangle, \langle \epsilon, c2, u \rangle, \langle \epsilon, \epsilon, \epsilon \rangle\}$ (Fig. 2.a).*

Expression 8 (Intersection). $i \triangleq c1.c2$ *(i is the* intersection *of c1 and c2) is represented by the synchronized product of $Clock_{c1}$, $Clock_{c2}$ and $Clock_i$ with respect to the synchronization constraint $I = \{\langle c1, c2, i \rangle, \langle c1, \epsilon, \epsilon \rangle, \langle \epsilon, c2, \epsilon \rangle, \langle \epsilon, \epsilon, \epsilon \rangle\}$ (Fig. 2.b).*

Those two expressions are stateless (one state). Other expressions are stateful and require building dedicated LTS to express their semantics.

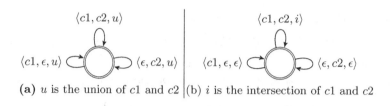

(a) u is the union of $c1$ and $c2$ **(b)** i is the intersection of $c1$ and $c2$

Fig. 2. Union and intersection of clocks

Expression 9 (Binary delay). *The* binary delay *(delayed* $\triangleq$ *base* $\$$ *n) is represented by a dedicated labeled transition system* $Delay(n) = \langle S, T, s0, \alpha, \beta, \lambda \rangle$ *over* $A = \{init, steady, \epsilon\}$ *with* $n+1$ *states such that*

- $S = \{d_0, d_1, \ldots, d_n\}$, $T = \{t_0, t_1, \ldots, t_n, e_0, \ldots, e_n\}$, $s0 = d_0$,
- $\alpha(t_i) = d_i$ *and* $\alpha(e_i) = d_i$ *for* $i \in \{0 \ldots n\}$,
- $\beta(t_i) = d_{i+1}$ *for* $i \in \{0 \ldots n\}$ *and* $\beta(t_n) = d_n$,
  $\beta(e_i) = d_i$ *for* $i \in \{0 \ldots n\}$,
- $\lambda(t_i) = init$ *for* $i \in \{0 \ldots n-1\}$ *and* $\lambda(t_n) = steady$ *and* $\lambda(e_i) = \epsilon$ *for* $i \in \{0 \ldots n\}$.

init denotes a preliminary phase during which the *base* clock must tick alone. *steady* is a phase where both clocks *base* and *delayed* become synchronous for ever.

The binary delay is a particular case of a more general synchronous expression called *FilteredBy* (denoted ▼). $f \triangleq c$ ▼ $u.(v)^\omega$ defines the clock f as a subclock of c according to two binary words u and v.

Definition 10 (Binary word). *A* binary word *w is a function,* $w : \mathbb{N}^* \to \{0, 1, \perp\}$*, such that* $(\exists l \in \mathbb{N}^*, w(l) = \perp) \implies ((\forall i > l)(w(i) = \perp))$*.*

Definition 11 (Length of a binary word). *If w is a binary word,* $len(w)$ *(denoted* $|w|$*) is called its* length*.* $len : (\mathbb{N}^* \to \{0, 1, \perp\}) \to \mathbb{N} \cup \{\omega\}$*. If* $\forall i \in \mathbb{N}^*, w(i) \neq \perp$ *then* $|w| = \omega$ *and w is said to be an* infinite *word, otherwise w is a* finite *word. When w is finite,* $|w| = min(i \in \mathbb{N}, w(i+1) = \perp)$*.*

Definition 12 (Exponentiation of a binary word). *Let n be a positive natural number (*$n \in \mathbb{N}^*$*). Let v be a finite binary word.* $w = v^n$ *is a finite binary word such that* $|w| = n * |v|$ *and* $\forall i \in 1..n, \forall j \in \{1..|v|\}, w(i * j) = v(j)$*.*

Definition 13 (Infinitely periodic binary word). *Let v be a finite binary word.* $w = (v)^\omega$ *is an infinite binary word such that* $\forall i \in \mathbb{N}, \forall j \in \{1..|v|\}, w(i * |v| + j) = v(j)$*.*

Definition 14 (Concatenation of binary words). *Let u and v be two binary words, u is finite.* $w = u.v$ *is a binary word such that* $(i \leq |u| \implies w(i) = u(i)) \wedge (i > |u| \implies w(i) = v(i - |u|))$*,* $\forall i \in \mathbb{N}^*$*. If v is infinite, then w is infinite. If v is finite, then w is finite and such that* $|w| = |u| + |v|$*.*

Expression 15 (Filtering). *If u and v are two finite binary words, the LTS for CCSL expression* FilteredBy *is defined as follows.* $f \triangleq c \blacktriangledown u.(v)^{\omega}$ *is the LTS* $Filter(u, v) = \langle S, T, s0, \alpha, \beta, \lambda \rangle$ *over* $A = \{zero, one, \epsilon\}$ *with* $n + 1$ *states s.t.,*

- $S = \{s_1, \ldots, s_{|u|+|v|}\}$, $T = \{t_1, \ldots, t_{|u|+|v|}, e_1, \ldots, e_{|u|+|v|}\}$, $s0 = s_1$,
- $\alpha(t_i) = s_i$ *for* $i \in \{1 \ldots |u| + |v|\}$,
- $\beta(t_i) = s_{i+1}$ *for* $i \in \{1 \ldots |u| + |v| - 1\}$ *and* $\beta(t_{|u|+|v|}) = s_{|u|+1}$,
- $\lambda(t_i) = zero$ *if* $u(i) = 0$ *and* $\lambda(t_i) = one$ *if* $u(i) = 1$, *for* $i \in \{1 \ldots |u|\}$
- $\lambda(t_{i+|u|}) = zero$ *if* $v(i) = 0$ *and* $\lambda(t_{i+|u|}) = one$ *if* $v(i) = 1$, *for* $i \in \{1 \ldots |v|\}$
- $\alpha(e_i) = s_i$ *and* $\beta(e_i) = s_i$ *and* $\lambda(e_i) = \epsilon$ *for* $i \in \{1 \ldots |u| + |v|\}$.

The label *one* denotes instants where both f and c tick together. The label *zero* when c ticks alone. Actually, Delay is just a particular case of filter with $u = 0^n$ and $v = 1$. Another interesting special case is when $u = 0^d$ and $v = 1.0^{p-1}$, for $d \in \mathbb{N}^*$ and $p \in \mathbb{N}$. This defines a **periodic pattern** $Periodic(d, p)$, where d is called the *offset* and p the *period*. $Delay(n)$ is also a particular periodic case with an offset of n and a period of 1.

Expression 16 (Sampling). *sampled* $\triangleq$ *trigger* ***sampledOn*** *base is the LTS* $Sampled = \langle S, T, s0, \alpha, \beta, \lambda \rangle$ *over* $A = \{base, trig, sample, all\epsilon\}$ *with 2 states such that,*

- $S = \{s_1, s_2\}$, $T = \{b, bs, sa_1, sa_2, t_1, t_2, e_1, e_2\}$, $s0 = s_1$,
- $\alpha(b) = \beta(b) = s_1$ *and* $\lambda(b) = base$,
- $\alpha(sa_i) = \beta(sa_i) = s_i$ *and* $\lambda(sa_i) = all$ *for* $i \in \{1 \ldots 2\}$,
- $\alpha(t_i) = s_i$ *and* $\beta(t_i) = s_2$ *and* $\lambda(t_i) = trig$ *for* $i \in \{1 \ldots 2\}$,
- $\alpha(bs) = s_2$ *and* $\beta(bs) = s_1$ *and* $\lambda(bs) = sample$,
- $\alpha(e_i) = \beta(e_i) = s_i$ *and* $\lambda(e_i) = \epsilon$ *for* $i \in \{1 \ldots 2\}$.

SampledOn is an expression that produces a clock s if and only if a *trigger* has ticked since the previous tick of a sampling clock (*base*). Labels *base* and *trig* respectively denote instants where clocks *base* and *trigger* tick alone. Label *sample* denotes instants where both clocks *base* and *sampled* tick simultaneously. Label *all* denotes instants where all the three clocks *base*, *trigger* and *sampled* tick simultaneously.

2.4   Unbounded Relations

Unbounded operators can be modeled with labeled transition systems that have an infinite but countable number of states.

Relation 17 (Precedence). *Precedence* $left \boxed{\prec} right$ *is a labeled transition system* $Precedes = \langle S, T, s0, \alpha, \beta, \lambda \rangle$ *over* $A = \{left, right, both, \epsilon\}$ *s.t.,*

- $S = \{p_i | i \in \mathbb{N}\}$, $T = \{l_i, r_i, lr_i, e_i | i \in \mathbb{N}\}$, $s0 = p_i$,
- $\alpha(l_i) = \alpha(e_i) = \alpha(lr_i) = p_i \wedge \alpha(r_i) = p_{i+1}, \forall i \in \mathbb{N}$,
- $\beta(l_i) = p_{i+1} \wedge \beta(r_i) = \beta(e_i) = \beta(lr_i) = p_i, \forall i \in \mathbb{N}$,
- $\lambda(l_i) = left \wedge \lambda(r_i) = right \wedge \lambda(lr_i) = both \wedge \lambda(e_i) = \epsilon, \forall i \in \mathbb{N}$.

Label *left* denotes instants where clock *left* must tick alone. Label *right* denotes instants where clock *right* must tick alone. Label *both* denotes instants where the two clocks must tick simultaneously. This operator is called *unbounded* because the drift between a and b is not bounded, *i.e.*, a can tick infinitely often without b ticking at all. This operator is not symmetrical. Even though a is unconstrained, b on the contrary is constrained to be always a little late compared to a. b is said to be slower than a, or a is faster than b.

2.5 Unbounded Expressions

In CCSL, there are two unbounded expressions that constrain neither a nor b: **Inf** and **Sup**.

Expression 18 (Infimum). $Inf(a, b)$ *is the labeled transition system* $Inf = \langle S, T, s0, \alpha, \beta, \lambda \rangle$ *over* $A = \{left, right, both, left\_inf, right\_inf, \epsilon\}$ *such that*

- $S = \{s_i | i \in \mathbb{Z}\}$, $T = \{inc_i, dec_i, t_i, e_i | i \in \mathbb{Z}\}$, $s0 = s_0$,
- $\alpha(inc_i) = \alpha(dec_i) = \alpha(both_i) = \alpha(e_i) = s_i$, $\forall i \in \mathbb{Z}$,
- $\beta(both_i) = \beta(e_i) = s_i$ *and* $\beta(inc_i) = s_{i+1}$ *and* $\beta(dec_i) = s_{i-1}$, $\forall i \in \mathbb{Z}$,
- $\lambda(inc_i) = left\_inf$ *if* $i \geq 0$, *and* $\lambda(inc_i) = left$ *if* $i < 0$, $\forall i \in \mathbb{Z}$
- $\lambda(dec_i) = right\_inf$ *if* $i \leq 0$, *and* $\lambda(dec_i) = right$ *if* $i < 0$, $\forall i \in \mathbb{Z}$
- $\lambda(both_i) = both$ *and* $\lambda(e_i) = \epsilon$, $\forall i \in \mathbb{Z}$

$Inf(a, b)$ is the slowest clock that is faster than both a and b. In most cases, $Inf(a, b)$ is neither a nor b but a clock that sometimes tick simultaneously with a (when a is in advance over b), sometimes it ticks simultaneously with b (when a is late compared to b) and sometimes it ticks simultaneously with a and b (when none of them precedes the other one). This LTS is infinite on both sides. By definition $Inf(a, b) \boxed{\preccurlyeq} a$ and $Inf(a, b) \boxed{\preccurlyeq} b$, which means that if $Inf(a, b)$ is somehow constrained (*i.e.*, by a synchronous operator like filter), then this propagates the constraint on both a and b. Additionally, the tickings of $Inf(a, b)$ are constrained (and bounded) by all the clocks faster than either a or b.

Expression 19 (Supremum). $Sup(a, b)$ *is a labeled transition system* $Sup = \langle S, T, s0, \alpha, \beta, \lambda \rangle$ *over* $A = \{left, right, both, left\_sup, right\_sup, both\_sup, \epsilon\}$ *such that*

- $S = \{s_i | i \in \mathbb{Z}\}$, $T = \{inc_i, dec_i, t_i, e_i | i \in \mathbb{Z}\}$, $s0 = s_0$,
- $\alpha(inc_i) = \alpha(dec_i) = \alpha(both_i) = \alpha(e_i) = s_i$, $\forall i \in \mathbb{Z}$,
- $\beta(both_i) = \beta(e_i) = s_i$ *and* $\beta(inc_i) = s_{i+1}$ *and* $\beta(dec_i) = s_{i-1}$, $\forall i \in \mathbb{Z}$,
- $\lambda(inc_i) = left$ *if* $i \geq 0$, *and* $\lambda(inc_i) = left\_sup$ *if* $i < 0$, $\forall i \in \mathbb{Z}$
- $\lambda(dec_i) = right$ *if* $i \leq 0$, *and* $\lambda(dec_i) = right\_sup$ *if* $i < 0$, $\forall i \in \mathbb{Z}$
- $\lambda(both_i) = both$ *if* $i \neq 0$ *and* $\lambda(e_i) = \epsilon$, $\forall i \in \mathbb{Z}$, *and* $\lambda(both_0) = both\_sup$

$Sup(a, b)$ is defined as the fastest clock that is slower than both a and b. In most cases, $Sup(a, b)$ is neither a nor b. By definition $a \boxed{\preccurlyeq} Sup(a, b)$ and $b \boxed{\preccurlyeq} Sup(a, b)$, which means that the constraints imposed on $Sup(a, b)$ do not directly impact neither a or b. However, whenever a clock c is known to be slower than either a or b, then it is also slower than $Sup(a, b)$, *i.e.*, $(\exists c$ such that $a \boxed{\preccurlyeq} c \lor b \boxed{\preccurlyeq} c) \implies Sup(a, b) \boxed{\preccurlyeq} c$.

3   Boundness Issues on CCSL Specifications

When several CCSL constraints are put in parallel, the composition is defined as
the synchronized product of the LTSs of the operators. However, since some of
the LTSs for the primitive operators are infinite (*e.g.,* Relation 17, or Expressions 18-19), the synchronized product might end up being infinite. However,
even though the product is potentially infinite, in some cases, only a finite subset of the synchronized product is reachable from the initial state. Section 3.1
shows a case where the product of infinite LTSs is finite. The algorithm used
in that subsection only terminates when the product is actually finite. The following section discusses a sufficient condition to decide whether the product
is actually finite and therefore whether the algorithm proposed in Section 3.1
actually terminates.

3.1   Finite Synchronized Product of Infinite LTSs

Considering n LTSs such that, for $i = 1, \ldots, n$, $\mathcal{A}_i = \langle S_i, T_i, s0_i, \alpha_i, \beta_i, \lambda_i \rangle$ and
one synchronization constraint $I \subseteq A_1 \times \ldots \times A_n$, the synchronized product of
$\mathcal{A}_i$ with respect to I is a labeled transition system $\langle S, T, s0, \alpha, \beta, \lambda \rangle$ over the set
I constructed as described in Algorithm 1.

Algorithm 1. Synchronized product through reachability analysis
Let $S \leftarrow \emptyset$, $T \leftarrow \emptyset$,
Let $s0 \leftarrow s0_1 \times \ldots \times s0_n$
Let $S' \leftarrow \{s0\}$
while S' *is not empty* {
    Let $st = st_1 \times \ldots \times st_n$ *be one element of* S'
    Let $S \leftarrow S \cup \{st\}$
    Let $S' \leftarrow S' \setminus \{st\}$
    $\forall t = \langle t_1, \ldots, t_n \rangle \in T_1 \times \ldots \times T_n$ *such that*
        $(\forall i \in \{1 \ldots n\})(\alpha_i(t_i) = st_i)$ *and* $\lambda_1(t_1) \times \ldots \times \lambda_n(t_n) \in I$ {
        Let $st' = \beta_1(t_1) \times \ldots \times \beta_n(t_n)$
        if $st' \notin S$ *then* $S' \leftarrow S' \cup \{st'\}$
        $T \leftarrow T \cup \{t\}$, $\alpha(t) = st$, $\beta(t) = st'$, $\lambda(t) = \lambda_1(t_1) \times \ldots \times \lambda_n(t_n)$,
    }
}

Theorem 1. *Algorithm 1 terminates if and only if the product has a finite number of states.*

Proof. S' is initialized with one state. At each iteration, one state st is removed
from S' and added to S. All the outgoing transitions of st are computed. If
C is the set of clocks, there are at most $2^{|C|}$ outgoing transitions. Some of
these transitions may be inconsistent. For each transition the target state st' is
computed and added to S' if not already present in S. This condition guarantees
that the same state is not visited twice. The algorithm terminates when S' is
empty. S' becomes empty when all the targeted state are already in S (have

already been visited). If the set of reachable states is finite then when all the states are in S then S' is necessarily empty. Therefore, when the set of reachable states is finite the algorithm terminates.

If there is an infinite number of reachable states, then S' is never empty and the algorithm never terminates.   □

Let us take as an example the following CCSL specification: $(a \boxed{\prec} b) \wedge (a' \triangleq a \$ 1) \wedge (b \boxed{\prec} a')$. This specification is defined as the synchronized product of *Precedes* (Relation 17), *Delay*(1) (Expression 9), *Precedes* (Relation 17 again).

Initially, $s0 = p_0 \times d_0 \times p_0$. The first *precedes* (state p_0) imposes b not to tick, the second *precedes* (state p_0) prevents a' from ticking whereas the *delay* (state d_0) only allows a to tick alone without a'. Therefore the only outgoing transition consists in making a ticks alone going into the state $s1 = p_1 \times d_1 \times p_0$. At this stage $S' = \{s1\}$ and $S = \{s0\}$. From $s1$, the first *precedes* (state p_1) does not impose any constraint while the second one (state p_0) still prevents a' from ticking. The *delay* (state $d1$) only allows making a and a' tick simultaneously. Since a' cannot tick, then a cannot tick either, so only b can tick leading to state $s2 = p_0 \times d_1 \times p_1$. Therefore $S = \{s0, s1\}$ and $S' = \{s2\}$. From $s2$, the first *precedes* prevents b from ticking, the second relation also prevents b from ticking. The *delay* only allows a and a' to tick simultaneously. Taking this (sole) solution leads to $s1$, which is already in S, so no new state is added to S'. S' being therefore empty, the algorithm terminates with $S = \{s0, s1, s2\}$ (Fig. 3).

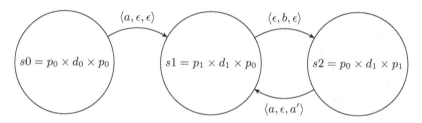

Fig. 3. CCSL alternation: synchronized product of two precedences and one delay

This particular construction is very frequent, it has been called **Alternation** and is denoted $a \boxed{\sim} b$. Increasing the delay from 1 to n makes a particular relation, called **bounded precedence** and denoted as $a \boxed{\prec_n} b$: $a \boxed{\sim} b \equiv a \boxed{\prec_1} b$. Previous works on CCSL were always assuming a bound for all CCSL operators, whereas here the bound is computed by reachability analysis. However, the (semi) algorithm sketched above may not terminate when the synchronized product is not finite.

3.2   A Sufficient Condition for Having a Bounded CCSL Specification

We have seen in the previous subsection that knowing in advance whether the synchronized product is finite is important. Indeed, when it is not finite,

Algorithm 1 does not terminate. This section discusses ways to determine whether the system is finite or not. The problem is similar to safety issues in process networks [9]. In process networks, a channel is *k-safe* it the channel can contain at most k tokens. A process network is k-safe if all its channels are k-safe. However, testing that a process network is k-safe is undecidable in the general case [10]. However, the problem becomes decidable if we restrict to a special kind of process networks, *i.e.*, the marked graphs [11] or their extension, the synchronous data flow (SDF) graphs [12].

So the idea here is to transform the CCSL specification into a Marked Graph (MG). Since MGs do not have any notion of simultaneous action, the full semantics of CCSL cannot be captured but it can still capture an abstraction of relative rates at which the clocks execute. Then, if the resulting MG is safe, the corresponding CCSL specification would be bounded. If it is not safe, then it does not say much of the CCSL specification since we consider only an approximation of CCSL semantics. Therefore, the safety of the underlying MG would only be a sufficient condition for a CCSL specification to be bounded.

For instance, let us look at Figure 4. The boxes are computation nodes (here clocks). The circles are unbounded channels working as a FIFO with non-blocking writes and blocking reads. CCSL clocks define triggering conditions just like MG computation nodes. CCSL constraints impose conditions that determine the relative rates at which each clock can tick. Similarly, MG edges also determine some dependencies and evolution rates between the MG actions.

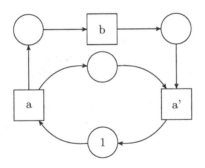

Fig. 4. CCSL delay as a Marked Graph

The arc (channel + edges) from a to b captures the specification $a \boxed{\prec} b$. Every time the node a executes, it produces one token (data) into its output communication channel. The node b can only execute if at least one token is available in its input channel. When b executes it consumes one token from its input channel. Therefore, the node b can compute its ith execution only after a has computed its ith execution. This is the exact same semantics as $a \boxed{\prec} b$ except that there is no temporal notion associated with MGs, and no notion of simultaneity, only of data dependency or causality.

The whole figure actually captures as a MG the CCSL specification used in the previous section: $(a \boxed{\prec} b) \wedge (a' \triangleq a \$ 1) \wedge (b \boxed{\prec} a')$. Each operator brings its own data/rate dependencies. The parallel composition of the operators consists in putting together all these dependencies. The cycle (a-a') at the bottom captures the delay. Both clocks must tick at the same rate but a is always one tick ahead of a'.

Classical results on data flow process networks show that this graph is 1-safe since all nodes are within a cycle and both cycles (a-b-a'-a and a-a'-a) have exactly one initial token. This means that the three clocks a, b and a' must execute at the same speed and therefore that the corresponding CCSL specification has a finite number of states. The state being the differences of ticks between the different clocks (the number of tokens in the places).

4   Example: CCSL for Capturing the Architecture, Application and Allocation

To illustrate the approach, we take an example inspired by [13], that was used for flow latency analysis on AADL[3] specifications [14]. However, with CCSL we are conducting different kinds of analyses, section 5 discusses some common points with classical real-time scheduling analysis.

4.1   Application

Figure 5 (on the top) considers a simple application described as a UML structured class. This application captures two inputs $in1$ and $in2$, performs some calculations (*step1*, *step2* and *step3*) and then produces a result *out*. This application has the possibility to compute *step1* and *step2* concurrently depending on the chosen execution platform. This application runs in a streaming-like fashion by continuously capturing new inputs and producing outputs.

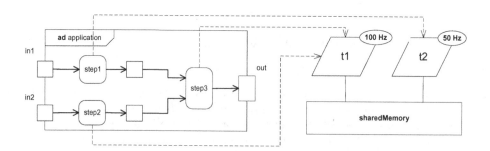

Fig. 5. Simple application

---

[3] AADL stands for Architecture & Analysis Description Language.

To abstract this application as a CCSL specification, we assign one clock to each action. The clock has the exact same name as the associated action (*e.g.,* *step1*). We also associate one clock with each input, this represents the capturing time of the inputs, and one clock with the production of the output (*out*). The successive instants of the clocks represent successive executions of the actions or input sensing time or output release time. The basic CCSL specification is:

$$in1 \boxed{\preccurlyeq} step1 \wedge step1 \boxed{\prec} step3 \tag{1}$$

$$in2 \boxed{\preccurlyeq} step2 \wedge step2 \boxed{\prec} step3 \tag{2}$$

$$step3 \boxed{\preccurlyeq} out \tag{3}$$

Eq. 1 specifies that *step1* may begin as soon as an input *in1* is available. Executing *step3* also requires *step1* to have produced its output. Eq. 2 is similar for *in2* and *step2*. Eq. 3 states that an output can be produced as soon as *step3* has executed. Note that CCSL precedence is well adapted to capture infinite FIFOs denoted on the figure as object nodes. Such a specification is clearly unbounded, therefore TimeSquare cannot perform any kind of exhaustive analysis and can only produce a particular schedule that matches the specification.

One way to reduce the state-space is to bound the drift between the inputs and the outputs. This means limiting the parallelism by slowing down the production of outputs when several computations are still on-going. This can easily be done by adding a CCSL constraint like Eq. 4.

$$Sup(in1, in2) \boxed{\sim} out \tag{4}$$

Reachability analysis as described in Section 3 tells us that the composition is still not bounded because bounds on $Sup(in1, in2)$ do not imply bounds on both *in1* and *in2*. To have a complete finite systems, we can for instance replace Eq. 4 by Eq. 5.

$$Inf(in1, in2) \boxed{\sim} out \tag{5}$$

By doing so, our reachability analysis algorithm converges and produces a bounded state-space.[4].

This kind of analysis is useful to detect invalid CCSL specifications. For instance, had we replaced Eq. 4 by Eq. 6 instead of Eq. 5, we would have obtained a finite result but with a typical case of deadlock in CCSL. Indeed, if from the initial state s_0, we decide to fire *in1* (resp. *in2*) alone, then Eq. 6 prevents $in1 + in2$ from ticking again before *out* ticks. But since *in2* (resp. *in1*) was not produced and therefore *step2* was not executed, then *step3* cannot execute either since it requires both *step1* and *step2*. If *step3* cannot execute, then *out* cannot be produced, which then results in a deadlock.

$$in1 + in2 \boxed{\sim} out \tag{6}$$

---

[4] The algorithm is available as an Eclipse update site on
http://timesquare.inria.fr/sts/update_site/

4.2　Execution Platform and Allocation

Once the application is designed, then CCSL can also be used to capture the execution platform. Figure 5 (bottom part) shows the selected execution platform: two tasks with different activation periods. The basic CCSL specification of the execution platform is given as follows:

$$t1 \triangleq ms \; \blacktriangledown \; (1.0^9)^\omega \qquad (7)$$

$$t2 \triangleq t1 \; \blacktriangledown \; (1.0)^\omega \qquad (8)$$

Eq. 8 is a pure logical relationship between $t1$ and $t2$ that states that thread $t2$ is twice slower than thread $t1$, *i.e.*, it is periodic on $t1$ with period 2 and offset 0. Eq. 7 is also a periodic relation, but relative to ms, a particular clock that denotes milliseconds. Being periodic on ms with a period of 10 makes $t1$ a 100 Hz clock and therefore $t2$ a 50 Hz clock.

When the execution platform is specified, the remaining task is to map the application onto the execution platform. In MARTE, this is done through an allocation. In CCSL, this is done by refining the two specifications with new constraints that specify this allocation. Since both *step2* and *step3* are allocated on the same thread, then their execution is exclusive (Eq. 9). Then, the thread being periodic, the inputs are sampled according to the period of activation of the threads (Eqs. 10-11). Then *step3* needs inputs from both *step1* and *step2* before executing but it can execute only according to the sampling period of $t1$ since *step3* is allocated to $t1$ (Eq. 12). Finally, all steps can only execute when their input data have been sampled (Eq. 13).

$$step2 \; \boxed{\#} \; step3 \qquad (9)$$

$$in1\_s \triangleq in1 \; \textbf{sampledOn} \; t1 \qquad (10)$$

$$in2\_s \triangleq in2 \; \textbf{sampledOn} \; t2 \qquad (11)$$

$$d3\_s \triangleq \textbf{Inf}(step1, step2) \; \textbf{sampledOn} \; t1 \qquad (12)$$

$$in1\_s \; \boxed{\preccurlyeq} \; step1 \wedge in2\_s \; \boxed{\preccurlyeq} \; step2 \wedge d3\_s \; \boxed{\preccurlyeq} \; step3 \qquad (13)$$

All these new constraints do not change anything on the finiteness of the whole system. They only reduce the set of possible executions. If the application specification was finite, then its allocated version is still finite. If it was infinite, they it remains infinite. Whether it is finite or not, TimeSquare can produce an execution of this specification (see Fig. 6). On this schedule the dashed arrows denote precedence relations, while the (red) vertical lines denote coincidence relations. Note that the fact that ms is a physical clock does not impact the calculus, it only impacts the visual representation of the schedule.

5　Related Work

The transformation of CCSL into labeled transition systems has already been attempted in [15,16]. However, in those attempts, the CCSL operators were

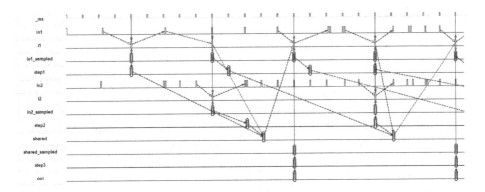

Fig. 6. A valid schedule for the allocated application (Fig. 5)

bounded because the underlying model-checkers cannot deal with infinite labeled transition systems. The purpose of this work is to deal with unbounded operators.

In [17], there was an initial attempt to provide a data structure suitable to capture infinite transition systems based on a lazy evaluation technique. A similar structure could be used in our case except that we consider clocks with only two states (instead of three): tick or stall. Clock death is still to be further explored.

The kind of applications addressed in section 4 is very close to models usually used in real-time scheduling theories. However, such theories usually rely on task models that abstract real applications. Originally they were rather simple (e.g., independent periodic tasks only for Rate Monotonic Analysis). Always more sophisticated models now appear in the literature. They are all based on numerous distinct parameters, providing numerical constraint values for timing aspects (dispatch time, period, deadline, jitter drift...). Tasks are considered as iterations of jobs (or jobs as instances of tasks). In our view, the successive timing values for characteristic feature of successive jobs can each be seen as a logical clock, and the time constraint relations between such clocks are usually expressed as simple equalities and bounded inequalities that fall well into the range of CCSL constructs descriptive power.

Classical (non real-time) scheduling, on its side, provides generally models where the initial constraints are less on timing and more on dependencies or on exclusive resource allocation. But resulting schedules are almost always of *modulo* periodic nature, here again matching the CCSL expressiveness.

Usually, authors [18,19,20] rely on "physical-by-nature" timing, found in theoretical models such as Timed Automata [21]. The distinctive difference is that timed automata assume a global physical time. Timed events are then constrained by value relations between so-called clocks (a different notion from our logical clocks), which are devices measuring physical time as it elapses.

Our work also bears some similarity with previous attempts by Alur and Weiss [22,23], which define schedules as infinite words expressed in regular expressions and then construct corresponding Büchi automata.

6   Conclusion

We have presented a state-based semantics of a kernel subset of CCSL, a language that relies on logical clocks to express logical and temporal constraints. Each CCSL operator (relation or expression) is defined as a label transition system, that may have either a finite or infinite number of states. The parallel composition of CCSL constraints is defined as the synchronized product of the primitive label transition systems. A (semi)algorithm is proposed to actually build the synchronized product of infinite transition systems by assuming that only a finite number of states are accessible in the product. The algorithm only terminates on that condition. Then a discussion is made on how data flow process networks could be used as a sufficient condition to decide that the synchronized product is actually finite. All the approach is illustrated on a simple example often used in AADL and where a simple application is allocated onto a two processor architecture. The work presented here improves on previous attempts to support exhaustive analyses of CCSL specifications. Indeed, previous works were only considering *a priori* bounded CCSL operators to guarantee the finiteness of the composition, while here no assumption is made on the boundness of primitive operators.

As a future work, we should extend and prove that data flow process networks can actually be used to detect finite compositions of any unbounded CCSL operators. Whereas it is pretty much clear that synchronous operators and regular asynchronous operators (like precedes, inf, sup) are always covered by synchronous data flow graphs, it is much less clear for mix operators like sampledOn. This aspect has only been briefly touched here to underline the fact that on simple examples our algorithm is actually useful.

References

1. OMG: UML Profile for MARTE, v1.0. Object Management Group. (November 2009) formal/2009-11-02
2. André, C., Mallet, F., de Simone, R.: Modeling time(s). In: Engels, G., Opdyke, B., Schmidt, D.C., Weil, F. (eds.) MODELS 2007. LNCS, vol. 4735, pp. 559–573. Springer, Heidelberg (2007)
3. André, C.: Syntax and semantics of the Clock Constraint Specification Language (CCSL). Research Report 6925, INRIA (May 2009)
4. DeAntoni, J., Mallet, F.: Timesquare: Treat your models with logical time. In: Furia, C.A., Nanz, S. (eds.) TOOLS 2012. LNCS, vol. 7304, pp. 34–41. Springer, Heidelberg (2012)
5. Benveniste, A., Caspi, P., Edwards, S.A., Halbwachs, N., Le Guernic, P., de Simone, R.: The synchronous languages 12 years later. Proc. of the IEEE 91(1), 64–83 (2003)
6. Le Guernic, P., Talpin, J.P., Le Lann, J.C.: Polychrony for system design. Journal of Circuits, Systems, and Computers 12(3), 261–304 (2003)
7. Lee, E.A., Sangiovanni-Vincentelli, A.L.: A framework for comparing models of computation. IEEE Transactions on Computer-Aided Design of Integrated Circuits and Systems 17(12), 1217–1229 (1998)
8. Arnold, A.: Finite transition systems - semantics of communicating systems. Int. Series in Computer Science. Prentice Hall (1994)

9. Kahn, G.: The semantics of simple language for parallel programming. In: IFIP Congress, pp. 471–475 (1974)
10. Buck, J.T.: Scheduling Dynamic Dataflow Graphs with Bounded Memory Using the Token Flow Model. PhD thesis, U.C. Berkeley (1993)
11. Commoner, F., Holt, A.W., Even, S., Pnueli, A.: Marked directed graphs. J. Comput. Syst. Sci. 5(5), 511–523 (1971)
12. Lee, E., Messerschmitt, D.: Synchronous data flow. Proceedings of the IEEE 75(9), 1235–1245 (1987)
13. Feiler, P.H., Hansson, J.: Flow latency analysis with the architecture analysis and design language. Technical Report CMU/SEI-2007-TN-010, CMU (June 2007)
14. Society of Automotive Engineers, SAE Architecture Analysis and Design Language (AADL) (June 2006) document number: AS5506/1
15. Yin, L., Mallet, F., Liu, J.: Verification of MARTE/CCSL time requirements in Promela/SPIN. In: ICECCS, pp. 65–74. IEEE Computer Society (2011)
16. Gascon, R., Mallet, F., DeAntoni, J.: Logical time and temporal logics: Comparing UML MARTE/CCSL and PSL. In: Combi, C., Leucker, M., Wolter, F. (eds.) TIME, pp. 141–148. IEEE (2011)
17. Romenska, Y., Mallet, F.: Lazy parallel synchronous composition of infinite transition systems. In: ICTERI. CEUR Workshop Proc., vol. 1000, pp. 130–145 (2013)
18. Amnell, T., Fersman, E., Mokrushin, L., Pettersson, P., Yi, W.: Times: A tool for schedulability analysis and code generation of real-time systems. In: Larsen, K.G., Niebert, P. (eds.) FORMATS 2003. LNCS, vol. 2791, pp. 60–72. Springer, Heidelberg (2004)
19. Krčál, P., Yi, W.: Decidable and undecidable problems in schedulability analysis using timed automata. In: Jensen, K., Podelski, A. (eds.) TACAS 2004. LNCS, vol. 2988, pp. 236–250. Springer, Heidelberg (2004)
20. Abdeddaim, Y., Asarin, E., Maler, O.: Scheduling with timed automata. Theoretical Computer Science 354(2), 272–300 (2006)
21. Alur, R., Dill, D.L.: A theory of timed automata. Theor. Comput. Sci. 126(2), 183–235 (1994)
22. Alur, R., Weiss, G.: Regular specifications of resource requirements for embedded control software. In: IEEE Real-Time and Embedded Technology and Applications Symp., pp. 159–168. IEEE CS (2008)
23. Alur, R., Weiss, G.: Rtcomposer:a framework for real-time components with scheduling interfaces. In: Int. Conf. on Embedded Software, EMSOFT 2008, pp. 159–168. ACM (2008)

Mining Dataflow Sensitive Specifications

Zhiqiang Zuo and Siau-Cheng Khoo

School of Computing, National University of Singapore
{zhiqiangzuo,khoosc}@nus.edu.sg

Abstract. Specification mining has become an attractive tool for assisting in numerous software development and maintenance tasks. The majority of these techniques share a common assumption: *significant program properties occur frequently*. Unfortunately, statistical inference alone produces too many program properties, many of which are found to be either insignificant or meaningless. Consequently, it becomes a laborious task for developers to separate semantically meaningful specifications from the rest. In this paper, we present a *semantic-directed specification mining* framework that injects in-depth semantics information into mining input. Specifically, we investigate the introduction of *dataflow semantics* to extract dataflow related sequences from execution traces, and demonstrate that mining specifications from these dataflow related sequences reduces a great number of meaningless specifications, resulting in a collection of specifications which are both semantically relevant and statistically significant. Our experimental results indicate that our approach can effectively filter out insignificant specifications and greatly improve the efficiency of mining. In addition, we also show that our mined specifications reflect the essential program behavior and can practically help program understanding and bug detection.

Keywords: specification mining, dataflow, dynamic analysis.

1 Introduction

Program comprehension has been found to be a crucial and time-consuming component of software maintenance task. While the comprehension task can be made easier by the presence of program specifications, the short time-to-market constraints, changing requirements, and poorly managed product evolution reduce the availability of such specifications, causing them to be incomplete, incorrect and obsoletely documented. One approach to address this challenge, which has been gaining much recognition by the software development community, is to automatically infer specifications of a system from its execution traces by a dynamic analysis process referred to as *specification mining* (see e.g., [2,9]).

The majority of these specification mining techniques adopt a statistical approach, and share a common assumption: *significant program properties occur frequently*. Unfortunately, statistical inference of program properties remains unsatisfactory. A prevalent obstacle to these specification mining techniques is that a great amount of meaningless specifications could be produced. It is painful

L. Groves and J. Sun (Eds.): ICFEM 2013, LNCS 8144, pp. 36–52, 2013.

and laborious to separate them from those semantically meaningful specifications. Consequently, the presence of these meaningless specifications will seriously weaken the quality of inferred specifications, and diminish the value of their use. Moreover, generating these meaningless patterns can consume enormous amount of mining time.

The underlying reason for these shortcomings is that statistical significance does not usually correlate to semantic significance. Some (in fact, many) semantically insignificant program specifications may be statistically significant, and get generated. As a case study, we investigated the behavioral change resulted from a bug fix from Compress revision 922299 to 922309. We attempted to understand the bug fix from the significant patterns which discriminate the two versions. Using traditional miner such as Iterative Pattern Miner [9], we obtain 63 discriminative patterns, many of which provide little value to our understanding of the change. On the other hand, by ensuring that calls in the patterns are dataflow related, we obtain just 4 discriminative patterns, all of which display the expected behavioral change of the revisions. We will elaborate this case study in more detail in Section 6.3.

Several researchers [17,15,14,12] have attempted to address this semantic-deficiency issue. However, none of these remedies proposed really incorporate in-depth semantic information (e.g., dataflow semantics) into specification mining. To address the lack of semantic significance and further improve the efficiency of specification mining, we introduce semantics information into mining, and propose a *semantic-directed specification mining* approach to discover semantically significant specifications from execution traces. The essential idea lies on the assumption that *semantically significant specification should be both semantically relevant and statistically significant*. Specifically, we first extract semantically relevant sequences from execution traces according to user-specific semantics. We next employ

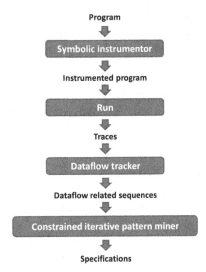

Fig. 1. Architecture of dataflow sensitive specification mining system

frequent pattern mining algorithm on these sequences to generate semantically significant specifications. We only extract semantically relevant sequences satisfying the user-specific semantics. All the semantically irrelevant events are filtered out in advance. Therefore, the mined specifications are all semantically significant. Moreover, the search space of frequent pattern mining is drastically reduced; hence mining becomes more efficient.

Here, we demonstrate this concept by focusing on a particular in-depth semantic-directed specification mining system called *dataflow sensitive specification mining*. A particular *dataflow semantic* over the runtime events is taken into consideration. We propose a dynamic, inter-procedural dataflow tracking analysis, which analyzes traces to extract dataflow related sequences. Lastly, we perform a novel constrained iterative pattern mining over these sequences to discover semantically significant iterative patterns. *Iterative pattern* is an important specification formalism [9]; it can be interpreted as interaction diagrams between classes/objects, and can be used to construct high-level scenario-based models such as live sequence chart (LSC) [3]. The architecture of our system is shown as Figure 1. The contributions of our work are as follows:

- We propose an in-depth semantic-directed specification mining approach, *dataflow sensitive specification mining* which injects dataflow semantics into mining to mine semantically significant specifications.
- We present an *dynamic, inter-procedural dataflow tracking analysis* to extract all the dataflow related sequences from execution traces.
- We develop a novel Apriori-like *constrained iterative pattern mining* algorithm to discover frequent patterns from a set of dataflow related sequences.
- We conduct experiments on five real-world subjects using our implemented prototype. The results show that our approach produces high-quality semantically significant specifications and scales to large real-world programs.

The remainder is organized as follows: We first discuss the literature in Section 2. Instrumentation is presented in Section 3. Section 4 and 5 introduce dataflow tracking analysis and constrained iterative pattern mining, respectively. We evaluate our approach in Section 6. Finally, Section 7 concludes.

2   Related Work

Semantics-Based Specification Mining: Ammons et al. [2] first coin the term *specification mining*. They collect execution traces and annotate them with intra-procedural data dependency information. Their technique then infers call interaction patterns as finite state machines. Thummalapenta and Xie [15] also analyze intra-procedural data dependency to filter out unrelated calls, while mining common exception-handling behavior. At the object-level semantics, Pradel and Gross [12] and Wasylkowski et al. [17] use object sharing relations to infer object usage models; Lee et al. [8] propose specification mining parameterized by object interactions. At predicate-level semantics, Ernst et al. develop Daikon [4] to discover from execution traces value-based invariants at specific program points. Our work differs from the above in the granularity of semantics information involved. Specifically, we track *fine-grained inter-procedural* dataflow information, and attempt to leverage complete dataflow relation to ensure that mined specifications are guaranteed to be dataflow relevant. We mine specifically *iterative patterns* introduced by Lo et al. [9], and extend their mining technique to ensure that patterns mined possess dataflow relations.

Program Slicing: Our work is related to dynamic data slicing [18,16] where only dynamic data dependences are considered ignoring control dependences. There are however differences: (1) Our mined patterns are both dataflow related and *statistically frequent*. (2) Mined patterns are viewed as program properties as they are derived from multiple traces, contrary to slices which are obtained from a single execution trace. (3) Mined patterns contain more abstract information than traditional slices as they only record method calls and returns. (4) Mined patterns capture more concrete runtime execution information than slices, because it can consist of multiple occurrences of the same statement in source code, whereas program slices record each statement uniquely. (5) Our result is a sequence or path of events instead of set or graph of statements for slicing.

3   Symbolic Instrumentation

The symbolic instrumentor conducts static instrumentation on the programs under analysis. The footprint produced by the instrumentor during execution is a sequence of *symbolic statements*, which enables tracking and reasoning of dataflow relations. Our trace is in Jimple format (refer to [13] for the formal Jimple grammar), which is a 3-address intermediate representation of Java in Soot framework[1].

```
public class Demo {
    public int invoke(int a, int b){
        int sa = square(a);
        int sb = square(b);
        return max(sa, sb) / 2;
    }

    private int square(int r){
        return r * r;
    }

    static int max(int i, int j){
        if(i > j) {return i;}
        else {return j;}
    }

    static void main(String[] args){
        new Demo().invoke(2, −1);
    }
}
```

Fig. 2. Demo

```
1:   $r1 = new Demo
2:   invoke $r1.<Demo:int invoke(int,int)>(2,−1)
3:       r0 := @this: Demo
4:       i0 := @parameter0: int
5:       i1 := @parameter1: int
6:       i2= invoke r0.<Demo:int square(int)>(i0)
7:           r0 := @this: Demo
8:           i0 := @parameter0: int
9:           $i1 = i0 * i0
10:          return $i1
11:      i3= invoke r0.<Demo:int square(int)>(i1)
12:          r0 := @this: Demo
13:          i0 := @parameter0: int
14:          $i1 = i0 * i0
15:          return $i1
16:      $i4= invoke <Demo:int max(int,int)>(i2,i3)
17:          i0 := @parameter0: int
18:          i1 := @parameter1: int
19:          return i0
20:      $i5 = $i4 / 2
21:  return $i5
```

Fig. 3. Trace

In this work, the events used to form iterative patterns are method calls and method returns. In order to capture precise and inter-procedural dataflow relations among events, we instrument five kinds of statements, namely IdentityStmt (e.g., statements 3, 4, 5), AssignStmt (9, 20), InvokeStmt (2, 6), ReturnStmt (10) and ThrowStmt, as they either contain dataflow information or represent

---

[1] http://www.sable.mcgill.ca/soot/

the desired events. They are necessary to be instrumented and included in the execution traces. Figure 2 and 3 show a demo program and its trace fragment, respectively.

4 Dataflow Tracking Analysis

We introduce our semantic analysis, called *dataflow tracking analysis* which takes as arguments the execution traces and produces a set of dataflow related sequences in this section.

4.1 Concepts

Consider the data dependence graph (Figure 4) of the example trace (Figure 3). As defined in [5], a statement s_1 is *data dependent* on a statement s_2 iff there is a variable x and a control flow path P from s_2 to s_1 such that x is defined at s_2, used at s_1, and not redefined along any subpath of P. In a data dependence graph, if s_1 is data dependent on s_2, then there is an edge (solid arrow line in Fig. 4) from s_2 to s_1. A *dataflow path* is a sequence of statements such that from each statement there is a data dependency edge to the next statement in the sequence. For instance, the graph

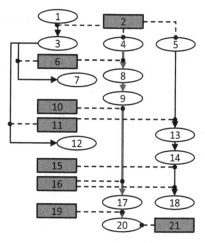

Fig. 4. Dynamic data dependence graph

(Figure 4) contains four dataflow paths. One of them is the sequence of statements $\langle 4, 8, 9, 17, 20 \rangle$ whose data dependency edges are marked as bold (and red).

While dataflow paths are defined over symbolic statements in the execution trace, our expected final results are sequences of events; i.e., method calls and method returns, shown as rectangles (with blue background) in the above graph. As an example, InvokeStmt 2 and ReturnStmt 21 represent a call event and a return event, respectively. We call the set of all events associated with a trace T an *event set*, and denote it by $E_{(T)}$. Considering the trace T in Figure 3, the event set $E_{(T)}$ contains those events which are highlighted in bold in Figure 3.

An event can have some arguments. For a call event, its arguments include the callee, its actual parameters, and all the class variables and instance variables used during method execution. Similarly, the arguments of a return event constitute the value returned by ReturnStmt, as well as all the defined or redefined class variables and instance variables during this method execution. The argument set of an event e is denoted by $A(e)$. An event e is *dataflow associated* with a dataflow path F iff there exists a statement s in F such that at least one argument of e is defined or used at s. In Figure 4, the dashed line shows this association. For example, the event $\langle Demo : int\ invoke\ (int, int)\rangle\_2^2$ in $E_{(T)}$ is dataflow associated with $F\ \langle 4, 8, 9, 17, 20\rangle$, since its first argument is used in statement 4.

Definition 1 ((Maximum) Dataflow Related Sequence). *Given a trace T, a dataflow path F of T, and the event set $E_{(T)}$, a sequence of events S ($\langle e_1, e_2, \ldots, e_n\rangle$) is a* dataflow related sequence *with respect to F iff $\forall e_k(k \in [1, n]), e_k \in E_{(T)}$ and $\forall e_i, e_j(i, j \in [1, n] \wedge i < j)$, the following holds:*

- *Temporal relation: e_i appears before e_j in T;*
- *Dataflow relation: e_i and e_j are both dataflow associated with F.*

Furthermore, S with respect to F is a maximum dataflow related sequence *iff there exists no dataflow related sequence S' of F such that S' is a super-sequence of S.*

From the above example, we can derive that the event sequence $\langle Demo : int\ invoke\ (int, int)\rangle\_2$, $\langle Demo : int\ square\ (int)\rangle\_6$, $R :\langle Demo : int\ square\ (int)\rangle\_10^3$, $\langle Demo : int\ max\ (int, int)\rangle\_16$, $R :\langle Demo : int\ max\ (int, int)\rangle\_19$, $R :\langle Demo : int\ invoke\ (int, int)\rangle\_21$ is a maximum dataflow related sequence with respect to F $\langle 4, 8, 9, 17, 20\rangle$.

4.2 Approach

The objective of the dataflow tracking analysis is to obtain all maximum dataflow related sequences by analyzing the symbolic traces. A naive way is to first construct the dynamic data dependence graph as an intermediate data and then traverse all the paths in the graph to get all dataflow related sequences. However, such an intermediate data is usually quite big. Its generation can severely affect the scalability of our analysis. Instead, our tracking analysis eliminates the generation of such intermediate data by directly outputting the dataflow related sequences while tracking each dataflow path. Briefly, we keep track of each dataflow path through analyzing the *use-def pairs*[4] statement by statement in chronological order. At the same time, we maintain one specific event list for each dataflow path. During the dataflow tracking, upon encountering an event which is associated with the currently tracked dataflow path, we append it to the end of the corresponding event list. When this dataflow path is completely tracked, the event list we maintain constitutes the desired maximum dataflow related sequence.

Our dataflow tracking analysis is called *stack-based scoped* because it dynamically maintains an "analysis stack" of "scopes" to help emulate the actual runtime execution. A scope mimics an activation record, which is pushed onto the

---

[2] It indicates the call event $\langle Demo : int\ invoke(int, int)\rangle$ represented by statement 2.

[3] "R" denotes the corresponding return event.

[4] A *use-def* pair (u, d), associates a statement in a program where variable u is used in defining variable d. For example, given the AssignStmt 14 in Figure 3, there is a *use-def* pair associated with this statement: $(i0, \$i1)$.

stack during method invocation and popped out at call return. It contains *triples* representing dataflow paths which are currently tracked by the analysis. Specifically, a triple is denoted (v_s, L, v_c) , where L is an event list forming a dataflow related sequence spanning across procedures with respect to the dataflow path currently tracked, v_s refers to the start variable of this dataflow path, v_c refers to the currently arrived variable. For efficiency, each scope is represented by a hash set consisting of triples, with hash keys constructed from the currently arrived variable of the triple.

Algorithm 1. Scoped Dataflow Tracking Analysis

Data: the trace T
Result: output all the maximum dataflow related sequences

```
1  foreach statement s in chronological order in trace T do
2      switch s do
3          case InvokeStmt(s)
4              S ← ∅;
5              push(S, Stack);
6              break;
7          case ReturnStmt(s)
8              Su ← pop(Stack);
9              Sd ← peek(Stack);
10             killAndGen(Su, Sd, s) ;        /* the top element Sd of Stack is updated */
11             for each t(vs, L, vc) ∈ Su do
12                 if isComplete(t) then output L;
13             break;
14         case IdentityStmt(s)
15             Su ← peek2nd(Stack) ;        /* peek at the second top element of Stack */
16             Sd ← peek(Stack);
17             killAndGen(Su, Sd, s);
18             break;
19         case AssignStmt(s)
20             Su ← collapse(Stack);
21             Sd ← peek(Stack);
22             killAndGen(Su, Sd, s);
```

As shown in Algorithm 1, the analyzer handles the trace statements in chronological order. When encountering an InvokeStmt, the analyzer pushes a new scope S into $Stack$ (lines 4-5). On the other hand, ReturnStmt indicates the end of the existing scope, and the analyzer pours out all the dataflow related sequences associated with the complete dataflow paths (lines 11-12). $isComplete(t)$ determines if t represents a complete dataflow path (i.e., completely tracked dataflow path). For each kind of statements encountered, the analyzer handles each variable (used variable and defined variable) active at the statement in its legitimate scope. Specifically, for ReturnStmt, the legitimate scope S_u for used variables is the scope popped from Stack. The legitimate scope S_d for defined variable is the top scope of $Stack$ (lines 8-10). For IdentityStmt, S_u is the second top element of $Stack$ (line 15). The top element of $Stack$ corresponds to S_d (line 16). Similarly, as for AssignStmt, S_d is the currently top element of $Stack$ (line 21). S_u is likely to be any scope in the $Stack$ (due to the liveness of instance variables or class variables). The analyzer searches $Stack$ from top towards bottom to obtain the desired triples; this is performed by the function `collapse`($Stack$).

Given a statement s and the corresponding legitimate scopes S_u and S_d, the analyzer uses the typical "kill-and-gen" dataflow analysis mechanism to update the stack by modifying the scope S_d at its top. More specifically, for each use-def pair (v_u, v_d) contained in statement s (where v_d is defined in s), the algorithm tries to extend the relevant dataflow paths in S_d (or create new dataflow paths when necessary) by generating new triples or to remove some paths the ending variable of which is redefined by killing the corresponding triples. Going through the algorithm, Lines 4-7 handle the case where a new dataflow path is created due to a constant or new instance; lines 9-14 extend the current dataflow paths through composing def-use chains. Lines 16-19 remove the triples whose currently arrived variable is redefined, and simultaneously output all the dataflow related sequences if t represents a complete dataflow path. Lastly, all generated triples are added into S_d (Line 20).

Algorithm 2. killAndGen(S_u, S_d, s)

Data: statement s, scope for used variable S_u, scope for defined variable S_d
Result: update the scope S_d which is the currently top element of $Stack$

```
1   P ← get_UD_Pairs(s) ;                    /* get the use-def pairs associated with s */
2   foreach use-def pair p(vu, vd) ∈ P do
3   |   GS ← ∅;
4   |   if vu is a constant or a new instance then
5   |   |   L' ← [ ];
    |   |   // A(e) is the set containing all the arguments of event e
6   |   |   if ∃ event e associated with s, vu ∈ A(e) then L' ← L' ++ [e];
7   |   |   GS ← GS ∪ {(vu, L', vd)} ;                     /* generate the new triple */
8   |   else
9   |   |   foreach t'(vs, L, vu) ∈ Su do   /* the currently arrived variable of t' is vu */
10  |   |   |   mark t' as incomplete;
11  |   |   |   L' ← L;
12  |   |   |   if ∃ event e associated with s, vu ∈ A(e) then L' ← L' ++ [e];
    |   |   |   // extend the tracked dataflow path and generate the new triple
13  |   |   |   GS ← GS ∪ {(vs, L', vd)}
14  |   |   end
15  |   end
16  |   foreach t(v*, L*, vd) ∈ Sd do          /* the currently arrived variable of t is vd */
17  |   |   if isComplete(t) then output L*;
18  |   |   Sd ← Sd − {t(v*, L*, vd)} ;                     /* kill the old triple */
19  |   end
20  |   Sd ← Sd ∪ GS;
21  end
```

---

5   Constrained Iterative Pattern Mining

In this section, we present constrained iterative pattern mining which mines the generated dataflow related sequences for final specifications.

5.1   Background

The concept of *iterative pattern* was first introduced by Lo et al. [9] to capture program behaviors involving repeated event occurrences (possibly caused by loop iterations). It forms the basis for temporal rules, which have been used to formulate specifications such as Live Sequence Chart (LSC) [3]. An iterative pattern is a sequence of events which must satisfy total-ordering [6] and one-to-one correspondence [7] properties. It can be identified by a set of instances, and one sequence can contain multiple instances. The following definition proposed in [9] expresses an iterative pattern instance in the form of Quantified Regular Expression [11] with ';' as concatenation operator, '[-]' as exclusion operator ([$-p, q$] means any event except p and q) and '*' as Kleene closure.

Definition 2 (Iterative Pattern Instance – QRE). *Given a pattern p^n ($\langle e_1 e_2 \ldots e_n \rangle$), a substring ($\langle f_1 f_2 \ldots f_m \rangle$) of a temporal sequence t ($\langle t_1 t_2 \ldots t_{end} \rangle$) in a sequence database SeqDB is an instance of p^n iff it can be expressed by the following QRE expression:*

$$e_1; [-e_1, \ldots, e_n]*; e_2; \ldots; [-e_1, \ldots, e_n]*; e_n.$$

Consider the following sequence representing a trace $\langle a,b,a,c,b,a,c,b \rangle$. The only three instances found in it for the iterative pattern $\langle a, b \rangle$ are substrings: $\langle a, b \rangle$ at index 1, $\langle a, c, b \rangle$ at index 3, and $\langle a, c, b \rangle$ at index 6. Note that $\langle a, b, a, c, b \rangle$ is not an iterative pattern instance, according to Definition 2.

The *support* of an iterative pattern P with respect to a sequence database *SeqDB* is the number of instances of pattern P in *SeqDB*. A pattern P is *frequent* if its support $sup(P)$ exceeds a specified threshold *min_sup*.

5.2   Constrained Iterative Pattern

We analyze traces to derive dataflow related sequences which constitute a sequence database in last section. Our goal is to mine all *dataflow relevant* and *frequent* iterative patterns from the derived *dataflow related sequence database*. For example, consider the trace (Fig. 3), the original sequence of events occurring in it is shown in Table 1(a)[5]. The generated dataflow related sequences by analyzing the trace are listed in Table 1(b). In order to track the origins of events in the dataflow sequences, we tag each event by the index with which the event is associated in the original event sequence (Table 1(a)). Let T be a trace. The sequence of all the events occurring in T is denoted by $L_{(T)}$. We refer to the ith event in $L_{(T)}$ as $L_{(T)}(i)$. We use $D_{(T)}$ to denote the dataflow related sequence database obtained

Table 1. (a).Sequence; (b).Database

(a)

Index	1	2	3	4	5	6	7	8
Event	a	c	d	c	d	e	f	b

(b)

Tid	Transaction					
0	1	2				
	a	c				
1	1	4				
	a	c				
2	1	2	3	6	7	8
	a	c	d	e	f	b
3	1	4	5	6		
	a	c	d	. e		

---

[5] For brevity, we use a single character to represent an event.

by analyzing the trace T. There are two problems we need take into account, which are not present in the original iterative pattern mining context.

The first problem is *Duplication*. Since one event in the trace may be involved in multiple dataflow paths, it may occur multiple times in the sequence database $D_{(T)}$. These duplicated events confuse the miner when it attempts to calculate the support of an event. In Table 1, the support for the event a, as determined from the trace, is 1; however, it appears 4 times in $D_{(T)}$. A normal miner working on the sequence database will count it as 4, instead of 1.

Another problem is *Correspondence*. Since we focus solely on dataflow relation, some events in traces may be omitted in dataflow related sequences. Therefore, an iterative pattern instance detected from the sequence database may not be a valid instance in the original trace. For instance, given the 2-pattern $\langle a, d \rangle$, we scan sequence transaction 3 in $D_{(T)}$ to obtain an iterative pattern "instance", $\langle 1, 5 \rangle$. But in fact, this "instance" does not correspond to a valid instance due to the additional 3rd event d in the trace. To address the above two problems, we introduce a novel definition of iterative pattern instance, called *constrained iterative pattern instance*.

Definition 3 (Constrained Iterative Pattern Instance). *Given a trace T and its event sequence $L_{(T)}$, an ordering number subsequence $\langle o_1 o_2 \ldots o_n \rangle$ of a sequence in $D_{(T)}$ is a* constrained iterative pattern instance *of $p^n(\langle e_1 e_2 \ldots e_n \rangle)$ iff the following conditions hold:*

- $\forall q \in [1, n], L_{(T)}(o_q) = e_q;$
- $\forall i \in [1, n-1], (\forall j \in (o_i, o_{i+1}), L_{(T)}(j) \notin p^n).$

Let's look at some examples. Consider sequence 3 in Table 1(b), the ordering number subsequence $\langle 1, 6 \rangle$ is a constrained iterative pattern instance of pattern $\langle a, e \rangle$. Specifically, $n = 2, o_1 = 1, o_2 = 6, \forall q \in [1, 2], L_{(T)}(o_q) = e_q$ and $\forall j \in (1, 6), L_{(T)}(j) \notin \langle a, e \rangle$ hold. On the other hand, $\langle 1, 5 \rangle$ is not a constrained iterative pattern instance of pattern $\langle a, d \rangle$, since for $3 \in (1, 5), L_{(T)}(3) = d \in \langle a, d \rangle$, which contradicts the second condition in the definition. Every constrained iterative pattern instance is represented by a unique ordering number subsequence. Each unique number indexes one unique event occurrence in the trace. Therefore, we can determine the duplication by comparing the instances (sequences of ordering numbers). Besides, in our definition, we do not only check the events in sequences (i.e. the first condition), but also consider the events discarded by the sequences (i.e. the second condition). We can ensure that any constrained iterative pattern instance is an iterative pattern instance in the original trace. The correspondence problem is thus solved.

5.3 Apriori Property

Apriori property has been introduced to prune the search space of mining algorithm [1]. It states that if a pattern p is not frequent, then it is not possible for any super-pattern of p to be frequent. Thus, it is unnecessary to search for any frequent super-pattern of p. Due to the specific constraints of iterative patterns, the original Apriori property does not hold. Here, we propose a special Apriori property to prune search space. We first provide some definitions.

Definition 4 (Prefix_pattern, Suffix_pattern, Infix_pattern). *For a k-pattern $p^k(\langle e_1, e_2, \ldots, e_k \rangle)$, its prefix_pattern is defined as $pre\_p^{k-1}(\langle e_1, e_2, \ldots, e_{k-1} \rangle)$; its suffix_pattern as $suf\_p^{k-1}(\langle e_2, e_3, \ldots, e_k \rangle)$; and its infix_pattern as $in\_p^{k-1}(\langle e_1, \ldots, e_{i-1}, e_{i+1}, \ldots, e_k \rangle)$, where $i \in [2, k-1]$ and $e_i \notin in\_p^{k-1}$.*

For example, given a 5-pattern $p^5(\langle A, B, C, D, B \rangle)$, it has the prefix_pattern $pre\_p^4(\langle A, B, C, D \rangle)$, suffix_pattern $suf\_p^4(\langle B, C, D, B \rangle)$, and infix_patterns $in\_p_4^4(\langle A, B, D, B \rangle)$ and $in\_p_2^4(\langle A, B, C, B \rangle)$. However, $\langle A, C, D, B \rangle$ is not an infix_pattern of p^5 since $B \in \langle A, C, D, B \rangle$. Having the above definitions, we arrive at the following specific Apriori property possessed by the (constrained) iterative pattern. We here omit the proof due to space constraint.

Theorem 1 (Apriori Property). *If a pattern p^k is frequent, then its prefix_pattern, suffix_pattern and all infix_patterns are frequent.*

5.4   Algorithm

Algorithm 3. CIPM($D_{(T)}, min\_sup, min\_den$)

Input: sequence database $D_{(T)}$, support threshold min_sup, density threshold min_den
Output: a set containing all frequent closed patterns F_{closed}

1 $F_1 \leftarrow \{p^1 \mid sup(p^1) \geq min\_sup\}$;
2 **for** $(k \leftarrow 2; F_{k-1} \neq \emptyset; k++)$ **do**
3 $\quad$ $C_k \leftarrow$ **apriori_gen**(F_{k-1});
4 $\quad$ $F_k \leftarrow$ **apriori_count**(C_k, min_sup);
5 $\quad$ $F_k \leftarrow$ **prune_density**(F_k, min_den);
6 $\quad$ $F_{closed} \leftarrow$ **process_closed**(F_k, F_{closed});
7 **end**
8 **return** F_{closed};

Algorithm 3 gives the mining algorithm involving two main phases. The first phase simply scans the sequence database once to detect all frequent singleton patterns (Line 1). The second phase is an iterative phase (Lines 2-7), which consists of four subprocedures. Firstly, the set of frequent $(k-1)$-patterns F_{k-1} is used to generate candidate k-patterns C_k using the apriori_gen function. Secondly, an apriori_count function is called to count the support of each candidate pattern in C_k. A set of frequent patterns F_k is thus generated. Next, we apply a density-based pruning strategy to prune the search space further and finally discard all non-closed iterative patterns.

Apriori Candidate Generation. This procedure consists of two steps, namely *join* and *prune*. First, in the *join* step, we check each pair of frequent $(k-1)$-patterns $p_i^{k-1}(\langle e_1, e_2, \ldots, e_{k-1} \rangle)$ and $p_j^{k-1}(\langle f_1, f_2, \ldots, f_{k-1} \rangle)$ in F_{k-1} to see if the prefix_pattern $pre\_p_i^{k-2}\langle e_1, e_2, \ldots, e_{k-2} \rangle$ of p_i^{k-1} is same as suffix_pattern $suf\_p_j^{k-2}\langle f_2, f_3, \ldots, f_{k-1} \rangle$ of p_j^{k-1}. If so, the candidate k-pattern $\langle f_1, f_2, f_3, \ldots, f_{k-1}, e_{k-1} \rangle$ will be generated by joining the two frequent $(k-1)$-patterns p_i^{k-1}

and p_j^{k-1}. Besides the prefix_pattern and suffix_pattern, all the infix_patterns of the given frequent pattern must be also frequent according to the Apriori Property. Next, in the *prune* step, we delete all candidate patterns whose infix_patterns are not all in F_{k-1}.

Apriori Support Counting. In order to address the duplication problem described earlier, we maintain an instance set $V(p^k)$ for each candidate pattern p^k, which contains all the already generated instances of p^k. We scan each sequence transaction to find all the constrained iterative pattern instances $Ins(p^k, tid)$ of pattern p^k in sequence tid. We then check each instance in $Ins(p^k, tid)$ to see if it has already been in $V(p^k)$ (*i.e.* whether it is duplicate or not). If not, we add the instance to $V(p^k)$ and increment the support of p^k. After scanning all the transactions, we compare the support of each candidate pattern p^k with the threshold *min_sup*. Finally, the frequent pattern set F_k is returned.

Density Pruning. We observed that the patterns whose density are low do not contain much information. In addition, mining these patterns can be costly. We elect to perform pruning on the basis of patterns' density[6]. The pattern whose density is lower than a threshold *min_den* is pruned out.

Closed Iterative Pattern Processing. The closed iterative pattern processing addresses the "compactness" issue of mined patterns by substantially reducing patterns reported while preserving the complete information on frequent patterns. We only keep closed iterative patterns based on the definition 5.

Definition 5 (Closed Iterative Pattern). *A frequent k-pattern p^k is closed iff there exists no super-pattern p^{k+1} such that: p^k and p^{k+1} has the same support and p^k is the prefix_pattern or suffix_pattern or infix_pattern of p^{k+1}.*

6   Empirical Evaluation

We conducted the experiments on five real-world programs using our implemented prototype. Table 2 shows the subjects used. All experiments were conducted on an Intel Quad 2.83GHz PC with 4GB main memory running Windows XP Professional.

Table 2. Characteristics of subject programs

Subject	Version	#LOC	#Class	#Method	Description
JDepend	2.9.1	2,723	18	224	Java dependency analyzer
Libsvm	3.1	3,188	21	98	SVM implementation
Compress	1.3	9,629	59	502	Commons Compress library
PMD	4.2.5	66,881	720	4,991	Java source code analyzer
Fop	0.95	185,186	1,313	9,840	XSL-FO to PDF transformer

---

[6] $den(p^k) = $ #(distinct events in p^k) / k.

6.1   Runtime Performance of Dataflow Tracker

Table 3 provides the detailed information on trace generation and dataflow tracking analysis. Even though the number of events (#Event) or statements (#Stmt)
in traces is huge, our analysis managed to complete its task for each subject
within a minute. Figure 5 shows the execution time of dataflow tracker against
the number of statements analyzed in traces. It shows that the time required
to track the dataflow is roughly linear with respect to the number of analyzed
statements. Our dataflow tracking analysis is scalable to large traces.

Table 3. Performance of dataflow tracking analysis

Subject	#Test	#Trace	#Stmt	#Event	Size(MB)	Time(s)	#Seq	AL^0	Time(s)
JDepend	5	5	494k	93k	57.4	5	73k	6.9	5
Libsvm	5	5	854k	36k	75.3	7	8k	5.7	5
Compress	5	5	949k	254k	155	10	156k	4.7	10
PMD	4	8	2119k	498k	235	17	299k	26.8	20
Fop	5	5	3480k	621k	417	42	535k	10.6	53

In the table the top spanning headers are: Trace Generation (over #Stmt, #Event, Size(MB), Time(s)) and Dataflow Analysis (over #Seq, AL^0, Time(s)).

6.2   Performance Comparison

Table 4 demonstrates the performance comparison of two different specification mining
schemes in terms of number of patterns mined
and time taken by mining. One is our dataflow
sensitive specification mining (DSSM), which
mines only semantically significant patterns
over the generated dataflow related sequences
using our constrained iterative pattern miner.
Another directly performs the original itera-

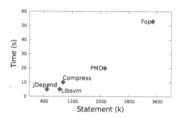

Fig. 5. Execution time against the
number of statements

tive pattern mining (IPM) over the original sequence of events occurring in the
trace. We further verified that *the set of patterns generated by DSSM is a proper
subset of that generated by IPM.*

For each subject, we choose three absolute support thresholds to carry out
the experiments. We choose the same density value (0.6) in all experiments. The
asterisk "*" denotes a number which is more than 10 times bigger than the
corresponding number of patterns generated by DSSM. The dash "-" denotes
a time longer than 3600 seconds. As can be seen from Table 4, the number of
patterns mined by IPM is much larger than that mined by DSSM. The ratios are
mostly greater than 10. This indicates that our approach can effectively filter
out dataflow irrelevant patterns. As a result, the effectiveness of the specifications will be substantially increased. We will further verify it in Section 6.3. In
addition, the time cost of DSSM is much lower than that of IPM, at least 10
times faster in most cases. This shows that the efficiency of specification mining
can be greatly improved.

---

^{0} "AL" represents the average length of these generated dataflow related sequences.

Table 4. Performance comparison

		DSSM		IPM		Ratio(IPM/DSSM)	
Subject	Support	#Pattern	Time(s)	#Pattern	Time(s)	#Pattern	Time
JDepend	15	221	17	*	-		
	30	181	15	*	-	>10	
	50	54	9	*	-		
Libsvm	5	130	16	*	-	>10	
	10	115	15	*	-		
	30	48	7	175	99	3.6	>10
Compress	15	79	22	*	-		
	50	44	19	*	-	>10	
	100	32	18	*	-		
PMD	150	205	97	*	-	>10	
	250	100	45	*	-		
	450	32	35	149	-	4.7	>10
Fop	400	211	171	*	-		
	1000	70	81	*	-	>10	
	1500	21	60	636	1342		

6.3   Case Studies

Through two case studies, we shall demonstrate how dataflow sensitive specifications can be used to highlight changes in software evolution.

Compress Revision 922299-922309: Figure 6 illustrates the code changes between revision 922309 and 922299 in class ZipUtil in order to fix a bug (COMPRESS-100). "+" denotes the additional code in new revision. "-" denotes the code deleted from the old revision. Specifically, it primarily involves two methods: the added method *supportsDataDescriptorFor* and changed method *supportsEncryptionOf*.

```
+   static boolean supportsDataDescriptorFor(ZipArchiveEntry entry){
+       return !entry.getGeneralPurposeBit().usesDataDescriptor()
+          || entry.getMethod() == ZipArchiveEntry.DEFLATED;
+   }

    static boolean supportsEncryptionOf(ZipArchiveEntry entry){
-       return !entry.isEncrypted();
+       return !entry.getGeneralPurposeBit().usesEncryption();
    }
```

Fig. 6. Code changes between revision 922309 and 922299 in ZipUtil

We perform our dataflow sensitive specification mining (DSSM) on two revisions using the same input and derive 4 discriminative patterns shown in Table 5 (against the common patterns mined from both revisions). The first three are additional patterns mined from the new revision. The fourth pattern is deleted from the old revision. Apparently, the first two additional patterns capture the added behavior of method *supportsDataDescriptorFor*. The third additional pattern and the deleted pattern correspond to the changes of *supportsEncryptionOf*.

To further demonstrate the applicability of our approach (DSSM), we compare with the original iterative pattern mining (IPM). Similarly, we employ IPM

Table 5. Four discriminative patterns between revision 922309 and 922299

⟨ZipUtil: supportsDataDescriptorFor(...)⟩; ⟨ZipArchiveEntry: getGeneralPurposeBit()⟩; R: ⟨ZipArchiveEntry: getGeneralPurposeBit()⟩; ⟨GeneralPurposeBit: usesDataDescriptor()⟩;	⟨ZipUtil: supportsDataDescriptorFor(...)⟩; ⟨ZipArchiveEntry: getMethod()⟩; R: ⟨ZipArchiveEntry: getMethod()⟩;
⟨ZipUtil: checkRequestedFeatures(...)⟩; ⟨ZipUtil: supportsEncryptionOf(...)⟩; ⟨ZipArchiveEntry: getGeneralPurposeBit()⟩; R: ⟨ZipArchiveEntry: getGeneralPurposeBit()⟩; ⟨GeneralPurposeBit: usesEncryption()⟩;	⟨ZipUtil: checkRequestedFeatures(...)⟩; ⟨ZipUtil: supportsEncryptionOf(...)⟩; ⟨ZipArchiveEntry: isEncrypted()⟩; R: ⟨ZipArchiveEntry: isEncrypted()⟩;

to two revisions using the same input. With the same threshold setting, IPM generates much more discriminative patterns (48 additional and 15 deleted patterns) than DSSM (3 additional and 1 deleted pattern). Although these patterns include the four semantically significant patterns, other semantically meaningless patterns would seriously weaken the efficacy of inferred specifications.

Compress Revision 911465-911467: Table 6 shows an additional pattern we discovered from revision 911467 for Compress. It describes a scenario that *fill* should call *count* to update the number of bytes read. It corresponds to a bug fixing. Specifically, in the previous revision 911465, *fill* missed calling *count* (COMPRESS-74).

From another perspective, this case shows that our approach can assist in detecting bugs to some extent. When performing our approach on the older buggy revision (911465), we failed to discover the above pattern. Specifically, 7 dataflow related patterns are produced. None of them contain method *fill* or *count*. A programmer with knowledge of how *fill* and *count* interact will easily find this bug due

Table 6. An additional pattern from revision 911467

⟨zip.ZipArchiveInputStream: void fill()⟩;
⟨ArchiveInputStream: void count(int)⟩;
⟨ArchiveInputStream: void count(long)⟩;
R: ⟨ArchiveInputStream: void count(long)⟩;
R: ⟨ArchiveInputStream: void count(int)⟩;
R: ⟨zip.ZipArchiveInputStream: void fill()⟩;

to lack of the pattern by checking the mining results. Compared with our approach, IPM reports much more patterns (151 patterns) under the same setting. 11 of them involve method *fill*. Clearly, manually checking 11/151 patterns needs much more efforts than checking 0/7 patterns.

6.4   Discussion

Threats to Validity: The number of subjects tested remains small, possibly causing a threat to external validity of our experiments. To mitigate this, we ensure that they are all real-world programs from different domains with varying sizes. A potential threat to internal validity lies with the choice of the support and density thresholds used during mining. Here, we take into account the characteristics of the sequence data (e.g., number of sequences, average sequence length) while choosing these absolute support values, to limit the unnecessary randomness. Lastly, we note that the effectiveness of applying dataflow sensitive specifications to characterize program changes is prominent only when the program change is indeed dataflow related, and can be represented at call level.

Limitations: Firstly, we notice that symbolic instrumentation may suffer from high time and space overheads, especially for long-running programs. This can be circumvented by eliminating trace generation through fusing dataflow tracking analysis with instrumentation. In addition, we can restrict instrumentation activities only on entrances to basic blocks (in the sense of control flow graph), thus minimizing the cost. Secondly, we did not instrument JVM's library, and assume that there is no dataflow through JVM calls. On the other hand, our experiments do not indicate any loss of valuable specifications due to this approximation. Thirdly, duplication of events at multiple dataflow paths can affect the scalability of our approach, and we intend to apply incremental mining [10] to eliminate this limitation. Finally, the approach does not discover interactive behavior among multiple threads, which will remain one of the future work.

7   Conclusion

We propose a novel semantic-directed specification mining scheme called *dataflow sensitive specification mining*. Using this approach, we discover frequent dataflow related iterative patterns from the program executions as specifications. The empirical evaluation shows that our approach is (1) effective in filtering off semantically irrelevant patterns, (2) efficient in generating semantically significant patterns, and (3) practical in program understanding and bug detection.

Acknowledgments. We are grateful to Wei-Ngan Chin and Jin Song Dong for their valuable comments and suggestions on the early GRP version of this work. Thanks also go to David Lo, Sandeep Kumar, Chengnian Sun, Narcisa Milea, Anh Cuong Nguyen, Yongzheng Wu and Xingliang Liu for their insightful discussions during our group meeting or lunch time. This work is partially supported by a research grant R-252-000-484-112.

References

1. Agrawal, R., Srikant, R.: Mining sequential patterns. In: ICDE 1995 (1995)
2. Ammons, G., Bodík, R., Larus, J.R.: Mining specifications. In: POPL 2002 (2002)
3. Damm, W., Harel, D.: Lscs: Breathing life into message sequence charts. Tech. rep.
4. Ernst, M.D., Cockrell, J., Griswold, W.G., Notkin, D.: Dynamically discovering likely program invariants to support program evolution. TSE (2001)
5. Horwitz, S., Reps, T., Binkley, D.: Interprocedural slicing using dependence graphs. In: PLDI 1988, NY, USA (1988)
6. ITU-T: Itu-t recommendation z.120: Message sequence chart (msc) (1999)
7. Kugler, H., Harel, D., Pnueli, A., Lu, Y., Bontemps, Y.: Temporal logic for scenario-based specifications. In: Halbwachs, N., Zuck, L.D. (eds.) TACAS 2005. LNCS, vol. 3440, pp. 445–460. Springer, Heidelberg (2005)

8. Lee, C., Chen, F., Roşu, G.: Mining parametric specifications. In: ICSE 2011, NY, USA (2011)
9. Lo, D., Khoo, S.C., Liu, C.: Efficient mining of iterative patterns for software specification discovery. In: KDD 2007, New York, NY, USA (2007)
10. Masseglia, F., Poncelet, P., Teisseire, M.: Incremental mining of sequential patterns in large databases. Data Knowl. Eng. (2003)
11. Olender, K.M., Osterweil, L.J.: Cecil: A sequencing constraint language for automatic static analysis generation. IEEE Trans. Softw. Eng. (1990)
12. Pradel, M., Gross, T.R.: Automatic generation of object usage specifications from large method traces. In: ASE 2009. IEEE Computer Society, USA (2009)
13. Raja, V.R.: Soot: A Java Bytecode Optimization Framework. Master's thesis, School of Computer Science, McGill University, Montreal (2000)
14. Thummalapenta, S., Xie, T.: Alattin: Mining alternative patterns for detecting neglected conditions. In: ASE 2009. IEEE Computer Society, USA (2009)
15. Thummalapenta, S., Xie, T.: Mining exception-handling rules as sequence association rules. In: ICSE 2009, Washington, DC, USA (2009)
16. Tip, F.: A survey of program slicing techniques. Tech. rep. (1994)
17. Wasylkowski, A., Zeller, A., Lindig, C.: Detecting object usage anomalies. FSE 2007 (2007)
18. Zhang, X., Gupta, R., Zhang, Y.: Precise dynamic slicing algorithms. In: ICSE 2003 (2003)

A Proof Slicing Framework for Program Verification

Ton Chanh Le, Cristian Gherghina, Razvan Voicu, and Wei-Ngan Chin

Department of Computer Science, National University of Singapore

Abstract. In the context of program verification, we propose a *formal frame-work* for *proof slicing* that can aggressively reduce the size of proof obligations as a means of performance improvement. In particular, each large proof obliga-tion may be broken down into smaller proofs, for which the overall processing cost can be greatly reduced, and be even more effective under *proof caching*. Our proposal is built on top of existing automatic provers, including the state-of-the-art prover Z3, and can also be viewed as a re-engineering effort in proof decomposition that attempts to avoid large-sized proofs for which these provers may be particularly inefficient. In our approach, we first develop a calculus that formalizes a *complete proof slicing* procedure, which is followed by the devel-opment of an *aggressive proof slicing* method. Retaining completeness is impor-tant, and thus in our experiments the complete method serves as a backup for the cases when the aggressive procedure fails. The foundations of the aggressive slicing procedure are based on a novel lightweight annotation scheme that cap-tures *weak links* between sub-formulas of a proof obligation; the annotations can be inferred automatically in practice, and thus both methods are fully automated. We support our theoretical developments with experimental results, which show significant improvements in the verification of complex programs, where richer specifications are often captured via loosely connected static properties.

1 Introduction

A significant challenge in the area of program verification is posed by the ever in-creasing number and complexity of proof obligations that need to be discharged by automated theorem provers. To overcome this challenge, a number of previous investi-gations have considered the approach of "shrinking" the generated proof obligations as a means of speeding up the solvers. [14] splits the proof obligations based on control flow to get smaller proofs. [16,22,23] detect and discard information that is not relevant to the problem at hand, thus streamlining the proof process. When this streamlining is performed aggressively, the size of the resulting proof obligations may be greatly reduced, leading to opportunities for significant performance improvement. In this con-text, an important technique is that of *proof caching* [10], which reuses proof results when multiple instances of the same sub-formulas are encountered. While the idea of *proof slicing* is not new in the context of automatic theorem provers, we believe that the procedure is more effectively carried out in the larger scope of program verification. In this regards, we make new contributions in three key directions, namely (i) the develop-ment of a *formal foundation* for proof slicing mechanisms, (ii) a general application of proof slicing that is *prover-independent* and tailored to *program verification*, and (iii) an

L. Groves and J. Sun (Eds.): ICFEM 2013, LNCS 8144, pp. 53–69, 2013.
© Springer-Verlag Berlin Heidelberg 2013

annotation scheme that allows a more aggressive application of the mechanism, leading to improved performance.

A formal foundation in proof slicing is important for providing an avenue towards a more rigorous investigation into the field. To that end, we first develop a *complete* calculus for automatic slicing, which serves as a foundation for the implementation of our tool. Importantly, apart from completeness, this calculus also enjoys properties of convergence and completeness, which are crucial for its trustworthiness, and its potential for efficient implementation.

One important application area is that of program verification, whereby a typical approach is to employ a program verifier that processes the code of interest, annotated with pre/post-conditions, in order to produce a set of proof obligations that are subsequently passed on to off-the-shelf theorem prover. These proof obligations are fundamentally of the form $P \implies Q$, whereby each P is an antecedent that captures some current program state, while Q is a goal (or assertion) that has to be proven. Since proof slicing remains complete only when the antecedent is satisfiable, and since satisfiability checks typically add a non-negligible overhead, existing state-of-the-art theorem provers, with formula reduction techniques such as relevancy propagation [4], or labelled splitting [8], do not employ this mechanism. However, with our slicing mechanism placed in-between the verifier and the theorem prover, we ensure that the satisfiability checks of antecedents are *incremental* and with low overhead, which is key to good performance.

As a further improvement, we designed an *annotation scheme* that captures *constraint linking properties*, that is, variable-sharing dependencies between interpreted atoms (*i.e.*, constraints) of a proof obligation; this scheme enables an *aggressive slicing* procedure. We believe that such an approach allows proof slicing to be viewed as a modular and extensible mechanism, rather than as a black box with limited functionality. This point is particularly poignant, as a good annotation scheme is also the basis for effective *annotation inference mechanisms*. These mechanisms can, in general, be completely automatic; several examples can be found in the experimental results section.

We summaries our research contributions, as follows:

- A formal and general framework for uniformly describing different proof slicing mechanisms (Sec. 3). We prove the proposed slicing mechanisms to be both sound and convergent, in the sense that, while non-deterministic, the framework always produces the same result for a given input. The immediate application of this framework is a *complete slicing* procedure (Sec. 4).
- An annotation scheme for slicing that is suitable for a variety of logics (Sec. 5). This is aimed at allowing parts of formulas to be identified as carrying information *linking* distinct properties. Then, an *aggressive proof slicing* mechanism can leverages on annotation schemes to obtain further reductions of the proof slices (Sec. 6). This also creates the opportunity for applying proof caching, which is particularly effective with smaller-sized proofs.
- An implementation of the both proof slicing mechanisms within an existing automated program verification system (Sec. 7). Our experiments show compelling performance gain of about 61% for complete proof slicing, and a further gain of 74% for aggressive proof slicing (see Fig. 7).

2   Proof Slicing for Program Verification

Depending on the context, we shall use the term "slicing" to denote either formula slicing or proof slicing. Formula slicing is the partitioning of a formula into "slices" – sub-formulas that group together related constraints. Two slices are said to be *disjoint* if they do not share any common variables, otherwise they are said to be *overlapping*. Proof slicing is the partitioning of a proof obligation into smaller sub-proofs to reduce the proof's complexity, thus improving performance of discharging proofs.

In the context of program verification, there are typically two major kinds of proof obligations, namely: (i) *Entailment checking*, of the form $P \vdash Q$ and (ii) *Unsatisfiability checking*, of the form $UNSAT(P)$ or $P \vdash \texttt{false}$. For unsatisfiability checking, the proof slicing mechanism partitions the initial formula P into a set of disjoint slices $\{P_1, \ldots, P_n\}$ whereby $P \leftrightarrow P_1 \wedge \cdots \wedge P_n$, and then incrementally applies unsatisfiability checks on some of these slices, *i.e.*, the slices that have been recently modified since the last unsatisfiability checks.

For entailment checking, proof slicing is the division of an initial, large entailment formula into smaller ones, obtained by slicing the original formula's antecedent with respect to each of its consequent. Given an antecedent P and a conjunctive consequent $Q_1 \wedge \cdots \wedge Q_n$, we partition P into possibly overlapping slices $\{P_1, \ldots, P_n\}$ such that each slice P_i is sufficient to prove the corresponding consequent Q_i. That is, the original entailment is replaced by a set of smaller entailments $\{P_i \vdash Q_i\}_{i=1}^n$. Importantly, this slicing step assumes that the sequent's antecedent is satisfiable, *i.e.*, it has been subjected to a prior unsatisfiability check. Loss of completeness occurs when weakening an unsatisfiable antecedent into a satisfiable one, and is the main reason for the limited adoption of this optimization in mainstream theorem provers.

Let consider the implication checks of the form $P_1 \wedge \cdots \wedge P_n \implies Q_1 \wedge \cdots \wedge Q_m$. Without proof slicing, a theorem prover needs to prove the unsatisfiability of $P_1 \wedge \cdots \wedge P_n \wedge (\neg Q_1 \vee \cdots \vee \neg Q_m)$. Due to the possibility of $P_1 \wedge \cdots \wedge P_n$ being unsatisfiable, the prover could not drop any constraint of the antecedents, unless it is willing to risk a loss of precision. By explicitly distinguishing between two kinds of proof obligations, our framework can avoid this problem by a prior unsatisfiable checking of the antecedents. Moreover, this distinction also allows us to exploit more aggressive pruning of irrelevant constraints from the antecedents with a novel annotation scheme (see Sec. 5).

Let us demonstrate how proof slicing can be applied to help with verifying the code snippet in Fig. 1(a). The pre- and post-conditions are provided by the `assume` and `assert` statements, respectively. To prove the total correctness of this program, we use the loop invariant $x = 2y \wedge n \geq 0$ for partial correctness proof, and the variant n as a well-founded measure for termination proof. The set of generated verification conditions are shown in Fig. 1(b). Observe that in these verification conditions, the constraints of x and y and the constraints of n are disjoint. As a result, they can be proven independently by the proof slicing mechanism, resulting in simpler proof obligations. For example, the verification condition VC_4 can be split into two separate entailments

$$VC_{4a}: x = 2y \vdash x + 2 = 2(y+1) \qquad VC_{4b}: n \geq 0 \wedge n > 0 \wedge n = N_0 \vdash n - 1 \geq 0 \wedge n - 1 < N_0$$

by partitioning the antecedent into two slices (i) $x = 2y$ and (ii) $n \geq 0 \wedge n > 0 \wedge n = N_0$. Prior to the entailment checks, each new antecedent is subjected to a satisfiability check, if

1: assume(n ≥ 0);	$Inv(x, y, n) \equiv x{=}2y \land n{\geq}0$
2: x = 0; y = 0;	
3: while (n > 0) {	$VC_1: x{=}0 \land y{=}0 \land n{\geq}0 \vdash Inv(0, 0, n)$
4: x = x + 2;	$VC_2: Inv(x, y, n) \land \neg(n{>}0) \vdash x{=}2y \land n{=}0$
5: y = y + 1;	$VC_3: Inv(x, y, n) \land n{>}0 \vdash n{\geq}0$
6: n = n − 1; }	$VC_4: Inv(x, y, n) \land n{>}0 \land n{=}N_0$
7: assert(x = 2 ∗ y ∧ n = 0);	$\vdash Inv(x{+}2, y{+}1, n{-}1) \land n{-}1{<}N_0$
(a)	(b)

Fig. 1. A code snippet and its verification conditions for total correctness proof

its slice has changed when compared to an earlier program point. We note that only formula slice (ii) has changed, with its invariant strengthened by the extra constraints $n{>}0 \land n{=}N_0$. Thus, for VC_4, we only need to check the satisfiability of the slice (ii), instead of the whole antecedent.

In summary, the division of proof obligations into two classes, of entailments and unsatisfiability checks, both of which benefit in performance from proof slicing, distinguishes our work from the techniques employed in current theorem provers. In entailment checks, the size of the antecedent can be greatly reduced when subjected to a prior unsatisfiability check. A similar mechanism is used for unsatisfiability checks, where only changed slices need be re-checked. Without this early analysis on the potential satisfiability of antecedents, current theorem provers would have to process much larger sets of constraints[1] when discharging proof obligations produced by a verification system.

3   A Framework for Proof Slicing

The starting point of our formalization is that of entailment or unsatisfiability obligations whose left hand side is an unquantified conjunction of constraints and uninterpreted predicates. For reasons of simplicity, we shall confine our presentation to unquantified formulas; the system is, nevertheless, capable of handling quantifiers. Informally, the slicing mechanism will preprocess the input by always floating outwards the constraints that appear under quantifiers but are independent of the corresponding quantified variables, and treat the remaining quantified constraints as atomic.

$$(\land N) \frac{X_{i_0}{=}X'_{j_0}}{\bigwedge_i X_i \lor \bigwedge_j X'_j \hookrightarrow X_{i_0} \land (\bigwedge_{i \neq i_0} X_i \lor \bigwedge_{j \neq j_0} X'_j)}$$

Consequently, we consider a first-order language with equality and interpreted function symbols. The atoms of the language are formed in the usual way, and denote *constraints*, *i.e.*, predicates

$$(\land R) \frac{P \vdash Q_1 \quad P \vdash Q_2}{P \vdash Q_1 \land Q_2} \qquad (\lor L) \frac{P_1 \vdash Q \quad P_2 \vdash Q}{P_1 \lor P_2 \vdash Q}$$

that have a fixed interpretation with respect to an external automated reasoning tool. Sequents are denoted by $P \vdash Q$, where P and Q are formulas. Our slicing mechanism

---

[1] A theorem prover might group relevant constraints into classes, such as congruence classes in the theory of equality, or classes of different theories in the Nelson-Oppen theory combination, or more generally, classes of constraints which share some common symbols.

$$\boxed{\text{SPLIT–E2}}$$

$$\begin{array}{c} \text{SPLIT}(P) = R \quad P_1 = \{Q \in R \mid \exists \beta \in Q.\text{SAMESLICE}(\alpha, \beta)\} \\ P_2 = \{Q \in R \mid \neg \exists \beta \in Q.\text{SAMESLICE}(\alpha, \beta)\} \\ \hline \text{SPLIT}(\{\alpha\} \cup P) = P_2 \cup \{\{\alpha\} \cup \bigcup_{X \in P_1} X\} \end{array}$$

$$\boxed{\text{SPLIT–E1}}$$
$$\overline{\text{SPLIT}(\emptyset) = \emptyset}$$

$$\boxed{\text{GETCTR–E2}}$$

$$\boxed{\text{GETCTR–E1}}$$
$$\overline{\text{GETCTR}_0(Q, PS) = \emptyset}$$
$$\frac{\{S \in PS \mid \text{ISRELEVANT}(Q, S)\} = \emptyset}{\text{GETCTR}_n(Q, PS) = \emptyset}$$

$$\boxed{\text{GETCTR–E3}}$$

$$\begin{array}{c} S_1 = \{S \in PS \mid \text{ISRELEVANT}(Q, S)\} \\ R = \bigcup_{X \in S_1} X \quad R' = \text{GETCTR}_{n-1}(R, PS \setminus S_1) \\ \hline \text{GETCTR}_n(Q, PS) = R \cup R' \end{array}$$

$$\boxed{\text{P–ENTAIL}}$$
$$\begin{array}{c} \text{SPLIT}(\{P_i\}_{i=0}^m) = PS \\ \text{GETCTR}_n(Q, PS) \Rightarrow Q \\ \hline \bigwedge_{i=0}^m P_i \vdash Q \end{array}$$

$$\boxed{\text{P–UNSAT}}$$
$$\begin{array}{c} \text{SPLIT}(\{P_i\}_{i=0}^m) = PS \\ \exists X \in PS \cdot \text{GETCTR}_n(X, PS) \Rightarrow \texttt{false} \\ \hline \text{UNSAT}(\bigwedge_{i=0}^m P_i) \end{array}$$

Fig. 2. Framework for Proof Slicing Mechanisms

is specified by the rules in Fig. 2, and works by taking in a sequent, and outputting a set of sliced sequents that are meant to be discharged by off-the-shelf provers. However, the input sequent must first undergo a pre-processing stage with the beside rewrite rule $(\wedge N)$ and two structural rules $(\wedge R)$ and $(\vee L)$, which yields a set of sequents in a form where the effect of the slicing rules in Fig. 2 is maximized, while retaining completeness. The result of this decomposition is a set of sequents whose LHS is a conjunctive formula and RHS is either a disjunctive or atomic formula. However, to avoid increasing the number of sub-sequents when these rules are applied, that may lead to some performance loss, rule $(\wedge N)$ should take precedence over rules $(\wedge R)$ and $(\vee L)$, if applicable, and rule $(\wedge R)$ can be stopped early if the pair of conjunctive consequents in the RHS share the same set of variables.

We distinguish between two calculi: a *complete slicing* calculus, and an *aggressive slicing* calculus. Both calculi formalize mechanisms for partitioning the conjuncts of a sequent, yielding sets of smaller sequents whose discharge is sufficient for establishing the proof of the original sequent. The assumption here is that the total effort of proving the set of smaller sequents by means of external provers is, in general, lighter than the effort of proving the original sequent by the same means. In the optimal case, the application of slicing decomposes the entailment $P_1 \wedge \ldots \wedge P_n \models Q$ into several sub-formulas, of the form $\bigwedge_{P \in X_i} P \models Q$, such that the sets X_i satisfy three properties: (i) *inclusion*: $\forall i. X_i \subseteq \{P_1, \ldots, P_n\}$, (ii) *relevance*: all X_i constraints are relevant to Q, *i.e.*, $\forall R. R \in X_i \rightarrow \bigwedge_{P \in X_i \setminus \{R\}} P \not\models Q$ and (iii) *correlation*: for each pair of constraints $P, P' \in X_i$, there exists a chain $P = P_1, \ldots, P_k = P'$ such that every two consecutive constraints P_j, P_{j+1} are overlapping. Similarly, an unsatisfiability check for a formula $P_1 \wedge \ldots \wedge P_n$ is sliced into several unsatisfiability checks for $\bigwedge_{P \in X_i} P$ such that X_i satisfies the inclusion and correlation properties.

Unfortunately, this formulation is not practical, as even establishing the relevance for a given slice is costly, let alone discovering the slices. Our proposal relies on a more syntactic formulation for the relevance and correlation properties, by using two meta-predicates, IsRELEVANT and SAMESLICE, as approximations of the relevance and correlation tests. The actual definitions dictate the slicing strategies each calculus uses. In the following sections, we expand more on their formulation and usage.

The complete and aggressive slicing calculi share the set of rules given in Fig. 2, which we shall call the *slicing framework* and differ in the definitions used for the two meta-predicates. Specifically, to obtain the *complete* (or *aggressive*) slicing calculus, we add the rules in Fig. 3 (or in Fig. 5, resp.) to the framework. We shall discuss the framework in the remainder of this section, and we shall devote Sec. 4 and 6 to each of the two calculi.

The conjunct partitioning procedure SPLIT calculates PS, a set of slices, from a set of conjuncts. Each slice is either extended with a new conjunct or not, in accordance with the SAMESLICE meta-predicate. This meta-predicate's role is to establish if two conjuncts should be kept in the same slice or not. Intuitively, it works by checking how information is shared between its two arguments. The result of applying the SPLIT relation to a formula P is a set of sets of constraints that represent the partitioning into *slices* of P. Each set of constraints can be interpreted as a formula that is formed by a conjunction of its constraints. Propertywise, we have:

$$\bigcup \text{SPLIT}(P) = P \wedge (\forall X, Y \in \text{SPLIT}(P) \cdot X \neq Y \to X \cap Y = \{\})$$

The formulation of $\boxed{\text{SPLIT–E2}}$ allows for arbitrary slicing decisions from the picking of α. Nevertheless, the slicing mechanism needs to be *convergent*, that is, to yield the same set of sliced sequents upon termination. Slicing convergence can be ensured by requiring the rewrite system formed by $\boxed{\text{SPLIT}}$ to be confluent. In the following sections, we shall investigate convergence properties for the complete and aggressive slicing calculi.

Another operation of interest is the computation of relevant slices for a given formula from a set of slices. $\boxed{\text{GETCTR–E3}}$ and $\boxed{\text{GETCTR–E2}}$ describe a family GETCTR_n of such functions that differ only in the exhaustiveness of the relevance computation. All start by picking the slices that are in the IsRELEVANT relation with the input formula Q. This step can be repeated using each of the previously selected slices as input for the next iteration. Such a refinement is important because, depending on the actual definition used for SAMESLICE, a single step might not be sufficient to gather all relevant constraints[2]. The default GETCTR function to use is GETCTR_1, but we can gradually increase its coverage through GETCTR_2, GETCTR_3, ..., if needed. This family of operators satisfies the following two properties

(i) $\text{GETCTR}_n(Q, PS) \subseteq PS$ (ii) $\text{GETCTR}_n(Q, PS) \subseteq \text{GETCTR}_{n+1}(Q, PS)$

Continuing on with the description of the slicing rules in Fig. 2, the rule $\boxed{\text{P–UNSAT}}$ defines slicing for unsatisfiability obligations. The formula P is first partitioned, and then a search is performed for an unsatisfiable slice. Each slice is considered together

---

[2] Such is the case for the *aggressive slicing calculus* with an *annotation scheme* that will be introduced later.

with its relevant counterparts as computed by GETCTR_n. The $\Rightarrow$ notation signifies the invocation of an external prover.

Similarly, [P-ENTAIL] defines the treatment of entailment obligations. The rule prescribes partitioning of the antecedent and the consequent, pairing consequent slices with relevant antecedent slices, and enforcing the implication relation on the resulting pairs. The [P-ENTAIL] rule corresponds to the conjunction introduction rules of Gentzen's sequent calculus [3]. Intuitively, a sequent with conjunctions on the right hand side can be split into separate sequents, each retaining one conjunct. Similarly, sequents with conjunctions on the left hand side can have any number (desirably, all but one) of conjuncts discarded. We state the lemma for soundness as follows , its proof can be found in the full version of the paper [13].

Lemma 1 (Soundness). *All sequents proven using the rules of the slicing framework are true.*

4   Complete Proof Slicing

In this section we introduce a completely automatic slicing mechanism. This mechanism uses the slicing framework rules given in Fig. 2, together with the meta-predicates SAMESLICE and ISRELEVANT given in Fig. 3. Essentially, this mechanism produces slices whose sets of free variables are disjoint. This is based on the idea that if a hypothesis and the conclusion of a proof obligation have disjoint sets of free variables, then the hypothesis cannot be directly contributing to the proof of the conclusion, and can thus be discarded.

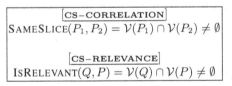

Fig. 3. Complete Slicing Mechanism

Whenever two conjuncts of the hypothesis share free variables, we say that they are *correlated*, and under the current slicing scheme, they should belong to the same slice. This is reflected in the rule [CS-CORRELATION], where the meta-predicate SAMESLICE is defined to keep two conjuncts together if their sets of free variables are correlated. Here, the symbol $\mathcal{V}$ denotes a function that returns the set of free variables from its input.

Similarly, if a conjunct in the hypothesis shares variables with the consequent, we say that the conjunct is *relevant* to proving the conclusion. The definition of the meta-predicate ISRELEVANT given in the rule [CS-RELEVANCE] captures precisely this idea. We have taken the approach of utilizing these two rules to make our proof slicing framework more general. In the next section, we shall define a new variant of our proof slicing framework with annotation guidance, by simply redefining these two rules, without having to change any of the rules in Fig. 2.

In the previous section, we mentioned that [SPLIT] rules are expected to be convergent. This can be ensured by the convergence of our calculi. The following lemma substantiates this claim.

Lemma 2. $[\text{SPLIT}]$ *with* $[\text{CS–CORRELATION}]$ *is confluent.*

An important property of the complete slicing mechanism is that it does not alter the level of completeness of the underlying solver. The slicing mechanism converts provable sequents into new sequents that are still provable in the same logic, provided that the antecedent of the sequent at hand is satisfiable. To formalize this claim, we assume that the underlying prover is formalized as a calculus LK^T, obtained from Gentzen's calculus LK [3], augmented with a theory T capable of handling the interpreted symbols of the language. Moreover, we assume that the axioms of T do not discharge sequents of the form $P \vdash Q$ when $\mathcal{V}(P) \cap \mathcal{V}(Q) = \emptyset$.

Lemma 3 (Relative completeness). *Let $P' \vdash Q$ be the sequent obtained by applying the complete slicing rules to the sequent $P \vdash Q$, where Q is atomic. Let LK^T be a sequent calculus obtained from LK by augmenting it with rules from a theory T that can handle the interpreted symbols of our formulas. If $P \vdash Q$ is provable, and P is satisfiable in LK^T, then $P' \vdash Q$, is also provable in LK^T.*

5   An Annotation Scheme for Proof Slicing

The complete proof slicing mechanism is particularly effective in the case of formulas that can be neatly partitioned into disjoint slices. It is, however, not as effective in the presence of constraints that seemingly link together sub-formulas that would otherwise be disjoint; for such cases, slicing needs to be applied more aggressively. To highlight this need, let us now consider a more expressive logic, capable of specifying and verifying heap-manipulating programs, with the possibility of generating more complex proof obligations. Consider the following definitions of a binary tree node and an inductive predicate that specifies an AVL tree rooted at its first argument and height-balanced.

```
data node { int val; node left; node right; }
avl(root,n,h,B) ≡ root=null∧n=0∧h=0∧B={}
  ∨ ∃v,p,q,n₁,n₂,h₁,h₂ · root↦node(v,p,q)
    * avl(p,n₁,h₁,B₁) * avl(q,n₂,h₂,B₂)
  ∧ n=1+n₁+n₂∧h=1+max(h₁,h₂)∧−1≤h₁−h₂≤1
  ∧ B={v}∪B₁∪B₂∧(∀a∈B₁·a<v)∧(∀b∈B₂·v≤b)
  inv n≥0 ∧ h≥0 ∧ n≥h;
```

This predicate captures four aspects of the AVL tree property. Parameter `root` is a pointer to the root of the tree, whereas `n`, `h`, and `B` (and their subscripted variants) capture, respectively, numbers of nodes in trees, their heights, and their sets of values. The constraint $-1 \le h_1 - h_2 \le 1$ states that the tree is nearly height-balanced, whereas the quantified set constraint $(\forall a \in B_1 \cdot a < v) \land (\forall b \in B_2 \cdot v \le b)$ enforces the binary search tree property. The formula specified after the **inv** keyword denotes the invariant property that holds for all instances of the predicate. Moreover, the *separating conjunction* operator $*$ (cf. [19]) is used to concisely capture the memory disjointness property.

To prove an invariant of the AVL predicate (*e.g.*, $n \ge 0$), the entailment proof (*e.g.*, $\text{avl}(x, n, h, B) \vdash n \ge 0$, resp.) can be discharged inductively by applying the definition of the predicate `avl`. For example, the below LHS is the resulting proof obligations (after each points-to $\mapsto$ is approximated by a non-null constraint, and each predicate is approximated by its invariant) while RHS is the same two entailments after applying *complete* proof slicing. For brevity, we use $n_i, h_i \ge 0$ to denote the conjunction $n_i \ge 0 \land h_i \ge 0$.

$$x=\text{null} \wedge n=0 \wedge h=0 \wedge B=\{\} \vdash n \geq 0 \qquad\qquad n=0 \vdash n \geq 0$$

$$x \neq \text{null} \wedge (n_1, h_1 \geq 0 \wedge n_1 \geq h_1) \wedge (n_2, h_2 \geq 0 \wedge n_2 \geq h_2) \qquad (n_1, h_1 \geq 0 \wedge n_1 \geq h_1) \wedge (n_2, h_2 \geq 0 \wedge n_2 \geq h_2)$$
$$\wedge\, n=1+n_1+n_2 \qquad\qquad\qquad\qquad\qquad\qquad\qquad\quad \wedge\, n=1+n_1+n_2$$
$$\wedge\, h=1+\max(h_1, h_2) \wedge -1 \leq h_1 - h_2 \leq 1 \qquad\qquad\quad \wedge\, h=1+\max(h_1, h_2) \wedge -1 \leq h_1 - h_2 \leq 1$$
$$\wedge\, B=\{v\} \cup B_1 \cup B_2 \wedge (\forall a \in B_1 \cdot a < v) \wedge (\forall b \in B_2 \cdot v \leq b)$$
$$\vdash n \geq 0 \qquad\qquad\qquad\qquad\qquad\qquad\qquad\qquad\qquad\qquad \vdash n \geq 0$$

Though sound, the second (sliced) entailment is unnecessarily verbose due to the presence of constraints $n_1 \geq h_1$ and $n_2 \geq h_2$ which act to link the constraints relating to size and height for the avl predicate. We refer to such constraints as *weakly linking* constraints, and propose to deploy a more aggressive proof slicing mechanism that can selectively disregard the relationship between variables occurring in such linkages. Though this decision may suffer from a risk of losing completeness, it would allow for a more aggressive application of the slicing mechanism. Applying this mechanism, we are able to obtain the following more compact entailment proof (*e.g.*, $n_1 \geq 0 \wedge n_2 \geq 0 \wedge n=1+n_1+n_2 \vdash n \geq 0$). To provide a systematic way to deal with weakly linking constraints, we propose the following annotation scheme.

Informal Definition 1 (Weakly Linking Constraint). *A constraint ϕ can be annotated as a* weakly linking *constraint $\phi\#$ if it is a weak constraint, such as inequality constraint (e.g., $\leq$ or $\neq$), that links together multiple variables from disjoint properties.*

In addition, for proving the invariant $\vdash n \geq h$ of the AVL predicate, our annotated proof slicing mechanism would keep the constraints related to both the size and the height properties and their weakly linking constraints, as follows:

$$n_1, n_2 \geq 0 \wedge h_1, h_2 \geq 0 \wedge (n_1 \geq h_1)\# \wedge (n_2 \geq h_2)\#$$
$$\wedge\, n=1+n_1+n_2 \wedge h=1+\max(h_1, h_2) \wedge -1 \leq h_1 - h_2 \leq 1 \vdash n \geq h$$

Aside from weakly linking constraints, we propose to support two additional kinds of weak linkages, namely:

Informal Definition 2 (Weakly Linking Variable). *A variable occurrence v can be annotated as a* weakly linking *variable $v\#$ if it does not belong to any particular property, but appears in the constraints of multiple distinct properties.*

Informal Definition 3 (Weakly Linking Expression). *An expression e can be annotated as a* weakly linking *expression $e\#$ if its definition has been captured by another variable, in a constraint such as $v=e$. This variable (or property) is only weakly linked with variables inside the linking expression.*

We note here that each weakly linking annotation is added only once (mostly in predicate definitions and specifications), with the intent of being used across the entire program verification process.

In summary, the key points on the use of weakly linking annotations in support of more aggressive proof slicing are: (i) Proof obligations containing multiple weakly linked properties are commonly generated from richer specifications. (ii) The use of weakly linking annotations leads to loosely connected partitions that can be split when necessary, thus easily regaining the performance benefits of proof slicing. (iii) Multiple instances of the same (small) slice are frequently encountered in practice, which are shown in our experiments; thus, the use of proof caching would yield further performance gains.

Moreover, in a goal driven approach, it is possible to select only a small set of (loosely connected) partitions that have a higher chance of being relevant for the current proof obligation. Should this attempt fail, the algorithm can retry with a broader set of partitions, preserving the precision of the approach. Since failure rate is small in practice, this aggressive approach yields a significant improvement in efficiency. In our experiments, we have obtained multi-fold reductions in prover execution times.

6 Aggressive Proof Slicing

In this section, we propose a novel *annotation* mechanism, capable of pinpointing locations where proof slicing can be applied more aggressively.

6.1 Annotation Scheme

As mentioned in Sec. 3, the target of our framework is a first-order language with equality and interpreted function symbols. This language, more precisely described in Fig. 4, imposes no restrictions on the versatility of our framework. Without loss of generality we can safely assume that the annotations described in Sec. 5 will be transparently translated into annotations in our target language.

6.2 Annotation Reduction

To simplify the formulation of our core calculus, we shall restrict our annotations for proof slicing to only weakly linking variables. Through a preprocessing step, we can transform each weakly linking constraint and each weakly linking expression into weakly linking variables, by transferring the weakly linking annotation to the free variables of a linking constraint or linking expression. Such a translation, named *red*, can be formalized as follows:

$$
\begin{array}{llll}
\pi & ::= \alpha_{\mathcal{L}} \mid \neg\alpha_{\mathcal{L}} \mid \pi_1 \wedge \pi_2 \\
\alpha_{\mathcal{L}} & ::= \alpha \mid (\alpha)\# & v_{\mathcal{L}} ::= v \mid v\# \\
\alpha & ::= \mathtt{true} \mid f_{\mathcal{L}}(v_{\mathcal{L}}^*) \mid v_{\mathcal{L}} = f_{\mathcal{L}}(v_{\mathcal{L}}^*) \mid v_{\mathcal{L}1} = v_{\mathcal{L}2} \\
f_{\mathcal{L}}(v_{\mathcal{L}}^*) & ::= f(v_{\mathcal{L}}^*) \mid (f(v_{\mathcal{L}}^*))\#
\end{array}
$$

where # *is the annotated slicing label;*
          α *denotes atomic predicates;*
          π *denotes pure formulas;* v *is a variable;*
          $v_{\mathcal{L}}$ *is a variable with or without # label;*
          $f_{\mathcal{L}}$ *is an interpreted symbol, possibly labeled;*

Fig. 4. Support Logic with Annotation Scheme

$$
\begin{array}{llll}
red_\beta(\pi_1 \wedge \pi_2) & \hookrightarrow red_\beta(\pi_1) \wedge red_\beta(\pi_2) & red_\beta(f_{\mathcal{L}}(v_{\mathcal{L}}^*)) & \hookrightarrow f_{\mathcal{L}}(red_\beta(v_{\mathcal{L}})^*) \\
red_\beta(\neg\alpha_{\mathcal{L}}) & \hookrightarrow \neg red_\beta(\alpha_{\mathcal{L}}) & red_\beta(v_{\mathcal{L}} = f_{\mathcal{L}}(v_{\mathcal{L}}^*)) & \hookrightarrow red_\beta(v_{\mathcal{L}}) = f_{\mathcal{L}}(red_\beta(v_{\mathcal{L}})^*) \\
red_\beta((\alpha)\#) & \hookrightarrow red_{\mathtt{true}}(\alpha) & red_\beta(v_{\mathcal{L}1} = v_{\mathcal{L}2}) & \hookrightarrow red_\beta(v_{\mathcal{L}1}) = red_\beta(v_{\mathcal{L}2}) \\
red_\beta(\mathtt{true}) & \hookrightarrow \mathtt{true} & red_\beta(v\#) & \hookrightarrow v\# \\
red_\beta(f(v_{\mathcal{L}}^*)) & \hookrightarrow f(red_\beta(v_{\mathcal{L}}^*)) & red_{\mathtt{true}}(v) & \hookrightarrow v\# \\
red_\beta((f(v_{\mathcal{L}}^*))\#) & \hookrightarrow f(red_{\mathtt{true}}(v_{\mathcal{L}}^*)) & red_{\mathtt{false}}(v) & \hookrightarrow v
\end{array}
$$

With this translation scheme, the free variable set of each constraint is divided into two disjoint sets, namely *weakly* and *strongly linking* variables. The set of *weakly linking* variables of a constraint can be computed by a simple function $\mathcal{V}_\mathcal{W}$ over the structure of the constraint α that picks up all (weakly) annotated variables, $\mathcal{V}_\mathcal{W}(v\#) = \{v\}$ while the set of *strongly linking* variables of a constraint α is its complement, namely $\mathcal{V}_\mathcal{S}(\alpha) = \mathcal{V}(\alpha) \setminus \mathcal{V}_\mathcal{W}(\alpha)$, where $\mathcal{V}(\alpha)$ returns the free variable set (without annotation) of the constraint α.

The translation scheme described above converts away all non-variable annotations. Nevertheless, a weakly linking constraint can still be distinguished from a constraint with weakly linking expressions or a constraint with a mix of weakly and strongly linking variables. At this point, we can make the following general observations: (i) a strongly linking constraint expresses knowledge specific to one property, and does not have any weakly linking variables; (ii) a weakly linking constraint encodes only weakly linking information, and thus has an empty set of strongly linking variables; (iii) constraints with weakly linking expressions or some weakly linking variables will express some relation between weakly linking entities and some other variables; thus neither set of weakly or strongly linking variables is empty. These observations allow us to support a uniform way of handling different kinds of linkages using a simpler variable-only annotation scheme.

6.3 Slicing Criterion

$$
\boxed{\text{AS}-\text{CORRELATION}}
$$
$$
\text{SAMESLICE}(P_1, P_2) = \begin{array}{l} \mathcal{V}_\mathcal{W}(P_1) = \mathcal{V}_\mathcal{W}(P_2) \wedge \\ \mathcal{V}_\mathcal{S}(P_1) \cap \mathcal{V}_\mathcal{S}(P_2) \neq \emptyset \end{array}
$$

$$
\boxed{\text{AS}-\text{RELEVANCE}}
$$
$$
\text{ISRELEVANT}(Q, P) = \begin{array}{l} (\mathcal{V}(Q) \cap \mathcal{V}_\mathcal{S}(P) \neq \emptyset) \vee \\ (\mathcal{V}_\mathcal{S}(P) = \emptyset \wedge \mathcal{V}_\mathcal{W}(P) \subseteq \mathcal{V}(Q)) \end{array}
$$

Fig. 5. Annotated Slicing Mechanism

To take advantage of weakly connected components, our aggressive slicing mechanism will create partitions (or slices) by ignoring links that are due to solely weakly linking variables. This is achieved by allowing two constraints to be in the same slice if they satisfy the following two conditions: (i) they share one or more strongly linking variables, and (ii) they have the same set of weakly linking variables. These two conditions are captured in a new definition for the SAMESLICE meta-predicate in Fig. 5. According to this definition, each weakly linking constraint will be kept as a separate slice. Furthermore, two constraints that share the same set of weakly linking variables will only be kept in the same slice if they share one or more strongly linking variables.

The following lemma establishes the convergence of our splitting procedure in the presence of the new meta-predicate.

Lemma 4. $\boxed{\text{SPLIT}}$ *with* $\boxed{\text{AS}-\text{CORRELATION}}$ *is convergent.*

6.4 Relevance Criterion

In the case of complete proof slicing, the constraints referring to a given property are spread across multiple slices. To have a good balance between precision and efficiency,

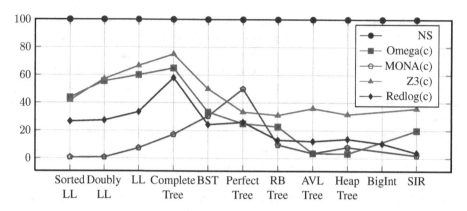

Fig. 6. Relative Comparison (%) of CS over NS with various theorem provers

we should ideally find the smallest set of hypotheses that ensure the success of the entailment check, whenever possible. To properly exploit the weakly linking annotations, we propose a two-step approach to finding relevant hypotheses. First, we employ aggressive slicing, which uses GETCTR$_2$, in order to obtain constraints that are most closely linked to the given goal. In case this first step fails, we may apply a subsequent exhaustive search step in order to identify additional constraints using a higher-level operator GETCTR$_n$, where n is the cardinality of our set of slices. Using n as a limit, our aggressive proof slicing mechanism has a similar behavior to that of complete proof slicing. We can formalize these two steps as instances of the slicing framework defined in Sec. 3.

Given a goal Q, the aggressive slicing mechanism would consider a slice *relevant* if either of the following holds:

1. It contains strongly linking variables that overlap with the free variables of Q.
2. It contains weakly linking constraints whose set of variables are entirely subsumed by the set of free variables of Q.

In order to collect these two categories of constraints, the calculus need only use GETCTR$_2$ in the aggressive search mechanism. The formalization of the aggressive search relevance check is given by [AS–RELEVANCE] in Fig. 5. The condition $\mathcal{V}_\mathcal{S}(P) = \emptyset$ in the meta-predicate ISRELEVANT indicates that P is a slice of a weakly linking constraint.

7   Experiments

We have integrated the proposed proof slicing mechanisms into a separation logic-based program verification system [18], where proof obligations are soundly approximated by formulas in heap-free pure logic that can be discharged by off-the-shelf back-end theorem provers. The theorem provers used in our current evaluation are the Omega Calculator [21], MONA [11], Reduce/Redlog [7] and Z3 [5]. The proof slicing mechanisms are implemented as intermediate layers between the verifier and the theorem

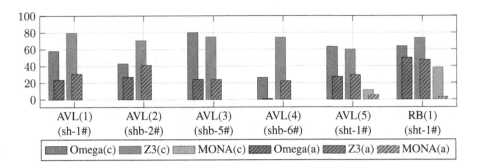

Fig. 7. Comparison of CS (c) and AS (a) over NS on examples with Weakly Linking Components (s: size, h: height, b: balance factor, t: sets, n#: number of (annotated) weakly linking components)

provers, effectively acting as prover-independent pre-processors for the back-end. In our measurements, we were careful to quantify the sole effect of applying the slicing procedures on the running time of the theorem provers (including overheads of the proof slicing mechanisms, if any) and show the relative comparison (on percentage) of timings by charts. The detailed timings (in seconds) and additional information are given as appendix in the long version of this paper [13]. For brevity, we use NS, CS and AS to indicate no, complete or aggressive proof slicing mechanism, respectively.

We used several benchmarks for evaluating the resulting system. The first benchmark includes a set of heap-manipulating programs, implementing typical operations for singly and doubly linked lists, as well as more complex tree data structures such as AVL and Red-Black trees. The benchmark also includes the BigInt program, which uses linked list to implement infinite precision integers and their arithmetic operations as well as the Karatsuba's fast multiplication method. The program is verified with non-linear constraints, which currently can only be handled by the Redlog prover. The second benchmark consists of programs taken from the SIR/Siemens test suite [6] with some data structures mentioned above and arrays.

Fig. 6 shows the comparison on percentage between the time spent on each underlying prover plus slicing overhead when CS is on (indicating by the prover name with the postfix (c)) and the time spent on the same prover without proof slicing mechanism (NS) for the first two benchmarks. [3] As can be seen, CS benefits all provers in general, especially on complex programs (*e.g.*, BigInt and SIR) with over 60% reduction. Moreover, on less scalable provers like Omega, MONA or Redlog, CS helps to reduce about 90% of the total prover time (or 10x faster). Those significant improvements come from the reduction on proof size for both unsatisfiability and entailment proofs by the effect of proof slicing. For Z3, the total reduction on the prover time is about 60% despite its own optimization mechanisms (*e.g.*, the relevancy propagation technique). Because our proof slicing mechanisms focus on the *higher level* tasks of checking entailments and detecting unsatisfiability, they are able to filter out irrelevant constraints more effectively whenever the relationships between constraints are preserved. Moreover, with

---

[3] We did not pay attention to the verification overhead because it is almost constant across different provers with and without proof slicing.

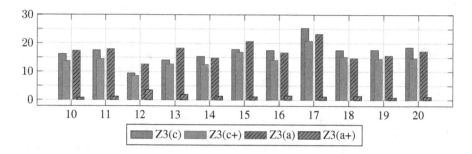

Fig. 8. Comparison (%) of CS and AS over NS on the Spaguetti Benchmark with the number of heap variables from 10 to 20 (+ indicates caching used)

proof slicing, the unsatisfiability checks on the antecedents of entailment proofs are performed incrementally and non-redundantly, thus bringing more performance gains.

The next set of experiments concerns annotated formulas, and the application of AS. The inductive predicates of data structures used in this benchmark are augmented with additional *linking constraints* that enhance their precision to move towards verification of full functional correctness but also greatly increase the complexity of the derived proof obligations. Annotations for those linking constraints are inferred automatically, via a number of heuristics. For example, each parameter of a heap predicate is regarded as an independent property, unless it is mutually-dependent on another parameter, leading to an approach where every constraint between two distinct properties is always marked as *weakly linking*. Due to space limitation, the heuristics for annotation inference are discussed in [13]. Fig. 7 illustrates the performance benefits of AS over CS in the relative comparison with NS. It shows that in the presence of more complex specifications, AS performs better than its complete counterpart. In these examples, proof obligations with set constraints are discharged by MONA.

The fourth benchmark, called *Spaguetti*, came from the SLP tool [17]. It includes a set of heap-based test cases; each of them comprises 1000 randomly-generated, parameterized by the number of heap variables, UNSAT checks of the form F ⊢ false with the success rate about 50%. The SLP tool is an optimized paramodulation prover, hardwired to support only the list segment predicate, together with equality and disequality constraints on heap addresses and thus yielding a very good performance (under 3 seconds for each Spaguetti test case). With the help of AS together with a simple heuristic that automatically marks each disequality as a weakly linking constraint, our generalpurpose separation logic-based prover is expected to achieve comparable performance while allowing a much more expressive specification language.

Unfortunately, as shown in Fig. 8, while the use of CS helps reduce the prover times with Z3 (by about 76.2% in total), AS has only little extra effect due to high numbers of (smaller) proofs generated. To obtain further improvements, we have augmented our proof slicing framework with a simple *proof caching mechanism* that memoizes on string representations of normalized proof obligations. This brought about over 90% reduction (after including overheads of both caching and slicing) when AS is used; thus the performance is now comparable to the SPL tool. This outcome is supported by a much higher hit rate (over 99%) from caching of smaller proofs generated by AS, as compared to the hit rate from the combination of proof caching and CS. This effective result highlights the synergistic interplay between the proof caching and AS although the idea of proof caching is not new. Moreover, with the help of AS, an obsolete prover like Omega can catch up the performance of the advanced prover Z3 because the number of disequalities, which are expensively handled by Omega, is considerably reduced.

To investigate the portability of our proof slicing mechanisms, we have equipped AS for the Frama-C verification system [24]. For evaluation, we designed a family of contrived procedures, parameterized by the number of their parameters, that do computation on these independent variables, so as to illustrate the potential of AS. A version comprising two parameters is shown in Fig 9. Our AS (without proof caching) is interposed between the Frama-C verifier and the default Alt-Ergo prover. AS is supported by an annotation heuristic marking simple constraints of the form $v=2$ as weakly linking constraints. As can be seen from Fig. 10, the use of AS achieved good performance gains in conjunction with the default prover. We have also evaluated our proof slicing mechanism on a set of 20 small examples obtained from the Frama-C distribution, on which the use of proof slicing did not yield any noticeable gain. It remains our thesis that larger, more complex examples would, in general, benefit more from our proof slicing methods.

```
void spring2 (int *x0, int *x1)
/*@ requires *x0>2 ∧ *x1>2;
    ensures *x0=old(*x0)+2
           ∧ *x1=old(*x1)+2 */
{ int v = 2;
  *x0=*x0+v; *x1=*x1+v;
  if (*x0>4) {
    *x0++; *x1++;
    if (*x1>4) {
      *x0--; *x1--; }}}
```

Fig. 9. A simple contrived procedure

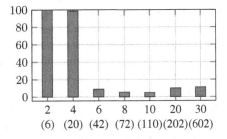

Fig. 10. Comparison (%) of AS over NS on the Spring Benchmark with Frama-C. The number of parameters ranges from 2 to 30 and the number of generated proof obligations are given in the parentheses.

8 Related Work and Conclusion

The problem of filtering irrelevant information has been studied under different guises in several research areas. In [12], the authors focus on filtering out non-relevant information in knowledge bases. They discuss the concept of free variable independence for a conservative partitioning scheme and the concept of forgetting constraints, by which they eliminate irrelevant variables and produce the strongest consequent of the initial formula containing only relevant variables. However, the lack of an aggressive slicing mechanism (which in our case was supported by annotating weak links between distinct properties) leads to higher overheads in both the elimination and the solving phases.

Huang et al. [10] focus on slicing proofs for the infeasibility of counterexamples generated from a model checking process. The insight of this work is that global proofs can be sliced into independent proofs of atomic predicates, and memoization can be used to store the smaller proofs. While the general slicing technique has also been refined via a myriad of proposals (such as combined with abstract interpretation [22]), no mechanism has been proposed to allow a more flexible tradeoff of effectiveness versus conservatism in the slicing process.

Yet another direction of related research focuses on conservatively slicing formulas in connected components in order to simplify the satisfiability and entailment checks. In [1], Amir et al. introduce a methodology for representing large knowledge bases, namely sets of axioms, as trees of loosely connected partitions. They also define a message passing mechanism for reasoning over individual partitions. This has the effect of maintaining the linking information, but leading to higher overheads.

Simpler schemes, *e.g.*, conservative partitioning, have been proposed for SAT solvers. The benefits of an union-find approach over the depth first search in identifying partitions are emphasized in [2]. In [25], a hypergraph cut method partitions the problem, then checks individual partitions and corroborates the results based on the assignments of the linking variables. In [20], SAT solvers are employed for each subproblem while delaying the assignments of linking variables to reduce the search space. In contrast to these methods, our approach refrains from converting implication checks into SAT checks, thus doing a better job at identifying weak linking constraints, and consequently yielding smaller proof slices. We also introduce customizable formula slicing capabilities that facilitate the exploration of new strategies. Our experiments shows that the approach is capable of speed gains without loss of completeness.

Finally, we mention Craig interpolation-based approaches, such as [9], that use interpolation to infer relevant predicates as a way of implementing abstraction refinement more efficiently. In these approaches, the notion of relevance is encoded in entailments and detected by an interpolating prover [15]. In contrast, relevance detection in our approach is largely syntactic, allowing the development of a generic proof slicing framework for automated program verification that would be effective for a broad range of off-the-shelf theorem provers used as back-end.

Conclusion. We have proposed a formal framework that allows the development of modular and extensible proof slicing mechanisms. Our proposal has been validated by an implementation and several experiments. Our technique shows considerable performance gains especially when weakly linking constraints are properly identified. Our aggressive proof slicing mechanism, based on the premise that a simple annotation scheme is sufficient to highlight weakly linking information, allowed us to develop a guided proof slicing process with surprisingly good performance. Experiments showed multi-fold reductions in verification times for each of the state-of-the-art provers used as back-end. We believe that our proposal is of importance for automated verification systems that are geared towards full functional correctness, where proof obligations are not only large and complex but may also be highly intertwined.

Acknowledgement. This work is supported by the research grant MOE2009-T2-1-063.

References

1. Amir, E., McIlraith, S.: Partition-based logical reasoning for first-order and propositional theories. Artificial Intelligence 162, 49–88 (2005)
2. Biere, A., Sinz, C.: Decomposing SAT problems into connected components. JSAT (2006)
3. Buss, S.R.: An introduction to proof theory. In: Handbook of Proof Theory (1998)
4. de Moura, L., Bjørner, N.: Relevancy propagation. Technical report, MSR (2007)
5. de Moura, L., Bjørner, N.: Z3: An Efficient SMT Solver. In: Ramakrishnan, C.R., Rehof, J. (eds.) TACAS 2008. LNCS, vol. 4963, pp. 337–340. Springer, Heidelberg (2008)
6. Do, H., Elbaum, S.G., Rothermel, G.: Supporting controlled experimentation with testing techniques: An infrastructure and its potential impact. In: ESE, vol. 10 (2005)
7. Dolzmann, A., Sturm, T.: Redlog: computer algebra meets computer logic. SIGSAM Bulletin 31, 2–9 (1997)
8. Fietzke, A., Weidenbach, C.: Labelled splitting. Annals of MAI 55 (2009)
9. Henzinger, T.A., Jhala, R., Majumdar, R., McMillan, K.L.: Abstractions from proofs. In: POPL (2004)
10. Huang, H., Tsai, W.-T., Paul, R.A.: Proof slicing with application to model checking web services. In: ISORC, pp. 292–299 (2005)
11. Klarlund, N., Moller, A.: MONA Version 1.4 - User Manual. BRICS Notes Series (2001)
12. Lang, J., Liberatore, P., Marquis, P.: Propositional independence: formula-variable independence and forgetting. Journal of Artificial Intelligence Research 18 (2003)
13. Le, T.C., Gherghina, C., Voicu, R., Chin, W.N.: A Proof Slicing Framework for Program Verification (2013), http://www.comp.nus.edu.sg/~chanhle/icfem13-long.pdf
14. Leino, K.R.M., Moskal, M., Schulte, W.: Verification condition splitting (2008)
15. McMillan, K.L.: An interpolating theorem prover. In: Jensen, K., Podelski, A. (eds.) TACAS 2004. LNCS, vol. 2988, pp. 16–30. Springer, Heidelberg (2004)
16. Meng, J., Paulson, L.C.: Lightweight relevance filtering for machine-generated resolution problems. Journal of Applied Logic, 41–57 (2009)
17. Navarro Pérez, J.A., Rybalchenko, A.: Separation logic + superposition calculus = heap theorem prover. In: PLDI, pp. 556–566 (2011)
18. Nguyen, H.H., David, C., Qin, S.C., Chin, W.N.: Automated Verification of Shape And Size Properties via Separation Logic. In: VMCAI, pp. 251–266 (2007)
19. O'Hearn, P.W., Reynolds, J., Yang, H.: Local Reasoning about Programs that Alter Data Structures. In: Fribourg, L. (ed.) CSL 2001. LNCS, vol. 2142, pp. 1–19. Springer, Heidelberg (2001)
20. Park, T.J., Gelder, A.V.: Partitioning methods for satisfiability testing on large formulas. In: McRobbie, M.A., Slaney, J.K. (eds.) CADE 1996. LNCS, vol. 1104, pp. 748–762. Springer, Heidelberg (1996)
21. Pugh, W.: The Omega Test: A fast practical integer programming algorithm for dependence analysis. Communications of the ACM 8, 102–114 (1992)
22. Hong, H.S., Lee, I., Sokolsky, O.: Abstract slicing: A new approach to program slicing based on abstract interpretation and model checking. In: SCAM (2005)
23. Sørensen, U.: Slicing for Uppaal. Technical report, AALBORG University (2008)
24. Frama-C Software Analyser System (2012), http://frama-c.com
25. Torres-Jimenez, J., Vega-Garcia, L., Coutino-Gomez, C.A., Cartujano-Escobar, F.J.: SSTP: An approach to Solve SAT instances Through Partition. In: WSEAS (2004)

Formally Verified System Initialisation

Andrew Boyton[1,2], June Andronick[1,2], Callum Bannister[1,2],
Matthew Fernandez[1,2], Xin Gao[1], David Greenaway[1,2], Gerwin Klein[1,2],
Corey Lewis[1], and Thomas Sewell[1,2]

[1] NICTA, Sydney, Australia*
[2] School of Computer Science and Engineering, UNSW, Sydney, Australia
`first-name.last-name@nicta.com.au`

Abstract. The safety and security of software systems depends on how they are initially configured. Manually writing program code that establishes such an initial configuration is a tedious and error-prone engineering process. In this paper we present an automatic and formally verified initialiser for component-based systems built on the general-purpose microkernel seL4. The construction principles of this tool apply to capability systems in general and the proof ideas are not specific to seL4. The initialiser takes a declarative formal description of the desired initialised state and uses seL4-provided services to create all necessary components, setup their communication channels, and distribute the required access rights. We provide a formal model of the initialiser and prove, in the theorem prover Isabelle/HOL, that the resulting state is the desired one. Our proof formally connects to the existing functional correctness proof of the seL4 microkernel. This tool does not only provide automation, but also unprecedented assurance for reaching a desired system state. In addition to the engineering advantages, this result is a key prerequisite for reasoning about system-wide security and safety properties.

Keywords: System Initialisation, seL4, Isabelle.

1 Introduction

Verification and validation of embedded software systems usually concentrate on the operational running state of the system. For example, the recent proof of non-interference for the seL4 microkernel [7] assumes the presence of a system state that corresponds to a high-level access control and information flow policy. It then shows that all executions from this state satisfy the non-interference property. Clearly, this operational running state is the interesting case for such proofs, but the question remains how to satisfy the initial assumption that the system is in a well-known state that corresponds to some specific policy.

* NICTA is funded by the Australian Government as represented by the Department of Broadband, Communications and the Digital Economy and the Australian Research Council through the ICT Centre of Excellence program. This work was in part funded by AOARD grant #FA2386-11-1-4070.

L. Groves and J. Sun (Eds.): ICFEM 2013, LNCS 8144, pp. 70–85, 2013.

More generally, this is the question of system initialisation: how does one bring a system from an empty power-off or boot state into a well-defined desired configuration from which it can operate normally, and how does one prove that this state is reached? For traditional operating systems, initialisation is mostly a question of initialising devices, loading binary code images, and running a manually created start-up script. For system security, the access control protection state of the initialised system is obviously critical. Such protection states can be large and intricate. Security policy descriptions in SELinux systems for instance, can have over 100,000 access control rules. Such policy descriptions are coarse grained compared to capability-based systems that control access to individual kernel objects. While the system is already constrained by a given security policy during operation, the initial startup code usually runs with elevated access and possesses the power to violate the policy. Its purpose is to bring the system into a state that conforms to the policy and then to relinquish its own access. Manually writing such a program for a sizeable policy is a daunting engineering task. Formally verifying that it does so correctly is even less appealing.

The main contribution of this paper is to demonstrate a technique for automatic and formally verified initialisation of capability-based systems. In particular, we show (a) an automatic initialiser for systems based on the formally verified seL4 microkernel, (b) a formal Isabelle/HOL model of this initialiser and its interaction with the kernel, (c) a formal Isabelle/HOL proof that this model leads to correctly initialised system states, (d) a formal connection of the system description that the initialiser takes as input to existing security policy formalisations and proofs for seL4 [7, 12], and (e) a formal proof that the seL4 invocations used by the initialiser model are refined by the exisiting functional specification of seL4 [4].

The initialiser takes as input a declarative description of the desired protection state in capDL [6], a capability distribution language, and automatically brings the system from the boot state into an initialised state that conforms with this desired protection state. While capDL descriptions can be large and complex, they can be generated from higher-level descriptions of the system, for instance from a component setup for MILS-style security architectures [1].

Our initialiser theorem is crucial for instantiating the existing seL4 security theorems [7, 12] that show the kernel enforces isolation of components running on top. This isolation allow us to establish that such MILS architectures are enforced correctly by the microkernel [3], which in turn enables us to reason modularly about user-level applications in the system.

The initialiser model directly connects to the seL4 API specification, which the binary of the kernel is proven to implement correctly [4, 11]. This is to our knowledge the first proof of a user-level model that directly links to a formally verified kernel implementation. This shows that such full realistic kernel API formalisations are usable for application-level proofs. The initialiser model has been implemented by straightforward translation into C code. We plan to prove that this translation is a correct implementation in future work. The focus in this paper is on the correctness of the algorithm and its use of the seL4 API.

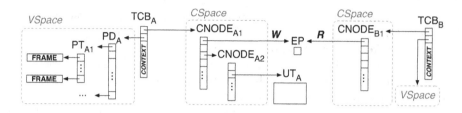

Fig. 1. seL4-based system with two threads that can communicate via an *endpoint*

We begin the remainder of this paper in Sec 2 with a short overview of the seL4 kernel. Sec 3 describes the capDL [6] language and associated proofs. Sec 4 presents the formalisation of the initialiser itself, while Sec 5 summarises the correctness proof. Sec 6 discusses experience and limitations.

2   seL4

The seL4 microkernel is a general-purpose operating system (OS) kernel designed as a secure and reliable foundation for a wide variety of applications. An OS kernel is the only software running in the *privileged* mode of the processor. The seL4 microkernel is formally verified for full functional correctness to the binary level [4, 11]. This means that there exists a machine-checked proof that the C code and binary of seL4 are a correct refinement of its functional, abstract specification.

As a microkernel, seL4 provides a minimal number of OS services: threads, inter-process communication, virtual memory, and capability-based access control. Fig 1 shows a trivial example system on seL4, composed of two threads, a sender A and a receiver B, communicating via an *endpoint* EP. Each thread is represented by its *thread control block* (TCB), which stores its context, virtual address space (VSpace) and capability space (CSpace). A VSpace defines the memory accessible to the thread; it is represented by a set of frames, generally organised in a hierarchical, architecture-dependent structure of page tables and page directories. CSpaces are kernel managed storage for *capabilities*. A capability is an unforgeable token that confers authority and that is stored in a graph of capability nodes (CNodes). In seL4, when a thread invokes an operation on an object, it needs to provide an index into its CSpace pointing to a capability for that object with sufficient authority. For instance, sender A needs a *write* capability to the endpoint, while receiver B needs a *read* capability to the same endpoint.

The allocation of kernel objects in seL4 is performed by retyping *untyped memory*, an abstraction of a region of physical memory. Possession of a capability to untyped memory confers the authority to allocate kernel objects in this region: sender A can request the kernel to transform UT_A into, say, a new CNode.

At boot time, seL4 first pre-allocates memory for itself and then gives the remainder to the initial user task in the form of capabilities to untyped memory. This user task is the initialiser we are targeting in this paper. Its aim is first to use these untyped capabilities for creating the required objects, such as TCB$_A$, TCB$_B$, CNode$_{A1}$, and then to initialise them appropriately, e.g. to set TCB$_A$'s CSpace field to CNode$_{A1}$. This includes setting up communication channels, e.g. storing the *write* capability to EP in TCB$_A$'s CSpace.

3 CapDL

We formally specify the desired initial system configuration as a *capDL system description*. The aim of the capability distribution language capDL [6] is to unify all aspects of the protection state of the system as explicit capabilities, allowing us to describe complete access control system configurations by capability distributions alone.

A capDL system description is both the input of our initialiser and its target: our initial user task must terminate in an initialised state corresponding to the description given as input. In the example of Fig 1, the description would be a formal and complete enumeration of all the kernel objects and the capabilities between them.

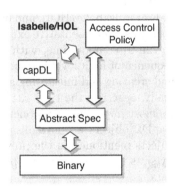

In addition to the language itself, which describes snapshots of system states, we have developed kernel semantics for this language that describes the effect of each kernel operation on such states, and showed that this *capDL kernel model* is a formally correct abstraction of existing models of seL4, with a complete refinement chain to the binary level, as shown in Fig 2. This ensures that the seL4 operations in the capDL model behave as the real kernel does.

Fig. 2. CapDL model in the seL4 refinement chain (where arrows denote formal proof)

We have also shown that capDL descriptions can be mapped to a corresponding access control policy: Let *s* be a kernel state from the abstract kernel specification level by Klein et al [4], `transform` be the state relation from abstract states to capDL states used in the refinement between these levels, `pas_refined P s` be the predicate that decides if *s* satisfies the access control policy *P* by Sewell et al [12], and `pcs_refined P c` be the predicate that decides whether a capDL state *c* satisfies the same policy *P*.

Theorem 1. *If the kernel invariants* `inv` *hold on* *s*, *then* `pas_refined P s = pcs_refined P (transform s)`.

The theorem implies that a capDL state description captures all information relevant to the protection state of an access control policy, i.e. instead of having to know the precise memory content of the machine, it is enough to reason about the information present in a capDL description.

```
init_system spec bootinfo obj_ids ≡
do (ut_cpts, free_cpts) ← parse_bootinfo bootinfo;
   (orig_caps, free_cpts) ← create_objs spec obj_ids ut_cpts free_cpts;
   dup_caps ← duplicate_caps spec orig_caps obj_ids free_cpts;
   init_vspace spec orig_caps obj_ids;
   init_tcbs spec orig_caps obj_ids;
   init_cspace spec orig_caps dup_caps obj_ids;
   start_threads spec dup_caps obj_ids
od
```

Fig. 3. The top-level definition of the system initialiser model

4   System Initialisation

In this section, we present an overview of our formal model of the system initialiser in Isabelle/HOL, and examine in detail the initialisation of the capability spaces as a representative example. Recall that the initialiser is the first user task to run after boot time, with access to all available memory. We model it as a sequence of high-level instructions, taking a capDL specification *spec* as input, and creating and initialising all objects and capabilities as specified by *spec*. Formally, *spec* has the type `cdl_state`, i.e. a full state of the capDL kernel model. Its most important component is the kernel `heap` of type `obj_id ⇒ cdl_object`. CapDL objects are formalisations of the TCBs, CNodes, Endpoint, and other objects mentioned in the previous section. They consist of a map from capability slots to capabilities and potentially additional payload such as further TCB data.

The top-level definition `init_system`, shown in Fig 3, is purposely divided into well-defined separate phases which simplifies reasoning as we will see in Sec 5. The additional input `bootinfo` is given by the kernel to the initial user task and specifies the location of untyped memory and free capability slots in the initialiser's CSpace. The final parameter to the initialiser is the list of object names `obj_ids` mentioned in *spec*. The `do x← f; g x od` notation is syntactic sugar for the monadic binding `f >>= (λx. g x)` where `f` is executed, potentially changing the underlying state, with its return value passed into `g`, bound to the variable `x`.

In the first phase of the initialiser, we extract from `bootinfo` the list `ut_cpts` of pointers to the untyped memory regions the initialiser has access to and can use to create new objects, as well as the list of free slots `free_cpts` in its CSpace it can use to store capabilities to these new objects.

In the second phase, we create all objects listed in the capDL specification by invoking seL4's *retype* operation on the provided untyped memory. During this operation, the kernel will create a capability to each object and store it in the provided free slot in the initialiser's CSpace. This original capability can then be given to other threads, either by moving it or by copying it (with full or diminished rights). Note that an original capability confers more authority than derived ones; it allows the revocation of derived capabilities and full destruction of the object. This creates a subtle dependency for the order in which the initialiser has to distribute capabilities: it eventually needs to give away original capabilities, and at the same time keep access to the objects to finish their initialisation.

For this reason, we duplicate, in a third phase, all original capabilities `orig_caps` into `dup_caps`, also stored in the initialiser's CSpace.

At this stage we can start the initialisation, per object type, including installing the capabilities into the capability storage objects. VSpaces are initialised by mapping in the required entries in page directories, and then page tables; TCBs are each initialised atomically; CSpaces are initialised similarly to VSpaces with the added complication of needing to distinguish between capabilities that are *moved* and the ones that are *copied*; Moreover, unlike VSpaces which are fixed, two-level data structures, CSpaces can be arbitrary directed acyclic graphs.

The final step of the initialisation is to set all threads to be runnable, from which point the initialiser becomes dormant and the system is ready to run.

We describe the initialisation of CSpaces more deeply and use it as a running example in this paper. The initialisation of CSpaces consists of putting the desired capability in every slot of every CNode appearing in *spec*. This occurs in two phases, depending on whether *spec* requires the capability to be the original one or not. For all capabilities that need not be originals, we *copy* the initialiser's original capability into the target CNode (we actually *mint* it, diminishing the access rights to those specified in *spec*). For the ones that need to be original, we *move* the initialiser's original capability (we actually *mutate* it with the appropriate rights specified in *spec*, except for endpoint capabilities which cannot be mutated in seL4). Each phase maps over the full list of all CNode slots, but does nothing to slots not concerned with that phase.

```
init_cspace spec orig_caps dup_caps obj_ids ≡
do cnode_ids ← return [obj←obj_ids. cnode_at obj spec];
   mapM (init_cnode spec orig_caps dup_caps Copy) cnode_ids;
   mapM (init_cnode spec orig_caps dup_caps Move) cnode_ids
od
```

The `return` function just returns its argument without modifying the state; `[a←xs. P a]` denotes a filter returning all elements of the list *xs* for which `P a` holds; `mapM f xs` is the standard map function over state monads, executing a monadic function *f* on each element of the list *xs* in order.

In each phase, we initialise the capability slots one by one.

```
init_cnode spec orig_caps dup_caps mode cnode_id ≡
do cnode_slots ← return $ slots_of_list spec cnode_id;
   mapM (init_cnode_slot spec orig_caps dup_caps mode cnode_id)
cnode_slots
od
```

The initialisation of a single capability slot `cnode_slot` of a CNode `cnode_id` is shown in Fig 4. This could for instance be the first slot of CNode$_{A1}$ in our example of Fig 1, which needs to contain a (not necessarily original) capability to

```
init_cnode_slot spec orig_caps dup_caps mode cnode_id cnode_slot ≡
do target_cap ← assert_opt (opt_cap (cnode_id, cnode_slot) spec);
   target_cap_obj ← return (cap_object target_cap);
   target_cap_rights ← return (cap_rights target_cap);
   target_cap_data ← return (cap_data target_cap);
   is_orig_cap ← return (is_orig_cap spec (cnode_id, cnode_slot));
   dest_obj ← get_spec_object spec cnode_id;
   dest_size ← return (object_size_bits dest_obj);
   dest_root ← assert_opt (dup_caps cnode_id);
   dest_index ← return cnode_slot;
   dest_depth ← return dest_size;
   src_root ← return seL4_CapInitThreadCNode;
   src_index ← assert_opt (orig_caps target_cap_obj);
   src_depth ← return 0x20;
   if target_cap = NullCap then return True
   else if mode = Move ∧ is_orig_cap
        then if ep_related_cap target_cap
            then seL4_CNode_Move dest_root dest_index dest_depth
                 src_root src_index src_depth
            else seL4_CNode_Mutate dest_root dest_index dest_depth
                 src_root src_index src_depth target_cap_data
        else if mode = Copy ∧ ¬ is_orig_cap
            then seL4_CNode_Mint dest_root dest_index dest_depth
                 src_root src_index src_depth target_cap_rights
                 target_cap_data
            else return True
od
```

Fig. 4. Initialisation of a single capability slot

the endpoint EP with a *write* right. In this definition, we first extract the target capability `target_cap` that `spec` requires in `cnode_slot`. The function `opt_cap` returns an `option` type, i.e. either `Some cap` or `None`. The function `assert_opt` asserts that this value is of the form `Some cap` and returns `cap`; otherwise it fails. From `target_cap`, we extract the target object `target_cap_obj` (say EP), the desired rights `target_cap_rights` (say *write*), and additional data `target_cap_data` (e.g. for endpoints, a so-called *badge*). We store in `is_orig_cap` whether `spec` requires the capability to be original for that slot.

In order to be able to invoke seL4's `seL4_CNode_Move`, `seL4_CNode_Mutate` and `seL4_CNode_Mint` operations, the initialiser needs to hold, in its CSpace, both the target capability to be moved or copied, and a capability to the destination slot. We compute the destination information (`dest_root`, `dest_index` and `dest_depth`) from the (duplicated) capability that the initialiser holds for the destination slot. (We use the duplicate capabilities in case the original capability to the destination slot has already been given away.) We compute the source information (`src_root`, `src_index` and `src_depth`) from the (original) capability that the initialiser holds for the target capability. We then can invoke the appropriate seL4 opération depending if the target capability needs to be original or not. These operations directly connect to the capDL-level API model of the kernel.

5   Correctness

In this section, we summarise the proof of system initialiser correctness. We present the separation logic we instantiated for this proof, state the top-level theorem, show how the proof is decomposed, and describe how it is connected to the seL4 kernel proofs.

5.1   Separation Logic Instance

We begin by setting up the basic reasoning framework we use in the proof of the initialiser. As described in Sec 4, we initialise each object in isolation, and within an object, each capability slot in isolation. Ideally, the proof about these executions follows the same pattern. Separation logic [10] is a good fit for this style of reasoning, at least if the specific flavour of separation logic allows us to decompose heaps, and objects within heaps, across exactly these boundaries. In addition to the local state of the user-level initialiser, we will have to reason about the internal state of the kernel comprising the various objects we create. This means, if we want to use a specific style of separation logic, we will have to retro-fit it onto the existing capDL-level kernel model.

Usually, a separation logic is defined in terms of a heap and the concepts of disjointness and separating conjunction. We can shortcut this stack of definitions by building on an Isabelle type class for abstract separation algebra [5]. This previous development allows us to merely define the concepts of a heap, heap addition, and heap disjointness. After proving their basic axioms, we get the development of separation logic for free, including basic Isabelle/HOL automation.

As mentioned, we want the heap in our separation algebra to be fine-grained enough to split objects into individual capability slots and other object data. The heap in the existing kernel model had no such requirement and therefore has no such concept. Instead of enriching the state space of the existing model with partial object ownership as described in [5] (and then having to re-prove refinement to the code), we *lift* the existing state space into a larger one that allows us to perform the desired decomposition easily. Our lifted heap is of type

```
sep_state = obj_id × cdl_component ⇒ sep_entity option
```

The `obj_id` is the same as in the heap mentioned in Sec 4. The `cdl_component` specifies which part of an object we are addressing — a single capability slot of an object, or the fields (non-capability data) of an object. A `sep_entity` is either a single capability, or an object with payload only. In the lifting from `obj_id` ⇒ `cdl_object` to `sep_state`, we also set the so-called `intent` field of TCBs to a default value. The `intent` models the contents of a thread's IPC buffer storing the parameters of the next kernel call it is about to make — a detail we can ignore, because the initialiser is the only thread that can make system calls.

In terms of separation algebra, the resulting `sep_state` is a standard heap structure and is instantiated in the standard manner [5]. The tradeoff is that we are not reasoning about the real state of the system, but about the lifted state. The lifted state space is larger than the original state space, and due to resetting the `intent` field, the mapping is not even injective. Neither effect impacts our verification: our predicates only talk about well-formed states that exist in reality and the states that are identified only differ in TCB intent which we can ignore.

To apply this lifting to the kernel state and phrase separation predicates about it, we use the syntax `<P>`. To apply separation predicates to the user-level initialiser state, which subsumes the kernel state, we use the syntax `«P»`.

Given this lifted heap and the automatic setup for separating conjunction $\wedge^*$ etc, we can define the classic maps-to predicates of separation logic. For instance, we define the predicate `ptr ↦ₒ object` that specifies that the state consists of the object `object` at position `ptr`. We can divide it into two predicates that extract the fields and capability slots of an object separately:

$$ptr \ \mapsto_o \ object \ = \ (ptr \ \mapsto_f \ object \ \wedge^* \ ptr \ \mapsto_S \ object)$$

Following our heap structure, we can further divide the predicate $\mapsto_S$ on the capability storage of an object into predicates $\mapsto_c$ about its individual capability slots.

One key reasoning principle in separation logic is the *frame rule*. Because the kernel API model is a shallow Isabelle/HOL embedding, we cannot prove the frame rule as a generic rule of the logic. We can, however, bake-in the frame rule to any statement we make about the kernel API, proving it about the leaf functions and then passing it up through to the API top level. For instance, we proved the following Hoare triple for the kernel-internal operation `set_cap`, which bakes in the frame rule by adjoining $\wedge^*$ `R`. The rule states that `set_cap` changes only a single capability slot of a single object, and leaves everything else unchanged, including other parts or other capability slots of the same object.

$$\{<ptr \ \mapsto_c \ old\_cap \ \wedge^* \ R>\} \ set\_cap \ ptr \ cap \ \{<ptr \ \mapsto_c \ cap \ \wedge^* \ R>\}$$

Making sure that our flavour of separation logic matches the verification problem gives us a convenient tool for reasoning about loops — a common operation in the system initialiser. We can reduce a global map of an operation such as `set_cap` over a list of capability slots to local reasoning about each slot simply by using the following rule.

$$(\bigwedge R \ x. \ x \in xs \implies \{«P \ x \ \wedge^* \ R»\} \ f \ x \ \{«Q \ x \ \wedge^* \ R»\}) \implies$$
$$\{«\bigwedge{}^* \ map \ P \ xs \ \wedge^* \ R»\} \ mapM \ f \ xs \ \{«\bigwedge{}^* \ map \ Q \ xs \ \wedge^* \ R»\}$$

In this rule, the big $\bigwedge$ is universal quantification and the big $\bigwedge^*$ is separating conjunction over a list of predicates in the usual way.

In the following sections we will see how these predicates and rules are applied to make statements about the initialiser behaviour.

5.2   Top-Level Statement

The correctness statement for the system initialiser is that, at the end of the initialisation, all objects in the system either belong to the initialiser itself and are inactive, or are initialised in conformance with the capDL specification.

In capDL specifications, systems are described as a mapping from object identifiers to objects. An object, identified by `spec_object_id` in the capDL specification `spec`, is said to be initialised in conformance to `spec`, defined by the predicate `object_initialised spec φ spec_object_id`, if the object `spec_object` it points to in the resulting state is the one `spec` requires it to point to.

```
object_initialised spec φ spec_object_id ≡
λs. ∃kernel_object_id spec_object.
        φ spec_object_id = Some kernel_object_id ∧
        (kernel_object_id ↦₀ spec2s φ spec_object) s ∧
        cdl_objects spec spec_object_id = Some spec_object
```

The injection φ captures the subtlety that the kernel decides memory addresses at runtime. It maps names in `spec` to these memory addresses. Therefore the predicate `object_initialised` requires that `spec_object_id` maps to a `kernel_object_id` via the injection φ and that `kernel_object_id` points to `spec_object` where all object identifiers have been renamed by φ — including those within the capabilities of each object, defined by `spec2s`. The function `cdl_objects spec` extracts the mapping from `obj_id` to object from `spec`.

The top-level theorem of the system initialiser is:

Theorem 2. *If* `well_formed spec` *and* `obj_ids = dom (cdl_objects spec)` *and* `distinct obj_ids` *then*

```
{⟪valid_boot_info bootinfo spec ∧* R⟫}
init_system spec bootinfo obj_ids
{λs. ∃φ. ≪∧* map (object_initialised spec φ) obj_ids ∧*
            si_objects spec φ ∧* R≫ s ∧
            injective φ ∧ dom φ = obj_ids}
```

It states that, given a `well_formed` capDL specification, the system initialiser, if it terminates, transforms a boot state described by `boot_info`, into a state containing (a) each object in the specification correctly initialised and (b) the data structures of the initialiser.[1] Additionally, it states that the mapping φ is injective and covers all specification objects.

The assumptions about the capDL system description encoded in the predicate `well_formed` exclude infeasible specifications by describing constraints on seL4-based system configurations. The formal definition of these constraints is too long for this paper but are summarised as follows.

- There is only a finite number of objects in the system.
- Every object is of the correct size, with the correct number of capability slots.
- Every capability points to an object, and there is a capability in the system for every object. The types of the object and corresponding capability match.
- Each object only possess capabilities of the right type, e.g. page tables only store Frame capabilities, whereas CNodes can contain most capability types.

---

[1] The initialiser presently does not delete the capabilities it duplicated.

- Capability rights are well formed, e.g. frames cannot have write without read permissions.
- Each capability has a unique original capability that it is derived from.
- Page tables cannot be shared.
- Page tables must be empty, or mapped in a page directory.

There are further constraints in `well_formed` that encode current limitations of the initialiser, not fundamental constraints. We describe these in Sec 6.

5.3 Decomposition

The key to this proof is the ability to decompose it along the functionality of the initialiser. There are two aspects to this decomposition — decomposing the proof itself along function boundaries and decomposing predicates about objects such as `object_initialised` into smaller predicates. The former is provided by the frame rule, the latter by our heap structure.

The proof of the system initialiser is divided into three sections. The first part ensures that parsing the kernel provided `bootinfo` structure correctly extracts information about untyped memory and free capability slots in the boot state. The second part ensures that the `create_objs` function creates all objects described by the specification in their default state and stores the corresponding capabilities in the slots that later parts of the initialiser expect. This involves some internal book-keeping and looping over the collection of untyped capabilities.

In the last, most complex part of the proof, we show that each object is transformed from this default state (`object_empty`) to its fully initialised state (`object_initialised`). We further divide this last part into separate proofs about the initialisation of each type of object by showing the following rewrite rule.

$$
\begin{aligned}
&[\![\texttt{well\_formed spec; obj\_ids = dom (cdl\_objects spec)}]\!] \\
&\implies \ll\!\bigwedge{}^{*} \texttt{ map P obj\_ids } \wedge^{*} R\!\gg \ = \\
&\quad \ll\!\bigwedge{}^{*} \texttt{ map P [obj}\!\leftarrow\!\texttt{obj\_ids. table\_at obj spec] } \wedge^{*} \\
&\quad \ \bigwedge{}^{*} \texttt{ map P [obj}\!\leftarrow\!\texttt{obj\_ids. tcb\_at obj spec] } \wedge^{*} \\
&\quad \ \bigwedge{}^{*} \texttt{ map P [obj}\!\leftarrow\!\texttt{obj\_ids. cnode\_at obj spec] } \wedge^{*} \\
&\quad \ \bigwedge{}^{*} \texttt{ map P [obj}\!\leftarrow\!\texttt{obj\_ids. stateless\_at obj spec] } \wedge^{*} R\!\gg
\end{aligned}
$$

Expanding this map of an arbitrary predicate over all objects into maps by type allows us to use the frame rule for looking at each type in isolation. As an example, consider the rules in Fig 5 for `init_tcbs` and `init_cspace`. It is not important to understand these predicates in detail. However, we can note that each of them talk about a separate part of the overall object map, both mention some side conditions about the presence of capabilities in the initialiser itself (`si_cap_at` φ `caps spec obj_id` and `si_cspace`), and both have a frame condition R than can be suitably instantiated to join them up.

Continuing in this trend, we decompose the problem of initialising a single object into the separate parts of an object, namely its fields and its individual capability slots. This is embodied in the following rule.

⟦well_formed spec; obj_ids = dom (cdl_objects spec); distinct obj_ids⟧
⟹ {⟪objects_empty spec φ [obj←obj_ids. tcb_at obj spec] ∧*
   ∧* map (si_cap_at φ orig_caps spec) obj_ids ∧* si_cspace ∧* R≫}
   init_tcbs spec orig_caps obj_ids
   {⟪objects_initialised spec φ [obj←obj_ids. tcb_at obj spec] ∧*
   ∧* map (si_cap_at φ orig_caps spec) obj_ids ∧* si_cspace ∧* R≫}

⟦well_formed spec; obj_ids = dom (cdl_objects spec); distinct obj_ids;
 distinct free_cptrs; orig_caps = map_of (zip obj_ids free_cptrs);
 length obj_ids ≤ length free_cptrs⟧
⟹ {⟪objects_empty spec φ [obj←obj_ids. cnode_at obj spec] ∧*
   ∧* map (si_cap_at φ orig_caps spec) obj_ids ∧*
   ∧* map (si_cap_at φ dup_caps spec)
        [obj←obj_ids. cnode_or_tcb_at obj spec] ∧*
   si_cspace ∧* R≫}
   init_cspace spec orig_caps dup_caps obj_ids
   {⟪objects_initialised spec φ [obj←obj_ids. cnode_at obj spec] ∧*
   ∧* map (λcptr. (si_cnode_id, cptr) ↦c NullCap)
        (take (length obj_ids) free_cptrs) ∧*
   ∧* map (si_cap_at φ dup_caps spec)
        [obj←obj_ids. cnode_or_tcb_at obj spec] ∧*
   si_cspace ∧* R≫}

Fig. 5. Individual rules for init_tcbs and init_cspace

⟦dom (slots_of obj_id spec) = slots; distinct slots⟧
⟹ object_initialised spec φ obj_id =
   (object_fields_initialised spec φ obj_id ∧*
   ∧* map (object_slot_initialised spec φ obj_id) slots ∧*
   object_empty_slots_initialised spec φ obj_id)

Such a decomposition is not necessarily true for any separation logic and any concept of partly initialised object. Being able to prove the rule above as an equality was one of the design goals of our separation logic. In particular, the definition of object_initialised (see Sec 5.2) contains an existential quantifier over kernel_object_id and spec_object which needs to be well-behaved enough to lift over the separating conjunction on the right hand side of the rule.

The proof of CNode initialisation is representative of the proofs of other object types. Capability slots in CNodes are initialised in a two-step process as described in Sec 4. We define a predicate cnode_half_initialised to describe this intermediate state and use the above decomposition rule for object_initialised, decomposing cnode_half_initialised in a similar way, combined with the mapM rule described in Sec 5.1 to reduce reasoning about loops to single capability slots. Arriving at the leaf kernel calls of the init_cnode function, the initialiser extracts the capabilities that authorise it to make these calls. These capabilities are mentioned in Fig 5 as si_cap_at φ caps spec obj_id in a map over all such capabilities. The following rule allows us to extract the specific one we need.

$$\llbracket x \in xs; \; \text{distinct } xs; \; \bigwedge R. \; \{\!\!\{\ll\!P \wedge^* I \; x \wedge^* R\!\gg\}\!\!\} \; f \; \{\!\!\{\ll\!Q \wedge^* I \; x \wedge^* R\!\gg\}\!\!\}\rrbracket$$
$$\implies \{\!\!\{\ll\!P \wedge^* \bigwedge^* \text{map } I \; xs \wedge^* R\!\gg\}\!\!\} \; f \; \{\!\!\{\ll\!Q \wedge^* \bigwedge^* \text{map } I \; xs \wedge^* R\!\gg\}\!\!\}$$

We join the initialiser proof with formal specifications of the seL4 API that are explained in the next section.

5.4   seL4 API Specification

It is a universal hazard in formal specification that the specification does not meet requirements, is inconsistent or does not match the code. We narrow the requirements gap by proving a high-level correctness statement. We address the latter two by the formal connection of the system initialisation proof to the capDL model of the seL4 kernel, which formally abstracts the seL4 binary as illustrated in Fig 2.

While we re-use the existing capDL kernel model, we did have to prove new properties about it. Existing proofs about seL4 mostly concerned global invariants and all possible, potentially malformed or malicious inputs. Exercising the kernel API from a user-level proof, however, requires a different perspective: given a specific good pre-state for an API call, show the effect of the API call on this state, and determine which other parts of the kernel state are (not) affected. Separation logic proved a good match for this kind of specification. This style of proof does not tell us anything about invariant preservation within the kernel, but it gives us the information we need for user-level proofs. We expect the separation logic triples we proved about the seL4 API to be useful in other user-level proofs as well; they were not specific to the initialiser. These triples are typically large, around 30–50 lines each, because they capture the precise conditions needed for a specific kernel call to succeed.

The system model we use to connect to the kernel formalisation is somewhat simplistic: it assumes that only one thread in the system can make kernel calls and affect the system state. This allows the initialiser model to treat the kernel as a library that embeds the kernel state in the initialiser state. It also allows us to avoid reasoning about interleaved user executions. This works for our one-thread initialiser, but obviously would have to be generalised for more complex systems.

6   Experience, Limitations, and Assumptions

This section describes some of the lessons learnt in this verification and discusses the limitations and assumptions of the current version of the proof.

The size of the initialiser model is relatively small: roughly 400 lines of Isabelle definitions. It connects to the seL4 capDL-level kernel model of about 4,150 lines. This connection to the fully realistic kernel model is the main source of complexity in the proof. As can be seen in Sec 4, the initialiser has to deal with a full kernel API with all its real-life complexities and wrinkles.

The proof specific to the user-level initialiser measures 8,100 lines of Isabelle, the separation logic proofs about kernel functions another 10,500 lines, coming to a total of 18,500 lines overall. This compares to 25,300 lines for the refinement proof between the capDL kernel model and the functional specification, and 200,000 lines for the functional specification to the C code of the kernel [4].

Previous verifications based on seL4 were either refinement proofs where one full specification layer is connected to another such layer [4], or proofs of global security properties [7,12]. The use of specific API functions in our setting, combined with local separation logic statements about them, gives our proofs a distinctly different flavour. While previous proofs had to show global invariants that are inconvenient to express in separation logic, we could get away without stating any global kernel-level invariants at all. The local separation logic specifications were sufficient.

Our compositional state space and the corresponding separation algebra was crucial for reasoning about individual components of each object separately. Another difference between the initialiser and previous seL4 proofs was the heavy use of nested loops. Again, our separation logic setup enabled us to decompose these loops into local steps without stating complex invariants.

These benefits of separation logic reasoning were not an accident. We expended considerable effort fine-tuning and designing the underlying separation algebra instance such that the higher-level proofs would later fall out relatively conveniently. This design was iterative, leading through a number of rather complex instantiations with the simple state space lifting presented here as the final result. The Isabelle-enforced abstraction layer, which the separation algebra type class brought, enabled us to change the algebra instantiation and heap structure several times underneath the kernel proofs. We only had to re-prove the basic axioms and frame properties of the leaf functions.

We share a frequent experience in separation logic proofs: more automation would have been welcome. While the generic separation logic setup in Isabelle/HOL provided basic proof tactics, higher-level automation such as frame computation/matching would have improved productivity. We are currently investigating how such support can be implemented.

Despite our comprehensive top-level correctness statement, there are still a number of limitations in the initialiser and corresponding proof.

A general limitation of this style of proof is that it shows a safety, not a liveness property: only if the initialiser finishes successfully do we know that the resulting state is correctly initialised. Since almost all loops in the initialiser are (potentially nested) maps over finite lists, termination is not an issue. However, the initialiser may legitimately fail, e.g. because of insufficient memory. This limitation could be lifted with further explicit assumptions about the bootinfo structure provided by the kernel. An assumption of the original seL4 verification was that the kernel boots correctly. We further assume that the bootinfo structure provides correct information about the layout of memory and capabilities.

Sec 5.2 mentions fundamental constraints on system configurations formalised in the predicate well_formed on the input specification. We also use this predicate to encode specific limitations of our current initialiser model. We currently do not allow the system configuration to mention untyped capabilities, IRQ capabilities and ASID pool capabilities. This corresponds to static system configurations as used in a separation-kernel setting [7]. With the basic reasoning framework set up, we think these limitations can be lifted easily in future work.

At present, capDL only models the protection state of the system, not its memory content. This means we also do not model the loading of program code. This limitation is less severe than it may sound, because in the envisioned application space, the system image loaded from disk already contains all application binaries. That is, loading program code is reduced to mapping the right memory frames into the right virtual address spaces, which we do model.

Finally, we do not model the kernel scheduler in our proofs, because the capDL kernel model does not provide enough detail on it. Our underlying execution model implicitly assumes that the initialiser is the only running thread in the system. Since the initialiser runs with highest priority and only produces threads with lower priority this assumption is trivially satisfied until the initialiser terminates. We do prove that the initialiser always remains runnable.

7   Conclusion and Related Work

Initialising systems according to a given configuration, and guaranteeing that the initialisation is correct, are both hard and critical tasks. Security requirements for high-assurance certification of separation kernels (SKPP) for instance include providing evidence that the initialisation function establishes the system in a secure state consistent with the configuration data [8]. Configuration data describes high-level partitions and authorised information flows between partitions.

SELinux policies allow fine grained MLS security, but the richness of these policies makes it difficult to understand them. Hicks et al. [2] developed a formal semantics for SELinux policies in Prolog and demonstrated that it was possible to show information flow properties of SELinux policies.

The EROS kernel partially side-steps the initialisation problem by persistence; it simply restarts at the last saved checkpoint. The initial system image is constructed by hand and the creation and instantiation of confined subsystems uses *constructors* that are part of the trusted computing base [13]. The proof of the correctness of these constructors is with respect to a high-level model of EROS only, not formally linked to the EROS code.

The OKL4 microkernel [9] moves the initialisation problem almost entirely to offline processing and runs the initialisation phase once, before the system image is built. Similarly to EROS, when the machine starts, it loads a fully pre-initialised state. While this makes it possible to inspect the initialised state offline, a full assurance case must be made for each system. In our approach, assurance about system initialisation is now reduced to reasoning about static, formal capDL system descriptions.

In this paper we presented the formalisation and correctness proof of a generic, automatic system initialiser that brings an seL4-based system from boot state into a desired access control configuration. From such a configuration, we can then reason with confidence about the security of the resulting system.

We have shown a general separation logic framework that can be used to reason about such user-level systems, we have produced a proof framework to reason about user-level executions on top of a formally verified microkernel API, and we have applied it to show the correctness of the initialiser model.

While the initialiser we present here is specific to seL4, we think that the general principle and pattern of reasoning would generalise to other capability-based systems. Future work includes the functional correctness proof down to the C code level of the initialiser. We expect this proof to be simpler than the seL4 correctness, because the initialiser code itself is much simpler. Its complexity lies in the interaction with the kernel, which we have treated here.

Acknowledgements. We are grateful to Mark Staples and Toby Murray for their feedback on drafts of this paper.

References

1. Alves-Foss, J., Oman, P.W., Taylor, C., Harrison, S.: The MILS architecture for high-assurance embedded systems. Int. J. Emb. Syst. 2, 239–247 (2006)
2. Hicks, B., Rueda, S., Clair, L.S., Jaeger, T., McDaniel, P.D.: A logical specification and analysis for SELinux MLS policy. In: Lotz, V., Thuraisingham, B.M. (eds.) SACMAT, pp. 91–100. ACM Press, New York (2007)
3. Klein, G.: From a verified kernel towards verified systems. In: Ueda, K. (ed.) APLAS 2010. LNCS, vol. 6461, pp. 21–33. Springer, Heidelberg (2010)
4. Klein, G., Elphinstone, K., Heiser, G., Andronick, J., Cock, D., Derrin, P., Elkaduwe, D., Engelhardt, K., Kolanski, R., Norrish, M., Sewell, T., Tuch, H., Winwood, S.: seL4: Formal verification of an OS kernel. In: 22nd SOSP, pp. 207–220. ACM (2009)
5. Klein, G., Kolanski, R., Boyton, A.: Mechanised separation algebra. In: Beringer, L., Felty, A. (eds.) ITP 2012. LNCS, vol. 7406, pp. 332–337. Springer, Heidelberg (2012)
6. Kuz, I., Klein, G., Lewis, C., Walker, A.: capDL: A language for describing capability-based systems. In: 1st APSys, New Delhi, India, pp. 31–36 (August 2010)
7. Murray, T., Matichuk, D., Brassil, M., Gammie, P., Bourke, T., Seefried, S., Lewis, C., Gao, X., Klein, G.: seL4: from general purpose to a proof of information flow enforcement. In: IEEE Symp. Security & Privacy, Oakland, CA (May 2013)
8. National Security Agency. U.S. government protection profile for separation kernels in environments requiring high robustness, version 1.3 (June 2007)
9. Open Kernel Labs. OKL4 microkernel, reference manual (September 2008), http://wiki.ok-labs.com/downloads/release-3.0/okl4-ref-manual-3.0.pdf
10. Reynolds, J.C.: Separation logic: A logic for shared mutable data structures. In: Proc. 17th IEEE Symposium on Logic in Computer Science, pp. 55–74 (2002)
11. Sewell, T., Myreen, M., Klein, G.: Translation validation for a verified OS kernel. In: Proc. 34th PLDI, pp. 471–481. ACM (June 2013)
12. Sewell, T., Winwood, S., Gammie, P., Murray, T., Andronick, J., Klein, G.: seL4 enforces integrity. In: van Eekelen, M., Geuvers, H., Schmaltz, J., Wiedijk, F. (eds.) ITP 2011. LNCS, vol. 6898, pp. 325–340. Springer, Heidelberg (2011)
13. Shapiro, J.S., Weber, S.: Verifying the EROS confinement mechanism. In: IEEE Symposium on Security and Privacy, pp. 166–176. IEEE Computer Society (2000)

Verifying an Aircraft Proximity Characterization Method in Coq

Dongxi Liu, Neale L. Fulton, John Zic, and Martin de Groot

CSIRO Computational Informatics, Australia
{dongxi.liu,neale.fulton,john.zic,martin.degroot}@csiro.au

Abstract. In this paper, we present a verification of an aircraft proximity characterization method in the proof assistant Coq. Our verification covers aircraft kinematics, foundational geometric objects, and real analysis, which are all used in the proximity characterization method. These subjects from different areas make our verification complicated. Through the verification, all proximity characteristics in that method are formalized and provided with machine-checkable proofs. We have identified and corrected several mistakes in the informal description of the method, and improved the accuracy of proximity characteristics by explicitly defining their conditions in the formalization. Our verification shows the effectiveness of using Coq to increase the trust to the aircraft proximity characterization method.

1 Introduction

An increase in air traffic is anticipated due to growth in traditional air travel, together with anticipated increases in the operation of uninhabited aerial vehicles, and of small personalized jets. To guarantee the safety of aircraft, the minimum standards of spatial and temporal proximity must not be violated. However, with an increase in air traffic, aircraft proximity incidents can also be anticipated to occur more frequently. For this reason, the engineering specifications underpinning aircraft proximity management functions are currently under scrutiny.

The proximity management function requires a number of characteristics to be examined and captured as airspace design requirements. Fulton and Huynh [1] developed a proximity characterization method based on the Apollonius circle in planar conditions or the Apollonius sphere in a three-dimensional setting. Using this method, they give two sets of fundamental characteristics of proximity: conflict-in-time and conflict-in-space.

The proximity characterization method [1] identifies that the Apollonius circle or sphere can be a unifying functional theme underpinning many different applications. For example, it provides a refinement of analysis for cockpit displays [2], and provides a more general interpretation the earliest intercept point concept [3]. The proximity characterization based on the Apollonius circle also can serve as a basis for the design of a fault-tolerant reversionary mode for the guidance laws applicable to aircraft in a proximity situation.

L. Groves and J. Sun (Eds.): ICFEM 2013, LNCS 8144, pp. 86–101, 2013.

Since the proximity characterization method [1] is used in safety-critical systems, it is crucial to guarantee the method's correctness. As completed for many similar systems [4–8], a rigorous formal analysis is desirable to guarantee the correctness and accuracy of the method. By accuracy, we mean the proximity characteristics and their correctness conditions should be expressed explicitly, such that the application of the proximity characteristics cannot violate such conditions.

In this paper, we verify the proximity characterization method [1] in the proof assistant Coq [9]. The Coq formal language permits the definition of mathematical specifications, algorithms and theorems and provides an interactive environment for developing machine-checkable proofs. Using Coq, we formalize the proximity characterization method by defining the aircraft kinematics (e.g. the aircraft position, velocity and the intercept condition), the foundational geometric objects (e.g., circles and triangles) and the conflict-in-space characteristics (e.g., the non-allowed steering directions, limits and monotonicity of aircraft distances). More importantly, the formalized characteristics are expressed as theorems, which are all proved interactively in Coq. It is our contribution of applying Coq to verify a practical application that covers subjects from several different areas (aircraft kinematics, geometric objects and real analysis).

During the verification, we found several mistakes in the initial transcript of the method and improved the accuracy of the method by explicitly giving the correctness conditions for each characteristic in its corresponding theorem. In addition, the dependency relationships among characteristics are recognized. For example, some characteristics are needed in the construction of the proof for other characteristics. Identifying such relationships improves the understanding to the proximity characteristics.

The paper is presented as follows. In Section 2, we give a brief review of the proximity characterization method to be verified. Then, we present the details of our Coq formalization in Section 3. In Section 4, we report our experiences of verification and the modularization of Coq proofs. Finally, we discuss related works in Section 5 and conclude the paper in Section 6.

2   Overview of Apollonius Intercept Circle

The proximity characterization method [1] describes both conflict-in-space and conflict-in-time characteristics of aircraft proximity based on the Apollonius circle. In this paper, we present the verification of the conflict-in-space characteristics, and hence only conflict-in-space characteristics are introduced below.

2.1   The Apollonius Circle

The method considers the proximity of two aircraft: a Pursuer aircraft and an Evader aircraft. The Pursuer aircraft, initially at a position $P_p(0)$, is the point of reference and the Evader aircraft is initially at a position $P_e(0)$. The two aircraft have uniform velocities V_P and V_E, respectively. Let $P_p(t)$ and $P_e(t)$ denote the positions of the Pursuer and the Evader at time t, respectively. Then, the vector equations of their flightpaths from their initial positions to their positions at time t are given by:

$$P_p(t) = P_p(0) + V_p t \quad \text{and} \quad P_e(t) = P_e(0) + V_e t$$

The ratio of linear speeds is a canonical characteristic of the geometric construction of the Apollonius circle. Let $\|V_P\|$ and $\|V_E\|$ denote the linear speeds of the Pursuer and the Evader, respectively (i.e., the norms of the velocity vectors V_p and V_E). Then, the ratio of the Pursuer's speed and the Evader's speed is represented as follows.

$$\frac{\|V_P\|}{\|V_E\|} = k$$

The proximity characterization method considers the case where $k \geq 1$. Without loss of generality, if the Pursuer is slower than the Evader the aircraft roles can be exchanged.

Suppose an intercept point I will be reached by the Pursuer and the Evader at some time. Then the Euclidean distance PI will be in the speed ratio k to the distance EI, as shown below, where P and I denote the initial points of the Pursuer and the Evader, respectively, corresponding to their initial positions.

$$\frac{PI}{EI} = k$$

Let the point P have the coordinate $(0,0)$, and assume that the points E and I have the coordinates $(x_E, 0)$, where $x_E > 0$, and (x_I, y_I), respectively. Then, the above distance ratio can be refined as follows:

$$\frac{PI}{EI} = \frac{\sqrt{x_I^2 + y_I^2}}{\sqrt{(x_I - x_E)^2 + y_I^2}} = k$$

This equation, expressed in terms of (x_I, y_I), is the equation of a circle (non-degenerate case with $k > 1$):

$$\left(x_I - \frac{k^2 x_E}{k^2 - 1} \right)^2 + y_I^2 = \left(\frac{k x_E}{k^2 - 1} \right)^2$$

with centre:

$$\left(\frac{k^2 x_E}{k^2 - 1}, 0 \right)$$

and radius:

$$\frac{k x_E}{k^2 - 1}$$

Pictorially, this circle is shown in Figure 1, where C is the circle centre and R denotes the radius. The x coordinate of C is denoted by xc. The line of sight distance between the two aircraft is denoted by R_{LOS}, which is equal to x_E. Other characteristics regarding angles and distances will be introduced below.

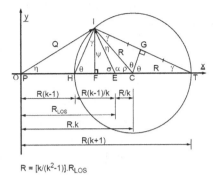

Fig. 1. The Apollonius Intercept Circle

2.2 Characteristic Distances

In addition to the ratio between PI and EI, the ratios between CI and EC, PC and CI are also k. The meanings of distances CI,EC and PC are illustrated in Figure 1. The ratio was originally expressed as $1/k$, which is corrected into k during verification.

$$\frac{CI}{EC} = \frac{PC}{CI} = k$$

The relation between the radius R and the line of sight R_{LOS} is described by the following equation.

$$R = \left(\frac{k}{k^2 - 1}\right) R_{LOS}$$

2.3 Characteristic Angles

In Figure 1, a number of triangles are presented. It is worth noting that several triangles have congruent angles sharing the same value. For example, there are two η angles and three θ angles. Some characteristic angles are given in Table 1.

The non-allowed steering directions (NASD) are calculated from a relationship between the aspect angle α of the Evader aircraft and the collision angle η of the Pursuer aircraft in Table 1.

The angle ψ is originally defined as $\alpha - \pi/2$ without being bounded by any condition. This definition applies only when $\dfrac{\pi}{2} < \alpha < \pi$. During verification, this mistake is found and then the definition of ψ is refined into cases as in Table 1.

The proximity characterization method also performs real analysis of some characteristics, such as the limits and monotonicity of CH and PH with respect to k. Due to space limitation, we do not introduce them and their verification (also the verification of the limit of ψ in Table 1).

Table 1. Characteristic Angles in terms of α and η

ψ	$\psi = \dfrac{\pi}{2} - \alpha$	$0 < \alpha < \dfrac{\pi}{2}$
	$\psi = \alpha - \dfrac{\pi}{2}$	$\dfrac{\pi}{2} < \alpha < \pi$
	$\psi \rightarrow \dfrac{\pi}{2}$	$\alpha \rightarrow 0$ or $\alpha \rightarrow \pi$
η	$\sin(\eta) = \dfrac{\sin(\alpha)}{k}$	$\max(|\sin(\eta)|) = \dfrac{1}{k}$

3   Formalization in Coq

In this section, we present the formalization of the aircraft proximity characterization method in Coq. As described before, the proximity characterization based on the Apollonius circle is a geometric method representing the position and movement relation between two aircraft. Correspondingly, the formalization starts with the kinematics of the aircraft then moves the geometric objects which are subsequently used to build the formal proximity characterization.

3.1   Aircraft Dynamics

Parameters and Assumptions. The proximity characterization method takes three parameters: the velocity of the Pursuer aircraft, the velocity of the Evader aircraft, and the initial position of the Evader with respect to the Pursuer aircraft. We formalize the aircraft kinematics in a two-dimensional space (i.e., in a plane) and assume the following:

1. The initial position of the Pursuer is assumed as the origin of a Cartesian coordinate system;
2. The initial position of the Evader is assumed on the x-axis of the coordinate system.

Based on these assumptions, the parameters for the proximity characterization are expressed below, where R is a Coq type, denoting the set of real numbers.

```
Parameter xe : R.
Parameter Vxp Vyp : R.
Parameter Vxe Vye : R.
```

The parameter xe is used to describe the x-coordinate of the Evader's position. The parameters Vxp and Vyp determine the velocity of the Pursuer in a two-dimensional space, and similarly Vxe and Vye are for the velocity of the Evader.

Aircraft Positions. Aircraft proximity depends on the absolute positions of the aircraft involved. In the two dimensional space, the aircraft positions are determined by the coordinates of the aircraft. In addition, a position should reflect the time at which an aircraft is at that position. The type for an aircraft position is defined below.

```
Inductive Position (t : R) : Type :=
   | position : R -> R -> Position t.
```

A value of this type `position t x y` means that at time `t` the aircraft is located at `(x,y)`. The initial positions of Pursuer and Evader , `Pp0` and `Pe0`, are given below. The initial time is indicated by the number 0.

```
Definition Pp0 : Position 0 := position 0 0 0.
Definition Pe0 : Position 0 := position 0 xe 0.
```

Aircraft Velocity and Movement. The collision of two aircraft occurs only when the aircraft are moving. Hence, an aircraft velocity is a necessary metric for the proximity characterization. To represent the velocity, we define the following `Velocity` type. Each value of this type is a velocity. A velocity `velocity x y` indicates the speed components `x` and `y` with respect to the x-axis and the y-axis, respectively.

```
Inductive Velocity :Type :=
 | velocity : R -> R -> Velocity.
```

The following are the definitions of the respective velocities for the Pursuer and the Evader. The definitions take the parameters `Vxp, Vyp` and `Vxe, Vye`.

```
Definition Vp : Velocity := velocity Vxp Vyp.
Definition Ve : Velocity := velocity Vxe Vye.
```

Suppose an aircraft is flying at a velocity `v` and its position at time 0 is denoted by `start`. Then, its new position at time `t` is computed by the function `CurPosition`.

```
Definition CurPosition (start: Position 0)
                       (t:R)(v:Velocity) : Position t :=
  match start with
  | position x0 y0 =>
    match v with
    | velocity vx vy => position t (x0+vx*t) (y0+vy*t)
    end
  end.
```

Using the `CurPosition` function, we can define the new positions of the Pursuer and the Evader at time `t`, as shown below.

```
Definition Ppt (t:R) : Position t := CurPosition Pp0 t Vp.
Definition Pet (t:R) : Position t := CurPosition Pe0 t Ve.
```

Given the velocity v of an aircraft, its flying distance after time t is defined by the function FlyingDist.

```
Definition FlyingDist (t:R) (v:Velocity) : R:=
  match v with
  | velocity vx vy => sqrt ((vx*t)*(vx*t)+(vy*t)*(vy*t))
  end.
```

Aircraft Intercept Condition and Position. At some time t, two aircraft may intercept, meaning that the two aircraft at time t are at the same position. This intercept condition is expressed as as a Coq predicate below.

```
Definition Intercepted (t:R) (p0:Position t)
                       (p1:Position t) : Prop :=
  match p0 with
  | position x0 y0=>
    match p1 with
    | position x1 y1 => x0 = x1 /\ y0 = y1
    end
  end.
```

That is, the positions p0 and p1 of two intercepting aircraft at time t have the same x-coordinate and the same y-coordinate. If the Pursuer and the Evader are intercepted at time t, the position is calculated by the function InterceptPos. The second parameter of InterceptPos is a proof that shows the Pursuer and the Evader intercept at time t, ensuring the returned position is a real intercept position. The name of the proof does not matter, indicated by a underscore _.

```
Definition InterceptPos (t:R)
           (_:Intercepted t (Ppt t) (Pet t)) : Position t :=  Ppt t.
```

Since the positions Ppt t or Pet t are the same at the time of intercept, so there is no difference in using either Ppt t or Pet t to represent the intercept position.

Aircraft Speed Ratio. The ratio of the Pursuer's speed to the Evader's speed, denoted by k, is an important parameter used in the proximity characterization method. The speed of an aircraft is the magnitude of its velocity, as defined below by MagVp and MagVe, respectively.

```
Definition MagVp : R := sqrt (Vxp*Vxp+Vyp*Vyp).
Definition MagVe : R := sqrt (Vxe*Vxe+Vye*Vye).
```

Then, their speed ratio k is expressed as MagVp/MagVe. A constant speed ratio for the two aircraft implies that the ratio of their flying distances will be the same value, given a specified time period. Formally, the ratio of flying distances of the Pursuer and the Evader is expressed by the theorem FlyingDisRatio.

```
Theorem FlyingDisRatio : forall t:R, t>0  ->
                  FlyingDist t Vp/FlyingDist t Ve = k.
```

3.2   Geometric Objects and Their Properties

In this section, we formalize the geometric objects that are used by the proximity characterization method. Some properties on geometric objects, such as the Law of Sines and the Pythagorean theorem, are stated axiomatically.

Points and Line Segments. In the two dimensional plane, a point is determined by two real numbers, indicating its x-coordinate and y-coordinate, respectively. As such, the type `Point` allows to construct a point value from two real numbers.

```
Inductive Point : Type :=
  | point : R -> R -> Point.
```

From an aircraft position, we can build a geometric point by using the function `mkPoint`. This function simply links the kinematics of each aircraft with their respective static geometric objects.

```
Definition mkPoint (t:R)(p:Position t) : Point :=
  match p with
  | position x y => point x y
  end.
```

Thus, assume `Ipf` is a proof of the intercept condition `Intercepted (Ppt t) (Pet t)`. Then, the specific geometric point, at time `t`, that the Pursuer and the Evader will intercept at can be obtained by evaluating `mkPoint t (InterceptPos t Ipf)`.

The length of the line segment between two points `p0` and `p1` is computed by the `length` function.

```
Definition length (p0 p1: Point) : R :=
  match p0 with
  | point x0 y0 =>
    match p1 with
    | point x1 y1 =>
      sqrt ((x0-x1)*(x0-x1)+(y0-y1)*(y0-y1))
    end
  end.
```

Circles, Angles and Triangles. The Apollonius circle plays a central role in the proximity characterization method. In our formalization, we define a circle not only by its center point and radius, but also explicitly requiring that the radius of a valid circle be positive, as shown in the `Circle` type. This requirement prevents the construction of invalid circles (i.e., the circles with non-positive radius).

```
Inductive Circle : Type :=
  | circle (c:Point) (r:R) (rPos:r>0): Circle.
```

The proximity characterization method describes the relations between angles, such as the aspect angle and the collision angle. As defined below, an angle is constructed with the constructor **ang** by specifying three points, say `p0`, `p1` and `p2`, where point `p1` is the vertex of the angle, and the two line segments between p0 and p1 and between p2 and p1 are the sides of the angle constructed.

```
Inductive Angle : Type :=
| ang : Point ->Point->Point->Angle.
```

To be flexible, our angle definition allows the three parameter points in an angle to be the same. This flexibility is necessary for the formalization since the points I and H, points I and T, points F and E and C in Figure 1 may overlap, which lead to angles with overlapped parameter points.

A triangle can be determined by its three vertexes. Given three points p0, p1 and p2, the definition below allows a triangle to be constructed by tri p0 p1 p2. This definition does not require the difference of three parameter points. Still, this flexibility is necessary for our formalization since the triangles in the proximity characterization method might have overlapped vertexes. For example, in Figure 1, F can overlap other points like C, H, E and T.

```
Inductive Triangle : Type :=
| tri : Point->Point->Point->Triangle.
```

The congruence between two triangles is needed when proving the relationship between angles (e.g., the equality between angles of two triangles). In our formal setting, triangle similarity is defined as follows. The predicate DiffPoint means its two parameter points are not the same and hence the resulting line segment is not zero in length.

```
Definition SimilarTriangle (ABC : Triangle)
                           (DEF : Triangle) : Prop :=
  match ABC with
  | tri A B C =>
    match DEF with
    | tri D E F =>
      let r := length A B/length E D in
      DiffPoint A B /\ DiffPoint B C /\
      DiffPoint A C /\ DiffPoint D E /\
      DiffPoint E F /\ DiffPoint D F /\
      r = length C B/length E F /\ r = length A C/length F D
    end
  end
```

Angular Radian and Its Properties. In the proximity characterization method, the radian is used as the measure for angles. For our formalization purpose, we do not directly calculate this measure. Instead, we axiomatically characterize the properties of the radian measure, which will be then used in the proofs of the theorems and the lemmas regarding the aircraft proximity characterization. That is, the proofs need the properties of the measure rather than the concrete value of the measure. We define a function variable AngRadian for representing the radian measure of angles.

```
Variable AngRadian: Angle -> R.
```

Thus, given an angle ang, the expression AngRadian ang represents the radian measure of ang. The properties of the radian measure by axioms. The following is the axiom for the Pythagorean theorem, as an example.

```
Axiom Pyth: forall t:Triangle,
 match t with
 | tri A C B => let angC := ang A C B in
    AngRadian angC = Pi/2 ->
      length C B * length C B + length C A * length C A =
                                 length A B * length A B
 end.
```

3.3   Formalized Characterization of Aircraft Proximity

In this section, the proximity characterization is formalized by expressing and proving the relations 1) between the Apollonius circle and the intercept point, 2) between specified angles (e.g., the aspect angle and the collision angle), and 3) between specified line segments related to the position of each aircraft.

The Apollonius Circle. By using the concepts just defined, the Apollonius circle ACircle is now defined below.

```
Definition ACircle (Kpf: k >1) (XePos: xe>0): Circle :=
 let c : Point := point ((k*k*xe)/(k*k-1)) 0 in
 let r : R := k*xe/(k*k-1) in
   circle c r (RadiusPos xe k Kpf XePos).
```

The center and the radius of this circle are described in the proximity characterization method. However, in the formal definition, we need to provide an explicit proof that the radius is positive. This proof is constructed by applying the lemma RadiusPos.

```
Lemma RadiusPos:forall x k':R, k'>1 -> x>0 -> k'*x/(k'*k'-1) > 0.
```

To construct the proof of positive radius, the definition ACircle needs the conditions k > 1 and xe > 0. If k < 1, a valid Apollonius circle can only be constructed after the roles of the Pursuer and the Evader are exchanged, as suggested by the proximity characterization method.

In Figure 1, the proximity characterization method claims the intercept point is in the Apollonius circle. Before formalizing this claim, we first define the InCircle property, which gives the condition as to whether a point belongs to a circle. That is, if the length between a point and a circle center is the same as the circle radius, then this point is in the circle.

```
Definition InCircle (p:Point) (c:Circle) : Prop :=
  match c with
  | circle cen r _  => length p cen = r
  end.
```

The following theorem formalizes the claim that the intercept point is in the Apollonius circle. The definition of this theorem is dependent on the InCircle property. Note that the condition Ipf explicitly gives one condition of the theorem, that is, that the Pursuer and the Evader must intercept. The function InterceptPnt t Ipf is defined as `mkPoint t (InterceptPos t Ipf)`. This theorem combines the aircraft kinematics with the geometrical objects.

```
Theorem InterceptCircle : forall (t:R) (Kpf:k>1)
  (Ipf: Intercepted t (Ppt t) (Pet t)) (XePos:xe>0), t>0 ->
    let I : Point := InterceptPnt t Ipf in
    InCircle I (ACircle Kpf XePos).
```

The Formalized Angle Relations. The most important angle relation is between the aspect angle and the collision angle. This relation is the basis for the non-allowed steering directions (NASD). In Figure 1, the aspect angle is represented α, the collision angle η, and their relation is represented as $\sin \eta = \sin \alpha / k$. Formally, this relation is represented in the `AlphaEta` theorem.

```
Theorem AlphaEta : forall (t:R) (H0:Intercepted t (Ppt t) (Pet t)),
  t>0 -> xe>0 -> k>1 ->
    let P := mkPoint 0 Pp0 in
    let E := mkPoint 0 Pe0 in
    let I := InterceptPnt t H0 in
    let C := point xc 0 in
    let eta := AngRadian (ang I P E) in
    let alpha := AngRadian (ang C E I) in
    sin eta = sin alpha/k.
```

The proximity characterization method defines the maximum of $\sin \eta = 1/k$. This characteristic is expressed by the `MaxEta2` theorem. This theorem explicitly gives the condition (`Vxe = 0`$\bigwedge$`Vye <> 0`), at which $\sin \eta$ takes its maximum value $1/k$. We also provide a theorem for $\sin \eta \leq 1/k$. Thus, we know $1/k$ is the maximal value of $\sin \eta$.

```
Theorem MaxEta2 : forall (t:R) (H0:Intercepted t (Ppt t) (Pet t)),
  t>0 -> xe>0 -> k>1 -> (Vxe = 0/\Vye <>0)->
    let P := mkPoint 0 Pp0 in
    let E := mkPoint 0 Pe0 in
    let I := InterceptPnt t H0 in
    let C := point xc 0 in
    let eta := AngRadian (ang I P E) in
    let alpha := AngRadian (ang C E I) in
    sin eta = 1/k.
```

In addition, when the Pursuer and the Evader will intercept after time t, η is an angle in the triangle `PIE`, such that its radian measure is between 0 and Pi. Hence, the conditions of `MaxEta2` theorem ensures $|\sin \eta| = \sin \eta$ and the `MaxEta2` theorem formalizes $\max(|\sin \eta|) = 1/k$ in Table 1.

In Figure 1 there are a number of unique triangles, some of which have identical angles. There are two triangles with an angle η, three triangles with an angle γ and three with an angle θ. The proximity characterization method does not present adequate proofs to show that the corresponding angles are the same. To formalize the equality of corresponding angles, we prove theorems on triangle similarity, since two similar triangles have the same corresponding angles.

The equality of two η angles is reflected by the `PICIECSimilar` theorem, which proves the similarity of the two triangles `tri P I C` and `tri I E C`. Consequently, the η angle in the triangle `tri P I C` (i.e., the angle `ang I P C`) is the same as the η angle in the triangle `tri I E C` (i.e., the angle `ang E I C`).

```
Theorem PICIECSimilar:forall (t:R)(H0:Intercepted t (Ppt t)(Pet t)),
   t>0 -> xe>0 -> k>1 ->
     let P := mkPoint 0 Pp0 in
     let E := mkPoint 0 Pe0 in
     let I := InterceptPnt t H0 in
     let C := point xc 0 in
     SimilarTriangle (tri P I C) (tri I E C).
```

The equality of the angles γ and θ is verified by proving similarity of the triangles `tri I G C` and `tri T G C`, and the similarity of triangles `tri I F H` and `tri I G C`, where G is the midpoint of the line from point I to T. The details of such similarity are elided here.

In Table 1, the relation between α and ψ is represented in two cases when $0 < \alpha < \pi/2$ and $\pi/2 < \alpha < \pi$, together with the limit of ψ when α is infinitely close to 0 or π. We first present the theorem `AlphaPsi2`, which formalizes the case when $\pi/2 < \alpha < \pi$ through the condition `Vxe < 0 /\ Vye <> 0`. This condition ensures that the angles ψ and σ are in one right triangle. The condition is not given in the original proximity characterization method.

```
Theorem AlphaPsi2 : forall (t:R) (Ipf:Intercepted t (Ppt t)(Pet t)),
   t>0 -> (Vxe<0/\Vye<>0 )-> xe>0 -> k>1 ->
   let I := InterceptPnt t Ipf in
   let F := point (xfi t Ipf) 0 in
   let E := point xe 0 in
   let C := point xc 0 in
   let psi := ang F I E in
   let alpha := ang C E I in
   Pi/2 + AngRadian psi = AngRadian alpha.
```

Based on the first failure attempt to prove the `AlphaPsi2` theorem without the condition `Vxe < 0 /\ Vye <> 0`, we realized that when `Vxe>=0`, the above relation between ψ and α is not true, since the angles ψ and α are in one right triangle and hence $\psi + \alpha = \pi/2$. Then, the proximity characterization method is refined to include the case $\psi + \alpha = \pi/2$ with the condition $0 < \alpha < \pi/2$. This case is formalized in the `AlphaPsi4` theorem.

```
Theorem AlphaPsi4: forall (t:R) (Ipf:Intercepted t (Ppt t) (Pet t)),
   t>0 -> (Vxe >0/\Vye <>0)-> xe>0 -> k>1 ->
   let I := InterceptPnt t Ipf in
   let F := point (xfi t Ipf) 0 in
   let E := point xe 0 in
   let C := point xc 0 in
   let alpha := ang C E I in
   let psi := ang F I E in
   AngRadian alpha + AngRadian psi = Pi/2.
```

Relations Between Line Segments. The proximity characterization method defines the lengths of the line segments (e.g., CE, EH, etc.) by representing these lengths in terms of Radius and RLos, respectively. RLos is a new name for xe (i.e. RLos = xe).

Before formalizing these lengths, we first characterize the relation between Radius and RLos in the lemma RRLos. Thus, after we prove a segment length in terms of Radius, this relation makes it easier to prove the length in terms of RLos.

```
Lemma RRLos : k>1 -> Radius = RLos*k/(k*k-1).
```

The proximity characterization method also describes three ratios between line segment lengths: PI and EI, EC and CI, and CI and PC. The lemma defining the ratio PI and EI is given as an example.

```
Lemma PIEIRatio : forall t:R, t>0->
  let PI:= length (mkPoint 0 Pp0) (mkPoint t (Ppt t)) in
  let EI:= length (mkPoint 0 Pe0) (mkPoint t (Pet t)) in
      PI/EI = k.
```

These lemmas about length ratios are used in the proofs of some theorems, such as InterceptCircle and PIEIECSimilar. Though the proximity characterization method describes these ratios, it was not clear at the first instance in developing the formal proofs as to why they were defined. Our formalization provides clarity of how these ratios are used in the proofs of proximity characterization theorems.

4   Our Experiences: The Coq Proofs Modularization

We present the complete definitions and proofs in a CSIRO technical report [10]. In this section, we report our experiences of performing formal proofs in Coq.

There are more than 4500 lines of Coq (version 8.3) code for the definitions and proofs. Each line in proof contains a Coq tactic, which instructs Coq on how to deal with the contexts and goals for that proof. Coq is a proof assistant and cannot automate the process of the proofs like a proof planning system [11]. Hence, The main challenge that was faced when proving a theorem or lemma was in finding a suitable proof tactic for the current contexts and goals. A wrong tactic can lead Coq to a proof goal that cannot be proved.

The proximity characterization method uses arithmetic operations on the set of Real numbers, as shown in the definitions of the centre and radius of the Apollonius circle. To deal with Real numbers, we imported the Coq Real library, which defines the Real numbers as a set. Operations (e.g. plus, multiplication, division, comparison) were then defined over this set as axioms such that the set has an algebraic ring structure.

In addition to the axioms provided in the Coq Real library, we also define axioms over real numbers to improve our efficiency of performing proofs. In the procedure of proofs, we define an intermediate axiom over the operations on real numbers, when the property stated by the axiom is true according to laws of real number algebra, but needs a number of steps to prove in Coq. An example of intermediate axiom is shown below.

```
Axiom Rplus_sqr: forall x0 x1: R,
  (x0-x1)*(x0-x1) = x0*x0 - 2*x0*x1 + x1*x1.
```

In this way, we can focus on our main target of proving the lemmas and theorems related to the proximity characterization. These intermediate axioms can be changed to lemmas and proved by using axioms from the Coq library. Thus, the verification is modularized into two parts: one is to formalize the proximity characterization method, and the other is to provide formalized properties on real numbers to facilitate the work in the first part. Through modularization, we improve our efficiency of performing complex verification tasks.

5 Related Research

The development of algorithms to detect and resolve potential aircraft conflicts in air traffic management systems is an important activity to ensure aircraft safety, and such algorithms must be highly trusted. These algorithms are developed using mathematical models which are then formally verified using tools like PVS, as described in [4–6]. Our research differs from these approaches in that our focus has been to formalize and prove various geometric and kinematic relationships of a new mathematical model. This research has resulted in a verified mathematical model based on the Apollonius geometry.

NASA's Small Aircraft Transportation System (SATS) defines an operational model and protocol for aircraft arrivals and departures at airports. The SATS High Volume Operations has been formalized and verified in [12], with one major design flaw found. In [7], the proofs for the safety properties of the SATS landing protocol were presented. Both [7, 12] formalize the states of aircraft, as well as state transitions specified by the SATS. In [13], a communication protocol between a ground station and a remotely operated aircraft was verified.

Platzer et al [8] formulate aircraft collision avoidance maneuvers in terms of a hybrid system that can take into account the interaction between the discrete control and the continuous aircraft dynamics. In particular, a specialised hybrid systems verification tool has been developed and used to show correctness of roundabout collision avoidance maneuvers. This tool is used to verify systems whose behaviors are partially described in differential equations. It is not applicable to our case, since our formalization and analysis does not rely on any differential equations to describe aircraft kinematics.

Many authors have formalized geometric objects and proofs on geometric theorems [14–16]. However, it is not easy to incorporate their geometric objects directly into our formalization. For example, the geometric objects formalized in [14–16] are coordinate-free; that is, a point is a primitive object, rather than (as in our case) being constructed from the coordinates that represent the point on a plane that describes an aircraft position. Similarly, our formalization of the proximity characterization method relies on specific requirements of geometric objects, such as a triangle that can have two overlapping vertexes.

In [14] and [17], new Coq tactics are implemented for automatic theorem proving in geometry, based on the area method [18] or Wu's method [19]. The new tactics are used to prove geometric theorems such as the Pythagorean theorem and the Law of Sines, which are defined as axioms in our formalization.

Cruz-Filipe [20] used Coq to formalize constructive real analysis. The formalization includes continuity, differentiability, integration, Taylor's theorem and the Fundamental Theorem of Calculus. However, this formalization is based on Cauchy sequences, thereby making it difficult to apply to our formulation of geometric and kinematic relationships based on the Apollonius geometry.

6 Conclusion

The safety of aircraft flight requires that the minimum standards of spatial and temporal proximity must not be violated. The proximity characterization method based on the Apollonius circle is a novel and effective method for determining both the non-allowed steering directions and other proximity characteristics. To guarantee the correctness of this method, we formalized the proofs of the proximity method in a proof assistant Coq. During this process, we used Coq's specification language to develop proofs supporting the aircraft kinematics, geometric objects and theorems about proximity characteristics and interactively proved all theorems using Coq's proof environment. Our formalization, including definitions and proofs, is machine-checkable using Coq. By taking this approach we have raised the confidence and trust to the novel aircraft proximity characterization method.

References

1. Fulton, N.L., Huynh, U.: A survey of aircraft proximity applications based on the Apollonius intercept. Report EP103115, CMIS, CSIRO, Canberra, ACT 2601, Australia (2010)
2. Ellerbroek, J., Visser, M., van Dam, S.B.J., Mulder, M., van Paassen, M.M.R.: Design of an airborne three-dimensional, separation assistance display. IEEE Trans. Systems, Man, and Cybernetics - Part A: Systems and Humans 41(5), 2787–2794 (2011)
3. Robb, M., White, B., Tsourdos, A.: Earliest intercept line guidance: a novel concept for improving mid-course guidance in area air defence. In: AIAA Guidance, Navigation, and Control Conference and Exhibit, San Francisco, California (August 2005)
4. Muñoz, C., Carreño, V., Dowek, G., Butler, R.W.: Formal verification of conflict detection algorithms. International Journal on Software Tools for Technology Transfer 4(3), 371–380 (2003)
5. Dowek, G., Muñoz, C., Carreño, V.: Provably safe coordinated strategy for distributed conflict resolution. In: AIAA Guidance, Navigation, and Control Conference and Exhibit, San Francisco, California (August 2005)
6. Dowek, G., Muñoz, C.: Conflict detection and resolution for 1,2,. . . ,n aircraft. In: 7th AIAA Aviation Technology, Integration and Operations Conference, Belfast, Northern Ireland (September 2007)
7. Umeno, S., Lynch, N.: Proving safety properties of an aircraft landing protocol using I/O automata and the PVS theorem prover: A case study. In: Misra, J., Nipkow, T., Sekerinski, E. (eds.) FM 2006. LNCS, vol. 4085, pp. 64–80. Springer, Heidelberg (2006)
8. Platzer, A., Clarke, E.M.: Formal verification of curved flight collision avoidance maneuvers: A case study. In: Cavalcanti, A., Dams, D.R. (eds.) FM 2009. LNCS, vol. 5850, pp. 547–562. Springer, Heidelberg (2009)
9. The Coq Deleopment Team: The Coq Proof Assistant, http://coq.inria.fr (accessed May 30, 2012)
10. Liu, D., Fulton, N.L., Zic, J., de Groot, M.: Formalization of aircraft proximity characterization in coq. Report EP125569, ICT Centre and CMIS, CSIRO, Marsfield, NSW 2122, Australia (2012)

11. Siekmann, J.H., Benzmüller, C., Autexier, S.: Computer supported mathematics with omegamega. J. Applied Logic 4(4), 533–559 (2006)
12. Muñoz, C.A., Dowek, G., Carreño, V.: Modeling and verification of an air traffic concept of operations. In: Proceedings of the 2004 ACM SIGSOFT International Symposium on Software Testing and Analysis, ISSTA 2004, pp. 175–182. ACM, New York (2004)
13. Goodloe, A., Muñoz, C.: Compositional verification of a communication protocol for a remotely operated aircraft. Science of Computer Programming (2011) (in press)
14. Janicic, P., Narboux, J., Quaresma, P.: The area method - a recapitulation. J. Autom. Reasoning 48(4), 489–532 (2012)
15. Pham, T.-M., Bertot, Y., Narboux, J.: A Coq-based library for interactive and automated theorem proving in plane geometry. In: Murgante, B., Gervasi, O., Iglesias, A., Taniar, D., Apduhan, B.O. (eds.) ICCSA 2011, Part IV. LNCS, vol. 6785, pp. 368–383. Springer, Heidelberg (2011)
16. Slind, K., Bunker, A., Gopalakrishnan, G. (eds.): TPHOLs 2004. LNCS, vol. 3223. Springer, Heidelberg (2004)
17. Génevaux, J.D., Narboux, J., Schreck, P.: Formalization of Wu's simple method in Coq. In: Jouannaud, J.-P., Shao, Z. (eds.) CPP 2011. LNCS, vol. 7086, pp. 71–86. Springer, Heidelberg (2011)
18. Chou, S.C., Gao, X.S., Zhang, J.Z.: Automated production of traditional proofs for constructive geometry theorems. In: Proceedings of Eighth Annual IEEE Symposium on Logic in Computer Science, pp. 48–56 (June 1993)
19. Wu, W.T.: On the decision problem and the mechanization of theorem proving in elementary geometry. Scientia Sinica 21(2), 159–172 (1978)
20. Cruz-Filipe, L.: A constructive formalization of the fundamental theorem of calculus. In: Geuvers, H., Wiedijk, F. (eds.) TYPES 2002. LNCS, vol. 2646, pp. 108–126. Springer, Heidelberg (2003)

Assisting Specification Refinement by Random Testing

Mengjun Li*

School of Computer Science, National University of Defense Technology,
Changsha, China

Abstract. Program invariants play a major role in program analysis, the specification refinement technique has the capability to generating all the required program invariants for verifying a specification. The refinement invariants generation is the main obstacles of the specification refinement. Based on random testing, this paper presents a practical assistant approach for specification refinement. The effectiveness of the approach is demonstrated on examples.

Keywords: Program Invariant, Specification Refinement, Random Testing.

1 Introduction

A key problem in automatic software verification system is the inference of program invariants. Many different approaches have been developed for inferring loop invariants. These approaches include:

(i)techniques based on abstract interpretation such as [1][2].
(ii)template-based techniques, such as [3][4][5][6].
(iii)algebraic techniques such as [7][8][9][10][11][12].

The above techniques are utilized to generate program invariants in the appointed forms, such as linear invariants, polynomial equational invariants etc.

Loop invariant is a weakened form of the loop's postcondition, taking advantage of this observation, in [13],Carlo A. Furia and Bertrand Meyer presented the work by using the postcondition as the basis and using various heuristics such as uncoupling for invariant inference. Thanks to these heuristics, the technique is able to infer invariants for a large variety of loop programs. This work indicates that inferring invariants is relevant to the specification of programs.

The specification refinement technique has the capability to generating all the required program invariants for verifying a specification. The refinement invariants generation is the main obstacles of the specification refinement.

Dynamic techniques have been applied to invariant inference. The Daikon approach of Ernst et al. [14][15] showed that dynamic inference is practical. The

* This work was supported by the National Natural Science Foundation of China (Grant Nos. 60703075, 90718017).

L. Groves and J. Sun (Eds.): ICFEM 2013, LNCS 8144, pp. 102–114, 2013.

dynamic approach consists in testing a large number of candidate properties against several program runs, the properties that are not violated in any of the executions are retained as "likely" invariants.

With the goal of reducing the burden of generating refinement invariants, based on random testing, this paper presents a practical assistant approach for specification refinement. The candidate refinement invariants are acted as the candidate properties, since they may be or may not be the program invariants of the program, the random testing technology is utilized to test the candidate properties against several program runs, the candidate properties that are not violated in any of the executions are retained as likely refinement invariants. Particularly, when the candidate refinement invariants can be described as equational parameter templates, the values of the parameters in the templates will be computed by random testing and solving linear equation system with Gaussian elimination method. Finally, the effectiveness of the approach is demonstrated on examples.

The rest of this paper is structured as follows: section 2 presents the Event-B method and the Rodin Platform, section 3 presents the random testing technique, section 4 presents the motivation, the algorithm for assisting specification refinement by random testing is presented in section 5, results of the experiments are shown in section 6, section 7 discusses the related work, and section 8 concludes this paper.

2   Event-B Method and the Rodin Platform

Event-B is a widely-used formal method for modeling and reasoning about complex systems. Event-B models are described in terms of contexts and machines, see Figure1.

Contexts[16][17][18] contain the static parts of an Event-B model. Besides carrier sets and constants, each context may consist of theorems and axioms which are used to describe the properties of carrier sets and constants. Contexts can be extended by other contexts and seen by more than one machines, see Figure2.

Machines[16][17][18] contain the dynamic parts of an Event-B model. Each machine may consist of variables, invariants, theorems and events. Variables are

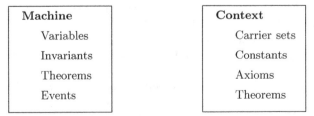

Fig. 1. Machines and Contexts

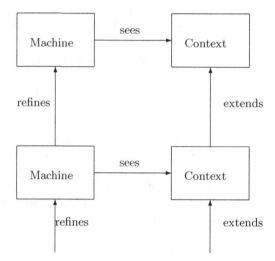

Fig. 2. Relationship between machines and contexts

constrained by invariants and theorems, the invariants must be proved through the discharge of proof obligations[16]. Each event is composed of three elements: an event name, guards and actions. The guard is the enabled condition. The actions determine the way the variables evolves[16]. The atomic action may be performed only when its guard holds. Machine can be refined by other machines, but each machine can refine at most one machine, see Figure2.

The Rodin platform[19] is an open and extensible tool for Event-B modeling and reasoning. Rodin also provides useful plug-ins such as a proof-obligation generator, provers etc.

3   Random Testing

In the random testing technique, the pseudo random numbers are generated as inputs of programs. In this paper, the random testing technique is illustrated using the integer square root algorithm program shown in Figure3. The considered imperative loop implements an algorithm for computing the integer square root k for a given integer number n.

For the integer square root algorithm program, we utilize the Mathematica program IntegerSquareRoot.m in Figure4. to randomly test whether $m = (k+1)^2$ is a likely program invariants.

In IntegerSquareRoot.m, the variable *sample* denotes the number of the pseudo random generated as inputs, and the variable *counter* denotes the sampling number of values of program variables. $RandomInteger[\{i_{min}, i_{max}\}]$ is a Mathematica function utilized to generate a pseudo-random integer number in the range $\{i_{min}, i_{max}\}$. The random testing technology is utilized to test

```
k := 0;
j := 1;
m := 1;
while (m ≤ n) do
{
    k := k + 1;
    j := j + 2;
    m := m + j;
}
```

Fig. 3. The integer square root algorithm program

```
sample = 5;
flag = true;
counter = 1;
While[counter ≤ sample,
    n = RandomInteger[{1, 1000}];
    k = 0;
    j = 1;
    m = 1;
    While[m ≤ n,
        k = k + 1;
        j = j + 2;
        m = k + j;
    ];
    If[flag == true,
        If[Simplify[m' == (k' + 1)², n' == n&&k' == k&&
        j' == j&&m' == m], , flag = false];
    ];
    counter = counter + 1];
```

Fig. 4. The Mathematica program IntegerSquareRoot.m

whether $m = (k + 1)^2$ is a likely program invariant at the exit of the loop with the Mathematica function $Simplify[expr, assum]$, which is utilized to simplify the expression $expr$ using the assumptions $assum$, for instance, the statement $If[Simplify[m' == (k' + 1)^2, n' == n\&\&k' == k\&\&j' == j\&\&m' == m], , flag = false]$ simplify the expression $m' == (k' + 1)^2$ under the assumption n', k', j', m' are assigned values n, k, j, m, and if the result is $false$, then the value of $falg$ is modified with $false$.

For the program IntegerSquareRoot.m, only if the output value of the variable $flag$ is $true$, $m = (k + 1)^2$ is retained as a likely program invariant at the exit of the loop.

4   Motivation

The assistant approach for specification refinement by random testing is illustrated using the integer square root algorithm program shown in Figure3. The specification of the program is specified by using the Hoare-triple in Figure5.

pre: $n \geq 0$
post: $k^2 \leq n < (k+1)^2$

Fig. 5. The specification of the integer square root algorithm program

In Figure5, *pre* denotes the precondition of the program, while *post* denotes its postcondition. The precondition defines the condition assumed concerning the parameters of the program, and the postcondition denotes what expected concerning the outcome of the program.

It is easy to encode an Hoare-triple equivalently as the initial Event-B model. The parameters in precondition are constants and the precondition are the axioms of these constants. The results are variables and the postcondition is represented by an event containing the postcondition in its guard together with a *skip* action. And the specification in Figure5. is encoded as the following initial Event-B model described in Figure6.

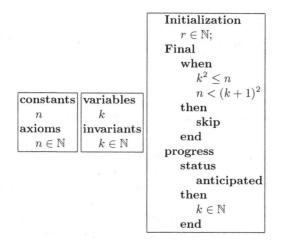

Fig. 6. The initial model

For the specification described in Figure5, the candidate refinement invariant may be $k^2 \leq n$ or $(k+1)^2 < n$, the Mathematica program IntegerSquareRoot-a.m in Figure7. is utilized to decide which one is the likely refinement invariant. Since the returned result of $flag$ is *true*, then $k^2 \leq n$ is the likely refinement

```
sample = 5;
flag = true;
counter = 1;
While[counter ≤ sample,
    n = RandomInteger[{1, 1000}];
    k = 0;
    j = 1;
    m = 1;
    If[flag == true,
        If[Simplify[k'² ≤ n', n' == n&&k' == k&&
            j' == j&&m' == m],, flag = false];
    While[m ≤ n,
        k = k + 1;
        j = j + 2;
        m = k + j;
    ];
    If[flag == true,
        If[Simplify[k'² ≤ n', n' == n&&k' == k&&
            j' == j&&m' == m],, flag = false];
    ];
    counter = counter + 1];
```

Fig. 7. The Mathematica program IntegerSquareRoot-a.m

invariant. The initial model in Figure6. is refined by introducing the invariant $k^2 \leq n$ on k. And the first refinement model is described in Figure8.

The specification $(k+1)^2 < n$ will be refined. Note that the loop condition of the integer square root algorithm program is $m \leq n$, assumes that the candidate refinement invariant template is $c_1 + c_2 k^2 + c_3 k + c_4 j + c_5 m = 0$. How to compute the value of the unknown coefficients $c_i (i = 1, \cdots, 5)$?

By the definition of loop invariant, all the values of n, k, j, m at the exit of the loop satisfy the template, for instance, if we have $n = 0$ at the entry of the loop, then we have $k = 0, j = 1, m = 1$ at the exit, since the values of n, k, j, m at the exit satisfy the template $c_1 + c_2 k^2 + c_3 k + c_4 j + c_5 m = 0$, we have $c_1 + c_4 + c_5 = 0$.

Sampling s copies $n_i, k_i, j_i, m_i (i = 1, \cdots, s)$ of values of n, k, j, m, a linear equation system as follows will be obtained:

$$\begin{pmatrix} 1 & k_1^2 & k_1 & j_1 & m_1 \\ \vdots & \vdots & \vdots & \vdots & \vdots \\ 1 & k_s^2 & k_s & j_s & m_s \end{pmatrix} \begin{pmatrix} c_1 \\ c_2 \\ c_3 \\ c_4 \\ c_5 \end{pmatrix} = \begin{pmatrix} 0 \\ 0 \\ 0 \\ 0 \\ 0 \end{pmatrix}$$

With the knowledge of linear equation system, among all the vectors $\langle 1, k_l^2, k_l, j_l, m_l \rangle$
$(l = 1, \cdots, s)$, if there exist five vectors $\langle 1, k_{i_v}^2, k_{i_v}, j_{i_v}, m_{i_v} \rangle (v = 1, \cdots, 5)$ are linear independent, then the solutions of all the unknown coefficients $c_i (i =$

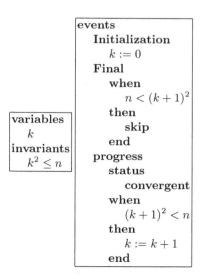

Fig. 8. The first refinement model

$1, \cdots, 5)$ are 0. And if there exist $t(1 \leq t < 5)$ vectors $\langle 1, k_{i_v}^2, k_{i_v}, j_{i_v}, m_{i_v} \rangle (v = 1, \cdots, t)$ are linear independent, then the solutions of the linear equation system are linear combination of $n - t$ linear independent vectors.

The above observation indicates that if there exist $l(l \geq 5)$ linear independent vectors $\langle 1, k_{i_v}^2, k_{i_v}, j_{i_v}, m_{i_v} \rangle (v = 1, \cdots, l)$ among all the vectors $\langle 1, k_u^2, k_u, j_u, m_u \rangle (u = 1, \cdots, s)$, the above loop has no loop invariant in the form $c_1 + c_2 k^2 + c_3 k + c_4 j + c_5 m = 0$. If there exist $l(1 \leq l < 5)$ vectors $\langle 1, k_{i_v}^2, k_{i_v}, j_{i_v}, m_{i_v} \rangle (v = 1, \cdots, l)$ are linear independent, then the linear equation system has solutions, replace the unknown coefficients $c_i (i = 1, \cdots, 5)$ in the template $c_1 + c_2 k^2 + c_3 k + c_4 j + c_5 m = 0$ with their solutions, we obtain a likely refinement invariant.

We use random testing technique to automatically sample values of n, k, j, m. For the integer square root algorithm program, we utilize the Mathematica program IntegerSquareRoot-b.m in Figure9. to random testing it and discover the likely refinement invariant.

In IntegerSquareRoot-b.m, the variable *sample* denotes the number of the generated pseudo random inputs, and the variable *counter* denotes the sampling number of values of program variables, $array1, array2, array3$ and $array4$ are arrays recording the values of n, k, j, m respectively, $Table[expr, \{i, i_{max}\}]$ is a Mathematica function used to generate a list of values of $expr$ when i runs from 1 to i_{max}, $Solve[eqns, vars]$ is a Mathematica function used to solve an equation or a set of equations for the variables $vars$.

In Table 1, the solutions of the linear equation systems induced by different samples are listed. From Table 1, we find the solutions are all equal when the sampling number *counter* ≥ 3:

$$C_1 = -C_4 - C_5, C_2 = -C_5, C_3 = -2C_4 - 2C_5,$$

Table 1. Solutions

Counter	Solutions
3	$C_1 = -C_4 - C_5, C_2 = -C_5, C_3 = -2C_4 - 2C_5$
4	$C_1 = -C_4 - C_5, C_2 = -C_5, C_3 = -2C_4 - 2C_5$
5	$C_1 = -C_4 - C_5, C_2 = -C_5, C_3 = -2C_4 - 2C_5$
50	$C_1 = -C_4 - C_5, C_2 = -C_5, C_3 = -2C_4 - 2C_5$
100	$C_1 = -C_4 - C_5, C_2 = -C_5, C_3 = -2C_4 - 2C_5$

where C_4, C_5 are free variables. Replace the unknown coefficients $c_i (i = 1, \cdots, 5)$ in the template $c_1 + c_2 k^2 + c_3 k + c_4 j + c_5 m = 0$ with the stable solution, we obtain the likely refinement invariants $C_4(-1 - 2k + j) + C_5(-1 - k^2 - 2k + m) = 0$. Note that C_4, C_5 are free variables, then $-1 - 2k + j = 0$ and $-1 - k^2 - 2k + m = 0$ are both likely refinement invariants.

The second refinement of the model is by introducing the new invariants $j = 2k + 1$ and $m = (k + 1)^2$ and refining the event progress, the refinement results is described in Figure10.

5   Assisting Specification Refinement By Random Testing

The algorithm for assisting specification refinement by random testing is described in Figure.11.

```
counter=5;
array1=Array[nValue,counter];
array2=Array[kValue,counter];
array3=Array[jValue,counter];
array4=Array[mValue,counter];
s=1;
While[s≤ counter,
  n=RandomInteger[{1, 1000}];
  k=0;
  j=1;
  m=1;
  While[m≤ n,
    k=k+1;
    j=j+2;
    m=k+j];
    Part[array1,l]=n;
    Part[array2,l]=k;
    Part[array3,l]=j;
    Part[array4,l]=m;
    s=s+1];
m=Table[C1+C2*Part[array2,tj]²+C3*Part[array2,tj]+C4*Part[array3,tj]
          +C5*Part[array4,tj]==0,{tj,counter}];
solutions=Solve[m,{C1,C2,C3,C4,C5}];
```

Fig. 9. The Program IntegerSquareRoot-b.m

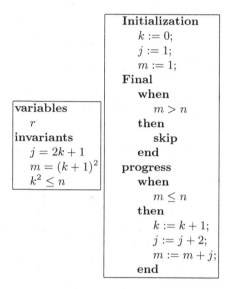

variables
r
invariants
$j = 2k + 1$
$m = (k + 1)^2$
$k^2 \leq n$

Initialization
$k := 0;$
$j := 1;$
$m := 1;$
Final
when
$\quad m > n$
then
$\quad$ **skip**
end
progress
when
$\quad m \leq n$
then
$\quad k := k + 1;$
$\quad j := j + 2;$
$\quad m := m + j;$
end

Fig. 10. The second refinement model

input
$\quad P :$ a program;
$\quad \eta :$ a candidate refinement invariant or an equational template with parameters $\mathcal{P}$
output
$\quad \eta' :$ *a likely refinement invariant or NULL*
begin
$\quad valueArray := randomSampling(P, varList, n);$
$\quad$ **If**$(\eta$ *is not an equational template*)
$\quad\quad$ **If**$(Simplify(\eta, varList, valueArray) == true)$
$\quad\quad\quad$ *return* $\eta;$
$\quad\quad$ **else**
$\quad\quad\quad$ *return NULL;*
$\quad$ **else**
$\quad$ {
$\quad\quad \Psi := generatingLinearSystem(valueArray, \eta)$
$\quad\quad \mathcal{P}^* := solvingLinearSystem(\Psi)$
$\quad\quad$ **If** $\mathcal{P}^* = 0$ **or** $\mathcal{P}^* = NULL$
$\quad\quad\quad$ **return**$NULL;$
$\quad\quad$ **else**
$\quad\quad\quad$ **return** $\eta[\mathcal{P}^*/\mathcal{P}];$
$\quad$ }
end

Fig. 11. Algorithm for assisting specification refinement by random testing

In Figure11, the input parameters of the algorithm include a program p and η, which is a candidate refinement invariant or a candidate refinement invariant in the form of equational template with parameters $\mathcal{P}$. The output is a likely refinement invariant η'.

In Figure11, the function $randomSampling(P, varList, n)$ denotes the program P is random tested n times, and the sampled values of program variables in $varList$ are stored in the array $valueArray$, $Simplify(\eta, varList, valueArray)$ simplify the expression η under the assumption the variables in $varList$ are assigned values in $valueArray$ respectively, the function $generatingLinearSyatem$

$(valueArray, \eta)$ denotes the linear equation constraint system Ψ is established with the sampling values $valueArray$ and the template η, and the function $solvingLinearSystem(\Psi)$ denotes the linear equation constraint system Ψ is solved and the solution is $\mathcal{P}^*$, if the solution is 0(denoted by $\mathcal{P}^* = 0$) or Ψ has no solution(denoted by $\mathcal{P}^* = NULL$), then the algorithm returns $NULL$ as output, otherwise $\eta[\mathcal{P}^*/\mathcal{P}]$ will be returned as output.

6   Experimental Results

The approach is evaluated by discovering program invariants for some imperative programs. The experiment is implemented on a laptop having Intel(R) Core(TM) M620 2.67GHz CPU and 3G memory.

In the experiment, the specifications of programs are refined with the platform Rodin 2.4, most of the generated proof obligations are discharged automatically by Rodin, few are discharged interactively.

The experimental results are listed in Table 2. For a given program, the specification, the generated likely refinement invariants are listed in the columns labeled by Specification, Refinement Invariants respectively, and the number of the generated total proof obligations and the number of proof obligations which are discharged automatically are listed in the column labeled by T(A).

In our experiment, all the retained likely refinement invariants are actually refinement invariants. The experimental results demonstrate that assisting specification refinement by random testing is effective.

7   Related Work

In [21], the mathematical techniques equation solving, polyhedra construction and SMT solving are combined to bring new capabilities to dynamic invariant detection. These methods are used to show how to find equalities and inequalities among nonlinear polynomials over program variables, and linear relations among array variables of multiple dimensions.

In [22], a practical approach for generating equality loop invariants using random testing, constraint solving and verification is presented. Given a template of equality loop invariants, by sufficiently random testing the given loop, a linear equation constraints system on the unknown coefficients in the template is established, by solving the equation system, a likely loop invariant is generated,

Table 2. Experimental Results

Example	Specification	Refinement Invariants	T(A)
Division	$pre: \ x \geq 0, y > 0$ $post: 0 \leq rem < y$ $quo \times y + rem = x$	$quo \times y + rem = x$ $rem \geq 0$	8(8)
Gaussian Sum	$pre: \ n \geq 0$ $post: s = n(n-1)/2$	$s = i(i-1)/2$	7(6)
Factorial	$pre: \ n \geq 0$ $\forall v.(v >= 1 \Rightarrow$ $v * (v-1)! = v!)$ $post: f = n!$	$f = v!$	10(5)
Integer Square Root	$pre: \ n \geq 0$ $post: k^2 \leq n$ $n < (k+1)^2$	$j = 2k+1$ $m = (k+1)^2$ $k^2 \leq n$	12(10)
Search	$pre: \ n \geq 1$ $f \in 1..n \to N$ $v \in f[1..n]$ $post: v = f(r)$	$r \in 1..n$ $v \notin f[1..r-1]$	5(2)
LCM-GCD	$pre: \ a > 0, b > 0$ $post: x = GCD(a,b)$ $(u+v)/2 = LCM(a,b)$	$xu + yv = 2ab$	11(11)
Binary Search	$pre: \ n \geq 1$ $f \in 1..n \to N$ $v \in f[1..n]$ $\forall i, j.i \in 1..n \land j \in 1..n$ $\land i \leq j \Rightarrow f(i) \leq f(j)$ $post: v = f(r)$	$r \in [p..q]$ $v \in f[p..q]$ $p <= q$	34(29)
ArrayPartition	$pre: \ n \geq 0, x \geq 0$ $f \in 1..n \to N$ $post: k \in 1..n$ $g \in 1..n \to N$ $ran(f) = ran(g)$ $\forall m(m \in 1..k \Rightarrow$ $g(m) \leq x)$ $\forall m(m \in k+1..n \Rightarrow$ $g(m) > x)$	$j \in 1..n$ $k \leq j$ $\forall s(s \in 1..k \Rightarrow$ $g(s) \leq x)$ $\forall s(s \in k+1..n \Rightarrow$ $g(s) > x)$	46(43)

and its validity is verified by computing its finite differences over all program transitions.

To sum up, the dynamic approach is utilized to discover program invariants in the appointed forms. Given the specification of a program, the program invariants in the appointed forms discovered by the dynamic approach may not occur in the verification of correctness of the program against the specification. In another word, the discovered program invariants may not be useful for the verification.

Refinement is a powerful mechanism for mastering the complexities that arise when formally modeling systems. In [13],Carlo A. Furia and Bertrand Meyer presented the work by using the postcondition as the basis for invariant inference and using various refinement heuristics. Thanks to these heuristics, the technique is able to infer invariants for a large variety of loop programs.

In [20], Maria Teresa Llano, Andrew Ireland and Alison Pease have investigated how a general purpose theory formation tool, HR, can be used to automate the discovery of such properties within the context of Event-B. They develop a heuristic approach to the automatic discovery of invariants and report upon a series of experiments. The set of heuristics developed provides systematic guidance in tailoring HR for a given Event-B development.

Based on random testing, this paper presents an assistant approach for specification refinement. Specification refinement and random testing are combined to discover likely refinement invariants. These discovered likely refinement invariants will be sufficient to verify the correctness of the program against its specification.

8   Conclusions

Based on random testing, this paper presents a practical assisting approach for specification refinement. The effectiveness of the approach is demonstrated on examples.

References

1. Cousot, P., Halbwachs, N.: Automatic discovery of linear restraints among variables of a program. In: Aho, A.V., Zilles, S.N., Szymanski, T.G. (eds.) POPL 1978, pp. 84–96. ACM Press, Tucson (1978)
2. Mine, A.: The octagon abstract domain. Higher-Order and Symbolic Computation 19(1), 31–100 (2006)
3. Colón, M.A., Sankaranarayanan, S., Sipma, H.B.: Linear invariant generation using non-linear constraint solving. In: Hunt Jr., W.A., Somenzi, F. (eds.) CAV 2003. LNCS, vol. 2725, pp. 420–432. Springer, Heidelberg (2003)
4. Gulwani, S., Srivastava, S., Venkatesan, R.: Program analysis as constraint solving. In: Gupta, R., Amarasinghe, S.P. (eds.) PLDI 2008, pp. 281–292. ACM Press, Tucson (2008)
5. Sankaranaryanan, S., Sipma, H.B., Manna, Z.: Non-Linear Loop Invariant Generation using Gröbner Bases. In: Jones, N.D., Leroy, X. (eds.) POPL 2004, pp. 318–329. ACM Press, Tucson (2004)
6. Chen, Y., Xia, B., Yang, L., Zhan, N.: Generating polynomial invariants with DISCOVERER and QEPCAD. In: Jones, C.B., Liu, Z., Woodcock, J. (eds.) Formal Methods and Hybrid Real-Time Systems. LNCS, vol. 4700, pp. 67–82. Springer, Heidelberg (2007)
7. Rodriguez-Carbonell, E., Kapur, D.: Generating All Polynomial Invariants in Simple Loops. J. of Symbolic Computation 42(4), 443–476 (2007)
8. Kovács, L.: Automated Invariant Generation by Algebraic Techniques for Imperative Program Verification in Theorema. PhD thesis, RISC, Johannes Kepler University Linz (2007)

9. Kovács, L.: Aligator: A Mathematica Package for Invariant Generation (System Description). In: Armando, A., Baumgartner, P., Dowek, G. (eds.) IJCAR 2008. LNCS (LNAI), vol. 5195, pp. 275–282. Springer, Heidelberg (2008)

10. Müller-Olm, M., Seidl, H.: Precise interprocedural analysis through linear algebra. In: Jones, N.D., Leroy, X. (eds.) POPL 2004, pp. 330–341. ACM Press, Tucson (2004)

11. Müller-Olm, M., Seidl, H.: Computing polynomial program invariants. Inf. Process. Lett. 91(5), 233–244 (2004)

12. Müller-Olm, M., Petter, M., Seidl, H.: Interprocedurally Analyzing Polynomial Identities. In: Durand, B., Thomas, W. (eds.) STACS 2006. LNCS, vol. 3884, pp. 50–67. Springer, Heidelberg (2006)

13. Furia, C.A., Meyer, B.: Inferring Loop Invariants Using Postconditions. In: Blass, A., Dershowitz, N., Reisig, W. (eds.) Fields of Logic and Computation. LNCS, vol. 6300, pp. 277–300. Springer, Heidelberg (2010)

14. Ernst, M.D., Cockrell, J., Griswold, W.G., Notkin, D.: Dynamically discovering likely program invariants to support program evolution. IEEE Transactions of Software Engineering 27(2), 99–123 (2001)

15. Perkings, J.H., Ernst, M.D.: Efficient incremental algorithms for dynamic detection of likely invariants. In: Taylor, R.N., Dwyer, M.B. (eds.) SIGSOFT FSE 2004, pp. 23–32. ACM Press, Tucson (2004)

16. Damchoom, K., Butler, M., Abrial, J.-R.: Modelling and proof of a tree-structured file system in Event-B and Rodin. In: Liu, S., Araki, K. (eds.) ICFEM 2008. LNCS, vol. 5256, pp. 25–44. Springer, Heidelberg (2008)

17. Abrial, J.-R.: Modeling in Event-B: System and Software Engineering. Cambridge University Press (2010)

18. Abrial, J.-R., Hallerstede, S.: Refinement, Decomposition, and Instantiation of Discrete Models: Application to Event-B. Fundam. Inform. 77(1-2), 1–28 (2007)

19. Abrial, J.-R., Butler, M.J., Hallerstede, S., Hoang, T.S., Mehta, F., Voisin, L.: Rodin: an open toolset for modelling and reasoning in Event-B. STTT 12(6), 447–466 (2010)

20. Llano, M.T., Ireland, A., Pease, A.: Discovery of Invariants through Automated Theory Formation. In: Derrick, J., Boiten, E.A., Reeves, S. (eds.) Refine 2011. EPTCS, vol. 55, pp. 1–19 (2011)

21. Nguyen, T., Kapur, D., Weimer, W., Forrest, S.: Using dynamic analysis to discover polynomial and array invariants. In: Glinz, M., Murphy, G.C., Pezzè, M. (eds.) ICSE 2012, pp. 683–693. IEEE Computer Society Press, Los Alamitos (2012)

22. Li, M.: A Practical Loop Invariant Generation Approach Based on Random Testing, Constraint Solving and Verification. In: Aoki, T., Taguchi, K. (eds.) ICFEM 2012. LNCS, vol. 7635, pp. 447–461. Springer, Heidelberg (2012)

Generation of Checking Sequences Using Identification Sets

Faimison Rodrigues Porto, Andre Takeshi Endo, and Adenilso Simao

Instituto de Ciências Matemáticas e de Computação,
Universidade de São Paulo (USP)
PO Box 668, 13560-970 São Carlos, SP, Brazil
{faimison,aendo,adenilso}@icmc.usp.br

Abstract. Finite state machine-based testing aims at generating checking sequences that guarantee the conformance between the implementation and the specification of a system. For that purpose, several methods have been proposed to generate checking sequences which ensure full coverage of possible faults in the implementation. Many existing methods are based on a special sequence, called distinguishing sequence, which does not exist for every minimal machine. Some methods are based on characterization sets since they exist for every machine. However, these methods generate checking sequences exponentially long. In this paper, we propose a method to generate checking sequences using identification sets. These sets exist for every minimal FSM and also lead to shorter checking sequences. We conducted an experimental study to compare the proposed method with the existing methods. The results show that on average our method generates checking sequences 31.7% to 99.9% shorter than the ones produced by existing methods.

Keywords: checking sequence, FSM testing, test generation methods, identification set.

1 Introduction

Testing, an important activity in the software development process, aims at improving the quality of a system by revealing existing faults. There are numerous techniques, methods and tools proposed in software testing to cover different application domains. Notable examples are the pervasive and mission-critical applications that demand more rigorous testing approaches in order to guarantee a high level of software reliability. In this context, formal techniques have been used to express test models, since they may contribute to more automated and, consequently, efficient and effective testing [10]. When a formal model is used to automatically generate test cases, this approach is called *Model-Based Testing* (MBT). A model represents the behavior of a system through states and transitions connecting states. Among a large universe of state-transition models, *Finite State Machines* (FSMs) have been frequently studied to support

L. Groves and J. Sun (Eds.): ICFEM 2013, LNCS 8144, pp. 115–130, 2013.
© Springer-Verlag Berlin Heidelberg 2013

the testing activity. Test generation from an FSM (a Mealy machine) is an active research topic with numerous contributions over decades, starting with the seminal work of Moore [13] and Hennie [8].

Given a specification FSM M and a black box implementation which is assumed to modeled by an unknown FSM N, the problem consists of deriving a test suite T from M, such that the application of T is able to check whether N behaves correctly according to M. In other words, T is able to detect all faults in N. This test suite can be generated from a specification, basing on some assumptions. When it is assumed that the implementation can be modeled by an FSM with at most the same number of states of M, the generated test suite is called n-complete. Another assumption is the existence of a reliable reset operation that brings the implementation to its initial state. This operation enables the execution of test cases always starting from the same state. However, a reliable reset may not be available or may be too expensive to use. Therefore, some methods aim at generating n-complete test suites formed by a single input sequence. This sequence is called *checking sequence*. The execution of a checking sequence does not require the assumption of an existing reliable reset.

Many methods for generating checking sequences have been proposed [8,7,2,15,18,11,3,19,9,16,17]. A crucial issue for these methods is how to guarantee that a black box implementation is in a known state after some input sequence is applied. This problem is somewhat simplified if the specification M has a distinguishing sequence. This is a special input sequence for which different states of M produce different outputs [16]. The application domain of methods that rely on distinguishing sequences, e.g., [7,18,11,3,19,9], is restricted since these sequences do not exist for every machine. Furthermore, constructing such sequences and determining their existence are non-trivial problems, in which only exponential algorithms are known [12]. On the other hand, characterization sets exist for every minimal FSM and can be found by polynomial algorithms [6]. A characterization set (or W set) for M is a set of input sequences for which distinct states of M produce distinct sets of outputs. In this context, some methods, e.g., [8,15], generate sequences based on W sets, since they can be applied on a broader domain of machines. However, the existing methods in this context are not efficient since the checking sequences generated are exponentially long in relation to the length of W [12].

In this paper, we propose a method that generates shorter checking sequences from FSMs without relying on distinguishing sequences. The method is based on the fact that the state identification can be provided by only a subset of the W set (instead of using the entire set to check each reached state of M as in [8] and [15]). This set is called identification set and provides optimizations in relation to the use of the entire characterization set. Experimental results show that the proposed method generates checking sequences shorter than existing methods. The results show that on average our method generates checking sequences from 31.7% to 99.9% shorter than Hennie's [8] and Rezaki and Ural's [15] methods.

This paper is organized as follows. Section 2 provides the necessary definitions. Section 3 introduces the proposed method by means of a formal algorithm along with a step-by-step example. Section 4 shows an experimental evaluation of the method. The related work is discussed in Section 5. Finally, Section 6 concludes the paper and sketches future work.

2 Preliminaries

This section introduces well-known notations and definitions used in the researched topic [15,12,16,4]. A Finite State Machine (FSM) is a deterministic (Mealy) machine, defined as follows. An FSM M is a 7-tuple $(S, s_0, I, O, D, \delta, \lambda)$, where:

- S is a finite set of states with initial state s_0,
- I is a finite set of inputs,
- O is a finite set of outputs,
- $D \subseteq S \times I$ is a specification domain,
- $\delta : D \to S$ is a transition function, and
- $\lambda : D \to O$ is an output function.

Tuple $(s, x) \in D$ is a *defined transition* in state s, which consumes input x. The form (s_i, x, y, s_j) can also be used to represent a transition from s_i to $s_j = \delta(s_i, x)$ that consumes input x and produces output $y = \lambda(s_i, x)$. In transition $t = (s_i, x, y, s_j)$, s_i and s_j are said to be the *head* and the *tail* states, respectively; t is an incoming transition for s_j and an outgoing transition for s_i. An FSM is complete if all states have defined transitions for each input, i.e., $D = S \times I$; otherwise, it is partial. A sequence $\alpha = x_1...x_k \in I^*$ is an input sequence defined for state $s \in S$, if there exist states $s_1, ..., s_{k+1}$ such that $s = s_1$, $(s_i, x_i) \in D$, and $\delta(s_i, x_i) = s_{i+1}$ for all $1 \leq i \leq k$. We say that α is a *transfer sequence* from s to s_{k+1} and that s_{k+1} is *reachable* from s. An FSM is strongly connected if every state is reachable from all states. Figure 1 illustrates a state diagram representation of an FSM.

Notation $\Omega(s)$ denotes all input sequences defined for state s and Ω_M is an abbreviation for $\Omega(s_0)$. Therefore, Ω_M is the set of all defined sequences for the FSM M. Given any two sequences α and ω, notation $\alpha\omega$ represents the concatenation of both. Sequence α is a prefix of sequence β, denoted by $\alpha \leq \beta$, if $\beta = \alpha\omega$, for some sequence ω. Sequence α is a proper prefix of β, denoted by $\alpha < \beta$, if $\beta = \alpha\omega$ and ω is not an empty sequence, i.e., $\omega \neq \epsilon$. In these cases, ω is a suffix of β. Given two sets of sequences D_1 and D_2, $D_1.D_2$ represents the set of sequences obtained by concatenating all sequences in D_1 with all sequences in D_2, i.e., $D_1.D_2 = \{\alpha\beta \mid \alpha \in D_1 \wedge \beta \in D_2\}$. Given a sequence ω and an integer n, notation $(\omega)^n$ represents n concatenations of ω, i.e., $(\omega)^n = \omega.(\omega)^{n-1}$ and $(\omega)^0 = \epsilon$, for $n \geq 0$. Given a sequence $\beta = \alpha\omega$, notation $\beta\backslash\omega$ represents sequence α obtained after suffix ω is removed from β.

The transition and output functions are extended to include defined input sequences and the empty sequence ϵ as follows. For a state $s_i \in S$, $\delta(s_i, \epsilon) = s_i$ and $\lambda(s_i, \epsilon) = \epsilon$; given an input sequence $\alpha x \in \Omega(s_i)$ such that $\alpha \in I^*$ and $x \in I$, we have $\delta(s_i, \alpha x) = \delta(\delta(s_i, \alpha), x)$ and $\lambda(s_i, \alpha x) = \lambda(s_i, \alpha)\lambda(\delta(s_i, \alpha), x)$. Notation

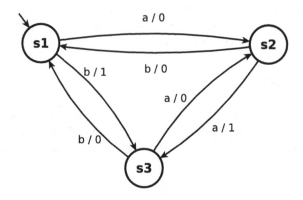

Fig. 1. Example of an FSM

$(s_i, \alpha, \lambda(s_i, \alpha), \delta(s_i, \alpha))$ is used to represent an input sequence $\alpha \in \Omega(s_i)$ that takes the FSM from s_i to $\delta(s_i, \alpha)$ and produces the output $\lambda(s_i, \alpha)$.

Two different states $s_i, s_j \in S$ are *distinguishable* if there exists a *separating sequence* $\gamma \in \Omega(s_i) \cap \Omega(s_j)$, such that $\lambda(s_i, \gamma) \neq \lambda(s_j, \gamma)$. An FSM M is reduced (or minimal) if all states are pairwise distinguishable. Given a different FSM $N = (Q, q_0, I, O, \Delta, \Lambda)$ with the same sets of inputs and outputs, we say that two machines M and N are distinguishable, if there exists a sequence $\gamma \in \Omega_M \cap \Omega_N$, such that $\lambda(s_0, \gamma) \neq \Lambda(q_0, \gamma)$.

A test case of M is an input sequence $\alpha \in \Omega_M$. A test suite of M is a finite set of test cases of M. The length (number of symbols) of a sequence α is represented by $|\alpha|$. For instance, given test case *babb* for the FSM in Figure 1, its length is 4, $|babb| = 4$, since it contains four symbols.

Given a specification M, notation $\Im$ denotes the set of all deterministic FSMs with the same input alphabet as M for which all sequences in Ω_M are defined, i.e., for each machine $N \in \Im$, $\Omega_M \subseteq \Omega_N$. Set $\Im$ is called a *fault domain* for M. Let $m \geq 1$ be an integer, $\Im_m$ denotes all FSMs of $\Im$ with at most m states. Given a specification M with n states, a test suite $T \subseteq \Omega_M$ is m-complete, $m \geq n$, if, for each $N \in \Im_m$ distinguishable from M, there exists a test in T that distinguishes M from N. An m-complete test suite has *full fault coverage* for the defined domain and is able to detect all faults in any implementation with at most m states. In this work, we consider n-complete test suites that represent the case in which $m = n$. A *checking sequence* of M is an n-complete test suite formed by a single sequence that distinguishes M from any FSM in $\Im_n$.

A *distinguishing sequence* (DS) is a defined input sequence that works as a separating sequence for each pair of states in the FSM, i.e., for every pair of $s_i, s_j \in S$, $i \neq j$ implies that $\lambda(s_i, DS) \neq \lambda(s_j, DS)$. A *characterization set*, also known as W set, is a set of defined input sequences for which the output sequences produced by M in response to the set of input sequences are different for each state of M, i.e., let $W = \{w_1, w_2, ..., w_r\}$, for every pair of $s_i, s_j \in S$, $i \neq j$, there exists at least one $\tau \in \{1, 2, ..., r\}$ such that $\lambda(s_i, w_\tau\} \neq \lambda(s_j, w_\tau\}$.

The elements of a characterization set are called *characterization sequences*. Given a set of input sequences $W_i = \{w_1^i, w_2^i, ..., w_p^i\} \subseteq W$, W_i is an *identification set* of $s_i \in S$ if and only if for each state $s_j \in S$, $i \neq j$, there exists an input sequence $\alpha \in W_i$ such that $\lambda(s_i, \alpha) \neq \lambda(s_j, \alpha)$ and no subset of W_i has this property [5]. Although a DS yields an efficient way to identify a state, this sequence does not exist for every minimal FSM [6]. For instance, for the FSM in Figure 1, no distinguishing sequence exists. Indeed, any input sequence starting with a produces the same output for states s_1 and s_2 and reach the same state, whereas any input sequence starting with b produces the same output for states s_1 and s_3 and reach the same state. On the other hand, a W set always exists for a minimal FSM and can be found by polynomial algorithms [6]. For the FSM presented in the Figure 1, the set $W = \{a, b\}$ produces distinct outputs for states s_1, s_2 and s_3. Given that $W_i \subseteq W$, identification sets also exist for every minimal FSM. For the FSM in Figure 1, the identification sets are $W_1 = \{b\}$, $W_2 = \{a\}$, and $W_3 = \{a, b\}$.

2.1   Locating Sequence

During the construction of checking sequences, it is necessary to guarantee that the black box implementation is in a known state after the application of some input sequence. To do so, most of the existing methods, e.g., [7], [18], [11], [3], and [19], are based on distinguishing sequences since they are an efficient way to recognize the actual state in the implementation. However, this kind of sequence cannot be found for every FSM. In this context, an alternative solution to generate checking sequences is to use W sets. Since a W set can be found for every minimal FSM, methods based on characterization sets can be applied to a broader domain. The basic idea to identify a state using the W set is applying every sequence of W over the same state. However, considering that a checking sequence is composed by a single sequence and does not rely on the reset operation, it is a problem to guarantee that all the sequences of W will be applied on the same state. Given an implementation of M with at most n states, one can realize that at most n distinct states can produce the same output for a specific input sequence. Thus, if an input sequence is applied repeatedly for $n+1$ times and always produce the same output, one can guarantee that the state reached immediately after the $(n+1)$-th time is a state already traversed and produces a known output for that specific sequence [8]. A *locating sequence* L_i for state s_i is based on this fact and enables us to identify a state in an implementation of M that behaves just like s_i with respect to the characterizing sequences derived from M [8]. We formally define locating sequences based on the work of Rezaki and Ural [15], as follows. Let $W = \{w_1, w_2, ..., w_r\}$ be a characterization set for M where w_τ is a characterizing sequence in W, $1 \leq \tau \leq r$. Furthermore, let U_k^i, $1 \leq k \leq r-1$, be some input sequence that has w_k as its prefix and that takes M from state s_i back to state s_i, i.e., $U_k^i = w_k.I_i^k$ where I_i^k is a transfer sequence from $\delta(s_i, w_k)$ to s_i. Also, let U_r^i be an input sequence that has w_r as its prefix and take M from state s_i back to state s_i, i.e., $U_r^i = w_r I_i^r$, where I_i^r is a transfer sequence from $\delta(s_i, w_r)$ to s_i. I_i^r can be the empty sequence if $\delta(s_i, w_r) = s_i$.

Definition 1. *A locating sequence for state s_i is $L_i = F(r, \{U_1^i, U_2^i, ..., U_r^i\})$ where $F : \mathbb{N} \times 2^{\Omega(s_i)} \to \Omega(s_i)$ is a recursive function so that $F(2, \{a_1, a_2\}) = (a_1)^{n+1}.a_2$, $F(k, \{a_1, a_2, ..., a_k\}) = (F(k-1, \{a_1, a_2, ..., a_{k-1}\}))^{n+1} \cdot F(k-1, \{a_1, a_2, ..., a_{k-2}, a_k\})$, $3 \le k \le r$, and a_i, $1 \le i \le k$ is an input sequence for M.*

A locating sequence L_i for state s_i has the property that the set of input sequences $w_1, w_2, ..., w_r$ is applied to the state $\delta(s_i, L_i \backslash U_r^i)$. State $\delta(s_i, L_i \backslash U_r^i)$ is defined as the L_i-related state. Let $L = \{L_1, L_2, ..., L_n\}$ be a set of locating sequences for M where L_k denotes the locating sequence for state $s_k \in S$, $1 \le k \le n$.

To exemplify, consider a set $W = \{w_1, w_2, w_3\}$ for an FSM M. A locating sequence for s_i is $L_i = F(3, \{U_1^i, U_2^i, U_3^i\}) = F(3, \{w_1 I_i^1, w_2 I_i^2, w_3 I_i^3\}) = ((w_1 I_i^1)^{n+1} w_2 I_i^2)^{n+1}.(w_1 I_i^1)^{n+1} w_3 I_i^3$. Consider the set $W = \{a, b\}$ for the FSM shown in Figure 1, the locating sequence for state s_1 is $L_1 = F(2, \{ab, bb\}) = (ab)^4 bb = ababababbb$ producing the output $(00)^4 10$. For this sequence, the L_1-related state is $\delta(s_1, L_1 \backslash bb) = \delta(s_1, ababab)$.

2.2 Checking Sequences Generation Using W-Sets

The locating sequence is the basic concept used to generate checking sequences based on W sets and was introduced by Hennie [8]. In this process, it is assumed that M is a minimal, complete, and strongly connected FSM and an implementation N of M can be modeled by an FSM with at most n states. In his work, Hennie [8] presents a method to generate checking sequences based on locating sequences. Basically, the method generates an input sequence where all the states and transitions of M are recognized and verified, respectively. The construction of the checking sequence is based on a local best choice procedure. The concepts of recognizing a state and verifying a transition are formally presented in Rezaki and Ural [15]. Let ω be an input sequence in Ω_M:

1. Suppose that $(s_a, L_a, \lambda(s_a, L_a), \delta(s_a, L_a))$ is a subsequence of ω where $\delta(s_a, L_a \backslash U_r^a) = s_i$. Then, s_i is l-recognized in ω as state s_a of M, i.e., s_i is an L_a-related state.
2. Suppose that each $(s_{x_\tau}, w_\tau, \lambda(s_a, w_\tau), \delta(s_{x_\tau}, w_\tau))$, $1 \le \tau \le r$, are subsequences of ω, and $s_{x_\tau} = \delta(u_{x_\tau}, I_\tau)$, where each u_{x_τ} is l-recognized in ω as the same state of M and I_τ is the same transfer sequence, $1 \le \tau \le r$. Then, s_{x_τ} is w-recognized in ω as state s_a of M.
3. Suppose that $(s_q, I, \lambda(s_q, I), s_i)$ and $(s_{j_\tau}, I, \lambda(s_{j_\tau}, I), s_{k_\tau})$, $1 \le \tau \le r$, are subsequences of ω such that s_q and s_{j_τ} are l-recognized in ω as some state s_a of M, and suppose that s_{k_τ} are w-recognized in ω as state s'_a of M. Then s_i is t-recognized in ω as state s'_a of M.
4. A transition (s_a, x, y, s_b) of M is verified in ω if:
   (a) There are subsequences $(s_{i_\tau}, x_i, y_i, s_{j_\tau})$, $1 \le \tau \le r$, of ω such that s_{i_τ} are t-recognized in ω as state s_a of M and s_{j_τ} are w-recognized in ω as state s_b of M;
   (b) $x_i/y_i = x/y$; and

(c) There are subsequences $(s_k, L_k, \lambda(s_k, L_k), s_m)$ of ω, for each $s_k \in S$, i.e., there must be a state $s_i = \delta(s_k, L_k \backslash U_r^k)$ in ω which is l-recognized in ω as state s_k of M.

In [15], Rezaki and Ural present and prove sufficient conditions based on the concepts aforementioned. The sufficient conditions guarantee that if all the transitions of M are verified in ω, then ω is a checking sequence of M. The authors also propose a general model for checking sequence construction based on graphs. In the model presented, an FSM M is represented by a directed graph $G = \{V, E\}$ where a set of vertexes $V = \{1, 2, ..., n\}$ represents the set of states S, and a set of directed edges $E = \{(s_j, s_k; x/y) : s_j, s_k \in V\}$ represents all the specified transitions of M [15]. Basically, the model consists of constructing an auxiliary graph G' which contains some sets of edges generated from G. Two sets of edges are essential: (i) α-set contains input sequences that provide the w-recognition of each state of M; and (ii) β-set contains input sequences which guarantee the verification of every transition of M. Thus, the model aims at find a path P in G' which contains necessarily all the sequences of α-set and β-set. The input portion of P (denoted as Q) represents a single test sequence which is proved to be a checking sequence of M. The model of Rezaki and Ural [15] generalizes the method proposed by Hennie [8].

3 Checking Sequences Generation using Identification Sets

In this section we propose a method that optimizes the length of checking sequences generated using W sets. This method assumes that (i) M is minimal, complete and strongly connected, and (ii) an implementation N of M can be modeled by an FSM and has the same number of states of M, as in [8,15,18,11,3,19,9,16,17]. The reduction proportioned by this method is based on the fact that, in certain cases, the state identification can be provided by only a subset of the W set (instead of using the entire set to check each reached state of M).

The use of identification sets instead of the W set can optimize the checking sequence length. The main optimization is on the length of sequences used to locate a state. The length of a locating sequence is exponentially proportional to the number of characterization sequences in W [8]. As a consequence, the reduction of the number of characterization sequences used in the construction of the locating sequence can reduce the final length of the checking sequence generated. Furthermore, the reduction of the locating sequence leads to a global optimization proportional to the domain of M, since both the state recognition and the transition verification of M depend on the application of locating sequences.

While existing generation methods for FSMs without DS are based on locating sequences (as in [8,15]), the method introduced in this paper uses a new type of sequence so-called *recognizing sequence*. Let $W_i = \{w_1^i, w_2^i, ..., w_p^i\}$ be an identification set for state $s_i \in S$ where w_r^i is an characterization sequence in

W_i, $1 \leq \tau \leq p$. Furthermore, let S_k^i, $1 \leq k \leq p-1$, be some input sequence that has w_k^i as its prefix and that takes M from state s_i back to state s_i, i.e., $S_k^i = w_k^i I_i^k$ where I_i^k is a transfer sequence from $\delta(s_i, w_k^i)$ to s_i. Also, let S_p^i be an input sequence that has w_p^i as its prefix and take M from state s_i back to state s_i, i.e., $S_p^i = w_p^i I_i^p$, where I_i^p is a transfer sequence from $\delta(s_i, w_p^i)$ to s_i. I_i^p is not an empty sequence except in the case that $\delta(s_i, w_p^i) = s_i$.

Definition 2. *A recognizing sequence for state s_i, denoted by P_i, is the sequence $P_i = F'(p, \{S_1^i, S_2^i, ..., S_p^i\})$ where $F' : \mathbb{N} \times 2^{\Omega(s_i)} \to \Omega(s_i)$ is a recursive function so that $F'(1, \{a_1\}) = a_1$, $F'(2, \{a_1, a_2\}) = (a_1)^{n+1}.a_2$, $F'(k, \{a_1, a_2, ..., a_k\}) = (F'(k-1, \{a_1, a_2, ..., a_{k-1}\}))^{n+1} . F'(k-1, \{a_1, a_2, ..., a_{k-2}, a_k\})$, $3 \leq k \leq p$, and a_i, $1 \leq i \leq k$ is an input sequence for M.*

The sequence defined above is similar to the one in Definition 1, except for two points. First, the sequence is derived from the identification set instead of the entire characterization set. Second, function F' covers the case when the identification set is formed by one sequence.

Let $N = (Q, q_0, I, O, \Delta, \Lambda)$ be a possible implementation of M in $\Im_n$ and $W = \{w_1, w_2, ..., w_r\}$ be a characterization set of M. The states of M are *identifiable* in N if for each state $s \in S$ there exists a state $q \in Q$ such that $\lambda(s, w_\tau) = \Lambda(q, w_\tau)$, $1 \leq \tau \leq r$. The concept of identifiable states is important to understand the property explained as below.

A recognizing sequence P_i for state s_i has the property that all the set of input sequences $w_1^i, w_2^i, ..., w_p^i$ is applied to the state $\delta(s_i, P_i \backslash S_p^i)$. This property enables us to use P_i to locate a state $q_i \in Q$ in N which has a behavior equivalent to s_i, in relation to W_i. However, this property does not guarantee that there exists only one state in N which behaves as s_i, in relation to W_i. On the other hand, assuming that all states of M are identifiable in N, P_i can be used to locate a state q_i in N with the guarantee that if q_i behaves as s_i in relation to W_i, then q_i also behaves as s_i in relation to the entire W. In other words, based on this assumption, we can use P_i to locate q_i in N and guarantee that q_i is unique in relation to W.

The assumption above is satisfied in the first step of the proposed method. For this, the entire W set is applied over each state of M. As a consequence, we conclude that recognizing sequences can be used instead of locating sequences during the checking sequence generation. In this way, some reductions are obtained. Moreover, from this assumption, the tail state of each transition can be verified by applying the correspondent identification set instead of the entire characterization set.

Thereby, the basic idea of the proposed method is to construct a checking sequence by concatenating two groups of sequences that recognize all states and verify all transitions of M, respectively. The method proposed produces a checking sequence in which every transition of M is verified according to the sufficient conditions proposed by Rezaki and Ural [15]. The method is composed of three main steps:

1. For each state s_i it is generated a sequence α_i in which all characterization sequences of W are applied over the tail state of P_i. These sequences ensure that each state of M is identifiable in the implementation. In addition, both the tail state of P_i and $\delta(s_i, P_i \backslash S_p^i)$ are recognized in the implementation as state s_i of M. Then, P_i is concatenated at the end of α_i in order to keep the generated sequence in a known state.

2. Each transition $(s_i, x) \in D$ is verified by the application of the identification set W_k over the reached state $s_k = \delta(s_i, x)$. The verification of the tail state of a transition can be made by only applying the correspondent identification set (instead of the entire W set) since the states of M are identifiable in the implementation (first step). In order to keep the sequence in a known state, the application of each sequence $w_\tau^k \in W_k$ is followed by the corresponding P_q, where $s_q = \delta(s_k, w_\tau^k)$. The state reached by P_q is known (recognized) once each characterization sequence of W is applied over s_q in the first step.

3. The input sequences generated in the previous steps are concatenated using appropriate transfer sequences.

The method is formally defined in Algorithm 1.

3.1   Example

In this section, we illustrate the method for the FSM M in Figure 1, also represented in Table 1. There is no DS for this machine and we consider the characterization set $W = \{w_1, w_2\} = \{a, b\}$ in the process. Table 2 shows the identification sets (column W_i), the recognizing sequences (column P_i), and the outputs produced by P_i for each $s_i \in S$ (column $P_i / \lambda(s_i, P_i)$).

Table 1. Transition table of the FSM in Figure 1

States	$\delta(s_i, a), \lambda(s_i, a)$	$\delta(s_i, b), \lambda(s_i, b)$
s_1	$s_2, 0$	$s_3, 1$
s_2	$s_3, 1$	$s_1, 0$
s_3	$s_2, 0$	$s_1, 0$

Table 2. Identification sets and recognizing sequences of M

States	W_i	P_i	$P_i / \lambda(s_i, P_i)$
s_1	$W_1 = \{b\}$	$P_1 = bb$	$P_1/10$
s_2	$W_2 = \{a\}$	$P_2 = aa$	$P_2/10$
s_3	$W_3 = \{a, b\}$	$P_3 = (aa)^4 bb$	$P_3/(01)^4 01$

The set of sequences A generated in the first step of Algorithm 1 is: $A = \{\alpha_1, \alpha_2, \alpha_3\}$ where $\alpha_1 = P_1 w_1 b P_1 w_2 b P_1$, $\alpha_2 = P_2 w_1 a P_2 w_2 a P_2$, and $\alpha_3 = P_3 w_1 a P_3 w_2 b P_3$. These sequences guarantee the recognition of each state of M

Algorithm 1. Checking sequence generation method.

Input: Minimal FSM $M = (S, s_0, I, O, D, \delta, \lambda)$,
       Characterization set W of M,
       Identification set W_i for each $s_i \in S$, and
       P_i for each $s_i \in S$.
Output: Checking sequence ω for M.

```
//Step 1
```
$A \leftarrow \emptyset$
foreach $s_i \in S$ **do**
    Let I_i^l, $1 \leq l \leq r$, be transfer sequences from $\delta(s_i, P_i w_l)$ to s_i
    $\alpha_i \leftarrow P_i w_1 I_i^1 P_i w_2 I_i^2 ... I_i^{r-1} P_i w_r I_i^r P_i$
    $A \leftarrow A \cup \{\langle s_i, \alpha_i \rangle\}$
endforeach

```
//Step 2
```
$B \leftarrow \emptyset$
foreach $(s_i, x) \in D$ **do**
    $s_k \leftarrow \delta(s_i, x)$
    foreach $w_\tau^k \in W_k$ **do**
        $\beta_{i,x,w_\tau^k} \leftarrow x w_\tau^k P_{\delta(s_k, w_\tau^k)}$
        $B \leftarrow B \cup \{\langle s_i, \beta_{i,x,w_\tau^k} \rangle\}$
    endforeach
endforeach

```
//Step 3
```
$\omega \leftarrow \epsilon$
$C \leftarrow A \cup B$
while $C \neq \emptyset$ **do**
    if there exists $\langle s, \gamma \rangle \in C$ such that $s = \delta(s_0, \omega)$ **do**
        $\omega \leftarrow \omega \gamma$
        $C \leftarrow C \backslash \{\langle s, \gamma \rangle\}$
    else
        determine the shortest transfer sequence θ from state
            $\delta(s_0, \omega)$ to some state $s \in S$, such that there exists
            $\langle s, \gamma \rangle \in C$
        $\omega \leftarrow \omega \theta$
    endif
endwhile

return ω

---

since every characterization sequence of W is applied over the same state. In each sequence α_i, state s_i recognized corresponds to the same state reached after the application of P_i. Thus, this process recognizes the state reached in further applications of P_i.

The sequences of B represent the input sequences that verify each defined transition. These sequences are generated in the second step of Algorithm 1 and are presented in Table 3. Since the verification of the tail state of a transition is based on the identification set instead of the entire characterization set, the cells filled with $-$ represent the spared characterizing sequences. For instance, in the transition (s_1, a), the reached state $s_2 = \delta(s_1, a)$ is recognized by applying the correspondent identification set $W_2 = \{a\}$ instead of the entire $W = \{a, b\}$, sparing sequence β for $w_\tau^k = b$. Then, it is applied the recognizing sequence $P_{\delta(s_1, aa)} = P_3$ to bring the machine to a known state. During the method, the cells filled with "-" result in optimizations on the checking sequence length.

Table 3. Set B generated by Step 2

Transitions	β_{i,x,w_1}	β_{i,x,w_2}
(s_1, a)	$\beta_{1,a,a} = aaP_3$	—
(s_1, b)	$\beta_{1,b,a} = baP_2$	$\beta_{1,b,b} = bbP_1$
(s_2, a)	$\beta_{2,a,a} = aaP_2$	$\beta_{2,a,b} = abP_1$
(s_2, b)	—	$\beta_{2,b,b} = bbP_3$
(s_3, a)	$\beta_{3,a,a} = aaP_3$	—
(s_3, b)	—	$\beta_{3,b,b} = bbP_3$

Finally, the sequences in A and B are concatenated. When necessary, the shortest transfer sequence is chosen to bring the machine to the appropriate state. In this example, we choose the sequences of A over sequences of B when transfer sequences have the same length. Thus, it is generated the checking sequence $\omega = \alpha_1\beta_{1,a,a}\alpha_3\beta_{3,a,a}\beta_{3,b,b}a\alpha_2\beta_{2,a,a}\beta_{2,a,b}\beta_{1,b,a}\beta_{2,b,b}bb\beta_{1,b,b}$ with length $|\omega| = 120$. For the same FSM, the methods proposed by Hennie [8] and Rezaki and Ural [15] generate checking sequences with lengths $|\omega_h| = 171$ and $|\omega_r| = 248$, respectively.

4   Experimental Results

In this section, we compare the proposed method with the methods of Hennie [8] and Rezaki and Ural [15]. The experiment involved randomly generated FSMs. Since the methods compared are designed to generate checking sequences for FSMs without distinguishing sequences, only such machines were considered. Complete, strongly connected, and minimal FSMs without a distinguishing sequence were generated as in [16]. We used machines with two inputs, two outputs, and number of states n ranging from 3 to 12; for each value of n, we randomly generated 100 machines. For each FSM, Algorithm 1 was executed, generating checking sequence ω. Then, we executed Hennie's method [8] obtaining checking sequence ω_h, and Rezaki and Ural's method [15] resulting in sequence ω_r. Notation $\mu(|\omega|)$ represents the average length of checking sequences ω generated by the proposed method. This notation is extended for the sequences ω_h and ω_r which are represented by $\mu(|\omega_h|)$ and $\mu(|\omega_r|)$, respectively.

Figure 2 shows how the ratios $\mu(|\omega|/|\omega_h|)$ and $\mu(|\omega|/|\omega_r|)$ vary in function of the number of states. The data is presented in a logarithmic scale for better visualisation. The experimental data indicate that ω represents, in general, just a small portion of the checking sequences generated by the two other methods. Notice that the reduction provided by the proposed method in relation to the other two existing methods is greater than 99% for machines with 7 and more states. Another ratio showed in this graphic is $\mu(|\omega_h|/|\omega_r|)$ which presents a reduction of up to 85% for the average length of $\mu(|\omega_h|)$ in relation to $\mu(|\omega_r|)$. This information becomes important if we consider that some optimizations provided by the Hennie's method also can be aggregated to the proposed method. Thus, even more reductions can be obtained.

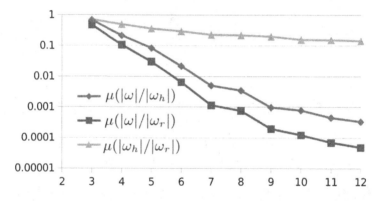

Fig. 2. Ratios $\mu(|\omega|/|\omega_h|)$, $\mu(|\omega|/|\omega_r|)$ and $\mu(|\omega_h|/|\omega_r|)$ presented in logarithmic scale in function of the number of states

The results aforementioned bring a general overview about the reductions provided by the proposed method. However, the results obtained from the average length can be affected by existing outliers in the data. Considering that, Figure 3 shows the boxplots[1] of ratios $|\omega|/|\omega_h|$ and $|\omega|/|\omega_r|$ obtained for three, eight, and 12 states; notice that the three boxplots are in different scales.

In general, notice that greater reduction ratios are obtained for greater numbers of states. For three states, the boxplot presents a median of 32% and 53% in relation to the methods of Hennie [8] and Rezaki and Ural [15], respectively. The

---

[1] Boxplots are useful graphs to show dispersion of numerical populations, representing the median, upper and lower quartiles, whiskers, and outliers; this graph was generated using the toolkit R [14].

reduction increases for eight states. Considering the upper quartile, the boxplot presents reductions of 88% in relation to the method of Hennie and 98% for the method of Rezaki and Ural. The boxplot referring to 12 states presents reductions greater than 99.5% in relation to both of the methods compared, when analyzed the upper quartile. In the worst case, when the identification sets are equals to the W set, no reduction is obtained for the proposed method. Nevertheless, these cases correspond just to a small portion of the data. In general, the obtained results show a high reduction of the checking sequence length with respect to the existing methods.

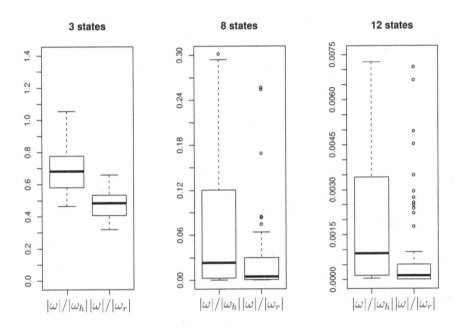

Fig. 3. Boxplots of the ratios $|\omega|/|\omega_h|$ and $|\omega|/|\omega_r|$ for three, eight, and 12 states

5   Related Work

In FSM-based testing, the checking sequence generation pioneered by Hennie [8] has been an active research topic with contributions in the past decades [7,2,15,18,11,12,3,19,9,16,17]. Hennie discusses an approach based on distinguishing sequences to generate checking sequences; his method is divided in two parts. First, the shortest distinguishing sequence is applied over every state of M starting from the initial state. The states are supposed to be ordered and subsequent states are reached by transfer sequences. Second, every transition (s, x) is checked. To do so, the machine is brought to a known state. Then, the distinguishing sequence is applied over the tail state of the transition to be checked. This method inspired other ones, e.g., [7,18,11,3,19,9], since distinguishing sequences yield an efficient way to identify an unknown state. Boute

[2] shows that shorter sequences can be obtained if, instead of distinguishing sequences, distinguishing sets are used, and the overlapping among the identification sequences is exploited. This kind of set is also the base for a method proposed by Simao and Petrenko [16]. The authors present a method based on a local choice procedure that leads to shorter checking sequences. A distinguishing set can be obtained from a distinguishing sequence and can exist for an FSM without a distinguish sequence. However, both distinguishing sequence and distinguishing set do not exist for every minimal FSM [17]. As a consequence, all these methods have a restricted domain of application.

Thus, checking sequence generation methods have been proposed using alternative ways that lead to a broader domain of application. These methods are based on the W set since it always exists for a minimal FSM [6]. In the Hennie's work [8], a nontrivial construction of checking sequences is discussed for a situation in which a machine does not have a distinguishing sequence; in general however, the produced checking sequences are exponentially long. According to Lee and Yannakakis [12], constructing checking sequences is widely assumed to be an easier problem if the machine has a distinguishing sequence and a harder one, otherwise. In his work, Hennie also defines a new sequence, constructed from the W set, called locating sequence. This sequence ensures the identification of a state of M in the implementation. From this sequence, the method consists of constructing a checking sequence in which all the states and transitions of M are recognized and verified, respectively. This is made by a best local choice procedure where optimizations can be applied to reduce the final length.

In this context, another method is proposed by Rezaki and Ural [15]. Their method is also based on locating sequences and the construction of the checking sequence is based on graphs. The specification is represented by a graph G where the vertices represent the states and the edges represent the transitions of M. Basically, the method consists of constructing an auxiliary graph G' which contains some sets of edges generated from G. Among these, two sets of edges are essential: (i) α-set contains input sequences that provides the recognition of each state of M; and (ii) β-set contains input sequences which guarantee the verification of every transition of M. Thus, the model aims to found a path P in G' which contains necessarily all the sequences of α-set and β-set. The problem is then cast as a Rural Chinese Postman Problem (RCPP), as previously proposed by Aho et al. [1]. The RCPP is an NP-complete problem that aim to find a minimal tour which traverses some required edges in a graph. This approach provides a global optimization with respect to the transfer sequences. However, this optimization is not significant in relation to the exponentially long length of the generated checking sequence.

In this context, the method proposed in this paper presents optimizations that reduce the final length of the checking sequences generated. The optimizations are provided from the use of identification sets, defined by Fujiwara et al. [5], instead of W sets, during the construction of checking sequences. Since the identification set is derived from the W set, it also exists for every minimal FSM.

6   Conclusion and Future Work

In this paper, we have proposed a method for generating checking sequence. In this method, the construction of checking sequences is based on identification sets, while most of the existing methods are based on distinguishing sequences. As a consequence, the method can be applied in a broader domain since not every FSM has a distinguishing sequence. Moreover, the use of identification sets instead of characterization sets provides some optimizations on the checking sequence length.

We experimentally compared the proposed method with existing generation methods based on characterization sets: Hennie [8] and Rezaki and Ural [15]. In the experiments, complete FSMs without distinguishing sequences were randomly generated. The results indicate that on average the proposed method generates checking sequences shorter than the methods of Hennie [8] and Rezaki and Ural [15]. Considering machines with seven states or more, the proposed method generates checking sequences up to 99.9% shorter than both methods compared.

In future work, extensions of the current work are manifold. The optimizations applied in the Hennie's method can be applied to the proposed method, improving even more its performance. Furthermore, theoretical analyses of the proposed method have been investigated to demonstrate its fault detection capabilities. Concerning the experiments, the method can be compared with other methods based on distinguishing sequences or in the context of FSMs that rely on the reset operation. These evaluations can lead to an interesting notion of how feasible the checking sequences generated by the proposed method are.

Acknowledgments. The authors acknowledge the support granted by CNPq and FAPESP to the INCT-SEC (National Institute of Science and Technology - Safety-Critical Embedded Systems – Brazil), process 573963/2008-9 and 2008/57870-9. Faimison Porto was financially supported by CAPES (grant DS-7490463/M). Andre T. Endo is financially supported by FAPESP (grant 2012/21083-9). Adenilso Simao is financially supported by FAPESP (grant 2012/02232-3).

References

1. Aho, A., Dahbura, A., Lee, D., Uyar, M.: An optimization technique for protocol conformance test generation based on uio sequences and rural chinese postman tours. IEEE Transactions on Communications 39, 1604–1615 (1991)
2. Boute, R.T.: Distinguishing sets for optimal state identification in checking experiments. IEEE Transactions on Computers 23, 874–877 (1974)
3. Chen, J., Hierons, R.M., Ural, H., Yenigun, H.: Eliminating redundant tests in a checking sequence. In: Khendek, F., Dssouli, R. (eds.) TestCom 2005. LNCS, vol. 3502, pp. 146–158. Springer, Heidelberg (2005)
4. Endo, A.T., Simao, A.: Evaluating test suite characteristics, cost, and effectiveness of FSM-based testing methods. Information and Software Technology 55(6), 1045–1062 (2013)

5. Fujiwara, S., van Bochmann, G., Khendek, F., Amalou, M., Ghedamsi, A.: Test selection based on finite state models. IEEE Transactions on Software Engineering 17, 591–603 (1991)
6. Gill, A.: Introduction to the theory of finite state machines. McGraw-Hill, New York (1962)
7. Gonenc, G.: A method for the design of fault detection experiments. IEEE Transactions on Computers 19, 551–558 (1970)
8. Hennie, F.C.: Fault detecting experiments for sequential circuits. In: Annual IEEE Symposium on Foundations of Computer Science, pp. 95–110 (1964)
9. Hierons, R.M., Ural, H.: Optimizing the length of checking sequences. IEEE Transactions on Computers 55, 618–629 (2006)
10. Hierons, R.M., Bogdanov, K., Bowen, J.P., Cleaveland, R., Derrick, J., Dick, J., Gheorghe, M., Harman, M., Kapoor, K., Krause, P., Lüttgen, G., Simons, A.J.H., Vilkomir, S., Woodward, M.R., Zedan, H.: Using formal specifications to support testing. ACM Computing Surveys 41, 1–76 (2009)
11. Hierons, R.M., Ural, H.: Reduced length checking sequences. IEEE Transactions on Computers 51, 93–99 (2002)
12. Lee, D., Yannakakis, M.: Principles and methods of testing finite state machines-a survey. Proceedings of the IEEE 84, 1090–1123 (1996)
13. Moore, E.F.: Gedanken Experiments on Sequential Machines. In: Automata Studies. Annals of Mathematical Studies, vol. 34, pp. 129–153 (1956)
14. R-Project: The R project for statistical computing (2013), http://www.r-project.org/
15. Rezaki, A., Ural, H.: Construction of checking sequences based on characterization sets. Computer Communications 18, 911–920 (1995)
16. Simão, A.S., Petrenko, A.: Generating checking sequences for partial reduced finite state machines. In: Suzuki, K., Higashino, T., Ulrich, A., Hasegawa, T. (eds.) TestCom/FATES 2008. LNCS, vol. 5047, pp. 153–168. Springer, Heidelberg (2008)
17. Simao, A., Petrenko, A.: Checking sequence generation using state distinguishing subsequences. In: The IEEE International Conference on Software Testing, Verification, and Validation Workshops, pp. 48–56 (2009)
18. Ural, H., Wu, X., Zhang, F.: On minimizing the lengths of checking sequences. IEEE Transactions on Computers 46, 93–99 (1997)
19. Ural, H., Zhang, F.: Reducing the lengths of checking sequences by overlapping. In: Uyar, M.Ü., Duale, A.Y., Fecko, M.A. (eds.) TestCom 2006. LNCS, vol. 3964, pp. 274–288. Springer, Heidelberg (2006)

The *Circus* Testing Theory Revisited in Isabelle/HOL

Abderrahmane Feliachi, Marie-Claude Gaudel,
Makarius Wenzel, and Burkhart Wolff

Univ. Paris-Sud, Laboratoire LRI, UMR8623, Orsay, F-91405, France
CNRS, Orsay, F-91405, France
{feliachi,gaudel,wenzel,wolff}@lri.fr

Abstract. Formal specifications provide strong bases for testing and bring powerful techniques and technologies. Expressive formal specification languages combine large data domain and behavior. Thus, symbolic methods have raised particular interest for test generation techniques.

Integrating formal testing in proof environments such as Isabelle/HOL is referred to as "theorem-prover based testing". Theorem-prover based testing can be adapted to a specific specification language via a representation of its formal semantics, paving the way for specific support of its constructs. The main challenge of this approach is to reduce the gap between pen-and-paper semantics and formal mechanized theories.

In this paper we consider testing based on the *Circus* specification language. This language integrates the notions of states and of complex data in a Z-like fashion with communicating processes inspired from CSP. We present a machine-checked formalization in Isabelle/HOL of this language and its testing theory. Based on this formal representation of the semantics we revisit the original associated testing theory.

We discovered unforeseen simplifications in both definitions and symbolic computations. The approach lends itself to the construction of a tool, that directly uses semantic definitions of the language as well as derived rules of its testing theory, and thus provides some powerful symbolic computation machinery to seamlessly implement them both in a technical environment.

Keywords: Formal Testing, Symbolic Computations, Isabelle/HOL, *Circus*.

1 Introduction

Test generation from formal specifications is an active research area. Several theoretical frameworks and tools have been proposed for various kinds of formal testing techniques and their resulting conformance and coverage notions [9].

We develop a formal test generation framework and tool for the *Circus* specification language. This language combines elements for the description of complex data and behavior specifications, via an integration of Z and CSP with a refinement calculus[18]. *Circus* has a denotational semantics [14], which is based on

L. Groves and J. Sun (Eds.): ICFEM 2013, LNCS 8144, pp. 131–147, 2013.
© Springer-Verlag Berlin Heidelberg 2013

UTP [10], and an operational semantics that can be found in [2]. Here we present an environment for *Circus* -based testing in the line of [2].

Formal environments like Isabelle/HOL [12] are usually applied for formal proof developments. Integrating formal testing in such environments is referred to as "theorem-prover based testing". Theorem-prover based testing can be adapted to a specific specification language via a representation of its formal semantics, paving the way for specific support of its constructs. The main challenge of this approach is to reduce the gap between pen-and-paper semantics and formal mechanized theories, especially to one amenable to efficient symbolic computing. We present such a semantic theory for *Circus*, develop formally its testing theory in Isabelle/HOL and integrate the result in an own testing environment called HOL-TESTGEN/*CirTA*. Our environment comes with some basic test selection criteria, and was applied to an industrial case study extracted from an operational remote sensing system.

The main contribution of this paper is the representation of the symbolic testing theory of *Circus* in Isabelle using the symbolic infrastructure of the prover. We show how the original formalization can be much simplified using shallow symbolic computations.

The paper is organised as follows: Section 2 briefly recalls the context of this work, namely essential issues on *Circus* and *Circus*-based testing, the Isabelle/HOL formal environment, and Isabelle/Circus, an embedding of the denotational semantics of *Circus* in Isabelle/HOL, which makes it possible to reason on *Circus* specifications; Section 3 discusses and describes our main choices for embedding the symbolic notions necessary for generating symbolic tests from *Circus* specifications; on these bases, Section 4 explains how the operational semantics and the *Circus* testing theories have been formulated as Isabelle/HOL definitions and theories, leading to some Isabelle/HOL tactics for symbolic test generation; moreover, the definition of two basic test selection criteria is presented, as well as the instantiation of symbolic tests into concrete ones.

2   Context

2.1   *Circus* and *Circus*-Based Testing

Circus is a formal specification language which combines the notions of states and complex data types in a Z-like style with a process-algebra in the tradition of CSP. The language comes with a formal notion of refinement allowing a formal development ranging from abstract specifications and to executable models and programs. *Circus* has a denotational semantics [14] presented in terms of the UTP [10], and a corresponding operational semantics [2]. UTP is essential for providing a seamless semantic framework for states and processes. A simple example of a *Circus* specification is given in fig. 1; it describes a Fibonacci-number generator.

In [2] the foundations of testing based on *Circus* specifications are stated for two conformance relations: *traces inclusion* and *deadlocks reduction* (usually called *conf* in the area of test derivation from transition systems). The basis

channel *out* : $\mathbb{N}$

process *Fibonacci* $\widehat{=}$ **begin**
state *FibState* $==$ $[\,x, y : \mathbb{N}\,]$
InitFibState $\widehat{=}$ $x := 1$; $y := 1$
InitFib $\widehat{=}$ *out*!1 $\rightarrow$ *out*!1 $\rightarrow$ *InitFibState*
OutFibState $\widehat{=}$ **var** *temp* : $\mathbb{N}$ $\bullet$ (*temp* := y; $y := x + y$; $x := temp$)
OutFib $\widehat{=}$ $\mu\, X$ $\bullet$ *out*!$(x + y)$ $\rightarrow$ *OutFibState*; X
$\bullet$ *InitFib*; *OutFib*
end

Fig. 1. The Fibonacci generator in *Circus*

of this work is an operational semantics that expresses in a symbolic way the evolution of systems specified in *Circus*. Using this operational semantics, symbolic characterizations of traces, initials, and acceptance sets have been stated and used to define relevant notions of tests. Two symbolic exhaustive test sets have been defined respectively for traces refinement and *deadlocks reduction*: proofs of exhaustivity guarantee that, under some basic testability hypotheses, a system under test (SUT) that would pass all the concrete tests obtained by instantiation of the symbolic tests of the symbolic exhaustive test set satisfies the corresponding conformance relation.

Testability hypotheses are assumptions on the SUT that are essential to prove that the success of a testing campaign entails correctness. In the *Circus* testing theory, the first testability hypothesis is that the SUT behaves like some unknown *Circus* process SUT_{Circus}. This means that, in any environment, the execution of the SUT and SUT_{Circus} give the same observations. In this context, even though the SUT is not a *Circus* process, one can use refinement to compare it to a given *Circus* specification. This requires, however, that events used in the specification are perceived as atomic and of irrelevant duration in the SUT.

The tests are defined using the following notions:

- *cstraces* : a constrained symbolic trace is a pair composed of a symbolic trace *st* and a constraint *c* on the symbolic variables of *st*.
- *csinitials*: the set *csinitials* associated with a cstrace (st, c) of a *Circus* process P contains the constrained symbolic events that represent valid continuations of (st, c) in P, i.e. events that are initials of P after (st, c).
- $\overline{csinitials}$: given a process P and one of its cstraces (st, c), the set $\overline{csinitials}$ contains the constrained symbolic events that represent the events that are not initials of P for any of the instances of (st, c).
- *csacceptances*: a *csacceptances* set associated with a cstrace (st, c) of a *Circus* process P is a set of sets SX of symbolic acceptances. An acceptance is a set of events in which at least one event must be accepted after (st, c).

Examples of a constrained symbolic trace of *Fibonacci* and of a constrained symbolic event in $\overline{csinitials}$ after this cstrace is:

$$([out.1, out.1, out.a, out.b], a = 2 \wedge b = 3) \qquad (out.a, a \neq 5)$$

Symbolic Tests for Traces Inclusion. *traces inclusion* refers to inclusion of trace sets: process P_2 is a *traces inclusion* of process P_1 if and only if the set of traces of P_2 is included in that of P_1. Symbolic tests for *traces inclusion* are based on some cstrace *cst* of the Circus process P used to build the tests, followed by a forbidden symbolic continuation, namely a constrained symbolic event *cse* belonging to the set $\overline{csinitials}$ associated with *cst* in P. Such a test passes if its parallel execution with the SUT blocks before the last event, and fails if it is completed. A test that, if successful, deadlocks at the end, is used to check that forbidden traces cannot be executed. An example of a test for *traces inclusion* for *Fibonacci* in given by:

$$([out.1, out.1, out.a, out.b], a = 2 \wedge b \neq 3)$$

Given a Circus process P the set of *all* the symbolic tests described above is a symbolic *exhaustive* test set with respect to *traces inclusion*: a SUT that would pass all the instances of all the symbolic tests is a *traces inclusion* of P, assuming some basic testability hypotheses that are given in [2], where the proof can also be found.

Symbolic Tests for *Deadlocks Reduction*. *deadlocks reduction* (also called *conf*) requires that deadlocks of process P_2 are deadlocks of process P_1. The definition of symbolic tests for *deadlocks reduction* is based on a cstrace *cst* followed by a choice over a set SX, which is a symbolic acceptance of *cst*. Such a test passes if its parallel execution with the SUT is completed and fails if it blocks before the last choice of events. An example of a test for *deadlocks reduction* in *Fibonacci* is given by:

$$([out.1, out.1, out.a], a = 2) \{out.3\}$$

Given a Circus process P the set of all the symbolic tests described above is a symbolic exhaustive test set with respect to *deadlocks reduction* [2] under the same testability hypotheses as above. This is also proved in [2].

2.2   The Isabelle/HOL Formal Environment

Isabelle. [12] is a generic theorem prover implemented in SML. Built upon a small trusted logical kernel, it is possible to provide logical and technical extensions by user-programmed procedures in a logically safe way. These days, the most commonly used logical extension is **Isabelle/HOL** supporting classical Higher-order Logics (HOL), i.e. a logic based on typed λ-calculus including a Haskell-style type-system. HOL provides the usual logical connectives as well as the object-logical quantifiers; in contrast to first-order logic, quantifiers may range over arbitrary types, including total functions of type $\alpha \Rightarrow \beta$. Isabelle/HOL comes with large libraries, where thousands of theorems have been proven from definitional axioms; this covers theories for sets, pairs, lists, relations, partial functions, orderings, and arithmetics. We use the HOL-notation throughout this paper (instead of, for example, the Z notation) in order to avoid confusion. The empty list is written $[]$ and the constructor $\#$; lists of the form $a\#b\#[]$ were denoted $[a, b]$. The @-operator denotes list concatenation, the projections into lists are the usual $hd[a, b] = a$ and $tl[a, b] = [b]$. **Isabelle/HOL-TestGen**[1] is a technical extension providing support for formal test generation.

Isabelle/*Circus* is a formalization of UTP and the denotational semantics of the *Circus* language[6] in Isabelle/HOL. For the work presented in this paper, we will use the operational semantics and the testing theory of *Circus*, and formalize it on top of Isabelle/*Circus*. We will discuss in detail the impact of the symbolic representation of the language for symbolic execution.

3   Shallow Symbolic Computations with Isabelle

The test sets introduced in section 2.1 are defined in [2] using symbolic variables and traces. *Symbolic variables* are syntactic names that represent some values without any type information. These symbolic variables are introduced to represent a set of values (or a single, loosely defined, value), possibly constrained by a predicate. An alphabet *a* is associated to all symbolic definitions of the testing theory. This alphabet enumerates the symbolic variable names.

A deep symbolic representation would require the definition of these symbolic notions on top of Isabelle/HOL. This would rather be heavy to realize and may introduce some inconsistency in the theory. The main problem is that symbolic variables are just names. They are syntactic not typed entities and the type information recorded in *Circus* variables is not present at this stage. Moreover, constraints would also be syntactic entities, and thus, have to be presented in a side-calculus mimicking *Circus* substitution and type-checking.

As an alternative to this deep symbolic execution, we opt for a so-called *shallow embedding*. This embedding is based directly on the Isabelle symbolic representation and computation facilities. Isabelle, as a formal framework, provides powerful symbolic computation facilities that can be reused directly for our purpose. This requires symbolic variables to be HOL variables, which are semantic typed entities manipulated by the prover. Expressions over these variables are written using HOL predefined operators or logical connectives, constraints are entities directly represented as HOL predicates. With our representation, all the symbolic execution is carried out by Isabelle's symbolic computations.

This representation choice is natural since symbolic computations and higher-order manipulations (definitions, theories, rules, ...) are not of the same nature. They correspond to two different abstraction levels. This is not the case for deep symbolic execution, which would be represented at higher order abstraction level. In shallow representations, low-level symbolic computations are the basis of high-level formal definitions.

This choice of embedding strongly influences the definition and representation of the operational semantics and testing theory. The impacts of this choice are explained in various places in the following sections. In the sequel, we use "symbolic execution" to refer to the explicit (deep) symbolic manipulations as defined in [2]; we use "symbolic computations" to refer to the (shallow) implementation in Isabelle of these symbolic notions. A more detailed development of these issues can be found in [5].

4   Revisiting the *Circus* Testing Theories

The embedding of the testing theories of *Circus* essentially depends on its operational semantics. Thus, we start by introducing a shallow embedding of the *Circus* symbolic operational semantics in Isabelle/HOL.

4.1   Operational Semantics

The *configurations* of the transition system for the operational semantics of *Circus* are triples $(c \mid s \models A)$ where c is a constraint over the symbolic variables in use, s a symbolic state, and A a *Circus* action. The transition rules over configurations have the form: $(c_0 \mid s_0 \models A_0) \xrightarrow{e} (c_1 \mid s_1 \models A_1)$, where the label e represents the performed symbolic event or ε.

The transition relation is also defined in terms of UTP and *Circus* actions. The formalization of the operational semantics is realized on top of Isabelle/*Circus*. In order to introduce the transition relation for all *Circus* actions, configurations must be defined first. Following the shallow symbolic representation, we introduce the following definitions in Isabelle/HOL.

Constraints. In the *Circus* testing theory [2], the transition relation of the operational semantics is defined symbolically. The symbolic execution system is based on UTP constructs. Symbolic variables (values) are represented by UTP variables with fresh names generated on the fly. The (semantics of the) constraint is represented by a UTP predicate over the values of these symbolic variables.

In our shallow symbolic representation, symbolic values are given by HOL variables, that can be constrained in proof terms, by expressing predicates over them in the premises. This makes the symbolic configuration defined on free HOL variables that are globally constrained in the context. Thus, the explicit representation of the constraint in the configuration is not needed. It will be represented by a (globally constrained) symbolic state and an action.

Actions. The action component of the operational semantics as defined in [2] is a syntactic characterization of some *Circus* actions. This corresponds to the syntax of actions defined in the denotational semantics. In our representation of the operational semantics, the action component is a semantic characterization of *Circus* actions. The *Circus* action type is given by (Θ, σ) action where Θ and σ are polymorphic type parameters for *channels* and *alphabet*; these type parameters are instantiated for concrete processes.

Labels. All the transitions over configurations are decorated with labels to keep a trace of the events that the system may perform. A label may refer to a communication with a symbolic input or output value, a synchronization (without communication) or an internal (silent) transition ε. In our representation, channels are represented by constructor functions of a data-type specific for a *Circus* process specification. For our symbolic trace example in Section 2.1, we will have the datatype `Fibonacci_channels = out int`, where `Fibonacci_channels` is the concrete instance of the channel alphabet Θ, and `out` the only typed channel constructor of the `Fibonacci`-process. A symbolic event is obtained by applying the corresponding channel constructor to a HOL term, thus `out(3)` or `out(a)`. Labels are then defined either by one symbolic event or by ε.

States. In the *Circus* testing theory [2], the state is represented by an assignment of symbolic values to all *Circus* variables in scope. Scoping is handled by variable introduction and removal and nested scopes are avoided using variable renaming.

As explained in section 3, symbolic variables are represented by HOL terms. Consequently, the symbolic state can be represented as a symbolic binding (variable name $\mapsto$ HOL term). Following the representation of bindings by extensible records, the symbolic state corresponds to a record that maps field names to values of an arbitrary HOL type. In order to keep track of nested statements, each *Circus* variable in the state binds to a *stack* of values.

Operational Semantics Rules Revisited. The operational semantics is defined by a set of inductive inference rules over the transition relation of the form:

$$\frac{C}{(s_0 \models A_0) \xrightarrow{e} (s_1 \models A_1)}$$

where $(s_0 \models A_0)$ and $(s_1 \models A_1)$ are configurations, e is a label and C is the applicability condition of the rule. Note that the revised configurations are *pairs* where s_1 and s_2 are symbolic states in the sense above, and the constraints are no longer kept inside the configuration, but in a side-condition C of the entire operational rule. This way, we can constrain on the HOL-side these symbolic states. A lot of explicit symbolic manipulations (e.g. fresh symbolic variable introduction) are built-in quantifiers managed directly by prover primitives. Thus, the shallow representation reduces drastically the complexity of the rules [5].

The entire operational relation is defined inductively in Isabelle covering all *Circus* constructs. Isabelle/HOL uses this specification to define the relation as least fixed-point on the lattice of powersets (according to Knaster-Tarski). From this definition the prover derives three kinds of rules:

- the introduction rules of the operational semantics used in the inductive definition of the transition relation,
- the inversion of the introduction rules expressed as a huge case-splitting rule covering all the cases, and
- an induction principle over the inductive definition of the transition relation.

4.2   Testing Theories

As seen in Section 2.1, testing from *Circus* specifications is defined for two conformance relations: *traces inclusion* and *deadlocks reduction*. These conformance relations are based on the notion of *cstraces*. As explained in section 3, we will represent the "symbolic" by the "shallow"; consequently, all symbolic notions defined in [2] are mapped to shallow computations from Isabelle's point of view.

Symbolic Traces Definition. let $cstraces(P)$ the set of constrained symbolic traces of the process P. A *cstrace* is a list of symbolic events associated with a constraint defined as a predicate over the symbolic variables of the trace. Events are given by the labels, different from ε, of the operational semantics transitions. Let us consider the relation noted "$\Longrightarrow$" defined by:

$$\frac{\qquad}{cf_1 \overset{[]}{\Longrightarrow} cf_1} \qquad \frac{cf_1 \overset{\varepsilon}{\longrightarrow} cf_2 \quad cf_2 \overset{st}{\Longrightarrow} cf_3}{cf_1 \overset{st}{\Longrightarrow} cf_3} \qquad \frac{cf_1 \overset{e}{\longrightarrow} cf_2 \quad cf_2 \overset{st}{\Longrightarrow} cf_3 \quad e \neq \varepsilon}{cf_1 \overset{e\#st}{\Longrightarrow} cf_3} \quad (*)$$

where cf_1, cf_2 and cf_3 are configurations.

The *cstraces* set definition is given in [2] using the relation (*) as follows:

Definition 1. *for a given process P, an initial constraint c_0, an initial state s_0*

$$cstraces^a(c_0, s_0, P) =$$
$$\{(st, \exists(\alpha c \setminus \alpha st) \bullet c) \mid s\, P_1 \bullet \alpha st \le a \wedge (c_0 \mid s_0 \models P) \overset{st}{\Longrightarrow} (c \mid s \models P_1)\}$$
$$cstraces^a(\textbf{begin } state[x : T]P \bullet \textbf{end}) = cstraces^a(w_0 \in T, x := w_0, P)$$

One can read: the constrained symbolic traces of a given configuration are the constrained symbolic traces that can be reached using the operational semantics rules starting from this configuration.

The shallow symbolic representation of this definition is simpler since the symbolic alphabet a is not addressed explicitly. It is also the case for the symbolic constraint because it is described by the characteristic predicate of the set of these traces. Therefore, the *cstraces* set is defined in our theory as follows:

Definition 2. cstraces P = {st. ∃ s P1. (s_0 ⊨P) =st⇒ (s ⊨P1)}

Since the operational semantics rules contain premises that ensure the validity of the target constraint, the trace constraint is embedded in the set predicate: in our formalization, a constrained symbolic trace is seen as a concrete trace, i.e. a trace with symbolic HOL variables, restricted by rules premises. Thus, the constraint of a constrained symbolic trace can be retrieved using set membership.

4.3 Test-Generation for *Traces Inclusion*

The first studied conformance relation for *Circus*-based testing corresponds to the traces-inclusion refinement relation. This relation states that all the traces of the SUT belong to the traces set of the specification, or in other words, the SUT should not engage in traces that are not traces of the specification.

As seen in Section 2.1, a forbidden *cstrace* is defined by a prefix which is a valid *cstrace* of the specification followed by a forbidden symbolic event (continuation). The set of forbidden continuations is called $\overline{csinitials}$, the set of valid continuations is $csinitials$. Because of the constrained symbolic nature of the *cstraces* and events, $\overline{csinitials}$ is not exactly the complement of $csinitials$.

***csinitials* Definition.** *csinitials* is the set of constrained symbolic events a system may perform after a given trace. It is defined in [2] as follows:

Definition 3. *For every* $(st, c) \in cstraces^a(P)$

$$csinitials^a(P, (st, c)) =$$
$$\{(se, c \wedge c_1) \mid (st@[se], c_1) \in cstraces^a(P) \wedge (\exists a \bullet c \wedge c_1)\}$$

Symbolic initials after a given constrained symbolic trace are symbolic events that, concatenated to this trace, yield valid constrained symbolic traces. Only events whose constraints are compatible with the trace constraint are considered.

We introduce the shallow symbolic representation of this definition as follows:

Definition 4. csinitials (P, tr) = {e. tr@[e] $\in$ cstraces (P)}

All explicit symbolic manipulations are removed, since they are implicitly handled by the prover. The constraint of the trace is not considered, since at this level *tr* is considered as a single concrete trace.

$\overline{csinitials}$ Definition. In order to generate tests for the *traces inclusion* relation, we need to introduce the definition of $\overline{csinitials}$. This set contains the constrained symbolic events the system must refuse to perform after a given trace. These elements are used to lead the SUT to execute a prohibited trace, and to detect an error if the SUT do so.

Definition 5. *for every* $(st, c) \in cstraces^a(P)$

$$\overline{csinitials}^a(P, (st, c)) =$$
$$\left\{ (d.\alpha_0, c_1) \mid \begin{pmatrix} \alpha_0 = a(\#st + 1) \wedge \\ c_1 = c \wedge \neg \bigvee \{c_2 \mid (d.\alpha_0, c_2) \in csinitials^a(P, (st, c))\} \end{pmatrix} \right\}$$

The $\overline{csinitials}$ set is built from the *csinitials* set: if an event is not in *csinitials* it is added to $\overline{csinitials}$, constrained with the constraint of the trace. If the event is in *csinitials* it is added with the negation of its constraint. The new symbolic variable α_0 is defined as a fresh variable in the alphabet a, the next after the symbolic variables used in the symbolic trace *st*.

In our theories, the symbolic execution is carried out by the symbolic computations of the prover. Consequently, all explicit symbolic constructs are removed in the representation of $\overline{csinitials}$. This representation is introduced as follows:

Definition 6. csinitialsb (P, tr) = {e. ¬Sup {e $\in$ csinitials(P, tr)}}

where the *Sup* operator is the supremum of the lattice of booleans which is predefined in the HOL library, i.e. generalized set union. No constraint is associated to the trace *tr* because it is globally constrained in the context. Symbolic $\overline{csinitials}$ are represented by sets of events where the constraint can be retrieved by negating set membership over the *csinitials* set.

4.4   Test-Generation for *Deadlocks Reduction*

The *deadlocks reduction* conformance relation, also known as *conf*, states that all the deadlocks must be specified. Testing this conformance relation aims at verifying that all specified deadlock-free situations are dead-lock free in the SUT. A deadlock-free situation is defined by a cstrace followed by the choice among a set of events the system must not refuse, i.e. if the SUT is waiting for an interaction after performing a specified trace, it must accept to perform at least one element of the proposed *csacceptances* set of this trace.

csacceptances **Definition.** In order to distinguish input symbolic events from output symbolic events in the symbolic acceptance sets, the set *IOcsinitials* is defined. This set contains, for a given configuration, the constrained symbolic initials where input and output information is recorded. Since inputs and outputs are considered separately in the labels of the transition relation, the set of *IOcsinitials* is easy to define. It contains the set of labels (different from ε) of all possible transitions of a given configuration.

Definition 7. *for a given process P_1*

$$IOcsinitials_{st}^a(c_1, s_1, P_1) =$$
$$\left\{ \begin{array}{l} (l, \exists (\alpha c_2 \setminus (\alpha(st@[l]))) \bullet c_2) \mid s_2, \ P_2 \bullet \\ (c_1 \mid s_1 \models P_1) \overset{l}{\longrightarrow} (c_2 \mid s_2 \models P_2) \wedge l \neq \varepsilon \wedge \alpha(st@[l]) \leq a \end{array} \right\}$$

A symbolic acceptance set after a given trace must contain at least one symbolic event from each *IOcsinitials* set obtained from a stable configuration after this trace. In our representation of this definition the alphabets a and $\alpha(st)$ are not addressed explicitly, and the constraint is defined as the set predicate.

Definition 8. *IOcsinitials cf = {e. ∃ cf'. cf -e→ cf' ∧ e ≠ε}*

The general definition of *csacceptances* was introduced in [2] as follows:

Definition 9. *for every $(st, c) \in cstraces^a(P_1)$ we define*

$$csacceptances^a(c_1, s_1, P_1, (st, c)) =$$
$$\left\{ SX \mid \left(\begin{array}{l} \forall c_2, s_2, P_2 \bullet \left(\begin{array}{l} (c_1 \mid s_1 \models P_1) \overset{st}{\Longrightarrow} (c_2 \mid s_2 \models P_2) \wedge \\ (\exists a \bullet c_2 \wedge c) \wedge stable(c_2 \mid s_2 \models P_2) \end{array} \right) \bullet \\ \exists iose \in SX \bullet iose \in IOcsinitials_{st}^a(c_2, s_2, P_2) \upharpoonright^a c \end{array} \right) \right\}$$

where
$$stable(c_1 \mid s_1 \models P_1) = \neg \ \exists c_2, s_2, P_2 \bullet (c_1 \mid s_1 \models P_1) \overset{\varepsilon}{\longrightarrow} (c_2 \mid s_2 \models P_2)$$
$$S \upharpoonright^a c = \{(se, c \wedge c_1) \mid (se, c_1) \in S \wedge (\exists a \bullet c \wedge c_1)\}$$

The *csacceptances* are computed using the *IOcsinitials* after a given stable configuration of the specification. A configuration is stable if no internal silent evolution is possible directly for its action. Only *IOcsinitials* whose constraints are compatible with the constraint of the tested trace are considered. A filter function $\upharpoonright$ is introduced in order to remove unfeasible initials.

The *csacceptances* set defined above is infinite and contains redundant elements since any superset of a set in *csacceptances* is also in *csacceptances*. A minimal symbolic acceptances set $csacceptances_{min}$ can be defined to avoid this problem. The $csacceptances_{min}$ set after a given *cstrace* must contain exactly one element from each *IOcsinitials* set. Unlike *csacceptances*, the $csacceptances_{min}$ contain only elements that are possible *IOcsinitials*. It is defined as follows:

Definition 10.

```
csacceptances_min tr s A =
      cart (⋃{SX. ∃ t∈(after_trace tr s A). SX ∈IOcsinitials t})
```

where `after_trace` is defined by:

```
after_trace tr s A = {t. (s ⊨A) =tr⇒A t ∧stable t}
```

and `cart` operator defined below is a generalized Cartesian product whose elements are sets, rather than tuples. It takes a set of sets *SX* as argument, and defines also a set of sets, characterized as follows:

```
cart SX = {s1. (∀ s2∈SX. s2 ≠{} ⟶(∃ e. s2 ∩s1 = {e}))
                            ∧ (∀ e∈s1. ∃ s2∈SX. e∈s2)}
```

The resulting $csacceptances_{min}$ of this definition is minimal (not redundant), but can still be infinite. This can come from some unbound internal nondeterminism in the specification that leads to infinite possibilities. In this case, the set cannot be restricted and all elements must be considered.

Each element of the resulting $csacceptances_{min}$ set is a set of symbolic events. A symbolic acceptance event is represented as a set of concrete events. The instantiation of these sets is done using the membership operator.

4.5   The *CirTA* System

CirTA stands for *Circus* Testing Automation, which is a test-generation environment for *Circus*. It defines some general tactics for generating, *cstraces* and test-cases for the two conformance relations introduced earlier.

cstraces **Generation Tactic.** Test definitions are introduced as test specifications that will be used for test-generation. For trace generation a proof goal is stated to define the traces a given system may perform. This statement is given by the following rule, for a given process P:

$$\frac{length(tr) \leq k \quad tr \in cstraces(P)}{Prog(tr)} \tag{1}$$

where k is a constant used to bound the length of the generated traces.

While in a conventional automated proof, a tactic is used to refine an intermediate step (a "subgoal") to more elementary ones until they eventually get "true", in prover-based testing this process is stopped when the subgoal reach a certain normal form of clauses, in our case, when we reach logical formulas of the form: C $\Longrightarrow$ Prog (tr), where C is a constraint on the generated trace. Note that different simplification rules are applied on the premises until no further simplification is possible. The shallow symbolic definition of *cstraces* makes it possible to simplify the set membership operator into a predicate in the premises. The final step of the generation produces a list of propositions, describing the generated traces stored by the free variable *Prog*. The trace generation tactic is described by the following algorithm:

> **Data**: k : the maximum length of traces
> Simplify the test specification using the *cstraces* Definition 2;
> **while** *length* $\leq k \wedge$ *more traces can be generated* **do**
> > Apply the rules of (*) on the current goal;
> > Apply the rules of the operational semantics on the resulting subgoals;
> **end**

The test specification 1 is introduced as a proof goal in the proof configuration. The premise of this proof goal is first simplified using the definition of *cstraces* given in 2. The application of the elimination rules (*) on this proof goal generates the possible continuations in different subgoals. The elimination rules of the operational semantics are applied to these subgoals in order to instantiate the trace elements. Infeasible traces correspond to subgoals whose premises are *false*. In this case, the system is able to close these subgoals automatically.

Specifications may describe unbounded recursive behavior and thus yield an unbounded number of symbolic traces. The generation is then limited by a given trace length k, defined as a parameter for the whole generation process. The list of subgoals corresponds to all possible traces with length smaller than this limit.

The trace generation process is implemented in Isabelle as a tactic. The trace generation tactic can be seen as an *inference engine* that operates with the derived rules of the operational semantics and the trace composition relation.

***csinitials* Generation Tactic.** The generation of *csinitials* is done using a similar tactic as for *cstraces*. In order to capture the set of all possible *csinitials*, the test theorem is defined in this case as follows:

$$\frac{S = csinitials(P, tr)}{Prog\ S} \tag{2}$$

the free variable *Prog* records the set S of all *csinitials* of P after the trace tr.

***c̄sinitials* Generation Tactic.** The generation of tests for *traces inclusion* is done in two stages. First, the trace generation tactic is invoked to generate the symbolic traces. For each generated trace, the set of the possible *csinitials* after this trace is generated using the corresponding generation tactic. Using this set, the feasible *c̄sinitials* are generated and added as a subgoal in the final generation state. This tactic can be represented in the following algorithm:

Data: k : the maximum length of tests

Generate *cstraces* using trace generation tactic for a length k;

foreach *generated trace tr* **do**

> Simplify the test specification (2) using the $\overline{csinitials}$ Definition 6;
>
> Generate the *csinitials* after *tr* using *csinitials set* generation tactic;
>
> Apply case-splitting and simplification rules to generate the $\overline{csinitials}$;

end

csacceptances **Generation Tactic.** test-generation in this case is based on the generation of the $csacceptances_{min}$ set. For a given symbolic trace generated from the specification, the generation of the sets of $csacceptances_{min}$ is performed in three steps. First, all possible stable configurations that can be reached by following the given trace are generated. In the second step, all possible *IOcsinitials* are generated for each configuration obtained in the first step. Finally, the generalized Cartesian product is computed from all resulting *IOcsinitials*. The generation tactic is defined in the following algorithm:

Data: k : the maximum length of tests

Generate *cstraces* using trace generation tactic for a length k;

foreach *generated trace tr* **do**

> Simplify the test specification using the $csacceptances_{min}$ Definition 10;
>
> Generate all stable configurations after *tr* using the derived rules;
>
> **foreach** *generated stable configuration cf* **do**
>
> > Generate all *IOcsinitials* after this configuration cf;
>
> **end**
>
> Introduce the definition of $\otimes$ for the resulting set;
>
> Apply simplification rules to generate the sets $csacceptances_{min}$;

end

4.6 Some Test Selection Hypotheses

Symbolic tests cannot be used directly for testing. A finite number of concrete (executable) tests must be instantiated from them. However, in some situations, there is an infinite number of instances: it may come from infinite types, or from symbolic tests with unbounded length, as mentioned in section 4.5. Some selection criteria must be used to choose a finite subset of concrete finite tests. They are formalized as test selection hypotheses on the SUT: assuming these hypotheses the selected tests form an exhaustive test set [2, 8].

Selection hypothesis that can be used in the case of unbounded tests are *regularity hypotheses*. The simplest one allows to bound the traces length: it states that if the SUT behaves correctly for traces shorter than a given length, it will then behave correctly for all the traces. Other selection criteria are needed to choose a finite subset of concrete tests among the instances of symbolic tests. *uniformity hypotheses* can be used to state that the SUT will behave correctly for all the instances if it behaves correctly for some subset of them. Such a subset can be obtained using on-the-fly constraint solving as, for instance, in [1]

Test selection hypotheses can be explicitly stated in our test-generation framework *CirTA*. Currently, the classical regularity hypothesis on traces length is used, where the maximum regularity length is provided as parameter. Moreover, for each resulting symbolic test, a uniformity hypothesis is stated to extract a *witness* value for each symbolic value in the test. Concrete (*witness*) values are represented by Isabelle *schematic variables* representing arbitrary (but constrained) values. These uniformity and regularity hypotheses are respectively defined as introduction rules as follows:

$$\frac{P \ ?x_1...?x_n \quad THYP((\exists\, x_1,...,x_n \bullet P \ x_1...x_n) \to (\forall\, x_1,...,x_n \bullet P \ x_1...x_n))}{\forall\, x_1,...,x_n \bullet P \ x_1...x_n}$$

$$\frac{\begin{matrix}[length(tr) < k]\\ \vdots \\ P \ (tr)\end{matrix} \quad THYP((\forall\, tr \mid length(tr) < k \bullet P \ (tr)) \to (\forall\, tr \bullet P \ (tr)))}{\forall\, tr \bullet P \ (tr)}$$

P is the predicate of a (symbolic) test case, tr is a (symbolic) trace and $THYP$ is a constant used to preserve test hypotheses from automatic simplifications. Schematic variables are represented in Isabelle with ? prefixing their name.

4.7   Test Instantiations

The last step of test-generation is the selection of actual witness values corresponding to schematic variables produced by the uniformity hypothesis. Constraint solvers that are integrated with Isabelle are used for this instantiation, in the same way as what was done in [1]. Two kind of solvers can be used: random solvers and SMT solvers. The random constraint solving is performed using QuickCheck, that instantiates randomly the values of the schematic variables. An integration of QuichCheck with the Isabelle simplifier defined for HOL-TestGen can also be used for more efficient random solving. The second kind of integrated constraint solvers are SMT solvers and especially Z3 [4].

5   Conclusion

Related Work. There exists quite a variety of tools for supporting test generation. Symbolic evaluation and constraint solving are widely used, as well as model checkers or similar techniques. The LOFT tool performed test generation from algebraic specifications, essentially based on narrowing. TGV [11] performs test generation from IOLTS (Input Output LTS) and test purposes for the *ioco* conformance relation. TGV considers finite transition systems, thus enumerative techniques are used to deal with finite data types. Some symbolic extension of TGV, STG has been enriched by constraint solving and abstract interpretation techniques [3]. The FDR model-checker was used [13] for generating test cases from CSP specifications for a conformance relation similar to *ioco*. In Spec Explorer [16], the underlying semantic framework are abstract state machines (ASM) and the conformance relation is alternating refinement. The techniques are similar to those used for explicit model-checking. The ASM framework provides foundation to deal with arbitrarily complex states, but the symbolic extension, based on constraint solving, is still experimental. JavaPathFinder [17] has been used for generating test input from descriptions of method preconditions. The approach combines model checking, symbolic execution, constraint solving and improves coverage of complex data structures in Java programs. A very strong tool in this line of white-box test systems using symbolic execution and model-checking is the Pex tool [15].

In our case, the use of a theorem prover, namely Isabelle/HOL, is motivated by the fact that test generation from rich specification languages such as *Circus* can greatly benefit from the automatic and interactive symbolic computations and proof technology to define sound and flexible test generation techniques. Actually, this is extremely useful and convenient to deal with infinite state spaces. TGV does not possess symbolic execution techniques and is thus limited to small data models. Our approach has much in common with STG, however its development was abandoned since the necessary constraint solving technologies had not been available at that time. In contrast, *CirTA* uses most recent deduction technology in a framework that guarantees its seamless integration. On the other hand, Symbolic JavaPathFinder and Pex are white-box testing tools which are both complementary to our black-box approach.

Summary. We have described the machine-checked formalization *CirTA* of the operational semantics and testing theory of *Circus*. Our experience has been developed for Isabelle/HOL, but could be reused for other HOL systems (like HOL4). Our formal reconstruction of the *Circus* theory lead to unforeseen simplifications of notions like channels and configurations, and, last but not least, to the concept of typing and binding inside the operational semantics rules, as well as the derived rules capturing the deductive construction of symbolic traces. In fact, since the original *Circus* theory is untyped, in a sense, Isabelle/*Circus* is an extension, and the question of the "faithfulness" of our semantic representation has to be raised. While a direct, formal "equivalence proof" between a machine-checked theory on the one hand and a mathematically rigorous paper-and-pencil development on the other is inherently impossible, nevertheless, we would argue that *CirTA* captures the *essence* of the *Circus* testing theory. Besides hands-on simulations in concrete examples, there is the entire architecture of similar definitions leading to closely related theorems and proofs that does establish a correspondence between these two. This correspondence would be further strengthened if we would complete the theory by a (perfectly feasible, but laborious) equivalence proof between the operational and denotational semantics (for the time being, such a proof does neither exist on paper nor in Isabelle). The correspondence could again be strengthened, if the existing paper-and-pencil proof of equivalence between the conformance relations and the refinement relation (given in [2]) could be reconstructed inside *CirTA*.

CirTA has been validated by a concrete case study. We developed, for a message monitoring module stemming from an industrial partner, an Isabelle/*Circus* model and derived tests for the real system. The component under test is embedded in not less than 5k lines of Java code. It binds together a variety of devices and especially patients pacemaker controllers, via sophisticated data structures and operations which was the main source of complexity when testing. More details about this case study can be found in [5, 7].

Isabelle/HOL is a mature theorem prover and easily supports our requirements for add-on tools for symbolic computation, but substantial efforts had to be invested for building our formal testing environment nonetheless. With regard to the experience of the last 10–20 years of the interactive theorem proving community, this initially steep ascend is in fact quite common, and we can anticipate eventual pay-off for more complex examples at the next stage. HOL as a logic opens a wide space of rich mathematical modeling, and Isabelle/HOL as a tool environment supports many mathematical domains by proof tools, say for simplification and constraint solving. Many of these Isabelle tools already incorporate other external proof tools, such as Z3. Thus we can benefit from this rich collection of formal reasoning tools for our particular application of *Circus* testing, and exploit the full potential of theorem prover technology for our work.

The Isabelle/HOL source code of Isabelle/*Circus* is already available in the Archive of Formal Proofs [1]. The source code of the *CirTA* environment will be distributed with the next release of HOL-TESTGEN.

Future Work. Besides the perspective to complete *CirTA* by the discussed equivalence theorems, our short term perspectives is to validate the environment on larger *Circus* specifications, and then integrate the *Circus* test generation framework with HOL-TestGen in order to benefit of its techniques for data-oriented case-splitting, test-driver generation and (on-the-fly) constraint-solving techniques. Moreover, we plan to study, develop and experiment with various test selection strategies and criteria for *Circus*.

References

[1] Brucker, A.D., Wolff, B.: On Theorem Prover-based Testing. In: Formal Aspects of Computing, FAOC (2012)
[2] Cavalcanti, A., Gaudel, M.-C.: Testing for refinement in circus. Acta Inf. 48(2), 97–147 (2011)
[3] Clarke, D., Jéron, T., Rusu, V., Zinovieva, E.: STG: A symbolic test generation tool. In: Katoen, J.-P., Stevens, P. (eds.) TACAS 2002. LNCS, vol. 2280, pp. 470–475. Springer, Heidelberg (2002)

---

[1] http://afp.sourceforge.net/entries/Circus.shtml

[4] de Moura, L., Bjørner, N.S.: Z3: An efficient SMT solver. In: Ramakrishnan, C.R., Rehof, J. (eds.) TACAS 2008. LNCS, vol. 4963, pp. 337–340. Springer, Heidelberg (2008)

[5] Feliachi, A.: Semantics-Based Testing for Circus. PhD thesis, Université Paris-Sud 11 (2012)

[6] Feliachi, A., Gaudel, M.-C., Wolff, B.: Isabelle/*Circus*: A process specification and verification environment. In: Joshi, R., Müller, P., Podelski, A. (eds.) VSTTE 2012. LNCS, vol. 7152, pp. 243–250. Springer, Heidelberg (2012)

[7] Feliachi, A., Gaudel, M.-C., Wolff, B.: Exhaustive testing in hol-testgen/cirta – a case study. Technical Report 1562, LRI (July 2013)

[8] Gaudel, M.-C., Gall, P.L.: Testing data types implementations from algebraic specifications. In: Hierons, et al (eds.) [9], pp. 209–239

[9] Hierons, R.M., Bowen, J.P., Harman, M. (eds.): FORTEST. LNCS, vol. 4949. Springer, Heidelberg (2008)

[10] Hoare, C., He, J.: Unifying theories of programming. Prentice Hall (1998)

[11] Jard, C., Jéron, T.: TGV: theory, principles and algorithms, a tool for the automatic synthesis of conformance test cases for non-deterministic reactive systems. In: STTT, vol. 6 (October 2004)

[12] Nipkow, T., Paulson, L.C., Wenzel, M.: Isabelle/HOL — A Proof Assistant for Higher-Order Logic. LNCS, vol. 2283. Springer, Heidelberg (2002)

[13] Nogueira, S., Sampaio, A., Mota, A.: Guided test generation from CSP models. In: Fitzgerald, J.S., Haxthausen, A.E., Yenigun, H. (eds.) ICTAC 2008. LNCS, vol. 5160, pp. 258–273. Springer, Heidelberg (2008)

[14] Oliveira, M., Cavalcanti, A., Woodcock, J.: A denotational semantics for Circus. Electron. Notes Theor. Comput. Sci. 187, 107–123 (2007)

[15] Tillmann, N., Schulte, W.: Parameterized unit tests. SIGSOFT Softw. Eng. Notes 30(5), 253–262 (2005)

[16] Veanes, M., Campbell, C., Grieskamp, W., Schulte, W., Tillmann, N., Nachmanson, L.: Model-based testing of object-oriented reactive systems with spec explorer. In: Hierons, R.M., Bowen, J.P., Harman, M. (eds.) FORTEST. LNCS, vol. 4949, pp. 39–76. Springer, Heidelberg (2008)

[17] Visser, W., Pasareanu, C.S., Khurshid, S.: Test input generation with Java PathFinder. In: ISSTA 2004, pp. 97–107. ACM (2004)

[18] Woodcock, J., Cavalcanti, A.: The semantics of *circus*: In: Bert, D., Bowen, J.P., Henson, M.C., Robinson, K. (eds.) ZB 2002. LNCS, vol. 2272, pp. 184–203. Springer, Heidelberg (2002)

A CSP Timed Input-Output Relation and a Strategy for Mechanised Conformance Verification

Gustavo Carvalho, Augusto Sampaio, and Alexandre Mota

Universidade Federal de Pernambuco - Centro de Informática
50740-560, Pernambuco, Brazil
{ghpc,acas,acm}@cin.ufpe.br

Abstract. Here we propose a timed input-output conformance relation (named CSPTIO) based on the process algebra CSP. In contrast to other relations, CSPTIO analyses data-flow reactive systems and conformance verification is mechanised in terms of a high-level strategy by reusing successful techniques and tools: refinement checking (particularly, using the FDR tool) and SMT solving (using Z3). Therefore, conformance verification does not require the implementation of specific algorithms or the manipulation of complex data structures. Furthermore, the mechanisation is proved sound. To analyse the usefulness of CSPTIO, we first consider a toy example. Then we analyse critical systems from two different domains: aeronautics and automotive. CSPTIO detected all undesired behaviours in the analysed implementation models.

Keywords: Conformance Relation, Time, Data, CSP, Constraint Solver.

1 Introduction

The continuous growth of software size and complexity demands more accurate verification processes to guarantee systems correctness. High trustworthiness levels are usually achieved by using Formal Verification and Model-Based Testing (MBT) techniques. From a few decades ago, formal testing approaches have been proposed to compare, by defining a suitable conformance relation, the behaviour of an Implementation Under Test (IUT) with respect to its Specification.

A conformance relation assumes that the specification is stated in formal models, such as Finite State Machines (FSM) or Labelled Transition Systems (LTS), and that the implementation can also be modelled using the same underlying formal representation. This last premise is called the *Testability Hypothesis*. Conformance is then defined as a mathematical relation between these models.

Most works initially proposed in the literature focused on relations that address only functional (qualitative) system behaviour [13], and thus are unable to tackle non-functional real-time (quantitative) properties. However, more recently, the research community have proposed time-based conformance relations.

Here we propose a *timed input-output* conformance relation, named CSPTIO, based on the process algebra CSP. We assume that delays only up to an arbitrary

L. Groves and J. Sun (Eds.): ICFEM 2013, LNCS 8144, pp. 148–164, 2013.

bound (k) are observable. In contrast to other relations, our relation analyses data-flow reactive systems. According to [10], a data-flow reactive system interacts cyclically with its environment by means of an input and output set of events. These events are modelled as input (monitored) and output (controlled) variables that might obey timing constraints. Changes in the input variables trigger particular changes in the output variables.

The verification that an implementation conforms to its specification, based on CSPTIO, is mechanised in terms of a high-level strategy by reusing successful techniques and tools: refinement checking (FDR[1]) and SMT solving (Z3[2]). Therefore, its mechanisation does not require the implementation of specific algorithms or the manipulation of complex data structures. Furthermore, our mechanisation is sound with respect to the CSPTIO definition. Previous works have explored the use of CSP to define conformance relations for testing, such as [3,6,7], but none of them have considered time aspects.

Differently from other relations, CSPTIO considers both specification and IUT described in CSP, in contrast to more operational models like LTSs. This eases the proof of soundness of the mechanisation of conformance verification; also, it is potentially suitable to explore compositional properties, which we consider as an important topic for future work. CSPTIO assumes that the specification and the IUT have as normal-form a non-terminating loop composed by three stages: (i) evolving the specification/IUT behaviour, (ii) interacting with the environment, and (iii) time passing. We model time and quiescence as symbolic events in such a way that they are later instantiated by the SMT solver (Z3).

We first evaluate CSPTIO using a toy example: a *Vending Machine*. Afterwards we use CSPTIO to analyse critical systems from two different domains: (i) a *Priority Command* function provided by our industrial partner (Embraer), and (ii) part of the *Turn Indicator System* (TIS) of Mercedes vehicles. In summary, the main contributions of this work are:

1. A CSP characterisation of data-flow reactive systems with time constraints;
2. A timed input-output conformance relation based on CSP (CSPTIO);
3. A sound mechanisation of CSPTIO conformance verification using FDR/Z3;
4. An analysis concerning the applicability of CSPTIO.

Section 2 shows how we model data-flow reactive systems in CSP, using a Vending Machine as a running example. Section 3 presents CSPTIO and its sound and mechanised strategy for conformance verification. Section 4 discusses the application of CSPTIO to analyse two critical systems. Section 5 addresses related work, and presents our conclusions and future work.

2   Data-Flow Reactive Systems in CSP

CSP is a formal language designed to describe behavioural aspects of systems. The fundamental element of a CSP specification is a process. CSP has two primitive processes: one that represents successful termination (*SKIP*) and another

---

[1] http://www.cs.ox.ac.uk/projects/concurrency-tools/
[2] http://z3.codeplex.com/

that stands for an abnormal termination ($STOP$), also interpreted as a dead-lock. The behaviour of a process is described by the set of sequences of events it can communicate to other processes (and its environment). Events are atomic. To define a process as a sequence of events, we use the prefix process ($ev \rightarrow P$), where ev is an event and P a process. We can use the prefix process to create an infinite (recursive) process such as $P = a \rightarrow b \rightarrow P$. A *channel* can be declared to denote a particular set of events. The term $c!e$, where c is a channel, denotes the event resulting from the evaluation of e, which is any CSP valid expression, whereas the term $c?v$ denotes any value of this particular set (e.g., for *channel c* : $\{0,1,2\}$, $c?v$ means $c.0$, $c.1$ or $c.2$). It is also possible to interpret these symbols (! and ?) as sending or receiving a value through a channel, respectively.

To define alternating behaviours, CSP offers (external, internal, or conditional) choice operators. An external choice ($\square$) represents a deterministic choice between two processes, whereas the internal one ($\sqcap$) involves a non-deterministic choice. The conditional (*if*) choice operator is similar to the conditionals of standard programming languages. Two other relevant operators are the sequential and parallel composition operators. For example, the following sequential composition $P = P1;P2$ states that the behaviour of P is equivalent to the behaviour of $P1$ followed by the behaviour of $P2$, exactly if and when $P1$ terminates successfully. Concerning the parallel composition, CSP allows a composition with ($\|$) or without ($\|\|$) synchronisation between the composed processes. CSP processes synchronise between themselves by means of common events.

From a CSP specification written in its machine-readable version called CSP_M, the *Failures-Divergences Refinement* (FDR) tool can check desirable properties, such as: (1) deadlock-freedom, (2) divergence-freedom, (3) deterministic behaviour, and (4) refinement according to different semantic models (e.g., *traces*, *failures*, and *failures-divergences*). See [11] for more information.

Def. 1. *A data-flow reactive system is a tuple (I, O, T, B, b_0, gc, F, M), where:*

- *I is a non-empty set of input variables;*
- *O is a non-empty set of output variables;*
- *T is a set of timers ($I \cap O \cap T = \emptyset$);*
- *B is a binding for input/output variables and timers;*
- *b_0 is the initial binding (an initial state);*
- *gc is the system global clock;*
- *F is a set of functions, one per reactive component of the system. Each function ($f_i \in F$) is defined as ($\Phi_{D_i} \times \Phi_{T_i} \rightarrow Act_i$), where Φ_{D_i} is a set of discrete boolean expressions ($\phi_{D_{i,j}}$), Φ_{T_i} a set of timed boolean expressions ($\phi_{T_{i,j}}$), and Act_i is a set of assignments, as detailed below.*
  - *$\phi_{D_{i,j}}$ is a boolean expression formed of terms $v \dagger value$ ($v \in I \cup O$), where $\dagger$ stands for $<, \leq, =, >, \geq$, and value is an Integer/Floating-point number or a Boolean value. As this expression does not consider timers, we say it represents a discrete guard.*
  - *$\phi_{T_{i,j}}$ is a boolean expression formed of terms $gc-t \dagger value$ ($t \in T$), where $\dagger$ stands for $<, \leq, =, >, \geq$, and value is a positive Integer/Floating-point number. In other words, it evaluates the elapsed time since the last reset*

of t (see explanation below). As this expression considers timers, we say it represents a timed guard.

- $Act_{i,j}$ is a set of assignments $(v := value\,;\, v \in O)$ or $(t := gc\,;\, t \in T)$, where value is an Integer/Floating-point number or a Boolean value. This last form of assignment is referred to as "reset of t". It is equivalent to assigning the current global time to t. Each assignment can be seen as $B' = B \oplus \{v \mapsto value\}$. Let eval be a function that evaluates a discrete or timed expression, the actions $Act_{i,j}$ are performed when both $eval(\phi_{D_{i,j}})$ and $eval(\phi_{T_{i,j}})$ evaluate to true.
- M represents the model (states and transitions) similar to the one defined in [9]. The element F is used to construct M from the initial state.

The behaviour of a DFRS is encoded by means of a transition relation. We adopt the RT-Tester transition relation solution [9]. This choice was taken since the RT-Tester tool as well as its transition relation have already been proved to scale up for different industrial-size examples of data-flow reactive systems [8]. In this way, we expect to describe a considerable set of reactive systems as well. However, our structure is not semantically equivalent to this transition relation, as long as we are modelling some aspects beyond it. For instance, the RT-Tester transition relation assumes deterministic behaviour and absence of race conditions. In our case, we do not impose these restrictions.

The RT-Tester transition relation relates pre- and post-states by means of first order predicates over unprimed and primed symbols that might be system variables and timers. Unprimed symbols refer to the values in the pre-state, and primed symbols to post-state values. This relation distinguishes between *discrete* and *timed transitions*, allowing the model execution time to advance and inputs to change, while the system variables remain unchanged. Discrete transitions take place whenever the system has an enabled transition, and its execution has some side-effect, modifying the system state (memory). The formal definition of this transition relation can be found in [9].

As a running example, we consider the Vending Machine (VM) presented in Figure 1 as a timed statechart. Actually, this example is an adaptation of the Coffee Machine presented in [5]. Initially, the VM is in an *idle* state. It may remain in this state indefinitely. When the system receives a coin, it goes to the *choice* state and resets the *reqTimer* (r in Figure 1) clock. This is equivalent to assigning the current global time (gc) to this variable. After inserting a coin, when the user selects the coffee option, the system goes to one of these two states: *weak* or *strong* coffee. If the user has selected coffee within 30 seconds after inserting the coin, the system goes to the *weak coffee* state. Otherwise, it goes to the *strong coffee* state. Therefore, if the user selects the coffee option too quickly, a weak coffee is dispensed instead of a strong one.

The time required to produce a weak coffee is different from that of a strong coffee. The machine outputs a weak coffee between 10 to 30 seconds after a user request, whereas 30 to 50 seconds are necessary for a strong coffee. After producing a weak or strong coffee, the system goes back to the idle state. To model the VM as a DFRS, we represent the system inputs as input

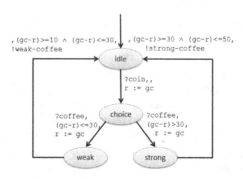

Fig. 1. The Vending Machine Specification

variables, and the system outputs, as well as the system states, as output variables. Therefore, concerning this example, we have the following DFRS.

- $I = \{$ *coin, coffee* $\}$, where *true* means the *coin* (*coffee*) button is pressed;
- $O = \{$ *mode, output* $\}$, where *mode* can be assigned to 0, 1, 2 or 3, to represent the states *idle, choice, weak, strong*, respectively and *output* to 0, 1 or 2 to represent the output of an undefined, weak, or strong coffee;
- $T = \{$ *reqTimer* $\}$;
- $b_0 = \{$ *coin* $\mapsto$ *false, coffee* $\mapsto$ *false, mode* $\mapsto$ *0, output* $\mapsto$ *0, reqTimer* $\mapsto$ *0* $\}$;
- $F = \{f_1\}$,
  $f_1 = \{...,($ *coffee=true, (gc-reqTimer)* $\leq$ *30* $\mapsto \{$ *mode:=2, reqTimer:=gc* $\}),...\}$.
  As the VM has one component, F has only one function. The element that is shown represents the transition from the *choice* to the *weak* state when the coffee button is pressed within 30 seconds since the last reset of *reqTimer*

In the following subsections, we explain how we model a DFRS using CSP. First, we represent the DFRS components I, O and B as a memory process. Then, we model the system interaction with its environment to update the I component. After that, we create a CSP process to model the F component and another one to model the time passing. Finally, we combine these elements to represent the cyclic evolution of the system over time.

2.1   Memory Representation

Among the different ways of representing state information (values of inputs, outputs and timers) in CSP, we adopt an alternative that creates an interleaving of processes, each one representing a single variable (memory cell). As discussed in [11], this solution is appropriate for concurrent access. Moreover, FDR has compression algorithms suitable for minimising the state-space for such a representation. The general outline of the memory definition is:

datatype VAR = ...
datatype TYPE = B.Bool | I.INTEGER_VALUES
channel get, set : VAR.TYPE

$$MCELL(var,val) = get!var!val \rightarrow MCELL(var,val)$$
$$\square \; set!var?val' : range(tag(val)) \rightarrow MCELL(var,val')$$
$$MEMORY(binding) = ||| \; (var,val) : binding @ MCELL(var,val)$$

The datatype VAR represents the system variable names, and the datatype $TYPE$ represents the possible values: Boolean and Integer values preceded by a tag (B or I, respectively). Although it is possible to represent floating-point numbers in CSP, this is out of the scope of this paper.

The memory is represented as an interleaving of memory cells ($MCELL$). Each cell represents one variable, which is initialised according to the *binding* set. This set is the CSP representation of the B component of a DFRS excluding the timers that are symbolically modelled (later explained). The value stored in each cell can be read or updated by the channels *get* and *set*, respectively. Therefore, the $MCELL$ process offers an external choice between these two possibilities (read/write). It is worth mentioning that it is only possible to write a value compatible to the type of the variable stored in the corresponding memory position. This restriction is imposed by the *range* function. We omitted the definitions of *tag* and *range* because they are simple functions that yield the type associated with a cell and its possible values, respectively.

Defining a $MEMORY$ for one particular DFRS requires the definition of VAR and *binding*. For the VM example, these definitions can be seen in Code 1.1. The variable names declared in line 2 are auxiliary variables (later described).

Code 1.1. Memory for the Vending Machine

```
1 datatype VAR = coin | coffee | mode | output |
2     pMode | pOutput | disTrans | memUpdate | eta1 | eta2 | eta3 | eta4
3 binding = {(coin,B.false), (coffee,B.false), (mode,I.0), (output,I.0),
4     (pMode,I.0), (pOutput,I.0), (disTrans,B.false), (memUpdate,B.false),
5     (eta1,B.false), (eta2,B.false), (eta3, B.false), (eta4, B.false)}
```

2.2 Environment Interaction

The interaction of a system with its environment is responsible for updating the system inputs. This communication is performed by CSP channels, each one representing the signals sent to the system. When the channels are declared, it is necessary to list the values that can be communicated through them. These values represent the data carried by the signals. This list may comprise all values of a particular type (e.g., *Integer*), a user-defined set (e.g., $\{80,\ 81\}$) or even a list returned by an SMT solver to exercise a certain portion of the system. We assume a failures-free environment and a single-rate system. In other words, the system is cyclically receiving system inputs, and all the system components perceive these input signals at the same time. The process $ENVIRONMENT\_SYNC$ represents the interaction with the environment. The outline of this CSP process is:

$$channel \; memory\_state : VAR.TYPE$$
$$ENVIRONMENT\_SYNC = c_i?val \rightarrow set!var_{c_i}!val \rightarrow$$
$$memory\_state!var_{c_i}!val \rightarrow SKIP$$

When a value (*val*) is received from the environment over a particular channel (let c_i be the channel associated with the i-th system input), this CSP process updates the memory position mapped to the variable that is related to this system input (var_{c_i}). Afterwards, this process communicates over the channel *memory_state*, which is defined similarly to the *get* and *set* channels, the value that has just been read. As we later explain, this communication is used by CSPTIO to assess whether an implementation is in conformance with respect to its specification. For the VM, we have the concrete CSP presented in Code 1.2. Note that $->$ is the CSP_M version of $\rightarrow$ (prefix) [11].

Code 1.2. Vending Machine Environment

```
1  channel coinButton  : Bool
2  channel coffeeButton : Bool
3  channel memory_state  : VAR.TYPE
4  ENVIRONMENT_SYNC = coinButton?newVCoin -> set!coin!B.newVCoin ->
5    memory_state!coin!B.newVCoin -> SKIP ; coffeeButton?newVCoffee ->
6    set!coffee!B.newVCoffee -> memory_state!coffee!B.newVCoffee -> SKIP
```

2.3   System Behaviour

Regarding a DFRS, a CSP process is derived for each function of F. Let P_i be the CSP process that represents f_i. The overall structure of P_i is:

$$P_i = get!var_1\,?I.varLocal_1 \rightarrow ... \rightarrow get!var_n\,?I.varLocal_n \rightarrow get!\eta_{i,1}\,?B.\eta Local_{i,1} \rightarrow$$
$$... \rightarrow get!\eta_{i,k}\,?B.\eta Local_{i,k} \rightarrow (\ (if\ eval(\phi_{D_{i,1}}) \wedge \eta Local_{i,1}\ then\ set!disTrans!B.true$$
$$\rightarrow Act_{i,1} \rightarrow MS_{Act_{i,1}} \rightarrow SKIP\ else\ STOP)\ \Box\ ...\ \Box\ (if\ eval(\phi_{D_{i,k}}) \wedge \eta Local_{i,k}$$
$$then\ set!disTrans!B.true \rightarrow Act_{i,k} \rightarrow MS_{Act_{i,k}} \rightarrow SKIP\ else\ STOP)\ \Box\ (if$$
$$\neg(eval(\phi_{D_{i,1}}) \wedge \eta Local_{i,1}) \wedge ... \wedge \neg(eval(\phi_{D_{i,k}}) \wedge \eta Local_{i,k})\ then\ SKIP\ else\ STOP))$$

First, P_i gets from the memory the current value of each system variable (var_1 ... var_n) and binds these values to the corresponding local variables ($varLocal_1$ ... $varLocal_n$). The same is done for $\eta_{i,k}$ (eta) variables. The timed guards are symbolically associated to these $\eta_{i,k}$ variables. An $\eta_{i,k}$ variable becomes true when the elapsed time makes the corresponding timed guard true (later explained). These values are then used to evaluate each guard.

The different actions of the i-th process are composed using the external choice operator. When one or more guards are true, the i-th process changes the memory according to the assignments contained in the corresponding actions, and it also communicates over the *memory_state* channel the assignments performed ($MS_{Act_{i,k}}$). Before doing this, the i-th process sets *true* to the auxiliary variable *disTrans* (discrete transition). This means that at least one guard was evaluated to true, and thus a discrete transition was taken. Later, we explain how this auxiliary variable is used to model the system evolution over time. When all guards are false (last external choice), the process behaves as *SKIP*.

Concerning the VM example, its CSP process is shown in Code 1.3. Note that [ ] is the CSP_M version of $\Box$, and that *condition & P* is a shortcut to *if condition then P else STOP* [11]. In line 1 the memory is read and the current value of each variable is bound to the corresponding local variable. Then we have the guards and actions of the VM. These actions are performed considering the primed version of the variables (for instance, *pOutput*). Primed variables concern the value after performing the corresponding actions, whereas the unprimed versions have the value prior to the actions. This is the reason for the variables *pMode* and *pOutput* in Code 1.1. It is also worth noting the communications over the *memory_state* channel. They are necessary to the definition of CSPTIO, as we explain in Section 3.

Code 1.3. Vending Machine CSP Specification

```
1  VM = get!mode?I.vMode -> ... -> get!eta1?B.vEta1 -> ... -> ( ...
2     [] (vMode == 2 and vEta3 & set!disTrans!B.true ->
3        set!pOutput!I.1 -> memory_state!output!I.1 ->
4        set!pMode!I.0 -> memory_state!mode!I.0 -> SKIP)
5     [] (vMode == 3 and vEta4 & set!disTrans!B.true ->
6        set!pOutput!I.2 -> memory_state!output!I.2 ->
7        set!pMode!I.0 -> memory_state!pMode!I.0 -> SKIP))
8     [] (... not(vMode == 2 and vEta3) and not(vMode == 3 and vEta4) & SKIP)
```

In particular, lines 2-7 show the guards for the transitions that dispense weak and strong coffees. This happens when the system is in the *weak* and *strong* states and a certain time has elapsed. The local variables *vEta3* and *vEta4* store the values of *eta3* and *eta4* (previously declared in the memory process - see Code 1.1), and they symbolically represent the timed guards $(gc - reqTimer) \geq 10 \wedge (gc - reqTimer) \leq 30$ and $(gc - reqTimer) \geq 30 \wedge (gc - reqTimer) \leq 50$, respectively. As time is symbolically modelled, the action of resetting a timer (e.g., *reqTimer:=gc*) is mapped to an event (*reset_*, e.g., *reset_reqTimer*) instead of changing the memory. This case is not shown in Code 1.3. It only happens in the first three transitions of the VM.

2.4   Time Passing

In our time framework, we assume, as usual, time additivity: time cannot rewind, and the elapsed time is always greater than 0. We support both discrete and dense time by capturing time aspects in a CSP process symbolically. Concrete values are just given later by an SMT solver. Therefore, if we want to analyse the system behaviour according to a discrete time model, we just need to configure the solver to work with Integer numbers. However, if we want a dense time analysis, the solver shall consider Real numbers. Regarding time priority, we assume all timed transitions are *delayable*. That is, once enabled, they must occur before they become disabled. The process *TIME_PASSING* is responsible for determining the amount of elapsed time.

$$TIME\_PASSING = time\_update\_started \rightarrow set!\eta_{1,1}!B.false \rightarrow ... \rightarrow$$
$$set!\eta_{i,k}!B.false$$
$$\rightarrow get!var_1?I.varLocal_1 \rightarrow ... \rightarrow get!var_n?I.varLocal_n \rightarrow$$
$$(\forall i,k : \exists \phi_{T_{i,k}} \bullet (\Box \ if \ eval(\phi_{D_{i,k}}) \ then \ set!\eta_{i,k}!B.true \rightarrow SKIP \ else \ STOP)$$
$$\Box \ if \ \forall i,k : \exists \phi_{T_{i,k}} \bullet \neg(eval(\phi_{D_{i,k}})) \ then \ \zeta \rightarrow SKIP \ else \ STOP)$$
$$; time\_update\_finished \rightarrow SKIP$$

The events *time_update_started* and *time_update_finished* are later used to synchronise this process with the others previously defined. For each timed guard we introduce a variable named $\eta_{i,k}$. Initially, this process sets false to all $\eta_{i,k}$ variables and reads from the memory the value of system variables. Afterwards, this process analyses if the system is in a state where the discrete guard ($\phi_{D_{i,k}}$) is true and there is a corresponding timed guard ($\phi_{T_{i,k}}$). If this is the case, it means that the amount of elapsed time influences if this transition is taken or not. Due to the underlying delayable priority, we say that some amount of time has elapsed that makes this guard true. Then we set to true the corresponding $\eta_{i,k}$ variable. Therefore, when the process P_i evaluates this condition, as $\eta_{i,k}$ will be true, the corresponding actions will be performed. The concrete amount of elapsed time is determined later by the solver. However, this amount shall respect the temporal constraints associated with $\eta_{i,k}$, that is $\phi_{T_{i,k}}$.

If the system is in a state where the amount of elapsed time has no influence (i.e., there is not a timed constraint ($\phi_{i,k}$) related to time passing), we say the system might diverge in time. Therefore, any amount of time can elapse without seeing any output. This means that the system is time quiescent at this state. This behaviour is captured by the last external choice: the process performs an ζ (zeta) event without setting true to any $\eta_{i,k}$ variable. Therefore, as a consequence of the time additivity assumption, the elapsed time shall be greater than 0, but it does not have an upper bound.

Regarding the VM, the *TIME_PASSING* definition can be seen in Code 1.4. Initially, it sets all $\eta_{i,k}$ variables to false. For the VM, we have four variables (*eta1, eta2, eta3, eta4*—see the memory definition in Code 1.1). Then it reads from the memory values that are stored in local variables (e.g., *vMode*). Lines 3 and 4 show the code that sets to true *eta3* or *eta4* if the system is in the *weak* or *strong* state, respectively. In these cases, the concrete value of elapsed time later determined by the solver shall adhere to the corresponding constraints (e.g., $(gc - reqTimer) \geq 10 \wedge (gc - reqTimer) \leq 30$ for *eta3*).

Code 1.4. Representing Timed Transitions

```
1  TIME_PASSING = time_update_started ->
2    set!eta1!B.false -> ... -> get!mode?I.vMode -> ... ->
3    ( ... [] (vMode == 2 & set!eta3!B.true -> SKIP)
4      [] (vMode == 3 & set!eta4!B.true -> SKIP)
5      [] (... not(vMode == 2) and not(vMode == 3) & zeta -> SKIP))
6    ; time_update_finished -> SKIP
```

2.5 Cyclic Behaviour

As previously said, a data-flow reactive system cyclically interacts with its environment. So far, we showed isolated processes. Now, we compose them to capture this cyclic behaviour over time. This cyclic behaviour is captured by the process *SPECIFICATION*.

> *SPECIFICATION = ((DISCRETE_TRANS ; ENVIRONMENT_SYNC ;*
> *time_update_started → time_update_finished → SKIP) ‖ TIME_PASSING)*
> *; SPECIFICATION*

First, the process *DISCRETE_TRANS* (later described) remains in a loop while discrete transitions can occur. At this point, it terminates successfully and passes control to the environment. The system interacts with the environment (*ENVIRONMENT_SYNC*) updating its internal state. Then the amount of elapsed time over the last environment interaction is determined by the *TIME_PASSING* process, which is composed in parallel and synchronises with the events *time_update_started* and *time_update_finished*. This enforces a sequential behaviour of time passing immediately after environment synchronization. In any case, we decided to specify time passing as an independent process. Finally, the process *SPECIFICATION* recurses, restarting this cyclic interaction with the environment. The process *DISCRETE_TRANS* is defined as follows.

DISCRETE_TRANS = set!disTrans!B.false → (P₁||| ... |||Pᵢ) ; get!disTrans?B.engaged
→ (if engaged then INSPECT_MEM ; get!memUpdate?B.changed → (if changed
then UPDATE_MEM ; DISCRETE_TRANS else SKIP) else SKIP)

Initially, this process sets *disTrans* to false, then it behaves as the interleaving of each P_i, which denotes the process derived from each function (f_i) of F (see Section 2.3). Considering the VM example, it is just the process *VM* (Code 1.3). When this interleaving finishes, that is, when each process P_i finishes, it is analysed whether at least one component has engaged on a transition. However, as previously said, engaging on a discrete transition is not a sufficient requirement to remain in the loop of performing discrete transitions. The transition must also have had a side-effect (memory change). Therefore, the process *INSPECT_MEM* performs this analysis. If there is a side-effect, the variable *memUpdate* (see the memory definition in Code 1.1) is set to true, and the effect of the transition is applied to the memory. In other words, the process *UPDATE_MEM* copies the value of the primed variables (p_-) to the corresponding variables. Finally, we declare a process *SYSTEM* as the parallel composition of the specification with the *MEMORY* process. This captures data-flow reactive systems in CSP.

$$SYSTEM = SPECIFICATION \underset{\{|get,set|\}}{\parallel} MEMORY(initialBinding)$$

3   A CSP Timed Input-Output Conformance Relation

As we use the CSP process algebra, a natural choice for a conformance relation would be one of the traditional CSP refinement notions (for traces, failures or failures-divergences). However, we considered a different approach influenced by some needs of our industrial partner (Embraer). First, the systems considered by them can be seen as data-flow reactive systems, and thus have a clear separation between inputs and outputs. Second, they find it useful to specify the system behaviour incrementally. Therefore, partial specifications should be taken into account. As the relation **ioco** [13] naturally handles these two aspects, we considered it as a basis for our work.

CSPTIO can be seen as a timed extension of *cspio* [6], which was inspired by *ioco* [13] and is formalised in terms of the CSP process algebra. In contrast to *cspio*, however, we consider *(time) quiescence*. CSPTIO assumes that the specification (S) and the implementation (IUT) are data-flow reactive systems (DFRS) modelled as described in Section 2 (*Testability Hypothesis*). Furthermore, their alphabets are assumed to be known, and split into two disjoint sets: inputs and outputs. The input alphabet (A_I) is determined by communications over the channel *memory_state* concerning the variables of the DFRS component I (see Code 1.2). The output alphabet (A_O) is defined analogously (see Code 1.3). The events that are not considered as inputs nor outputs are hidden. A CSP Timed I/O process is defined as follows. Despite not dealing with time directly, we use the term *timed* since the CSP process has events that symbolically represent time elapsing.

Def. 2. *Let SYSTEM be a CSP process for the specification of a data-flow reactive system S, A the alphabet of SYSTEM, A_{I_S}/A_{O_S} the input/output alphabet of SYSTEM, $P_S = SYSTEM \setminus (A \setminus (A_I \cup A_O))$. The 3-tuple (P_S, A_{I_S}, A_{O_S}) represents the CSP Timed I/O process corresponding to S.*

The alphabet of *IUT* is assumed to be compatible with that of *S*.

Def. 3. *Let S and IUT be two CSP Timed I/O processes. Their alphabets are compatible iff $A_{I_S} \subseteq A_{I_{IUT}}$ and $A_{O_S} \subseteq A_{I_{IUT}}$.*

The specification does not need to be *input enabled* (ready to accept any input at any time); and we allow partial specifications. However, as usual, we assume the implementation model to be input enabled. Both specification and implementation might have quiescent behaviour. We say a process P is time quiescent iff a ζ event can occur. It is a natural property with respect to timed systems since sometimes it is needed to model non-forced inputs (the input might be received within any amount of time). In other words, the elapsed time before seeing the input can be as great as one wishes, and it is possible to never observe an output after this situation.

Def. 4. *Let P be a CSP Timed I/O process, and $\mathcal{T}(SYSTEM)$ the set all sequences of events SYSTEM, which is the CSP specification of S, can perform. S is quiescent iff $\exists s \in \mathcal{T}(SYSTEM) \bullet (\exists j \bullet s_j = \zeta)$.*

We assume that all timed guards are time satisfiable. If a timed guard is not satisfiable we would generate a CSP process with a transition that would not happen in the actual system. This happens because in the CSP model we consider time aspects symbolically. Therefore, if this property is not respected, we would be analysing an LTS that would not be equivalent to the actual system behaviour. Considering the VM, the timed guard $((gc-reqTimer) \geq 10 \wedge (gc-reqTimer) \leq 5)$ is not time satisfiable, and thus is invalid. To state this property, we use the auxiliary function *elapsed*.

Let P be a CSP Timed I/O process and s a trace of the respective *SYSTEM*; the function *elapsed(P,s)* yields the set of all delays that might have elapsed in *SYSTEM* concerning the last time passing associated with the trace s. The delays can be positive Integer or Real numbers. It depends on the solver configuration. Here, without loss of generality, we assume the delays are positive Real numbers. If the last event in trace s is $set!\eta_{i,k}!B.true$, then the set yielded by the function *elapsed* shall include all solutions of the corresponding timed guard $(\phi_{T_{i,k}})$. For a ζ event we have as solutions all positive Real numbers. In any other situation, *elapsed* searches for the last $set!\eta_{i,k}!B.true$ or ζ event performed.

Def. 5. $elapsed(P,s) = \{\!|SAT(s, \phi_{T_{i,k}})|s = t^\frown\langle a\rangle \wedge a = set!\eta_{i,k}!B.true|\!\} \cup \{\!|\mathbb{R}^+| s = t^\frown\langle a\rangle \wedge a = \zeta|\!\} \cup \{\!|elapsed(t)|s = t^\frown\langle a\rangle \wedge a \neq set!\eta_{i,k}!B.true \wedge a \neq \zeta|\!\}$, where $SAT(s,\phi_{T_{i,k}})$ represents the set of solutions of $\phi_{T_{i,k}}$, which is related to SYSTEM, after performing the trace s.

Based on this definition, we say that a CSP Timed I/O process is time satisfiable if for all traces that have at least one time elapsing event $(set!\eta_{i,k}!B.true$ or $\zeta)$, the elapsed time is a non-empty set. That is, some time have elapsed.

Def. 6. *Let P be a CSP Timed I/O process. P is time satisfiable iff $\forall s \in \mathcal{T}(SYSTEM)|(\exists j \bullet s_j = set!\eta_{i,k}!B.true \vee s_j = \zeta) \bullet elapsed(P,s) \neq \emptyset$.*

We also assume time determinism: the amount of elapsed time only activates one timed guard. If this property is not respected, we also create a CSP process that does not correspond to the actual system behaviour. Considering the VM, suppose we have the following two timed guards $(gc - reqTimer) \leq 10$ and $(gc - reqTimer) \leq 5$, and the corresponding η variables (η_1, η_2). In this case, whenever the elapsed time satisfies the latter guard, the former one is also satisfied. However, in the CSP model, as time is symbolically modelled, we would have only one η variable being set to true. Therefore, we would be again with an LTS that would not be equivalent to the actual system behaviour.

Def. 7. *Let P be a CSP Timed I/O process. P is time deterministic iff $\forall i, j, k, l \mid eval(\phi_{D_{i,k}}) \wedge eval(\phi_{D_{j,l}}) \wedge SAT(\phi_{T_{i,k}}) \cap SAT(\phi_{T_{j,l}}) \neq \emptyset \bullet i = j \wedge k = l$.*

Despite the restriction imposed by this last assumption, we believe it is not restrictive as non-satisfiable behaviour are usually avoided in implementations of reactive systems.

3.1   Conformance Relation

The conformance relation CSPTIO is defined in terms of the traces semantics. In order to define CSPTIO we need two auxiliary functions: *out* and *elapsed* (previously defined). Let P be a CSP Timed I/O process and s a trace of P_S; the function *out(P,s)* yields the set of output events that P_S can perform after the trace s.

Def. 8. $out(P,s) = \{a \in A_{O_P}|s^\frown\langle a\rangle \in \mathcal{T}(P_S)\}$

As a consequence of the cyclic behaviour of a CSP Timed I/O process, the set of traces is infinite. When analysing the system static behaviour, it is not a problem since the corresponding LTS is finite. However, when analysing the temporal behaviour, we can infinitely analyse the system. Therefore, we define an arbitrary k that provides a limit to the analysis: we only consider traces where the time has elapsed up to k times. In other words, the number of events $set!\eta_{i,k}!B.true$ and ζ is lower than or equal to k.

Def. 9. $\mathcal{T}_k(P) = \{s \in \mathcal{T}(SYSTEM) \mid t = s \upharpoonright \{set!\eta_{i,k}!B.true, \zeta\} \wedge \#t = k\}$

Based on these previous definitions, we formally define **csptio** as follows.

Def. 10. *Consider two CSP Timed I/O processes S and IUT, such that the alphabets of S and IUT are compatible. Then:*

$$IUT \ \mathbf{csptio}_k \ S \triangleq \forall s : \mathcal{T}(S) \bullet out(IUT, s) \subseteq out(S, s)$$
$$\wedge \ \forall s : \mathcal{T}_k(S) \bullet elapsed(IUT, s) \subseteq elapsed(S, s)$$

The intuition behind this definition is that, after a trace s of the specification, the implementation shall output a subset of the expected outputs allowed by the specification. Furthermore, the implementation cannot have an amount of elapsed time not allowed in the specification.

3.2   A Sound Mechanisation of CSPTIO

Theorem 1. *Consider two CSP Timed I/O processes S and IUT, such that the alphabets of S and IUT are compatible.* $IUT \ \mathbf{csptio}_k \ S$ *holds iff the following expression holds:*

$$P_S \sqsubseteq_{\mathrm{T}} (P_S \ \triangle \ ANY(A_{O_{IUT}}, STOP)) \ \underset{A_{I_{IUT}} \cup A_{O_{IUT}}}{\|} \ P_{IUT}$$
$$\wedge \forall s : \mathcal{T}_k(S) \bullet (\nexists d \in \mathbb{R} \bullet (d \in elapsed(IUT, s) \wedge d \notin elapsed(S, s)))$$

The second term of Theorem 1 is just another way, which is more appropriate for a constrain solver, of expressing set inclusion. The first term is a consequence of Theorem 5.1 that is presented in [6], which includes a comprehensive proof that this refinement expression is equivalent to $out(IUT, s) \subseteq out(S, s)$. Differently from our work, in [6] it is assumed that S and IUT are CSP I/O processes (without time). However, as our CSP Timed I/O processes hide all symbolic time events (only input/output events are visible), and our work respects the assumptions of [6], the CSP Timed I/O process is equivalent to the CSP I/O process defined in [6], and thus we reuse the results of their Theorem 5.1.

To understand the intuition behind Theorem 1, let us analyse separately the conjunction terms. The first term is a refinement expression such that if an input event occurs in the implementation, but not in the specification, on the right-hand side of the refinement, the parallel composition does not progress through this event (this event is refused). As the refinement considers the traces model, refused events are not taken into account. Therefore, new input events in the implementation are allowed. The goal of the process

$ANY(alphabet, P) = \Box\, event : alphabet @ event \rightarrow P$ is to avoid that the right-hand side refuse output events that the implementation can perform but the specification cannot. Therefore, if after a common trace the implementation performs output events not expected in the specification, these events will appear in the traces of the implementation and the refinement expression will be false.

The second term concerns the time analysis. For each trace of the specification, this term verifies if there is an amount of elapsed time that is allowed by the implementation but not by the specification. To perform this check we need to compute $SAT(s, \phi_{T_{i,k}})$. Here we present just an overview of how it is done (the idea is similar to the one reported in [9]). We create a *Constraint Satisfaction Problem* that considers the following variables: gc_S^i, gc_I^i, t_S^i, t_I^i, d_S^i, and d_S^i. These variables represent the system global clock, the system timers, and time delays in an i-th instant of the system for a specification S and an implementation I, respectively. Then, we add to this problem the constraints related to the *eta* events as well as the symbolic reset events.

For example, considering the VM, let *eta2* be related to the time constraint required to go to the state *strong*: *(gc-reqTimer)>30* for the specification and *(gc-reqTimer)≤30* for the implementation. The trace "$<..., zeta, ..., reset\_reqTimer, ..., set.eta2.B.true>$" generates the following constraints regarding the implementation: $\{gc_I^1 = 0, r_I^1 = 0, d_I^1 > 0, gc_I^2 = gc_I^1 + d_I^1, r_I^2 = gc_I^2, d_I^2 > 0, gc_I^3 = gc_I^2 + d_I^2, (gc_I^3 - r_I^2) \leq 30\}$, where r is an abbreviation of *reqTimer*. For the specification we do the same, but we analyse if there is a delay in the implementation that is not allowed in the specification: $\{gc_S^1 = 0, r_S^1 = 0, d_S^1 > 0, gc_S^2 = gc_S^1 + d_S^1, r_S^2 = gc_S^2, gc_S^3 = gc_S^2 + d_I^2, \neg((gc_S^3 - r_S^2) > 30)\}$. Finally, we give these constraints to Z3 and check whether there is a solution. In this case, there is a solution: $d_I^2 = 1$ is allowed in the implementation but $d_S^2 = 1$ is not allowed in the specification.

4   Empirical Analyses

First, we used the VM example to evaluate CSPTIO. Based on the specification (S), three implementation models in CSP were created: (1) a wrong implementation with respect to its static behaviour, (2) a wrong implementation with respect to its temporal behaviour, and (3) a correct implementation with a new behaviour. As expected, CSPTIO holds only for the last implementation. Afterwards, we considered a simplification of the *Turn Indicator System*[3] (TIS) specification that is currently used by Daimler for automatically deriving test cases. It serves well as a proof of concept because it represents a safety-critical system portion with real-time and concurrent aspects. After specifying the TIS as a CSP Timed I/O process, we created three implementations similarly as we did to the VM example. Here, as expected, CSPTIO holds only for the last implementation. Analogously, we did the same for an example provided by our industrial partner (Embraer): the *Priority Command* (PC) function.

---

[3] The original model is presented in [8].

For these examples[4], we collected some metrics (see Table 1) using an Intel Quad-Core @ 2,66 GHz (4GB of RAM; 1TB of disk) running Ubuntu. The TIS specification is the most complex: it considers 17 variables and 18 (discrete and timed) guards ($\#\text{dom}(f_i)$). Therefore, its LTS is the largest one. In particular, its third implementation, which adds a new variable/behaviour/guard, has more than 200 million of states/transitions. Concerning the TIS, FDR performed its classical analyses within about 60s, and the verification of CSPTIO, which holds for this particular example, took about 97s. As expected the other examples (VM and PC) required less time since they are simpler. Concerning Z3, we only measured the time to find a counter-example (provided a trace that exhibits the undesired temporal behaviour) as the enumeration of traces were done by hand (its implementation is a work in progress). These traces can be identified with $k=2$. Z3 quickly found the solution (about 80ms). Therefore, the time required to verify CSPTIO does not seem to be a difficulty. This time might be lower, when there is a counter-example, if we use a CSP on-the-fly model checker such as PAT[5]. This evaluation remains as a future work.

Table 1. Results for the Verification of CSPTIO

METRIC	VM				PC				TIS			
	S	1	2	3	S	1	2	3	S	1	2	3
Lines of Code	139	151	151	159	145	161	161	170	224	236	236	245
Variables	15	15	15	17	11	11	11	12	17	17	17	18
$\#\text{dom}(f_i)$	5	5	5	6	9	9	9	10	18	18	18	19
States ($\pm$)	7K	7K	7K	50K	8K	7K	8K	18K	63K	118K	63K	246K
Transitions ($\pm$)	7K	7K	7K	53K	8K	7K	8K	19K	65K	122K	65K	253K
$\mu_{Deadlock}$	227ms	225ms	230ms	842ms	89ms	88ms	89ms	159ms	29.5s	30.7s	28.2s	60.2s
$\mu_{Determinism}$	179ms	184ms	182ms	488ms	56ms	56ms	58ms	74ms	26.1s	26.8s	28.6s	60.8s
$\mu_{Divergence}$	260ms	256ms	260ms	1.17s	116ms	111ms	116ms	232ms	29.1s	30.6s	26.6s	62.7s
$\mu_{csptio,FDR}$	-	797ms	2.28s	846ms	-	162ms	1.21s	176ms	-	61.2s	83.9s	97.2s
$\mu_{csptio_2,Z3}$	-	-	80ms	-	-	-	82ms	-	-	-	81.9ms	-

The time required to generate the CSP specification was not measured since this translation was so far done manually. After the implementation of this translation, which will be based on the overall structures presented in Section 2, this metric will also be measured.

5   Conclusions

We presented a timed input-output conformance relation (name CSPTIO) based on the process algebra CSP. Our experiments provide some evidence that CSPTIO is suitable for analysing data-flow reactive systems, and its mechanisation is performed in terms of refinement checking (using FDR) and SMT solving (using Z3). Therefore, conformance verification does not require the implementation of specific algorithms or the manipulation of complex data structures.

---

[4] The CSP/Z3 codes are available at http://www.cin.ufpe.br/~ghpc/ ICFEMdata.zip

[5] http://www.comp.nus.edu.sg/~pat/

Moreover, the mechanisation of CSPTIO is sound with respect to its definition. CSPTIO was used to analyse examples from different domains, and it detected all undesired behaviours in the analysed implementation models.

Considering relations that segregate inputs from outputs, we can identify two types of timed relations. The first one comprises relations that assume that all delays are observable (e.g., $tioco_{TTG}$ [4], $rtioco$ [5]), whereas for the second type only delays up to some bound are observable (e.g., $tioco_M$ [1], $tioco_\varsigma$ [12]). The relation $tioco_\varsigma$ considers an unbounded delay, whereas $tioco_M$ considers an arbitrary delay M. CSPTIO is more related to $tioco_M$ since it defines an arbitrary upper bound k. Differently from these relations, we do not need to handle operational models like LTSs nor rely upon new algorithms. An evidence of the modularity of a process algebraic approach is that [6] shows how to deal with control aspects and then considers data as a conservative extension. Handling time as we do here is also a conservative extension of the theory presented in [6]. Particularly, Theorem 1 is an orthogonal extension of Theorem 5.1 (from [6]), which allowed us to reuse both the refinement assertion and the proof of the untimed conformance verification. Furthermore, our algebraic and symbolic approach seems more suitable to explore compositional properties, which we plan to develop as future work. However, we still do not have a test generation strategy, whereas $tioco_M$, for instance, already considers one.

As future work, we intend to: (1) analyse the soundness of our DFRS encoding in CSP, (2) propose a test generation strategy based on CSPTIO, (3) integrate the FDR enumeration of traces with the Z3 tool, (4) further investigate the scalability of CSPTIO by means of analysing parametrised systems, and (5) adapt the strategy described in [2] to automatically infer a DFRS from the corresponding natural language specification.

Acknowledgments. This work was supported by INES[6], and the grants: EU FP7 COMPASS 287829, FACEPE 573964/2008-4, APQ-1037-1.03/08, CNPq 573964/2008-4 and 476821/2011-8.

References

1. Briones, L.B., Brinksma, E.: A test generation framework for *quiescent* real-time systems. In: Grabowski, J., Nielsen, B. (eds.) FATES 2004. LNCS, vol. 3395, pp. 64–78. Springer, Heidelberg (2005)
2. Carvalho, G., Falcão, D., Barros, F., Sampaio, A., Mota, A., Motta, L., Blackburn, M.: Test case generation from natural language requirements based on SCR specifications. In: Proceedings of ACM SAC, vol. 2, pp. 1217–1222 (2013)
3. Cavalcanti, A., Gaudel, M.-C.: Testing for refinement in CSP. In: Butler, M., Hinchey, M.G., Larrondo-Petrie, M.M. (eds.) ICFEM 2007. LNCS, vol. 4789, pp. 151–170. Springer, Heidelberg (2007)
4. Krichen, M., Tripakis, S.: Black-box conformance testing for real-time systems. In: Graf, S., Mounier, L. (eds.) SPIN 2004. LNCS, vol. 2989, pp. 109–126. Springer, Heidelberg (2004)

[6] www.ines.org.br

5. Larsen, K., Mikucionis, M., Nielsen, B.: Online Testing of Real-time Systems using Uppaal: Status and Future Work. In: Dagstuhl Seminar Proceedings: Perspectives of Model-Based Testing, vol. 04371 (2004)
6. Nogueira, S., Sampaio, A., Mota, A.: Test generation from state based use case models. Formal Aspects of Computing, 1–50 (2012)
7. Peleska, J., Siegel, M.: Test automation of safety-critical reactive systems. South African Computer Journal 19, 53–77 (1997)
8. Peleska, J., Honisch, A., Lapschies, F., Löding, H., Schmid, H., Smuda, P., Vorobev, E., Zahlten, C.: A Real-World Benchmark Model for Testing Concurrent Real-Time Systems in the Automotive Domain. In: Wolff, B., Zaïdi, F. (eds.) ICTSS 2011. LNCS, vol. 7019, pp. 146–161. Springer, Heidelberg (2011)
9. Peleska, J., Vorobev, E., Lapschies, F., Zahlten, C.: Automated model-based testing with RT-Tester. Tech. rep., Universität Bremen (2011)
10. Piel, É., Gonzalez-Sanchez, A., Gross, H.-G.: Built-in data-flow integration testing in large-scale component-based systems. In: Petrenko, A., Simão, A., Maldonado, J.C. (eds.) ICTSS 2010. LNCS, vol. 6435, pp. 79–94. Springer, Heidelberg (2010)
11. Roscoe, A.W.: Understanding Concurrent Systems. Springer (2010)
12. Schmaltz, J., Tretmans, J.: On conformance testing for timed systems. In: Cassez, F., Jard, C. (eds.) FORMATS 2008. LNCS, vol. 5215, pp. 250–264. Springer, Heidelberg (2008)
13. Tretmans, J.: Testing concurrent systems: A formal approach. In: Baeten, J.C.M., Mauw, S. (eds.) CONCUR 1999. LNCS, vol. 1664, pp. 46–65. Springer, Heidelberg (1999)

Deadline Analysis of AUTOSAR OS Periodic Tasks in the Presence of Interrupts

Yanhong Huang[1], João F. Ferreira[2,3], Guanhua He[2],
Shengchao Qin[2,4,*], and Jifeng He[1]

[1] East China Normal University
[2] Teesside University
[3] HASLab/INESC TEC, Universidade do Minho
[4] Shenzhen University
{yhhuang,jifeng}@sei.ecnu.edu.cn,
{jff,g.he,s.qin}@tees.ac.uk

Abstract. AUTOSAR, the open and emerging global standard for automotive embedded systems, offers a timing protection mechanism to protect tasks from missing their deadlines. However, in practice, it is difficult to predict when a deadline is violated, because a task missing its deadline may be caused by unrelated tasks or by the presence of interrupts. In this paper, we propose an abstract formal model to represent AUTOSAR OS programs with timing protection. We are able to determine schedulability properties and to calculate constraints on the allowed time that interrupts can take for a given task in a given period. We implement our model in *Mathematica* and give a case study to illustrate the utility of our method. Based on the results, we believe that our work can help designers and implementors of AUTOSAR OS programs check whether their programs satisfy crucial timing properties.

Keywords: AUTOSAR, timing protection, interrupts, periodic fixed priority scheduling, real-time operating systems.

1 Introduction

The increasing complexity of automobile Electronic Control Units (ECUs) demands standards and methods that support a systematic and reliable approach to the development of automotive software systems. One of such emerging standards is AUTOSAR [1], an initiative led by major automotive OEMs, suppliers and tool vendors to standardize an automotive software architecture. It contains a list of specifications to describe the architecture, including the AUTOSAR Operating System (OS) specification which presents the essential requirements that AUTOSAR OS implementations must follow.

One of the main novelties in AUTOSAR OS is a timing protection mechanism, whose main goal is to prevent tasks from missing their deadlines. The specification suggests the configuration of certain time constraints, like bounding

---

* Corresponding author.

L. Groves and J. Sun (Eds.): ICFEM 2013, LNCS 8144, pp. 165–181, 2013.
© Springer-Verlag Berlin Heidelberg 2013

the execution time of each task and interrupt service routine (ISR). However, in practice, it is difficult to predict when a deadline is violated, because a task missing its deadline may be caused by delays in unrelated tasks. The problem becomes even more challenging when interrupts are enabled, because interrupts can occur at anytime and it is difficult to estimate the time they may take.

In recent works, Bertrand et al. [9] pay attention to the AUTOSAR OS timing protection mechanism. They analyze the mechanism and compare it with other similar mechanisms used in comparable real-time operating systems. They implement the mechanism in a simulation tool and find that "smart configurations" allow better results. However, they do not provide a model that can be directly used by developers to predict deadline faults. Moreover, they do not consider the possibility of interrupts occurring. Hladik et al. [10] provide AUTOSAR OS designers with some usable analysis techniques and corresponding design guidelines. Their work is close to ours, but we focus on periodic tasks. We define a formal model for periodic tasks that can be interrupted by ISRs; our healthiness conditions can directly help the designers configuring the time constraints of periodic tasks mentioned in the specification of the AUTOSAR OS timing protection mechanism. In another work, Schwarz et al. [20] have considered the problem of interrupts occurring in OSEK/VDX OSes. They provide a static analysis for detecting data races between tasks running with different priorities as well as methods to guarantee transactional execution of procedures. However, their focus is on memory safety problems caused by interrupts, whilst our focus is on timing safety.

In this paper, we develop an abstract formal model to represent AUTOSAR OS periodic tasks and to help designers and implementors of AUTOSAR OS programs to analyze and predict deadline faults in their programs. In summary, the main contributions of our work are:

– An abstract formal model that can be used to analyze and predict deadline faults in AUTOSAR OS programs. We define two healthiness conditions, depending on whether interrupts are enabled. Developers of AUTOSAR OS programs can use these healthiness conditions to statically check whether their programs will miss any deadline.
– Based on the model that we develop, we show how to compute the time that interrupts (including sporadic tasks triggered by interrupts) are allowed to take during the execution of tasks. Given that in practice specifications usually mention time intervals (e.g., "interrupt service routines can take n ms, as long as n is between 1ms and 5ms"), rather than showing how to obtain particular times, we show how to derive general time constraints; by focusing on general constraints, developers can consider time intervals.
– To illustrate the practicality of our model, we implement it in *Mathematica* [8]. This allows the automatic calculation of time constraints for interrupts. We also analyze a simple, yet non-trivial, case study. Based on the results, we believe that the work presented in this paper can help designers and implementors of AUTOSAR OS programs check that their programs satisfy crucial timing properties.

The remainder of the paper is organized as follows: Section 2 introduces AU-TOSAR OS, its timing protection mechanism, and the goals and assumptions that we have made. We conclude that section with a simple example illustrating the underlying challenges. In Section 3, we define an abstract model to represent AUTOSAR OS periodic tasks. We define two healthiness conditions that can be used to predict deadline faults in Section 4 and Section 5 respectively. Section 5 also presents how to calculate the maximum available time that interrupts can take during the execution of a given task in a given period. In Section 6, we put the method developed into practice to analyze a case study. Finally, we conclude the paper in Section 7, where we discuss related work and further directions to develop the work presented.

2   Background

In this section, we explain the main characteristics of AUTOSAR OS [1] and of its timing protection mechanism. We also present and justify the assumptions that we have made. We conclude with an example that illustrates the problem we want to tackle and may help the reader understand subsequent sections.

On AUTOSAR OS.

AUTOSAR (AUTomotive Open System ARchitecture) is an open and standard-ized automotive software architecture, jointly developed by automobile manu-facturers, suppliers and tool developers. One of the specifications included in AUTOSAR is AUTOSAR OS, which specifies AUTOSAR operating systems.

The two main identities discussed in AUTOSAR OS are tasks and interrupt service routines (ISR). Each task and ISR are statically associated with a pro-gram. There are two types of tasks: basic and extended tasks. The difference is that the AUTOSAR OS event mechanism is only applied to extended tasks. In other words, basic tasks do not block whereas extended tasks can block until a given event happens. Each task has a priority and AUTOSAR OS suggests a priority-based scheduling policy. Because two tasks cannot occupy the same resource at the same time, AUTOSAR OS prescribes a priority ceiling protocol. As a result, each resource is given a *ceiling priority* that is set at least to the highest priority of all tasks that access a resource or any of the resources linked to this resource. If a task requires a resource, and its current priority is lower than the ceiling priority of the resource, the priority of the task is raised to the ceiling priority of the resource. The priority of the task is reset to its initial pri-ority after releasing the resource. Regarding ISRs, there are also two categories: category 1 and category 2. The main difference is that ISRs of category 1 (ISR1) cannot be controlled by the kernel, while ISRs of category 2 (ISR2) are similar to basic tasks. Contrary to ISR2, ISR1 cannot use any operating system services. That means ISR2 may activate tasks.

On AUTOSAR OS Timing Protection Mechanism.

AUTOSAR is derived from OSEK/VDX [2], an open and widely used indus-try standard for automotive embedded systems that does not offer any protec-tion mechanism. One of the novelties is that AUTOSAR extends OSEK/VDX

with memory and timing protection mechanisms. Before the publication of AU-
TOSAR, two extensions were proposed to equip OSEK/VDX with timing protection: OSEK-time and HiS OSEK. Both extensions used deadline monitoring,
which allows recovery when a failure is detected. However, deadline monitoring
is insufficient to correctly identify what caused a deadline fault. As explained in
the AUTOSAR OS specification, a deadline can be violated due to a deadline
fault introduced by an unrelated task or by the interference of an interrupt. The
fault in this case lies with the unrelated task or interrupt and will propagate
through the system until a task misses its deadline. A task that misses a deadline is therefore not necessarily the task that has failed at runtime; it is simply
the earliest point at which a timing fault is detected.

The AUTOSAR OS timing protection mechanism protects tasks and interrupt
service routines of category 2. It suggests three ways of preventing timing faults:

1. bound the execution time of each task and ISR2;
2. bound the locking time (e.g., the time that resources are held by tasks);
3. guarantee inter-arrival time (e.g., the time for successive activation of tasks
   and ISR2s).

In practice, these bounds are set statically. At runtime, the bounds are used by
the kernel to control the execution of tasks and ISRs. To give a concrete example,
in *Arctic Core* [3], the leading open-source implementation of AUTOSAR OS,
each task and ISR2 control block have a reference to a *OsTimingProtectionType*
structure where the bounds are defined:

```
typedef struct OsTimingProtection {
    // ROM, worst case execution budget in ns
    uint64   executionBudget;
    // ROM, the frame in ns that timelimit may
    // execute in.
    uint64 timeFrame;
    // ROM, time in ns that the task/isr may
    // with a timeframe.
    uint64 timeLimit;
    // ROM, resource/interrupt locktimes
    OsLockingtimeType *lockingTime;
} OsTimingProtectionType;
```

Note the reference to "ROM" in the comments, meaning that these values should
be set initially by the programmer and never changed during execution.

On Our Goals and Assumptions.
In this paper, we focus on the timing protection mechanism introduced in AU-
TOSAR OS. The specification gives the three suggestions above, but it does
not mention how to set the time constraints. The goal is to define an abstract
formal model to represent AUTOSAR OS periodic tasks and to help designers
of AUTOSAR OS programs to analyze and predict deadline faults in their programs. Based on the model, we present how to calculate time constraints on

the allowed time that interrupts can take for a given task in a given period. We introduce a model heavily inspired by an implementation provided by the company *iSoft* (iSoft Infrastructure Software CO.), so we make the assumptions described below.

Assumption 1: In AUTOSAR OS, the tasks that have deadlines are usually periodic tasks (periodicity is achieved by a mechanism called *Schedule Tables*). As a result, all the tasks we discuss in this paper are periodic tasks with a given period. We also assume each task's deadline equals its own period and that all the tasks are ready at the very beginning. Moreover, we assume that the priority and the worst case execution time (WCET) of all tasks are known. The calculation of WCETs is out of the scope of this paper (for details on methods and tools to calculate WCETs, we refer the reader to [4]).

Assumption 2: We assume that any task activated by ISR2 will execute and terminate before ISR2 concludes. When ISR2 terminates, the preempted task is resumed. We consider the total time taken by ISR2 as time spent by interrupts, even if it was running a sporadic task.

Assumption 3: We do not consider AUTOSAR OS resources in this paper, so we assume that the priority of tasks will not change during execution. In other words, we do not discuss the locking time introduced in the timing protection specification.

We now give an example that illustrates the sort of system we will discuss and the sort of problem we want to solve in this paper.

Example 1. Suppose that there are three tasks in the system: A, B, and C; the characteristics of each task, like their priority and deadline (which is the same as their period), are configured statically as shown in Table 1.

Table 1. Properties of the tasks shown in Example 1

Task	Priority	Execution time	Deadline (same as Period)
A	3	1	5
B	2	3	10
C	1	5	15

Figure 1 presents the execution of the three tasks when no interrupts happen. Assuming a fixed priority preemptive scheduling policy and assuming higher priority tasks run before lower priority tasks, task A runs at the very beginning, then B runs, and C starts at the fifth time unit. Because the period of A is 5, task C is preempted and control passes to task A at the sixth time unit. C resumes after the execution of A. In this example, all the tasks meet their own deadlines.

Now we consider an example where interrupts occur during the execution of tasks. We assume the existence of an interrupt called *Isr* that costs one time unit and that can happen at any time. To help with the presentation, in this

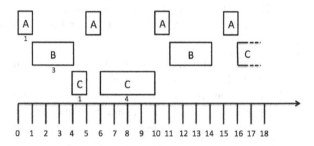

Fig. 1. The execution of tasks without interrupts

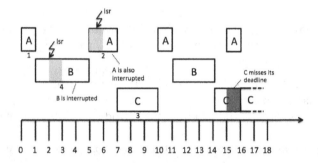

Fig. 2. The execution of tasks with interrupts

example, we assume that *Isr* happens during the execution of both *A* and *B*. Figure 2 shows that task *C* cannot execute until the eighth time unit because the higher priority tasks *A* and *B* finish later due to the time taken by *Isr*. As the figure shows, the late start of *C* leads to a timing fault, as *C* does not meet its deadline. This example shows that although *A* and *B* are interrupted, both of them still meet their deadlines. However, *C* misses its deadline even though it was never interrupted.

In order to avoid the deadline errors mentioned above, the AUTOSAR OS specification advices to bound the execution time of each task, which is actually the sum of the time taken by task own execution and interrupts execution. Assuming that the worst case execution time of tasks are given (assumption 1), we only need to bound the maximum allowed time taken by interrupts for each task in its given period. For example, to guarantee that the tasks shown meet all their deadlines, task *A* cannot be interrupted for more than 1 time units, and tasks *B* and *C* cannot be interrupted at the same time.

3   Tasks Model

In this section, we present an abstract language to specify AUTOSAR OS periodic tasks that can be interrupted. Later, we also define two healthiness conditions that allow to determine when programs can safely execute without any task missing its deadline. Altogether, we can see our formalization as a model that allows the analysis of the AUTOSAR OS timing protection mechanism in the presence of interrupts.

In our model, a *system* is composed by three components: a set of periodic tasks, a set of ISRs, and a list of functions providing static information. We use the notation $\mathsf{Sys} ::= \{\mathsf{Prog}, \mathsf{ISR}, \mathsf{Funs}\}$ to describe a system, where Prog and ISR denote a set of periodic tasks and a set of ISRs respectively, and Funs represents information about tasks and ISRs. A system with m tasks and n ISRs can be represented as:

$$\mathsf{Prog} ::= \{T_1, T_2, ..., T_m\}$$
$$\mathsf{ISR} ::= \{I_1, I_2, ..., I_n\}$$

Each task has its own priority and period which are configured statically and do not change during execution. Recall that the tasks we consider are periodic and their deadlines are equal to their periods (assumption 1). Each ISR also has a priority, which we assume to be always higher than all the tasks' priorities, so that ISRs can interrupt any running task. In our model, we allow a higher priority ISR to interrupt a lower priority ISR. Moreover, we also assume that the worst case execution time of both tasks and ISRs are given.

To facilitate the expression of properties in our model, we make use of the following functions Funs (we assume that T is an element of Prog and I is an element of ISR):

- **Priority Function.**
  $Pr : T \cup I \to \mathbb{N}$ is used to get the priority of a given task or ISR. Different tasks can have the same priority, but no task can have a higher priority than that of an ISR.
- **Deadline Function.**
  $De : T \to \mathbb{N}$ is used to get the deadline (or period) of a given task. Furthermore, we assume that task T_i in its kth period is ready at time $(k-1) \times De(T_i)$, where $k \in \mathbb{N}^+$, and it must finish before $k \times De(T_i)$.
- **Worst Case Execution Time Function.**
  $ET : T \cup I \to \mathbb{N}$ is used to get the worst case execution time of a given task or ISR. We assume the worst case execution time analysis has been already done, so it is not considered in this paper.
- **Maximum Interrupt Time Function.**
  $IT : T \to \mathbb{N}$ is used to get the maximum allowed time taken by interrupts for a given task. It is the total time that the system allows ISRs to take during one period of a given task.

All systems should define the four functions above. But as we mentioned in the previous section, it is difficult to set a reasonable value for the maximum interrupt time. One of our goals in this paper is to help the designers set this value, so we allow the designers to omit this value, and we can calculate that based on the other three values. Of course, if the designers have given all of them, we can also determine whether the maximum interrupt time is suitable to make all tasks meet their deadlines.

Example 2. We use our language to describe the system mentioned in Example 1. There are three tasks: A, B and C, so we set Prog as Prog $::= \{A, B, C\}$. There is only one ISR, so we set ISR as ISR $::= \{Isr\}$. The whole system is represented as Sys $::= \{\text{Prog}, \text{ISR}, \text{Funs}\}$.

Now we define the priority function so that $Pr(A) = 3$, $Pr(B) = 2$, $Pr(C) = 1$, and $Pr(Isr) = 4$; the deadline function is defined as $De(A) = 5$, $De(B) = 10$, $De(C) = 15$; finally, the worst case execution time function is defined as $ET(A) = 1$, $ET(B) = 3$, $ET(C) = 5$ and $ET(Isr) = 1$.

In this example, the maximum allowed time taken by interrupts for each task, $IT(T_i)$, is not given. Later, in Section 5, we show how the function IT can be defined.

4   Timing Protection without Interrupts

In this section, under the assumption that interrupts are disabled, we show conditions under which a collection of tasks can safely execute without missing deadlines.

Given that tasks are periodic, we are interested in evaluating the behaviors of tasks in their shortest repeating cycle[1], which is given by the least common multiple of the periods of all tasks. Given a program Prog, we denote the shortest repeating cycle of its tasks as lcm(Prog). In Example 2, we have lcm(Prog)=30, because the periods of A, B, and C are, respectively, 5, 10, and 15. In other words, the executing pattern shown in Figure 1 repeats itself after 30 time units.

To ensure that a system can run safely without any task missing its deadline, the requirement that we need to guarantee is:

Requirement. *Each task T_i is expected to have a complete execution in each period from $(k-1) \times De(T_i)$ to $k \times De(T_i)$, for all $k \in \mathbb{N}^+$.*

For instance, in Example 1, we want to guarantee that task C starts running and terminates within the periods from $(k-1) \times 15$ to $k \times 15$, for all $k \in \mathbb{N}^+$. However, in the scenario shown in Figure 2 this property is violated because C is not able to terminate within its first period (from 0 to 15).

To formalize the requirement above we start by analyzing the time available for a given task to execute during a given period. Given that our model assumes a fixed priority preemptive scheduling[2], to calculate the time available for task T_i during its kth period (denoted by $\mathbf{AT}_k(T_i)$), we subtract from T_i's deadline the amount of time units taken by all the tasks that have a higher priority than T_i. There is a special case that needs to be considered: if a task T_i has several higher priority tasks with the same period, we combine these tasks

---

[1] The shortest repeating cycle is the smallest amount of time after which the executing pattern repeats itself (when interrupts are disabled).

[2] A fixed priority preemptive scheduler always chooses the highest priority task that is ready to execute.

into one task when calculating the time available for T_i. For example, suppose that tasks $T_{j_1},..., T_{j_n}$ have the same period, i.e., $De(T_{j_1})=...=De(T_{j_n})$. When calculating the time available for task T_i whose priority is lower than all of those tasks $T_{j_1},..., T_{j_n}$, we define a new task T_j with period $De(T_j)=De(T_{j_1})$, priority $Pr(T_j)=min(Pr(T_{j_1}), ..., Pr(T_{j_n}))$ and the worst case execution time $ET(T_j)=ET(T_{j_1})+...+ET(T_{j_n})$. Assuming that $\mathbf{TT}(T_j, l)$ represents the total time taken by task T_j up to the time unit l, we define $\mathbf{AT}_k(T_i)$ as follows:

$$\mathbf{AT}_k(T_i) =_{df} De(T_i) - \sum_{\substack{Pr(T_i) \leq Pr(T_j) \\ \wedge \ j \neq i}} (\mathbf{TT}(T_j, k \times De(T_i)) - \mathbf{TT}(T_j, (k-1) \times De(T_i)))$$

Clearly, the value of $\mathbf{TT}(T_j, k \times De(T_i)) - \mathbf{TT}(T_j, (k-1) \times De(T_i))$ corresponds to the time taken by task T_j between the time unit $(k-1) \times De(T_i)$ and the time unit $k \times De(T_i)$; in other words, it corresponds to the time taken by task T_j during the kth period of T_i. To define $\mathbf{TT}(T_j, l)$ we first observe that the number of times that T_j executes up to time unit l is at least $\lfloor \frac{l}{De(T_j)} \rfloor$. As a result, the total time that T_j takes up to time unit l is at least $\lfloor \frac{l}{De(T_j)} \rfloor \times ET(T_j)$. To determine the exact amount of time, we need to analyze the value of $l \bmod De(T_j)$: if it is long enough for T_j to execute, then T_j executes once; otherwise, T_j will run for $l \bmod De(T_j)$ time units. Put more formally, we have:

$$\mathbf{TT}(T_j, l) =_{df} \begin{cases} \lfloor \frac{l}{De(T_j)} \rfloor \times ET(T_j) + ET(T_j) & \text{if } l \bmod De(T_j) \geq ET(T_j) \\ \lfloor \frac{l}{De(T_j)} \rfloor \times ET(T_j) + l \bmod De(T_j) & \text{if } l \bmod De(T_j) < ET(T_j) \end{cases}$$

Example 3. Based on Example 2, we show how to calculate each task's available time in each period in the shortest repeating cycle. The shortest repeating cycle is 30 time units, task A will execute 6 times, task B will execute 3 times, and task C will execute 2 times.

$AT_i(A) = 5 - 0 = 5 \qquad$ where $i \in \{1, 2, 3, 4, 5, 6\}$
$AT_1(B) = 10 - \lfloor \frac{10 \times 1}{5} \rfloor \times 1 = 10 - 2 = 8$
$AT_2(B) = 10 - (\lfloor \frac{10 \times 2}{5} \rfloor \times 1 - \lfloor \frac{10 \times 1}{5} \rfloor \times 1) = 10 - (4 - 2) = 8$
$AT_3(B) = 10 - (\lfloor \frac{10 \times 3}{5} \rfloor \times 1 - \lfloor \frac{10 \times 2}{5} \rfloor \times 1) = 10 - (8 - 6) = 8$
$AT_1(C) = 15 - (\lfloor \frac{15 \times 1}{5} \rfloor \times 1 + \lfloor \frac{15 \times 1}{10} \rfloor \times 3 + 3) = 15 - (3 + 6) = 6$
$AT_2(C) = 15 - ((\lfloor \frac{15 \times 2}{5} \rfloor \times 1 - \lfloor \frac{15 \times 1}{5} \rfloor \times 1) + (\lfloor \frac{15 \times 2}{10} \rfloor \times 3 - (\lfloor \frac{15 \times 1}{10} \rfloor \times 3 + 3)))$
$\qquad = 15 - ((6 - 3) + (9 - 6)) = 15 - (3 + 3) = 9$

Example 4. We use this example to explain the special issue we mentioned before. A system has three tasks, two of them have a same period. We set Prog $::= \{T_1, T_2, T_3\}$. The priority function is defined as $Pr(T_1) = 3$, $Pr(T_2) = 2$, and $Pr(T_3) = 1$. The deadline function is defined as $De(T_1) = De(T_2) = 8$ and $De(T_3) = 10$. The worst case execution time is defined as $ET(T_1) = 2$, $ET(T_2) = 2$, and $ET(T_3) = 4$. When calculating $AT(T_3)$, we combine T_1 and T_2 into T_{12} which $De(T_{12}) = 8$, $Pr(T_{12}) = 2$, and $ET(T_{12}) = 4$. Hence, i.e., the time is available for task T_3 in its first period: $AT_1(T_3) = 10 - (\lfloor \frac{10 \times 1}{8} \rfloor \times 4 + 10 \ mod \ 8) = 10 - (4 + 2) = 4$.

Now that we have a formal definition for $\mathbf{AT}_k(T_i)$, we can use it to formalize conditions under which a collection of tasks can safely execute without any deadline being missed. We first show how to formalize the situation where no interrupts can occur; we then extend it to the situation where interrupts are enabled.

Definition 1 (Healthiness $\mathcal{H}_1$). We say that a system is in $\mathcal{H}_1$ if in the absence of interrupts, all the tasks meet their respective deadlines in their shortest repeating cycle. Formally, given a system Sys, containing m tasks $T_1, \ldots, T_m$, we define the healthiness predicate $\mathcal{H}_1$:

$$\mathcal{H}_1(\mathsf{Sys}) =_{df} \forall i \in \{1, \ldots, m\}, k \in \{1, \ldots, \frac{\mathsf{lcm}(\mathsf{Prog})}{De(T_i)}\} \bullet \mathbf{AT}_k(T_i) \geq ET(T_i)$$

Using the values calculated in Example 3, we can conclude that the system described in Example 1 is an $\mathcal{H}_1$ system.

5   Timing Protection with Interrupts

In the previous section, we have defined $\mathcal{H}_1$ systems, which are systems where no deadlines are missed, as long as there are no interrupts. In this section, we study the case when interrupts can occur.

To consider interrupts, we redefine the functions shown in the previous section to include the time taken by interrupts. First, we define $\mathbf{ATI}_k(T_i)$, which represents the time available for a given task T_i during its kth period when interrupts are allowed to occur[3].

$$\mathbf{ATI}_k(T_i) =_{df} De(T_i) - \sum_{\substack{Pr(T_i) \leq Pr(T_j) \\ \wedge \ j \neq i}} (\mathbf{TTI}(T_j, k \times De(T_i)) - \mathbf{TTI}(T_j, (k-1) \times De(T_i)))$$

where $\mathbf{TTI}(T_j, l)$ represents the total time taken by task T_j and by interrupts up to time unit l. Following the discussion in the previous section, we observe that the value of $\mathbf{TTI}(T_j, k \times De(T_i)) - \mathbf{TTI}(T_j, (k-1) \times De(T_i))$ corresponds to the time taken by task T_j and by interrupts during the kth period of T_i. The function $\mathbf{TTI}$ is defined below.

Functions $\mathbf{ATI}$ and $\mathbf{TTI}$ are similar to functions $\mathbf{AT}$ and $\mathbf{TT}$. The difference is that the former two consider the execution time $ET(T)$ and the maximum allowed time for interrupts $IT(T)$, while the latter two only consider the execution time $ET(T)$. Note that the sum of the worst case execution time of a task and the maximum allowed time for interrupts for that task is the actual bounding execution time mentioned in AUTOSAR OS timing protection mechanism.

---

[3] The special case discussed in the previous section should be also considered here.

$$\mathbf{TTI}(T_j, l) =_{df} \begin{cases} \lfloor \frac{l}{De(T_j)} \rfloor \times (ET(T_j) + IT(T_j)) + (ET(T_j) + IT(T_j)) \\ \qquad \text{if } l \bmod De(T_j) \geq (ET(T_j) + IT(T_j)) \\ \lfloor \frac{l}{De(T_j)} \rfloor \times (ET(T_j) + IT(T_j)) + l \bmod De(T_j) \\ \qquad \text{if } l \bmod De(T_j) < (ET(T_j) + IT(T_j)) \end{cases}$$

The time available for a given task may be different in its different periods; we use the notation $\mathbf{minATI}(T_i)$ to denote the minimum time available for task T_i in the repeating cycle of the system:

$$\mathbf{minATI}(T_i) = \min(\mathbf{ATI}_1(T_i), \ldots, \mathbf{ATI}_k(T_i)), \quad where \; k = \frac{\mathsf{lcm}(\mathsf{Prog})}{De(T_i)}$$

We now use $\mathbf{minATI}$ to extend Definition 1 for the case where interrupts can occur.

Definition 2 (Healthiness $\mathcal{H}_2$). We say that a system is in $\mathcal{H}_2$ if (1) a system is in $\mathcal{H}_1$ and (2) when in the presence of interrupts, the system guarantees that all tasks can meet their deadlines. Formally, given a system as described in Definition 1, we define the healthiness predicate $\mathcal{H}_2$:

$$\mathcal{H}_2(\mathsf{Sys}) =_{df} \left(\mathcal{H}_1(\mathsf{Sys}) \wedge \forall i \in \{1, ..., m\} \bullet \mathbf{minATI}(T_i) \geq ET(T_i) + IT(T_i) \right)$$

$\mathcal{H}_2$ systems guarantee that all tasks will meet their deadlines even if interrupts occur. According to the definition above, healthiness condition $\mathcal{H}_1$ is subsumed by $\mathcal{H}_2$, meaning that an $\mathcal{H}_2$ system must be an $\mathcal{H}_1$ system. In other words, when a system wants to guarantee all tasks meet their deadlines in the presence of interrupts, the system must guarantee all tasks meet their deadlines in the absence of interrupts at first. However, we should note that in practice, it is difficult to set a reasonable maximum allowed time for each task to be interrupted, because we always have to consider the whole system. We can overcome this difficulty by observing that Definition 2 gives us a system of inequations that can be used to calculate the values for function IT:

$$\forall i \in \{1, ..., m\} \bullet IT(T_i) \leq \mathbf{minATI}(T_i) - ET(T_i) \tag{1}$$

We will use this system of inequations in the next section.

As a concluding remark, we observe that the function IT can be defined according to different requirements. For example, three cases are suggested as below:

- **Case 1.** The system allows only one task to be interrupted at runtime. For example, task T_i is the only task that can be interrupted; the value of IT for other tasks is set to 0: $\forall j, j \neq i \bullet IT(T_j) = 0$.
- **Case 2.** The system allows every task to be interrupted the same amount of time, so we define $\forall i \bullet IT(T_i) = t$, for some t. One implementation of AUTOSAR OS developed by *iSoft* adopts this kind of timing protection mechanism.

– **Case 3**. The system allows every task to be interrupted, but distributes them into different groups according to the amount of time allowed for interrupts. Every two tasks in the same group have the same allowed time for interrupts, i.e., if task T_i and task T_j are in the same group, then $IT(T_i) = IT(T_j)$.

To illustrate how IT can be used, we give an example based on Example 3.

Example 5. Based on Example 3, we assume task C is the only task that can be interrupted (like case 1 above), so we set $IT(A) = IT(B) = 0$. In this case, $\forall k \bullet \mathbf{ATI}_k(C) = \mathbf{AT}_k(C)$ and $\mathbf{minATI}(C) = \min(6,9) = 6$. So $IT(C) \leq (6-5) = 1$. In fact, looking at Figure 1, we see that if C is interrupted for more than one time unit, task C will miss its deadline.

6   A Case Study

In this section, we use a more complex example to illustrate the utility of our method. The tricky part of the example is that the deadline of a lower priority task is less than that of a higher priority task. Moreover, the higher priority task may not finish in one period of lower priority task, but in two, which makes it difficult to predict the *healthiness* of the system.

Implementation.
We have implemented all the functions and healthiness conditions in *Mathematica* [8] and evaluated our method. The user can define a system using the prototype; when the priority, deadline and worst case execution time of all the tasks of a program are given, the prototype can determine whether a system is in $\mathcal{H}_1$. If the maximum allowed time taken by interrupts for all the tasks is given as additional input (i.e., function IT), our prototype can determine whether a system is in $\mathcal{H}_2$. Otherwise, it can calculate a set of time constraints to help the

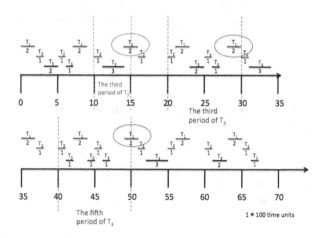

Fig. 3. The scheduling of tasks in case study

designers configure the maximum allowed time for interrupts (according to the system of inequations (1) shown in Section 5).

Example.

The example we use is shown in Table 2. We present the scheduling of tasks without interrupts in Figure 3. In the example, the priority of task T_2 is lower than that of T_1, but the deadline of T_2 is less than that of T_1. In the third period of task T_2 and in the fifth period of task T_3, T_1 starts at the last time unit, and does not finish in one period of the lower priority tasks. In the third period of task T_3, T_1 finishes its execution in one period of T_3. But when interrupts are enabled, T_1 may finish in next period of T_3. Moreover, we can see that the time available for the same task in different periods is different. That is why we should consider the shortest repeating cycle.

Table 2. Properties of the tasks shown in the case study

Task	Priority	Execution time	Deadline (same as Period)
T_1	3	200	700
T_2	2	100	500
T_3	1	300	1000

$AT_i(T_1) > 700 - 0 = 700$
$AT_i(T_1) > ET(T_1)$ where $i \in \{1, ..., 10\}$
$AT_1(T_2) = 500 - 200 = 300$
$AT_1(T_2) > ET(T_2)$
$AT_2(T_2) = 500 - (\lfloor \frac{500*2}{700} \rfloor * 200 + 200 - 200) = 500 - (400 - 200) = 300$
$AT_2(T_2) > ET(T_2)$
$AT_3(T_2) = 500 - ((\lfloor \frac{500*3}{700} \rfloor * 200 + 500 * 3 \bmod 700 - (\lfloor \frac{500*2}{700} \rfloor * 200 + 200))$
$\quad = 500 - ((400 + 100) - 400) = 400$
$AT_3(T_2) > ET(T_2)$
$AT_4(T_2) = 500 - (\lfloor \frac{500*4}{700} \rfloor * 200 + 200 - (\lfloor \frac{500*3}{700} \rfloor * 200 + 500 * 3 \bmod 700))$
$\quad = 500 - (600 - 500) = 400$
$AT_4(T_2) > ET(T_2)$
$\qquad ...$
$AT_1(T_3) = 1000 - (\lfloor \frac{1000*1}{700} \rfloor * 200 + 200 + \lfloor \frac{1000*1}{500} \rfloor * 100) = 1000 - (400 + 200) = 400$
$AT_1(T_3) > ET(T_3)$
$\qquad ...$
$AT_6(T_3) = 1000 - ((\lfloor \frac{1000*6}{700} \rfloor * 200 + 200 - (\lfloor \frac{1000*5}{700} \rfloor * 200$
$\quad + 1000 * 5 \bmod 700)) + (\lfloor \frac{1000*6}{500} \rfloor * 100 - \lfloor \frac{1000*5}{500} \rfloor * 100))$
$\quad = 1000 - ((1800 - 1500) + (1200 - 1000)) = 1000 - (300 + 200) = 500$
$AT_6(T_3) > ET(T_3)$
$AT_7(T_3) = 1000 - ((\lfloor \frac{1000*7}{700} \rfloor * 200 - (\lfloor \frac{1000*6}{700} \rfloor * 200 + 200)) + (\lfloor \frac{1000*7}{500} \rfloor * 100 - \lfloor \frac{1000*6}{500} \rfloor * 100))$
$\quad = 1000 - ((2000 - 1800) + (1400 - 1200)) = 1000 - (200 + 200) = 600$
$AT_7(T_3) > ET(T_3)$

Fig. 4. The calculation details for the case study

Healthiness $\mathcal{H}_1$. To evaluate whether this example is an $\mathcal{H}_1$ system, we have to make sure all the tasks can meet their deadlines when there are no interrupts (according to Definition 1). Using our implementation in *Mathematica*, we conclude that this system is in $\mathcal{H}_1$. We also list some details in Figure 4 to help the reader understand our method.

The shortest repeating cycle of this example is 7000 time units. So we should consider 10 periods of task T_1 (because the period is 700), 14 periods of task T_2 (because the period is 500), and 7 periods of T_3 (because the period is 1000). Here, we only list a few.

Healthiness $\mathcal{H}_2$. We calculate the maximum allowed time taken by interrupts for each task by following the constraints given in the previous section. More specifically, the values of $IT(T_1)$, $IT(T_2)$ and $IT(T_3)$ should satisfy the inequality $2IT(T_1) + 2IT(T_2) + IT(T_3) \leq 100$ (calculated by the implementation in *Mathematica*). We can use this inequality to set the interrupt time $IT(T_i)$ for task T_i. For example, if we want to make the maximum allowed time that interrupts can take the same for all tasks (as described in Case 2 above), we can set $IT(T_1)=IT(T_2)=IT(T_3)=20$ at most. Moreover, if the system has already set the function IT, we can use this inequality to evaluate whether this system is in $\mathcal{H}_2$.

7   Related Work and Conclusion

Related Work.

Many researchers have done much work on fixed priority scheduling of periodic tasks. The problem of scheduling periodic tasks with hard deadlines on a uniprocessor was first studied by Liu and Layland in 1973 [11]. Later, Lehoczky developed an exact schedulability criterion for the fixed priority scheduling of periodic tasks with arbitrary deadlines [12]. Harbour et al. presented a generalized model of fixed priority scheduling of periodic tasks where each task's execution priority may vary [13]. Katcher et al. developed scheduling models for four generic scheduler implementations that represent the spectrum of implementations found in real-time kernels [14]. In many respects, there is an overlap of concerns between these works and this paper. However, the focus and novelty of our work is on estimating the available time for interrupts that can occur in periodic AUTOSAR OS programs.

A related line of research is presented in [15,16,17,18], where timed automata are used to analyze different problems about scheduling. We plan to reuse parts of these works to extend our model with support for AUTOSAR resources (see discussion on future work below).

There has also been a considerable amount of work on interrupt-based programs. For example, the works [5,20,21] deal with the analysis and verification of memory safety properties. More related to this paper is the work presented in [19], where a tool for deadline analysis of interrupt-driven Z86-based software is presented. Other works give advice and introduce models to guarantee that interrupts do not cause timing faults: in [6], the number of the interruptions during certain time intervals is limited; in [7], tasks and interrupts are integrated to provide predictable execution times in real-time systems.

The work presented in this paper can be seen as a continuation of our previous work. In [22], we have developed a formal model of interrupt-based programs from a probabilistic perspective: we designed a probabilistic operational semantics able to capture the potential properties, and specified the time constraint of interrupt programs. In [23], we have analyzed and verified ORIENTAIS, an operating system based on OSEK/VDX and developed by *iSoft*.

Conclusion.

This paper proposes a simple and abstract formal model to represent AUTOSAR OS programs that need to ensure certain timing properties. The model can be used to predict if a given periodic task will miss its deadline. We present two healthiness conditions: condition $\mathcal{H}_1$ is used to check if tasks meet their deadlines when interrupts are disabled; condition $\mathcal{H}_2$ is used to check if tasks meet their deadlines when interrupts are enabled. To have a definitive answer to the question "is a given system an $\mathcal{H}_2$ system?", we need to know what is the time taken by interrupts, so we use *Mathematica* to compute time constraints for interrupts. Rather than assuming specific times for interrupts, we are able to give answers of the type "the given system is an $\mathcal{H}_2$ system, provided that task T_1 is not interrupted for more than 5 time units *and* task T_2 is not interrupted for more than 3 time units". It is worth saying that, although our focus is on interrupt-based programs, the timing constraints developed are general enough to be used for other purposes. For example, the theory applies if instead of interrupts we consider delays; saying that a given task can be interrupted for at most 5 time units is the same as saying that the task can be delayed by at most 5 time units.

We believe that the work presented in this paper can help designers and implementors of AUTOSAR OS programs check that their programs satisfy crucial timing properties.

As for future work, we plan to extend the model to consider the locking time of resources mentioned in the AUTOSAR OS timing protection specification. The difficulty of adding resources in the model is related with the *priority ceiling protocol*, which causes the priority of tasks to change during execution. The extended model should be able to cope with dynamic changes of priority (i.e., functions like **AT** and **ATI** will need to be redefined). We also plan to generalize the model so that periods and deadlines do not coincide. Finally, we will construct software tools that automatically construct models from the source code of AUTOSAR OS programs. We envisage these tools to be integrated into tool chains specifically designed for AUTOSAR OS developers.

Acknowledgments. This work was partly supported by the Danish National Research Foundation and the National Natural Science Foundation of China (Grant No. 61061130541) for the Danish-Chinese Center for Cyber Physical Systems. And, it is also supported by National Basic Research Program of China (Grant No. 2011CB302904), National High Technology Research and Development Program of China (Grant Nos. 2011AA010101 and 2012AA011205).

The majority of the work reported in this paper was done while Yanhong Huang was a visiting researcher at Teesside University (funded by the Teesside University Research Fund). The support of Teesside University is gratefully acknowledged.

References

1. AUTOSAR. Specification of Operating System V3.1.1 R3.1 Rev 0002 (2012), http://www.autosar.org/ (last accessed: July 1, 2013)
2. OSEK/VDX, http://www.osek-vdx.org/ (last accessed: July 1, 2013)
3. Arctic Core — the open-source AUTOSAR embedded platform, http://www.arccore.com/ (last accessed: July 1, 2013)
4. Wilhelm, R., Engblom, J., Ermedahl, A., Holsti, N., Thesing, S., Whalley, D., Bernat, G., Ferdinand, C., Heckmann, R., Mitra, T., Mueller, F., Puaut, I., Puschner, P., Staschulat, J., Stenström, P.: The worst-case execution-time problem—overview of methods and survey of tools. ACM Trans. Embed. Comput. Syst. 7(3) (2008)
5. Tuch, H.: Formal Memory Models for Verifying C Systems Code. Ph.D. Thesis. University of NSW, Australia (2008)
6. Regehr, J., Reid, A., Webb, K.: Eliminating stack overflow by abstract interpretation. In: EMSOFT (2003)
7. Leyva-del-Foyo, L.E., Mejia-Alvarez, P., de Niz, D.: Predictable Interrupt Management for Real Time Kernels over conventional PC Hardware. In: RTAS (2006)
8. Wolfram Research, Inc., Mathematica, Version 8.0, Champaign, IL (2010).
9. Bertrand, D., Faucou, S., Trinquet, Y.: An analysis of the AUTOSAR OS timing protection mechanism. In: ETFA (2009)
10. Hladik, P.E., Deplanche, A.M., Faucou, S., Trinquet, Y.: Adequacy between AUTOSAR OS specification and real-time scheduling theory. In: SIES (2007)
11. Liu, C.L., Layland, J.W.: Scheduling Algorithms for Multiprogramming in a Hard-Real-Time Environment. Jounal of the Assocaition for Computing Macheinery 20(1) (1973)
12. Lehoczky, J.P.: Fixed priority scheduling of periodic task sets with arbitrary deadlines. In: RTSS (1990)
13. Harbour, M.G., Klein, M.H., Lehoczky, J.P.: Fixed Priority Scheduling of Periodic Tasks with Varying Execution Priority. In: RTSS (1991)
14. Katcher, D.I., Arakawa, H., Strosnider, J.K.: Engineering and analysis of fixed priority schedulers. IEEE Transactions on Software Engineering (1993)
15. Amnell, T., Fersman, E., Mokrushin, L., Pettersson, P., Wang, Y.: TIMES: a Tool for Schedulability Analysis and Code Generation of Real-Time Systems. In: Larsen, K.G., Niebert, P. (eds.) FORMATS 2003. LNCS, vol. 2791, pp. 60–72. Springer, Heidelberg (2004)
16. Fersman, E., Wang, Y.: A Generic Approach to Schedulability Analysis of Real Time Tasks. Nordic Journal of Computing 11(2) (2004)
17. Krcal, P., Wang, Y.: Decidable and Undecidable Problems in Schedulability Analysis Using Timed Automata. In: Jensen, K., Podelski, A. (eds.) TACAS 2004. LNCS, vol. 2988, pp. 236–250. Springer, Heidelberg (2004)
18. Fersman, E., Mokrushin, L., Pettersson, P., Wang, Y.: Schedulability Analysis of Fixed-Priority Systems Using Timed Automata. Journal of Theoretical Computer Science 354(2) (2006)
19. Brylow, D., Palsberg, J.: Deadline Analysis of Interrupt-Driven Software. IEEE Transactions on Software Engineering (2004)
20. Schwarz, M.D., Seidl, H., Vojdani, V., Lammich, P., Muller-Olm, M.: Static analysis of interrupt-driven programs synchronized via the priority ceiling protocol. In: POPL (2011)

21. Feng, X., Shao, Z., Guo, Y., Dong, Y.: Certifying Low-Level Programs with Hardware Interrupts and Preemptive Threads. J. Autom. Reasoning 42(2-4) (2009)
22. Zhao, Y., Huang, Y., He, J., Liu, S.: Formal Model of Interrupt Program from a Probabilistic Perspective. In: ICECCS (2011)
23. Shi, J., Zhu, H., He, J., Fang, H., Huang, Y., Zhang, X.: ORIENTAIS: Formal Verified OSEK/VDX Real-Time Operating System. In: ICECCS (2012)

Improving Model Checking Stateful Timed CSP with non-Zenoness through Clock-Symmetry Reduction

Yuanjie Si[1], Jun Sun[2], Yang Liu[3], and Ting Wang[1]

[1] College of Computer Science, Zhejiang University, China
{siyuanjie,qdw}@zju.edu.cn
[2] Information System Technology and Design,
Singapore University of Technology and Design, Singapore
sunjun@sutd.edu.sg
[3] School of Computer Engineering, Nanyang Technological University, Singapore
yangliu@ntu.edu.sg

Abstract. Real-time system verification must deal with a special notion of 'fairness', i.e., clocks must always be able to progress. A system run which prevents clocks from progressing unboundedly is known as Zeno. Zeno runs are infeasible in reality and thus must be pruned during system verification. Though zone abstraction is an effective technique for model checking real-time systems, it is known that zone graphs (e.g., those generated from Timed Automata models) are too abstract to directly infer time progress and hence non-Zenoness. As a result, model checking with non-Zenoness (i.e., existence of a non-Zeno counterexample) based on zone graphs only is infeasible. In our previous work [23], we show that model checking Stateful Timed CSP with non-Zenoness based on zone graphs only is feasible, due to the difference between Stateful Timed CSP and Timed Automata. Nonetheless, the algorithm proposed in [23] requires to associate each time process construct with a unique clock, which could enlarge the state space (compared to model checking without non-Zenoness) significantly. In this paper, we improve our previous work by combining the checking algorithm with a clock-symmetry reduction method. The proposed algorithm has been realized in the PAT model checker for model checking LTL properties with non-Zenoness. The experimental results show that the improved algorithm significantly outperforms the previous work.

1 Introduction

Timed Automata [2,11] are popular for real-time system modeling and verification. Verification tools for Timed Automata based models have proven to be successful [15,5]. Nonetheless, modeling hierarchical timed systems in Timed Automata is not trivial. The proposed remedies include extensions of Timed Automata [6,8,4,9] or alternative languages [29,16,23]. In our previous work [23], a new language named Stateful Timed CSP (STCSP) is proposed to model hierarchical real-time systems, which combines compositional language constructs from process algebra community (i.e., Timed CSP [20]) with imperative programs and timed constructs like *delay*, *timeout*, and *deadline*, etc. For instance, we write *P timeout[d] Q* in STCSP to denote that process *P* must perform an action (e.g., a data operation or channel communication) within *d*

L. Groves and J. Sun (Eds.): ICFEM 2013, LNCS 8144, pp. 182–198, 2013.

time units or otherwise process Q takes over the control and starts executing; we write *P deadline*[d] to denote that P must terminate within d time units.

Like model checking Timed Automata, model checking STCSP models must deal with the emptiness checking problem, i.e., the problem of checking whether a timed model accepts at least one non-Zeno run. An infinite run is non-Zeno if and only if it takes an unbounded amount of time. Zeno runs are infeasible in reality and thus must be pruned during system verification. That is, it is necessary to check whether a run is Zeno so as to avoid presenting Zeno runs as counterexamples. For instance, given a model *P deadline*[1] where $P = a \rightarrow P \mid b \rightarrow Skip$. If property 'eventually event b occurs' is verified without non-Zenoness, then a counterexample with infinitely many a events will be generated. A close look reveals that the counterexample is Zeno since infinitely many a events must occur within 1 time unit. We thus need a method to check whether a run is Zeno or not. Furthermore, the reason that the non-Zenoness checking is particularly interesting is that it is infeasible with zone abstraction [13], which is an effective technique for model checking Timed Automata (which has been employed by many tools including UPPAAL [15]) and STCSP [23]. Zone abstraction, which constructs zone graphs, is too abstract to directly infer time progress and hence non-Zenoness. This issue has attracted much attention recently. The proposed remedies include either introducing an additional clock [24] or additional accepting states in zone graphs [13]. The state-of-art emptiness checking algorithm [12] for Timed Automata has a complexity of $(|C| + 1)^2 \cdot |ZG|$ where $|C|$ is the number of clocks and $|ZG|$ is the size of the zone graph.

Unlike Timed Automata, model checking with non-Zenoness in STCSP can be achieved based on the zone graphs only. It has been shown that zone abstraction can be applied to STCSP, by explicitly associating clocks with the timed constructs, dynamically activating/de-activating clocks and constructing the zone graph [23]. STCSP is different from Time Automata as it relies on implicit clocks which cannot be modified directly. We observe that clocks in STCSP (which are implicit) always have constant upper bounds. For instance, if a clock c is used to model a 'timeout' at time d, c is associated with an upper bound d which will remain constant. Based on this observation, we develop an efficient emptiness checking algorithm for STCSP in [23], based on zone graphs only without introducing extra clocks or states. The algorithm is then applied to model checking STCSP models with the non-Zenoness assumption.

Our Contribution. In this work, we significantly improve [23] by combining the emptiness checking algorithm with a clock-symmetry reduction method. We show that emptiness checking can be performed even without maintaining the clock names (since the clock names in [23] are implicit and 'introduced' anyway), which implies that a clock symmetry reduction method can be applied. That is, the emptiness problem for STCSP can be solved based on a quotient zone graph, which potentially reduces the size of the zone graph by a factor of K factorial, where K is the maximum number of *overlapping* clocks. The experimental results confirm that our method improves previous approaches significantly and allows model-checking with non-Zenoness with minor overheard compared to model checking without non-Zenoness. In summary, we make the following new contributions. First, we develop a clock-symmetry reduction method and combine it with the emptiness checking algorithm for STCSP, which significantly improves the

$P = Stop \mid Skip \mid e \rightarrow P \mid a\{program\} \rightarrow P \mid \textbf{if} (b) \{P\} \textbf{ else } \{Q\} \mid P \mid Q \mid P; Q$
    $\mid P \setminus X \mid P \parallel Q \mid Wait[d] \mid P \; timeout[d] \; Q \mid P \; interrupt[d] \; Q \mid P \; within[d]$
    $\mid P \; deadline[d] \mid Q$

Fig. 1. Process constructs

performance. Second, we extend the PAT model checker [23] to support LTL checking with non-Zenoness assumption for STCSP, and compare our algorithm with previous approaches by verifying a number of benchmark systems.

2 Stateful Timed CSP

STCSP [23] is a recently proposed real-time modeling language, which extends Timed CSP [19] with shared variables and additional timed process constructs. An STCSP model is a 3-tuple (Var, σ_0, P_0) where Var is a set of *finite-domain* global variables; σ_0 is the initial valuation of Var (which maps one variable to one value only) and P_0 is a process. A variable can be of a pre-defined type like Boolean, bounded integer, array of bounded integers or any user-defined data type[1]. Process P models the control logic of the system using a rich set of process constructs. A process can be defined by the grammar presented in Figure 1. For simplicity, we assume that P is not parameterized.

Process *Stop* does nothing but idling. Process *Skip* terminates, possibly after idling for some time. Process $e \rightarrow P$ engages in event e first and then behaves as P. Note that e may serve as a synchronization barrier, if combined with parallel composition. In order to seamlessly integrate data operations, we allow sequential programs to be attached with events. Process $a\{program\} \rightarrow P$ performs data operation a (i.e., executing the sequential *program* whilst generating event a) and then behaves as P. The *program* may be a simple procedure updating data variables (written in the form of $a\{x := 5; y := 3\}$) or a complicated sequential program. A conditional choice is written as **if** (b) $\{P\}$ **else** $\{Q\}$. Process $P \mid Q$ offers an (unconditional) choice between P and Q[2]. Process $P; Q$ behaves as P until P terminates and then behaves as Q immediately. $P \setminus X$ hides occurrences of events in X. Parallel composition of two processes is written as $P \parallel Q$, where P and Q may communicate via event synchronization (following CSP rules [14]) or shared variables. Notice that if P and Q do not communicate through event synchronization, then it is written as $P \mid\mid\mid Q$, which reads as 'P interleaves Q'. Additional process constructs (e.g., while or periodic behaviors) can be defined using the above. In order to focus on the central issue in this paper, we keep the un-timed process compositions minimal and focus only on sequential composition, conditional choice and parallel composition in the following.

In addition, a number of timed process constructs are designed to capture common real-time system behavior patterns. Let $d \in \mathbb{R}^+$. Process $Wait[d]$ idles for exactly d time units. Process $P \; timeout[d] \; Q$ behaves as P if P performs an action before d time units

---

[1] Refer to PAT user manual on how to define a type in C# or Java.
[2] For simplicity, we omit external and internal choices [14] in the discussion.

elapsed since the process starts, or as Q after idling for d time units. Notice that when exactly d time units have elapsed, either P or Q may execute. Process P *interrupt*$[d]$ Q behaves as P for exactly d time units (during the time P may perform multiple actions) and then behaves as Q. Process P *within*$[d]$ constrains that P must *react* (by performing an action) within d time units. Process P *deadline*$[d]$ constrains that P must terminate within d time units. Notice that a timed process construct is always associated with an *integer* constant d which is referred to as its parameter. Furthermore, a process expression Q can be given a name P, written as $P = Q$, and recursion can be defined through process referencing.

Example 1. Let δ and ϵ be two constants. Fischer's mutual exclusion algorithm is a model $(Var, \sigma_0, Protocol)$. *Var* contains one integer variable named *turn* recording the process which attempts to access the critical section most recently. Valuation σ_0 maps *turn* to -1, indicating that no process is attempting initially. Process *Protocol* is defined as $Pro(0) \parallel Pro(1)$ where

$$
\begin{aligned}
Pro(i) = \ &if \ (turn = -1) \ \{ \\
&\quad (set.i\{turn := i\} \to Wait[\epsilon]) \ within[\delta]; \\
&\quad if \ (turn = i) \ \{ \\
&\quad\quad cs.i \to exit.i\{turn := -1\} \to Pro(i) \\
&\quad \} \\
&\quad else \ \{Pro(i)\} \\
&\} \\
&else \ \{ \\
&\quad Pro(i) \\
&\}
\end{aligned}
$$

Process $Pro(i)$ models a process with a unique integer identify i. If *turn* is -1, the process starts attempting to enter the critical section. Firstly *turn* is set to be i (indicating that the i-process is now attempting). Note that this must occur within δ time units (captured by *within*$[\delta]$). Next, the process idles for ϵ time units (captured by *Wait*$[\epsilon]$). It then checks whether *turn* is still i. If so, it enters the critical section. Otherwise, it restarts from the beginning. Mutual exclusion is guaranteed if $\delta < \epsilon$.   □

Given a model (Var, σ_0, P_0), its concrete operational semantics is defined through a set of firing rules. We omit the rules here and refer interested readers to [23]. Based on the firing rule, we can systematically construct a labeled transition system (LTS) $CG = (S, init, \Sigma, T)$ such that a state in S is of the form (σ, P) where σ is a valuation function of *Var* and P is a process; $init = (\sigma_0, P_0)$; Σ is the alphabet; and a transition in T of the form $(s, (d, e), s')$ such that $s, s' \in S$ and $(d, e) : \mathbb{R}^+ \times \Sigma$ is the transition label. Note that d is a real number that denotes the time elapsed (since s is reached) before the transition is taken and e is the event name. A (rooted) non-Zeno run of the model is an infinite sequence $\langle s_0, (d_0, e_0), s_1, (d_1, e_1), \cdots \rangle$ of CG such that $s_0 = (\sigma_0, P_0)$ and $(s_i, (d_i, e_i), s_{i+1})$ is a transition of CG for all i and the sum of $d_0, d_1, \cdots$ is unbounded. The sequence $\langle s_0, e_0, s_1, e_1, \cdots \rangle$ is called a timed-abstract run. A model is non-empty if and only if it contains at least one non-Zeno run.

STCSP differs from Timed Automata as it relies on implicit clocks. For instance, intuitively, a clock starts ticking whenever a process *Wait*$[d]$ is activated. Semantically, it has been shown in [23] that STCSP has the same expressiveness as closed timed safety automata with invisible transitions (i.e., τ transitions), which is strictly less expressive than Timed Automata with invisible transitions and more expressive than closed timed safety automata. More importantly, because clocks in STCSP are implicit and there is no direct way to access the clocks, *the bounds associated with the clocks always remain constant.*

3 Emptiness Checking of Stateful Timed CSP

In the following, we describe the emptiness checking algorithm for STCSP developed in [23]. First we summarize dynamic zone abstraction developed for STCSP and then introduce the emptiness checking approach.

3.1 Dynamic Zone Abstraction

Implicitly, each timed process *instance* is associated with a *unique* clock. For instance, it can be viewed that the clock associated with $Wait[3]$ starts ticking as soon as it is *activated* and expires as soon as it reaches 3. Notice that different instances of the same process are associated with different clocks. For instance, given process $P = Wait[3]$; P, each invocation of P will generate a different instance of $Wait[3]$ with a different clock. For simplicity, we write $Wait_c[d]$ (P $timeout_c[d]$ Q and so on) to denote that the associated clock is c. The clock is activated as soon as the process is activated (i.e., the process receives the control). For instance, in process $Wait_{c_1}[5]$; $Wait_{c_2}[4]$, only c_1 is activated and c_2 is activated as soon as $Wait_{c_1}[5]$ is terminated. Given a process P, the set of *activated* clocks of P is written as $clock(P)$.

In the abstract zone graph, a node is of the form (σ, P, Z) where σ is a valuation of Var; P is a process; and Z is a zone which is a constraint on values of $clock(P)$. We write $clock(Z)$ to denote the clocks used in Z. For now, we say that two abstraction configurations (σ_0, P_0, Z_0) and (σ_1, P_1, Z_1) are equivalent if $\sigma_0(x) = \sigma_1(x)$ for all x in Var; and P_0 and P_1 are equivalent processes *associated with the same clocks*; and Z_0 and Z_1 share the same canonical form if they are represented as DBMs(Difference Bound Matrices). An abstract transition is of the form $(\sigma, P, Z) \overset{e}{\to} (\sigma', P', Z')$. Notice that $clock(P)$ and $clock(P')$ could be different, i.e., some process constructs may be pruned and some new ones may be activated. For instance, given process $(e \to Wait_{c_2}[3])$ $timeout_{c_1}[4]$ Q, the transition labeled with e results in a configuration where c_1 is pruned (see the abstract firing rule below) and c_2 is activated. Clocks that are not in $clock(P)$ are irrelevant to future behaviors of (σ, P, Z). Therefore, we always prune those clocks from Z. Given a set of clocks X, we write $Z[X]$ to denote the zone obtained by projecting Z onto X. This operator can be realized based on DBM [23]. Furthermore, we define a function $clean(\sigma, P, Z)$ that returns the abstract configuration (σ, P, Z') where Z' is the conjunction of $Z[clock(P)]$ and $c = 0$ for each $c \in (clock(P) \backslash clock(Z))$. Notice that $Z[clock(P)]$ prunes irrelevant clocks and $(clock(P) \backslash clock(Z))$ contains the newly activated clocks. It can be seen that $clock(P) = clock(Z')$.

The abstract operational semantics is defined through a set of abstract firing rules. We present sample abstract firing rules P $timeout_c[d]$ Q in the following. The rest can be found in [23].

$$\frac{(\sigma, P, Z) \xrightarrow{e} (\sigma', P', Z')}{(\sigma, P \ timeout_c[d] \ Q, Z) \xrightarrow{e} (\sigma', P', Z' \wedge c \le d)}$$

$$\overline{(\sigma, P \ timeout_c[d] \ Q, Z) \xrightarrow{\tau} (\sigma, Q, Z^\uparrow \wedge c = d \wedge idle(\sigma, P, Z))}$$

The first rule states if a transition of P occurs no later than d time units since the process is enabled, the *timeout* is resolved. Otherwise, if P may delay until $c = d$ (captured by $idle(\sigma, P, Z)$), time out occurs when $c = d$. Function $idle(\sigma, P, Z)$ returns the zone that can be reached by idling from the abstract system configuration (σ, P, Z). For instance, the following shows how the *idle* function is defined for process $P \ timeout[d] \ Q$.

$$idle(\sigma, P \ timeout_c[d] \ Q, Z) = Z^\uparrow \wedge c \le d \wedge idle(\sigma, P, Z)$$

Intuitively, process $P \ timeout_c[d] \ Q$ can idle as long as P can idle and the reading of clock c is less than or equal to d. Similarly, we can define *idle* for all process types. The detailed definition is presented in [23]. *It is important to notice that all the timing constraints are in the form of $c \le d$ or $c = d$.*

Given a model (Var, σ_0, P_0), using the abstract firing rules, we can build an abstract zone graph $AG = (S, init, \Sigma, T)$ such that S is a set of abstract states (σ, P, Z) such that Z is not empty; $init = clean(\sigma_0, P_0, true)$ is the initial configuration; Σ is the alphabet; and T contains a transition $((\sigma, P, Z), e, clean(\sigma', P', Z'))$ iff $(\sigma, P, Z) \xrightarrow{e} (\sigma', P', Z')$.

It has been shown that CG and AG share the same set of time-abstract runs [23] and therefore we can model check AG against temporal properties like LTL formulae. The number of states in AG is bounded by $\#\sigma \times \#P \times \#Z$ where $\#\sigma$ is the number of valuations of Var; $\#P$ is the number of process expressions and $\#Z$ is the number of zones. $\#\sigma$ is finite by assumption. $\#P$ is infinite for two reasons. Firstly, due to unbounded recursion, P can be infinitely long. For example, define $P_0 = e \rightarrow (P_0 \parallel P_{new})$ which forks a process P_{new} every time e occurs. The resultant process therefore may contain unboundedly many copies of P_{new}. In this work, we assume that P always has a bounded length, following existing approaches [17]. Secondly, because different timed process instances have different clocks, unboundedly many clocks are used. As a result, there are infinitely many different P and Z. Because P has a bounded length by assumption, there is a bound K on the number of overlapping activated clocks (since every clock is associated with one timed process instance in P). Hence, we can systematically rename the clocks in P (and correspondingly in Z) to a set of reserved K clocks.

Let $C = \{x_1, x_2, \cdots, x_K\}$ be the set of reserved clocks. Given any state (σ, P, Z), for any clock x in $clock(P)$, if $x \notin C$, then x is renamed to an available clock in $C \backslash clock(P)$. As a result, only K clocks are necessary and thus $\#P$ is finite. Lastly, it can be shown that all clocks in STCSP have upper bounds (i.e., $c \le d$ for all clock c and some integer d) and hence $\#Z$ is finite if the number of clocks is finite. Notice that zone normalization is not necessary. This is exactly the approach proposed in [23]. We refer to the LTS constructed in the above way as RAG (short for renamed abstract graph).

3.2 Emptiness Check

In [23], we present an algorithm to solve the emptiness problem based on *RAG*, with a complexity linear in the size of *RAG*. The next theorem reduces the emptiness checking problem to an SCC search problem, the proof of which can be found in [23].

Theorem 1. *A model is non-empty if and only if RAG contains a reachable (maximum) strongly connected component (SCC) scc such that*

† *not all transitions connecting two states in scc are instantaneous; and*
‡ $\{clock(P) \mid (\sigma, P, Z) \ in \ scc\} = \varnothing$.   □

Intuitively, the second condition states that every clock is pruned eventually. The above theorem implies that in order to solve the emptiness problem, we need to test each SCC against two conditions: whether it contains a transition which can be locally delayed; and whether every clock is reset later. Notice that both checks have a complexity linear in the size of the SCC. This leads to the algorithm shown in Algorithm 1. It takes a

---

Algorithm 1. Previous emptiness checking algorithm for STCSP

Algorithm *NonEmptinessChecking* {
1.   **while** (there are un-explored states) {
2.   find a new SCC *scc*;
3.   **if** (*scc* satisfies † and ‡) { **return** true; }
4.   }
5.   **return** false;
6. }

STCSP model as input, and constructs *RAG* on-the-fly while applying Tarjan's algorithm to identify SCCs. Once an SCC is found, we check whether it satisfies † and ‡. If yes, it returns true at line 3. After checking all SCCs, it returns false. The complexity of the algorithm is linear in time $|RAG|$ (which is due to Tarjan's algorithm for identifying SCC). The overhead of checking † and ‡ is minor.

4 Improved Emptiness Checking Algorithm

In this work, we show that we can improve the performance of emptiness checking using a clock symmetry reduction method.

4.1 Clock Symmetry Reduction

The zone abstraction presented above relies on associating timed processes with explicit clocks. Note that the clock names are irrelevant, except for distinguishing different timed processes. Consider two configurations (σ, P, Z) and (σ, P', Z') such that

$$P = Wait_{c_1}[5] \parallel (Q_0 \ timeout_{c_2}[6] \ Q_1) \ \text{and} \ Z = c_2 \leq c_1$$
$$P' = Wait_{c_2}[5] \parallel (Q_0 \ timeout_{c_1}[6] \ Q_1) \ \text{and} \ Z' = c_1 \leq c_2$$

They are exactly the same if we interchange clock c_1 and c_2. In fact, *all clocks are fully symmetric*, since they are implicit and 'introduced' anyway. In the following, we present a method which systematically detects such equivalent states, and potentially reduces the state space by a factor of K factorial. Later, we show that it can be combined with our algorithm for emptiness check.

Observe that there is a fixed ordering on the clocks in $clock(P)$ for any process P, e.g., from left to right as they appear in P. For instance, P as defined above has the sequence $\langle c_1, c_2 \rangle$, where P' has the sequence $\langle c_2, c_1 \rangle$. Let $\langle c_1, c_2, \cdots \rangle$ be the sequence of clocks in $clock(P)$ with the ordering. Recall that $C = \{x_1, x_2, \cdots, x_K\}$ is the set of reserved clocks. We define a function *map* such that $map(c_i) = x_i$ for all i, i.e., mapping the first clock in the sequence to the first reserved clock x_1 and the second to x_2, etc. In an abuse of notation, we write $map(\sigma, P_1, Z_1)$ to denote the abstract configuration (σ, P_2, Z_2) such that any clock c_i in $clock(P_1)$ is renamed to x_i in P_2 and Z_2. It is easy to see that (σ, P_1, Z_1) and (σ, P_2, Z_2) are equivalent. For instance, the above two configurations are mapped to the same configuration (σ, P'', Z'') such that P'' is $Wait_{x_1}[5] \parallel (Q_0 \ timeout_{x_2}[6] \ Q_1)$ and Z'' is $x_2 \leq x_1$.

Given a model (Var, σ_0, P_0) and its abstract zone graph AG, we obtain a QAG (short for quotient abstract graph) after applying function *map* to every state of AG, i.e., an abstract LTS $(S, init, \Sigma, T)$ such that S is a set of abstract states (σ, P, Z) such that Z is not empty; $init = map(clean(\sigma_0, P_0, true))$ is the initial state; Σ is the alphabet; and T contains a transition $((\sigma, P, Z), e, (\sigma', P', Z'))$ if and only if $(\sigma, P, Z) \xrightarrow{e} (\sigma', P'', Z'')$ and $(\sigma', P', Z') = map(clean(\sigma', P'', Z''))$. Lastly, since the clocks in P always appear in the same ordering, we can re-order the clocks in Z such that they follow the same order. *Afterwards, the clock names are irrelevant and the clocks can be anonymized.*

Corollary 1. *AG and QAG are time-abstract bi-similar.* □

Two zone graphs are time-abstract bi-similar if and only if there exists a time-abstract bi-simulation relation between them [23]. In [23], we proved that CG and AG are time-abstract bi-similar. Corollary 1 can be proved similarly.

4.2   *QAG* Extension

Notice that Theorem 1 requires to check whether a clock is pruned in order to determine whether an SCC is non-Zeno, anonymizing the clocks in QAG makes it infeasible to track which clock is pruned. To solve this problem, we extend QAG with two transition labels. One is a set of resetting clocks to tell whether a clock is reset later. The other is a Boolean flag to tell whether a transition can be delayed locally. We start with the former.

Let x_0 be another reserved clock, which is not in the set C of reserved clocks presented before. We define a new function *newclean* that satisfies the following: for every (σ, P, Z), $newclean(\sigma, P, Z) = (\sigma, P, Z' \wedge x_0 = 0)$ if $clean(\sigma, P, Z) = (\sigma, P, Z')$. Intuitively, function *newclean* is the same as function *clean* except that it introduces a new clock x_0. The idea is to have a clock at 0 for every state so that by looking at the value of x_0 after a transition, we can infer whether the transition is required to occur immediately. For instance, given $(\sigma_0, Q_0, Z_0) \xrightarrow{e} (\sigma_1, Q_1, Z_1)$ (where x_0 is set to 0 in Z_0), we can infer that the transition must occur immediately if Z_1 implies $x_0 = 0$.

Notice that given a system run in STCSP, a transition that can be *locally* delayed may in fact be constrained to occur immediately *globally*. Consider the following example: $(e \rightarrow Wait[5])$ *deadline*$[5]$. If we only consider event e, it is only constrained to occur within 5 time units. However, because the process $e \rightarrow Wait[5]$ is constrained to terminate within 5 time units, e must occur immediately.

In the following, we augment *QAG* so as to solve the emptiness problem. Given any transition $((\sigma, P, Z), e, (\sigma', P'', Z''))$ in *QAG*, by definition there exists P' and Z' such that $(\sigma, P, Z) \xrightarrow{e} (\sigma', P', Z')$ and $map(newclean(\sigma', P', Z')) = (\sigma', P'', Z'')$. We associate the transitions with three additional labels. Let $\langle x_1, x_2, \cdots, x_m \rangle$ be the sequence of clocks appearing in P; and $\langle x_1, x_2, \cdots, x_n \rangle$ be the sequence of clocks appearing in P''. Notice that all clocks in P and P'' have been mapped to the set of reserved clocks. The additional labels are:

- a Boolean flag b to indicate whether the transition can be locally delayed.
- a set of indices $R = \{i_1, i_2, \cdots\}$ such that for all i in the set, x_i is in $clock(P)$ but not $clock(P')$, i.e., the indices of clocks which are removed.
- a mapping f such that $f(i) = j$ if $map(x_i) = x_j$ for all $i \notin R$.

A run is then $\langle s_0, (e_0, b_0, R_0, f_0), s_1, (e_1, b_1, R_1, f_1), \cdots \rangle$. With the label R and f, given any state $s_k = (\sigma_k, P_k, Z_k)$ in the sequence, and the i-th clock x_i in the sequence of clocks in P_k, we can check whether x_i is removed later. A clock is removed later if it is removed immediately or renamed to a clock which is removed later. That is, x_i at s_k is removed if and only if there exists $l \geq k$ such that $l = k$ and $i \in R_k$; or $f_k(i) = j$ and clock x_j at s_{i+1} is removed later.

Theorem 2. *Let* $\pi = \langle s_0, (e_0, b_0, R_0, f_0), s_1, (e_1, b_1, R_1, f_1), \cdots \rangle$ *be a run of QAG.* π *is non-Zeno if and only if*

* *there exists infinitely many k such that $b_k = true$;*
⋆ *and for all m, every $x_i \in clocks(P_m)$ is removed later.*   □

Proof : Recall that every clock is associated with a timed process and every clock is bounded from above. A clock thus puts an upper bound on the execution time of every transition of a segment of the run, i.e., from the moment the clock is activated to the moment the clock is removed.

(**only-if**) If π is non-Zeno, * is trivially true. Since every clock is bounded from above, every clock must be removed since by definition its value goes unbounded along the run; otherwise, we have an empty zone and thus an infeasible run. Hence, ⋆ is true.

(**if**) In the following, we show that if * and ⋆ are true, thus π is progressive [2] and thus non-Zeno. Let the following be a segment of π.

$$\langle s_i, (e_i, b_i, R_i, f_i), s_{i+1}, \cdots, (e_{i+k}, b_{i+k}, R_{i+k}, f_{i+k}), s_{i+k+1} \rangle$$

such that $b_i = true$ and all clocks in the process of s_i are removed before or at the last transition of the segment. Because there are infinitely many such segments, in order to prove that the run is progressive, it is sufficient to show that the segment takes a positive integer amount of time. Let y_j denote the number of time units that can elapse from state s_j to s_{j+1} where $i \leq j \leq i + k$. For each clock c used in the segment (including those not in s_i), assume that clock c is present at state s_m and not removed until state s_{m+n+1} where $i \le m \le m+n \le i+k$ (i.e., its life-span in the segment). We have a constraint of the following form, which puts an upper bound on the total time of a part of the segment.

$$ y_m + y_{m+1} + \cdots + y_{m+n} \sim d_c \qquad - (C1) $$

where $\sim \in \{\le, =\}$. Because b_i is true, it is implied that $d_c > 0$ if $m = i$ (by assumption $b_i = true$). In the following, we analyze all three cases and show the theorem holds.

- If $d_c = 0$ (which implies $m > i$), $y_m, \cdots, y_{m+n}$ must all be 0. For the constraint on any clock c', we can substitute $y_m, \cdots, y_{m+n}$ with 0 and get a constraint in the same form but with $d_{c'} > 0$. Notice that by $*$, it is guaranteed that not all $d_{c'}$ is 0.
- If $d_c > 0$ for all constraints and if $\sim$ is $=$, then the segment takes at least d (which is a positive integer) time and therefore we conclude that π is non-Zeno.
- If $d_c > 0$ for all constraints and $\sim$ is $\le$, the constraints are satisfiable with $y_i = d_{min}$ (i.e., y_i equals the minimum of all ds and the rest of the variables equal to 0). Therefore, we conclude that π is non-Zeno.

With the above, we conclude that the theorem holds.   □

4.3   Improved Emptiness Check

In the following, we extend Algorithm 1 for STCSP. Notice that emptiness check based on QAG is more complicated as we do not maintain clock names (and hence telling whether a clock is removed later is not as straightforward). By Theorem 2, every clock of every state in a run must be checked in order to determine whether the run is non-Zeno or not. The following theorem simplified the task by showing that it is sufficient to check *any* state which is visited infinitely often.

Theorem 3. *A model is non-empty iff QAG contains a reachable (maximum) SCC such that*

  † *it contains a transition $(s, (e, b, R, f), s')$ where $b = true$;*
  ‡ *and there is a state (σ, P, Z) in the SCC satisfies that for every clock in $clock(P)$, there is a path from (σ, P, Z) in the SCC such that the clock is removed along the path.*   □

Proof: (**only-if**) Assume that QAG is non-empty, since QAG is finite-state, there must be a non-Zeno run and the run must visit a set of states/transitions X infinitely often. There must be an SCC which contains X. X must contain a transition with a label b being true (by contradiction) and therefore † is trivially true. Similarly, every clock of a state in X (which is a state in the SCC) must be removed later (by definition). Thus, there exists some states (σ, P, Z) in the SCC such that every clock in $clock(P)$ is removed later. For every other state (σ', P', Z') in the SCC, because (σ', P', Z') can always reach (σ, P, Z), every clock in $clock(P')$ is removed too (either before reaching (σ, P, Z) or after).

(**if**) Assume there exists an SCC satisfying † and ‡. Let π be a run that visits every

---

Algorithm 2. Algorithm for STCSP emptiness check

Algorithm *NonEmpty* {	**Algorithm** *IsRemoved(s, x)* {
1. **while** (there are un-explored states) {	1. **return** false if (s, x) has been explored;
2. find a new SCC *scc*;	2. **foreach** transition $(s, (e, b, R, f), s')$ {
3. **if** (*scc* satisfies †) {	3. **if** ($x \in R$ or *IsRemoved(s', f(x))*) {
4. **let** $s = (\sigma, P, Z)$ be a state in *scc*;	4. **return** true; }
5. **foreach** clock x in *clock(P)* {	5. }
6. **if** (!IsRemoved(s, x)){	6. **return** false;
7. **goto** line 1; }	}
8. }	
9. **return** true;	
10. }	
11. }	
12. **return** false;	
}	

---

state/transition in the SCC infinitely often. It is straightforward to see that π satisfies $*$ of Theorem 2 because of †. By ‡, there exists a state s such that every clock c at s is removed later (by visiting s multiple times and each time choosing a path which removes a different clock). For every other state s' in the SCC, there exists a path from s' to s. A clock at s' is either removed before reaching s or removed afterwards (since all clocks at s are removed later). Therefore, $\star$ is satisfied. Thus, π is non-Zeno by Theorem 2 and *QAG* is non-empty.

Therefore, we conclude that the theorem holds.   □

The above theorem implies that in order to solve the emptiness problem, we need to check each SCC to see whether it contains a transition that can be locally delayed; and whether all clocks of *any* state are removed later. This leads to the algorithms shown in Algorithm 2. Given a model (Var, σ_0, P_0), algorithm *NonEmpty* constructs *QAG* on-the-fly while applying Tarjan's algorithm to identify SCCs. Once an SCC is found, we check whether it satisfies † (line 3). Lines 4 to 10 then check whether ‡ is satisfied. Notice that at line 4, any state can be picked. For efficiency, we always pick the state in the SCC which has the least number of clocks (since it is sufficient to check any state). The inner loop from line 5 to 8 then checks whether every clock of the state is removed later using algorithm *IsRemoved*. Given a state s and a clock x at the state, algorithm *IsRemoved* returns true if and only if x is removed later. Line 1 of algorithm *IsRemoved* prevents the same pair (a state and a clock) from being explored again, so that the algorithm becomes terminating. Lines 2 to 5 check whether x is removed along any of the outgoing transitions or the renamed clock $f(x)$ is removed at the post-state s' (through a recursive call). If yes, it returns true at line 4. Otherwise, it returns false at line 6. Notice that at line 6 of algorithm *NonEmpty*, if any clock is not removed, then by Theorem 3 there is no non-Zeno run visiting states of the SCC infinitely often and therefore we drop the SCC and go on with checking other unexplored SCCs. If all

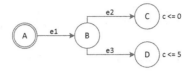

Fig. 2. A general Timed Automaton example

clocks are removed, we return true at line 9 since the run which visits all states and transitions in the SCC infinitely often must be non-Zeno.

The correctness of algorithm can be established based on Theorem 3 straightforwardly. Given that it has been established that QAG is finite, it is obvious that the algorithm is terminating. In the worst case, the algorithm runs in time $\mathcal{O}(|QAG|+K^2\cdot|QAG|)$ where $|QAG|$ is the number of transitions in QAG and K is the maximum number of clocks in any state. Firstly, Tarjan's algorithm runs in time $|QAG|$. Secondly, the overhead of checking † is negligible. Lastly, given an SCC in QAG, the algorithm for checking ‡ run in time $\mathcal{O}(K_{min} \cdot K_{max} \cdot |SCC|)$ where K_{min} (and K_{max}) is the minimum (and maximum) number of clocks in any state of the SCC and $|SCC|$ is the number of transitions in the SCC. In particular, if there exists a state with no clock (i.e., $K_{min} = 0$), we conclude ‡ is satisfied right away.

In practice, the algorithm performs better than the upper bound complexity for several reasons. Firstly, the algorithm often terminates early as it constructs the state space on-the-fly and terminates as soon as an SCC satisfying † and ‡ is found. Secondly, the overhead of checking ‡ is reduced when (A) we find that a clock is not removed later (in which case we conclude ‡ is not satisfied by the SCC); (B) or we find a transition satisfying a constraint of the form $c = d$ where c is a clock activated at some state in the SCC (in which case we conclude ‡ is true, as at least d time units have elapsed since c is activated). In addition, notice that not all SCCs need to be checked against ‡. For instance, only SCCs which satisfy † (and acceptance conditions from the property, e.g., containing a Büchi accepting state if the property is LTL) are to be checked.

Notice that our approach does not work for Timed Automata in general. Because for every clock in our model, the constraints on the clocks remain the same throughout its life-span, *along any path in the graph*. This allows us to obtain a set of constraints on segments of a run in the form of $(C1)$ (refer the proof of Theorem 2) and also allows us to detect whether a transition can be locally delayed, without referring to a particular path. In the setting of Timed Automata, given any state, the constraints on a clock differ if different paths are taken from the state. For instance, given a Timed Automaton shown in Figure 2, where state A is the initial state and c is a clock. The transition from A to B can be delayed given the path from A to D but not the path from A to C. Interested readers are referred to [22] on how to extend Algorithm 1 to Timed Automata. This work is however orthogonal to [22] as the clock-symmetry reduction is specific to STCSP.

5   Evaluation

We extend PAT model checker [23] to support model checking with non-Zenoness using our method. We evaluate its efficiency using five examples. The first three are benchmark systems modeled in STCSP: Fischer's mutual exclusion algorithm, the railway control system, and the CSMA/CD protocol. In addition, we model and verify two hierarchical systems: a simplified pacemaker [3], and a multi-lift system. All models are available online [21]. We remark that modeling the latter two systems in Timed Automata could be non-trivial due to system hierarchy.

The pacemaker example models an electronic implanted device which functions to regulate the heart beat by electrically stimulating the heart to contract and thus to pump blood throughout the body. Quantitative timing is crucial for pacemakers. A pacemaker can operate in many different modes according to the implanted patient's heart problem. We skip the details and refer the readers to [21]. The verified property is that always either a heart beat is detected or the pacemaker eventually stimulates one. The lift system is a standard case study used to demonstrate the power of various specification/verification techniques. It is hierarchical, i.e., the system contains multiple lifts, floors, users, and a central controller; each lift contains a local controller, a button panel; and each local controller is composed of multiple processes (for controlling the shaft, maintaining the request queue, etc.); etc. Furthermore, real-time is an important aspect of the system, e.g., a lift door opens for a certain number of time units; a lift travels at certain speed; etc. The verified property is that a lift door eventually closes.

In our experiments, in order to focus on the reduction obtained using the new method, simple LTL properties which are true are chosen. Notice that because the model checking algorithm is on-the-fly, its performance depends on the searching order in the presence of a counterexample. Table 1 summarizes the experimental results, obtained on a server running 64-bit Windows with Intel Xeon CPU at 2.13GHz and 32GB RAM. Column *RZG* shows the verification statistics based on constructing *RZG* (which renames clocks but not anonymize them). Column K shows the maximum number of overlapping clocks. Column *+Zeno* shows the verification time *without* the non-Zenoness assumption, and *−Zeno* shows the verification time *with* the non-Zenoness assumption. Similarly, column *QAG* shows the verification statistics based on constructing *QAG*. Column *OH* shows the overhead of non-Zenoness check and column *Speedup* shows the improvement. Note that '-' means that the data is not available (either out of memory or running for more than 8 hours). The memory consumption in PAT cannot be measured accurately due to limitation of managed memory in .NET framework. The number of states can reflect the real memory usage.

A few observations can be made based on the results. Firstly, it can be shown from the data that non-Zenoness checking incurs some overhead. The theoretical study shows that in the worst case the state space could be enlarged by a factor of $1 + K^2$, whereas in all the experiments, model checking with non-Zenoness takes three times less than the time needed for model checking without non-Zenoness. In average, the overhead is 58% of the verification time without non-Zenoness. Secondly, the experiment results confirm that the verification is significantly faster compared to [23] in all cases, because clock symmetry reduction is combined with non-Zenoness check. The speedup ranges from 2 to 90.25 times. In average, the speedup is 17 for this set of experiments. It can be further noticed that though in theory that the more clocks, the more potential speedup there is, the actual speedup depends on the particular models.

Table 1. Experiment results for STCSP model checking with non-Zenoness

Model	K	RZG			QAG				Speedup	
		States	+Zeno(s)	-Zeno(s)	States	+Zeno(s)	-Zeno(s)	OH	+Zeno	-Zeno
Fischer*5	5	1.1M	180	361	36K	3	4	33%	60	90.25
Fischer*6	6	-	-	-	291K	50	73	46%	-	-
Fischer*7	7	-	-	-	2.6M	1557	4522	190%	-	-
Railway*6	4	158K	14	16	74K	6	6	0%	2.33	2.67
Railway*7	4	1.1M	143	203	527K	44	53	15%	3.25	3.83
Railway*8	4	9.1M	4895	8104	4.3M	818	1339	64%	5.98	13.55
CSMA*6	5	30K	4	5	15K	2	2	0%	2	2.5
CSMA*8	5	237K	46	54	119K	20	21	5%	2.3	2.57
CSMA*10	5	1.6M	1012	1291	803K	239	338	64%	4.23	3.82
Pacemaker	-	-	-	-	1.2M	8711	-	-	-	-
Lift*2*2	4	8.7M	12271	22260	756K	297	728	145%	42.31	30.57

6 Related Work

This work is related to research on hierarchical real-time system modeling and verification. Compositional specification for real-time systems based on timed process algebras has been studied extensively [16,29,18,23]. The closely related work is STCSP [23] which integrates timed process constructs with data variables in order to model complex systems. In [23], zone abstraction, which has been proven successful for Timed Automata, is adopted and used to verify STCSP models. The idea is to explicitly associate clocks with each timed process constructs and use constraints to represent clock values. Furthermore, the approach in [23] is designed to minimize the number of clocks by sharing clocks among all process constructs which are activated at the same time. This work improves [23] by reducing the size of the zone graph significantly (through exploring the symmetry among the clocks). Furthermore, we show that the emptiness problem can be solved based on the reduced zone graph.

This work is also related to research on model checking with non-Zenoness. In [24], it has been shown that zone graphs generated from Timed Automata are too abstract to directly infer time progress and hence non-Zenoness. Syntactic conditions for Timed Automata to be free from Zeno runs have been identified. In [24,27], the authors showed that every Timed Automaton can be transformed into a strongly non-Zeno one, for which, the emptiness problem can be solved easily. The price to pay is an extra clock. Recently, it has been shown that adding one clock may result in an exponentially larger zone graph [13]. The proposed remedy is to transform the zone graph into a *guess zone graph* by introducing extra states. A path of the guess zone graph is non-Zeno if all clocks which are bounded from above are reset infinitely often during the run and the run visits an extra state such that the clocks can be strictly positive [13]. The guess zone graph is $|C| + 1$ times larger than the zone graph and the complexity of the proposed algorithm is $|ZG| \cdot (|C| + 1)^2$ where ZG is the size of the zone graph and $|C|$ is the number of clocks. In addition, this work is remotely related to the work on non-Zeno real-time game strategy [7], which however is not based on zone abstraction, whereas our work is on solving a problem on combining zone abstraction and non-Zenoness. In this work, we show that zone graphs generated from Stateful Timed CSP models are different as all clocks are bounded from above and cannot be reset arbitrarily. As a result, detecting Zeno runs based on zone graphs is feasible. In addition, this work is also related to the work on applying symmetry reduction technique in model checkers, e.g., adding symmetry reduction to UPPAAL [10], exploiting symmetry in RED [28], etc.

In terms of tool support for model checking with non-Zenoness, UPPAAL [15] and KRONOS [5] and RT Spin [26] allow some form of non-Zenoness detection. UPPAAL relies on test automata [1] and leads-to properties. The problem with this approach is that it is sufficient-only. KRONOS supports an expressive language for specifying properties, which allows encoding of a sufficient and necessary condition for non-Zenoness. Checking for non-Zenoness in KRONOS is expensive. The non-Zenoness checking algorithm implemented in RT Spin is unsound [26]. Furthermore, an alternative approach has been proposed by the author in [25]. It is however never implemented. As far as we know, our implementation in PAT is the only model checker that supports model checking LTL with the non-Zenoness assumption.

7   Conclusion

Our contribution in this work is threefold. Firstly, we improve our previous work for STCSP significantly by combining the emptiness checking algorithm with a clock-symmetry reduction method. Secondly, we realize our method in the context of model checking LTL through various benchmark systems and show that it can be used with minor overhead. Lastly, we develop a software toolkit to support model checking LTL with the non-Zenoness assumption.

As for future work, we are investigating how to check timed refinement relationship between two Stateful Timed CSP models with the assumption of non-Zenoness.

Acknowledgment. This work is jointly supported by the project "ZJURP1100105" from Singapore University of Technology and Design, by NSFC Program (No.61103032) and by the National 973 Fundamental Research and Development Program of China under the Grant 2009CB320701.

References

1. Aceto, L., Bouyer, P., Burgueño, A., Larsen, K.G.: The Power of Reachability Testing for Timed Automata. Theoretical Computer Science 300(1-3), 411–475 (2003)
2. Alur, R., Dill, D.L.: A Theory of Timed Automata. Theoretical Computer Science 126, 183–235 (1994)
3. Barold, S.S., Stroopbandt, R.X., Sinnaeve, A.F.: Cardiac Pacemakers Step by Step: an Illustrated Guide. Blachwell Publishing (2004)
4. Beyer, D., Rust, H.: Concepts of Cottbus Timed Automata. In: FBT, pp. 27–34 (1999)
5. Bozga, M., Daws, C., Maler, O., Olivero, A., Tripakis, S., Yovine, S.: Kronos: A Model-Checking Tool for Real-Time Systems. In: Vardi, M.Y. (ed.) CAV 1998. LNCS, vol. 1427, pp. 546–550. Springer, Heidelberg (1998)

6. Cattani, S., Kwiatkowska, M.Z.: A Refinement-based Process Algebra for Timed Automata. Formal Asp. Comput. 17(2), 138–159 (2005)

7. Chatterjee, K., Prabhu, V.S.: Synthesis of Memory-efficient "Real-time" Controllers for Safety Objectives. In: HSCC, pp. 221–230. ACM (2011)

8. David, A., Larsen, K.G., Legay, A., Nyman, U., Wąsowski, A.: ECDAR: An Environment for Compositional Design and Analysis of Real Time Systems. In: Bouajjani, A., Chin, W.-N. (eds.) ATVA 2010. LNCS, vol. 6252, pp. 365–370. Springer, Heidelberg (2010)

9. Dong, J.S., Hao, P., Qin, S., Sun, J.: Wang Yi. Timed Automata Patterns. IEEE Transactions on Software Engineering 34(6), 844–859 (2008)

10. Hendriks, M., Behrmann, G., Larsen, K., Niebert, P., Vaandrager, F.: Adding Symmetry Reduction to Uppaal. Springer (2004)

11. Henzinger, T.A., Nicollin, X., Sifakis, J., Yovine, S.: Symbolic Model Checking for Real-Time Systems. Information and Computation 111(2), 193–244 (1994)

12. Herbreteau, F., Srivathsan, B.: Efficient On-the-Fly Emptiness Check for Timed Büchi Automata. In: Bouajjani, A., Chin, W.-N. (eds.) ATVA 2010. LNCS, vol. 6252, pp. 218–232. Springer, Heidelberg (2010)

13. Herbreteau, F., Srivathsan, B., Walukiewicz, I.: Efficient Emptiness Check for Timed Büchi Automata. In: Touili, T., Cook, B., Jackson, P. (eds.) CAV 2010. LNCS, vol. 6174, pp. 148–161. Springer, Heidelberg (2010)

14. Hoare, C.A.R.: Communicating Sequential Processes. International Series in Computer Science. Prentice-Hall (1985)

15. Larsen, K.G., Pettersson, P., Wang, Y.: Uppaal in a Nutshell. International Journal on Software Tools for Technology Transfer 1(1-2), 134–152 (1997)

16. Nicollin, X., Sifakis, J.: The Algebra of Timed Processes, ATP: Theory and Application. Information and Computation 114(1), 131–178 (1994)

17. Ouaknine, J., Worrell, J.: Timed CSP = Closed Timed Safety Automata. Electr. Notes Theor. Comput. Sci. 68(2) (2002)

18. Reed, G.M., Roscoe, A.W.: A Timed Model for Communicating Sequential Processes. In: Kott, L. (ed.) ICALP 1986. LNCS, vol. 226, pp. 314–323. Springer, Heidelberg (1986)

19. Schneider, S.: Concurrent and Real-time Systems. John Wiley and Sons (2000)

20. Schneider, S., Davies, J., Jackson, D.M., Reed, G.M., Reed, J.N., Roscoe, A.W.: Timed CSP: Theory and Practice. In: Huizing, C., de Bakker, J.W., Rozenberg, G., de Roever, W.-P. (eds.) REX 1991. LNCS, vol. 600, pp. 640–675. Springer, Heidelberg (1992)

21. Si, Y.J., Sun, J., Liu, Y., Wang, T., Dong, J.S.: Improving Model Checking Stateful Timed CSP with non-Zenoness through Clock-Symmetry Reduction,
http://www.comp.nus.edu.sg/~pat/stcsp

22. Si, Y.J., Sun, J., Wang, X.Y., Wang, T., Liu, Y., Dong, J.S., Yang, X.H., Li, X.H.: An Analytical Study on Non-Zenoness Checking for Timed Automata. IEEE Transactions on Software Engineering (submitted, 2013)

23. Sun, J., Liu, Y., Dong, J.S., Liu, Y., Shi, L., André, É.: Modeling and verifying hierarchical real-time systems using stateful timed csp. ACM Transactions on Software Engineering and Methodology (TOSEM) 22(1), 3 (2013)

24. Tripakis, S.: Verifying Progress in Timed Systems. In: Katoen, J.-P. (ed.) ARTS 1999. LNCS, vol. 1601, pp. 299–314. Springer, Heidelberg (1999)

25. Tripakis, S.: Checking Timed Büchi Automata Emptiness on Simulation Graphs. ACM Trans. Comput. Log. 10(3) (2009)

26. Tripakis, S., Courcoubetis, C.: Extending Promela and Spin for Real Time. In: Margaria, T., Steffen, B. (eds.) TACAS 1996. LNCS, vol. 1055, pp. 329–348. Springer, Heidelberg (1996)

27. Tripakis, S., Yovine, S., Bouajjani, A.: Checking Timed Büchi Automata Emptiness Efficiently. FMSD 26(3), 267–292 (2005)

28. Wang, F., Schmidt, K.: Symmetric symbolic safety-analysis of concurrent software with pointer data structures. In: Peled, D.A., Vardi, M.Y. (eds.) FORTE 2002. LNCS, vol. 2529, pp. 50–64. Springer, Heidelberg (2002)

29. Wang, Y.: CCS + Time = An Interleaving Model for Real Time Systems. In: Leach Albert, J., Monien, B., Rodríguez-Artalejo, M. (eds.) ICALP 1991. LNCS, vol. 510, pp. 217–228. Springer, Heidelberg (1991)

A Modular Approach for Reusing Formalisms in Verification Tools of Concurrent Systems

Étienne André[1], Benoît Barbot[2], Clément Démoulins[3], Lom Messan Hillah[4], Francis Hulin-Hubard[2], Fabrice Kordon[4], Alban Linard[2], and Laure Petrucci[1]

[1] Université Paris 13, Sorbonne Paris Cité, LIPN, CNRS, UMR 7030, F-93430, Villetaneuse, France
[2] LSV, CNRS, INRIA & ENS Cachan, France
[3] EPITA Research and Development Laboratory (LRDE), France
[4] LIP6, CNRS UMR 7606, Université P. & M. Curie and Université P. Ouest, France

Abstract. Over the past two decades, numerous verification tools have been successfully used for verifying complex concurrent systems, modelled using various formalisms. However, it is still hard to coordinate these tools since they rely on such a large number of formalisms. Having a proper syntactical mechanism to interrelate them through variability would increase the capability of effective integrated formal methods. In this paper, we propose a modular approach for defining new formalisms by reusing existing ones and adding new features and/or constraints. Our approach relies on standard XML technologies; their use provides the capability of rapidly and automatically obtaining tools for representing and validating models. It thus enables fast iterations in developing and testing complex formalisms. As a case study, we applied our modular definition approach on families of Petri nets and timed automata.

Keywords: Formal methods, Model Driven Engineering, Interoperability, Reusability, Concurrent Systems, Model Checking.

1 Introduction

Research teams have built over the past two decades numerous verification tools that have successfully been applied to case studies. Formal models used by these tools are described by formalisms. We call *formalism* a metamodel for a formal notation. A formalism describes the entities to be found in the notation but it also associates these with a behavioural semantics.

In this work, we focus on formal notations that are all dedicated to the description of distributed and concurrent systems behaviour. Hence, their operational semantics (i.e. how they can be executed) must be mathematically founded to enable automated reasoning techniques such as model checking. Another characteristic of these notations is to be graph-based. This encompasses (but is not limited to) automata, Petri nets and their variants.

Each of these numerous tools handles its own set of formalisms, in its own set of syntactic formats, which makes it hard to harness their verification power into

L. Groves and J. Sun (Eds.): ICFEM 2013, LNCS 8144, pp. 199–214, 2013.
© Springer-Verlag Berlin Heidelberg 2013

integrated platforms. Some attempts have however been successful in integrating various model checking tools into a single platform. One notable instance is the CPN-AMI platform [10], used worldwide since the 1990's.

As part of the MeFoSyLoMa[1] community, we have had a long tradition of maintaining this platform. The continuous maintenance has become very costly and questionable recently, as new tools requirements in terms of new formalisms and interoperability dramatically increased the time and effort required to build adapters and wrappers for their integration. Moreover, the local syntax of CPN-AMI could no longer cope with the constructs in the new formalisms handled by the new tools. This is especially the case for the compositional and hierarchical aspects. Therefore, its extension in its current form turned out not to be a viable option.

Contribution. This context led us to start the development of a new, flexible and extensible syntactic framework for the integration of new formalisms. The supporting format is now XML-based, more specifically on the RELAX-NG standard [14]. We designed the new open format with extensibility in mind, to allow quick and easy definitions of new formalisms, by reusing existing constructs.

A major benefit of this approach is to provide the capability to rapidly and automatically obtain tools for representing and validating models. It thus also reduces the engineering effort to integrate new tools, as libraries to handle models of their formalisms are automatically generated.

We describe in this paper a modular approach for reusing syntactic definitions of formalisms, such as Petri nets and automata, in verification tools. We also report its successful implementation using XML technologies. This approach is implemented in a distributed and fully open platform, *CosyVerif* [3], making it possible for any research team to set up local tools in a server on their premises, and automatically register the provided services in the cloud of *CosyVerif*. The maintenance effort of several days required for CPN-AMI has now decreased to less than half a day for integrating formalisms and tools in *CosyVerif*. From the user point of the view, the use of any tool is greatly eased thanks to a user-intuitive graphical client.

Outline. Section 2 presents an overview of current techniques in modelling the abstract syntax of formal notations. With lessons learned from previous experiences, Section 3 describes our solution and details its implementation using standard XML-based technologies. An application to Petri nets and automata shows in Section 4 how we leveraged the combined use of these technologies to build an extensible and incremental architecture of interrelated formalisms. We also identify good practices for the definition and the reuse of formalisms. Section 5 presents the integration of our approach into the distributed platform *CosyVerif*. We identify future directions of research in Section 6.

---

[1] "Méthodes formelles pour les systèmes logiciels et matériels" (formal methods for software and hardware systems), see http://www.mefosyloma.fr

2   Related Work

Generally, tools work on models typed after a *formalism*. Tools taking as input the same formalism usually have a different syntax. For example, consider the case of timed automata [1]: among a few examples of tools taking as input (extensions of) timed automata – HyTech [11], Imitator [2], PAT [21] and Uppaal [20] – all have a very different input syntax. Manually translating a model from a given syntax into another one is cumbersome and error-prone; an automated translation can be performed, but must be defined for any pair of tools sharing the same input formalism. Hence unifying formalisms definitions is a necessary condition to an effective integration of heterogeneous tools.

Several approaches have attempted, with various degrees of success, to tackle this challenge, using model-based techniques, and sometimes backed by existing platforms.

2.1   Related Model-Based Approaches

A notable work using model-based techniques is the Petri nets standard, ISO/IEC 15909. Part 2 of this standard [16] defines the Petri Net Markup Language (PNML), a transfer format to foster interoperability among Petri net tools. The standard defines the abstract syntax of PNML using UML class diagram notation. It defines the format concrete representation using RELAX-NG. PNML is supported by PNML Framework [12], a generated Java library thanks to model-driven engineering techniques, relying on the Eclipse Modeling Framework [22].

OMDoc[2] is a markup format and data model for Open Mathematical Documents, defining an ontology language for mathematical knowledge. No platform is associated with this work, but interfaces to existing tools (such as PVS or Coq) are available.

MoWGLI[3] builds on previous standards for the management and publication of mathematical documents (MathML, OpenMath, OMDoc). It relies on XML-based technologies (XSLT, RDF, etc.). However, it seems that there is no associated platform, and it looks like it is not maintained anymore.

2.2   Related Platforms

Several platforms have been designed over the past decade in order to achieve similar goals. CASL (Common Algebraic Specification Language) is a general-purpose specification language. A tool named HetCASL[4](Heterogeneous Tool Set) has been proposed, that incorporates different theorem provers and different specification languages, hence allowing the designer to handle heterogeneous specifications. This approach is very much theorem prover oriented (including connections with Isabelle, Maude, etc.). In contrast, *CosyVerif* is more general.

---

[2] http://www.omdoc.org/
[3] http://mowgli.cs.unibo.it/
[4] http://www.informatik.uni-bremen.de/agbkb/forschung/
formal_methods/CoFI/hets/

Diabelli [24] is a heterogeneous proof system, allowing one to perform theorem proving with both diagrammatic and sentential formulae, and proof steps. It is shipped as a standalone tool combining Isabelle and Speedith. The tool does feature a graphical interface, but models are given in a textual form only. We believe that this tool does not provide a high degree of flexibility (because it requires translations), and apparently it does not work in the cloud, contrarily to *CosyVerif*.

LTSmin [6] is a meta toolkit that supports different input language modules (mCRL2, Promela, etc.) relying on labeled transition systems (LTS). LTSmin allows LTS-based semantic exchanges of state space between different tools (based on a Partitioned Next-State function). Furthermore, it allows the end user to apply alternative verification algorithms to their native tool. However, the tool only works with a LTS-based semantics, whereas we aim at considering a larger set of formalisms.

Rich-model Toolkit[5] is a standardisation of formal languages: it features common formats for systems, formulae, proofs and counterexamples. Contrarily to our approach, it is SAT- and SMT-oriented, and algorithms seem to be built-in, although it is hard to get a precise idea of the features, since this is a very recent initiative.

StarExec[6] is an initiative of the logic community to build a shared logic solving infrastructure (SAT, SMT), to enable researchers to manage libraries, provide solver execution on a large cluster, and facilitate translation between logics. According to their system architecture specification, users interface with the infrastructure via a Web application.

PAT [21] is a multi-formalisms platform based on modules. Each module relies on its own formalism and domain of application (e.g. real-time systems, probabilistic systems, network calculus, etc.), and must provide a semantics in the form of LTS. Then, common algorithms (deadlock-checking, LTL-checking) can be used for any of the modules, in addition to domain-specific algorithms. It also features graphical facilities, a simulator, syntactical checkers, counterexample exhibition, etc. Different from our approach, PAT is mainly LTS-based (with additional integration of Markov Decision Processes and Timed Transition Systems), and formalisms are not related to each other, i.e. the modules are independent.

2.3   Discussion

Our approach is similar to the ISO/IEC 15909 standard in terms of formalism definition, and to StarExec, in terms of supporting platform. However there are notable differences.

In ISO/IEC 15909, only most popular Petri nets types are considered: P/T (places/transitions) nets, Symmetric and High-Level nets. Moreover, the identification of features variability to enable extensibility is an issue not completely

---

[5] http://richmodels.epfl.ch/
[6] http://www.starexec.org/starexec/public/about.jsp

solved due to a large family of types in the Petri net community. Many Petri net types are ad-hoc variants of mainstream or exotic types, defined for specific research purposes. So the right level of granularity among such a large family is hard to figure out for defining a feature-proof extensible framework in the standard. We learnt from this case, and now consider the issue from a graph-based approach: any graph-based formalism, including Petri nets and automata (our case study in Section 4) should be adequately integrated in the framework.

The StarExec platform builds upon a grid engine (Oracle Grid Engine), where solvers and benchmarks jobs are scheduled and dispatched over worker nodes, in a typical grid computing fashion. *CosyVerif* is more cloud-based, since each participant can set up his/her own tools server and automatically register the services it provides in the cloud. Moreover *CosyVerif* does not mandate a Web-based user interface for jobs submission. Users can interface with tools via existing front ends like Coloane (available from [23]), or via their own tools using a provided library.

3   A Unified Representation

One of our main goals is to address the high variability in formalisms definitions. For example, since the original definition of timed automata [1], many variants and extensions have been proposed, among which: timed automata with stopwatches, parametric timed automata, interrupt timed automata, hybrid automata, etc. And each of these variants and extensions are themselves subject of variants and extensions. The same applies to other families of formalisms such as Petri nets.

Our model-based solution mainly and directly relies on XML technologies. We use XML as it provides a common, flexible, and very expressive syntax. We decided not to start with a model-based high-level notation such as UML for formalism definition, to keep a lightweight approach, accessible to most tool developers, easy and fast to implement and test. Although verbose, XML can be given a precise semantics and, as XML is both a mature and widely used technology, numerous tools and libraries for manipulating XML files are available.

We defined a two-layered XML-based modelling language, depicted in Fig. 1a:

1. FML (Formalism Markup Language), that specifies the concepts of any graph-based formalism and their relationships;
2. GrML (Graph Markup Language), that specifies how a graph-based model, complying with a given FML formalism, is structured.

A user-defined formalism must comply with FML constructs, as per the relationship between **User Formalism** and **FML**. A compliance procedure checks the consistency of the user-defined formalism and its structure. Any **User Formalism**, since it is graph-based, is structured by the GrML language.

GrML is a language that describes a specification in the context of a given formalism. In other words, the user domain specific language is defined using FML, and the models of the domain must be structured as graphs in the associated

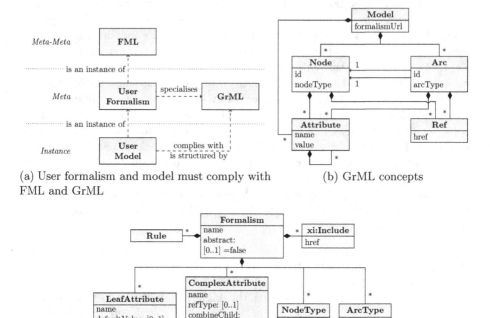

(a) User formalism and model must comply with FML and GrML

(b) GrML concepts

(c) FML concepts

Fig. 1. FML and GrML concepts

formalism, this being enforced by GrML. By analogy with a model-based specification language such as UML, FML defines the *superstructure* of our framework, while GrML defines its *infrastructure*.

We introduce in more details FML and GrML in the next two subsections.

3.1   FML: Formalism Markup Language

The characteristic elements of formalisms to be used are described using the FML language. FML caters for interdependent formalisms, allowing for hierarchical definitions.

The metamodel of FML, illustrated in Fig. 1c, defines the concepts of a graph-based formalism. When a **Formalism** is made *abstract*, it is intended to serve as the basis (root or intermediate) for a hierarchy of concrete formalisms of the same family. For instance, one may define the abstract graph of Petri nets (places, transitions and arcs), and then build the concrete type place/transition (P/T) net upon this primary definition. Note that "abstract: [0..1] = *false*" denotes that the attribute "abstract" is optional (its cardinality is 0 or 1); the notation "= *false*" indicates that its default value is false.

A **Formalism** is composed of **NodeType**, **ArcType**, **LeafAttribute** and **ComplexAttribute**. A **LeafAttribute** may have a scalar value (attribute "defaultValue"), and may refer to a concrete **NodeType** or **ArcType** (attribute "refType").

A **ComplexAttribute** is a structured attribute, which also allows for hierarchical composition of formalisms. In a Symmetric net for example, the marking of a place, composed of *tokens*, would be defined as an expression denoting a multiset of tuples where each token in a tuple may be a scalar value of a colour domain, or an expression using built-in Symmetric net functions (e.g. successor, predecessor, broadcast). This concept of tuple also exists in P/T nets, but refers there to a simple integer. This gives an example of reuse of the same notion (i.e. ComplexAttribute) with different definitions in different formalisms.

The hierarchy between formalism descriptions can be achieved by the relationship between **NodeType**, **ArcType** and **Ref**. Typically, in the Petri net model of a hierarchical system, submodels may be attached to a place or a transition.

Finally, reuse between formalisms to allow for compositional and incremental definitions is achieved thanks to the relationship between **Formalism** and the **xi:Include** construct. The latter represents the ability to use the XML XInclude technology[7] to import other formalisms. XInclude enables the inclusion of one or several XML documents into another one. This mechanism allows for defining new formalisms by simply composing one or several previously defined formalisms, and only defining the new features, in order to facilitate modularity. The grammar of FML (in RELAX-NG) is available on the *CosyVerif* Web page[8].

3.2   GrML: Graph Markup Language

The structure of a GrML model is described by the metamodel in Fig. 1b. A **Model** is a graph typed by a user formalism (referred to by the attribute "formalismUrl"). It consists of a set of **Node** and a set of **Arc**. The arcs connect the nodes. A node in a GrML model is typed by its "nodeType", declared in the corresponding formalism. The same principle applies to an arc (typed by its "arcType"). A **Ref** represents the link between two elements or between an element and a model (the reference is provided by its "href" attribute). Any referenced element must be identified by an "id" in the containing model file, and any referenced model is identified by the model file name. The reference ("href") value is an URI.

---

[7] http://www.w3.org/TR/xinclude/

[8] https://forge.cosyverif.org/projects/formalisms/
repository/entry/trunk/formalism.rng

A user model (Fig. 1a) is thus contained in a GrML document, an XML file describing a model and given in the form of an annotated graph. The model, its arcs and nodes can contain attributes given in the form of a tree and must comply with the associated FML description. The grammar of GrML (in RELAX-NG) is available on the *CosyVerif* Web page[9].

Finally note that verification tools implementing our approach can use GrML as an abstract syntax, and hence implement translation from/to their concrete syntax, or directly use GrML libraries.

3.3   Automated Compliance Checking

Our approach includes a mechanism for automatically checking the conformance of a GrML model with respect to its corresponding user-defined FML formalism and the FML language. It works as follows.

First, GrML and FML syntaxes are validated using RELAX-NG. Then, the content of a GrML file is checked against the corresponding description of its associated formalism. To do so, Schematron [15] rules are generated from the XML description of the formalism. Schematron is a rule-based validation language relying on XPATH[10] idioms to query and validate co-occurrence constraints in an XML file. We chose Schematron since an XML grammar cannot capture some particular constraints: for instance, "in a Petri net formalism, no arc should connect two nodes of the same type" (i.e. only arcs between a place and a transition – or vice versa – are allowed). Schematron is also used to perform consistency checks such as correspondence between the declaration of a variable and its usage.

This automated compliance checking is implemented in a freely available tool: GrML-Check[11].

3.4   Ease of Implementation for Data Structures

Since our approach relies on standard XML technologies that are well developed, we are able to easily generate the data structures representing the models, as well as the read and write operations.

The XML Schema is generated using the **trang**[12] utility from the RELAX-NG description. Then, tools are run to generate the API for loading, storing, and manipulating GrML models, in different programming languages:

- JAXB[13] for Java;
- Code Synthesis xsd[14] for C++;
- and other languages that could be made available, such as Python.

---

[9] https://forge.cosyverif.org/projects/formalisms/
   repository/entry/trunk/model.rng
[10] http://www.w3.org/TR/xpath20/
[11] https://forge.cosyverif.org/projects/grml-check
[12] http://www.thaiopensource.com/relaxng/trang.html
[13] http://jaxb.java.net/
[14] http://www.codesynthesis.com/products/xsd/

This approach has one drawback: it only generates APIs for the generic GrML models, not for a particular formalism. We have to write API generators to wrap the GrML API with the notions defined in each formalism. The automation of this work is currently being explored. It can be solved by writing only one generator per language, that takes a formalism as input and generates the wrapping of the GrML API.

The performance of the libraries is usually very good, as they can load big models very fastly within a reasonable amount of memory. For example, a JAXB-generated parser for PNML P/T models can load a 336 MiB PNML file in 7.90 seconds, with 1 GiB of memory allocated to the Java Virtual Machine (using the -Xmx option).

The next section instantiates this modular definition approach on a zoo of formalisms made up of the families of (timed) automata and Petri nets.

4   Application to Automata and Petri Nets

We leveraged the flexibility, compositional and incremental reuse characteristics of FML and GrML to build an architecture of interrelated formalisms, for Petri nets and automata. Our goal here is to obtain an architecture structuring these two families of graph-based formalisms.

4.1   Description

Our proposal is given in Fig. 2. In this proposal, formalisms can *reuse* existing formalisms: for example, Parametric Timed Automaton reuses the syntactic features of Timed Automaton. Other formalisms can be defined as a restricted version of an existing formalism: this is the case of Linear Hybrid Automaton that reuses the concepts of Hybrid Automaton, but adds *constraints*. Abstract formalisms as explained earlier, are meant to provide the bridge linking concrete formalisms of the same family, structured in a hierarchical architecture.

In Fig. 2, the composition and incremental reuse takes place from top to bottom. So, the core building blocks appear at the top of the figure, and each formalism (or abstract formalism) in a layer is a potential building block for the formalisms in the layer below[15].

For example, we will create the formalism Timed Automaton in this section. It is built upon Abstract Timed Automaton, which is itself built upon Automaton, described below:

```
<formalism name="Automaton" xmlns="http://cosyverif.org/ns/formalism">
    <leafAttribute name="initialState" />
    <leafAttribute name="finalState" />
    <complexAttribute name="type" refType="state">
        <child refName="initialState" minOccurs="0" maxOccurs="1" />
        <child refName="finalState" minOccurs="0" maxOccurs="1" />
```

---

[15] For the sake of readability and saving space, we sometimes depict different formalisms at the same level, although one includes another one (see, e.g. Stopwatch Automaton and Parametric Stopwatch Automaton).

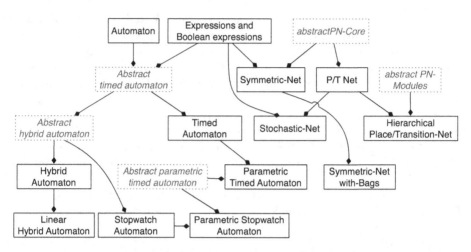

Fig. 2. An architecture of formalisms

```
    </complexAttribute>
    <leafAttribute name="name" refType="state"/>
    <leafAttribute name="label" refType="transition"/>
    <nodeType name="state"/>
    <arcType name="transition"/>
</formalism>
```

An automaton contains states (defined by the nodeType tag), and transitions (defined by the arcType tag). States have two attributes, "name" and "type" (defined by the leafAttribute and complexAttribute), where "type" is a combination of optional "initialState" and "finalState". Transitions have only a label.

Abstract Timed Automaton is defined above **Automaton** by:

```
<formalism abstract="true" name="Abstract timed automaton"
           xmlns="http://cosyverif.org/ns/formalism">
    <xi:include href="automaton.fml"/>
    <xi:include href="abstract_expression.fml"/>
    <complexAttribute name="declaration" refType="Abstract timed
        automaton">
        <child refName="clocks" minOccurs="0" maxOccurs="1"/>
    </complexAttribute>
    <complexAttribute name="clocks">
        <child refName="clock" minOccurs="0"/>
    </complexAttribute>
    <complexAttribute name="clock">
        <child refName="name" maxOccurs="1"/>
    </complexAttribute>
    <complexAttribute name="guard" refType="transition">
        <child refName="boolExpr" maxOccurs="1"/>
    </complexAttribute>
    <complexAttribute name="updates" refType="transition">
        <child refName="update" minOccurs="0"/>
    </complexAttribute>
    <complexAttribute name="update">
        <child refName="name" maxOccurs="1"/>
        <child refName="expr" maxOccurs="1"/>
    </complexAttribute>
</formalism>
```

This formalism includes the base `Automaton` formalism and another formalism that describes Boolean and Integer expressions. It defines clocks on the automaton and guards and updates of the clocks on the transitions.

This latter formalism instantiates the `Abstract Timed Automaton` as `Timed Automaton`.

```
<formalism name="Timed Automaton"
             xmlns="http://cosyverif.org/ns/formalism">
    <xi:include href="abstract_timed-automaton.fml"/>
</formalism>
```

Note that the `Abstract Timed Automaton` is useful to define others formalisms, like `Hybrid Automaton`. `Timed Automaton` itself becomes a building block for `Parametric Timed Automaton`.

Once the formalism has been defined, the developer can write models in GrML and check them using the GrML-Check tool. He/she can also manipulate models using the GrML library available in his programming language. In a near future, developers will also be able to generate an API for their specific formalisms and use it in their tools.

In this incremental definition approach, for two same concepts in two consecutive layers, the most recent one (in the layer below) subsumes (i.e. merges) the previous one. The XInclude technology allows to specify how to combine elements and attributes of the subsumed concept with those of the including one. Multiple composition is allowed.

Note that, although in theory Petri nets and automata do not share much syntax, we do not have two independent connected components in Fig. 2, as one could expect. Instead, the hierarchy of automata (on the left) and the hierarchy of Petri nets (on the right) share a common formalism, i.e. `Expressions` and `Boolean expressions`. Furthermore, if time(d) Petri nets are to be defined, they will certainly share some attributes with timed automaton (e.g. the definition of clocks), and hence both `Abstract Time Petri Nets` and `Abstract Timed Automaton` may build upon a new abstract formalism, e.g. `Abstract timed systems`. The same holds for the extension to the parametric case. This shows the interest of reusability in our solution, and of the notion of abstract formalisms.

All the formalisms defined in *CosyVerif* can be found on the *CosyVerif* Web page[16].

4.2 Discussion

Our aim is not only to describe formalisms, but also to ease the development of new formalisms possibly using parts of existing ones. Thus formalisms we use in this framework are not built independently of one another, but factor as much as possible their common features, as the above application shows. Most formalisms are extensions of other formalisms. Maintaining relations of hierarchy or dependency is also an important issue both to navigate through the zoo of formalisms and to ensure consistency in the long run.

---

[16] https://forge.cosyverif.org/projects/formalisms/repository/entry/trunk/

4.3   Towards Good Practices

While working on this structured architecture of formalisms, we identified a good practice for defining formalisms, based on *abstract* and *concrete* formalisms. Abstract formalisms (depicted in Fig. 2 in dotted red) define the core of our formalisms; they must be as organised (through inclusion) as possible. Each abstract formalism can include other abstract formalisms, and add new features. Concrete formalisms can include several abstract or concrete formalisms, but should not add new features. They can however add constraints. Of course, only concrete formalisms can be instantiated in a GrML model. This separation between concrete and abstract formalisms is inspired by the object-orientation paradigm.

Finally, an important issue to be addressed is to identify whether tools would still be compatible in case the hierarchy of formalisms is subject to modifications. We should find criteria to allow backward compatibility; in particular, modifications could be performed to the hierarchy, as long as the (abstract) syntax of the formalism supported by the tool remains unchanged.

5   Integration into the *CosyVerif* Platform

This work has been implemented in the *CosyVerif* verification environment [3]. *CosyVerif* aims at gathering within a common interface various existing tools for specification and verification. It has been designed in order to:

1. support different formalisms with the ability to easily create new ones;
2. provide a graphical interface for every formalism;
3. include verification tools called via the interface as Web services; in fact, the provided graphical front end in the *CosyVerif* platform wraps such Web services; any other client (third party product) able to wrap such Web services can be used as well;
4. offer the possibility for a developer to integrate his/her own tool without much effort, also allowing it to interact with the other tools.

5.1   Architecture

CosyVerif consists of two components:

- a distributed server (Alligator), which provides an integration framework based on Web Services;
- a client (Coloane), which provides a graphical front-end.

Users may either install the server (containing all verification tools) as a standalone binary, or only install the light client and connect to an existing server.

CosyVerif relies on the use of GrML files describing models that comply with FML describing formalisms. The Coloane client allows to graphically design a model, which is automatically translated into a GrML file.

The *CosyVerif* platform is OS-independent and entirely open source (server, client and verification tools). Alligator is published under the GNU Affero General Public License (AGPL) version 3. Coloane is published under the Eclipse Public License (EPL) version 1.

5.2   Advantages

Among the advantages of *CosyVerif* is the easy use of the platform: the end user can simply install the client, that will automatically connect to an existing server. For the tool developer, integrating a tool into the platform first requires the definition of a FML formalism (if it was not previously available), by reusing portions of formalisms. Then, (s)he only needs to write a parser taking GrML as input. Here again, much reuse can be performed: for formalisms reusing other formalisms, parts of their parser can be reused here as well . The whole operation usually requires less than half a day.

Finally, the platform is client-independent; although we provide Coloane, any home-made client using a provided library or using appropriately the Web service protocol can connect to an existing server as well and benefits from the services provided by the tools integrated in *CosyVerif*.

5.3   Integrated Tools

Up to now, 8 tools (that support GrML input) are available in *CosyVerif*:

- COSMOS [5], a statistical model checker for Petri net with general distribution against specification given as a linear hybrid automaton;
- Crocodile [7], a model checker for Symmetric nets with bags [9];
- CUNF [4], a toolset for carrying out unfolding-based verification of Petri nets extended with read arcs;
- IMITATOR [2], a tool for synthesising timing parameters for networks of timed automata augmented with stopwatches;
- ModGraph [19], a tool for the construction and analysis of modular state spaces;
- ObsGraph [17], a BDD-based tool implementing a verification approach for workflows using Symbolic Observation Graphs;
- PNXDD [13], a model checker for place/transition Petri nets based on hierarchically structured decision diagrams.

More details on the tools can be found in the publications related to the tools, as well as in [3]. The integration of other tools is still ongoing.

5.4   Banks of Formalisms and Models

Two major sets of FML formalisms are available so far: Petri nets and timed automata (see Fig. 2). They can be downloaded from the *CosyVerif* repository.

Using the translation facilities offered by some tools to convert models given in their native format to models in the GrML syntax, several lists of benchmarks are now available in the GrML format, and have been grouped on the *CosyVerif*'s Web site [23] (in Downloads → Repository).

A first list of case studies of parametric timed automata comes from IMITATOR [2]. These case studies concern hardware circuits (including original industrial case studies), communication protocols, scheduling problems, as well as some classical case studies from the literature. A second list of benchmarks consists of a large list of Petri nets models and their extensions (including coloured Petri nets), coming from the model checking contests in 2011, 2012 and 2013 at the International Conference on Application and Theory of Petri Nets and Concurrency [13,18].

6   Conclusion and Perspectives

This paper proposes a mechanism to integrate heterogeneous formalisms and associated tools, and enhance interoperability between tools, using a modular formalisms definition approach. Our solution relies on the FML language for describing formalisms, and the GrML language for describing models. An automated compliance check is performed between any GrML model and its corresponding FML formalism. We aim at emphasising the reusability of formalisms as much as possible, so as to ease the engineering of verification tools. Our approach was implemented in the *CosyVerif* platform. A hierarchy of FML formalisms for extensions of Petri nets and automata has been defined and implemented, and several lists of benchmarks are available.

We give below some directions for future research.

6.1   Properties

The approach described in this paper allows the modular definition of formalisms. It can be pushed one step further to cover not only the models, but also their properties and results of tools.

Researchers have defined properties for the models, for instance place bounds or invariants for Petri nets. These properties can be either filled by the modeler or computed by tools. Currently, the tools usually display the result but do not make it easily available to other tools. Thus, it is difficult to reuse the results of one tool into the computations of another tool. Such communication between tools is interesting though. For instance, the place bounds of a Petri net can be used by a model checker (especially those based on decision diagrams) to improve their efficiency.

As we propose a way to define modular formalisms, we propose to provide properties as formalism extensions in the future. It would benefit from an easy integration with the current approach, while allowing better communication and interaction between the tools. This important and much asked-for feature in the model checking community was totally missing in most platforms.

6.2 Semantics

An additional challenge is the ability of composing models defined using different formalisms (e.g. a Petri net with a finite state automaton). This requires semantic information (in order to define, e.g. what kind of variable of a first formalism corresponds to what kind of variable in a second formalism and hence be able to synchronise them). Attaching some semantic information to the FML formalisms is the subject of ongoing work.

Attaching more semantic information to FML formalisms will also make it possible to automatically translate a model described using any FML formalism into a model described using any other FML formalism. Of course, if these formalisms are incompatible (e.g. a timed Petri net can in general not be translated into a finite state automaton), this must be detected. Such a work can be related to the automated composition of logics, with automated feedback for consistency [8].

References

1. Alur, R., Dill, D.L.: A theory of timed automata. Theoretical Computer Science 126(2), 183–235 (1994)
2. André, É., Fribourg, L., Kühne, U., Soulat, R.: IMITATOR 2.5: A tool for analyzing robustness in scheduling problems. In: Giannakopoulou, D., Méry, D. (eds.) FM 2012. LNCS, vol. 7436, pp. 33–36. Springer, Heidelberg (2012)
3. André, É., Hillah, L.-M., Hulin-Hubard, F., Kordon, F., Lembachar, Y., Linard, A., Petrucci, L.: CosyVerif: An open source extensible verification environment. In: ICECCS. IEEE Computer Society (to appear, 2013)
4. Baldan, P., Bruni, A., Corradini, A., König, B., Rodríguez, C., Schwoon, S.: Efficient unfolding of contextual Petri nets. Theoretical Computer Science 449, 2–22 (2012)
5. Ballarini, P., Djafri, H., Duflot, M., Haddad, S., Pekergin, N.: HASL: An expressive language for statistical verification of stochastic models. In: VALUETOOLS, pp. 306–315 (2011)
6. Blom, S., van de Pol, J., Weber, M.: LTSmin: Distributed and symbolic reachability. In: Touili, T., Cook, B., Jackson, P. (eds.) CAV 2010. LNCS, vol. 6174, pp. 354–359. Springer, Heidelberg (2010)
7. Colange, M., Baarir, S., Kordon, F., Thierry-Mieg, Y.: Crocodile: A symbolic/symbolic tool for the analysis of symmetric nets with bags. In: Kristensen, L.M., Petrucci, L. (eds.) PETRI NETS 2011. LNCS, vol. 6709, pp. 338–347. Springer, Heidelberg (2011)
8. Ferré, S., Ridoux, O.: Logic functors: A toolbox of components for building customized and embeddable logics. Technical report, INRIA (2006), http://www.irisa.fr/LIS/ferre/logfun/doc/ResearchReportInria0000.pdf
9. Haddad, S., Kordon, F., Petrucci, L., Pradat-Peyre, J.-F., Trèves, N.: Efficient state-based analysis by introducing bags in Petri net color domains. In: ACC 2009, pp. 5018–5025. Omnipress IEEE (2009)
10. Hamez, A., Hillah, L.-M., Kordon, F., Linard, A., Paviot-Adet, E., Renault, X., Thierry-Mieg, Y.: New features in CPN-AMI 3: Focusing on the analysis of complex distributed systems. In: ACSD, pp. 273–275. IEEE Computer Society (2006)

11. Henzinger, T.A., Ho, P.-H., Wong-Toi, H.: HyTech: A model checker for hybrid systems. Software Tools for Technology Transfer 1, 110–122 (1997)
12. Hillah, L.M., Kordon, F., Petrucci, L., Trèves, N.: PNML framework: An extendable reference implementation of the Petri net markup language. In: Lilius, J., Penczek, W. (eds.) PETRI NETS 2010. LNCS, vol. 6128, pp. 318–327. Springer, Heidelberg (2010)
13. Hong, S., Kordon, F., Paviot-Adet, E., Evangelista, S.: Computing a hierarchical static order for decision diagram-based representation from P/T nets. In: Jensen, K., Donatelli, S., Kleijn, J. (eds.) ToPNoC 2012. LNCS, vol. 6900, pp. 121–140. Springer, Heidelberg (2012)
14. ISO/JTC1/SC34. ISO/IEC 19757-2:2008: Information Technology – Document Schema Definition Language (DSDL) – Part 2: Regular-grammar-based validation – RELAX NG. ISO/IEC, http://relaxng.org
15. ISO/JTC1/SC34. ISO/IEC 19757-3:2006: Information Technology - Document Schema Definition Languages (DSDL) - Part 3: Rule-based validation - Schematron. ISO/IEC, http://schematron.com/
16. ISO/JTC1/SC7/WG19. ISO/IEC 15909-2:2011. Systems and software engineering – High-level Petri nets – Part 2: Transfer format (2011)
17. Klai, K., Ochi, H.: Modular verification of inter-enterprise business processes. In: eKNOW, pp. 155–161 (2012)
18. Kordon, F., Linard, A., Buchs, D., Colange, M., Evangelista, S., Fronc, L., Hillah, L.-M., Lohmann, N., Paviot-Adet, E., Pommereau, F., Rohr, C., Thierry-Mieg, Y., Wimmel, H., Wolf, K.: Raw report on the model checking contest at Petri nets, 2012. Technical report, CoRR (2012)
19. Lakos, C., Petrucci, L.: Modular analysis of systems composed of semiautonomous subsystems. In: ACSD, pp. 185–196. IEEE Computer Society (2004)
20. Larsen, K.G., Pettersson, P., Yi, W.: UPPAAL in a nutshell. International Journal on Software Tools for Technology Transfer 1(1-2), 134–152 (1997)
21. Liu, Y., Sun, J., Dong, J.S.: PAT 3: An extensible architecture for building multi-domain model checkers. In: ISSRE, pp. 190–199. IEEE (2011)
22. Steinberg, D., Budinsky, F., Paternostro, M., Merks, E.: EMF: Eclipse Modeling Framework, 2nd edn. Eclipse Series. Addison-Wesley Professional (2008)
23. The CosyVerif group. CosyVerif Web page, http://www.cosyverif.org
24. Urbas, M., Jamnik, M.: Diabelli: A heterogeneous proof system. In: Gramlich, B., Miller, D., Sattler, U. (eds.) IJCAR 2012. LNCS(LNAI), vol. 7364, pp. 559–566. Springer, Heidelberg (2012)

A UTP Semantics for Communicating Processes with Shared Variables[*]

Ling Shi[1], Yongxin Zhao[1], Yang Liu[2], Jun Sun[3], Jin Song Dong[1], and Shengchao Qin[4]

[1] National University of Singapore
[2] Nanyang Technological University, Singapore
[3] Singapore University of Technology and Design
[4] Teesside University, UK

Abstract. CSP# (Communicating Sequential Programs) is a modelling language designed for specifying concurrent systems by integrating CSP-like compositional operators with sequential programs updating shared variables. In this paper, we define an observation-oriented denotational semantics in an *open* environment for the CSP# language based on the UTP framework. To deal with shared variables, we lift traditional event-based traces into *hybrid* traces which consist of event-state pairs for recording process behaviours. We also define refinement to check process equivalence and present a set of algebraic laws which are established based on our denotational semantics. Our approach thus provides a rigorous means for reasoning about the correctness of CSP# process behaviours. We further derive a *closed* semantics by focusing on special types of hybrid traces; this closed semantics can be linked with existing CSP# operational semantics.

1 Introduction

Communicating Sequential Processes (CSP) [6], a prominent member of the process algebra family, has been designed to formally model concurrent systems whose behaviours are described as process expressions together with a rich set of compositional operators. It has been widely accepted and applied to a variety of safety-critical systems [18]. However, with the increasing size and complexity of concurrent systems, it becomes clear that CSP is deficient to model non-trivial data structures (for example, hash tables) or functional aspects. To solve this problem, considerable efforts on enhancing CSP with data aspects have been made. One of the approaches is to integrate CSP (CCS) with state-based specification languages, such as Circus [8], CSP-OZ [4,13], TCOZ [9], CSP_σ [3], CSP$\|$B [11], and CCS+Z [5,16].

Inspired by the related works, CSP# [14] has been proposed to specify concurrent systems which involve *shared variables*. It combines the state-based program with the event-based specification by introducing non-communicating events to associate state transitions. CSP# integrates CSP-like compositional operators with sequential program

---

[*] This work is partially supported by project "ZJURP1100105" from Singapore University of Technology and Design.

L. Groves and J. Sun (Eds.): ICFEM 2013, LNCS 8144, pp. 215–230, 2013.

constructs such as assignments and while loops, for the purpose of expressive modelling and efficient system verification[1]. Besides, CSP# is supported by the PAT model checker [15] and has been applied to a number of systems available at the PAT website (www.patroot.com).

Sun *et al.* presented an operational semantics of CSP# [14], which interprets the behaviour of CSP# models using labelled transition systems (LTS). Based on this semantics, model checking CSP# models becomes possible. Nevertheless, the suggested operational semantics is not fully abstract; two behaviourally equivalent processes with respect to the operational semantics may behave differently under some process context which involves shared variables, for instance. In other words, the operational semantics of CSP# is not compositional and lacks the support of compositional verification of process behaviours. Thus there is a need for a compositional semantics to explain the notations of the CSP# language.

Related Work. The denotational semantics of CSP has been defined using two approaches. On one hand, Roscoe [10] and Hoare [6] provided a *trace* model, a *stable-failures* model and a *failures-divergences* model for CSP processes. In the trace model, every process is mapped to a set of traces which capture sequences of event occurrences during the process execution. In the stable-failures model, every process is mapped to a set of pairs, and each pair consists of a trace and a refusal. In the failures-divergences model, every process is mapped to a pair, where one component is the (extension-closed) set of traces that can lead to divergent behaviours, and the other component contains all stable failures which are all pairs, and each pair is in the form of a trace and a refusal. On the other hand, Hoare and He defined a denotational semantics for CSP processes using the UTP theory [7]. Each process is formalised as a relation between an initial observation and a subsequent observation; such relations are represented as predicates over observational variables which record process stability, termination, traces and refusals *before* or *after* the observation. Cavalcanti and Woodcock [2] presented an approach to relate the UTP theory of CSP to the *failures-divergences* model of CSP.

The original denotational semantics for CSP does not deal with complex data aspects. To solve this problem, much work has been done to provide the denotational semantics for languages which integrate CSP with state-based notations. For example, Oliveira *et al.* presented a denotational semantics for Circus based on a UTP theory [8]. The proposed semantics includes two parts: one is for Circus actions, guarded commands, etc., and the other is for Circus processes which contain an encapsulated state, a main action, etc. However, this proposed semantics assumes that the sets of variables in processes shall be *disjoint* when running in parallel or interleaving. Qin *et al.* formalised the denotational semantics of Timed Communicating Object Z (TCOZ) [9] based on the UTP framework. Their unified semantic model can deal with channel-based and sensor/actuator-based communications. However, shared variables in TCOZ are restricted to only sensors/actuators.

There exists some work on shared-variable concurrency. Brooks defined a denotational semantics for a shared-variable parallel language [1]. The semantic model only

---

[1] Most integrated formalisms are too expressive to have an automated supporting tool. CSP# combines CSP with C#-like program instead of Z.

considers state transitions, and it cannot be directly applied to the semantics of communicating processes. Zhu *et al.* derived an denotational semantics from the proposed operational semantics for the hardware description language Verilog [19]. In addition, they derived the denotational semantics from the algebraic semantics for Verilog to explore the equivalence of two semantic models [20]. Recently, they proposed a probabilistic language *PTSC* which integrates probability, time and shared-variable concurrency [22]. The operational semantics of PTSC is explored and a set of algebraic laws are presented via bisimulation. Furthermore, a denotational semantics using the UTP approach is derived from the algebraic laws based on the head normal form of PTSC constructs [21]. These semantic models lack expressive power to capture more complicated system behaviours like channel-based communications.

The above existing work cannot be applied to define the denotational semantics of CSP# which involves global shared variables. In this paper, we present an observation-oriented denotational semantics for the CSP# language based on the UTP framework in an *open* environment, where process behaviours can be interfered with by the environment. The proposed semantics not only provides a rigorous meaning of the language, but also deduces algebraic laws describing the properties of CSP# processes. To deal with shared variables, we lift traditional event-based traces into *hybrid* traces (consisting of event-state pairs) for recording process behaviours. To handle different types of synchronisation in CSP# (i.e., event-based and synchronised handshake), we construct a comprehensive set of rules on merging traces from processes which run in parallel/interleaving. These rules capture all possible concurrency behaviours between event/channel-based communications and global shared variables.

Contribution. We highlight our contributions by the three points below.

- The proposed semantic model deals with not only communicating processes, but also shared variables. It can model both event-based synchronisation and synchronised handshake over channels. Moreover, our model can be adapted/enhanced to define the denotational semantics for other languages which possess similar concurrency mechanisms.
- The semantics of processes can serve as a theoretical foundation to develop mechanical verification for CSP# specifications, for example, to check process equivalence based on our definition of process refinement, using conventional generic theorem provers like PVS. In addition, the proposed algebraic laws can act as auxiliary reasoning rules to improve verification automation.
- A *closed* semantics can be derived from our open denotational semantics by focusing on special types of hybrid traces. The closed semantics can be linked with the CSP# operational semantics in [14].

The remainder of the paper is organised as follows. Section 2 introduces the syntax of the CSP# language with informal descriptions. Section 3 constructs the observation-oriented denotational semantics in an open environment based on the UTP framework; healthiness conditions are also defined to characterise the semantic domain. Section 4 discusses the algebraic laws. Section 5 presents a closed semantics derived from the open semantics. Section 6 concludes the paper with future work.

2   The CSP# Language

Syntax. A CSP# model may consist of definitions of constants, variables, channels, and processes. A constant is defined by keyword *#define* followed by a name and a value, e.g., *#define max* 5. A variable is declared with keyword *var* followed by a name and an initial value, e.g., *var x* = 2. A channel is declared using keyword *channel* with a name, e.g., *channel ch*. Notice that we use T to denote the types of variables and channel messages and T will be used in Section 3.1.1. A process is specified in the form of $Proc(i_1, i_2, \ldots, i_n) = ProcExp$, where *Proc* is the process name, $(i_1, i_2, \ldots, i_n)$ is an optional list of process parameters and *ProcExp* is a process expression. The BNF description of *ProcExp* is shown below with short descriptions.

$P ::= Stop \mid Skip$	– primitives
$\mid a \rightarrow P$	– event prefixing
$\mid ch!exp \rightarrow P \mid ch?m \rightarrow P(m)$	– channel output/input
$\mid e\{prog\} \rightarrow P$	– data operation prefixing
$\mid [b]P$	– state guard
$\mid P \;\Box\; Q \mid P \sqcap Q$	– external/internal choices
$\mid P; Q$	– sequential composition
$\mid P \setminus X$	– hiding
$\mid P \parallel Q \mid P \;\vert\vert\vert\; Q$	– parallel/interleaving
$\mid p \mid \mu p \bullet P(p)$	– recursion

where P and Q are processes, a is an action, e is a non-communicating event, ch is a channel, exp is an arithmetic expression, m is a bounded variable, $prog$ is a sequential program updating global shared variables, b is a Boolean expression, and X is a set of actions. In addition, the syntax of *prog* is illustrated as follows.

$prog ::= x = exp$	– assignment
$\mid prog_1; prog_2$	– composition
$\mid$ if b then $prog_1$ else $prog_2$	– conditional
$\mid$ while b do $prog$	– iteration

In CSP#, channels are *synchronous* and their communications are achieved by a handshaking mechanism. Specifically, a process $ch!exp \rightarrow P$ which is ready to perform an output through ch will be enabled if another process $ch?m \rightarrow P(m)$ is ready to perform an input through the same channel ch simultaneously, and *vice versa*. In process $e\{prog\} \rightarrow P$, *prog* is executed *atomically* with the occurrence of e. Process $[b]P$ waits until condition b becomes *true* and then behaves as P. There are two types of choices in CSP#: external choice $P \;\Box\; Q$ is resolved only by the occurrence of a *visible* event, and internal choice $P \sqcap Q$ is resolved non-deterministically. In process $P \parallel Q$, P and Q run in parallel, and they synchronise on common communication events. In contrast, in process $P \;\vert\vert\vert\; Q$, P and Q run independently (except for communications through synchronous channels). Detailed descriptions of the CSP# syntax can be found in [14].

Concurrency. As mentioned earlier, concurrent processes in CSP# can communicate through shared variables or event/channel-based communications.

Shared variables in CSP# are globally accessible, namely, variables can be read and written by different (parallel) processes. They can be used in guard conditions, sequential programs associated with non-communicating events, and expressions in the channel outputs; nonetheless, they can only be updated in sequential programs. Furthermore, to avoid any possible data race problem when programs execute atomically, sequential programs from different processes are not allowed to execute simultaneously.

A synchronisation event, which is also called an action, occurs *instantaneously*, and its occurrence may require simultaneous participation by more than one processes. In contrast, a communication over a synchronous channel is two-way between a sender process and a receiver process. Namely, a handshake communication *ch.exp* occurs when both processes *ch!exp* $\rightarrow$ *P* and *ch?m* $\rightarrow$ *Q(m)* are enabled simultaneously. We remark that this two-way synchronisation is different from CSP_M where multi-way synchronisation between many sender and receiver processes is allowed [10].

3 The Observation-Oriented Semantics for CSP#

3.1 UTP Semantic Model for CSP#

UTP [7] uses relations as a unifying basis to define denotational semantics for programs across different programming paradigms. Theories of programming paradigms are differentiated by their *alphabet, signature* and a selection of laws called *healthiness conditions*. The alphabet is a set of observational variables recording external observations of the program behaviour. The signature defines the syntax to represent the elements of a theory. The healthiness conditions identify valid predicates that characterise a theory.

For each programming paradigm, programs are generally interpreted as relations between initial observations and subsequent (intermediate or final) observations of the behaviours of their execution. Relations are represented as predicates over observational variables to capture all aspects of program behaviours; variables of initial observations are undashed, constituting the input alphabet of a relation, and variables of subsequent observations are dashed, constituting the output alphabet of a relation.

The challenge of defining a denotational semantics for CSP# is to design an appropriate model which can cover not only communications but also the shared variable paradigm. To address this challenge, we blend communication events with states containing shared variables. Namely, we introduce *hybrid* traces to record the interactions of processes with the global environment; each trace is a sequence of communication events or (shared variable) state pairs.

3.1.1 Observational Variables

The following variables are introduced in the alphabet of observations of CSP# process behaviour. Some of them (i.e., *ok, ok', wait, wait', ref*, and *ref'*) are similar to those in the UTP theory for CSP [7]. The key difference is that the event-based traces in CSP are changed to hybrid traces consisting of event-state pairs.

- *ok, ok'*: Boolean describe the stability of a process.
  ok = true records that the process has started in a stable state, whereas *ok = false* records that the process has not started as its predecessor has diverged.
  ok' = true records that the process has reached a stable state, whereas *ok' = false* records that the process has diverged.

- *wait, wait'*: Boolean distinguish the intermediate observations of waiting states from the observations of final states.
  wait = true records that the execution of the previous process has not finished, and the current process starts in an intermediate state, while *wait = false* records that the execution of the previous process has finished and the current process may start.
  wait' = true records that the next observation of process is in an intermediate state, while *wait' = false* records that the next observation is in a terminated state.
- *ref, ref'*: $\mathbb{P}$ *Event* denote a set of actions and channel inputs/outputs that can be refused before or after the observation. The set *Event* denotes all possible actions and channel input/output directions (e.g., *ch?, ch!*). An input direction *ch?* denotes any input through channel *ch*, and a channel output direction *ch!* denotes any output through channel *ch*.
- *tr, tr'*: seq$((S \times S^{\perp}) \cup (S \times E))$ record a sequence of observations (state pairs or communication events) on the interaction of processes with the global environment.
  - S is the set of all possible mappings (states), and a state $s : \mathsf{VAR} \to \mathsf{T}$ is a function which maps global shared variables VAR into values of T.
  - E is the set of all possible events, including actions, channel inputs/outputs and synchronous channel communications. Note that non-communicating events are excluded from the set.
  - $S \times S^{\perp}$ is the set of state pairs, and each pair consists of a pre-state recording the initial variable values before the observation and a post-state recording the final values after the observation. $S^{\perp} \mathrel{\widehat{=}} S \cup \{\perp\}$ represents all states, where the improper state $\perp$ indicates non-termination. Remark that the state pair is used to record the observation for the sequential program.
  - $S \times E$ denotes a set of occurring events under the pre-states. The reason of recording the pre-state is that the value of the expression which may contain shared variables in a channel output shall be evaluated under this state.

3.1.2 Healthiness Conditions

Healthiness conditions are defined as equations in terms of an idempotent function ϕ on predicates. Every healthy program represented by predicate P must be a fixed point under the healthiness condition of its respective UTP theory, i.e., $P = \phi(P)$.

In CSP#, a process can never change the past history of the observations; instead, it can only extend the record, captured by function **R1**. We use predicate P to represent the semantics of the CSP# process below.

R1: $\mathbf{R1}(P) = P \land tr \leq tr'$

The execution of a process is independent of the history before its activation, captured by function **R2**.

R2: $\mathbf{R2}(P(tr, tr')) = \sqcap_s P(s, s \mathbin{\frown} (tr' - tr))$

As mentioned earlier, variable *wait* distinguishes an waiting state from the final state. A process cannot start if its previous process has not finished, or otherwise, the values of all observational variables are unchanged, characterised by function **R3**.

R3: $\mathbf{R3}(P) = I\!I \lhd wait \rhd P$

where $P \lhd b \rhd Q \mathrel{\widehat{=}} b \land P \lor \neg b \land Q$ and $I\!I \mathrel{\widehat{=}} (\neg ok \land tr \leq tr') \lor (ok' \land tr' = tr \land wait' = wait \land ref' = ref)$. Here $I\!I$ states that if a process is in a divergent state, then only the trace can be extended, or otherwise, it is in a stable state, and the values of all observational variables remain unchanged.

When a process is in a divergent state, it can only extend the trace. This feature is captured by function **CSP1**.

CSP1: $CSP1(P) = (\neg ok \wedge tr \leq tr') \vee P$

Every process is monotonic in the observational variable ok'. This monotonicity property is modelled by function **CSP2** which states that if an observation of a process is valid when ok' is false, then the observation should also be valid when ok' is true.

CSP2: $CSP2(P) = P; (ok \Rightarrow ok' \wedge tr' = tr \wedge wait' = wait \wedge ref' = ref)$

The behaviour of a process does not depend on the initial value of its refusal, captured by function **CSP3**.

CSP3: $CSP3(P) = Skip; P$

Similarly, when a process terminates or diverges, the value of its final refusal is irrelevant, characterised by function **CSP4**.

CSP4: $CSP4(P) = P; Skip$

If a deadlocked process refuses some set of events offered by its environment, then it would still be deadlocked in an environment that offers even fewer events, captured by function **CSP5**

CSP5: $CSP5(P) = P \parallel\parallel Skip$

We below use **H** to denote all healthiness conditions satisfied by the CSP# process.

$$H = R1 \circ R2 \circ R3 \circ CSP1 \circ CSP2 \circ CSP3 \circ CSP4 \circ CSP5$$

From the above definition, we can see that although CSP# satisfies the same healthiness conditions of CSP, observational variables tr, tr' in our semantic model record additional information for shared variable states. We adopt the same names for the idempotent functions used in CSP for consistency. In addition, function **H** is idempotent and monotonic [2,7].

3.2   Process Semantics

In this section, we construct an observation-oriented semantics for all CSP# process operators based on our proposed UTP semantic model for CSP#. The semantics is defined in an open environment; namely, a process may be interfered with by the environment. In Section 3.1.1, we have defined a hybrid trace to record the potential events and state transitions in which a process P may engage; for example, the trace $tr' = \langle (s_1, s_1') \rangle \frown \langle (s_2, a_2) \rangle$ describes the transitions of process P. In an open environment, tr' may contain an (implicit) transition (s_1', s_2) as the result of interference by the environment where states s_1' and s_2 can be different.

In the following, we first illustrate our semantic definitions of three important process operators: synchronous channel output/input, data operation prefixing, and parallel composition. These three process operators are non-trivial and frequently used in complex concurrent systems with the involvement of channel-based communications and shared variables. We further present the semantics of other process operators and refinement at the end; detailed semantic definitions of the complete CSP# language are available in our technical report [12].

3.2.1 Synchronous Channel Output/Input

In CSP#, messages can be sent/received synchronously through channels. The synchronisation is pair-wise, involving two processes. Specifically, a synchronous channel communication $ch.exp$ can take place only if an output $ch!exp$ is enabled and a corresponding input $ch?m$ is also ready.

$$
ch!exp \rightarrow P \mathrel{\hat=} \mathbf{H}\left(ok' \wedge \left(\begin{array}{l} ch? \notin ref' \wedge tr' = tr \\ \triangleleft wait' \triangleright \\ \exists s \in \mathbf{S} \bullet tr' = tr \frown \langle (s, ch!\mathcal{A}[\![exp]\!](s)) \rangle \end{array} \right) \right) ; P
$$

The above semantics of synchronous channel output depicts two possible behaviours: when a process is waiting to communicate on channel ch, it cannot refuse any channel input over ch provided by the environment to perform a channel communication (represented by predicate $ch? \notin ref'$), and its trace is unchanged; or a process performs the output through ch and terminates without divergence. Since the environment may interfere with the process behaviour and make a transition on the shared variable states, we use state s to denote the initial state before the observation (also named pre-state). The observation of the trace is recorded as a tuple $(s, ch!\mathcal{A}[\![exp]\!](s))$, where the value of the output message is evaluated under the pre-state s. Here function $\mathcal{A}$ defines the semantics of arithmetic expressions, and its definition is available in [12]. After the output occurs, the process behaves as P. Note that the semantics of sequential composition "; " is defined in Section 3.2.4.

$$
ch?m \rightarrow P(m) \mathrel{\hat=} \exists v \in \mathbf{T} \bullet \left(\mathbf{H}\left(ok' \wedge \left(\begin{array}{l} ch! \notin ref' \wedge tr' = tr \\ \triangleleft wait' \triangleright \\ \exists s \in \mathbf{S} \bullet tr' = tr \frown \langle (s, ch?v) \rangle \end{array} \right) \right) ; P(v) \right)
$$

As shown above, the semantics of synchronous channel input is similar to channel output except that when a process is waiting, it cannot refuse any channel output provided by the environment, and after the process receives a message v from channel ch, its trace is appended with a tuple $(s, ch?v)$. In addition, parameter m cannot be modified in process P; namely, it becomes constant-like and its value is replaced by value v.

3.2.2 Data Operation Prefixing

In CSP#, sequential programs are executed atomically together with the occurrence of an event, called data operation. The updates on shared variables are observed after the execution of all programs as illustrated below.

$$
e\{prog\} \rightarrow Skip \mathrel{\hat=} \mathbf{H}\left(ok' \wedge \left(\begin{array}{l} tr' = tr \frown \langle (s, \bot) \rangle \wedge wait' \\ \triangleleft \exists s \in \mathbf{S} \bullet (s, \bot) \in \mathcal{C}[\![prog]\!] \triangleright \\ \exists s' \in \mathbf{S} \bullet (tr' = tr \frown \langle (s, s') \rangle \\ \qquad \wedge (s, s') \in \mathcal{C}[\![prog]\!]) \wedge \neg wait' \end{array} \right) \right)
$$

If the evaluation of the program does not terminate (represented by predicate $(s, \bot) \in \mathcal{C}[\![prog]\!]$), then the process is in a waiting state, and its trace is extended with the record of non-termination. On the other hand, if the evaluation succeeds and terminates, then the process terminates and the state transition is recorded in the trace. In our definition, the non-communicating event is not recorded in the trace since such an event would not synchronise with other events; instead, its effect can be described by the updates on variable states. Thus the non-communicating event is used as a label to indicate the updates on shared variables. Note that post-state s' after the observation is associated with the pre-state s under the semantics of sequential programs ($(s, s') \in C[\![prog]\!]$). Function C defines the semantics of programs by structured induction [17] as follows.

$$
\begin{aligned}
C[\![x = exp]\!] &= \{(s, s[n/x]) \mid s \in S \land n = A[\![exp]\!](s)\} \\
C[\![prog_1; \ prog_2]\!] &= \{(s, s') \mid \exists s_0 \in S \bullet (s, s_0) \in C[\![prog_1]\!] \\
&\quad \land (s_0, s') \in C[\![prog_2]\!]\} \cup \\
&\quad \{(s, \bot) \mid (s, \bot) \in C[\![prog_1]\!]\} \\
C[\![\text{if } b \text{ then } prog_1 \text{ else } prog_2]\!] &= \{(s, s') \mid B[\![b]\!](s) = true \land (s, s') \in C[\![prog_1]\!]\} \cup \\
&\quad \{(s, s') \mid B[\![b]\!](s) = false \land (s, s') \in C[\![prog_2]\!]\} \\
C[\![\text{while } b \text{ do } prog]\!] &= \{(s, s') \mid (s, s') \in C[\![\mu X \bullet F(X)]\!]\}
\end{aligned}
$$

where, $F(X) \,\hat{=}\, \text{if } b \text{ then } prog; \ X \text{ else skip}$, $\mu X \bullet F(X) \,\hat{=}\, \bigcap_n F^n(true)$, $C[\![skip]\!] = \{(s, s) \mid s \in S\}$, and $C[\![true]\!] = \{(s, s') \mid s \in S, s' \in S^{\bot}\}$.

The data operation prefixing process $e\{prog\} \rightarrow P$ is thus defined as sequential composition of data operation and P.

$$e\{prog\} \rightarrow P \,\hat{=}\, (e\{prog\} \rightarrow Skip); \ P$$

3.2.3 Parallel Composition

The parallel composition $P \parallel Q$ executes P and Q in the following way: (1) common actions of P and Q require simultaneous participation, (2) synchronous channel output in one process occurs simultaneously with the corresponding channel input in the other process, and (3) other events of processes occur independently.

In CSP, the semantics of parallel composition is defined in terms of the merge operator $\parallel_M$ in UTP [7], where the predicate M captures how to merge two observations. To deal with channel-based communications and shared variable updates in CSP#, we here define a new merge predicate $M(X)$ to model the merge operation. The set X contains common actions of both processes (denoted by set X_1) and all synchronous channel inputs and outputs (denoted by set X_2). Namely,

$$
P \parallel Q \,\hat{=}\, \left(\begin{array}{l} P[0.ok, 0.wait, 0.ref, 0.tr/ok', wait', ref', tr'] \land \\ Q[1.ok, 1.wait, 1.ref, 1.tr/ok', wait', ref', tr'] \end{array} \right); \ M(X)
$$

where

$$
M(X) \,\hat{=}\, \left(\begin{array}{l} (ok' = 0.ok \land 1.ok) \land \\ (wait' = 0.wait \lor 1.wait) \land \\ (ref' = (0.ref \cap 1.ref \cap X_2) \cup ((0.ref \cup 1.ref) \cap X_1) \\ \qquad \cup ((0.ref \cap 1.ref) - X_1 - X_2)) \\ (tr' - tr \in (0.tr - tr \parallel_X 1.tr - tr)) \end{array} \right); \ Skip
$$

Our defined predicate $M(X)$ captures four kinds of behaviours of a parallel composition. First, the composition diverges if either process diverges (represented by predicate

$ok' = 0.ok \wedge 1.ok$). Second, the composition terminates if both processes terminate ($wait' = 0.wait \vee 1.wait$). Third, the composition refuses synchronous channel ouputs/inputs that are refused by both processes ($0.ref \cap 1.ref \cap X_2$), all actions that are in the set X_1 and refused by either process ($(0.ref \cup 1.ref) \cap X_1$), and actions that are not in the set X_1 but refused by both processes ($(0.ref \cap 1.ref) - X_1 - X_2$). Last, the trace of the composition is a member of the set of traces produced by the *trace synchronisation* function $\|_X$ as elaborated below.

Function $\|_X$ models how to merge two individual traces into a set of all possible traces; there are 9 cases from 6 groups. In the following definitions, $s, s', s_1, s'_1, s_2, s'_2$ are representative elements of variable states, a, a_1, a_2 are representative elements of actions, ch is a representative element of channel names, and v is a value with type T.

- When one of the input traces is empty, (1) if both input traces are empty, the result is a set of an empty sequence (denoted by **case-1**); (2) if only one input trace is empty, the result is determined based on the first observation of that non-empty trace: (i) if that observation is an action in the set X which requires synchronisation, then the result is a set containing only an empty sequence, or otherwise, the first observation is recorded in the merged trace (**case-2**); if the first observation is (ii) a channel input/output/communication (**case-3**) or (iii) a state pair (**case-4**), then the observation is recorded in the merged trace.

case-1 $\langle\rangle \|_X \langle\rangle = \{\langle\rangle\}$

case-2 $\langle(s, a)\rangle \frown t \|_X \langle\rangle = \begin{cases} \{\langle\rangle\} & \text{if } a \in X \\ \{\langle(s, a)\rangle \frown l \mid l \in t \|_X \langle\rangle\} & \text{otherwise} \end{cases}$

case-3 $\langle(s, h)\rangle \frown t \|_X \langle\rangle = \{\langle(s, h)\rangle \frown l \mid l \in t \|_X \langle\rangle\}$, where $h \in \{ch?v, ch!v, ch.v\}$

case-4 $\langle(s, s')\rangle \frown t \|_X \langle\rangle = \{\langle(s, s')\rangle \frown l \mid l \in t \|_X \langle\rangle\}$

- When a communication is over a synchronous channel, (1) if the first observations of two input traces match (see Definition 1 below), then a synchronisation may occur (denoted by the set $\mathcal{G}_1$) or at this moment a synchronisation does not occur (denoted by the set $\mathcal{G}_2$), or otherwise, a synchronisation cannot occur. Here, two observations are matched provided that both channel input and output from two processes respectively are enabled under the same pre-state.

Definition 1 (Match). *Given two pairs $p_1 = (s_1, h_1)$ and $p_2 = (s_2, h_2)$, we say that they are matched if both $s_1 = s_2$ and $\{h_1, h_2\} = \{ch?v, ch!v\}$ are satisfied, denoted as* $\mathsf{match}(p_1, p_2)$.

case-5 $\langle(s_1, h_1)\rangle \frown t_1 \|_X \langle(s_2, h_2)\rangle \frown t_2 = \begin{cases} \mathcal{G}_1 \cup \mathcal{G}_2 & \mathsf{match}((s_1, h_1), (s_2, h_2)) \\ \mathcal{G}_2 & \text{otherwise} \end{cases}$

where $h_1, h_2 \in \{ch?v, ch!v, ch.v\}$, $\mathcal{G}_1 \cong \{\langle(s_1, ch.v)\rangle \frown l \mid l \in t_1 \|_X t_2\}$, and $\mathcal{G}_2 \cong \{\langle(s_1, h_1)\rangle \frown l \mid l \in t_1 \|_X \langle(s_2, h_2)\rangle \frown t_2\} \cup \{\langle(s_2, h_2)\rangle \frown l \mid l \in \langle(s_1, h_1)\rangle \frown t_1 \|_X t_2\}$.

- When two actions (a_1 and a_2) are synchronised, there are five cases with respect to the initial states (s_1 and s_2) and actions from the first observation of two input traces: (1) both actions are in the set X but different, (2) actions from X are the same but under different pre-states, (3) actions from X are the same and under the same pre-state, (4) one of the actions is not in X, and (5) both actions are not in X. As shown in **case-6** below, the result is a set containing only an empty sequence for cases (1) and (2). A synchronisation occurs under case (3), although it is postponed to occur under case (4). Either action can occur for case (5).

case-6 $\langle (s_1, a_1) \rangle \frown t_1 \parallel_X \langle (s_2, a_2) \rangle \frown t_2 =$

$$
\begin{cases}
\{\langle \rangle\} & a_1, a_2 \in X \wedge a_1 \neq a_2 \\
\{\langle \rangle\} & a_1, a_2 \in X \wedge a_1 = a_2 \wedge s_1 \neq s_2 \\
\{\langle (s_1, a_1) \rangle \frown l \mid l \in t_1 \parallel_X t_2\} & a_1, a_2 \in X \wedge a_1 = a_2 \wedge s_1 = s_2 \\
\{\langle (s_1, a_1) \rangle \frown l \mid l \in t_1 \parallel_X \langle (s_2, a_2) \rangle \frown t_2\} & a_1 \notin X \wedge a_2 \in X \\
\{\langle (s_1, a_1) \rangle \frown l \mid l \in t_1 \parallel_X \langle (s_2, a_2) \rangle \frown t_2\} & \\
\cup & a_1 \notin X \wedge a_2 \notin X \\
\{\langle (s_2, a_2) \rangle \frown l \mid l \in \langle (s_1, a_1) \rangle \frown t_1 \parallel_X t_2\} &
\end{cases}
$$

- When the merge operation is on an action a and channel input $ch?v$, output $ch!v$, communication $ch.v$, or a post-state s_2', (1) if a is from the set X, then its occurrence is postponed ($\mathcal{G}_3$), (2) or otherwise, either observation from two processes occurs ($\mathcal{G}_3 \cup \mathcal{G}_4$).

case-7 $\langle (s_1, a) \rangle \frown t_1 \parallel_X \langle (s_2, h) \rangle \frown t_2 = \begin{cases} \mathcal{G}_3 & \text{if } a \in X \\ \mathcal{G}_3 \cup \mathcal{G}_4 & \text{otherwise} \end{cases}$

where $h \in \{ch?v, ch!v, ch.v, s_2'\}$, $\mathcal{G}_3 \stackrel{\frown}{=} \{\langle (s_2, h) \rangle \frown l \mid l \in \langle (s_1, a) \rangle \frown t_1 \parallel_X t_2\}$, and $\mathcal{G}_4 \stackrel{\frown}{=} \{\langle (s_1, a) \rangle \frown l \mid l \in t_1 \parallel_X \langle (s_2, h) \rangle \frown t_2\}$.

- When the merge operation is over two state pairs or the operation is on a state pair and a channel input/output/communication, either observation from two processes can occur as only one process can update shared variable(s) at a time when processes run in parallel.

case-8 $\langle (s_1, s_1') \rangle \frown t_1 \parallel_X \langle (s_2, h) \rangle \frown t_2 = \{\langle (s_1, s_1') \rangle \frown l \mid l \in t_1 \parallel_X \langle (s_2, h) \rangle \frown t_2\} \cup \{\langle (s_2, h) \rangle \frown l \mid l \in \langle (s_1, s_1') \rangle \frown t_1 \parallel_X t_2\}$ where $h \in \{s_2', ch?v, ch!v, ch.v\}$

- Finally , function $\parallel_X$ is symmetric.

case-9 $t_1 \parallel_X t_2 = t_2 \parallel_X t_1$

3.2.4 Other Processes and Refinement

The semantics of other processes is the same as those counterparts in the CSP model [7] except state guard ($[b]P$) and interleaving ($P \mathbin{|||} Q$) due to the involvement of shared variables as we illustrate below.

For process $[b]P$, shared variables can be read in the Boolean expression b, and b is evaluated simultaneously with the occurrence of the first event of process P. That is to say, the evaluation of b is under the pre-state of the first observation of process P ($\mathcal{B}[\![b]\!](\pi_1(head(tr' - tr)))$), and if the evaluation returns true, then the process behaves as P, or otherwise, the process behaves as process $Stop$. Here, function $\mathcal{B}$ defines the semantics of Boolean expressions, function π_1 selects the first element of a tuple, and function $head$ returns the first element of a sequence.

Process $P \mathbin{|||} Q$ runs independently except for the communications through synchronous channels. Thus, we define the semantics of the interleaving operator in a similar way of handling parallel operator (in Section 3.2.3) except that the set X contains only synchronous channel inputs/outputs.

$$P; \ Q \ \hat{=} \ \exists \, obs_0 \ \bullet \ (P[obs_0/obs'] \wedge Q[obs_0/obs])^2$$
$$[b]P \ \hat{=} \ P \triangleleft (tr < tr' \wedge \mathcal{B}(b)(\pi_1(head(tr' - tr))) = true) \triangleright Stop$$
$$P \ ||| \ Q \ \hat{=} \ P \ ||_{M(X)} \ Q$$

Refinement calculus is designed to produce correct programs, assisting in the software development. In the UTP theory, it is expressed as logic implication; an implementation (denoted as predicate P) satisfying a specification (denoted as predicate S) is formally expressed by universal quantification implication $\forall \, a, a', \cdots \bullet P \Rightarrow Q$, where $a, a', \cdots$ are all the variables of the alphabet, which must be the same for the specification and implementation. The universal quantification implication is usually denoted as $[P \Rightarrow Q]$. The definition of refinement in CSP# is given as below.

Definition 2 (Refinement). *Let P and Q be predicates for processes with the same shared variable state space, the refinement $P \sqsupseteq Q$ holds iff $[P \Rightarrow Q]$.*

The refinement ordering in our definition is strong; every observation that satisfies P must also satisfy Q. The observation includes all process behaviours, i.e., stability, termination, traces, and refusals. Moreover, the record of the trace considers both variable states and event occurrences. For example, given a process $P = [x = 2]b \to Skip \ \square \ [x \neq 2]c \to Skip$, and a process $Q = [x = 2]b \to Skip \ \square \ [x \neq 2]d \to Skip$, the refinement $P \sqsupseteq Q$ does not hold although one observation satisfies both processes when x is equal to 2. A counterexample is that when x is not equal to 2, processes P and Q perform action c and d, respectively.

Notice that we only allow that in the trace sequence of process P, every element shall be the same as its counterpart in Q. In other words, our refinement prevents atomic program operations updating shared variables from being refined by non-atomic program operations which make the same effect. For example, given a process $P = e\{x = x + 1\} \to e\{x = x + 1\} \to Skip$, and a process $Q = e\{x = x + 2\} \to Skip$, the refinement $P \sqsupseteq Q$ does not hold.

Definition 3 (Equivalence). *For any two CSP# processes P and Q, P is equivalent to Q if and only if $P \sqsupseteq Q \wedge Q \sqsupseteq P$.*

Lemma 1. *All process combinators defined in the CSP# language are monotonic.*

Theorem 1. *The open semantics of CSP# is compositional.*

The proofs of Lemma 1 and Theorem 1 are available in appendix.

4   Algebraic Laws

In this section, we present a set of algebraic laws concerning the distinct features of CSP#. All algebraic laws can be established based on our denotational model. That is to say, if the equality of two differently written processes is algebraically provable, then the two processes are also equivalent with respect to the denotational semantics. Moreover, these algebraic laws can be used as auxiliary reasoning rules to provide an easier

---

[2] The term *obs* represents the set of observational variables *ok*, *wait*, *tr*, and *ref*, as is the case of obs_0 and obs'.

way to prove process equivalence during the theorem proving procedures. Due to the space limitations, proofs that the algebraic laws are sound with respect to the denotational semantics are available in [12].

State Guard
guard - 1 $[b_1]([b_2]P) = [b_1 \wedge b_2]P$
guard - 2 $[b](P_1 \text{ op } P_2) = [b]P_1 \text{ op } [b]P_2$ where, $\text{op} \in \{\|, \Box, \sqcap\}$
guard - 3 $[false]P = Stop$
guard - 4 $[true]P = P$
guard - 1 enables the elimination of nested guards. **guard - 2** shows the distribution of the state guard through parallel composition, external choice and internal choice. **guard - 3** shows that process $[false]P$ behaves like $Stop$ because its guard can never be fired. **guard - 4** shows that process $[true]P$ always activates the process P.

Sequential Composition
seq - 1 $(P_1; P_2); P_3 = P_1; (P_2; P_3)$
seq - 2 $P_1; (P_2 \sqcap P_3) = (P_1; P_2) \sqcap (P_1; P_3)$
seq - 3 $(P_1 \sqcap P_2); P_3 = (P_1; P_3) \sqcap (P_2; P_3)$
seq - 4 $P = Skip; P$
seq - 5 $P = P; Skip$
seq - 1 shows that sequential composition is associative. **seq - 2, 3** show the distribution of sequential composition through external choice. **seq - 4, 5** show that process $Skip$ is the left and right unit of sequential composition, respectively.

Parallel Composition
par - 3 $Skip \| P = P = P \| Skip$
par - 1, 2 show that parallel composition is commutative and associative. Consequently, the order of parallel composition is irrelevant. **par - 3** shows that process $Skip$ is the unit of parallelism.

5   The Closed Semantics

So far, we have constructed an open semantics for CSP#. Namely, the denotational semantics is defined in an open environment. The interference by the environment is implicitly captured in the hybrid trace which collects the potential events or state transitions in which a process may engage. For example, given a trace $\langle (s_1, s_1') \rangle \frown \langle (s_2, e) \rangle$, the transition from state s_1' to s_2 is implicit, and it is performed by the environment. In addition, the environment can change the states, so it is not necessary to ensure that state s_1' is the same as s_2. Thus the system and environment alternate in making transitions. From Theorem 1, the open semantics maintains the compositionality of the processes. Therefore, it supports compositional verification of process behaviours.

However, if we look at it in another light, there is no need to retain all possible transitions from the environment if we have already built the model of the whole system or the behaviour of the environment has been modelled as a process. In this situation, we attempt to consider a closed semantics for the CSP# language. Fortunately, the closed semantics does not need to be defined from the scratch; it can be generated from the open semantics. Thus, we first introduce the definition of closed traces to judge which trace exactly describes the process behaviour in a closed environment.

Definition 4 (Closed Trace). *A hybrid trace tr is closed, represented as* cl(tr), *if it satisfies the following two conditions.*

(1) For any state pair which is not the last element in the trace, the post-state is passed as the pre-state of its immediate subsequent element, i.e., $\forall 0 \leq i < \#tr - 1, \exists s, s' \in \mathsf{S} \bullet (tr_i = (s, s') \Rightarrow s' = \pi_1(tr_{(i+1)}))^3$.

(2) For any event which is not the last element in the trace, it should share the same pre-state with its immediate subsequent element, i.e., $\forall 0 \leq i < \#tr - 1, \exists s \in \mathsf{S}, a \in \mathsf{E} \bullet (tr_i = (s, a) \Rightarrow s = \pi_1(tr_{(i+1)}))$.

Informally speaking, a closed trace has this property: two adjacent elements in the trace are associated by a common state; the post-state of the former equals to the pre-state of the latter if the former is a state transition; the pre-state is shared if the former is an event. Note that every element in a hybrid trace has a pre-state but only the state transition possesses a post-state because the pre-state is not changed when an event occurs. Since the environment cannot update the shared state, a closed trace is identified as the behaviour of the process in the closed environment. For convenience, given a set of hybrid traces, denoted as the set *HT*, we define CL(*HT*) to represent the set of all closed traces in *HT*. Obviously, we have CL(*HT*) ⊆ *HT*.

Now, we can generate the closed semantics (denoted by $[\![P]\!]_{closed}$) from the open semantics ($[\![P]\!]_{open}$) for any communicating process *P*. The relation between them is revealed by Definition 5.

Definition 5 (Closed Semantics). $[\![P]\!]_{closed} \mathrel{\hat{=}} [\![P]\!]_{open} \wedge \mathsf{cl}(tr) \wedge \mathsf{cl}(tr')$

According to the open semantics, two processes that are semantically equivalent can generate the same traces *tr*, *tr'*. Further, any two closed traces generated from their open traces are the same. Thus the equality with respect to the open semantics is preserved by the closed semantics, which is shown in Theorem 2.

Theorem 2. $[\![P]\!]_{open} = [\![Q]\!]_{open} \Rightarrow [\![P]\!]_{closed} = [\![Q]\!]_{closed}$

However, we cannot imply that $[\![P]\!]_{open} = [\![Q]\!]_{open}$ is true when $[\![P]\!]_{closed} = [\![Q]\!]_{closed}$ holds. Furthermore, given that $[\![P]\!]_{closed} = [\![Q]\!]_{closed}$, the law $P \parallel R = Q \parallel R$ may be invalid; the compositionality fails in the closed semantics as shown by Example 1.

Example 1. Given a process $P = a\{x = 2\} \rightarrow ([x = 2]b \rightarrow Skip \ \square \ [x \neq 2]c \rightarrow Skip)$, and a process $Q = a\{x = 2\} \rightarrow ([x = 2]b \rightarrow Skip \ \square \ [x \neq 2]d \rightarrow Skip)$, the closed semantics of processes *P* and *Q* is the same, while their open semantics is not the same because after executing the event *a*, process *P* may execute event *c*, and process *Q* may execute event *d* when the value of variable *x* is not equal to 2 in their pre-states. Therefore, given a process $R = e\{x = 3\} \rightarrow Skip$, there is a case that after executing the events *a* and *e* sequentially, process $P \parallel R$ will execute event *c* while process $Q \parallel R$ will execute event *d*, and thus the law $P \parallel R = Q \parallel R$ is not satisfied.

---

³ tr_i returns the $(i + 1)th$ element of the sequence *tr*.

6   Conclusion

In this work, we have proposed an observation-oriented semantics in an open environment for the CSP# language based on the UTP framework. The formalised semantics covers different types of concurrency, i.e., communications and shared variable parallelism. In addition, a set of algebraic laws have been proposed based on the denotational model for communicating processes involving shared variables. Furthermore, a *closed* semantics has been derived from the open denotational semantics by focusing on the particular hybrid traces. Our next step is to encode our proposed semantics into a generic theorem prover and in turn to validate the algebraic laws using the theorem proving techniques. Ultimately, we can verify the correctness of system behaviours in a theorem prover which may solve the common state space explosion problem.

Acknowledgements. The authors thank Jim Woodcock for insightful comments in the initial discussion.

References

1. Brookes, S.D.: Full abstraction for a shared-variable parallel language. Inf. Comput. 127(2), 145–163 (1996)
2. Cavalcanti, A., Woodcock, J.: A tutorial introduction to CSP in *unifying theories of programming*. In: Cavalcanti, A., Sampaio, A., Woodcock, J. (eds.) PSSE 2004. LNCS, vol. 3167, pp. 220–268. Springer, Heidelberg (2006)
3. Colvin, R., Hayes, I.J.: CSP with Hierarchical State. In: Leuschel, M., Wehrheim, H. (eds.) IFM 2009. LNCS, vol. 5423, pp. 118–135. Springer, Heidelberg (2009)
4. Fischer, C.: Combining Object-Z and CSP. In: FBT, pp. 119–128 (1997)
5. Galloway, A.J., Stoddart, W.J.: An Operational Semantics for ZCCS. In: ICFEM, pp. 272–282 (1997)
6. Hoare, C.: Communicating Sequential Processes. Prentice-Hall (1985)
7. Hoare, C., He, J.: Unifying Theories of Programming. Prentice-Hall (1998)
8. Oliveira, M., Cavalcanti, A., Woodcock, J.: A UTP Semantics for *Circus*. Formal Asp. Comput. 21(1-2), 3–32 (2009)
9. Qin, S., Dong, J.S., Chin, W.-N.: A Semantic Foundation for TCOZ in Unifying Theories of Programming. In: Araki, K., Gnesi, S., Mandrioli, D. (eds.) FME 2003. LNCS, vol. 2805, pp. 321–340. Springer, Heidelberg (2003)
10. Roscoe, A.W.: The Theory and Practice of Concurrency. Prentice Hall (1997)
11. Schneider, S., Treharne, H.: CSP Theorems for Communicating B Machines. Formal Asp. Comput. 17(4), 390–422 (2005)
12. Shi, L.: A UTP Semantics for Communicating Processes with Shared Variables. Technical report, NUS (2013), http://www.comp.nus.edu.sg/~shiling/Tech13.pdf
13. Smith, G.: A Semantic Integration of Object-Z and CSP for the Specification of Concurrent Systems. In: Fitzgerald, J.S., Jones, C.B., Lucas, P. (eds.) FME 1997. LNCS, vol. 1313, pp. 62–81. Springer, Heidelberg (1997)
14. Sun, J., Liu, Y., Dong, J.S., Chen, C.: Integrating Specification and Programs for System Modeling and Verification. In: TASE, pp. 127–135 (2009)
15. Sun, J., Liu, Y., Dong, J.S., Pang, J.: PAT: Towards Flexible Verification under Fairness. In: Bouajjani, A., Maler, O. (eds.) CAV 2009. LNCS, vol. 5643, pp. 709–714. Springer, Heidelberg (2009)
16. Taguchi, K., Araki, K.: The State-Based CCS Semantics for Concurrent Z Specification. In: ICFEM, pp. 283–292 (1997)

17. Winskel, G.: The Formal Semantics of Programming Languages: An Introduction. MIT Press, Cambridge (1993)
18. Woodcock, J., Larsen, P.G., Bicarregui, J., Fitzgerald, J.S.: Formal Methods: Practice and Experience. ACM Comput. Surv. 41(4) (2009)
19. Huibiao, Z., Bowen, J.P., Jifeng, H.: From Operational Semantics to Denotational Semantics for Verilog. In: Margaria, T., Melham, T.F. (eds.) CHARME 2001. LNCS, vol. 2144, pp. 449–464. Springer, Heidelberg (2001)
20. Zhu, H., He, J., Bowen, J.P.: From algebraic semantics to denotational semantics for verilog. In: ISSE, vol. 4(4), pp. 341–360 (2008)
21. Zhu, H., Qin, S., He, J., Bowen, J.P.: PTSC: probability, time and shared-variable concurrency. In: ISSE, vol. 5(4), pp. 271–284 (2009)
22. Zhu, H., Yang, F., He, J., Bowen, J.P., Sanders, J.W., Qin, S.: Linking Operational Semantics and Algebraic Semantics for a Probabilistic Timed Shared-Variable Language. J. Log. Algebr. Program. 81(1), 2–25 (2012)

Appendix

A   Proof of Lemma 1

Proof. We show here the proof of monotonicity for the parallel composition operator, and the proofs of monotonicity for other operators are available in our technical report [12].

Case: Parallel Composition Given any two processes P and Q such that $P \sqsupseteq Q$ and synchronisation events of process $P \parallel R$ and process $Q \parallel R$ are the same (denoted as set X), $P \parallel R \sqsupseteq Q \parallel R$ holds.

First, we have two auxiliary lemmas in our proof, whose proofs are available in [12].

Lemma 2. $(P \wedge R) \sqsupseteq (Q \wedge R)$, provided that $P \sqsupseteq Q$.

Lemma 3. $(P;\ R) \sqsupseteq (Q;\ R)$, provided that $P \sqsupseteq Q$.

$$
\begin{aligned}
& P \sqsupseteq Q && [\textit{Definition 2}] \\
={} & [P \Rightarrow Q] && [\textit{predicate calculus}] \\
={} & [P[0.obs/obs'] \Rightarrow Q[0.obs/obs']] && [\textit{Definition 2}] \\
={} & P[0.obs/obs'] \sqsupseteq Q[0.obs/obs'] && [\textit{Lemma 2}] \\
={} & \begin{array}{l} (P[0.obs/obs'] \wedge R[1.obs/obs']) \sqsupseteq \\ (Q[0.obs/obs'] \wedge R[1.obs/obs']) \end{array} && [\textit{Lemma 3}] \\
\Rightarrow{} & \begin{array}{l} (P[0.obs/obs'] \wedge R[1.obs/obs']);\ M(X) \sqsupseteq \\ (Q[0.obs/obs'] \wedge R[1.obs/obs']);\ M(X) \end{array} && [3.2.3] \\
={} & P \parallel R \sqsupseteq Q \parallel R && \square
\end{aligned}
$$

In a similar proof, the predicate $R \parallel P \sqsupseteq R \parallel Q$ also holds given the same assumption as above.   □

B   Proof of Theorem 1

Proof. Given process combinator F and processes P, Q such that P and Q are equivalent with respect to the open semantics, we have $P \sqsupseteq Q$ and $Q \sqsupseteq P$ according to Definition 3. According to Lemma 1, both $F(P) \sqsupseteq F(Q)$ and $F(Q) \sqsupseteq F(P)$, which indicates $F(P) = F(Q)$, i.e., the open semantics is compositional.   □

Verification of Static and Dynamic Barrier Synchronization Using Bounded Permissions

Duy-Khanh Le, Wei-Ngan Chin, and Yong-Meng Teo

Department of Computer Science, National University of Singapore
{leduykha,chinwn,teoym}@comp.nus.edu.sg

Abstract. Mainstream languages such as C/C++ (with Pthreads), Java, and .NET provide programmers with both *static* and *dynamic barriers* for synchronizing concurrent threads in fork/join programs. However, such barrier synchronization in fork/join programs is hard to verify since programmers must not only keep track of the dynamic number of participating threads, but also ensure that all participants proceed in correctly synchronized phases. As barriers are commonly used in practice, verifying correct synchronization of barriers can provide compilers and analysers with important phasing information for improving the precision of their analyses and optimizations.

In this paper, we propose an approach for statically verifying correct synchronization of *static* and *dynamic barriers* in fork/join programs. We introduce the notions of *bounded permissions* and *phase numbers* for keeping track of the number of participating threads and barrier phases respectively. The approach has been proven sound, and a prototype of it (named VERIBSYNC) has been implemented for verifying barrier synchronization of realistic programs in the SPLASH-2 benchmark suite.

Keywords: Verification, Concurrency, Barrier, Logic, Permissions.

1 Introduction

Software barriers are a kind of collective operations available in Pthreads, Java, .NET, OpenMP, and others. Threads participating in a barrier proceed in *phases*. A typical usage of barriers is presented in Fig. 1. When a thread issues a barrier wait, it waits until a pre-defined number of threads (all threads or just a group of threads) have also issued a barrier wait; after that, all participating threads proceed to the next phase. SPMD (single program, multiple data) programs, such as those written in OpenMP, typically have a single barrier to coordinate all threads in the programs. On the other hand, fork/join programs written in Pthreads, Java, and .NET could use more than one barrier to coordinate different (possibly non-disjoint) groups of threads. In

```
//b has 2 participants
b = new barrier(2);

//Thread 1  ‖ //Thread 2
//Phase 0   ‖ //Phase 0
wait(b);    ‖ wait(b);
//Phase 1   ‖ //Phase 1
```

Fig. 1. Typical Usage of Barriers

L. Groves and J. Sun (Eds.): ICFEM 2013, LNCS 8144, pp. 231–248, 2013.
© Springer-Verlag Berlin Heidelberg 2013

Pthreads [1], barriers are *static*, i.e. the number of participants is fixed. In .NET framework [7], barriers are *dynamic* as the number of participants can vary during a program's execution. The java.util.concurrent library [9] supports both static and dynamic barriers (i.e. CyclicBarrier and Phaser respectively).

Barriers are commonly used in practice. For example, all twelve realistic programs in SPLASH-2 benchmark suite [22] use at least one barrier and four out of twelve programs use more than one barrier for synchronization, covering numerous application domains such as computer graphics (volrend), water molecule simulation (water-spatial), and engineering (radix) among others. Therefore, verifying correct synchronization of barriers is desirable because it can provide compilers and analysers with important phasing information for improving the precision of their analyses and optimizations such as reducing false sharing [11], may-happen-in-parallel analysis [15,24], and data race detection [12]. For example, given the information that a program is verified as correctly synchronized on a barrier, concurrency analysers [12,15,24] could significantly improve their analyses by exploiting the fact that two statements in different barrier phases cannot be executed in parallel. However, static verification of barrier synchronization in fork/join programs is hard because programmers must not only keep track of (possibly dynamic) number of participating threads, but also ensure that all participants proceed in correctly synchronized phases.

Verification approaches such as those based on separation logic [18] and implicit dynamic frames [21] often use an *access permission system*, such as fractional permissions [5] or counting permissions [4], as the basis for reasoning about race-free sharing of resources. There are *bounded resources* (e.g. barriers) which are typically shared among a *bounded* number (or a group) of concurrent threads. Unfortunately, when using existing permission systems [4,5], a resource could be split off an unbounded number of times and hence unintentionally shared among an *unbounded* number of concurrent threads. Therefore, existing permission systems are not suitable for reasoning about bounded resources.

In this paper, we first introduce a new permission system, called *bounded permissions*, to enable reasoning for bounded resources (§3). We then present a logical approach for statically verifying correct synchronization of *static* and *dynamic* barriers in fork/join programs. For verifying *static barriers*, the approach uses *bounded permissions* and *phase numbers* to keep track of the number of participants and barrier phases respectively (§4). For verifying *dynamic barriers*, the approach introduces *dynamic bounded permissions* to additionally keep track of the additions and/or removals of participants (§5). To the best of our knowledge, our paper is the first effort to verify synchronization of both *static* and *dynamic barriers* in fork/join programs.

2   Background

In this section, we first discuss some basic notations in separation logic [17,18]. We then present a fork/join programming language with barriers.

2.1   Concurrent Separation Logic and Permissions

Separation logic [18] is a resource logic for reasoning about heap-manipulating programs. In separation logic, the simplest *heaps* are the *empty heap* emp and the *heap node* $x \mapsto E$. The basic heap node $x \mapsto E$, pronounced x *points to* E, asserts that it consists of a single cell with integer address x and integer content E. We write $x \mapsto \_$ to describe a heap node with unknown content. Heaps are connected together to form larger heaps by using the *separation connective* $*$. In order to reason about race-free sharing of resources among concurrent threads, heaps are enhanced with *permissions* π [4,5]. A heap node $x \overset{\pi}{\mapsto} E$ indicates a permission to access the content E at the address x. A permission can be *partial* or *full* indicating read or write permission respectively. A permission (either full or partial) can be split into multiple partial permissions which can be shared among threads. Partial permissions can also be gathered back into a single full permission for accounting. A *memory state* consists of $*$-conjunctions of heaps and constraints on their addresses, contents, and permissions.

The beauty of separation logic lies under its *frame rule*:

$$\frac{\{\Phi_1\} \ \mathrm{s} \ \{\Phi_1'\} \qquad modifies(\mathrm{s}) \cap FV(\Phi_2) = \varnothing}{\{\Phi_1 * \Phi_2\} \ \mathrm{s} \ \{\Phi_1' * \Phi_2\}} \tag{1}$$

Informally, if a statement s is safe in a state Φ_1, then s is also safe in a larger state $\Phi_1 * \Phi_2$ given the side condition that s does not modify any free variables in Φ_2 [18]. The same principle applies when verifying concurrent threads, as indicated in the following *parallel composition rule*:

$$\frac{\{\Phi_1\} \ s_1 \ \{\Phi_1'\} \qquad modifies(s_1) \cap FV(\Phi_2, \Phi_2') = \varnothing}{\{\Phi_1 * \Phi_2\} \ s_1 \mid\mid s_2 \ \{\Phi_1' * \Phi_2'\}} \qquad \frac{\{\Phi_2\} \ s_2 \ \{\Phi_2'\} \qquad modifies(s_2) \cap FV(\Phi_1, \Phi_1') = \varnothing}{} \tag{2}$$

Since two concurrent threads s_1 and s_2 "mind their own business" and do not modify variables of each other, the combined state $\Phi_1' * \Phi_2'$ is safe [17]. This principle allows *local reasoning* as concurrent threads are verified independently. Note that the frame rule can be expressed in terms of the parallel composition rule as s is equivalent to s||no-op.

$P ::= proc^*$	Program
$proc ::= \mathbf{pn}((t \ v)^*) \ spec^* \ \{ \ s \ \}$	Procedure declaration
$spec ::= \mathbf{requires} \ \Phi_{pr} \ \mathbf{ensures} \ \Phi_{po};$	Pre/Post-conditions
$t ::= \mathbf{int} \mid \mathbf{bool} \mid \mathbf{void} \mid \mathbf{barrier}$	Type
$v = \mathbf{fork}(pn, v^*) \mid \mathbf{join}(v)$	
$\qquad \mid \mathbf{barrier} \ b = \mathbf{new} \ \mathbf{barrier}(n)$	
$s ::= \ \mid \mathbf{destroy}(b) \mid \mathbf{wait}(b)$	
$\qquad \mid \mathbf{add}(b, m) \mid \mathbf{remove}(b, m)$	Statement
$\qquad \mid s_1; s_2 \mid \mathbf{pn}(v^*) \mid \mathbf{if} \ e \ \mathbf{then} \ s_1 \ \mathbf{else} \ s_2$	
$\qquad \mid \ldots$	

Fig. 2. Fork/Join Programming Language with Specifications

2.2   A Fork/Join Programming Language with Barriers

Mainstream languages such as C/C++ (with Pthreads), Java, and .NET provide barriers for synchronizing a group of threads. As our approach is language-independent, we develop a core language with fork/join concurrency and barriers (Fig. 2). The language is straightforward (see [14] for details). Note that in this paper, for brevity of presentation, we often use the parallel composition $(s_1\|s_2)$; as an abbreviation for creating concurrent threads. The parallel composition is syntactic sugar and can easily be encoded via fork and join.

3   Bounded Permissions

In this section, we present our bounded permission system for reasoning about bounded resources. Although we place our bounded permissions in the context of separation logic, bounded permissions can be generally applied to other logics such as implicit dynamic frames [21].

A permission system should distinguish full permission for total control (read, write, and destroy) from partial permission for shared access (read only: no thread can write or destroy) [5]. Permission accounting (e.g. the ability to split a permission into multiple partial permissions for shared access and to combine partial permissions into a full permission for exclusive write) is critical for reasoning about fork/join programs [4]. Besides the above properties, our bounded permission system additionally provides the notion of "boundedness" as the guarantee for reasoning about bounded resources.

Bounded permission: $x \xmapsto{c,t} E$		
Permission count: c	Full permission: $c = t$	
Permission total: t	Partial permission: $c < t$	
Permission invariant: $0 < c \leq t$	Unit permission: $c = 1$	

Permission rules:

[SPLIT/COMBINE] $x \xmapsto{c,t} E \wedge c = c_1 + c_2 \iff x \xmapsto{c_1,t} E * x \xmapsto{c_2,t} E$

[SEP] $x_1 \xmapsto{c_1,t_1} E * x_2 \xmapsto{c_2,t_2} E \wedge (t_1 \neq t_2 \vee c_1 + c_2 > t_1) \implies x_1 \neq x_2$

Fig. 3. Bounded Permission System

Fig. 3 summarizes our bounded permission system. An assertion $x \xmapsto{c,t} E$ represents a bounded permission to access the content E at the address x. A permission quantity is a pair of integers (c,t) where $0 < c \leq t$; $c = t$ indicates a *full permission* while $c < t$ indicates a *partial permission*. Permissions with $c = 1$ are called *unit permissions*. A permission can be split into two permissions (reading from left to right of the rule [SPLIT/COMBINE]). In the other direction, heap nodes can be combined using $*$ iff their addresses coincide, they agree on their contents and their permissions can be combined arithmetically. Note that due to the invariant $0 < c \leq t$, a unit permission cannot be split off. Besides the ability

$$\{ \text{ emp } \}$$
$$\texttt{x = new(2)};$$
$$\{ x \xmapsto{2,2} \_ \}$$
$$\texttt{[x] = 5};$$
$$\{ x \xmapsto{2,2} 5 \}$$
$$//|\text{SPLIT}|$$

$$\left(\begin{array}{c} \{ x \xmapsto{1,2} 5 \} \\ \texttt{y=[x]+1}; \\ \{ x \xmapsto{1,2} 5 \land y = 6 \} \end{array} \middle\| \begin{array}{c} \{ x \xmapsto{1,2} 5 \} \\ \texttt{z=[x]-1}; \\ \{ x \xmapsto{1,2} 5 \land z = 4 \} \end{array} \middle\| \begin{array}{c} \{ \text{ emp } \} \\ \texttt{t=10}; \\ \{ t = 10 \} \end{array} \right) ;$$

$$//|\text{COMBINE}|$$
$$\{ x \xmapsto{2,2} 5 \land y = 6 \land z = 4 \land t = 10 \}$$
$$\texttt{destroy(x)};$$
$$\{ \text{ emp } \land y = 6 \land z = 4 \land t = 10 \}$$

Fig. 4. Example of Using Bounded Permissions

to split/combine permissions, the notion of separation ([SEP]) is important for reasoning about separation of resources [4,18]. Two heaps agreeing on their contents are separated ($x_1 \neq x_2$) if their permission totals are different or the sum of their permission counts is higher than the permission total.

We can create a new bounded-permission resource (with n is assigned to the permission total) and destroy it only in full permissions:

$$\{ n > 0 \} \texttt{ x = new(n)}; \{ x \xmapsto{n,n} \_ \} \tag{3}$$
$$\{ x \xmapsto{n,n} \_ \} \texttt{ destroy(x)}; \{ \text{ emp } \}$$

Given a full permission, we are sure that no other thread can access the shared resource. Therefore, we can safely destroy it. In languages with automatic garbage collection, such a destroy operation is not necessary, but the full permission is still useful in guiding the garbage collector for safe collection.

Similarly, we need a full permission for writing and any permission (full or partial) for reading:

$$\{ x \xmapsto{n,n} \_ \} \texttt{ [x] = E}; \{ x \xmapsto{n,n} E \} \tag{4}$$
$$\{ x \xmapsto{c,t} E \} \texttt{ y = [x]}; \{ x \xmapsto{c,t} E \land y = E \}$$

[x] is an abbreviation for accessing the content located at the address x. In the last rule, there is a side condition that y is not free in E.

Now, it is straightforward to verify the correctness of the program in Fig. 4, in which only two threads are intended to concurrently read the content at the location x. As a brief comparison, when using existing permission systems [4,5], there is nothing to prevent x from being split off into more than two partial permissions and hence unintentionally accessed by more than two threads.

The following lemma states our guarantee on boundedness property.

Lemma 1 (Boundedness). *Given a resource x with a full permission $x \xmapsto{n,n} \_$ ($n>0$), there are at most n concurrent accesses to x, i.e. x is shared among at most n concurrent threads at a given time.*

Proof. A thread needs at least a unit permission $x \overset{1,n}{\longmapsto} \_$ to access x and there are at most n such unit permissions.   □

4   Verification of Static Barriers

In this section, we present our approach to verifying correct synchronization of static barriers. We first define what it means for a program to be correctly synchronized.

Definition 1 (Correct Synchronization). *A program is correctly synchronized with respect to a static barrier b iff:*

- *There is exactly a predefined number of threads participating in the barrier b's wait operations.*
- *Participating threads operate on b in the same numbers of phases.*

$$\{ \text{ emp } \}$$
$$\text{barrier b = new barrier(2);}$$
$$\{ b \overset{2,2}{\longmapsto} \text{barrier}(0) \}$$

$\{ b \overset{1,2}{\longmapsto} \text{barrier}(0) \}$	$\{ b \overset{1,2}{\longmapsto} \text{barrier}(0) \}$
//phase 0;	//phase 0;
wait(b);	wait(b);
//phase 1;	//phase 1;
$\{ b \overset{1,2}{\longmapsto} \text{barrier}(1) \}$	$\{ b \overset{1,2}{\longmapsto} \text{barrier}(1) \}$

$$\{ b \overset{2,2}{\longmapsto} \text{barrier}(1) \}$$
$$\text{destroy(b);}$$
$$\{ \text{ emp } \}$$

(a) Correctly synchronized

$$\{ \text{ emp } \}$$
$$\text{barrier b = new barrier(2);}$$
$$\{ b \overset{2,2}{\longmapsto} \text{barrier}(0) \}$$

$\{ b \overset{1,2}{\longmapsto} \text{barrier}(0) \}$	$\{ b \overset{1,2}{\longmapsto} \text{barrier}(0) \}$
//phase 0;	//phase 0;
wait(b);	//no-op;
//phase 1;	
$\{ b \overset{1,2}{\longmapsto} \text{barrier}(1) \}$	$\{ b \overset{1,2}{\longmapsto} \text{barrier}(0) \}$

//FAIL
. . .

(b) Incorrectly synchronized

Fig. 5. Barrier Synchronization

For illustration, the program in Fig. 5a is correctly synchronized while the program in Fig. 5b is not because the two threads in Fig. 5b operate in different numbers of phases. As shown in Section 3, bounded permissions can be used to ensure that *at most* a predefined number of threads can access a resource at a given time. However, verification of barrier synchronization requires a stronger guarantee: *exactly* a predefined number of threads participates in a barrier wait. We enforce such a guarantee by requiring that a participating thread must hold a *unit permission* to perform a barrier wait. If a participant has more than a unit permission, it prohibits other participants from participating. An analogy is a meeting room with n keys distributed among n participants; a meeting takes place only when all participants have come. If a participant has more than one key, when he/she enters the room, at least one other participant will not be able to get in and the meeting cannot take place. We capture barrier phasing by using *phase numbers*, which increase by one after each barrier wait, and require that all participants end up with the same phase numbers. If participants have different phase numbers when completing their execution, some of them must have lost phasing and the program is not correctly synchronized.

A summary of our approach is presented in Fig. 6. An assertion $b \xmapsto{c,t} \mathsf{barrier}(p)$ indicates a bounded permission (c,t) to access the barrier b which is at phase p. When creating a new barrier with the number of participants n, a full permission (i.e. $c=t=n$) of barrier b is created. We can safely destroy a barrier in its full permission. Waiting on a barrier b requires a unit permission $(1,n)$. This is a contributing factor to certify that there is exactly a predefined number of threads participating in the barrier b. After finishing waiting, the phase number p is increased by 1 and threads proceed to the next phase. The permission rules for split/combine ([S–SPLIT] and [S–COMBINE]) and separation [S–SEP] are similar to those of standard bounded permissions.

Bounded permission: $b \xmapsto{c,t} \mathsf{barrier}(p)$

Permission count: c	Permission invariant:	$0 < c \le t$
Permission total: t	Full permission:	$c = t$
Phase number: p	Partial permission:	$c < t$
	Unit permission:	$c = 1$

Verification rules:

$$\{\, n > 0 \,\} \quad \mathtt{barrier\ b\ =\ new\ barrier(n);} \quad \{\, b \xmapsto{n,n} \mathsf{barrier}(0) \,\}$$

$$\{\, b \xmapsto{n,n} \mathsf{barrier}(\_) \,\} \quad \mathtt{destroy(b);} \qquad\qquad\qquad \{\, \mathsf{emp} \,\}$$

$$\{\, b \xmapsto{1,n} \mathsf{barrier}(p) \,\} \quad \mathtt{wait(b);} \qquad\qquad\quad \{\, b \xmapsto{1,n} \mathsf{barrier}(p+1) \,\}$$

Permission rules:

$$[\text{S–SPLIT}]$$
$$b \xmapsto{c,t} \mathsf{barrier}(p) \wedge c = c_1 + c_2 \;\Longrightarrow\; b \xmapsto{c_1,t} \mathsf{barrier}(p) * b \xmapsto{c_2,t} \mathsf{barrier}(p)$$

$$[\text{S–COMBINE}]$$
$$b \xmapsto{c_1,t} \mathsf{barrier}(p) * b \xmapsto{c_2,t} \mathsf{barrier}(p) \;\Longrightarrow\; b \xmapsto{c,t} \mathsf{barrier}(p) \wedge c = c_1 + c_2$$

$$[\text{S–SEP}]$$
$$b_1 \xmapsto{c_1,t_1} \mathsf{barrier}(p) * b_2 \xmapsto{c_2,t_2} \mathsf{barrier}(p) \wedge (t_1 \ne t_2 \;\vee\; c_1 + c_2 > t_1) \;\Longrightarrow\; b_1 \ne b_2$$

Fig. 6. Verification of Static Barriers

Our approach allows for local reasoning where each thread (more precisely each procedure) is verified separately. Intuitively, if threads participate in a barrier b, when they join together, their states must agree on the barrier b. Therefore, we enforce the requirement that concurrent threads must maintain a program in barrier-consistent (or *b-consistent*) states:

$$\frac{\{\Phi_1\}\; s_1\; \{\Phi_1'\} \qquad modifies(s_1) \cap FV(\Phi_2, \Phi_2') = \varnothing}{\{\Phi_2\}\; s_2\; \{\Phi_2'\} \qquad modifies(s_2) \cap FV(\Phi_1, \Phi_1') = \varnothing} \atop {\Phi_1 * \Phi_2\; is\; b-consistent \qquad \Phi_1' * \Phi_2'\; is\; b-consistent \over \{\Phi_1 * \Phi_2\}\; s_1 || s_2\; \{\Phi_1' * \Phi_2'\}}} \tag{5}$$

Compared with the original rule in (2), our parallel composition rule in (5) additionally requires that concurrent threads begin and end in b-*consistent* states. That is, starting from a consistent state with respect to barriers in the program, threads concurrently operate on the barriers; if they terminate, they do so in a consistent state with respect to the barriers. Informally, a memory state is b-*consistent* if its barrier nodes agree on the phase numbers. After completing their execution, if the threads end up in a joined state $\Phi_1' * \Phi_2'$ which is not b-consistent, the program is rejected as it is incorrectly synchronized. A similar consistency check is also required for the frame rule, which is omitted here since it can be derived from the parallel composition rule (see Section 2.1).

Definition 2 (Combined State). *A combined state Φ_c of a memory state Φ is achieved by repeatedly applying the* [S–COMBINE] *rule until a fixpoint is reached.*

Such a fixpoint always exists as the [S–COMBINE] rule can only reduce the number of heap nodes.

Lemma 2. *A memory state Φ and its combined state Φ_c are equivalent.*

Proof. Φ_c is derived from Φ using [S–COMBINE] rule and Φ can be derived from Φ_c using [S–SPLIT] rule. □

Definition 3 (b-consistency). *A combined state Φ_c is b-consistent iff for every pair of barrier nodes $b_1 \xmapsto{c_1, t_1}$ barrier(p_1) and $b_2 \xmapsto{c_2, t_2}$ barrier(p_2) in Φ_c, $b_1 = b_2 \implies p_1 = p_2$ holds.*

Corollary 1. *A memory state Φ is b-consistent iff its combined state Φ_c is b-consistent.*

Proof. It directly follows from Lemma 2 as Φ and Φ_c are equivalent. □

Example 1. The memory state $b_1 \xmapsto{1,2}$ barrier(p_1) * $b_2 \xmapsto{1,2}$ barrier(p_1) is b-consistent. However, the memory state $b_1 \xmapsto{1,2}$ barrier(p_1) * $b_2 \xmapsto{1,2}$ barrier(p_1+1) is not since, intuitively, it is possible for $b1$ and $b2$ to be aliased and thus the two aliased barrier nodes have inconsistent phase numbers on the same barrier.

We apply our approach to verification of the programs presented in Fig. 5. The program in Fig. 5a can be proven correctly synchronized. When verifying the program in Fig. 5b, our verification system reports a failure when joining the two threads because the joined state is not b-consistent.

Fig. 7 shows another example which is rather complex due to intricate phasing. Our bounded permissions ensure that there are exactly two threads participating

$$\{ \text{ emp } \}$$
$$\texttt{barrier b = new barrier(2);}$$
$$\{ b \xmapsto{2,2} \text{barrier}(0) \}$$

$$
\left(
\begin{array}{l}
\{ b \xmapsto{1,2} \text{barrier}(0) \} \\
\texttt{int i=0;} \\
\{ b \xmapsto{1,2} \text{barrier}(0) \wedge i = 0 \} \\
\texttt{while (i<10)\{ wait(b);i++;\}} \\
\texttt{i=0;} \\
\texttt{while (i<10)\{ wait(b);i++;\}} \\
\{ b \xmapsto{1,2} \text{barrier}(20) \wedge i = 10 \}
\end{array}
\middle\|
\begin{array}{l}
\{ b \xmapsto{1,2} \text{barrier}(0) \} \\
\texttt{int j=0;} \\
\{ b \xmapsto{1,2} \text{barrier}(0) \wedge j = 0 \} \\
\texttt{while (j<20)\{wait(b); j++; \}} \\
\\
\\
\{ b \xmapsto{1,2} \text{barrier}(20) \wedge j = 20 \}
\end{array}
\right) ;
$$

$$\{ b \xmapsto{2,2} \text{barrier}(20)\}$$

Fig. 7. More Complex Example

in the barrier b while the phase numbers capture exact phasing. Although the two threads operate in different while loops, our notion of phase numbers can certify that the two threads participate in the same numbers of phases. Therefore, the program is correctly synchronized. Our approach is also capable of verifying programs with more intricate sharing and nested fork/join (see [14] for more example programs).

5   Verification of Dynamic Barriers

This section presents our approach to verifying correct synchronization of dynamic barriers. In contrast to static barriers whose number of participants is fixed, dynamic barriers allow the number of participants to be changed during a program's execution. For example, .NET framework allows threads to add and remove m participants to/from a barrier b dynamically via $\mathbf{add}(b, m)$ and $\mathbf{remove}(b, m)$.[1] We first present a variant of bounded permissions (called *dynamic bounded permissions*) to keep track of the additions and/or removals of barrier participants of each thread. We then introduce a set of verification and permission rules to reason about dynamic behaviors of dynamic barriers.

A summary of our approach is presented in Fig. 8. Compared to the bounded permission in Section 3, a dynamic bounded permission of a barrier $b \xmapsto{c,t,a}$ barrier(p) adds an additional component a, called *permission addition*, to keep track of the additions and/or removals of barrier participants issued by each thread. Permission addition a is a rational number since when splitting a dynamic bounded permission, we require that the split-off permissions have proportional shares of a (details to be presented soon). We also introduce the notion of *zero permission* to capture the fact that a thread has dropped its participation to a barrier ($c=0$) but still retained its information about the addition and/or removals of participants. Our approach guarantees that zero permission can only

---

[1] .NET indeed uses AddParticipants() and RemoveParticipants(); we write add() and remove() for brevity.

Dynamic bounded permission: $b \xmapsto{c,t,a}$ barrier(p)	
Permission count: $\quad c$	Permission invariant: $\quad 0 \le c \le t+a$
Permission total: $\quad t$	Full permission: $\quad c = t+a$
Permission addition: a	Partial permission: $\quad 0 < c < t+a$
Phase number: $\quad p$	Unit permission: $\quad c = 1$
	Zero permission: $\quad c = 0$

Verification rules:

$$\{n>0\} \ \texttt{b = new barrier(n);} \ \{b \xmapsto{n,n,0} \text{barrier}(0)\}$$

$$\{b \xmapsto{c,t,a} \text{barrier}(\_) \wedge c=t+a\} \ \texttt{destroy(b);} \qquad \{emp\}$$

$$\{b \xmapsto{1,t,a} \text{barrier}(p)\} \ \texttt{wait(b);} \qquad \{b \xmapsto{1,t,a} \text{barrier}(p+1)\}$$

$$\{b \xmapsto{c,t,a} \text{barrier}(p) \wedge c>0 \wedge m>0\} \ \texttt{add(b,m);} \qquad \{b \xmapsto{c+m,t,a+m} \text{barrier}(p)\}$$

$$\{b \xmapsto{c,t,a} \text{barrier}(p) \wedge c \ge m \wedge m>0\} \ \texttt{remove(b,m);} \qquad \{b \xmapsto{c-m,t,a-m} \text{barrier}(p)\}$$

Permission rules:

$$[\text{D--SPLIT}]$$

$$b \xmapsto{c,t,a} \text{barrier}(p) \wedge 0<c\le t+a \wedge 0<c_1<t+a_1 \wedge 0<c_2<t+a_2 \wedge c=c_1+c_2 \wedge a=a_1+a_2$$
$$\wedge \ a_1=\tfrac{c_1}{c}\cdot a \wedge a_2=\tfrac{c_2}{c}\cdot a \implies b \xmapsto{c_1,t,a_1} \text{barrier}(p) * b \xmapsto{c_2,t,a_2} \text{barrier}(p)$$

$$[\text{D--COMBINE--1}]$$

$$b \xmapsto{c_1,t,a_1} \text{barrier}(p) * b \xmapsto{c_2,t,a_2} \text{barrier}(p) \wedge c_1 \ne 0 \wedge c_2 \ne 0$$
$$\implies b \xmapsto{c,t,a} \text{barrier}(p) \wedge c=c_1+c_2 \wedge a=a_1+a_2$$

$$[\text{D--COMBINE--2}]$$

$$b \xmapsto{c_1,t,a_1} \text{barrier}(p_1) * b \xmapsto{c_2,t,a_2} \text{barrier}(p_2) \wedge c_1 \ne 0 \wedge c_2=0 \wedge p_2 \le p_1$$
$$\implies b \xmapsto{c,t,a} \text{barrier}(p_1) \wedge c=c_1+c_2 \wedge a=a_1+a_2$$

$$[\text{D--COMBINE--3}]$$

$$b \xmapsto{c_1,t,a_1} \text{barrier}(p_1) * b \xmapsto{c_2,t,a_2} \text{barrier}(p_2) \wedge c_1=0 \wedge c_2=0$$
$$\implies b \xmapsto{0,t,a} \text{barrier}(p) \wedge a=a_1+a_2 \wedge p=max(p_1,p_2)$$

$$[\text{D--FULL}]$$

$$b \xmapsto{c,t,a} \text{barrier}(p) \wedge c=t+a \wedge a \ne 0 \implies b \xmapsto{c,t+a,0} \text{barrier}(p)$$

$$[\text{D--SEP}]$$

$$b_1 \xmapsto{c_1,t_1,a_1} \text{barrier}(p_1) * b_2 \xmapsto{c_2,t_2,a_2} \text{barrier}(p_2) \wedge (t_1 \ne t_2 \ \vee \ c_1+c_2>t_1+a_1+a_2)$$
$$\implies b_1 \ne b_2$$

Fig. 8. Verification of Dynamic Barriers

be achieved by a thread deliberately removing its participation and cannot be produced by a permission split. A permission quantity (c, t, a) statically captures the local view of a thread on the barrier. With the presence of permission addition a, the full permission is achieved when $c = t + a$. Intuitively, the current number of participants is equal to the original number of participants plus the number of participants added or removed. One could recognize that dynamic bounded permission and bounded permission coincide when $a=0$.

The verification rules in Fig. 8 capture dynamic behaviors of dynamic barriers. Creating a new barrier results in a full permission of the barrier with $a=0$. Destroying a barrier requires a full permission ($c=t+a$). Waiting at a barrier requires a unit permission ($c=1$). Adding and removing m participants add and respectively subtract m from the permission count and the permission addition. The permission total t remains unchanged; it acts as a pivot for combining permissions when threads join together. A thread can only remove up to the permission count it has ($c \geq m$). If $c=m$, after removing, a thread is considered dropping its participation to the barrier. Adding participants requires $c>0$ to ensure that a drop-out thread could not re-participate in a barrier. This is necessary because when dropping out, a thread has lost phasing with other participants; therefore, it is unsafe to allow it to re-participate.

Due to the nature of dynamic barriers, a thread could either fully participate in a barrier (i.e. it does not drop out) or drop its participation in the middle of its execution. Permission rules in Fig. 8 capture those dynamic behaviors. The rule [D–SPLIT] never splits into zero permissions; therefore, it ensures that a zero permission only appears due to a thread's drop-out. The rule also ensures that a full permission is never created by splitting a partial permission since it requires that the two split-off permissions have proportional shares of a; that is $a_1 = \frac{c_1}{c} \cdot a$ and $a_2 = \frac{c_2}{c} \cdot a$. We provide the proof for this claim in [14]. When multiple threads join, some of them have fully participated in the barrier b while others might drop out midway. Therefore, the combine rules have to take into consideration several situations. First, combining two fully participating threads ($c_1 \neq 0$ and $c_2 \neq 0$) adds up their permission counts and permission additions ([D–COMBINE–1]). Because of their full participation, their phase numbers should be equal (both are p). Second, in order to combine one fully-participating thread ($c_1 \neq 0$) and a drop-out ($c_2=0$), the phase number of the latter is at most that of the former ([D–COMBINE–2]). Intuitively, if a thread has dropped its participation in the middle of an execution, it did not participate in some later phases; therefore, its phase number is at most that of a fully-participating thread. Lastly, combining two drop-outs ($c_1=0$ and $c_2=0$) retains their total number of additions/removals ($a=a_1+a_2$) and picks up the maximum between their phase numbers ([D–COMBINE–3]). The rule [D–FULL] reshuffles the full permission into an equivalent form. The rule [D–SEP] introduces the notion of separation in the context of dynamic bounded permissions.

Similar to static barriers, in order to ensure correct synchronization of dynamic barriers and to support local reasoning, our approach requires that concurrent threads maintain a program in dynamic-barrier-consistent (*db-consistent*) states. *Db-consistency* is mostly similar to *b-consistency*; it additionally considers the cases where the phase numbers of barrier nodes of the same barrier are not the same (due to the removal of participants). Due to space limitation, we refer interested readers to our technical report [14] for more details.

Fig. 9 presents the proof outline of a program with dynamic barriers. The leftmost thread fully participates in b while the right thread participates in one phase, then adds another participant (line 8), and creates two child threads operating on b. The left child thread drops out after one phase while the right child thread drops out without participation. At the end of the parallel compositions, the permissions are combined together into a full permission. In our approach,

```
 1                        { emp }
 2              barrier b = new barrier(2);
 3                  { b 2,2,0⟶ barrier(0) }
 4                  //[D−SPLIT]
 5   { b 1,2,0⟶ barrier(0) }              { b 1,2,0⟶ barrier(0) }
 6   wait(b);                             wait(b);
 7   { b 1,2,0⟶ barrier(1) }              { b 1,2,0⟶ barrier(1) }
 8                                        add(b,1);
 9                                        { b 2,2,1⟶ barrier(1) }
10                                        //[D−SPLIT]
11
12                    ⎛ { b 1,2,½⟶ barrier(1) }  ‖  { b 1,2,½⟶ barrier(1) } ⎞
13   wait(b);          ⎜   wait(b);                      remove(b,1);        ⎟
14   { b 1,2,0⟶ barrier(2) }  { b 1,2,½⟶ barrier(2) }                        ⎟
15                    ⎜   remove(b,1);                                        ⎟
16                    ⎜ { b 0,2,−1/2⟶ barrier(2) } ‖ { b 0,2,−1/2⟶ barrier(1) } ⎟
17   wait(b);          ⎝                                                      ⎠
18                              //[D−COMBINE−3]
19   { b 1,2,0⟶ barrier(3) }      { b 0,2,−1⟶ barrier(2) }

19                  //[D−COMBINE−2]
20                  { b 1,2,−1⟶ barrier(3) }
21                      destroy(b);
22                        { emp }
```

Fig. 9. An Example of Verifying Synchronization of Dynamic Barriers

for local reasoning, each thread is verified separately and is unaware of operations (such as add/remove) performed by other threads until they join together. Although sound (as proven in Section 6), our approach is incomplete since it could reject programs that are correct at run-time. However, we believe that our static verification is generally a good practice for programmers to follow in order to avoid unexpected run-time behaviors (see [14] for detailed discussions).

6   Soundness

We show that our proposed approach guarantees correct synchronization of dynamic barriers. As dynamic barriers are more general than static barriers, the soundness also implies correct synchronization of static barriers. We first present an encoding of join operations in terms of barrier operations. This encoding simplifies the proof rules and soundness arguments to only focusing on barrier operations. We then proceed to the main soundness arguments of our approach.

Lemma 3 (Soundness of Verifying Barrier Synchronization). *Given a program with a barrier b and a set of procedures P^i together with their corresponding pre/post-conditions $(\Phi_{pr}^i/\Phi_{po}^i)$, if our verifier derives a proof for every* procedure P^i, i.e. $\{\Phi^i_{pr}\}P^i\{\Phi^i_{po}\}$ is valid, then the program is correctly synchronized with respect to the barrier b.

Proof. Detailed definitions and proofs can be found in [14].   □

7 Implementation and Experimental Results

We implemented our approach into a prototype tool, named VERIBSYNC[2]. We applied VERIBSYNC to verifying static[3] barrier synchronization of all twelve simplified[4] programs of SPLASH-2 suite [22]. SPLASH-2 suite is one of the most widely used benchmarks for evaluating shared-memory systems. The suite consists of twelve realistic programs covering numerous application domains such as computer graphics (`volrend`), signal processing (`fft`), water molecule simulation (`water-spatial`), and general engineering (`radix`) among others. Besides the theoretical contributions, the empirical question we investigate is how well our approach handles realistic barrier synchronization. The results were promising as our approach was able to verify all but one program in SPLASH-2 suite with modest annotation. All experiments were done on a 3.20GHz Intel Core i7-960 processor with 16GB memory running Ubuntu Linux 10.04. The suite of benchmark programs and other examples are provided in our project website.

The experimental results are presented in Table 1. The column *#Bar* shows the number of barriers used in the corresponding program. The column *LOC* shows the total number of non-blank, non-comment, non-annotation lines of source code, counted by `sloccount` (v2.26). The column *LOAnn* shows the total number lines of annotation. Annotation *overhead* is computed as $\frac{LOAnn}{LOC}$ (the lower, the better). Verification times are in seconds. VERIBSYNC was able to verify barrier synchronization of all but one program in SPLASH-2 suite with the verification time in several seconds. We discuss the reason why VERIBSYNC was not able to verify `radiosity` program in Section 8.1. The verification time and annotation overhead depend on characteristics of the programs. Programs that have complicated non-linear constraints and/or use barriers in many execution branches (such as `lu`, `barnes`, `water-*`, and `volrend`) require higher verification time and annotation overhead. On average, VERIBSYNC requires annotation overhead of 11%, which is modest compared with that of 100% reported in the

---

[2] The tool is available for both online use and download at
   `http://loris-7.ddns.comp.nus.edu.sg/~project/veribsync/`.

[3] As dynamic barriers have just been available recently since .NET 4.0 (April 2010) and Java 7 (July 2011), we are not aware of existing concurrency benchmarks that use dynamic barriers. Nonetheless, we applied our prototype on a set of textbook programs which represent typical usage of dynamic barriers. The programs are available in our project website.

[4] As verifying full functional correctness of these programs is beyond the scope of this paper, our experiments were conducted on a set of simplified programs where parts of programs that are not related to barriers were omitted. All related parts such as branching conditions and loops were retained to ensure that barrier synchronizations in the simplified programs are similar to those of the original programs.

Table 1. Annotation Overhead and Verification Time of SPLASH-2 Suite

Program	Description	#Bar	LOC	LOAnn	Overhead	Time
ocean	large-scale ocean simulation	1	60	5	8%	1.01
radix	integer radix sort	2	68	7	10%	3.11
lu	blocked LU decomposition	1	79	12	15%	14.33
barnes	Barnes-Hut for N-body problem	1	84	12	14%	2.35
raytrace	optimized ray tracing	1	94	7	7%	0.44
fft	complex 1D FFT	1	101	8	8%	0.69
water-nsquared	water simulation w/o spatial data structure	3	113	16	14%	13.23
water-spatial	water simulation w/ spatial data structure	3	117	18	15%	13.53
cholesky	blocked sparse cholesky factorization	1	131	10	8%	0.50
fmm	adaptive fast multipole for N-body problem	1	175	20	11%	0.79
volrend	optimized ray casting	2	232	36	16%	7.50
radiosity	hierarchical diffuse radiosity method	1	83	-	-	-
Average	-	-	-	-	11%	5.23

literature [10].[5] Much of the annotation and verification time are dedicated for functional correctness properties of the programs such as branching conditions and loops. As annotation efforts for these properties are also necessary for verifying functional correctness of concurrent programs, we believe that existing logics for verifying functional correctness can easily integrate our approach into their logics and benefit from our guarantee of correct barrier synchronization.

8   Discussion

This section discusses limitations and future extensions of our existing approach.

8.1   Functional Correctness vs. Barrier Synchronization

In our existing approach, threads are correctly synchronized if they end up with the same (determinable) phase numbers. However, there are programs (such as radiosity) where the phase numbers are tightly coupled with functional correctness. A fragment of radiosity program is shown in Fig. 10.

```
/* ... perform ray-gathering till
the solution converges */
while( init_ray_tasks(...) ) {
    wait(barrier);
    process_tasks(...);
}
```

Fig. 10. A Fragment of radiosity

The barrier barrier is used within the while loop which terminates only when the solution converges (by calling the procedure init_ray_tasks to check for convergence). The init_ray_tasks procedure only allows one thread (the first thread entering) to check for convergence and to update a global variable while other threads only read that variable. Such barrier phasing, therefore, is deeply correlated with functional correctness of the program (i.e. the convergence) which could not be captured by our existing approach. However, our approach could be extended to verify this type of programs by considering resource re-distribution that could be used to verify functional correctness, and the use of existential phase numbers. Details of such an extension will be more carefully investigated in the near future.

---

[5] To be precise, the annotation overhead in [10] also includes the specification for functional correctness. Although verifying functional correctness is not our main goal, we also need to specify them for verifying barrier synchronization.

8.2   Deadlock-Free Multiple Barriers

Correct synchronization is a property weaker than deadlock freedom: it ensures deadlock freedom in case of a single barrier. When using multiple barriers, their synchronization patterns could potentially lead to deadlocks. We plan to extend our existing approach with barrier expressions to capture patterns of participating in multiple barriers. Together with the phase numbers, by proving that the barrier expressions of different participants are compatible, we could guarantee deadlock freedom. Patterns of participating in multiple barriers have been used in verification of SPMD programs with static barriers [2,13,24]. However, adapting them to verification of fork/join programs with dynamic barriers is non-trivial. This is not only because we need to address the unstructured nature of fork/join programs (in SPMD programs, threads execute the same code while in fork/join programs, they execute different pieces of code), but also because we need to handle dynamic allocation/deallocation and addition/removals of participants in a modular way. We leave this topic for future investigation.

9   Related Work

This section discusses related works regarding access permission systems and static verification of barrier synchronization. Recently, other advanced forms of barriers such as X10's clocks [19] and phasers [20] have been introduced in the context of async/finish programs. For space reasons, we focus on standard barriers and provide an extended discussion of related works on those advanced forms of barriers in the companion technical report [14].

9.1   Access Permissions

Boyland first introduced fractional permissions for reasoning about non-interference of concurrent programs [5]. Bornat et. al. added counting permissions [4]. Recently, various permission systems such as binary tree share model [6], Plaid's permission system [3], and borrowing permissions [16] have been proposed. In a nutshell, they are akin to fractional and counting permissions.

   Importantly, not every program is suitable for fractional permissions and counting permissions. Programs that allow sharing resources among only a bounded number of threads need another alternative treatment. Fractional and counting permissions could not reason about those programs because, when using these permission systems, there is nothing to prevent a resource from being split off an unbounded number of times and shared among an unbounded number of threads. Given any fractional permission f where $0<f\leq1$, it is always possible to split f into two fractions f_1 and f_2 where $f_1+f_2=f$ and $f_1, f_2>0$. Similarly, in counting permissions, given a central *permission authority* holding a source permission n, it is always possible to split off into a new source permission $n+1$ (held by the central authority) and a read permission -1 for sharing. On the other hand, in our bounded permission system, any non-unit permission

(c, t) where $1 < c \leq t$ (either partial or full permissions) can be split off without the presence of a central authority, and a bounded permission can only be split off a bounded number of times (up to unit permissions). Therefore, bounded permissions enable reasoning about bounded resources such as barriers.

9.2   Verification of Barrier Synchronization

Most existing works on verifying barrier synchronization focus on SPMD programs [2,11,12,13,15,24,23]. In SPMD programs, the fact that threads execute the same code makes verification more tractable. SMPD programs also assume that barriers are global and all threads need to participate in barrier operations. Hence, existing techniques for SPMD programs cannot be directly applied to fork/join programs. This paper fills in the gap and addresses barriers in the context of fork/join concurrency where concurrent threads could execute different pieces of code while participating in barrier operations. Furthermore, we do not restrict that all threads should participate, i.e. a group of threads can participate on a certain barrier. We also support verification of dynamic barriers whose number of participants can vary during a program's execution. We are not aware of any related works capable of verifying dynamic barriers in fork/join programs.

To the best of our knowledge, the most closely related work is by Hobor and Gherghina [10]: they propose a specification logic for verifying partial correctness of programs with static barriers. Based on the global *phase transition specification* of a barrier, they can also verify that participants proceed in correct phases. However, there are several critical differences. First, they do not handle dynamic barriers. Second, they require a global specification of each barrier, whereby programmers have to specify pre-state and post-state for each thread for every phase transition over the barrier. However, there are programs (such as that in Fig. 7) where our approach using phase numbers can verify, but it is not possible to capture a global specification for its barrier [8]. Though the global specification of each barrier is an extra annotation burden, they can facilitate resource re-distribution at synchronization points to ensure functional partial correctness. Our current approach using phase numbers is considerably simpler, but has not yet been designed to support resource re-distribution. This may be important for more complex usage of barrier synchronization.

10   Conclusion

We described a specification and verification approach for ensuring correct synchronization of software barriers. Barriers, provided by many mainstream languages such as C/C++ (with Pthreads), Java, and .NET, are hard to handle in fork/join programs because programmers must not only pay special attention to the (possibly dynamic) number of participating threads, but also ensure that threads proceed in correctly synchronized phases. To our knowledge, this is the first work that statically ensures the correct synchronization of both *static* and *dynamic* barriers in fork/join programs. The keys of our approach are the *bounded permissions* and *phase numbers* to keep track of the number of participating threads and barrier phases respectively. Not restricted to only barriers, bounded permissions can be generally used to reason about any resources that are shared among a bounded number of concurrent threads. Our approach has been proven sound, and a prototype of it has been implemented for verifying barrier synchronization of realistic programs in SPLASH-2 benchmark suite.

Acknowledgement. We are grateful to our colleagues and the anonymous reviewers for their comments. Special thanks to C. Gherghina for many insightful discussions, and to H. D. Nguyen for suggesting the use of rational numbers for soundness. This work is supported by MOE Project 2009-T2-1-063.

References

1. The Open Group Base Specifications Issue 7 IEEE Std 1003 (January 2008), http://pubs.opengroup.org/onlinepubs/9699919799/basedefs/pthread.h.html
2. Aiken, A., Gay, D.: Barrier Inference. In: POPL, pp. 342–354 (1998)
3. Bierhoff, K., Aldrich, J.: Modular typestate checking of aliased objects. In: OOPSLA, pp. 301–320 (2007)
4. Bornat, R., Calcagno, C., O'Hearn, P., Parkinson, M.: Permission Accounting in Separation Logic. In: POPL, pp. 259–270. ACM, New York (2005)
5. Boyland, J.: Checking Interference with Fractional Permissions. In: Cousot, R. (ed.) SAS 2003. LNCS, vol. 2694, pp. 55–72. Springer, Heidelberg (2003)
6. Dockins, R., Hobor, A., Appel, A.W.: A Fresh Look at Separation Algebras and Share Accounting. In: Hu, Z. (ed.) APLAS 2009. LNCS, vol. 5904, pp. 161–177. Springer, Heidelberg (2009)
7. Freeman, A.: Pro.NET 4 Parallel Programming in C#. Apress (2010)
8. Gherghina, C.: Personal communication (April 2013)
9. González, J.F.: Java 7 Concurrency Cookbook. Packt. Pub. Limited (2012)
10. Hobor, A., Gherghina, C.: Barriers in concurrent separation logic: Now with tool support? Logical Methods in Computer Science 8(2) (2012)
11. Jeremiassen, T.E., Eggers, S.J.: Static Analysis of Barrier Synchronization in Explicitly Parallel Programs. In: PACT, pp. 171–180 (1994)
12. Kamil, A., Yelick, K.: Concurrency Analysis for Parallel Programs with Textually Aligned Barriers. In: Ayguadé, E., Baumgartner, G., Ramanujam, J., Sadayappan, P. (eds.) LCPC 2005. LNCS, vol. 4339, pp. 185–199. Springer, Heidelberg (2006)
13. Kamil, A., Yelick, K.: Enforcing Textual Alignment of Collectives Using Dynamic Checks. In: Gao, G.R., Pollock, L.L., Cavazos, J., Li, X. (eds.) LCPC 2009. LNCS, vol. 5898, pp. 368–382. Springer, Heidelberg (2010)
14. Le, D.K., Chin, W.N., Teo, Y.M.: Verification of Static and Dynamic Barrier Synchronization Using Bounded Permissions. Technical report, NUS (April 2013)
15. Lin, Y.: Static Nonconcurrency Analysis of OpenMP Programs. In: Mueller, M.S., Chapman, B.M., de Supinski, B.R., Malony, A.D., Voss, M. (eds.) IWOMP 2005/2006. LNCS, vol. 4315, pp. 36–50. Springer, Heidelberg (2008)
16. Naden, K., Bocchino, R., Aldrich, J., Bierhoff, K.: A Type System for Borrowing Permissions. In: POPL, pp. 557–570 (2012)
17. O'Hearn, P.W.: Resources, Concurrency and Local Reasoning. In: Schmidt, D. (ed.) ESOP 2004. LNCS, vol. 2986, pp. 1–2. Springer, Heidelberg (2004)

18. Reynolds, J.: Separation Logic: A Logic for Shared Mutable Data Structures. In: LICS, Copenhagen, Denmark (July 2002)
19. Saraswat, V.A., Jagadeesan, R.: Concurrent Clustered Programming. In: Abadi, M., de Alfaro, L. (eds.) CONCUR 2005. LNCS, vol. 3653, pp. 353–367. Springer, Heidelberg (2005)
20. Shirako, J., Peixotto, D.M., Sarkar, V., Scherer III, W.N.: Phasers: A Unified Deadlock-free Construct for Collective and Point-to-point Synchronization. In: ICS, pp. 277–288 (2008)
21. Smans, J., Jacobs, B., Piessens, F.: Implicit Dynamic Frames. In: TOPLAS (2012)
22. Woo, S.C., Ohara, M., Torrie, E., Singh, J.P., Gupta, A.: The SPLASH-2 Programs: Characterization and Methodological Considerations. In: ICSA (1995)
23. Zhang, Y., Duesterwald, E.: Barrier Matching for Programs with Textually Unaligned Barriers. In: PPoPP, pp. 194–204 (2007)
24. Zhang, Y., Duesterwald, E., Gao, G.R.: Concurrency Analysis for Shared Memory Programs with Textually Unaligned Barriers. In: Adve, V., Garzarán, M.J., Petersen, P. (eds.) LCPC 2007. LNCS, vol. 5234, pp. 95–109. Springer, Heidelberg (2008)

Formal Models of SysML Blocks

Alvaro Miyazawa[1], Lucas Lima[2], and Ana Cavalcanti[1]

[1] Department of Computer Science, University of York, York, UK
{alvaro.miyazawa,ana.cavalcanti}@york.ac.uk
[2] Centro de Informática, Universidade Federal de Pernambuco, Recife, Brazil
lal2@cin.ufpe.br

Abstract. In this paper, we propose a formalisation of SysML blocks based on a state-rich process algebra that supports refinement, namely, CML. We first establish a set of guidelines of usage of SysML block definition and internal block diagrams. Next, we propose a formal semantics of SysML blocks described by diagrams that conform to our guidelines. The semantics is specified by inductive functions over the structure of SysML models. These functions can be mechanised to support automatic generation of the CML models.

Keywords: CML, SysML, process algebra, refinement, semantics.

1 Introduction

SysML is an extension of UML 2.0 to support modelling for systems engineering. In recent years, it has increasingly been supported by a number of tool vendors such as IBM [13], Atego [1] and Sparx Systems [19].

Our aim is to support the application of formal analysis tools and techniques at the level of the graphical notations used in current industrial practice. In particular, in this paper, we present our results on formalising the notion of SysML blocks including their related elements such as associations, compositions, generalisations, ports, interfaces and connectors. This is achieved by a denotational semantics of SysML blocks in the COMPASS modelling language (CML) [22], a formal specification language that supports a variety of analysis techniques [4].

Whilst SysML is an informal graphical notation, CML builds on well known and widely used formal specification languages: VDM [9] and CSP [12]. Its approach to modelling reactive behaviour and its semantic model are those adopted in the *Circus* [3] family of refinement languages.

The semantics of both CML and *Circus* use the Unifying Theories of Programming to cater for object-orientation [17], time [18], and synchronicity [2], for instance.The distinguishing feature of CML and *Circus* is the support for modelling at various levels of abstraction, and compositional refinement, including formal derivation (or verification) of code.

We present a denotational semantics for blocks in SysML models using CML. Its main distinctive feature is the fact that it can be used as an integration context for formal models of other SysML elements such as state machine, activity and sequence diagrams. The semantic function is formalised via translation

L. Groves and J. Sun (Eds.): ICFEM 2013, LNCS 8144, pp. 249–264, 2013.

rules, which can be used to generate CML models of blocks automatically; they are presented in [14]; here we illustrate the modelling approach via examples. Currently, our translation rules are being used as a basis for an implementation of a CML semantics of SysML based on the Atego's Artisan Studio [1]. As far as we know, there are no formal accounts in the literature of the behavioural semantics of SysML blocks that support integration with other diagrams.

The CML semantics enables a variety of refinement-based analysis of SysML models. CML tools [4] include an Eclipse-based development environment (parser and type-checker) with links to Artisan Studio [1] to support design using SysML and RT-Tester [20] for test automation, and plug-ins that support the generation of proof obligations, simulation, theorem proving based on Isabelle/HOL [16], model checking, and the application of a refinement calculus. The use of CML to reason about systems of systems is discussed in [22], and compositional refinement-based reasoning techniques are described and formalised in [15].

In SysML, the behaviour of blocks may be specified by state machine diagrams, and operations may be specified by activity diagrams, which describe a form of flowchart. Sequence diagrams may be used to model particular scenarios of interaction between elements of the model. Our approach considers process models for state machine, activity and sequence diagrams. An approach to the construction of these models is described in [14].

This paper is structured as follows. Sections 2 and 3 briefly present CML and SysML. Section 4 describes our guidelines of usage of SysML blocks and the formal model of SysML blocks by means of a simple example. Section 5 discusses related work and Section 6 summarises our results and discusses future work.

2   CML

A CML specification consists of a number of paragraphs, which at the top level can declare types, classes, functions, values (i.e., constants), channels, channel sets, and processes. Both classes and processes declare state components, and may contain paragraphs declaring types, values, functions and operations. Processes also have actions, which provide a behavioural specification including data operations (using VDM) and interaction patterns (using CSP).

Processes are the main elements of a CML specification; systems and their components are both specified by processes that encapsulate some state and communicate with each other and the external environment via channels. A process may declare any number of actions, and must contain an anonymous main action, which specifies the behaviour of the process.

Other features of CML used in this paper are explained as necessary. For further details on CML, we refer to [21,22]. An example is presented in Figure 1.

This specification declares a type Item of natural numbers, a constant MAX, two channels put and get that communicate values of type Item, and four processes. The first process, Producer, has a state component i whose initial value is 0; it records the number of items sent through put. Its behaviour is defined by a recursive action that increments i, sends i through put (put.i) and waits one time

```
types
  Item = nat
values
  MAX = 5
channels
  put, get: Item
process Producer = begin
  state i: nat := 0
  @ mu X @ i := i+1; put!i -> Wait(1); X
end
process Consumer = begin
  @ mu X @ get?x -> Wait(2); X
end
process Buffer = begin
  state b: seq Item
  @ mu X @ ([len b > 0] & get!(hd b) -> b := tl b
           [] [len b < MAX] & put?x -> b := b^[x]
  ); X
process System = (Buffer [|{|put,get|}|]
                  (Producer ||| Consumer))\{|put,get|}
```

Fig. 1. CML excerpt

unit (`Wait(1)`) before recursing (`X`). `Consumer` reads a value x from `get` (`get?x`) and waits two time units before recursing. `Buffer` maintains a sequence b of values of type `Item`, and recursively allows a choice (`[]`) of communications on `put` and `get` depending on whether b is not empty (`len b > 0`) or not full (`len b < MAX`). The value output via `get` is the first element of b (`hd b`), and the value x input via `put` is appended to the end of b (`b := b^[x]`).

The overall specification is given by the process `System`, which composes in parallel the three previous processes. `Producer` and `Consumer` are composed in interleaving (`|||`), that is, without communication, and their composition is put in parallel (`[|{|put,get|}|]`) with `Buffer` synchronising on the channels `put` and `get`. Finally, these channels are made internal using the hiding operator (`\`).

Another example of a CML model is sketched in Section 4.

3   SysML

SysML is built as a UML profile, that is, it reuses part of the UML metamodel and extends it with some specific features from system engineering. The classic software-centric focus of UML, through class and composite structure diagrams, has been moved to the system level in SysML by the introduction of the block definition diagram (bdd) and internal block diagram (ibd). The UML notion of interfaces has been focused in SysML on system-level interfaces by the introduction of ports, which are located in the boundary of a block and may communicate

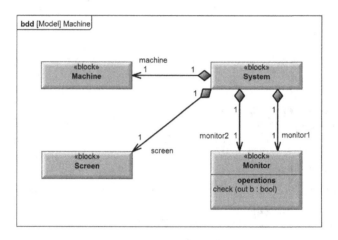

Fig. 2. Block Definition Diagram

service-based data and flow-based items; we identify two sides of a port with respect to the block that contains it: internal and external. Blocks are based on UML classes and composite structures with some changes and extensions. A block is defined in terms of a structural part, which can include constraints, properties (simple attributes), and parts (that may be typed by another block), and a behavioural part, which is defined in terms of operations and signals. Blocks can communicate with each other by sending events, which correspond to sending a signal or an operation call from one block to another. Whilst signals and operation calls are elements of the model, signal events and operation call events are occurrences of the model elements in a particular time point.

A bdd defines a structure of blocks and their relationships such as associations, generalisations, and dependencies. It is based on UML class diagrams with restrictions and extensions. Figure 2 shows an example where the block System is linked by a part-whole association (known in UML as composition) to three other blocks: Machine, Screen and Monitor. This diagram provides a view of the main components of the example we use here to illustrate our semantics. The actual configuration of the parts of System is described by the ibd in Figure 3.

An ibd is a modified version of a UML composite structure diagram. It captures the internal organization of a block in terms of its parts and the connection between them. Whilst in a bdd the blocks can be compared to classes, in an ibd the connected parts resemble instances of classes. Usually, these parts are typed by other blocks, hence, the diagram explains how the instances of blocks communicate with each other. Such communications can be represented by a direct link between the parts or by connected ports. For example, the ibd in Figure 3 shows that the blocks Monitor and Screen have each one port (p and p2, respectively), Machine has three ports (m1, m2 and p1), and System has one port (p3). Ports may restrict the kind of communication that can happen between blocks by specifying interfaces, which define the operations and signals that the

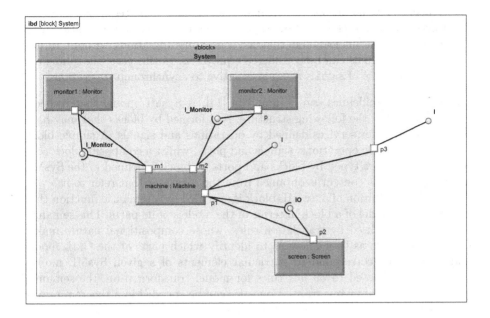

Fig. 3. Internal Block Diagram

block provides and requires. For instance, the port p1 in Figure 3 provides the interface I, which contains signals that control the machine, and requires the interface IO, which contains an operation that allows printing. Further details of our running example are presented where necessary.

In the next section, to explain our approach to define CML models of SysML blocks, we present the formal model of our running example.

4   Formal Models of SysML Blocks

We assume that the SysML model is sufficiently complete to allow the derivation of a well formed CML model. This assumption is decomposed in a number of guidelines that can be divided into three groups:

Entity Definition. These guidelines require that elements such as operations, blocks and associations are defined somewhere in the model. For instance, it requires that operations are defined either via the action language, a state machine or an activity diagram.

Instance Definition. These guidelines require that enough information about the instances of composite blocks is available. For instance, it requires that the parts of a composite block and their interconnections are specified.

Simplification Assumptions. These guidelines provide alternatives to the use of certain elements, where they have an equivalent counterpart, or define how they can be used. An example of such guidelines is the requirement that asynchronous operations are modelled as signals. This requirement stems from the fact that the meaning in SysML of an asynchronous operation with return value is unclear and that asynchronous operations without return values and signals can be considered equivalent. In this case, the guidelines propose the use of signals as an alternative to asynchronous operations.

The full list of guidelines can be found in [14]. A SysML model that respects our guidelines has the following structure. It is formed by blocks that may have properties and offer services defined by operations and signals. A simple block contains properties, operations, signals and ports, whilst a composite block contains parts that are typed by blocks and ports. A block is defined in the SysML metamodel and its content is obtained from the diagrams that refer to it.

Our CML definition of a SysML block is specified by a semantic function that calculates the model of a block in terms of the models of its parts. This semantic function is formalised by translation rules, whose compositional nature makes traceability viable as they allow us to identify which parts of the CML model that they define correspond to particular elements of a given SysML model. Moreover, as opposed to *ad hoc* rules for model transformation, the semantic function formalised by our translation rules can be encoded in a theorem prover to support both the validation of the semantics and the analysis of the model using techniques based on theorem proving.

4.1   Structure of Models

We model a block as a CML process, where the state characterised by its properties is encapsulated (not accessible externally). For this reason, access to properties as well as interaction via operations and signals are modelled as communications through channels. The CML process that models a block can receive requests to read and write to the block's properties, as well as signals and operation calls. Each of these requests are received through CML channels whose names are the names of the blocks properties prefixed by set_ and get_, or the name of the block appended with _op and _sig. Finally, a channel _addevent is used to delegate the treatment of event to the environment, which, for instance, can be a process that models an activity or a state machine diagram.

In general, a SysML model may contain a number of blocks that are not related to each other. In this case, our CML model consists of a number processes, one for each block, that are also not related to each other. An analysis needs therefore to focus on a particular process.

The model of a simple block is formed by the parallel composition of two or more basic processes: one specifying the behaviour of the block's parent, another called simple_ process, modelling the behaviour of the block itself, and the remaining modelling the block's ports. This allows the reuse of the model of the parent block to reflect the structure of the SysML model in CML. A CML process that models a composite block is defined in terms of the processes that model its parts and ports.

Table 1. SysML-CML correspondence

SysML element	CML element
Simple block	Process
Composite block	Process
Port	Process
Connector	Channel
Interface	Class
Operation call	Record type
Signal	Record Type
Event	Communication

A port is modelled by a process that uses four channels: ext_op, ext_sig, int_op and int_sig. The first two allow the port to interact with a component external to the block by sending and receiving signals and operation calls as well as responses to operation calls. The last two are used to communicate with the model of the block. The behaviour of a port is to restrict which values can be received at each channel, and relay the accepted values to the equivalent channel on the other side of the port.

Table 1 shows the correspondence between elements of a SysML model and elements of CML. In general, a SysML element that exhibits some form of behaviour, namely, blocks and ports, are modelled by CML processes; connectors, which specify communication links, are modelled by channels; static elements (i.e, without intrinsic behaviour), namely operational calls and signals, are modelled by record types, and interfaces, which are collections of static elements are modelled by classes. Operation calls are considered static because they specify the message that is sent to blocks, not the behaviour of the operation itself, which is usually specified by a state machine or activity diagram. Events, like the communication of signals, are modelled by CML communications.

4.2 Integration with other SysML Model Elements

In our approach, the processes that model state machine and activity diagrams accept events through a channel addevent. These events are added to an event pool and are processed according to the semantics of the element (state machine or activity diagram). The processing of events may lead to the generation of new events as well as to changes to the state of the block that is associated with state machine or activity diagram. The models of sequence diagrams use the channels of the blocks included in the diagram.

To obtain the integrated model of a block whose behaviour is specified by a state machine diagram or whose operations are specified by activity diagrams, the processes that model the state machine and activity diagrams are composed in parallel with the process that models the block. Each of these processes synchronise on the events associated with a channel _addevent whose parameters include the operations and signals treated by the activity or state machine diagrams. For instance, if a state machine diagram treats the operations check,

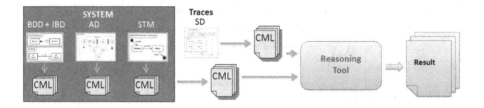

Fig. 4. Integrated Model Analysis Approach

and an activity diagram responds to a signal off, the synchronisation sets should be as follows. The first synchronisation set includes all events of the channel addevent where the first three parameters (representing the instance, source and target of a signal or operation call) are unrestricted and the fourth is limited to values whose type is the input record type of the operation check. Similarly, the second synchronisation set includes all events of the channel addevent where the first three parameters are unrestricted and the fourth is limited to values of the record type of the signal off.

Figure 4 illustrates an approach to the analysis of SysML models by establishing consistency between a sequence diagram, which describes possible valid traces, and the SysML model described by the blocks, and activity and state machine diagrams. The integrated CML model can be validated by reasoning tools, like a model checker, in order to check whether the system model is compatible with the flows of execution specified by the sequence diagram.

In the following sections, we present in more detail the model of blocks.

4.3 Structure of the CML Specification

Figure 5 gives an overview of the formal model of our example; it consists of a number of type declarations that encode the operations and signals found in the model, and classes that group some of these types. Additionally, channels and processes are declared to model SysML connectors and blocks.

A global type ID is used to identify instances of blocks as well as instances of model elements such as ports and states. It is declared as sequences of type token, which is the most unspecified type in CML, supporting only comparison. The use of sequences to identify instances allows us to produce unique identifiers based on the hierarchical structure of the models.

Next, a number of types are declared: two for each operation and one for each signal. These types encapsulate the parameter of the operations and signals. All the operation types are gathered in the type OPS, and similarly all signal types are gathered in the type S. These two types are then joined to form the type of all messages MSG. Next, classes are defined to declare the types of operations, signals and messages that correspond to the operations and signals of a block, port or interface. In the case of a port, the class is defined in terms of the interface classes and further distinguishes operations and signals according to the type of interface: provided or required.

```
types
    ID = seq of token
    check_I = <check_I> ... fix = <fix> ...
    OPS = check_I | check_O | print_I | print_O
    S = fix | on | off
    MSG = OPS | S
class I_types = ...
channels
    c_m1_p.ops: nat*ID*ID*OPS
    ...
    c_p1_p2.sig: nat*ID*ID*S
process Machine = ...
process Screen = ...
class Monitor_types ...
channels
  Monitor_op: nat*ID*ID*OPS Monitor_sig: nat*ID*ID*S
  Monitor_addevent: nat*ID*ID*MSG
process simple_Monitor = ...
process bare_Monitor = id: ID @ simple_Monitor(id)
process Monitor = ...
process System = ...
```

Fig. 5. Overview of the formal model of the example in Figure 2 and 3

Next, for each connector, two channels are declared. The values communicated by these channels correspond to instances of operation calls and signals dispatch; they identify the instance of the call or dispatch (using a natural number), the source and destination of the message (using ID values), and the message itself including any parameters (a value of type OPS or S).

Finally, the models of each of the blocks and ports are declared. These include new types and channel declarations as well as processes and channel sets.

4.4 Simple Blocks

The model of a simple block comprises a class, a number of channels and three processes. Figure 5 shows an overview of the declarations associated with the block Monitor in Figure 2. First, the class containing the types of signals and operations of the block is declared, and then the three channels previously described: _op, _sig, _addevent. Finally, the three processes that specify the behaviour of the block are declared.

The details of the process simple_Monitor are shown in Figure 6. This process is parametrised by a value that identifies an instance of the block. For example, the process that models the part monitor1 in Figure 3 is an instantiation of the process Monitor with an identifier id^[mk_token(monitor1)], where id is the identifier of an instance of the block System.

```
process simple_Monitor = id: ID @ begin
  state enabled: Bag := empty_bag
  actions
    Monitor_state = Skip
    Monitor_requests = mu X @ (
      Monitor_op?n?o!id?x:(is_Monitor_types'check_I(x)) -> (
        [is_Monitor_types'check_I(x)] &
          Monitor_addevent!n!o!id!x -> Skip;
          enabled := bunion(enabled, Monitor_types'check_O)
      ) [] Monitor_op?n?o!id?x:(in_bag(x,enabled)) -> (
        [is_Monitor_types'check_O(x)] &
          enabled := bdiff(enabled, Monitor_types'check_O)
      ) [] ...
    ); X
  @ Monitor_state [||{}|{enabled}||] Monitor_requests
end
```

Fig. 6. Process simple_Monitor

The process simple_Monitor declares a state containing all the properties of
the block, and an extra component enabled whose type is a bag of elements of the
type OPS. This component models the responses to operation calls that the block
can communicate, and since multiple calls to the same operation may occur, this
state component must be able to hold any number of identical values, thus the
use of a bag. The component enabled is initialised with the empty bag. Next,
two actions are declared: the first controls access to the state components that
model block properties, and the second controls the communication of operation
and signal messages. The two actions are composed in interleaving to specify the
overall behaviour of the process (main action).

Since Monitor does not have properties, the state of the process declares a
single component, namely enabled, and the action that controls the access to the
block properties is declared as Skip, that is, the action that terminates immediately. If a block has properties, the state declares corresponding components,
and this action recursively offers a choice between reading or writing to the state
components through the channels set_ and get_.

The second action Monitor_requests controls which signals and operation calls
can be accepted by the block, and which values can be communicated as a response to an operation call. This action is recursive; each cycle corresponds to the
handling of a signal or operation call, or the response to an operation call. Each
cycle offers a choice between receiving values of an input record type or sending
values of an output record type on the channel Monitor_op, and receiving values
of a signal record type on the channel Monitor_sig. The input types that can be
received are restricted to those in the class Monitor_types, which contains the
signal, input and output record types of the signals and operations in the block

Monitor. The restriction of the communication is achieved by constraining the parameter x of the communication `Monitor_op?n?o!id?x`, which corresponds to a signal or operation call, with the predicate `is_Monitor_types'check_I(x)`. The function `is_Monitor_types'check_I` becomes available in the CML specification when the type `Monitor_types'check_I` is declared.

After receiving any value x of the input record type of one of the operations in the block, the event is communicated through the channel `Monitor_addevent` (and can then be treated by the environment, perhaps characterised by state machine or activity diagrams, as explained in Section 4.2). Since values of output record types can only be communicated after a corresponding input record type value has been received (that is, an operation can only terminate after it has been started), after sending the event through `Monitor_addevent`, all the possible values of the output record type of the operation are added to the bag `enabled`.

The second possible communication in a cycle of the recursion restricts the possible values of output record types that can be communicated. Only values that are in the component `enabled` can be communicated as a response to an operation call. Once the communication is completed, one instance of each value of the appropriate output record type is removed from the bag. The third choice treats signals in a way similar to the treatment of operation calls just explained.

The two actions `Monitor_state` and `Monitor_requests` are composed in interleaving to define the main action of the process. The interleaving operator `[{}||{enabled}]` partitions the state between the actions to avoid race conditions. In the process `simple_Monitor`, the first action has no write access to the state, and the second action has write access to the state component `enabled`.

Processes prefixed by `bare_` model SysML's generalisation (inheritance) relation as interleaving. If a block A has parents B and C, the process `bare_A` is the interleaving of `simple_A`, `bare_B` and `bare_C`, renaming the channels of the last two processes to match those of `simple_A`. This is necessary to allow signals and operations defined in the parents' models to be communicated through the channel of A. The process `bare_Monitor` in Figure 7 is just the instantiation of `simple_Monitor` because Monitor does not have parents.

`Monitor`, depicted in Figure 7, is the parallel composition of `bare_Monitor` and the process modelling the port p (`port_p`) with its `p_int_op` and `p_int_sig` channels (see Section 4.6) renamed to the corresponding channels in the block Monitor. The renaming is necessary to synchronise these channels and the channels of the block to model the fact that values received in the port of a simple block are relayed to the block. This parallel composition synchronises on the channels `Monitor_op` and `Monitor_sig` where the source and destination of the communication are the block and the port, and vice-versa. That is, the events on those channels that communicate values between the port and the block. These events are then made internal through the hiding operator ($\backslash$) because the communication between a block and its ports is implicit in the SysML model.

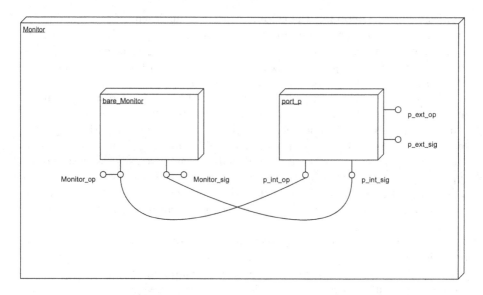

Fig. 7. Structure of the process `Monitor`

4.5   Composite Blocks

The model of a composite block is a process that composes in parallel the models
of its parts and ports. The pattern of communication within the parallelism
is determined by the connectors between the parts and ports. The channels
associated with a connector are used to rename the channels of processes that
model the blocks or ports to which the connector is attached. The renamed
processes are then composed in parallel synchronising on the channels associated
with the connectors. Figure 8 gives an overview of the structure of System.

The body of the process `System` is defined as the parallel composition of five
processes (four parts and one port), whose channels have been renamed with
the channels associated with any connectors reaching the block or its ports,
synchronising on the channels associated with the connectors. For instance, the
process `Machine(...)` has the external channels of the ports m1, m2 and p1
renamed to the channels of the connectors from m1 to p, m2 to p, p1 to p3, and
p1 to p2, and similarly the channels of the processes that model the ports p, p2
and p3 are renamed with the channels of these connectors. The synchronisation
between these channels is depicted in Figure 8 by the curves lines connecting the
processes (represented by boxes). Whilst in the case of ports in the parts of the
block the renaming occurs on the external channels of the port, in the case of
ports in the block itself, the renaming takes place on the channel associated with
the internal side of the port. This can be observed in Figure 8 by the connection
between the channels (straight lines with black dot) `p3_int_op` and `p1_ext_op`,
and the channels `p3_int_sig` and `p1_ext_sig`. The renaming of port channels by
connector channels is necessary because the ports of a block may be linked to

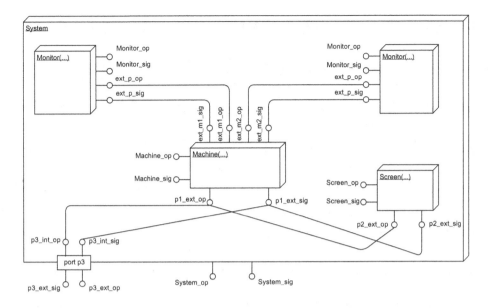

Fig. 8. Overview of the model of the block System

different connectors in different contexts, and thus the link must be established at the level of the port process instantiation, and not in its declaration.

4.6   Ports

The models of ports consist of a class, four channels and one process. The class differs from that of blocks and interfaces in that it distinguishes between operations and signals contributed by provided and required interfaces; it defines six types, three for provided interfaces and three for required interfaces. These types identify the input, output and signal record types that are defined in terms of the interfaces. For port p1, the type of provided signals is defined as the type S of the provided interface I.

The four channels declared for a port allow the communication of operation and signal records from both sides of the port (internal and external). These channels are used in the process `port_p1` to restrict the kind of message that can be received in the port depending on the direction, and also to relay the message to the appropriate destination. For instance, calls for provided operations (values of a provided input record type) can only be received on the external channel `p1_ext_op`. In this case, the port relays the message through the internal channel `p1_int_op`. Notice that whilst the message is received by the port (third parameter of the communication is `id`), it relays the message from the port to some unknown target (`?y`). This reflects the fact that the target of the message is not determined until the port is associated with a block. This is achieved through renaming as shown in Figure 8 by the connection between the channels.

```
process port_p1 = id: ID @ begin
  @ mu X @ (
    p1_ext_sig?i?o!id?x:(is_p1_types'P_S) ->
      p1_int_sig.i.id?y.x -> Skip
    [] p1_int_sig?i?o!id?x:(is_p1_types'R_S) ->
      p1_ext_sig.i.id?y.x -> Skip
    [] p1_ext_op?i?o!id?x:(is_p1_types'P_I) ->
      p1_int_op.i.id?y.x -> Skip
    [] p1_int_op?i?o!id?x:(is_p1_types'P_O) ->
      p1_ext_op.i.id?y.x -> Skip
    [] p1_ext_op?i?o!id?x:(is_p1_types'R_O) ->
      p1_int_op.i.id?y.x -> Skip
    [] p1_int_op?i?o!id?x:(is_p1_types'R_I) ->
      p1_ext_op.i.id?y.x -> Skip
  ); X
end
```

Fig. 9. Overview of the communication patterns of a port

The complete formalisation of the semantics of SysML blocks as well as state machine, activity and sequence diagrams can be found in [14].

5 Related Work

Graves [10] proposes a representation of a restricted subset of SysML block diagrams in OWL2, which is a language for knowledge representation based on a description logic. Ding and Tang [5] proposes a representation of SysML block diagrams directly in a description logic. In both cases, block diagrams are restricted to include only associations and simple blocks.

Graves and Bijan [11] extend [10] by encoding SysML diagrams into a type theory that axiomatises block diagram notions of types, properties and operators. Both bdds and ibds are covered, but dynamic aspects of SysML diagrams, such as the treatment of operation calls, are not.

All these works focus on generating a set of axioms that specify a system based on a SysML diagram, and then using techniques for the underlying logic to check properties. Although Graves and Bijan [11] describe model refinement as theory refinement (that is, modification of the knowledge base aiming at achieving consistency), they do not elaborate on the topic, and it is not clear what properties are preserved by this notion of refinement.

Evans and Kent [6] describes the pUML approach, which aims at strengthening the meta-model semantics of UML via a precise semantics. This work focusses on the semantics of generalisation and packages, and provides a number of extra well-formedness conditions. Dynamic aspects of UML models are not discussed, and it is not clear how the pUML approach tackles such aspects.

The work presented in [8] is the closest to ours. It formalises UML-RT structure diagrams in CSP-OZ [7], and whilst the treatment of composition and connectors is similar to ours, the semantics does not cover issues related to operation calls and integration with other diagrams.

6 Conclusions

In this paper, we have presented a behavioural model of SysML blocks that includes simple and composite blocks, generalisation, association and composition relations, standard ports and connectors, interfaces, operations, properties and signals. To the best of our knowledge, this is the first formalisation of the behavioural semantics of a comprehensive subset of the block notation.

The main characteristics of our approach are the compositionality of the generated models, the use of parallelism to compose different aspects of the system and the support for refinement. These aspects make it possible to apply compositional analysis techniques [15], and refinement strategies to obtain equivalent models better suited to alternative analysis techniques (e.g., model checking).

The most interesting aspects of our models are the treatment of operation calls, the use of interleaving to model inheritance, and the use of parallelism to model block composition. Finally, whilst the models of ports are simple, the use of interface classes in the specification of a port's communication protocol proved important to preserve the compositionality of our models.

The functions that characterise our semantics are specified by translation rules, which take elements of the SysML abstract syntax and produce the corresponding CML elements. The complete set of translation rules for SysML blocks can be found in [14]. These rules are currently being implemented in Artisan Studio to support the automatic generation of CML from SysML models. This work is being carried out by our industrial partners at Atego, and the revision of the rules by a SysML expert and the process of mechanising the rules have helped us partially validate our semantics.

As future work, we plan to further validate our semantics by completing the automation of the translation rules, simulating the models using the CML tools, applying refinement strategies for model simplification, and analysing models via model-checking. Finally, we plan to encode the translation rules in Isabelle/HOL and prove general properties of our semantics.

Acknowledgement. This work is supported by the EU FP7 Project COM-PASS (http://www.compass-research.eu).

References

1. Artisan Studio, http://atego.com/products/artisan-studio/ (accessed: April 11, 2013)
2. Gancarski, P., Butterfield, A.: The Denotational Semantics of slotted-*Circus*. In: Cavalcanti, A., Dams, D.R. (eds.) FM 2009. LNCS, vol. 5850, pp. 451–466. Springer, Heidelberg (2009)

3. Cavalcanti, A.L.C., Sampaio, A.C.A., Woodcock, J.C.P.: A Refinement Strategy for *Circus*. Form. Asp. Comp. 15(2-3), 146–181 (2003)
4. Coleman, J.W., Malmos, A.K., Larsen, P.G., Peleska, J., Hains, R., Andrews, Z., Payne, R., Foster, S., Miyazawa, A., Bertolini, C., Didier, A.: COMPASS Tool Vision for a System of Systems Collaborative Development Environment. In: 7th International Conference on System of Systems Engineering, pp. 451–456 (2012)
5. Ding, S., Tang, S.Q.: An approach for formal representation of SysML block diagram with description logic SHIOQ(D). Proceedings of the 2nd ICIIS 2, 259–261 (2010)
6. Evans, A., Caskurlu, B.: Core Meta-Modelling Semantics of UML: The pUML Approach. In: France, R.B. (ed.) UML 1999. LNCS, vol. 1723, pp. 140–155. Springer, Heidelberg (1999)
7. Fischer, C.: CSP-OZ: A combination of Object-Z and CSP. In: Bowmann, H., Derrick, J. (eds.) FormalMethods for Open Object-Based Distributed Systems (FMOODS 1997), vol. 2, pp. 423–438. Chapman & Hall, Ltd. (1997)
8. Fischer, C., Olderog, E.-R., Wehrheim, H.: A CSP View on UML-RT Structure Diagrams. In: Hussmann, H. (ed.) FASE 2001. LNCS, vol. 2029, pp. 91–108. Springer, Heidelberg (2001)
9. Fitzgerald, J., Larsen, P.G.: Modelling Systems – Practical Tools and Techniques in Software Development, 2nd edn. Cambridge University Press (2009)
10. Graves, H.: Integrating SysML and OWL. In: Proceedings of OWL: Experiences and Directions (2009)
11. Graves, H., Bijan, Y.: Using formal methods with SysML in aerospace design and engineering. Ann. Math. Artif. Intel., 1–50 (2011)
12. Hoare, C.A.R.: Communicating sequential processes. Prentice-Hall, Inc. (1985)
13. Rational Rhapsody Architect for Systems Engineers, http://www-142.ibm.com/software/products/us/en/ratirhaparchforsystengi (accessed: April 11, 2013)
14. Miyazawa, A., Albertins, L., Iyoda, J., Cornélio, M., Payne, R., Cavalcanti, A.: Final report on combining SysML and CML. Technical report, COMPASS (2013)
15. Oliveira, M., Sampaio, A., Antonino, P., Ramos, R., Cavalcanti, A., Woodcock, J.: Compositional analysis and design of CML models. Technical report, COMPASS (2013)
16. Paulson, L.C.: Isabelle: A Generic Theorem Prover. LNCS, vol. 828. Springer, Heidelberg (1994)
17. Santos, T., Cavalcanti, A., Sampaio, A.: Object-Orientation in the UTP. In: Dunne, S., Stoddart, B. (eds.) UTP 2006. LNCS, vol. 4010, pp. 18–37. Springer, Heidelberg (2006)
18. Sherif, A., Cavalcanti, A., Jifeng, H., Sampaio, A.: A Process Algebraic Framework for Specification and Validation of Real-time Systems. Form. Asp. Comp. 22, 153–191 (2010)
19. Sparx Systems' Enterprise Architect supports the Systems Modeling Language, http://sparxsystems.com/products/mdg/tech/sysml/ (accessed: April 11, 2013)
20. RT-Tester, http://verified.de/en/products/rt-tester (accessed: April 11, 2013)
21. Woodcock, J., Cavalcanti, A., Coleman, J., Didier, A., Larsen, P.G., Miyazawa, A., Oliveira, M.: CML Definition 0. Technical Report D23.1, COMPASS (2012)
22. Woodcock, J., Cavalcanti, A., Fitzgerald, J., Larsen, P., Miyazawa, A., Perry, S.: Features of CML: A formal modelling language for Systems of Systems. In: 7th International Conference on System of Systems Engineering, pp. 1–6 (2012)

Towards a Process Algebra Framework for Supporting Behavioural Consistency and Requirements Traceability in SysML

Jaco Jacobs and Andrew Simpson

Department of Computer Science, University of Oxford
Wolfson Building, Parks Road
Oxford OX1 3QD
{jaco.jacobs,andrew.simpson}@cs.ox.ac.uk

Abstract. The Systems Modeling Language (SysML), an extension of a subset of the Unified Modeling Language (UML), is a visual modelling language for systems engineering applications. At present, the semi-formal SysML, which is widely utilised for the design of complex hetero-geneous systems, lacks integration with other more formal approaches. In this paper, we describe how Communicating Sequential Processes (CSP) and its associated refinement checker, Failures Divergence Refinement (FDR), may be used to underpin an approach that facilitates the refine-ment checking of behavioural consistency of SysML diagrams; we also show how the proposed approach supports requirements traceability. We illustrate our contribution by means of a small case study.

Keywords: CSP, SysML, Requirements Traceability.

1 Introduction

State-of-the-art systems are typically organic, multi-disciplinary compositions of interconnecting components or systems, functioning as a whole in order to achieve a shared goal.

The *Systems Modeling Language* (SysML) [1], proposed by the Object Management Group (OMG)[1], is a graphical modelling notation that can be used to describe complex, heterogeneous systems comprised of various components. These, in turn, might be simple structural elements, or might themselves be viewed as systems comprised of various components working together.

One of the biggest challenges in the specification and design of a complex system, potentially composed of several subsidiary systems, is to ensure that the proposed design is logically consistent. There are, of course, various aspects to take into account when looking at the notion of consistency. For example, it is possible to consider whether the non-behavioural aspects — embodied by the structural constructs of the modelling language — are specified such that they are logically sound, and that the constraints imposed upon them, hold. It

---

[1] http://www.omg.org

L. Groves and J. Sun (Eds.): ICFEM 2013, LNCS 8144, pp. 265–280, 2013.

is also possible to consider more closely the behavioural aspects of a proposed design, and this is our focus in this paper. For this purpose, we utilise Communicating Sequential Processes (CSP) [2,3]. In contrast to SysML, which one might categorise as a semi-formal notation, CSP has a rigorous mathematical underpinning with an elegant means of specifying and reasoning about complex behaviour. Moreover, the Failures Divergence Refinement (FDR) [4] tool — a refinement checker for CSP — readily allows for the reasoning about correctness of designs and verification that asserted properties hold. Specifically, by translating SysML into CSP we can precisely define the intended behaviour of a given SysML model, by making use of the underlying formal semantics of CSP. Consequently, this allows refinement checking of the SysML model. However, when attempting to formalise behaviour, we still need to consider structural aspects: if we are to define a sensible behavioural semantics, we cannot be agnostic with respect to the static composition of the SysML model. Moreover, the resulting CSP process network and its associated communication configuration need to reflect the structural specification of the model. It is worth noting at this point that the intention here is not to propose a means of replacing SysML modelling tools, but, rather, to develop a formal framework that can be used in conjunction with SysML, with a view to complementing the modelling activity. The subsequent integration of graphical and formal notations would have the potential to allow the modeller to reap the benefits of both methods.

Modelling a system with SysML relies on the concept of blocks — each with an associated set of states — that communicate via events, possibly resulting in a change of state for one or more of the communicating blocks. The architecture of these systems allows a top-down design, starting from an abstract level with high level concepts, down to levels with increasingly more detail. These successive transformations allow replacing an abstract block with a composition of parts, but the big drawback of this decomposition is that it is at best semi-formal and cannot guarantee consistency between a block and its parts. Process algebras, like CSP, can help in this respect.

Requirements traceability plays an important role as part of any model-based systems engineering methodology. In SysML, requirements can be related to other requirements, as well as to other model elements via one or more relationships: a behavioural construct can be allocated to a particular requirement, and we can subsequently use FDR to ensure that the model satisfies it.

In Section 2, we define the necessary mathematical structures, based on the syntax of SysML, required to formulate behavioural CSP descriptions. (We assume that the reader is familiar with CSP.) Section 3 presents a bird's eye view of how CSP can be used in combination with SysML in order to create well-formed models and ensure that requirements are satisfied. To this end, we provide a formal semantics for state machines, within the context of SysML. In Section 4, we introduce a small case study which we use as a means of illustrating and validating the contribution. Finally, Section 5 summarises the contribution of this paper, places it in context with respect to other research, and outlines possible avenues of further work.

2   Syntactical Structures

In order to define a formal semantics for blocks, parts and state machines, we need a precise description of their syntax. To this end, we define simple mathematical constructs that are closely related to the syntactical structure of their corresponding SysML counterparts. Our purpose is not to formulate a complete syntactical specification of the considered constructs, but rather to employ these expositions to assist us in defining the formal behavioural semantics in a comprehensible and sympathetic fashion.

2.1   Model and Signals

Let the SysML model be a quintuple $(\mathcal{B}, \mathcal{P}, \mathcal{M}, \mathcal{R}, \mathcal{S})$, where $\mathcal{B}$ is the set of blocks, $\mathcal{P}$ is the set of parts, $\mathcal{M}$ is the set of state machines, and $\mathcal{R}$ is the set containing all requirements. $\mathcal{S}$ contains the set of all signals; these are used as a means of communication between state machines.

A *signal* $S_i \in \mathcal{S}$ is uniquely identified by a name, $N_{S_i} \in \mathcal{N_S}$, and contains a sequence of parameters. Let $\mathcal{N_S}$ contain the names of all signals. The function $name : \mathcal{S} \to \mathcal{N_S}$ returns the unique name of a signal. The sequence of parameters P_{S_i} of a signal S_i is given by $params(S_i) = P_{S_i}$.

2.2   Blocks and Parts

The fundamental modelling construct present in SysML is the *block*. Each block is assigned an associated main behaviour, called its *classifier* behaviour. Depending on the purpose of the block, the classifier behaviour can either be a state machine (for reactive, event-driven blocks) or an activity (for transformational blocks that take inputs to outputs via a sequence of actions).

A block $B_i \in \mathcal{B}$ is a classifier that describes common behavioural and structural features of its instances, and can be considered akin to a UML class. We assume that the classifier behaviour is specified using state machines, and given by the function $classifier : \mathcal{B} \to \mathcal{M}$. These blocks communicate via events (instances of signals) that act as stimuli for the respective state machines.

A block makes known the names of the *operations*, for method calls, or *receptions*, for signals, that: it responds to (i.e. the block provides the behaviour); or, alternatively, expects its SysML environment to respond to (i.e. the environment provides the behaviour). These behavioural features are designated as *provided* and *required behavioural features*. In this paper we consider only asynchronous communication using signal events, therefore all behavioural features are receptions. We define the functions $prov : \mathcal{B} \to \mathbb{P}\,\mathcal{S}$ and $reqd : \mathcal{B} \to \mathbb{P}\,\mathcal{S}$ to return provided and required receptions.

The *internal block diagram*, as per Figure 1, graphically sets out the internal structure of a block from its parts. In contrast, a *block definition diagram*, also presented in Figure 1, depicts the composition of a block, but abstracts away from the internal structure. A *part* is connected to another part via a connector; it is an instance of a block. As such, it represents a particular usage of its

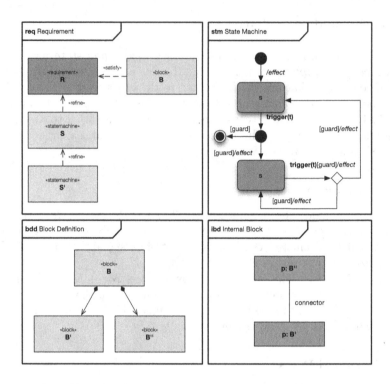

Fig. 1. Examples of a *requirement*, a *state machine*, a *block definition*, and an *internal block diagram*. Block definition and internal block diagrams are used to model static, structural aspects. In contrast, the state machine diagram models dynamic behaviour. Requirements and their relationship to other modelling constructs are shown on a requirement diagram.

classifying block within the context of its owning block. Each part $P_i \in \mathcal{P}$ is typed by a block $B_j \in \mathcal{B}$; the function $type : \mathcal{P} \to \mathcal{B}$ reflects this.

The *connector* serves as a bidirectional link between the block instances and is used to convey signals send between communicating block instances.

2.3   State Machines

We now define a structural model for non-hierarchical state machines, our main concern in this paper. Figure 1 presents an example of a *state machine diagram* with the modelling constructs we consider here.

A *state machine* $M_i \in \mathcal{M}$ consists of a finite set of *states*, denoted S_{M_i}, and *transitions* between those states, denoted T_{M_i}. We partition S_{M_i} such that $S_{M_i}^I$ represents the set of *initial states*, $S_{M_i}^F$ the set of *final states*, $S_{M_i}^S$ the set of *simple states*, $S_{M_i}^J$ the set of *junction states*, and finally $S_{M_i}^C$ the set of *choice states*. Assume that the aforementioned sets are mutually disjoint: we have $\forall s_j, s_k :$ $\{S_{M_i}^I, S_{M_i}^F, S_{M_i}^S, S_{M_i}^J, S_{M_i}^C\} \bullet s_j \neq s_k \Rightarrow s_j \cap s_k = \emptyset$. Furthermore, assume that

$S^I_{M_i}$ is the singleton set, that is, there is a unique initial state. In addition, we assume that a final state is optional: $S^F_{M_i}$ can be the empty set.

Refer to Figure 1. Diagrammatically, initial and final states are indicated by a solid circle and encircled solid circle, respectively, whereas junction and choice states are indicated using a solid circle and diamond shaped node. When labelling transitions, we use the following convention: **trigger**[guard]/*effect*.

A function *outgoing* : $S_{M_i} \to \mathbb{P}\, T_{M_i}$ returns the set of outgoing transitions for a state. In order to make the formalisation easier, assume the existence of *outgoing'* and *outgoing''*, where the former returns, for a particular state, all guarded outgoing transitions, and the latter returns all those that are not guarded. Thus,

$$\forall s : S_{M_i} \bullet outgoing(s) = outgoing'(s) \cup outgoing''(s)$$
$$\land$$
$$outgoing'(s) \cap outgoing''(s) = \emptyset$$

A transition consists of a *trigger*, a *guard*, and an *effect*. Additionally, a transition is defined to exist between a source and target state. We define the following functions, to return for a transition t:

- the source state, given by *source* : $T_{M_i} \to S_{M_i}$;
- the target state, given by *target* : $T_{M_i} \to S_{M_i}$;
- the trigger, given by *trigger* : $T_{M_i} \to \mathcal{S}$;
- the guard, given by *guard* : $T_{M_i} \to E_{M_i}$; and
- the effect, given by *effect* : $T_{M_i} \to \text{seq}\,\mathcal{S}$.

In the above, E_{M_i} represents a set of expressions. Let $eval(e, p)$ represent the evaluation of an expression e by considering the values of the instantiated parameter sequence p, returning a value from the set $\mathbb{B} = \{true, false\}$. Specifically, for a transition t, we substitute[2] the parameters passed on the receive signal event, $params(trigger(t))$, in the guard expression, $guard(t) \in E_{M_i}$. We write $eval(guard(t), params(trigger(t)))$ to denote this.

One take an alternative stance with respect to the guards of transitions. Specifically, the CSP non-deterministic choice operator can be used instead of conditional choice. We opt for conditional choice here, as we assume the parameters of the receive signal event to be of relevance when evaluating the conditions.

We distinguish between two types of transitions: *simple transitions* and *complex transitions* via junction and choice pseudo states, respectively. A simple transition exists between two simple states. A complex transition is treated as two separate transitions between a simple state and a pseudo state, and a pseudo state and a simple state, where the pseudo state is either a junction or choice state. Thus it allows for the specification of multiple paths between states, although only a single path can be taken in response to any event. Again, Figure 1 presents an example of this.

---

[2] In SysML, parameters are matched based on their names and types.

3   A CSP View of SysML

This section outlines an approach to integrate the semi-formal SysML notation with the process algebra CSP. Throughout, we make use of the structures defined in Section 2. First, we provide a formal process semantics for a set of communicating SysML blocks — a central aspect to any SysML model. We then consider how CSP and refinement can be utilised to support requirements traceability — a core SysML concept supported via the requirement diagram.

3.1   Signals and Events

In CSP, for a signal S_i, the name of the signal $name(S_i)$ is used as a component of the CSP event. In our formalisation, an effect corresponds to a sequence of *send signal events*, whereas a trigger corresponds to a *receive signal event*. We write $snd(S_i)$ for a send signal event, where the parameters of the event are communicated as outputs on the corresponding CSP channel. Conversely, for a receive signal event, written $rcv(S_i)$ the parameters are modelled as inputs. The signal types the corresponding send and receive signal events and this is reflected in the CSP channel definition. For a signal S_i, with parameter component given by $params(S_i) = \langle p_0, p_1, .., p_n \rangle$, we have (for a CSP channel c)

- $snd(S_i) = c.name(S_i)!p_0!p_1...!p_n$
- $rcv(S_i) = c.name(S_i)?p_0?p_1...?p_n$

For the base case where $params(S_i) = \langle \rangle$, the corresponding input and output components are simply omitted.

3.2   State Machines

Consider a state machine M_i. We provide mapping rules, starting from an initial state, using a translation function $\mathcal{T}$. Every rule, $\mathcal{T}(m, s)$, is defined such that it describes the behaviour of state machine m at state s. These rules define local process definitions, where each state and pseudo state is represented by a CSP process. This approach is similar to that taken by Ng and Butler [5].

Initial State. We start with the unique initial state $s_0 \in S_{M_i}^I$. In order for the state machine to be well-defined, the initial state must have a single outgoing transition that defines its unique starting point. The lone outgoing transition, $t \in outgoing(s_0)$, may optionally include a sequence of effects.

$$\mathcal{T}(M_i, s_0) = \textit{Effect}(effect(t)) \mathbin{\raise0.3ex\hbox{$\scriptstyle\circ$}\kern-0.4em\raise-0.3ex\hbox{$\scriptstyle\circ$}} \mathcal{T}(M_i, target(t))$$

In the above, the CSP process *Effect* takes a sequence of events and communicates them in order before successfully terminating.

$\textit{Effect}(s) =$
    if $null(s)$ then
        Skip
    else
        $snd(head(s)) \rightarrow \textit{Effect}(tail(s))$

Simple State. Consider a simple state $s \in S_{M_i}^S$. We define the following functions:

- $\forall s : S_{M_i}^S \bullet simple'(s) = \{t : outgoing'(s) \mid target(t) \in S_{M_i}^S\}$, that returns guarded transitions to simple states;
- $\forall s : S_{M_i}^S \bullet simple''(s) = \{t : outgoing''(s) \mid target(t) \in S_{M_i}^S\}$, that returns transitions with no guard condition that lead to simple states;
- $\forall s : S_{M_i}^S \bullet junction'(s) = \{t : outgoing'(s) \mid target(t) \in S_{M_i}^J\}$, that returns guarded transitions to junction states;
- $\forall s : S_{M_i}^S \bullet junction''(s) = \{t : outgoing''(s) \mid target(t) \in S_{M_i}^J\}$, that returns transitions with no guard condition that lead to junction states;
- $\forall s : S_{M_i}^S \bullet choice'(s) = \{t : outgoing'(s) \mid target(t) \in S_{M_i}^C\}$, that returns guarded transitions to choice states;
- $\forall s : S_{M_i}^S \bullet choice''(s) = \{t : outgoing''(s) \mid target(t) \in S_{M_i}^C\}$, that returns transitions with no guard condition that lead to choice states.

The arrival of a SysML signal event serves as the trigger; consequently this is made available as a CSP event. If the signal signature has a data component associated with it, this is made available as an input along with the channel modelling the event. Next, the guard (if it exists) is evaluated and if false the event is discarded without effect. Conversely, if the guard evaluates to true the effects are executed in order before behaving as the process associated with the destination state. Recall that in our formalisation, an effect corresponds to the sending of a series of send signal events, in the order prescribed by the sequence modelling the effect. In addition, we need to consider the eventuality where the state machine receives a signal event not expected in the current state s: that is, an instance of a signal event S_j such that $S_j \notin \{t : outgoing(s) \bullet trigger(t)\}$. Here, the state machine discards the unexpected event. In the following, assume that $unexpected(s)$ returns the set of unexpected events for state s (receive signal events that are valid in other states of S_M but not in s).

Junction or choice states are modelled as a parametrised CSP processes: we assume that the data component, i.e. the parameters, of the receive signal event that served as the trigger, will be used in the guard of the next leg of the compound transition. A choice state is distinct from a junction state in that a junction state only allows for a trigger and optional guard on the first leg of the compound transition, whereas a choice state allows a trigger, guard and effect.

The CSP channel *in* is used for communicating with the event queue of the state machine M_i.

$\mathcal{T}(M_i, s) =$
    $\Box\, t : simple'(s) \bullet in.rcv(trigger(t)) \rightarrow$
        (if $eval(guard(t), params(trigger(t)))$ then
            $Effect(effect(t)) \,\fatsemi\, \mathcal{T}(M_i, target(t))$
        else
            $\mathcal{T}(M_i, s))$
    $\Box$
    $\Box\, t : simple''(s) \bullet in.rcv(trigger(t)) \rightarrow$
        $Effect(effect(t)) \,\fatsemi\, \mathcal{T}(M_i, target(t))$

□

□ $t : junction'(s) \bullet in.rcv(trigger(t)) \rightarrow$
　　(if $eval(guard(t), params(trigger(t)))$ then
　　　$\mathcal{T}(M_i, target(t))[params(trigger(t))]$
　　else
　　　$\mathcal{T}(M_i, s))$

□

□ $t : junction''(s) \bullet in.rcv(trigger(t)) \rightarrow$
　　$\mathcal{T}(M_i, target(t))[params(trigger(t))]$

□

□ $t : choice'(s) \bullet in.rcv(trigger(t)) \rightarrow$
　　(if $eval(guard(t), params(trigger(t)))$ then
　　　$Effect(effect(t)) \,{}_9^{\,} \mathcal{T}(M_i, target(t))[params(trigger(t))]$
　　else
　　　$\mathcal{T}(M_i, s))$

□

□ $t : choice''(s) \bullet in.rcv(trigger(t)) \rightarrow$
　　$Effect(effect(t)) \,{}_9^{\,} \mathcal{T}(M_i, target(t))[params(trigger(t))]$

□

□ $t : unexpected(s) \bullet in.rcv(trigger(t)) \rightarrow \mathcal{T}(M_i, s)$

Junction or Choice State. Consider a junction state $s \in S_{M_i}^J$, or alternatively a choice state $s \in S_{M_i}^C$. Furthermore, assume a set of outgoing transitions such that $\forall\, t : outgoing(s) \bullet target(t) \in S_{M_i}^S$. The second leg of the complex transition (emanating from the choice or junction state) consists of a guard and optional sequence of effects. In order for the state machine to be well-defined, we assume that all guards must be mutually exclusive and that one of the guards always evaluates to true. The assumption here sits well with the notion that a state machine cannot stay indefinitely within a pseudo state and that it is merely a temporary point along a transition, designed to determine the next simple state. As such, one of the available transitions must be selected based on the guards, and the subsequent effects executed. In addition, note that there are no triggering events possible in a junction or choice state, because the triggering event is assumed to have occurred on the previous leg of the compound transition.

$\mathcal{T}(M_i, s)[params(trigger('t))]^3 =$
　　□ $t : outgoing'(s) \bullet$
　　　(if $eval(guard(t), params(trigger('t)))$ then
　　　　$Effect(effect(t)) \,{}_9^{\,} \mathcal{T}(M_i, target(t))$
　　　else
　　　　$Stop)$

---

[3] Formal parameters corresponding to the signal (parameter component thereof) that typed the send signal event that served as the trigger. The transition $'t$ is that of the first leg of the compound transition.

SysML allows a junction or choice state to have multiple incoming transitions, but these can always be recast into separate pseudo states, each with a single incoming transition. As such, our formalisation assumes a single incoming transition per pseudo state, as the definition of parametrised process is dependent on the triggering component of the transition.

Final State. Consider a final state $s_f \in S_{M_i}^F$. A final state has no outgoing transitions and is trivially modelled as the deadlocked process.

$$\mathcal{T}(M_i, s_f) = Stop$$

Process. The state machine as a whole is modelled with a single process that contains all the localised process descriptions defined above. The overall structure is similar to that given by Davies and Crichton [6]. The state machine receives all communications through an event queue, modelled as a CSP buffer of size 1. It communicates with this buffer on a CSP channel, *in*. Each of the localised processes have access to this channel in order to receive communications from the event queue. The overall process $\mathcal{T}(M_i)(queue, in)$ initially behaves as the process associated with the initial state $\mathcal{T}(M_i, s_0)$. The local process EQ models the event queue. Here, we assume a queue with a maximum capacity of 1; the queue blocks when full. Non-blocking semantics, where events are discarded when the queue becomes full, is conceivable; so are event queues with different capacities. A semantics with an unbounded queue is also conceivable, although this is not finite state, and therefore not amenable to verification with FDR.

$$
\begin{aligned}
&\mathcal{T}(M_i)(queue, in) = \\
&\quad \textbf{let} \\
&\qquad \mathcal{T}(M_i, s_0) = \ldots \\
&\qquad \vdots \\
&\qquad \mathcal{T}(M_i, s_f) = Stop \\
&\qquad EQ = queue?a \rightarrow in.a \rightarrow EQ \\
&\quad \textbf{within} \\
&\qquad \mathcal{T}(M_i, s_0) \; [| \{| \; in \; |\} |] \; EQ
\end{aligned}
$$

The state machine of a block B_i only receives (through its event queue) the provided receptions, $prov(B_i)$. The required features, $reqd(B_i)$, are communicated across the connectors linking parts. In our formalisation, the name of the part is used as the channel name. For example, if another part P_i provides a feature S_j that a part P_k requires, the state machine of P_k uses $name(P_i).snd(S_j)$ to model the event.

3.3 Blocks and Parts

The structure of the SysML model is described by a block $B_i \in \mathcal{B}$, composed from N constituent block instances, the parts $\{P_0 .. P_{N-1}\} \subseteq \mathcal{P}$. The classifier behaviour of each part P_j is modelled via a state machine M_j, given by $classifier(type(P_j))$.

The complete system, B_i, can be modelled by placing the processes corresponding to each of the state machines M_j, where $0 \leq j \leq N - 1$, in parallel:

$$B_i = \| \, j : \{0 \, .. \, N - 1\} \bullet [\alpha M_j] M_j$$

3.4 Requirements

A *requirement* $R_i \in \mathcal{R}$ is a SysML-specific modelling construct represented explicitly in the syntax of the language via the *requirement diagram*. Requirements, in their most basic form, are typically text-based, and allow for the description of conditions that must be satisfied by a particular system. Requirements can be related to other requirements and to modelling constructs via several relationships. For the purposes of this paper, we concern ourselves with the *satisfy* and *refine* relationship, which are defined as follows.

"The satisfy relationship describes how a design or implementation model satisfies one or more requirements" [1]

This relationship is used to state that a particular model element meets the associated requirement. This is merely an assertion and not a proof of fact.

"The refine requirement relationship can be used to describe how a model element or set of elements can be used to further refine a requirement" [1]

A text-based requirement can be captured in a SysML model, with the danger being that a textual description can often be ambiguous. Furthermore, such a description is, in general (and for obvious reasons), not well-suited to automated reasoning. A more precise definition is possible in SysML, which allows any behavioural formalism — for example, a state machine — to be assigned to a requirement using the *refine* relationship. This results in a more formal representation of the corresponding desired behaviour. If this behavioural requirement is subsequently mapped to CSP — as a corresponding characteristic process — we can utilise the refinement checker to assist in reasoning about whether this refinement holds for a given model. The characteristic process is therefore a CSP process that describes the patterns of behaviour of an associated textual requirement.

Consider Figure 1. Here, we assume that B, S and S' all denote behavioural constructs of SysML, and R represents a text-based requirement. In the case of a static modelling construct like a block, we assume the corresponding classifier behaviour. We base our treatment of the UML satisfy and refine relationships on that of the satisfaction and refinement relations of [3]. In the following, $CHAR_R$ denotes the characteristic process of a textual requirement R, and B, S, and S' are the CSP processes for B, S and S', respectively. For the satisfy relationship between a behavioural formalism B and a textual requirement R, we define:

B satisfy R $\Leftrightarrow$ $CHAR_R \sqsubseteq B$

The definition of the refine relationship is dependent on the model elements involved in the relationship. In the case where the relationship is between two behavioural formalisms S and S', we define:

S' refine S $\Leftrightarrow S \sqsubseteq S'$

Alternatively, in the case where the refine relationship is expressed between a behavioural formalism S and a textual requirement R, we define the corresponding process S of the behavioural formalism S to be the characteristic process $CHAR_R$ of R:

S refine R $\Leftrightarrow CHAR_R = S$

Therefore, using the definitions above (and substitution) we can check whether S holds in B by executing a refinement check (where the set *Hidden* consists of those events not present in S):

$S \sqsubseteq B \setminus Hidden$

If the refinement does not hold, FDR generates a *counterexample* that demonstrates where the behaviour of B deviates from S, prompting the designer to correct the design. Furthermore, we can check the refinement relation between S and S':

$S \sqsubseteq S' \setminus Hidden$

These successive transformations (assuming the refinements hold) are behavioural formalisms that we can think of as getting more specific as we move along the refinement chain: S' is more refined than S, which means that (if we only consider traces) $traces \llbracket S' \rrbracket \subseteq traces \llbracket S \rrbracket$ due to the reverse inclusion characteristic of refinement. The direction of the arrowhead in the requirement diagram, as per Figure 1, and its treatment in CSP is also of significance. In UML, the direction of the arrow is from the dependent model element to the independent model element. The state machine B is dependent on the requirement R: any change in R could impact B; CSP refinement honours this dependency.

The Requirement diagram is introduced in SysML and is a core part of the language. Requirements traceability is undoubtedly a good thing; a formal representation of requirement diagrams in CSP gives rise to a formal means of requirements traceability. This provides a formal foundation for this otherwise informal technique that serves as justification for the development of a formal framework. It should be noted that the above approach hinges on the characteristic process being specified correctly.

4   Case Study: An Access Control System

Our case study is a small control component for a physical access control system that can be used, for example, to manage admittance to a toll road. Each authorised user is assigned a *tag*; in order to gain access, the tag is placed on a *reader*. If the tag is valid, a *barrier* moves to the open position; otherwise, it remains closed.

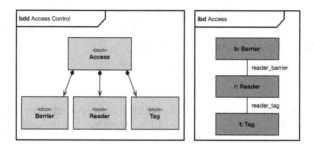

Fig. 2. The block definition diagram modelling the case study as an Access block, composed of aggregate blocks Barrier, Reader and Tag. The internal block diagram of Access shows the internal decomposition into constituent parts, with connectors indicating the links between block instances b, r and t.

4.1 Behavioural Consistency of Communicating Blocks

We now describe how state-based behaviour of blocks may be modelled in CSP, using the formalisms and translation approach defined in Section 2. We also consider how their combined behaviour may be verified using FDR.

The block Access is decomposed into constituent parts: the Barrier, Reader, and Tag block instances (see Figure 2). These parts need to communicate in an orchestrated fashion so as to incorporate the desired behaviour of the composing block, Access. Figure 2 shows a snapshot of the structural constructs used in the design: an instance of the block Reader, r, communicates with instances of the blocks Tag, t, and Barrier, b, using events, typed by signals, via the various connectors. The classifier behaviour of each block is modelled using a corresponding state machine, as per Figure 3.

> datatype $BarrierSignal = open \mid close$
> channel $barrier, blocal : BarrierSignal$
>
> $Barrier(queue, in) =$
>   let
> $INIT = CLOSE$
> $CLOSE =$
> $in.open \rightarrow OPEN$
> $\Box$
> $in?discard : \{close\} \rightarrow CLOSE$
> $OPEN =$
> $in.close \rightarrow CLOSE$
> $\Box$
> $in?discard : \{open\} \rightarrow OPEN$
> $EQ = queue?a \rightarrow in.a \rightarrow EQ$
>   within
> $INIT \; [\mid \{\mid in \mid\} \mid] \; EQ$

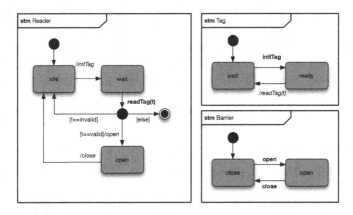

Fig. 3. The state machines modelling the classifier behaviour of the Barrier, Reader and Tag blocks

$$BARRIER = Barrier(barrier, blocal)$$
$$\alpha BARRIER = \{| \; barrier, blocal \; |\}$$

The definition of process *Barrier*, the CSP counterpart of the classifier behaviour of Barrier, is presented above. A datatype definition is used to type the provided receptions of the Barrier block; these serve as triggers for the classifying state machine.

datatype $TagValue = valid \mid invalid$
datatype $ReaderSignal = readTag.TagValue$
channel $reader, rlocal : ReaderSignal$

$Reader(queue, in) =$
    let
        $INIT = IDLE$
        $IDLE = tag.initTag \rightarrow WAIT$
        $WAIT = in.readTag?t \rightarrow JUNCTION(t)$
        $JUNCTION(t) =$
            if $(t == valid)$ then $barrier.open \rightarrow OPEN$
            elseif $(t == invalid)$ then $IDLE$
            else $ERROR$
        $OPEN = barrier.close \rightarrow IDLE$
        $ERROR = STOP$
        $EQ = queue?a \rightarrow in.a \rightarrow EQ$
    within
        $INIT \; [| \; \{| \; in \; |\} \; |] \; EQ$

$READER = Reader(reader, rlocal)$
$\alpha READER = \{| \; reader, rlocal, tag.initTag, barrier.close, barrier.open \; |\}$

Similarly, the process *Reader* models the classifier behaviour of the Reader block. In this case, an additional datatype definition is used to model the parameters passed with the signal. Definitions for *Tag*, *TAG* and αTAG are omitted: these are defined in a similar fashion to the above.

We use parallel composition to construct the system in terms of its constituent processes. The process *Access* is defined thus:

$$ACCESS = \|(p, a) : Parts \bullet [a]p$$

The set *Parts*, containing (*process*, *alphabet*) pairs, is given by:

$$Parts = \{(BARRIER, \alpha Barrier), (READER, \alpha Reader), (TAG, \alpha Tag)\}$$

These recursive decompositions sit extremely well with the process algebraic formalism CSP. Moreover, by utilising CSP in conjunction with SysML, we are able to describe, and reason about, complex patterns of interaction to an extent not currently possible using just SysML.

4.2 Requirements Traceability and Refinement

A text-based requirement can be formalised by allocating another SysML model element to the requirement in order to clarify its description and limit ambiguity. In addition, we can test whether a design satisfies the requirement. As an example, consider the following text-based requirement:

"The barrier will only open if a valid tag is presented"

This requirement can be refined by a behavioural modelling construct, e.g., a state machine, as shown in Figure 4, that enriches the textual description.

The associated process, *AccessRequirement*, is defined thus:

$$AccessRequirement =$$
$$\quad let$$
$$\quad\quad INIT = STATE$$
$$\quad\quad STATE = reader.readTag?t \rightarrow JUNCTION(t)$$
$$\quad\quad JUNCTION(t) =$$
$$\quad\quad\quad if\ (t == valid)\ then\ barrier.open \rightarrow STATE$$
$$\quad\quad\quad elseif\ (t == invalid)\ then\ STATE$$
$$\quad within$$
$$\quad\quad INIT$$

Using the hiding operator and refinement we can test if the design satisfies this requirement, which FDR confirms:

$$AccessRequirement \sqsubseteq_T ACCESS \setminus (\Sigma \setminus NotHidden) \qquad \text{[refinement holds]}$$

In the above, Σ denotes the set of all CSP events within the context of the specification. The set *NotHidden* is given by

$$NotHidden = \{reader.readTag.valid, reader.readTag.invalid, barrier.open\}$$

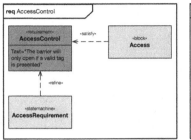
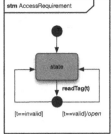

Fig. 4. The state machine AccessRequirement refining the textual description of the requirement AccessControl, which is satisfied by the Access block

5   Conclusions

SysML is a standard that has only recently matured, and, as such, efforts to integrate it with formal approaches are ongoing. Jacobs and Simpson [10] presented an approach to decompose an abstract SysML block into constituent, concrete blocks. Activity diagrams [7] and state machine diagrams [5] have both been given a formal semantics (considering a subset of the available modelling constructs) in CSP. Abdelhalim *et al.* presented an approach based on checking behavioural consistency between a UML state machine diagram and a corresponding fUML activity diagram [8]. The diagrams are given a formal semantics in CSP; FDR is then employed in order to ensure that a trace refinement holds between the abstract state machine diagram and the concrete activity diagram. Other noteworthy contributions include that of Davies and Crichton [6], which provides a behavioural semantics to combinations of class, object, and state machine diagrams using CSP. Behavioural conformance is formalised within the context of traces and failures refinement of CSP. As another example, Graves and Bijan integrated SysML with a higher order type theory logic in an incremental, top-down approach that aims to maintain the logical consistency of the design, with a case study from the aerospace industry [9].

We have presented a bird's eye view of how CSP and the associated refinement checker FDR can be used in conjunction with a model-based systems engineering approach to systems modelling. Our focus is on the high level integration of blocks, where the behavioural characteristics are modelled using SysML state machines. We cannot view these in isolation, but need to consider them in their context of use as to ensure that the complete system functions as intended. We showed how refinement can be utilised to facilitate requirements traceability and bestow a sense of confidence in the validity of the design.

The choice of CSP is due to a number of factors. First, the behavioural aspects of SysML can be modelled naturally by a process algebraic formalism such as CSP, resulting in a formal framework where assertions about requirements can be proved or refuted relatively straightforwardly. Second, CSP's approach to process composition, combined with the fact that refinement is preserved within

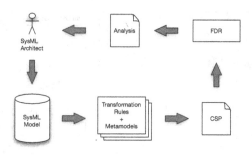

Fig. 5. High level overview of the approach

context, would allow us to decompose a complex design of a system (or system of systems) in such a way that the automated analysis is computationally feasible.

Future avenues of research will include the implementation of a formal refinement framework, using a model based approach similar to [8], where SysML and CSP are each defined using a meta-model, and transformations are subsequently used in order to translate from SysML to CSP, as per Figure 5.

References

1. Object Management Group: Systems Modelling Language Specification, version 1.3 (2012)
2. Hoare, C.A.R.: Communicating Sequential Processes. Prentice Hall (1985)
3. Roscoe, A.W.: Understanding Concurrent Systems. Springer (2010)
4. Department of Computer Science, University of Oxford & Formal Systems Europe: Failures Divergence Refinement User Manual, version 2.94 (2012)
5. Ng, M.Y., Butler, M.: Towards formalizing UML state diagrams in CSP. In: Proceedings of the 1st International Conference on Software Engineering and Formal Methods (SEFM 2003), pp. 138–147. IEEE (2003)
6. Davies, J.W.M., Crichton, C.R.: Concurrency and refinement in the Unified Modelling Language. Electronic Notes in Theoretical Computer Science 70(3), 217–243 (2002)
7. Dong, X., Philbert, N., Zongtian, L., Wei, L.: Towards formalizing UML activity diagrams in CSP. In: Proceedings of the International Symposium on Computer Science and Computational Technology (ISCSCT 2008), pp. 450–453. IEEE (2008)
8. Abdelhalim, I., Schneider, S.A., Treharne, H.: Towards a practical approach to check UML/fUML models consistency using CSP. In: Qin, S., Qiu, Z. (eds.) ICFEM 2011. LNCS, vol. 6991, pp. 33–48. Springer, Heidelberg (2011)
9. Graves, H., Bijan, Y.: Using formal methods with SysML in aerospace design and engineering. Annals of Mathematics and Artificial Intelligence 63(1), 53–102 (2011)
10. Jacobs, J., Simpson, A.C.: A process algebraic approach to decomposition of communicating SysML blocks. International Journal of Modeling and Optimization 3(2), 153–157 (2013)

Translation from Workflow Nets to MSVL*

Ya Shi, Zhenhua Duan**, and Cong Tian

ICTT and ISN Lab, Xidian University, Xi'an, China, 710071
y.shi@stu.xidian.edu.cn, zhenhua_duan@126.com,
tico_tools@163.com

Abstract. An automatic translation from Workflow nets (WFNs) to Modeling, Simulation and Verification Language (MSVL) is presented in this paper. As a result, WFNs can be simulated and verified through the well developed supporting tool named MSV for MSVL programs. To do so, annotations are added to WFNs first. Further, translating rules are presented w.r.t regular structures for the translation from Annotated WFNs to MSVL programs. Finally, a tool called PN2MSVL has been implemented for the automatic translation from WFNs to MSVL.

Keywords: Workflow Nets, MSVL, Modeling, Verification, Simulation.

1   Introduction

As a subset of Petri nets [16], Workflow Nets (WFNs) [1] have been widely adopted in modeling business processes. WFNs combine an intuitive graphical formalism with a mathematical sound foundation. The graphical representation is useful in capturing the intuition of a modeler faithfully while the formal foundation allows the verification of a variety of properties [8, 16]. However, as an abstract model, WFNs are not implementable although some tools, e.g. CPN [4], can support the simulation and verification of WFNs.

To implement WFNs, several transformations from WFNs to executable codes in Java, Ada, and BPEL have been investigated. Considering readability, extensibility and efficiency of the generated codes, structured translations [2, 10, 13–15, 17] draw much attention. Within structured translations, behavioral constructs, such as sequences, choices, and loops, are mapped into the corresponding structured statements of programming languages. The challenge is that some complex constructs are difficult to be translated into conventional structured statements directly. In the translations from WFNs to BPEL in [2, 15], some complex constructs are mapped to flow activities with control links to indicate the excepted execution order. These methods are unsuitable for common programming languages because of the usage of flow statements. In [2], manual translation is employed when a complex construct cannot be translated automatically. There are also other approaches [9, 12, 18, 19] through structured graph-oriented

---

* This research is supported by NSFC Grant Nos. 61133001, 61003078, 61272117, 61272118, and 61202038, National Program on Key Basic Research Project of China (973 Program) Grant No. 2010CB328102, and ISN Lab Grant No. ISN1102001.
** Corresponding author.

L. Groves and J. Sun (Eds.): ICFEM 2013, LNCS 8144, pp. 281–296, 2013.

models, since the structured translation from structured WFNs to programming languages is smooth. However, it is declared in [12] that there exist WFNs without any equivalent structured models. To sum up, there are still lots of difficulties in the structured transformation from WFNs to programming languages. In addition, most of the existing structured translations just aim at the implementation of WFNs without considering verification of correctness of the models.

Modeling, Simulation and Verification Language (MSVL) [6] is an executable subset of Projection Temporal Logic (PTL) [20]. In addition to common statements, eg, *assignment*, *sequence*, *condition* and *loop*, in C, C++, and Java, etc., concurrent statements like *await*, *parallel*, as well as *projection* are also provided in MSVL. As a modeling, simulation and verification language, MSVL can perform as a programming language for simulation, model a concurrent system like PROMELA [11], and verify critical properties of a system through model checking approaches. Meanwhile, supporting tool for simulation, modeling and verification with MSVL has been well developed [6].

Therefore, we are motivated to implement WFNs with MSVL such that WFNs models can be not only implemented but also verified with properties specified by Propositional Projection Temporal Logic formulas (PPTL) [6]. To the end of the translation from WFNs to MSVL programs, annotations are added to WFNs first. Further, translating rules are presented for the translation from Annotated WFNs (AWFNs) to MSVL programs and a tool called PN2MSVL is implemented for the automatic translation from WFNs to MSVL. The merits of the translation presented in this paper are in two folds: (1) the translation is structured and easy to be extended to other general programming languages; (2) when transformed as MSVL programs, critical properties of the original WFN models can be verified via model checking approaches.

The rest of the paper is organized as follows. In Section 2, preliminaries about WFNs and MSVL are presented. AWFNs and regular structures are presented in Section 3, and translating rules and algorithm from WFNs to MSVL are discussed in Section 4. In Section 5, translating tool PN2MSVL as well as case studies are presented. Finally, the conclusion is drawn and the future research directions are pointed out in Section 6.

2 Preliminaries

This section briefly presents the definitions of Workflow nets as well as MSVL.

2.1 Workflow Nets

Definition 1 (Workflow Nets). *A Petri net* $N = (P, T, F)$ *is a Workflow net if and only if: (1) there is one source place* $i \in P$ *such that* $^\bullet i = \emptyset$; *(2) there is one sink place* $o \in P$ *such that* $o^\bullet = \emptyset$; *(3) the net* $\overline{N} = (P, T \cup \{t_N\}, F \cup \{(o, t_N), (t_N, i)\})$, $t_N \notin T$, *is strongly connected.*

As usual, a WFN system $\Sigma = (P, T, F, M_0)$ always initially puts only one token into the source place, i.e. $M_0 = \{i\}$. A WFN $N = (P, T, F)$ is *sound* [3] iff (1) $\forall M$, $(\{i\} \xrightarrow{*} M) \Rightarrow (M \xrightarrow{*} \{o\})$; (2) $\forall M$, $(\{i\} \xrightarrow{*} M \wedge M \geq \{o\}) \Rightarrow (M = \{o\})$; (3) $\forall t \in T$, $\exists M, M', \{i\} \xrightarrow{*} M \xrightarrow{t} M'$. A net $N = (P, T, F)$ is a *free-choice net* [5] iff $\forall t_1, t_2 \in T$, if

$^{\bullet}t_1 \cap {}^{\bullet}t_2 \neq \emptyset$, then $^{\bullet}t_1 = {}^{\bullet}t_2$. Given a free-choice net N, a *complete choice* is a maximal subset of transitions with the same input places, and the set of all complete choices is denoted by CC_N.

In general only the models that have been verified will be useful in practice, and soundness is widely accepted as an essential attribute of well designed models. Further, free-choice nets are an important subclass of Petri nets. As a good compromise between expressive power and analyzability, free-choice nets have strong theoretical results and efficient analysis algorithms [5]. With these considerations, in this paper we only deal with sound free-choice WFNs.

2.2 MSVL

MSVL is an executable subset of PTL. Expressions of MSVL are presented below:

$$e ::= n|s|x$$
$$b ::= \text{true}|\text{false}|e_0 = e_1|\neg b|b_0 \text{ and } b_1$$

where n is an integer, s a string, and x a variable. The following are the statements in MSVL:

Assignment :	$x_1 <= e$	Sequential :	$p_1; p_2$
Conditional :	if b_1 then $\{p_1\}$ else$\{p_2\}$	While :	while b_1 do$\{p_1\}$
Guarded Conditional :	$(b_1 \rightarrow p_1)[] \ldots [](b_m \rightarrow p_m)$	Selection :	(p_1)or(p_2)
Interval Frame :	$frame(x_1, \ldots, x_n)$	Parallel :	$(p_1)\|(p_2)$
Await :	$await(b_1)$	Skip :	skip

where e stands for an arbitrary expression, each b_i a boolean expression, each p_i a statement, $i \in \{1, 2, \ldots, m\}$, and each x_j a statement of MSVL, $j \in \{1, 2, \ldots, n\}$. $x_1 <= e$ means that the value of variable x_1 is assigned to the value of expression e_1 and a proposition p_{x_1} combined with x_1, in the mean time, is set to true. The sequential, conditional, and while statements are the same as that of conventional imperative languages. $(b_1 \rightarrow p_1)[] \ldots [](b_m \rightarrow p_m)$ means that if none of the conditions is true, the program will abort; otherwise an arbitrary program p_i with a true guard b_i will be selected for execution. (p_1)or(p_2) means that either p_1 or p_2 is executed. $frame(x_1, \ldots, x_n)$ indicates that for every variable x_j the value of it keeps unchanged over an interval if no assignment to it is encountered. $(p_1)\|(p_2)$ means that p_1 and p_2 start simultaneously, execute parallelly, and can end asynchronously. $await(b_1)$ does not change any variable, but waits until the condition b_1 becomes true, at which point it terminates. *skip* specifies an interval of unit length.

Currently, a tool named MSV has been developed for MSVL. MSV can work in three modes: simulation, modeling, and verification. In the simulation mode, an MSVL program is executed with an interpreter; in the modeling mode, the whole state space of the program can be illustrated in terms of Normal Form Graph (NFG) [7]; and in the verification mode, a Propositional Projection Temporal Logic (PPTL) formula is used to specify the desired property of the model, then the unified model checking approach [6] is utilized to check whether the MSVL model can satisfy the PPTL formula.

3   Annotated Workflow Nets and Regular Structures

For the fluent translation from WFNs to MSVL, we introduce Annotated Workflow
Nets (AWFNs) and regular structures in AWFNs first.

3.1   Annotated Workflow Nets

Definition 2. *An* Annotated WFN (AWFN) *is a tuple* (P, T, F, G, L), *where* $N = (P, T, F)$
is a WFN, G and L are condition and statement annotations on a transition $t \in T$,
respectively. For each transition $t \in T$, *the condition annotation* $G(t)$ *of t is a boolean
expression, and the statement annotation* $L(t)$ *of t is a statement in MSVL.*

In an AWFN, a transition t is *enabled* iff for each place $p \in {}^{\bullet}t$, $M(p) > 0$ and $G(t)$ is
true. The statement annotation $L(t)$ will be executed while t is fired. AWFNs serve as
an intermediary in the translation from WFNs to MSVL.

Given a sound free-choice WFN $N = (P, T, F)$, an AWFN $AN = (P, T, F, G, L)$ can
be obtained by:

- $G(t) = $ true for each $t \in T$,
- $L(t) = (p_1 <= 0)$ and ... and $(p_m <= 0)$ and skip; $(q_1 <= 1)$ and ... and $(q_n <= 1)$ and skip, where ${}^{\bullet}t = \{p_1, \ldots, p_m\}$ and $t^{\bullet} = \{q_1, \ldots, q_n\}$.

Intuitively, for each place p of N, a variable p is utilized to record the number of tokens
in it, and for each transition t, a statement $L(t)$ is employed to describe the effect of the
transition t on places.

3.2   Regular Structures

Let $N = (P, T, F)$ be a Petri net. For two nodes $x, y \in P \cup T$, there exists a path from
x to y iff $(x, y) \in F^+$. N is *standard* iff there exist two distinct nodes, denoted by st_N
and end_N (means starting and ending node, respectively), such that every node appears
on a path from st_N to end_N. Let $X \subseteq P \cup T$ be a set of nodes. The *projection* of N
to X is a subnet $N|_X = (P|_X, T|_X, F|_X)$ of N, where $P|_X = P \cap X$, $T|_X = T \cap X$, $F|_X = F \cap ((P|_X \times T|_X) \cup (T|_X \times P|_X))$, and for each node $x \in X$, ${}^{\bullet}x|_X = {}^{\bullet}x \cap X$ and $x^{\bullet}|_X = x^{\bullet} \cap X$.
$N|_X$ is *autonomous* iff $N|_X$ is standard, $({}^{\bullet}st_{N|_X} \cup end_{N|_X}{}^{\bullet}) \cap X = \emptyset$, and ${}^{\bullet}X' \cup X'^{\bullet} = X$,
where $X' = X \backslash \{st_{N|_X}, end_{N|_X}\}$.

Now given a sound free-choice AWFN $N = (P, T, F, G, T)$ as well as a set of nodes
$X \subseteq P \cup T$. Some regular structures in AWFNs are defined as follows:

1. Redundant Place Structure: $N|_X$ is a *redundant place structure (RPS)* iff $X = \{p_1, p_2\} \subset P$, ${}^{\bullet}p_1 = {}^{\bullet}p_2$, and $p_1^{\bullet} = p_2^{\bullet}$. Fig. 1 (a) shows a RPS, where $M(q_1) = M(q_2)$ for any reachable marking M.
2. Sequence Structure: $N|_X$ is a *sequence structure (SS)* iff $T|_X = \{t_1, t_2\}$, $P|_X = \{p\} = t_1^{\bullet} = {}^{\bullet}t_2$, ${}^{\bullet}p = \{t_1\}$, and $p^{\bullet} = \{t_2\}$. Obviously, a sequence structure is a standard net. Fig. 2 (a) shows an SS, where t_1 and t_2 always occur sequentially.
3. Explicit Choice Structure: $N|_X$ is an *explicit choice structure (ECS)* iff $P|_X = P_1 \cup P_2$, $P_1 \cap P_2 = \emptyset$, $|P_1| > 0$, $|P_2| > 0$, $|T|_X| > 1$, and $\forall t \in T|_X$, ${}^{\bullet}t = P_1$, $t^{\bullet} = P_2$. Fig. 3 (a) shows an ECS, where the occurrences of t_1 and t_2 are mutually exclusive.

4. Simple Loop Structure: $N|_X$ is a *simple loop structure (SLS)* iff $T|_X = \{t\}$ and $P|_X = {}^\bullet t = t^\bullet$. Fig. 4 (a) shows a SLS, where t_0 can occur repeatedly.

5. Complex Loop Structure: $N|_X$ is a *complex loop structure (CLS)* iff $N|_X$ is connected, $|T|_X| > 1$, $\forall t \in T|_X$, $|{}^\bullet t| = |t^\bullet| = 1$, and $\forall p \in P|_X$, $|{}^\bullet p|_X| = |p^\bullet|_X| = 1$. Since N is a free-choice WFN, we have $\forall p \in P|_X$, $\forall t \in p^\bullet$, ${}^\bullet t = \{p\}$. The dashed rectangle in Fig. 5 (a) shows a CLS, where once one transition in the loop occurs, all transitions in the loop will occur iteratively.

6. Complex Choice Structure: $N|_X$ is a *complex choice structure (CCS)* iff $N|_X$ is a standard net, $st_{N|_X}, end_{N|_X} \in P|_X$, $\forall t \in T|_X$, $|t^\bullet| = |{}^\bullet t| = 1$, $\forall p \in P|_X \backslash \{st_{N|_X}, end_{N|_X}\}$, $|p^\bullet|_X| = |{}^\bullet p|_X| = 1$, $|st_{N|_X}{}^\bullet|_X| = |{}^\bullet end_{N|_X}|_X| = 2$, ${}^\bullet st_{N|_X} \neq \emptyset$, $end_{N|_X}{}^\bullet \neq \emptyset$, and $\forall t \in end_{N|_X}{}^\bullet$, $|{}^\bullet t| = 1$. Similarly, since N is a free-choice net, for all $p \in P|_X$ and $t \in p^\bullet$, we have ${}^\bullet t = \{p\}$. The dashed rectangle in Fig. 6 (a) presents a CCS where four cases: t_1 and t_2, or t_3 and t_4 fire together, or only t_1 or t_4 fires.

7. Concurrent Structure: $N|_X$ is a *concurrent structure (CoS)* iff $N|_X$ is autonomous, $st_{N|_X}, end_{N|_X} \in T|_X$, $\forall p \in P|_X$, $|{}^\bullet p| = |p^\bullet| = 1$, and $T|_X = {}^\bullet(P|_X) \cup (P|_X)^\bullet$. A *minimal CoS* is a CoS where no smaller CoS can be contained. Fig. 7 (a) presents a CoS, where after the occurrence of t_0, all the rest transitions in it will occur.

8. Irregular Structure: $N|_X$ is an *irregular structure (IS)* iff X is autonomous and containing no regular structures defined above. A *minimal IS* is an IS where no smaller IS can be contained. Since N is a sound net, once a transition in an IS $N|_X$ occurs, the occurrence of $N|_X$ will eventually end with no tokens left. Fig. 8 (a) shows an IS where once t_0 or t_1 occurs, t_3 will eventually occur.

4 Translation from AWFNs to MSVL

With respect to each regular structure, a translating rule is given for the transformation from AWFNs to the eventually MSVL programs.

4.1 RULE RRP: Removal of Redundant Places

For each reachable marking of a sound free-choice AWFN, the numbers of tokens contained in all places of a redundant place structure are the same. Thus, control-flow of the structure will not be changed in case any one of the places is removed. Accordingly, for a redundant place structure $N|_X$, we remove one of the two places in X.

Formally, for a redundant place structure $N|_X$ of a sound free-choice AWFN $N = (P, T, F, G, L)$, by RULE RRP, a new sound free-choice AWFN $N' = (P', T, F', G, L)$ is obtained, where $P' = P \setminus \{p\}$, $p \in X$, and $F' = (F \cap ((P' \times T) \cup (T \times P')))$.

As an example, for the redundant place structure illustrated in Fig. 1 (a), by RULE RRP, place q_2 is removed as depicted in Fig. 1 (b).

4.2 RULE FSS: Folding Sequence Structures

In a sequence structure, two transitions always occur sequentially. We fold them into one transition with statement annotation being the sequential composition of the two statement annotations on the two transitions.

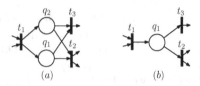

Fig. 1. Removal of Redundant Places

Formally, for a sequence structure $N|_X$ of a sound free-choice AWFN $N = (P, T, F, G, L)$, by RULE FSS, a new sound free-choice AWFN $N' = (P', T', F', G', L')$ is generated, where

- $P' = P \backslash X$;
- $T' = (T \backslash X) \cup \{d_X\}, d_X \notin P \cup T$;
- $F' = (F \cap ((P' \times T') \cup (T' \times P'))) \cup ({}^\bullet st_{N|_x} \times \{d_X\}) \cup (\{d_X\} \times end_{N|_x}{}^\bullet)$;
- $\forall t \in T' \backslash \{d_X\}, G'(t) = G(t)$, and $G'(d_X) = G(st_{N|_x})$;
- $\forall t \in T' \backslash \{d_X\}, L'(t) = L(t)$, and $L'(d_X) = L(st_{N|_x}); L(end_{N|_x})$.

For instance, by RULE FSS, the sequence structure in Fig. 2 (a) can be transformed as d_X in Fig. 2 (b) where $G'(d_X) = G(t_1)$, and $L'(d_X) = L(t_1); L(t_2)$.

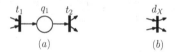

Fig. 2. Folding Sequence Structures

4.3   RULE FECS: Folding Explicit Choice Structures

In an explicit choice structure, the occurrences of transitions are mutually exclusive. The transitions are folded into one transition with a guarded conditional statement as the statement annotation.

Formally, for an explicit choice structure $N|_X$ of a sound free-choice AWFN $N = (P, T, F, G, L)$, by RULE FECS, a new sound free-choice AWFN $N' = (P, T', F', G', L')$ is produced, where

- $T' = (T \backslash X) \cup \{d_X\}, d_X \notin P \cup T$;
- $F' = (F \cap ((P \times T') \cup (T' \times P))) \cup ({}^\bullet(T|_X) \times \{d_X\}) \cup (\{d_X\} \times T|_X{}^\bullet)$;
- $\forall t \in T' \backslash \{d_X\}, G'(t) = G(t)$, and $G'(d_X) = OR_{d \in T|_X} G(d)$;
- $\forall t \in T' \backslash \{d_X\}, L'(t) = L(t)$, and $L'(d_X) = (G(t_0) \rightarrow L(t_0))[] \dots []G(t_n) \rightarrow L(t_n))$, where $T|_X = \{t_0, \dots, t_n\}$.

For example, by RULE FECS, the explicit choice structure in Fig. 3 (a) is folded as the transition d_X in Fig. 3 (b) where $G'(d_X) = G(t_1)$ or $G(t_2)$ and $L'(d_X) = (G(t_1) \rightarrow L(t_1))[](G(t_2) \rightarrow L(t_2))$.

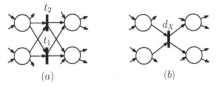

Fig. 3. Folding Explicit Choice Structures

4.4 RULE FSLS: Folding Simple Loop Structures

In a simple loop structure, the transition could occur repeatedly. We fold this structure into one transition with a while statement as the statement annotation.

Formally, for a simple loop structure $N|_X$ of a sound free-choice AWFN $N = (P, T, F, G, L)$, by RULE FSLS, a new sound free-choice AWFN $N' = (P', T', F', G', L')$ is obtained, where

- $P' = (P\backslash X) \cup P_0 \cup P_1$, where $P_0 \cap P_1 = \emptyset$, $(P_0 \cup P_1) \cap (P \cup T) = \emptyset$, and there exit bijective mappings μ_0, $P|_X \to P_0$, and μ_1, $P|_X \to P_1$;
- $T' = (T\backslash X) \cup \{d_X\}$, $d_X \notin P \cup T \cup P_0 \cup P_1$;
- $F' = (F \cap ((P' \times T') \cup (T' \times P'))) \cup (P_0 \times \{d_X\}) \cup (\{d_X\} \times P_1) \cup F_0 \cup F_1$, where $F_0 = \{(x, \mu_0(p))| \forall p \in P|_X, \forall (x, p) \in F|_X\}$ and $F_1 = \{(\mu_1(p), x)| \forall p \in P|_X, \forall (p, x) \in F|_X\}$;
- $\forall t \in T'\backslash\{d_X\}$, $G'(t) = G(t)$, and $G'(d_X) = \texttt{true}$;
- $\forall t \in T'\backslash\{d_X\}$, $L'(t) = L(t)$ and $L'(d_X) = over_X <= 0$ and $\texttt{skip; while}(over_X = 0$ and $G(t))\{(over_X <= 1$ and $\texttt{skip})$ or $(L(t))\}$, where $T|_X = \{t\}$.

For instance, by RULE FSLS, the simple loop structure in Fig. 4 (a) is folded as transition d_X in Fig. 4 (b), where $G'(d_X) = \texttt{true}$ and $L'(d_X) = over_X <= 0$ and $\texttt{skip; while}$ $(over_X = 0$ and $G(t_0))\{(over_X <= 1$ and $\texttt{skip})$ or $(L(t_0))\}$.

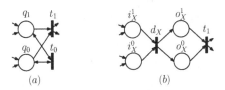

Fig. 4. Folding Simple Loop Structures

4.5 RULE FCLS: Folding Complex Loop Structures

In a complex loop structure, whenever a transition occurs, all transitions in it will occur iteratively. Accordingly, we fold a complex loop structure as a transition with a while statement as the statement annotation. Further, since it may have more than one entries or exits, two auxiliary variables $LPNext_X$ and $LPOut_X$ are utilized to mark the actual entry and exit in one occurrence.

Let $N|_X$ be a complex loop structure of a sound free-choice AWFN $N = (P, T, F, G, L)$. $entry_X$ and $exit_X$ denotes the set of entries and exits of $N|_X$, respectively. Formally, $entry_X = \{p| \forall p \in P|_X, {}^{\bullet}p\backslash X \neq \emptyset\}$ and $exit_X = \{p| \forall p \in P|_X, p^{\bullet}\backslash X \neq \emptyset\}$. Once a transition in $N|_X$ with an entry of $N|_X$ as input place occurs, the occurrence of $N|_X$ starts. While in case a transition outside of $N|_X$ with an exit of $N|_X$ as input place occurs, the occurrence of $N|_X$ ends. Therefore, when an exit q of $N|_X$ gets the token, the occurrence of $N|_X$ can end if one transition d, outside of $N|_X$, with q as input is enabled, i.e. $\mathrm{OR}_{t\in p^\bullet\setminus X}G(t)$ holds. For convenience, we use $EG_X(p)$ to indicate $\mathrm{OR}_{t\in p^\bullet\setminus X}G(t)$ for each place p in $exit_X$. To formally present the details of the transformation, notations below are defined first.

$LN_X \subseteq entry_X \times entry_X$ is a binary relation such that for any $(p_0, p_1) \in LN_X$, there exits a path in $N|_X$ from p_0 to p_1 containing no other entries of $N|_X$. $N|_Y$ is a segment of N_X iff $Y \subseteq X$, $N|_Y$ is a standard net, and $(st_{N|_Y}, end_{N|_Y}) \in LN_X$. Now we extend relation LN_X to segments, namely segments LN_X (SLN_X). Let $N|_{Y_1}$ and $N|_{Y_2}$ be two distinct segments. $(N|_{Y_1}, N|_{Y_2}) \in SLN_X$ iff $(st_{N|_{Y_1}}, st_{N|_{Y_2}}) \in LN_X$. For instance, in the complex loop structure $N|_X$ illustrated in the dashed rectangle of Fig. 5 (a), $entry_X = \{q_1, q_2\}$, $exit_X = \{q_1, q_3\}$, $EG_X(q_1) = G(t_5)$, $EG_X(q_3) = G(t_7)$, and $LN_X = \{(q_1, q_2), (q_2, q_1)\}$. There are two segments $N|_{X_1}$ and $N|_{X_2}$ of loop structure $N|_X$, where $X_1 = \{q_1, q_2, t_0\}$, $X_2 = \{q_2, q_3, q_1, t_1, t_2\}$, and $(N|_{X_1}, N|_{X_2}), (N|_{X_2}, N|_{X_1}) \in SLN_X$.

To construct the statement annotation of the transition formed by RULE FCLS, each segment of a complex structure is mapped into a conditional statement, and then a while statement is constructed such that an arbitrary conditional statement among them serves as the starting, and all conditional statements occur w.r.t to the relations of segments described in SLN_X.

Specifically, given a complex loop structure $N|_X$ of a sound free-choice AWFN $N = (P, T, F, G, L)$, a new sound free-choice AWFN $N' = (P', T', F', G', L')$ is obtained by RULE FCLS, where

- $P' = (P\setminus X) \cup \{i_X, o_X\}$ with $\{i_X, o_X\} \cap (P \cup T) = \emptyset$;
- $T' = (T\setminus X) \cup \{d_X\}$, where $d_X \notin P \cup T \cup \{i_X, o_X\}$;
- $F' = (F \cap ((P' \times T') \cup (T' \times P'))) \cup ((^\bullet entry_X\setminus X) \times \{i_X\}) \cup \{(i_X, d_X), (d_X, o_X)\} \cup (\{o_X\} \times (exit_X^\bullet\setminus X))$;
- $G'(t) = G(t)$, for each $t \in T'\setminus(exit_X^\bullet \cup \{d_X\})$; $G'(t) = G(t)$ and $LPOut_X = $ "p", for each $t \in exit_X^\bullet\setminus X$, where $^\bullet t = \{p\}$; and $G'(d_X) = \mathtt{true}$;
- $L'(t) = L(t)$, for each $t \in T'\setminus(^\bullet entry_X \cup exit_X^\bullet \cup \{d_X\})$, $L'(t) = L(t)$; $LPNext_X <= $ "p" and skip, for each $t \in {}^\bullet entry_X\setminus X$, where $t^\bullet \cap X = \{p\}$, $L'(t) = LPOut_X <= $ "$NULL$" and skip; $L(t)$, for each $t \in exit_X^\bullet\setminus X$, and $L'(d_X)$ is shown in Statement Annotation 1.

In Statement Annotation 1, for each segment $N|_Y$ of $N|_X$ there exists a conditional statement from line 3 to 16. The condition in line 3 is used to check whether the starting place $st_{N|_Y}$ of $N|_Y$ gets a token. If the condition does not hold, the conditional statement is skipped. Otherwise, $LPNext_X$ is assigned as "$end_{N|_Y}$", which makes the conditional statement of the subsequent segment executable. Thus, the statement annotation of transition t_Y^1 between $st_{N|_Y}$ and r_Y^1 is executed subsequently. Here r_Y^1 is the first exit in $N|_Y$. When r_Y^1 gets a token, a guarded conditional occurs. In case the assignment statement in line 5 is executed, the occurrence of $N|_X$ ends and the actual exit of this occurrence is marked by $LPOut_X$. Otherwise, the occurrence of $N|_X$ goes on. t_Y^2 is the transition between r_Y^1 and the successive exit r_Y^2. t_Y^3 is the transition between r_Y^2 and the subsequent exit. r_Y^k is the last exit in $N|_Y$ and t_Y^v is the transition between r_Y^k and $end_{N|_Y}$. All conditional statements occur w.r.t to the relations of segments described in SLN_X.

Statement Annotation 1.

1: while($\neg(LPNext_X = $ "$NULL$")) do{
2:     . . .
3:     if($LPNext_X = $ "$st_{N|y}$") then {
4:         $LPNext_X <= $ "$end_{N|y}$" and skip; $L(t_Y^1)$;
5:         ($EG_X(r_Y^1) \rightarrow LPNext_X <= $ "$NULL$" and $LPOut_X <= $ "r_Y^1" and skip)[]
6:         ($G(t_Y^2) \rightarrow L(t_Y^2)$);
7:             ($EG_X(r_Y^2) \rightarrow LPNext_X <= $ "$NULL$" and $LPOut_X <= $ "r_Y^2" and skip)[]
8:             ($G(t_Y^3) \rightarrow L(t_Y^3)$);
9:                 . . .
10:                     ($EG_X(r_Y^k) \rightarrow$
11:                         $LPNext_X <= $ "$NULL$" and $LPOut_X <= $ "r_Y^k" and skip
12:                     )[]($G(t_Y^v) \rightarrow L(t_Y^v)$))
13:                 . . .
14:         )
15:     )
16: }
17:     . . .
18: }

By RULE FCLS, the complex loop structure shown in Fig. 5 (a) is transformed as d_X in Fig. 5 (b), where

$G'(t_5) = G(t_5)$ and $LPOut_X = $ "q_1", $L'(t_5) = LPOut_X <= $ "$NULL$" and skip; $L(t_5)$,
$G'(t_7) = G(t_7)$ and $LPOut_X = $ "q_3", $L'(t_7) = LPOut_X <= $ "$NULL$" and skip; $L(t_7)$,
$L'(t_3) = L(t_3)$; $LPNext_X <= $ "q_1" and skip,
$L'(t_4) = L(t_4)$; $LPNext_X <= $ "q_1" and skip,
$L'(t_6) = L(t_6)$; $LPNext_X <= $ "q_2" and skip,
$G'(d_X) = $ true,
$L'(d_X) = $ while($\neg(LPNext_X = $ "$NULL$")) do{
        if($LPNext_X = $ "q_1") then{$LPNext_X <= $ "q_2" and skip;
        ($G(t_5) \rightarrow LPNext_X <= $ "$NULL$" and $LPOut_X <= $ "q_1" and skip)[]($G(t_0) \rightarrow L(t_0)$)}
        if($LPNext_X = $ "q_2") then{$LPNext_X <= $ "q_1" and skip; $L(t_1)$;
        ($G(t_7) \rightarrow LPNext_X <= $ "$NULL$" and $LPOut_X <= $ "q_3" and skip)[]($G(t_2) \rightarrow L(t_2)$)}}

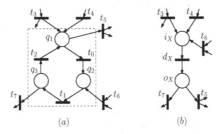

(a)   (b)

Fig. 5. Folding Complex Loop Structures

4.6   RULE FCCS: Folding Complex Choice Structure

We fold a complex choice structure $N|_X$ as a transition with a conditional statement as the statement annotation. Similar to complex loop structures, there may be more than one entries and exits in a complex choice structure. Thus, two auxiliary variables

$CCNext_X$ and $CCOut_X$ are utilized to mark the position where an occurrence of $N|_X$ starts and stops, respectively.

Let $N|_X$ be a complex choice of a sound free-choice AWFN $N = (P, T, F, G, L)$. The definitions of $entry_X$, $exit_X$, EG_X, and LN_X are the same as that of complex loop structures. $N|_Y$ is a *segment* of $N|_X$ iff $Y \subset X$, $N|_Y$ is a standard net, and (1) $(st_{N|_Y}, end_{N|_Y}) \in LN_X$, or (2) $Y \cap entry_X = st_{N|_X}$ and $end_{N|_Y} = end_{N|_X}$. Note that among the segments of $N|_X$, there are two starting at $st_{N|_X}$ as well as two ending at $end_{N|_X}$. The definition of SLN_X is the same as that of complex loop structures. For instance, for the complex choice structure $N|_X$ as shown in the dashed rectangle of Fig. 6 (a), $entry_X = \{q_0, q_2\}$, $exit_X = \{q_1, q_3\}$, $EG_X(q_1) = G(t_7)$, $EG_X(q_3) = G(t_5)$, $LN_X = \{(q_0, q_2), (q_2, q_3), (q_0, q_3)\}$. There are three segments $N|_{X_1}$, $N|_{X_2}$, and $N|_{X_3}$ of $N|_X$, where $X_1 = \{q_0, q_2, t_3\}$, $X_2 = \{q_2, q_3, t_4\}$, $X_3 = \{q_0, q_1, q_3, t_1, t_2\}$, and $SLN_X = \{(N|_{X_1}, N|_{X_2})\}$.

According to the definition of complex choice structure $N|_X$, there are two different pathes from $st_{N|_X}$ to $end_{N|_X}$. To construct the statement annotation of the transition formed by RULE FCCS, (1) for each path from $st_{N|_X}$ to $end_{N|_X}$, a sequential statement is constructed with conditional statements obtained from segments in it; (2) in each sequential statement, all conditional statements occur w.r.t to the relations of segments described in SLN_X; and (3) a new guarded conditional statement with these two sequential statements as branches is constructed.

Specifically, given a complex choice structure $N|_X$ of a sound free-choice AWFN $N = (P, T, F, G, L)$, a new sound free-choice AWFN $N' = (P', T', F', G', L')$ is obtained by RULE FCCS, where

- $P' = (P \backslash X) \cup \{i_X, o_X\}$, and $\{i_X, o_X\} \cap (P \cup T) = \emptyset$;
- $T' = (T \backslash X) \cup \{d_X\}$, where $d_X \notin P \cup T \cup \{i_X, o_X\}$;
- $F' = (F \cap ((P' \times T') \cup (T' \times P'))) \cup ((^\bullet entry_X \backslash X) \times \{i_X\}) \cup \{(i_X, d_X), (d_X, o_X)\} \cup (\{o_X\} \times (exit_X^\bullet \backslash X))$;
- $G'(t) = G(t)$, for each $t \in T' \backslash (exit_X^\bullet \cup \{d_X\})$; $G'(t) = G(t)$ and $CCOut_X = $ "p", for each $t \in exit_X^\bullet \backslash X$, where $^\bullet t = \{p\}$; and $G'(d_X) = \text{true}$;
- $L'(t) = L(t)$, for each $t \in T' \backslash (^\bullet entry_X \cup exit_X^\bullet \cup \{d_X\})$; $L'(t) = L(t)$; $CCNext_X <= $ "p" and skip, for each $\forall t \in {}^\bullet entry_X \backslash X$, where $t^\bullet \cap X = \{p\}$; $L'(t) = CCOut_X <= $ "$NULL$" and skip; $L(t)$, for each $t \in exit_X^\bullet \backslash X$; and $L'(d_X) =$

```
1 : (CCNextₓ = "a₀" and (G(t₀) or EGₓ(a₀)) or CCNextₓ = "a₁" or ... or CCNextₓ = "aₘ" →
2 :    ...)[]
3 : (CCNextₓ = "b₀" and (G(t₁) or EGₓ(b₀)) or CCNextₓ = "b₁" or ... or CCNextₓ = "bₙ" →
4 :    ...)
```

In $L'(d_X)$, each a_i and b_j, $i \in \{0, 1, \ldots, m\}$, $j \in \{0, 1, \ldots, n\}$, is an entry of the complex choice structure appearing in the two pathes from $st_{N|_X}$ to $end_{N|_X}$. Note that $a_0 = b_0 = st_{N|_X}$. t_0 and t_1 are the first transitions in the two pathes from $st_{N|_X}$ to $end_{N|_X}$. The two conditions are used to select a path from $st_{N|_X}$ to $end_{N|_X}$ for executing. For each segment of a path, in line 2 (or 4) there exists a conditional statement similar to the one from line 3 to 16 in Statement Annotation 1 with $LPNext_X$ and $LPOut_X$ being replaced by $CCNext_X$ and $CCOut_X$. All conditional statements in line 2 and 4 occur w.r.t to the relations of segments described in SLN_X. For segments $N|_Y$ ending at $end_{N|_X}$, the statement $CCNext_X <= $ "$end_{N|_Y}$" in line 4 of Statement Annotation 1 is replaced by $CCNext_X <= $ "$NULL$", and the codes in line 10 and 12 of Statement Annotation 1 are removed.

By RULE FCCS, the complex choice structure in Fig. 6 (a) is transformed as transition d_X in Fig. 6 (b), where

$G'(t_5) = G(t_5)$ and $CCOut_X$ = "q_3", $L'(t_5) = CCOut_X$ <= "NULL" and skip; $L(t_5)$,
$G'(t_7) = G(t_7)$ and $CCOut_X$ = "q_1", $L'(t_7) = CCOut_X$ <= "NULL" and skip; $L(t_7)$,
$L'(t_0) = L(t_0); CCNext_X$ <= "q_0" and skip,
$L'(t_6) = L(t_6); CCNext_X$ <= "q_2" and skip,
$G'(d_X)$ = true,
$L'(d_X) = (CCNext_X$ = "q_0" and $G(t_1) \rightarrow$
    if($CCNext_X$ = "q_0") then {$CCNext_X$ <= "NULL" and skip; $L(t_1)$;
    ($G(t_7) \rightarrow CCNext_X$ <= "NULL" and $CCOut_X$ <= "q_1" and skip)[]
    ($G(t_2) \rightarrow L(t_2); CCNext_X$ <= "NULL" and $CCOut_X$ <= "q_3" and skip)})[]
  ($CCNext_X$ = "q_0" and $G(t_3)$ or $CCNext_X$ = "q_2" $\rightarrow$
    if($CCNext_X$ = "q_0") then {$CCNext_X$ <= "q_2" and skip; $L(t_3)$};
    if($CCNext_X$ = "q_2") then {$L(t_4)$; $CCNext_X$ <= "NULL" and $CCOut_X$ <= "q_3" and skip})

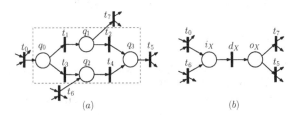

Fig. 6. Folding Complex Choice Structures

4.7   RULE FCoS: Folding Concurrent Structure

In a concurrent structure $N|_X$, once a transition $st_{N|_X}$ occurs, all other transitions will occur. Thus, it is folded into a transition with a parallel statement as the statement annotation. Furthermore, auxiliary variables and await statements are needed to control the occurrence order of transitions in it.

Given a sound free-choice AWFN $N = (P, T, F, G, L)$ with a minimal concurrent structure $N|_X$, for each $t \in T|_X$, $B_X(t)$ is used to indicate $L(t)$; $(B_X(t_1)\| \ldots \|B_X(t_m))$, where $\{t_1, \ldots, t_m\} = t^{\bullet\bullet} \cap (T|_X \backslash \{end_{N|_X}\})$. We first update $L(t)$ as await(vp_1 = 1 and $\ldots$ and vp_m = 1); vp_1 <= 0 and $\ldots$ and vp_m <= 0 and skip; $L(t)$, for each transition $t \in T|_X \backslash \{st_{N|_X}, end_{N|_X}\}$ with $|^{\bullet}t| > 1$, where $\{p_1, \ldots, p_m\} = {}^{\bullet}t \backslash \{p\}$, $p \in {}^{\bullet}t$, and remove input arcs of t excepting for (p, t). Secondly, for each transition $t \in T|_X$ with $\exists q \in t^{\bullet}$, $q^{\bullet} = \emptyset$, we update $L(t)$ as $L(t)$; vq_1 <= 1 and $\ldots$ and vq_n <= 1 and skip, where $\{q_1, \ldots, q_n\} = \{q|\forall q \in t^{\bullet}, q^{\bullet} = \emptyset\}$. Then it has $\forall t \in T|_X \backslash \{st_{N|_X}, end_{N|_X}\}$, $|^{\bullet}t| = 1$. Finally, we fold $N|_X$ and generate a new sound free-choice AWFN $N' = (P', T', F', G', L')$, where

- $P' = (P \backslash X) \cup \{i_X, o_X\}$, $\{i_X, o_X\} \cap (P \cup T) = \emptyset$;
- $T' = (T \backslash (X \backslash \{st_{N|_X}, end_{N|_X}\})) \cup \{d_X\}$, $d_X \notin P \cup T \cup \{i_X, o_X\}$;
- $F' = (F \cap ((P' \times T') \cup (T' \times P'))) \cup \{(st_{N|_X}, i_X), (i_X, d_X), (d_X, o_X), (o_X, end_{N|_X})\}$;
- $\forall t \in T' \backslash \{d_X\}$, $G'(t) = G(t)$, and $G'(d_X)$ = true;
- $\forall t \in T \backslash \{d_X\}$, $L'(t) = L(t)$, and $L'(d_X)$ = frame($vr_1, \ldots, vr_i$) and vr_1 <= 0 and $\ldots$ and vr_i <= 0 and$((B_X(t_1))\| \ldots \|(B_X(t_n)))$. Note that $\{t_1, \ldots, t_n\} \subseteq T|_X$ are the transitions that still have input places formed by output places of $st_{N|_X}$ after the first step. $vr_1, \ldots, vr_i$ are the auxiliary variables added in the rule.

By RULE FCoS, the concurrent structure in Fig. 7 (a) is transformed as transition d_X in Fig. 7 (b), where $G'(d_X) =$ true and $L'(d_X) = frame(vq_4)$ and $vq_4 <= 0$ and $((L(t_1); (L(t_3)\|(await(vq_4 = 1); vq_4 <= 0$ and $skip; L(t_4))))\|(L(t_2); vq_4 <= 1$ and $skip))$.

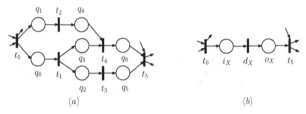

(a) (b)

Fig. 7. Folding Concurrent Structures

4.8   RULE FIS: Folding Irregular Structures

In an irregular structure $N|_X$, once a transition occurs, the occurrence of $N|_X$ will eventually ends with no tokens left. Although the control-flow of an irregular structure is complicated, it could still be folded as a transition with a parallel statement as the statement annotation, where the occurring order of the transitions is organized by auxiliary variables and await statements.

Let $N|_X$ be an irregular structure in a sound free-choice AWFN $N = (P, T, F, G, L)$. We define $stp_X = \{st_{N|_X}\} \cap P$, $endp_X = \{end_{N|_X}\} \cap P$, $stt_X = \{st_{N|_X}\} \cap T$, and $endt_X = \{end_{N|_X}\} \cap T$. Let $N|_X$ be a minimal irregular structure of N. We first add an auxiliary transition t_{over} to N such that $t_{over}{}^\bullet = \emptyset$, $L(t_{over}) = over_X <= 1$ and skip, ${}^\bullet t_{over} = {}^\bullet end_{N|_X} \cap X$ and $G(t_{over}) = G(end_{N|_X})$ if $endt_X \neq \emptyset$, ${}^\bullet t_{over} = \{end_{N|_X}\}$ and $G(t_{over}) = OR_{t \in end_{N|_X}{}^\bullet \setminus X} G(t)$ otherwise. Accordingly, a new sound free-choice AWFN $N' = (P', T', F', G', L')$ is obtained where,

- $P' = (P \setminus X) \cup \{i_X, o_X\}$, $\{i_X, o_X\} \cap (P \cup T \cup \{t_{over}\}) = \emptyset$,
- $T' = (T \setminus ((X \cup \{t_{over}\}) \setminus (stt_X \cup endt_X))) \cup \{d_X\}$, $d_X \notin P \cup T \cup \{t_{over}, i_X, o_X\}$,
- $F' = (F \cap ((P' \times T') \cup (T' \times P'))) \cup \{(i_X, d_X), (d_X, o_X)\} \cup F_i \cup F_o$, where $F_i = ({}^\bullet stp_X \times \{i_X\}) \cup (\{i_X\} \times (stp_X{}^\bullet \setminus X))$, if $stp_X \neq \emptyset$, otherwise $F_i = stt_X \times \{i_X\}$; $F_o = (({}^\bullet endp_X \setminus X) \times \{o_X\}) \cup (\{o_X\} \times endp_X{}^\bullet)$, if $endp_X \neq \emptyset$, otherwise $F_o = \{o_X\} \times endt_X$;
- $G'(t) = G(t)$, for each $t \in T' \setminus \{d_X\}$; $G'(d_X) =$ true, if $stp_X = \emptyset$, otherwise, $G'(d_X) = OR_{d \in stp_X{}^\bullet \setminus X} G(d)$;
- $\forall t \in T' \setminus \{d_X\}$, $L'(t) = L(t)$, and $L'(d_X) =$

$$
\begin{aligned}
&\cdots\\
&pro\ D() = \{\\
&\quad \texttt{while}(over_X = 0)\{await(vr_1 = 1\ \text{and}\ \cdots\ \text{and}\ vr_i = 1\ \text{or}\ over_X = 1);\\
&\quad \texttt{if}(over_X = 0)\ \texttt{then}\{vr_1 <= 0\ \text{and}\ \cdots\ \text{and}\ vr_i <= 0\ \text{and}\ skip;\\
&\qquad (G(t_1) \rightarrow L(t_1); vs_1 <= 1\ \text{and}\ \cdots\ \text{and}\ vs_{j_1} <= 1\ \text{and}\ skip)[]\\
&\qquad \cdots\\
&\qquad [](G(t_k) \rightarrow L(t_k); vs_1 <= 1\ \text{and}\ \cdots\ \text{and}\ vs_{j_k} <= 1\ \text{and}\ skip)\}\}\};\\
&\cdots\\
&\texttt{define}\ start_X() = \{vp_{j_1} <= 1\ \text{and}\ \cdots\ \text{and}\ vp_{j_k} <= 1\ \text{and}\ skip\};\\
&\texttt{define}\ end_X() = \{over_X <= 0\ \text{and}\ skip\};\\
&\texttt{frame}(vp_1, \ldots, vp_n, over_X)\ \text{and}\ vp_1 <= 0\ \text{and}\ \cdots\ \text{and}\ vp_n <= 0\ \text{and}\ over_X <= 0\ \text{and}\\
&(start_X(); (D_X^1()\| \ldots \| D_X^h()); end_X())
\end{aligned}
$$

In $L'(d_X)$, for each place $p \in P|_X$, an auxiliary variable vp is used to record the tokens in it. And $st^{\bullet}_{N|_X} = \{p_{j_1}, \ldots, p_{j_k}\}$, if $stt_X \neq \emptyset$, otherwise $k = 1$ and $p_{j_1} = st_{N|_X}$. For each complete choice $\{t_1, \ldots, t_k\} = D \in CC_{N|_X} = \{D^1_X, \ldots, D^h_X\}$, there exits a process $D()$ containing a while statement where transitions in D are executed repeatedly. In a complete choice D, all transitions have $\{r_1, \ldots, r_i\}$ as input. Thus, all of the transitions have to wait until $N|_X$ ends or each common input place gets a token. Once one of the transitions occurs, all tokens in the input are consumed, and each output place gets a token.

By RULE FIS, the irregular structure in Fig. 8 (a) is transformed as a transition in Fig. 8 (b), where $G'(d_X) = \texttt{true}$ and $L'(d_X) =$

```
pro D¹ₓ() = {
   while(overₓ = 0){await(vq₁ = 1 and vq₂ = 1 or overₓ = 1);
      if(overₓ = 0) then{vq₁ <= 0 and vq₂ <= 0 and skip;(G(t₃) → overₓ <= 1 and skip)}}};
pro D²ₓ() = {
   while(overₓ = 0){await(vq₃ = 1 or overₓ = 1);
      if(overₓ = 0) then{vq₃ <= 0 and skip;(G(t₂) → L(t₂);vq₁ <= 1 and skip)}}};
pro D³ₓ() = {
   while(overₓ = 0){await(vq₀ = 1 or overₓ = 1);
      if(overₓ = 0) then{vq₀ <= 0 and skip;
         (G(t₀) → L(t₀);vq₁ <= 1 and vq₂ <= 1 and skip)[]
         (G(t₁) → L(t₁);vq₂ <= 1 and vq₃ <= 1 and skip)}}};
define startₓ() = {vq₀ <= 1 and skip};
define endₓ() = {overₓ <= 0 and skip};
frame(vq₃,vq₂,vq₁,vq₀,overₓ) and vq₃ <= 0 and vq₂ <= 0 and vq₁ <= 0 and vq₀ <= 0
and overₓ <= 0 and (startₓ();(D¹ₓ()||D²ₓ()||D³ₓ()); endₓ())
```

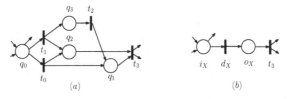

Fig. 8. Folding Irregular Structures

4.9 Translation Algorithm

Based on the translating rules, Algorithm PN2MSVL is presented for the translation from sound free-choice WFNs to MSVL programs.

In the MSVL program generated by Algorithm PN2MSVL, for each place $p_h \in P = \{p_1, \ldots, p_a\}$, a variable p_h is introduced in the final MSVL program. Especially, p_1 specifies the source place of N. $v_1, \ldots, v_b$ are the extra variables introduced by translating rules where $v^1_i, \ldots, v^j_i$ (or $v^1_s, \ldots, v^k_s$) are all integer (string) variables among them. For each transition t of T there exits a definition statement, where ${}^{\bullet}t = \{p^1_t, \ldots p^m_t\}$ and $t^{\bullet} = \{q^1_t, \ldots, q^n_t\}$.

Algorithm PN2MSVL:

Translation from sound free-choice WFNs to MSVL programs

Input: A sound free-choice WFN $N = (P, T, F)$;

Output: A MSVL program;

Translate N to the corresponding AWFN $AN = (P, T, F, G, L)$;

while $|T| > 1$

    if AN has a redundant place structure **then** Apply RULE RRP to AN; continue;

    if AN has a sequence structure **then** Apply RULE FSS to AN; continue;

    if AN has an explicit choice structure **then** Apply RULE FECS to AN; continue;

    if AN has a simple loop structure **then** Apply RULE FSLS to AN; continue;

    if AN has a complex loop structure **then** Apply RULE FCLS to AN; continue;

    if AN has a complex choice structure **then** Apply RULE FCCS to AN; continue;

    if AN has a concurrent structure **then** Apply RULE FCoS to AN; continue;

    if AN has an irregular structure **then** Apply RULE FIS to AN; continue;

Add initialization, frame and definition statements to $L(t)$;   /* Let $T = \{d\}$ */

return the final MSVL program shown as follows.

    $\mathbf{frame}(p_1, \ldots, p_a, v_1, \ldots, v_b)$ and $p_1 <= 1$ and $p_2 <= 0$ and $\ldots$ and $p_a <= 0$ and

    $v_i^1 <= 0$ and $\ldots$ and $v_i^j <= 0$ and $v_s^1 <= $ "$NULL$" and $\ldots$ and $v_s^k <= $ "$NULL$" and (

      $\mathbf{define}\ t() = \{p_t^1 <= 0$ and $\ldots$ and $p_t^m <= 0$ and $\mathbf{skip};$

              $q_t^1 <= 1$ and $\ldots$ and $q_t^n <= 1$ and $\mathbf{skip}\}$;

      $\ldots$

    $L(d))$

5 Experiments

We have realized Algorithm PN2MSVL as a tool named PN2MSVL (http://ictt.xidian.edu.cn/toolkit/). PN2MVSL gets a WFN in .g format that can be produced by Workcraft [21] and outputs an MSVL program.

For the sound free-choice WFN in Fig. 9, a MSVL program can be obtained by PN2MSVL as below.

    $\mathbf{frame}(p9, p8, p7, p6, p5, p4, p3, p2, p1, p0, LPNext0, LPOut0)$ and $p0 <= 1$ and $p9 <= 0$

    and $p8 <= 0$ and $p7 <= 0$ and $p6 <= 0$ and $p5 <= 0$ and $p4 <= 0$ and $p3 <= 0$ and $p2 <= 0$

    and $p1 <= 0$ and $LPNext0 <= $ "$NULL$" and $LPOut0 <= $ "$NULL$" and (

    $\mathbf{define}\ t8() = \{p8 <= 0$ and $p6 <= 0$ and $\mathbf{skip}; p9 <= 1$ and $\mathbf{skip}\}$;

    $\ldots$

    $t0()$;

    $\mathbf{frame}(vp7)$ and $vp7 <= 0$ and (

      $(\mathbf{await}(vp7 = 1); vp7 <= 0$ and $\mathbf{skip}; t6())||$

      (

        $(\mathbf{true} \rightarrow t5(); LPNext0 <= $ "$p4$" and $\mathbf{skip})[](\mathbf{true} \rightarrow t1(); LPNext0 <= $ "$p3$" and $\mathbf{skip})$;

        $\mathbf{while}(\neg(LPNext0 = $ "$NULL$"$))\{$

          $\mathbf{if}(LPNext0 = $ "$p3$"$)\mathbf{then}\{LPNext0 <= $ "$p4$" and $\mathbf{skip}; t2()\}$

          $\mathbf{if}(LPNext0 = $ "$p4$"$)\mathbf{then}\{LPNext0 <= $ "$p3$" and $\mathbf{skip}; t3()$;

            $(\mathbf{true} \rightarrow LPNext0 <= $ "$NULL$" and $LPOut0 <= $ "$p5$" and $\mathbf{skip})[](\mathbf{true} \rightarrow t7())\}\}$;

        $LPOut0 <= $ "$NULL$" and $\mathbf{skip}; t4(); vp7 <= 1$ and $\mathbf{skip}))$;

    $t8()$

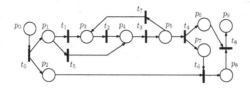

Fig. 9. A Workflow net

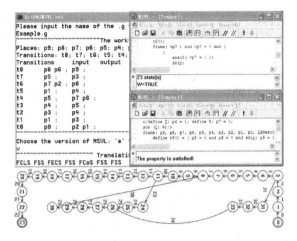

Fig. 10. Results in MSV

When implementing the MSVL program above within MSV, simulation result can be obtained as depicted in the upper right of Fig. 10, where $W = $ true means a successful execution of this program. Now we specify the desired property of the model in PPTL:

$$\Diamond(Q; W)$$

where Q and W means $p4 = 1$ and $p7 = 1$, respectively. The intuition of the formula is that if $p4 = 1$ holds sometimes, $p7 = 1$ will holds eventually. The verification result is shown in the lower right of Fig. 10. In addition, the model of the MSVL program can also be explored as illustrated at the bottom of Fig. 10.

6   Conclusion

An automatic translation from WFNs to MSVL is presented in this paper. The translation is structured and easy to be extended to other general programming languages. In the near future, we are going to further prove the completeness as well as the soundness of the translation. Also, we will try to improve readability of the generated MSVL programs by exploring more regular structures in AWFNs. As applications, we will translate some big systems modeled by WFNs to MSVL and verify the correctness of these systems with MSV.

References

1. van der Aalst, W.M.P.: The application of petri nets to workflow management. Journal of Circuits, Systems, and Computers 8(1), 21–66 (1998)
2. van der Aalst, W.M.P., Lassen, K.B.: Translating unstructured workflow processes to readable bpel: Theory and implementation. Information & Software Technology 50(3), 131–159 (2008)

3. van der Aalst, W.M.P.: Structural characterizations of sound workflow nets. Computing Science Reports 96/23, Eindhoven University of Technology (1996)
4. CPN, http://cpntools.org/
5. Desel, J., Esparza, J.: Free choice Petri nets. Cambridge tracts in theoretical computer science, vol. 40. Cambridge University Press (1995)
6. Duan, Z., Tian, C.: A unified model checking approach with projection temporal logic. In: Liu, S., Araki, K. (eds.) ICFEM 2008. LNCS, vol. 5256, pp. 167–186. Springer, Heidelberg (2008)
7. Duan, Z., Tian, C., Zhang, L.: A decision procedure for propositional projection temporal logic with infinite models. Acta Informatica 45(1), 43–78 (2008)
8. Esparza, J., Heljanko, K.: Implementing ltl model checking with net unfoldings. In: Dwyer, M.B. (ed.) SPIN 2001. LNCS, vol. 2057, pp. 37–56. Springer, Heidelberg (2001)
9. Hauser, R.: Analysis and transformation of behavioral models containing overlapped patterns. Journal of Object Technology 9(3), 105–124 (2010)
10. Hauser, R.: Automatic transformation from graphical process models to executable code. Eidgenössische Technische Hochschule Zürich (2010)
11. Holzmann, G.J.: Design and validation of protocols: A tutorial. Computer networks and ISDN systems 25(9), 981–1017 (1993)
12. Kiepuszewski, B., ter Hofstede, A.H.M., Bussler, C.J.: On structured workflow modeling. In: Wangler, B., Bergman, L.D. (eds.) CAiSE 2000. LNCS, vol. 1789, pp. 431–445. Springer, Heidelberg (2000)
13. Kleine, J., Reisig, W.: Transformation von offenen Workflow-Netzen zu abstrakten WS-BPEL-Prozessen (in German). Ph.D. thesis, Humboldt-Universität zu Berlin, Berlin (2007)
14. Lassen, K.B., Tjell, S.: Translating colored control flow nets into readable java via annotated java workflow nets. In: Jensen, K. (ed.) 8th Workshop and Tutorial on Practical Use of Coloured Petri Nets and the CPN Tools, pp. 127–146. Aarhus University, Aarhus (2007)
15. Lohmann, N., Kleine, J.: Fully-automatic translation of open workflow net models into simple abstract bpel processes. In: Kühne, T., Reisig, W., Steimann, F. (eds.) Modellierung 2008. Lecture Notes in Informatics, vol. 127, pp. 57–72. Gesellschaft für Informatik, Bonn (2008)
16. Murata, T.: Petri nets: properties, analysis and applications. Proceedings of the IEEE 77(4), 541–580 (1989)
17. Ouyang, C., Dumas, M., van der Aalst, W.M.P., ter Hofstede, A.H.M., Mendling, J.: From business process models to process-oriented software systems. ACM Transactions on Software Engineering and Methodology 19(1) (2009)
18. Polyvyanyy, A., García-Bañuelos, L., Dumas, M.: Structuring acyclic process models. Information Systems 37(6), 518–538 (2012)
19. Polyvyanyy, A., García-Bañuelos, L., Fahland, D., Weske, M.: Maximal structuring of acyclic process models. The Computing Research Repository abs/1108.2384 (2011)
20. Tian, C., Duan, Z.: Propositional projection temporal logic, buchi automata and ω-regular expressions. In: Agrawal, M., Du, D.-Z., Duan, Z., Li, A. (eds.) TAMC 2008. LNCS, vol. 4978, pp. 47–58. Springer, Heidelberg (2008)
21. Workcraft, http://www.workcraft.org/wiki/

Asymptotic Bounds for Quantitative Verification of Perturbed Probabilistic Systems[*]

Guoxin Su and David S. Rosenblum

National University of Singapore
{sugx,david}@comp.nus.edu.sg

Abstract. The majority of existing probabilistic model checking case studies are based on well understood theoretical models and distributions. However, real-life probabilistic systems usually involve distribution parameters whose values are obtained by empirical measurements and thus are subject to small perturbations. In this paper, we consider perturbation analysis of reachability in the parametric models of these systems (i.e., parametric Markov chains) equipped with the norm of absolute distance. Our main contribution is a method to compute the *asymptotic bounds* in the form of *condition numbers* for constrained reachability probabilities against perturbations of the distribution parameters of the system. The adequacy of the method is demonstrated through experiments with the Zeroconf protocol and the hopping frog problem.

1 Introduction

Probabilistic model checking is a verification technique that has matured over the past decade, and one of the most widely known and used probabilistic model checking tools is PRISM [1]. The majority of the reported case studies of probabilistic model checking, including those performed in PRISM, involve systems whose stochastic nature arises from well understood theoretical probabilistic distributions, such as the use of a fair coin toss to introduce randomization into an algorithm, or the uniform distribution of randomly chosen IP addresses in the Zeroconf protocol. More complex, realistic systems, on the other hand, involve behaviors or other system characteristics generated by empirical distributions that must be encoded via empirically observed parameters. In many cases, these distribution parameters are based on finite numbers of samples and are statistical estimations that are subject to further adjustments. Also, the stochastic nature of the model (e.g., the failure rate of some hardware component) may be varying over time (e.g., the age of the component). The conventional techniques and tools of probabilistic model checking, including PRISM, do not provide sufficient account for systems with distribution parameters. Consider, for instance,

---

[*] The work is supported by grant R-252-000-458-133 from Singapore Ministry of Education Academic Research Fund. The authors would like to thank Professor Mingsheng Ying for pointing them to perturbation theory and the anonymous referees for improving the draft of this paper.

L. Groves and J. Sun (Eds.): ICFEM 2013, LNCS 8144, pp. 297–312, 2013.

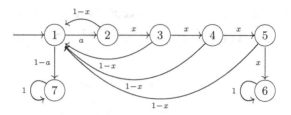

Fig. 1. Zeroconf protocol with noisy channels

the setting of automata-based model checking: Given a (probabilistic) model $\mathcal{M}$ and an LTL formula φ, the model checker returns a satisfaction probability p of φ in $\mathcal{M}$. However, $\mathcal{M}$ is just an *idealized* model of the probabilistic system under consideration, and because the real distribution(s) of its parameter(s) may be slightly different from those specified in $\mathcal{M}$, p is merely a *referential* result whilst the *actual* result may deviate from p to a small but non-trivial extent. We elaborate this pitfall in the following two concrete examples.

Motivating examples. We first consider an IPv4 Zeroconf protocol model for a network with noisy communication channels. Figure 1 presents the protocol model that uses a maximum of four "ok" message probes. Let a be the probability that the new host chooses an IP address that has been assigned already, and x be the probability that the probe or its reply is lost due to channel noise or some other reason (if any). If an IP address is randomly chosen, then a is equal to m/n, where $n = 60,534$ is the size of IP address space as specified in Zeroconf and m is number of hosts already connected. By contrast, x relies on an *ad hoc* statistical estimation of the loss rate of messages tested in experiments. In reality, it is less meaningful to specify a single, constant value of x, as the measurement could be affected by factors such as network load, environment noise, temperature, measurement time, etc. Instead, x may be given as the expression $x_0 \pm x_\Delta$, where x_0 is the mean value of the measured results and x_Δ specifies the maximal perturbation. It is therefore reasonable to express the probability that an address collision happens as $p = p_0 \pm y_\Delta$, where p_0 is a referential value for the result and y_Δ specifies the range of perturbation of p. However, although the standard model checking techniques allow one to obtain p_0 by inputting x_0, they provide little account for the relationship between y_Δ and x_Δ.

Another example is a variant of the classic hopping frog problem. A frog hopping between four rocks and the (i, j)-entry in the following *parametric transition matrix* provides the concrete or abstract probability of frog's movement from the ith rock to the jth rock:

$$\begin{array}{cccc} z_1 & z_2 & z_3 & z_4 \end{array}$$
$$\begin{pmatrix} \frac{3}{8} & \frac{1}{8} & \frac{1}{4} & \frac{1}{4} \\ 0 & \frac{1}{2} & \frac{1}{2} & 0 \\ \frac{1}{3} & 0 & \frac{1}{3} & \frac{1}{3} \end{pmatrix}$$

where the tuple of variables (z_1, z_2, z_3, z_4) satisfies that $z_i \geq 0$ for each $1 \leq i \leq 4$, $z_1 + z_2 + z_3 + z_4 = 1$ and

$$\left| z_1 - \frac{3}{8} \right| + \left| z_2 - \frac{1}{8} \right| + \left| z_3 - \frac{1}{4} \right| + \left| z_4 - \frac{1}{4} \right| \leq \Delta \tag{1}$$

with Δ a sufficiently small positive number. Intuitively, according to Equation (1), $(\frac{3}{8}, \frac{1}{8}, \frac{1}{4}, \frac{1}{4})$ is the idealized distribution of (z_1, z_2, z_3, z_4) and a small perturbation of (z_1, z_2, z_3, z_4) is allowed and measured. We call (z_1, z_2, z_3, z_4) a *distribution parameter* and $(\frac{3}{8}, \frac{1}{8}, \frac{1}{4}, \frac{1}{4})$ its *reference*. A typical model checking problem for this example can be stated as "what is the probability that the frog eventually reaches the fourth rock without landing on the third rock?" Again, well established model checking techniques do not provide a direct solution for this question.

Approach. In a nutshell, the aforementioned two examples demonstrate that a satisfactory model checking result for a probabilistic system with one or more perturbed distribution parameters should shed light on the *sensitivity* of the result to the distribution parameters. In this paper, we provide a method to compute the *asymptotic bounds* of the results in terms of *condition numbers* for reachability checking of probabilistic systems under perturbations. We model the probabilistic systems in discrete-time Markov chains (MCs)[1] with distribution parameters, which are coined as *parametric Markov chains* (PMCs), and introduce the *norm of absolute distance* to measure the deviation distances of their distribution parameters (as exemplified by equation (1)). The reachability checking is formalized as follows: Given a PMC $\mathcal{M}_*$ with state space $S_{\mathcal{M}_*}$ and two sets of states $S_?, S_! \subseteq S_{\mathcal{M}_*}$, a reachability problem is phrased as the probability of "reaching states in $S_!$ only via states in $S_?$". By adopting a notation from temporal logic, the problem is denoted by $S_? \, \mathcal{U} \, S_!$, where $\mathcal{U}$ refers to the "until" operator.[2] Two instances of the reachability problem class are mentioned in the two motivating examples above. The output of the reachability checking contains a referential probabilistic result $p \in [0, 1]$ and a condition number $\kappa_i \in \mathbb{R}$ where $i \in I$, an index set, for *each* distribution parameter. The significance of the output is that, if a sufficiently small perturbation Δ_i, measured by the norm of absolute distance, occurs on the parameter whose condition number is κ_i for each $i \in I$, then the actual result is asymptotically bounded by $p \pm \sum_{i \in I} \kappa_i \Delta_i$. A brief comparison of the reachability checking in MCs and PMCs in terms of input and output is presented in Table 1.

Perturbation bounds have be pursued for MCs in a line of research [2–5]. However, to the best of our knowledge, this paper is the first one devoted to the application of concepts and methods from perturbation theory to

---

[1] Throughout the paper, unless mentioned otherwise, by MCs we mean discrete-time Markov chains.

[2] In fact, the formulation of reachability in the present paper is sightly more general than the standard definition of reachability and sometimes is called *constrained reachability*, since the $S_?$ in $S_? \, \mathcal{U} \, S_!$ plays a constraining role.

Table 1. Reachability checking in MCs and PMCs

Model	Input	Output
$\mathcal{M}$	$S_? \, \mathcal{U} \, S_!$	p (idealized reachability probability)
$\mathcal{M}_*$	$S_? \, \mathcal{U} \, S_!$	p (referential reachability probability) and κ_i (condition numbers)

quantitative verification. To further explain our method, it is beneficial to compare it with a standard method for error estimation based on differentiation and linear approximation. Suppose a sphere (such as a prototype of balls produced by a sporting goods factory) is measured and its radius is $21cm$ with a possible small error within $0.05cm$. The dependence of the sphere volume on the radius is given by $V = \frac{4}{3}\pi r^3$. The problem is to compute volume error V_Δ given the radius error r_Δ. We recall a classic method for this problem: First, the differential function of V on r is given by $dV = 4\pi r^2 dr$. Second, let $dr = r_\Delta = 0.05cm$ (which is significantly small compared with $r = 21cm$) and we obtain $V_\Delta \approx dV = 4\pi \times 21^2 \times 0.05 \approx 277cm^3$. The sensitivity of V_Δ to r_Δ is approximated by the ratio $\frac{dV}{dr} = 4\pi r^2 \approx 5,542$ and this expression is useful if the value of r_Δ is unknown in advance. We aim to develop a similar methodology to estimate the perturbations of reachability in PMCs, which is comparable to the use of differentiation and linear approximation in estimating the error of the ball volume described above.

Organization. The remainder of the paper is organized as follows. The next section (Section 2) presents the formulations of PMCs and introduces the norm of absolute distance for probabilistic distributions. For presentation purposes, we separate the treatment of PMCs into that of basic PMCs, which have a single distribution parameter, and general PMCs, which have multiple distribution parameters. Section 3 deals with basic PMCs by establishing a method for computing their asymptotic bounds, in particular, condition numbers for the given reachability problems. Section 4 generalizes the computation method to handle non-basic PMCs. Our approach is evaluated by experiments in Section 5. Related work is discussed in Section 6. In Section 7, the paper is concluded and several future research directions are outlined. Proof details of the theorems are found in [6].

2   Parametric Markov Chains

In this section, we define the formal models of PMCs, which are parametric variants of MCs. Informally speaking, a PMC is obtained from an MC by replacing the *non-zero* entries in one or more rows of its probabilistic transition matrix by mutually distinct variables.

Let $\mathbf{x}$ be a symbolic vector of pair-wise distinct variables, called a *vector variable* for short. A *reference* $\mathbf{r}$ for $\mathbf{x}$ is a probabilistic vector such that $|\mathbf{r}| = |\mathbf{x}|$.

We use $\mathbf{x}[j]$ to denote the variable in the ith entry of $\mathbf{x}$. An extension of $\mathbf{x}$, denoted by $\mathbf{x}^*$, is obtained by inserting the number zero into $\mathbf{x}$, i.e.,

$$\mathbf{x}^* = (\underbrace{0,\ldots,0}_{l_0\ 0\text{'s}}, \mathbf{x}[1], \ldots, \mathbf{x}[j], \underbrace{0,\ldots,0}_{l_j\ 0\text{'s}}, \mathbf{x}[j+1], \ldots, \mathbf{x}[k], \underbrace{0,\ldots,0}_{l_k\ 0\text{'s}}) ,$$

where $l_0, \ldots, l_k$ are non-negative integers. Two vector variables are *disjoint* if they share no common variables. Let $(\mathbf{x}_i)_{i\in I}$ be a sequence of pair-wise disjoint vector variables for an index set $I \neq \varnothing$ of positive integers. We abbreviate the sequence $(\mathbf{x}_i)_{i\in I}$ as $\mathbf{x}_I$. Let $\mathcal{P}(\mathbf{x}_I)$ be a $k \times k$ abstract square matrix with parameters $\mathbf{x}_I$ such that (i) $k \geq \max(I)$, (ii) if $i \notin I$ then the ith row of $\mathcal{P}(\mathbf{x}_I)$ is a probabilistic vector and (iii) if $i \in I$ then the ith row of $\mathcal{P}(\mathbf{x}_I)$ is $\mathbf{x}_i^*$, an extension of $\mathbf{x}_i$. Here, the involvement of extensions of vector variable intends to be consistent with the replacement of non-zero entries by variables mentioned previously. Such an abstract matrix $\mathcal{P}(\mathbf{x}_I)$ is called a *parametric transition matrix* and each parameter $\mathbf{x}_i$ appearing in $\mathcal{P}(\mathbf{x}_I)$ is called a *distribution parameter*. We can view $\mathcal{P}(\mathbf{x}_I)$ as mapping from sequences of vectors to concrete matrices. As such, $\mathcal{P}\langle\mathbf{r}_I\rangle$, where $\mathbf{r}_I$ abbreviates $(\mathbf{r})_{i\in I}$, is the matrix obtained by replacing $\mathbf{x}_i$ with its reference $\mathbf{r}_i$ for each $i \in I$. Sometimes, especially in our running examples, it is cumbersome to present the distribution parameters $\mathbf{x}_I$ in $\mathcal{P}(\mathbf{x}_I)$; if so, we just write $\mathcal{P}$ and mention its distribution parameters in the text.

Definition 1. *A parametric Markov chain (PMC) is given by the tuple*

$$\mathcal{M}_* = (\iota, \mathcal{P}(\mathbf{x}_I), \mathbf{r}_I) ,$$

where ι is a probabilistic vector (for the initial distribution of $\mathcal{M}_*$), $\mathcal{P}(\mathbf{x}_I)$ is a $|\iota| \times |\iota|$ parametric transition matrix, and $\mathbf{r}_I$ contains references for vector variables in $\mathbf{x}_I$.

The underlying MC of $\mathcal{M}_*$ is $\mathcal{M} = (\iota, \mathcal{P}\langle\mathbf{r}_I\rangle)$. We do not specify the state space for $\mathcal{M}_*$ and $\mathcal{M}$. But throughout the paper, we assume that their state spaces $S_{\mathcal{M}_*} = S_{\mathcal{M}} = \{1, \ldots, |\iota|\}$.

As promised earlier, we introduce a statistical distance measurement between distribution parameters and their references, which is given by the norm of absolute distance (also called total variation).

Definition 2. *The statistical distance for $\mathcal{M}_*$ is given by $\|\cdot\|$ such that $\|\mathbf{v}\| = \sum_{i=1}^{n} |\mathbf{v}[i]|$ for any vector $\mathbf{v}$.*

By definition, the scalar function $\|\mathbf{x}^* - \mathbf{r}^*\|$ is the same as the scalar function $\|\mathbf{x} - \mathbf{r}\|$. If I is a singleton, we also call the PMC a *basic PMC*. In other words, a basic PMC is a PMC with a single distribution parameter.

We now present examples of PMCs. The first example is a PMC $\mathcal{M}_*^{\text{fg}}$ for the hopping frog. Its parametric transition matrix (the 4×4 symbolic matrix already presented in the Introduction) is denoted by $\mathcal{P}_*^{\text{fg}}$. In $\mathcal{P}_*^{\text{fg}}$, the tuple (z_1, z_2, z_3, z_4) is given as the only distribution parameter. We let the reference to the parameter be $(0.375, 0.125, 0.25, 0.25)$. In words, ideally, the probabilities for the frog to jump from the first rock to the first, second, third, and fourth rocks are 0.375, 0.125, 0.25, and 0.25, respectively. Such a PMC is denoted by $\mathcal{M}_*^{fg}$. Additionally, we let the initial distribution in $\mathcal{M}_*^{fg}$ be $\iota^{fg} = (0.25, 0.25, 0.25, 0.25)$, which means that all rocks have an equal probability to be the frog's initial position. Clearly, $\mathcal{M}_*^{fg}$ is a basic PMC.

Another example is PMC $\mathcal{M}_*^{zf}$ for the noisy version of Zeroconf. For illustration purposes, a probabilistic transition system with a parameter x is provided in Figure 1. The formulation of $\mathcal{M}_*^{zf}$ according to Definition 1 deviates from the transition system because of the use of distribution variables. Following the definition, we let the sequence of distribution parameters be $(x_i, x_i')_{i=1}^4$. The parametric transition matrix is given by the following 7×7 symbolic matrix:

$$
\mathcal{P}^{zf} = \begin{pmatrix}
0 & a & 0 & 0 & 0 & 0 & 1-a \\
x_1 & 0 & x_1' & 0 & 0 & 0 & 0 \\
x_2 & 0 & 0 & x_2' & 0 & 0 & 0 \\
x_3 & 0 & 0 & 0 & x_3' & 0 & 0 \\
x_4 & 0 & 0 & 0 & 0 & x_4' & 0 \\
0 & 0 & 0 & 0 & 0 & 1 & 0 \\
0 & 0 & 0 & 0 & 0 & 0 & 1
\end{pmatrix}
$$

The constant number a is calculated according to the number of addresses and that of the occupied ones. The reference for (x_i, x_i') in $\mathcal{M}_*^{zf}$ is $(0.75, 0.25)$ for each $1 \leq i \leq 4$. In other words, we suppose that under idealized conditions the chances of not receiving a reply in four probes are equivalently 0.25. The initial distribution ι^{zf} is $(1, 0, \ldots, 0)$, as state 1 is the initial state.

3   Perturbation Analysis of Basic PMCs

From this section, we commence the perturbation analysis of reachability problems in PMCs. For presentation purposes, in this section we deal with basic PMCs. Recall that a basic PMC has a single distribution parameter. Our main goal is to establish a method to compute an asymptotic bound, in particular, a condition number for a given reachability problem in a basic PMC against the perturbation of its sole distribution parameter. In the next section, we generalize the method to the setting of general PMCs.

3.1   Perturbation Function

Throughout this section, we assume $\mathcal{M}_*$ contain a single distribution parameter; thus, $\mathcal{M}_* = (\iota, \mathcal{P}(\mathbf{x}), \mathbf{r})$. Without loss of generality, let $\mathbf{x}$ appear in the first row of $\mathcal{P}(\mathbf{x})$. We consider the reachability problem $S_? \mathcal{U} S_!$ in $\mathcal{M}_*$ with state space $S_{\mathcal{M}_*} = \{1, \ldots, |\iota|\}$ such that $S_? \cup S_! \subseteq S_{\mathcal{M}_*}$. For convenience, we let $S_? = \{1, \ldots, n_?\}$ and $S_! = \{n_!, \ldots, |\iota|\}$, where $0 \leq n_? < n_! \leq |\iota|$. Thus, $S_? \cap S_! = \varnothing$.[3] We call $S_?$ the *constraint* set of $S_? \mathcal{U} S_!$ and $S_!$ its *destination* set. In the

---

[3] This assumption does not impose any theoretical restriction on the reachability problem, because if $S_? \cap S_! \neq \varnothing$ then we carry out the analysis based on $(S_? \backslash S_!) \mathcal{U} S_!$.

remainder of this subsection, our goal is to formulate a function that captures the effect of the perturbation of $\mathbf{x}$ on the probability of $S_? \,\mathcal{U}\, S_!$ being satisfied by $\mathcal{M}_*$. To motivate and explain the formulation, we recall the standard model checking techniques for reachability probabilities based on non-parametric MCs.

The underlying MC of the basic PMC $\mathcal{M}_*$ is $\mathcal{M} = (\iota, \mathcal{P}\langle \mathbf{r}\rangle)$ and the state space of $S_{\mathcal{M}} = S_{\mathcal{M}_*}$. Let $\mathcal{P}' = \mathcal{P}\langle \mathbf{r}\rangle$. We use $\mathcal{P}'[i,j]$ to denote the number in the (i,j)-entry of $\mathcal{P}'$. Let $\mathbf{p}$ be a vector such that $|\mathbf{p}| = n_?$ and, for each $1 \le i \le n_?$, $\mathbf{p}[i]$ is the probability of $S_? \,\mathcal{U}\, S_!$ satisfied in state i of $\mathcal{M}$. Thus,

$$\mathbf{p}[i] = \sum_{j=1}^{n_?} \mathcal{P}'[i,j] \cdot \mathbf{p}[j] + \sum_{j=n_!}^{|\iota|} \mathcal{P}'[i,j] \;, \tag{2}$$

for each $1 \le i \le n_?$. We rewrite the equation system given in (2) as

$$\mathbf{p} = \mathbf{A}' \cdot \mathbf{p} + \mathbf{b}' \;, \tag{3}$$

where $\mathbf{A}'$ is the up-left $n_? \times n_?$ sub-matrix of $\mathcal{P}'$ (thus, $\mathbf{A}[i,j] = \mathcal{P}[i,j]$ for each $1 \le i,j \le n_?$), and $\mathbf{b}'$ is a vector such that $|\mathbf{b}'| = n_?$ and $\mathbf{b}[i] = \sum_{j=n_!}^{|\iota|} \mathcal{P}[i,j]$ for each $1 \le i \le n_?$. Moreover, $\mathbf{p}$ is the least fixed point satisfying equation (3).

Lemma 3. $\mathbf{p}$ *is computed by* $\mathbf{p} = \sum_{i=0}^{\infty} \mathbf{A}'^i \cdot \mathbf{b}'$.

In the following, we define the parametric counterparts of $\mathbf{A}'$ and $\mathbf{b}'$ specified in Equation (3), namely, $\mathbf{A}(\mathbf{x})$ and $\mathbf{b}(\mathbf{x})$. It should be stressed that according to our notations not necessarily all variable in the vector variable $\mathbf{x}$ appear in each of $\mathbf{A}(\mathbf{x})$ and $(b)(\mathbf{x})$. There are two equivalent ways to obtain $\mathbf{A}(\mathbf{x})$ and $\mathbf{b}(\mathbf{x})$. One way is to define them by going over the aforementioned procedure for $\mathbf{A}'$ and $\mathbf{b}'$, and the other way is to directly parameterize $\mathbf{A}'$ and $\mathbf{b}'$. Here, the second way is chosen. Recall that the first row of $\mathbf{P}(\mathbf{x})$ is an extension $\mathbf{x}^*$ of $\mathbf{x}$. We let $\mathbf{x}^*|_{n_?}$ be the sub-vector of $\mathbf{x}^*$ that consists of the first $n_?$ components (variables or zeros) of $\mathbf{x}^*$, and $\vec{\mathbf{x}}_{n_!}$ be the expression $\mathbf{x}[n_!] + \ldots + \mathbf{x}[|\iota|]$. Then, $\mathbf{A}(\mathbf{x})$ is obtained by replacing the first row in $\mathbf{A}'$ with $\mathbf{x}^*|_{n_?}$ and $\mathbf{b}(\mathbf{x})$ is by replacing the first entry of $\mathbf{b}$ with $\vec{\mathbf{x}}_{n_!}$. If it is not necessary to mention the (possible) variables in $\mathbf{A}(\mathbf{x})$ or $\mathbf{b}(\mathbf{x})$, we just write $\mathbf{A}$ or $\mathbf{b}$.

As an example, consider the following model checking problem of the hopping frog (which has already been mentioned in Sections 1 and 2): What is the probability of reaching the fourth rock without landing on the third one? In this problem, the constraint set is $\{1,2\}$ and the destination set is $\{4\}$. Recall that the only distribution parameter in $\mathcal{M}_*^{\mathrm{fg}}$ is (z_1, z_2, z_3, z_4). Thus, the parametric matrix and the parametric vector are respectively given by

$$\mathbf{A}^{\mathrm{fg}} = \begin{pmatrix} z_1 & z_2 \\ \frac{3}{8} & \frac{1}{8} \end{pmatrix} \;, \quad \mathbf{b}^{\mathrm{fg}} = \begin{pmatrix} z_4 \\ \frac{1}{4} \end{pmatrix} \;.$$

Let $\mathbf{V} = [0,1]^k$ where $k = |\mathbf{x}|$ and $\mathbf{U} = \{\mathbf{v} \in \mathbf{V} \mid \sum_{i=1}^{n} \mathbf{v}[i] = 1\}$. Let $\iota_?$ be the first $n_?$ items in ι.

Definition 4. *The perturbation function of* $\mathbf{x}$ *for a basic PMC* $M_* = (\iota, \mathcal{P}(\mathbf{x}), \mathbf{r})$ *and with respect to the problem* $S_? \, \mathcal{U} \, S_!$ *such that* $S_?, S_! \subseteq S_{M_*}$ *is* $\rho : \mathbf{V} \to [-1, 1]$ *such that*

$$\rho(\mathbf{x}) = \iota_? \cdot \sum_{j=0}^{\infty} \left(\mathbf{A}(\mathbf{x})^j \cdot \mathbf{b}(\mathbf{x}) - \mathbf{A}\langle\mathbf{r}\rangle^j \cdot \mathbf{b}\langle\mathbf{r}\rangle \right) \ . \tag{4}$$

The perturbation function ρ captures the effect of any small variation of $\mathbf{x}$ with respect to $\mathbf{r}$ on the satisfaction probability of the problem $S_? \, \mathcal{U} \, S_!$ in M_*. For convenience, we call $\mathbf{r}$ the reference of ρ.

3.2   Asymptotic Bounds

There are various ways to express the asymptotic bounds. We adopt the most basic way: The bounds are given by the so-called *(absolute) condition numbers* [7]. In Section 6 we briefly discuss the terminologies of perturbation bounds and condition numbers in the context of related work.

Let $\Delta > 0$ represent the perturbation distance of a distribution parameter. In reality, we usually assume Δ to be a sufficiently small positive number. The following auxiliary definition captures the variation range of ρ with respect to the perturbation distance Δ of the distribution parameter $\mathbf{x}$.

Definition 5. *The variation range of* ρ *with reference* $\mathbf{r}$ *against* Δ *is the set*

$$\bar{\rho}(\Delta) = \{\rho(\mathbf{v}) \mid \|\mathbf{v} - \mathbf{r}\| \leq \Delta, \mathbf{v} \in \mathbf{U}\} \ . \tag{5}$$

It is not hard to see that $\bar{\rho}(\Delta)$ is an interval. The existence of a condition number for ρ depends on the differentiability of ρ. The following proposition confirms that ρ enjoys this property in a "neighborhood" of $\mathbf{r}$. Recall that we have assumed $|\mathbf{x}| = k$.

Proposition 6. ρ *is differentiable at* $\mathbf{r}$, *namely,* $\rho(\mathbf{x}) = \mathbf{h} \cdot (\mathbf{x} - \mathbf{r}) + \theta(\mathbf{x} - \mathbf{r})$, *for some* $\mathbf{h} \in \mathbb{R}^k$ *and* $\theta : \mathbb{R}^k \to \mathbb{R}$ *such that* $\lim_{\|\mathbf{y}\| \to 0} \theta(\mathbf{y})/\|\mathbf{y}\| = 0$.

In other words, $\mathbf{h} \cdot (\mathbf{x} - \mathbf{r})$ is used as the *linear approximation* of ρ at a point sufficiently close to $\mathbf{r}$, and we write $\rho(\mathbf{x}) \approx \mathbf{h} \cdot (\mathbf{x} - \mathbf{r})$. Later, we will provide an algorithmic method to determine $\mathbf{h}$. Let $\max(\mathbf{h}) = \max\{\mathbf{h}[i] \mid 1 \leq i \leq |\mathbf{h}|\}$ and $\min(\mathbf{h}) = \min\{\mathbf{h}[i] \mid 1 \leq i \leq |\mathbf{h}|\}$.

Theorem 7. *The asymptotic bound of* ρ *is given by the condition number*

$$\kappa = \lim_{\Delta \to 0} \sup \left\{ \frac{x}{\delta} \mid x \in \bar{\rho}(\delta), 0 < \delta \leq \Delta \right\} \ . \tag{6}$$

Then, the number κ *exists and, moreover,*

$$\kappa = \frac{1}{2}(\max(\mathbf{h}) - \min(\mathbf{h})) \ . \tag{7}$$

According to the definition of κ in Theorem 7 (in particular, equation (6)), mathematically, if the parameter $\mathbf{x}$ in a basic PMC $\mathcal{M}_*$ with reference $\mathbf{r}$ varies an infinitesimally small Δ from $\mathbf{r}$ in terms of the absolute distance, then the perturbation of the reachability checking result, $\rho(\Delta)$, is estimated to be within $\pm \kappa \Delta$, where κ is the condition number of ρ. We test the applicability of such κ in experiments in Section 5.

The definition of κ captures the sensitivity of ρ to $\mathbf{x}$: How does ρ change if we perturb $\mathbf{x}$? A closely related problem is phrased as this: How much do we have to perturb $\mathbf{x}$ to obtain an approximation of ρ—in other words, what is the backward error of ρ? The following proposition gives a "backward" characterization of the asymptotic bound κ, which, by its formulation, pursues the infimum of variations of $\mathbf{x}$ (or equivalently, the supremum of their reciprocals) that can cause the given perturbation of ρ.

Proposition 8. $\kappa = \lim_{x \to 0} \sup \{ \delta^{-1} y \mid 0 < y \leq x, \, y \in \overline{p}(\delta) \}$.

In the following, we present a method to compute the linear approximation of ρ. We write $\sum_{i=0}^{\infty} \mathbf{A}^i$ as $\sum \mathbf{A}$. Let $\mathbf{C}(\mathbf{x}) = \mathbf{A}(\mathbf{x}) - \mathbf{A}\langle \mathbf{r} \rangle$ and $\mathbf{d}(\mathbf{x}) = \mathbf{b}(\mathbf{x}) - \mathbf{b}\langle \mathbf{r} \rangle$.

Theorem 9. *Let*

$$\mathbf{e}(\mathbf{x}) = \sum \mathbf{A}\langle \mathbf{r} \rangle \cdot \mathbf{C}(\mathbf{x}) \cdot \sum \mathbf{A}\langle \mathbf{r} \rangle \cdot \mathbf{b}\langle \mathbf{r} \rangle + \sum \mathbf{A}\langle \mathbf{r} \rangle \cdot \mathbf{d}(\mathbf{x}) \; . \tag{8}$$

Then, $\rho(\mathbf{x}) \approx \iota_? \cdot \mathbf{e}(\mathbf{x})$.

Theorems 7 and 9 together provide algorithmic techniques for computing the condition number κ for $\mathcal{M}_*$ and the reachability problem $S_? \, \mathcal{U} \, S_!$.

4   Perturbation Analysis of General PMCs

In this section, we generalize the method developed in the previous section from basic PMCs to general PMCs that may have multiple distribution parameters. For general PMCs, perturbations of the parameters may vary either proportionally or independently, yielding two forms of asymptotic bounds, namely, two condition numbers. However, it turns out that the two kinds of bounds coincide.

4.1   Directional Conditioning

For general PMCs, we need to handle multiple distribution parameters. The reachability problem $S_? \, \mathcal{U} \, S_!$ in a PMC $\mathcal{M}_*$ is the same as for basic PMCs. In this subsection, we suppose their perturbations are subject to a prescribed ratio, i.e., proportionally. Hence, we associate a function $w : I \to [0, 1]$ to $\mathbf{x}_I$ such that $\sum_{i \in I} w(i) = 1$. Such w is called a *direction* of $\mathbf{x}_I$.

To enable the formal treatment, we first define some notations. For each $i \in I$, let $\mathbf{V}_i = [0, 1]^{k_i}$ and $\mathbf{U}_i = \{ \mathbf{v} \in \mathbf{V}_i \mid \sum_{j=1}^{k_i} \mathbf{v}[i] = 1 \}$ where $k_i = |\mathbf{x}_i|$. If $I = \{ i_1, \ldots, i_m \}$, then $\mathbf{V}_I$ denotes the cartesian space $\mathbf{V}_{i_1} \times \ldots \times \mathbf{V}_{i_m}$. Similarly,

$\mathbf{U}_I$ is $\mathbf{U}_{i_1} \times \ldots \times \mathbf{U}_{i_m}$. $\mathbf{A}(\mathbf{x}_I)$, $\mathbf{b}(\mathbf{x}_I)$, $\mathbf{A}\langle\mathbf{r}_I\rangle$ and $\mathbf{b}\langle\mathbf{r}_I\rangle$ are natural generalizations of their basic PMC counterparts. We stress that, unlike $\mathcal{P}(\mathbf{x}_I)$, some variables in $\mathbf{x}_I$ for each $i \in I$ may not appear at $\mathbf{A}(\mathbf{x}_I)$ and $\mathbf{b}(\mathbf{x}_I)$. We can also abbreviate $\mathbf{A}(\mathbf{x}_I)$ and $\mathbf{b}(\mathbf{x}_I)$ as $\mathbf{A}$ and $\mathbf{b}$ if $\mathbf{x}_I$ is clear in the context.

We illustrate these definitions by the example of noisy Zeroconf, whose model is a non-basic PMC. Clearly, the pursuit of the problem "what is probability of an address collision?" is equivalent to the problem "what is probability to avoid an address collision?" In the second problem, the constraint set is $\{1, \ldots, 5\}$ and the destination set is $\{7\}$. The sequence of parameters is $(x_i, 1 - x_i)_{i=1}^4$. Thus,

$$\mathbf{A}^{\mathrm{zf}} = \begin{pmatrix} 0 & a & 0 & 0 & 0 \\ 1 - x_1 & 0 & x_1 & 0 & 0 \\ 1 - x_2 & 0 & 0 & x_2 & 0 \\ 1 - x_3 & 0 & 0 & 0 & x_3 \\ 1 - x_4 & 0 & 0 & 0 & 0 \end{pmatrix}, \quad \mathbf{b}^{\mathrm{zf}} = \begin{pmatrix} 1 - a \\ 0 \\ 0 \\ 0 \\ 0 \end{pmatrix}$$

The following definition generalizes Definition 4.

Definition 10. *The perturbation function of $\mathbf{x}_I$ for a PMC $\mathcal{M}_* = (\iota, \mathcal{P}(\mathbf{x}_I), \mathbf{r}_I)$ and with respect to the problem $S_? \,\mathcal{U}\, S_!$ such that $S_?, S_! \subseteq S_{\mathcal{M}_*}$ is $\varrho : \mathbf{V}_I \to [-1, 1]$ such that*

$$\varrho(\mathbf{x}_I) = \iota_? \cdot \sum_{j=0}^{\infty} (\mathbf{A}(\mathbf{x}_I)^j \cdot \mathbf{b}(\mathbf{x}_I) - \mathbf{A}\langle\mathbf{r}_I\rangle^j \cdot \mathbf{b}\langle\mathbf{r}_I\rangle) \ . \tag{9}$$

The perturbation function ϱ captures the effect of the small variation of $\mathbf{x}_i$ with respect to $\mathbf{r}_i$ for each $i \in I$ on the reachability problem $S_? \,\mathcal{U}\, S_!$ in $\mathcal{M}_*$. We call vectors in $\mathbf{r}_I$ references of ϱ. The definition below generalizes Definition 5.

Definition 11. *The w-direction variation range of ϱ with reference in $\mathbf{r}$ against Δ is the set*

$$\overline{\varrho}_w(\Delta) = \{\varrho(\mathbf{v}_I) \mid \|\mathbf{v}_i - \mathbf{r}_i\| \le w(i)\Delta, \ \mathbf{v}_i \in \mathbf{U}_i, \ i \in I\} \ , \tag{10}$$

where $\mathbf{v}_I = (\mathbf{v}_i)_{i \in I}$.

Let $\mathbf{x}_I - \mathbf{r}_I$ be the sequence $(\mathbf{x}_i - \mathbf{r}_i)_{i \in I}$, supposing $|\mathbf{x}_i| = |\mathbf{r}_i|$ for each $i \in I$. Let $\|\mathbf{x}_I\|$ be $\sum_{i \in I} \|\mathbf{x}_i\|$. Similar to ρ, the following proposition holds for ϱ.

Proposition 12. *ϱ is differentiable at $\mathbf{r}_I$, namely, $\varrho(\mathbf{x}_I) = \sum_{i \in I} \mathbf{h}_i \cdot (\mathbf{x}_i - \mathbf{r}_i) + \theta'(\mathbf{x}_I - \mathbf{r}_I)$, for some $\mathbf{h}_i \in \mathbb{R}^k$ ($i \in I$) and $\theta' : \mathbb{R}^{k|I|} \to \mathbb{R}$ such that $\lim_{\|\mathbf{y}_I\| \to 0} \theta'(\mathbf{y}_I)/\|\mathbf{y}_I\| = 0$.*

We write $\varrho(\mathbf{x}_I) \approx \sum_{i \in I} \mathbf{h}_i \cdot (\mathbf{x}_i - \mathbf{r}_i)$ and call $\sum_{i \in I} \mathbf{h}_i \cdot (\mathbf{x}_i - \mathbf{r}_i)$ the *linear approximation* of ϱ at $\mathbf{r}_I$. The following theorem generalizes Theorem 7.

Theorem 13. *The w-direction asymptotic bound of ϱ is given by the directional condition number*

$$\kappa_w = \lim_{\Delta \to 0} \sup \left\{ \frac{x}{\delta} \ \middle| \ x \in \overline{\varrho}_w(\delta), 0 < \delta \le \Delta \right\} \ . \tag{11}$$

Then, κ_w exists and, moreover,

$$\kappa_w = \frac{1}{2} \sum_{i \in I} w(i)(\max(\mathbf{h}_i) - \min(\mathbf{h}_i)) \ . \tag{12}$$

If the distribution parameters vary a small Δ in the direction w, then we can estimate the perturbation of ρ as $\pm k_w \Delta$. In the case that $w(i) = 1/|I|$ for each $i \in I$, such k_w is called a *uniform* condition number. Like the asymptotic bounds for basic PMCs, a "backward" characterization of κ_w also exists, as follows.

Proposition 14. $\kappa_w = \lim_{x \to 0} \sup \{\delta^{-1} y \mid 0 < y \leq x, \ y \in \overline{\varrho}_w(\delta)\}$.

We provide a method to compute the linear approximation of ϱ. We define two specific parametric matrices: $\mathbf{C}(\mathbf{x}_I) = \mathbf{A}(\mathbf{x}_I) - \mathbf{A}\langle \mathbf{r}_I \rangle$ and $\mathbf{d}(\mathbf{x}_I) = \mathbf{d}(\mathbf{x}_I) - \mathbf{d}\langle \mathbf{r}_I \rangle$. We have the following generalized theorem of Theorem 9.

Theorem 15. *For each $i \in I$, let*

$$\mathbf{e}(\mathbf{x}_I) = \sum \mathbf{A}\langle \mathbf{r}_I \rangle \cdot \mathbf{C}(\mathbf{x}_I) \cdot \sum \mathbf{A}\langle \mathbf{r}_I \rangle \cdot \mathbf{b}\langle \mathbf{r}_I \rangle + \sum \mathbf{A}\langle \mathbf{r}_I \rangle \cdot \mathbf{d}(\mathbf{x}_I) \ . \tag{13}$$

Then, $\varrho(\mathbf{x}_I) \approx \iota_? \cdot \mathbf{e}(\mathbf{x}_I)$.

Theorems 13 and 15 together provide an algorithmic method for computing the directional condition number κ_w for $\mathcal{M}_*$ and the reachability problem $S_? \, \mathcal{U} \, S_!$.

4.2   Parameter-Wise Conditioning

The parameter-wise perturbation analysis handles the independent variations of distribution parameters. In this case, to facilitate perturbation estimation, we expect to obtain a condition number for each distribution parameter. It turns out that the parameter-wise analysis can be reduced to the directional analysis.

We use $\mathbf{r}_I[i := \mathbf{v}]$ denote the sequence of vectors obtained by replacing the ith vector in $\mathbf{r}_I$ by $\mathbf{v}$.

Definition 16. *The variation range of ϱ projected at $\mathbf{x}_i$ against Δ is the set*

$$\overline{\varrho}_i(\Delta) = \{\varrho(\mathbf{r}_I[i := \mathbf{v}]) \mid \|\mathbf{v} - \mathbf{r}_i\| \leq \Delta, \ \mathbf{v} \in \mathbf{U}_i\} \ . \tag{14}$$

The asymptotic bound of ϱ projected at $\mathbf{x}_i$ is given by the condition number

$$\kappa_i = \lim_{\Delta \to 0} \sup \left\{ \frac{x}{\delta} \mid x \in \overline{\varrho}_i(\delta), 0 < \delta \leq \Delta \right\} \ . \tag{15}$$

Let w_i be the direction such that $w_i(i) = i$ and $w_i(j) = 0$ for each $j \in I \backslash \{i\}$. It is easy to see that $\overline{\varrho}_i$ (resp. κ_i) is just $\overline{\varrho}_{w_i}$ (resp. κ_{w_i}). It means that parameter-wise bounds are special cases of directional bounds. Moreover, the following theorem states that any set of parameter-wise condition numbers conforms to a specific directional condition number.

Table 2. Experimental data of noisy Zeroconf ($\times 10^{-3}$)

Model	x_i	Probability	Distance	Condition Number	Variation Range
$\mathcal{M}_*^{zf}$	750	999.024	-	7.797	-
$\mathcal{M}_1^{zf}$	749	−.016	2	-	±.016
$\mathcal{M}_2^{zf}$	752	+.031	4	-	±.031
$\mathcal{M}_3^{zf}$	747	−.048	6	-	±.047

Theorem 17. *Let* $\Delta = \sum_{i \in I} \Delta_i$ *and* $w(i) = \Delta_i / \Delta$ *for each* $i \in I$. *Then,* $\sum_{i \in I} \kappa_i \Delta_i = \kappa_w \Delta$.

If the direction of perturbation may not be known in advance, it is more useful to present the set of parameter-wise bounds. Theorem 17 provides a mathematical characterization for parameter-wise perturbations in terms of directional perturbations.

5   Experiments

We evaluate by experiments, how well the condition numbers capture possible perturbations of reachability probabilities for some PMCs under consideration. Recall that the outcome of the reachability checking algorithm for a PMC consists of two parts, namely, a referential probabilistic result and one or more condition numbers (see Table 1). The probabilistic result is computed by a conventional numerical model checking algorithm. For the problems considered in this section, only a single condition number will be returned. The condition number is calculated by the method presented in the previous sections.

Our experiments proceed as follows. (i) We specify a reachability problem for a PMC $\mathcal{M}_*$ and compute the referential probabilistic result p and *one* condition number κ for the problem, although multiple condition numbers may be required in other contexts. (ii) By deliberately assigning concrete probability distributions to the distribution parameter(s) of $\mathcal{M}_*$, we construct several potential non-parametric models $\mathcal{M}_j$ with sufficiently small statistical distances from $\mathcal{M}_*$. (iii) We compute an actual probabilistic result p_j for each $\mathcal{M}_j$ and calculate the actual distance Δ_j between the reference(s) in $\mathcal{M}_*$ and the corresponding distribution(s) in $\mathcal{M}_j$. (iv) We compare $p - p_j$, the difference between the referential result and an actual result, and $\pm \kappa \Delta_j$, the perturbation estimation.

We performed experiments for the examples of noisy Zeroconf and hopping frog (the PMCs $\mathcal{M}_*^{zf}$ and $\mathcal{M}_*^{fg}$) in Matlab® [8]. Although Matlab is not a specialized tool for probabilistic model checking, it provides convenient numerical and symbolic mathematical operations that are necessary to compute the perturbation function. For the easier calculations in the noisy Zeroconf example, we let a in $\mathcal{P}_*^{zf}$, the parametric transition matrix of $\mathcal{M}_*^{zf}$, be 0.2. Moreover, for simplicity, it is assumed that each probe message and its reply are affected by the same channel noise level, namely, that the four distribution parameters of

Table 3. Experimental data of hopping frog $(\times 10^{-3})$

Model	Distribution	Probability	Distance	Condition Number	Variation Range
$\mathcal{M}_*^{\text{fg}}$	$(375, 125, 250, 250)$	500.000	-	312.500	-
$\mathcal{M}_1^{\text{fg}}$	$(374, 124, 251, 251)$	0	4	-	± 1.250
$\mathcal{M}_2^{\text{fg}}$	$(374, 124, 250, 252)$	$+.623$	4	-	± 1.250
$\mathcal{M}_3^{\text{fg}}$	$(377, 125, 248, 250)$	$+.627$	4	-	± 1.250
$\mathcal{M}_4^{\text{fg}}$	$(377, 125, 250, 248)$	$-.627$	4	-	± 1.250
$\mathcal{M}_4^{\text{fg}}$	$(375, 125, 248, 252)$	$+1.250$	4	-	± 1.250
$\mathcal{M}_5^{\text{fg}}$	$(375, 125, 252, 248)$	-1.250	4	-	± 1.250

$\mathcal{M}_*^{\text{zf}}$ are perturbed in a uniform direction. Several MCs in both experiments are generated by assigning different distributions to the distribution parameters in their PMCs. Because the infinite matrix series $\sum_{i=0}^{\infty} \mathbf{A}^j$ cannot be computed directly, we adopt an approximation by taking the sum of the first hundred items in each series encountered. There was no significant truncation error involved the numerical calculations in our experiments. We test the reachability problems $\{1, \ldots, 5\} \mathcal{U} \{7\}$ in the first experiment (which states "what is the probability to avoid an IP collision?") and $\{1, 2\} \mathcal{U} \{4\}$ in the second one (which states "what is the probability for the frog to reach the fourth rock without landing on the third rock?"). The experimental data are summarized in Tables 2 and 3, respectively. In Table 2, the distance of the perturbed models to the PMC increases. We observe that the condition number accounts for the result nicely if the perturbed distance is smaller than 0.006. When the distance exceeds 0.006, the perturbation of the probabilistic result may exceed the variation range. In Table 3, several perturbed models with the distance 0.004 to the PMC are presented. The data also demonstrate that the condition number bounds the reachability perturbation between a perturbed model and the PMC to a satisfactory degree. In particular, the difference between the result for $\mathcal{M}_4^{\text{fg}}$ (resp., $\mathcal{M}_5^{\text{fg}}$) and the referential result overlaps with the positive (resp., negative) predicted bound.

In short, we observe from the experiments that condition numbers adequately, although not rigorously, predict the bounds of the reachability checking results for probabilistic models under small perturbations.

6   Discussion and Related Work

The pursuit of perturbation bounds for MCs can be traced back to the 1960's. Schweitzer [2] gave the first perturbation bound, namely, an absolute condition number for the stationary distribution of an MC against its fundamental matrix (which is defined by the transition matrix of the MC), and this motivated a variety of subsequent work. Cho and Meyer [3] provided an excellent overview for various bounds of stationary distributions (all of which are condition numbers) up to the time of their publication, whilst more recent papers [4, 5] shed light on new definitions and techniques for perturbation bounds. In spite of its relatively long history, to the best of our knowledge, the present paper is the first paper that studies the perturbation problem in quantitative verification. Moreover, our approach is different from most of the works on the perturbation analysis for MCs in that, instead of formulating the bounds in terms of mathematically meaningful components, we adopt numerical computation to approximate the bounds. Therefore, our work is in mid of a broader branch of perturbation theory for numerical linear algebra [9], the goal of which is to investigate the sensitivity of a matrix-formulated problem with respect to one or more perturbed components in its formulation, and to provide various forms of perturbation bounds for the solution to the problem. One important group of such bounds is called asymptotic bounds (also called linear local bounds), which is further divided into two subgroups, namely, absolute condition numbers and relative condition numbers. Both subgroups of condition numbers have their own significance—absolute condition numbers enjoy a more elegant mathematical formulation and are easier to employ for practical problems, whilst relative ones are more important to the floating point arithmetic implemented in every computer, which is affected by relative rather than absolute errors. A detailed classification of these bounds is found in Konstantinov et al. [7] (Chapters 1 and 2). The condition numbers that we pursue in the present paper are absolute ones and we leave the analysis of our problem based on other kinds of bounds to future work.

Quantitative verification of Markov models with various formulations of uncertainty is a recently active field of research. Daws [10] proposed a symbolic PCTL model checking approach in which concrete or abstract transition probabilities in his parametric variant of a discrete-time MC are viewed as letters in an alphabet of a finite automaton. As such, the probability measure of a set of paths satisfying a formula is computed symbolically as a regular expression on that alphabet, which is further evaluated to its exact rational value when transition probabilities are rational symbolic expressions of variables. Hahn et al. [11] improved the approach of Daws for reachability checking (i.e., PCTL formulae without nested probability operators) by carefully intertwining the computation procedure and evaluation procedure of Daws. By definition, their parametric variants of MCs are more general than ours because they allow abstract transition probabilities to be expressed by rational symbolic expressions. But in order to introduce a metric to measure the perturbations for our PMCs, we let abstract transition probabilities be expressed as single variables. Another and more important difference is that, instead of pushing the symbolic computation to an extreme as they did, we calculate numbers in symbolic expressions numerically as in ordinary mathematical calculations.

Another group of research works addresses the undetermined transition probabilities in MCs by specifying their interval values. Sen et al. [12] considered two semantic interpretations for such models, which are either classes of MC or generalizations of Markov Decision Processes (MDPs). In the first interpretation, the PCTL model checking problem is to search for an MC within the MC class such that a PCTL formula is satisfied; in the second one, the problem can be reduced to a corresponding MDP of exponential size. Benedikt et al. [13]

considered the LTL model checking problem for the same models, which they defined as the search of an MC that meets the model constraint and optimizes the probability of satisfying an LTL formula. However, in our perturbation approach we specify a metric to measure the perturbed distances of the models but not their perturbed boundaries in terms of interval transition probabilities.

There have also been attempts to study perturbation errors in realtime systems, in particular, timed automata. For example, Alur *et al.* [14] defined a perturbed semantics for timed automata whose clocks might skew at some very small rates. They showed that if an automaton has a single clock, then the language accepted by it under the perturbed semantics is accepted by an equivalent deterministic automaton under the standard semantics. Bouyer *et al.* [15] provided another time perturbation notion, which expresses not the perturbations of the clock rates but those of the clock constraints. They developed model checking techniques for ω-regular properties based on their novel semantic relation, which captures—as argued—the intuition "whether the considered property holds for the same model implemented in a sufficient (but not infinitely) fast hardware".

7 Conclusions

Motivated by the pervasive phenomena of perturbations in the modeling and verification of real-life probabilistic systems, we studied the sensitivity of constrained reachability probabilities of those systems—which are modeled by parametric variants of discrete-time MCs—to perturbations of their distribution parameters. Our contribution is a method to compute the asymptotic bounds in terms of absolute condition numbers for characterizing the sensitivity. We also conducted experiments to demonstrate the practical adequacy of the computation method.

This paper is an initial step towards investigating the sensitivity and bounds for quantitative verification of perturbed systems, and we may identify several interesting directions for further research. First, reachability, in spite of its fundamental status in model checking, captures only a narrow group of practical verification problems (particularly in the probabilistic domain) and, therefore, it is desirable to extend the present method to accommodate the general model checking problems formalized, for instance, in LTL formulas. Second, we adopt the norm of absolute distance to measure the distance between two probability distributions; however, there exist other distance measures that are useful for problems in some specific domains. For example, the well-known Kullback-Leibler divergence is widely adopted in information theory [16]. Finally, condition numbers are among several other forms of perturbation bounds. An in-depth comparison of their pros and cons is left to future work.

References

1. Kwiatkowska, M., Norman, G., Parker, D.: PRISM 4.0: Verification of probabilistic real-time systems. In: Gopalakrishnan, G., Qadeer, S. (eds.) CAV 2011. LNCS, vol. 6806, pp. 585–591. Springer, Heidelberg (2011)

2. Schweitzer, P.J.: Perturbation theory and finite Markov chains. Journal of Applied Probability 5(2), 401–413 (1968)
3. Cho, G.E., Meyer, C.D.: Comparison of perturbation bounds for the stationary distribution of a Markov chain. Linear Algebra Appl. 335, 137–150 (2000)
4. Solan, E., Vieille, N.: Perturbed Markov chains. J. Applied Prob., 107–122 (2003)
5. Heidergott, B.: Perturbation analysis of Markov chains. In: 9th International Workshop on Discrete Event Systems, WODES 2008, pp. 99–104 (2008)
6. Su, G., Rosenblum, D.S.: Asymptotic bounds for quantitative verification of perturbed probabilistic systems, proof details (2013), http://arxiv.org/abs/1304.7614
7. Konstantinov, M., Gu, D., Mehrmann, V., Petkov, P.: Perturbation Theory for Matrix Equations. Elsevier, Amsterdam (2003)
8. MATLAB: version 8.0 (R2012b). The MathWorks Inc., Natick, Massachusetts (2012)
9. Trefethen, L.N., Bau, D.: Numerical Linear Algebra. SIAM: Society for Industrial and Applied Mathematics (1997)
10. Daws, C.: Symbolic and parametric model checking of discrete-time markov chains. In: Liu, Z., Araki, K. (eds.) ICTAC 2004. LNCS, vol. 3407, pp. 280–294. Springer, Heidelberg (2005)
11. Hahn, E., Hermanns, H., Zhang, L.: Probabilistic reachability for parametric Markov models. International Journal on Software Tools for Technology Transfer 13(1), 3–19 (2011)
12. Sen, K., Viswanathan, M., Agha, G.: Model-checking Markov chains in the presence of uncertainties. In: Hermanns, H., Palsberg, J. (eds.) TACAS 2006. LNCS, vol. 3920, pp. 394–410. Springer, Heidelberg (2006)
13. Benedikt, M., Lenhardt, R., Worrell, J.: LTL model checking of interval Markov chains. In: Piterman, N., Smolka, S.A. (eds.) TACAS 2013. LNCS, vol. 7795, pp. 32–46. Springer, Heidelberg (2013)
14. Alur, R., La Torre, S., Madhusudan, P.: Perturbed timed automata. In: Morari, M., Thiele, L. (eds.) HSCC 2005. LNCS, vol. 3414, pp. 70–85. Springer, Heidelberg (2005)
15. Bouyer, P., Markey, N., Reynier, P.-A.: Robust model-checking of linear-time properties in timed automata. In: Correa, J.R., Hevia, A., Kiwi, M. (eds.) LATIN 2006. LNCS, vol. 3887, pp. 238–249. Springer, Heidelberg (2006)
16. Cover, T.M., Thomas, J.A.: Elements of information theory. Wiley-Interscience, New York (1991)
17. Baier, C., Katoen, J.P.: Principles of Model Checking. The MIT Press (2008)

Verification of Functional and Non-functional Requirements of Web Service Composition*

Manman Chen[1], Tian Huat Tan[1], Jun Sun[2], Yang Liu[3], Jun Pang[4], and Xiaohong Li[5]

[1] School of Computing, National University of Singapore
{chenman,tianhuat}@comp.nus.edu.sg
[2] Singapore University of Technology and Design
sunjun@sutd.edu.sg
[3] Nanyang Technological University
yangliu@ntu.edu.sg
[4] Université du Luxembourg
jun.pang@uni.lu
[5] Tianjin University
xiaohongli@tju.edu.cn

Abstract. Web services have emerged as an important technology nowadays. There are two kinds of requirements that are crucial to web service composition, which are functional and non-functional requirements. Functional requirements focus on functionality of the composed service, e.g., given a booking service, an example of functional requirements is that a flight ticket with price higher than $2000 will never be purchased. Non-functional requirements are concerned with the quality of service (QoS), e.g., an example of the booking service's non-functional requirements is that the service will respond to the user within 5 seconds. Non-functional requirements are important to web service composition, and are often an important clause in service-level agreements (SLAs). Even though the functional requirements are satisfied, a slow or unreliable service may still not be adopted. In our paper, we propose an automated approach to verify combined functional and non-functional requirements directly based on the semantics of web service composition. Our approach has been implemented and evaluated on the real-world case studies, which demonstrate the effectiveness of our method.

1 Introduction

Based on Service Oriented Architecture (SOA), Web services make use of open standards, such as WSDL [1] and SOAP [2], that enable the interaction among heterogeneous applications. A real-world business process may contain a set of services. A web service is a single autonomous software system with its own thread of control. A fundamental goal of web services is to have a collection of network-resident software services, so that it can be accessed by standardized protocols and integrated into applications or composed to form complex services which are called *composite services*. A

---

* This research is supported in part by Research Grant IDD11100102 of Singapore University of Technology and Design, IDC and MOE2009-T2-1-072 (Advanced Model Checking Systems).

L. Groves and J. Sun (Eds.): ICFEM 2013, LNCS 8144, pp. 313–328, 2013.

composite service is constructed from a set of *component services*. Component services have their interfaces and functionalities defined based on their internal structures. While the technology for creating services and interconnecting them with a point-to-point basis has achieved a certain degree of maturity, there is a challenge to integrate multiple services for complex interactions. Web service composition standards have been proposed in order to address this challenge. The *de facto* standard for Web service composition is Web Services Business Process Execution Language (WS-BPEL) [3]. WS-BPEL is an XML-based orchestration business process language. It provides basic activities such as service invocation, and compositional activities such as sequential and parallel composition to describe composition of web services. BPEL is inevitably rich in concurrency and it is not a simple task for programmers to utilize concurrency as they have to deal with multi-threads and critical regions. It is reported that among the common bug types concurrency bugs are the most difficult to fix correctly, the statistic shows that 39% of concurrency bugs are fixed incorrectly [4]. Therefore, it is desirable to verify web services with automated verification techniques, such as model checking [5].

There are two kinds of requirements of web service composition, i.e., functional and non-functional requirements. Functional requirements focus on the functionalities of the web service composition. Given a booking service, an example of functional requirement is that a flight ticket with price higher than $2000 will never be purchased. The non-functional requirements are concerned with the Quality of Service (QoS). These requirements are often recorded in service-level agreements (SLAs), which is a contract specified between service providers and customers. Given a booking service, an example of non-functional requirements is that the service will respond to the user within 5 ms. Typical non-functional requirements include response time, availability, cost and so on. However, it is difficult for service designers to take the full consideration of both functional and non-functional requirements when writing BPEL programs.

Model checking is an automatic technique for verifying software systems [5], which helps find counterexamples based on the specification at the design time so that it could detect errors and increase the reliability of the system at the early stage. Currently, increasing number of complex service processes and concurrency are developed on web service composition. Hence, model checking is a promising approach to solve this problem. Given functional and non-functional requirements, existing works [6,7,8,9] only focus on verification of one aspect, and disregard the other, even though these two aspects are inseparable. Different non-functional properties might have different aggregation functions for different compositional structures, and this poses a major challenge to integrate the non-functional properties into the functional verification framework.

In this work, we propose a method to verify BPEL programs against combined functional and non-functional requirements. A dedicated model checker is developed to support the verification. We make use of the labeled transition systems (LTSs) directly from the semantics of BPEL programs for functional verification. For non-functional properties, we propose different strategies to integrate different non-functional properties into the functional verification framework. We focus on three important non-functional properties in this work, i.e., availability, cost and response time. To verify availability and cost, we calculate them on-the-fly during the generation of LTS, and associate calculated values to each state in the LTS. Verification of response time requires an additional preprocessing stage, before the generation of LTS. In the preprocessing stage, response time tag is assigned to each activity that is participated in the service composition. With such integration, we are able to support combined functional and non-functional requirements.

The contributions of our work are summarized as follows.

1. We support integrated verification of functional and non-functional properties for Web service composition. To the best of our knowledge, we are the first work on such integration.
2. We capture the semantics of web service composition using labeled transition systems (LTSs) and verify the web service composition directly without building intermediate or abstract models before applying verification approaches, which makes our approach more suitable for general web service composition verification.
3. Our approach has been implemented and evaluated on the real-world case studies, and this demonstrates the effectiveness of our method.

Paper Outline. The rest of paper is structured as follows. Section 2 describes the BPEL running example. Section 3 introduces QoS compositional model. Section 4 shows how to verify functional and non-functional propeties. Section 5 provides the evaluation of our work. Section 6 reviews the related work. Finally, Section 7 concludes the paper and outlines our future work.

2 Motivating Example

In our work, we assume that composite services are specified in the BPEL language. BPEL is the *de facto* standard for implementing composition of existing services by specifying an executable workflow using predefined activities. BPEL is an XML-based orchestration business process language for the specification of executable and abstract business processes. It supports control flow structures such as sequential and concurrency execution. In the following, we introduce the basic BPEL notations. <receive>, <invoke>, and <reply> are the basic communication activities which are defined to receive messages, execute component services and return messages respectively for communicating with component services. There are two kinds of <invoke> activities, i.e., synchronous and asynchronous invocation. Synchronous invocation activities are invoked and the process waits for the reply from the component service before moving on to the next activity. Asynchronous invocation activities are invoked and moving on to the next activity directly without waiting for the reply. The control flow of composite services is specified using the activities like <sequence>, <while>, <if> and <flow>. <sequence> is used to define the sequential ordering structure, <while> is used to define the loop structure, <if> is used to define the conditional choice structure, and <flow> is used to implement concurrency structure.

2.1 Computer Purchasing Services (CPS)

In this section, we introduce the computer purchasing service (CPS), which is designed to allow users to purchase a computer online using credit cards. The workflow of CPS is illustrated in Figure 1.

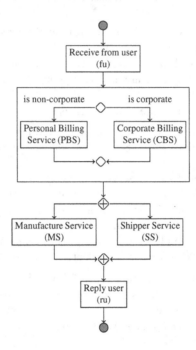

Fig. 1. Computer Purchasing Service

CPS has four component web services, namely Personal Billing Service (PBS), Corporate Billing Service (CBS), Manufacture Service (MS), Shipper Service (SS). CPS is initialized (donated by ●) upon receiving the request from the customer (fu) with the information of the customer and the computer that he wishes to purchase for. Subsequently, an $<if>$ activity (donated by ◇) is used for checking whether the customer is a corporate customer or non-corporate customer. If it is a corporate customer, CBS is invoked synchronously to bill the corporate customer, otherwise, PBS is invoked synchronously to bill the non-corporate customer with credit card information. Upon receiving the reply, a $<flow>$ activity (donated by ⊕) is triggered and MS and SS are invoked concurrently. MS is invoked synchronously to notify manufacture department for manufacturing the purchased computers. SS is invoked synchronously to schedule shipment for the purchased computers. Upon receiving the reply message from SS and MS, reply user (ru) is called to return the result of the computer purchasing to the customer. Then, the workflow of CPS has ended (donated by ●).

A property that CPS must fulfill is that it must invoke reply user (ru) within 5 ms. Notice that this property combines the functional (must invoke reply user (ru)) and non-functional (within 5 ms) requirements.

2.2   BPEL Notations

In order to present BPEL syntax compactly, we define a set of BPEL notations below:

– $rec(S)$ and $reply(S)$ are used to denote "receive from" and "reply to" a service S;

Table 1. QoS Attribute Values

QoS Attribute	PBS	CBS	MS	SS
Response Time(ms)	1	2	3	1
Availability(%)	90	80	80	80
Cost($)	3	2	2	2

- $sInv(S)$ (resp. $aInv(S)$) is used to denote synchronous (resp. asynchronous) invocation of a service S;
- $P_1 \| P_2$ is used to denote <flow> activity, i.e., the concurrent execution of BPEL activities P_1 and P_2;
- $P_1 \vartriangleleft b \vartriangleright P_2$ is used to denote <if> activity, where b is a guard condition. Activity P_1 is executed if b is evaluated true. Otherwise, activity P_2 will be executed;
- $P_1 \to P_2$ is used to denote <sequence> activity, where P_1 is executed followed by P_2.

We denote activities that contain other activities as *composite activities*, they are $P_1 \| P_2$, $P_1 \vartriangleleft b \vartriangleright P_2$ and $P_1 \to P_2$. For activities that do not contain any other activities, we denote them as *atomic activities*, they are $rec(S)$, $reply(S)$, $sInv(S)$ and $aInv(S)$.

3 QOS-Aware Compositional Model

In this section, we define the QoS compositional model used in this work and briefly introduce the semantics of BPEL, captured by labeled transition systems (LTSs). We introduce some definitions used in the semantic model in the following.

3.1 QoS Attributes

In this work, we deal with quantitative attributes that can be quantitatively measured using metrics. There are two classes of QoS Attributes, positive and negative attributes. Positive attributes (e.g., availability) have a good effect on the system, and therefore, they need to be maximized. Availability of the service is the probability of the service being available. Negative attributes (e.g., response time, cost) need to be minimized as they have the negative impact on the system. Response time of the service is defined as the delay between sending a request and receiving the response and cost of the service is defined as the money spent on the service. In this work, we assume the unit of response time, availability and cost to be millisecond (ms), percentage (%) and dollar ($). Table 1 shows the information of response time, availability and cost of each component service for the CPS example as described in Section 2.1.

Given a component service s with n QoS attributes, we use a vector $Q_s = \langle q_1(s), \ldots, q_n(s) \rangle$ to represent QoS attributes of the service s, where $q_i(s)$ represents the value of ith attribute of the component service s. Similarly, $Q'_{cs} = \langle q_1(cs)', \ldots, q_n(cs)' \rangle$ is used to denote the QoS attributes of the composite service cs, where $q_i(cs)'$ represents the ith attribute of the composite service cs.

Table 2. Aggregation Function

QoS Attribute	Sequential	Parallel	Loop	Conditional
Response Time	$\sum_{i=1}^{n} q(s_i)$	$\max_{i=1}^{n} q(s_i)$	$k * (q(s_1))$	$\max_{i=1}^{n} q(s_i)$
Availability	$\prod_{i=1}^{n} q(s_i)$	$\prod_{i=1}^{n} q(s_i)$	$(q(s_1))^k$	$\min_{i=1}^{n} q(s_i)$
Cost	$\sum_{i=1}^{n} q(s_i)$	$\sum_{i=1}^{n} q(s_i)$	$k * (q(s_1))$	$\max_{i=1}^{n} q(s_i)$

3.2 QoS for Composite Services

A composite service S is constructed using a finite number of component services to reach a business goal. Let $C = \langle s_1, s_2, \ldots, s_n \rangle$ be the set of all component services that are used by S. The QoS of composite services is aggregated from the QoS of the component services, based on the service internal compositional structure, and the type of QoS attributes. Table 2 shows the aggregation functions for each compositional structure. We consider three types of QoS attributes: response time, availability and cost. For response time, in sequential composition, the response time of the composite service is aggregated by summing up the response time of each component service. As for parallel composition, the response time of the composite service is the maximum response time among that of each participating component service. For loop composition, the response time of the composite service is obtained by summing up the response time of the participating component service for k times, where k is the number of maximum iteration of the loop. And for conditional composition, the response time of the composite service is the maximum response time of n participating component services since it is not known that which guard is satisfied at the design phase. For availability, in sequential composition, the availability of the composite service is the product of that of all component services in the sequence because it means all component services are available during the sequential execution. It is similar to parallel and loop composition for aggregation of availability of the composite services. For conditional availability of the composite service, since one component service will be chosen at execution, therefore, we denote the availability as the minimum availability among all component services participated in the conditional composition. For cost, in sequential composition, the cost of the composite service is decided by the total cost of component services. For the conditional composition, the cost of the composite service is the maximum cost of n participating component services. Other common QoS attribute types can be aggregated in the similiar way with these three attributes. For example, QoS attributes like reliability share the same aggregation function with availability.

3.3 Labeled Transition Systems

The QoS-aware composite model in this work is defined using labeled transition systems (LTS). In the following we define various terminologies that will be used in this work.

Definition 1 (System State). *A system state s is a tuple (P, V, Q), where P is the composite service process and V is a (partial) variable valuation that maps variables to their values, Q is a vector which represents QoS attributes of the composite service.*

Two states are equivalent iff they have the same process P, the same valuation V and the same QoS vectors Q. Given a system state $s = (P, V, Q)$, $Q = \langle r, a, c \rangle$ is a vector with three elements, where $r, a, c \in \mathbb{R}_{\geq 0}$, and $0 \leq a \leq 1$. r, a, c represent the response time, availability, and cost of the state s. The response time, availability, and cost are calculated from the execution that starts at initial state s_0 up to the state s. Henceforth, we use the notation $Q(ResponseTime)$, $Q(Availability)$ and $Q(Cost)$ to denote the value of r, a, and c of QoS vector Q, respectively.

Definition 2 (Composite Service Model). *A composite service model $\mathcal{M}$ is a tuple (Var, P_0, V_0, F), where Var is a finite set of variables, P_0 is the composite service process, and V_0 is an initial valuation that maps each variable to its initial value. F is a function which maps component services to their QoS attribute vectors.*

Given a composite service (Var, P_0, V_0, F), an example of valuation V is $\{var_1 \mapsto 1, var_2 \mapsto \perp\}$, where $var_1, var_2 \in Var$, and $var_2 \mapsto \perp$ is used to denote that var_2 is undefined.

Definition 3 (LTS). *An LTS is a tuple $\mathcal{L} = (S, s_0, \Sigma, \rightarrow)$, where*

- *S is a set of states,*
- *$s_0 \in S$ is the initial state,*
- *Σ is a set of actions,*
- *$\rightarrow : S \times \Sigma \times S$ is a transition relation.*

For convenience, we use $s \xrightarrow{a} s'$ to denote $(s, a, s') \in \rightarrow$ and we denote the LTS of a BPEL service $\mathcal{M}$ as $L(\mathcal{M})$. Given a composite service model $\mathcal{M} = (Var, P_0, V_0, F)$, $L(\mathcal{M}) = (S, (P_0, V_0, Q_0), \Sigma, \rightarrow)$. Q_0 is the QoS attribute vector of the initial state, where the availability is 1, cost and response time are equal to 0. Give a state $s \in S$, $Enable(s)$ is denoted as the set of states reachable from s by one transition; formally, $Enable(s) = \{s' | s' \in S \wedge a \in \Sigma \wedge s \xrightarrow{a} s' \in \rightarrow\}$. An *execution* π of $\mathcal{L}$ is a finite alternating sequence of states and actions $\langle s_0, a_1, s_1, \ldots, s_{n-1}, a_n, s_n \rangle$, where $\{s_0, \ldots, s_n\} \in S$ and $s_i \xrightarrow{a_{i+1}} s_{i+1}$ for all $0 \leq i < n$. We denote the execution π by $s_0 \xrightarrow{a_1} s_1 \xrightarrow{\cdots} s_{n-1} \xrightarrow{a_n} s_n$. A state s is called reachable if there is an execution that ends in s and starts in an initial state.

Assume a composite service model is $\mathcal{M} = (Var, P_0, V_0, F)$ and the LTS of $\mathcal{M}$ is $L(\mathcal{M}) = (S, s_0, \Sigma, \rightarrow)$. Every action $a \in \Sigma$ is triggered by an atomic activity. The atomic activities used in this work are $rec(S)$, $reply(S)$, $sInv(S)$, and $aInv(S)$, where S is the component service that the atomic activities are communicated with. For activities $rec(S)$ and $sInv(S)$, they are required to wait for reply from component service S before continuing, therefore their availability, cost and response time are equivalent to the availability, cost and response time of component service S. For activities $reply(S)$ and $aInv(S)$, they are not required to wait reply from the component service S, therefore they are regarded as internal operations. We assume the availability, cost and response time for an internal operations as 100%, \$0 and 0 ms respectively

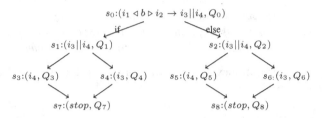

Fig. 2. LTS of CPS where i_1 is sInv(PBS), i_2 is sInv(CBS), i_3 is sInv(MS) and i_4 is sInv(SS)

(see Section 4.3 for discussion). Given two states $s = (P, V, Q)$, $s' = (P', V', Q')$, where $s, s' \in S$, $s \xrightarrow{a} s' \in \rightarrow$, and $a \in \Sigma$, we use the function $AtomAct(a)$ to denote the atomic activity that triggers the action a. As an example, given $s = (sInv(S) \rightarrow rec(S), V, Q)$ and $s' = (rec(S), V, Q)$, the function $AtomAct(a)$ returns the activity $sInv(S)$. We define the function $ResponseTime(a)$, $Availability(a)$ and $Cost(a)$ to map the action a to the response time, availability, and cost of the activity returned by $AtomAct(a)$. Using the previous example, $ResponseTime(a)$ is the response time of activity $sInv(S)$, which is essentially the response time of component service S.

The LTS of CPS as discussed in Section 2 is shown in Figure 2, where we omit the $Receive\ from\ user(fu)$, $Reply\ user(ru)$, all actions $a \in \Sigma$, and component V in the state for the reason of brevity. From state s_0, conditional activity $i_1 \lhd b \rhd i_2$ is enabled. Given that $\{b \mapsto \bot\}$, either i_1 or i_2 might be executed, therefore states s_1 and s_2 are evolved from state s_0. Noted that if guard b is defined, then only one branch is explored in the LTS. From state s_1, the flow activity $i_3 \| i_4$ is enabled, and both activities i_3 and i_4 are allowed to execute. This leads to states s_3 and s_4, respectively. State s_3 evolves into state s_7 after activity i_4 is executed. $stop$ activity in state s_7 is a special activity which does nothing. Other states in LTS could be reasoned similarly. We assume that the upper bound on the number of iterations for loop activities is known, therefore, there is no recursive activities in BPEL.

4 Verification of Functional and Non-functional Requirements

This section is devoted to discuss how to verify combined functional and non-functional requirements based on the LTS semantics of web service composition. Current works only verify one aspect of requirements, either functional or non-functional requirement, however, these two aspects are inseparable. For example, some property such as in the CPS example is required to reply the user within 5 ms, involves both functional and non-functional requirements. Therefore, we propose an approach to combine functional and non-functional requirements.

4.1 Verification of Functional Requirement

To verify functional requirements of a BPEL program, LTS of the BPEL program is built from composite service model. We support the verification of deadlock-freeness, reachability of a state. To verify the LTL formulae, we make use of automata-based on-the-fly verification algorithm [10], by firstly translating a formula to a Büchi automaton and then checking emptiness of the product of the system and the automaton. For fairness checking, we utilize the on-the-fly parallel model checking based on Tarjan strongly connected components (SCC) detection algorithms similar to [11].

4.2 Integration of Non-functional Requirement

In this section, we present our approach in integrating the non-functional requirements into verification framework. Different non-functional properties might have different aggregation functions for different compositional structures, and this poses a major challenge to integrate the non-functional properties into the functional verification framework. In the following, we adopt two different strategies in integrating the non-functional requirements. We first discuss our approach in integration of availability and cost, and following that, we discuss the integration of response time.

Integration of Availability and Cost.   In this section, we present our approach to integrate the availability and cost to the verification framework. Given two states $s = (P, V, Q)$, $s' = (P', V', Q')$, where $s, s' \in S$, $s \xrightarrow{a} s' \in \rightarrow$, and $a \in \Sigma$, the availability and cost of state s' is calculated using the following formulae:

$$\begin{cases} s'.Q(availability) = s.Q(availability) * Availability(a) \\ s'.Q(cost) = s.Q(cost) + Cost(a) \end{cases} \tag{1}$$

Example. We illustrate the integration using the LTS of CPS as shown in Figure 3. In state s_0, it has the initial availability of 1 and initial cost of \$0. From state s_0, it evolves into state s_1 after invocation of i_1. Since i_1 has availability of 0.9 and cost of \$3 (refer to Table 1), therefore the resulting QoS vector of state s_1 is $\langle r_1, 1 * 0.9, 0 + 3 \rangle = \langle r_1, 0.9, 3 \rangle$. From state s_1, it evolves into state s_3 after the invocation of i_3, and since i_3 has availability of 0.8 and cost of \$2, the resulting QoS vector of state s_3 is $\langle r_3, 1 * 0.9 * 0.8, 0 + 3 + 2 \rangle = \langle r_3, 0.72, 5 \rangle$. Other states are calculated similarly.

In general, given an execution $\pi = s_0 \xrightarrow{a_1} s_1 \xrightarrow{\cdots} s_{n-1} \xrightarrow{a_n} s_n$ in $L(\mathcal{M})$, where $\{s_0, \ldots, s_n\} \in S$ and $s_i \xrightarrow{a_{i+1}} s_{i+1} \in \rightarrow$, for all $0 \le i < n$

$$\begin{cases} s_{i+1}.Q(availability) = s_0.Q(availability) * \prod_{m=1}^{i} Availability(a_m) \\ s_{i+1}.Q(cost) = s_0.Q(cost) + \sum_{m=1}^{i} Cost(a_m) \end{cases} \tag{2}$$

with $s_0.Q = \langle 0, 1, 0 \rangle$.

Integration of Response Time.   One might naively think that we can adopt the method of calculating the cost as the method for calculating the response time. However, this would result in incorrect result. Refer to Figure 3, the value of response times r_2, r_5, r_6, and r_8 will be 2 ms, 5 ms, 3 ms, and 6 ms respectively by using the method of calculating the cost in Section 4.2. In such case the value of r_8 is incorrect. The reason

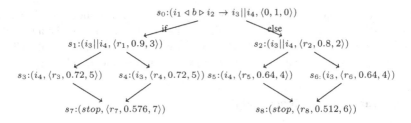

Fig. 3. LTS of CPS with Availability and Cost, where i_1 is sInv(PBS), i_2 is sInv(CBS), i_3 is sInv(MS) and i_4 is sInv(SS)

is that it should be calculated as maximum of value of r_5 and r_6, since parallelism allows both i_3 and i_4 to be executed simultaneously, and the total time for the response time is decided by the maximum response time of i_3 and i_4. A challenge to evaluate the maximum time in state s_8 is that the information of parallism in state s_2 ($i_3||i_4$) is removed in state s_5 and state s_6 (only left with i_3 or i_4). In order to retain this information, we preprocess the BPEL service model $\mathcal{M}$ to associate with a time tag which will be used to calculate the response time in the LTS generation stage.

Algorithm 1 presents the main algorithm for preprocessing. Given a BPEL process P_0, $TagTime(P_0, x)$ returns the process P_0' which is the process P_0 with its internal activities associated with time tags. Given each activity $Acv \in P_0$, a value $timetag \in \mathbb{R}_{\geq 0}$ is associated with Acv, denoted as $Acv.timetag$. $Acv.timetag$ represents the total time delay from the start of process P_0, up to the completion of activity Acv. In the following, we describe the Algorithm 1. The function $TagTime(P_0, x)$ is used to calculate the total time delay from the start of process P_0 up to the completion of activity Acv. Variable $x \in \mathbb{R}_{\geq 0}$ is the the total time delay from the start of process P_0 to the point just before the execution of activity Acv. Lines $1, 5, 9$ and 11 are used to detect the structure of the activities. At line 1, if P is detected to be a sequential activity, activity A will be tagged with the delay x (line 2) as A is triggered once P is triggered. Subsequently, activity B will be tagged. Since activity B is executed after the completion of activity A, therefore the x is set to be the value of $A.timetag$ (line 3). Finally, the $timetag$ of P is the same as $timetag$ of B, since the completion of activity B implies the completion of execution of process P (line 4). At line 5, if P is detected to be a concurrent or conditional activity, activity A and activity B will be tagged with value x (lines 6 and 7), since A and B are triggered at the same time once P is triggered. At line 8, the $timetag$ of P is the maximum value of $timetag$ of A and B (refer to Section 3.2 for details). If P is detected to be a synchronous receive activity or invocation activity, the $timetag$ of P is set to the sum of x and $ResponseTime(P)$ (line 10).

Example. In the following, we use an example to illustrate how to calculate the response time for each state in the LTS. Given initial service process $P_0 = sInv(PBS) \triangleleft b \triangleright sInv(CBS) \rightarrow (sInv(MS)||sInv(SS))$, we denote $P_0' = TagTime(P_0, 0)$ and

$$P_0' = [[[sInv(PBS)]^1 \triangleleft b \triangleright [sInv(CBS)]^2]^2 \rightarrow [[sInv(MS)]^5||[sInv(SS)]^3]^5]^5$$

Algorithm 1. Algorithm TagTime(P, x)

---

input : P, the BPEL process
input : x, the delay from the start to execution of process P
output: P', process P with time tag

1 **if** P *is* $A \rightarrow B$ **then**
2    $TagTime(A, x)$;
3    $TagTime(B, A.timetag)$;
4    $P.timetag \leftarrow B.timetag$;
5 **else if** P *is* $A \| B$ *or* $A \triangleleft b \triangleright B$ **then**
6    $TagTime(A, x)$;
7    $TagTime(B, x)$;
8    $P.timetag \leftarrow max(A.timetag, B.timetag)$;
9 **else if** P *is* $rec(S)$ *or* $sInv(S)$ **then**
10    $P.timetag \leftarrow x + ResponseTime(P)$;
11 **else if** P *is* $reply(S)$ *or* $aInv(S)$ **then**
12    $P.timetag \leftarrow x$;

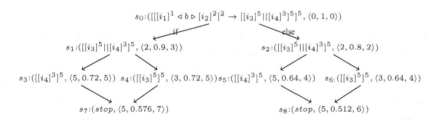

Fig. 4. LTS of CPS with Response Time, Availability and Cost, where i_1 is sInv(PBS), i_2 is sInv(CBS), i_3 is sInv(MS) and i_4 is sInv(SS)

where for each activity $A \in P$, $[A]^t$ is used to denote the activity A with $A.timetag = t$. Next, in the LTS generation stage, Algorithm 2 is used to calculate the response time for each state.

Given the process P of some state $s \in S$, $CalculateTime(P)$ in Algorithm 2 returns the total response time $t \in \mathbb{R}_{\geq 0}$ from the initial state s_0 to s'. The value t is assigned to Q($responseTime$) for state s'. Lines 1, 6, 11 are used to detect the structure of the activities. We introduce a special activity $skip$ to denote the completion of execution of an atomic activity. $skip$ is used for the purpose of calculating the response time, and it will be removed after the calculation. At line 1, if P is detected to be a sequential activity, the activity A is then checked whether it is a $skip$ activity. If it is (line 2), which implies that activity A has finished execution, $A.timetag$ is returned (line 3). Otherwise, $CalculateTime(A)$ is invoked in order to determine the response time (line 5). At line 6, if P is detected to be a concurrent activity or conditional activity, A and B will be determined whether both are $skip$ activities. If it is (line 7), which implies that P has finished execution, $P.timetag$ is returned (line 8).

Algorithm 2. Algorithm CalculateTime(P)

---

input : P, BPEL process with time tagged

output: $t \in \mathbb{R}_{\geq 0}$, the time delay from the start of initial process P_0 to the completion of P

1 **if** P *is* $A \rightarrow B$ **then**
2 | **if** A *is skip* **then**
3 | | **return** $A.timetag$;
4 | **else**
5 | | **return** $CalculateTime(A)$;
6 **else if** P *is* $A\|B$ *or* $A \triangleleft b \triangleright B$ **then**
7 | **if** A *is skip and* B *is skip* **then**
8 | | **return** $P.timetag$;
9 | **else**
10 | | **return** $CalculateTime(PreviousActive(P))$;
11 **else if** P *is skip* **then**
12 | **return** $P.timetag$;

Otherwise, $CalculateTime(PreviousActive(P))$ is invoked in order to obtain the response time (line 10) where $PreviousActive(P)$ is used to denote previous execution activity. For example, given $s = (i_1\|i_2, V, Q)$, $s' = (skip\|i_2, V', Q')$, and $s \xrightarrow{a} s' \in \rightarrow$, $PreviousActive(skip\|i_2)$ will return $AtomAct(a) = i_1$. At line 11, P is determined to be a $skip$ activity implies that P has finished execution, therefore, $P.timetag$ is returned (line 12). The value of $timetag$ for each BPEL process is obtained using Algorithm 1.

Example. In Figure 4, given the initial state s_0, there are two branches due to the conditional process. If sInv(PBS) is executed, it will evolved into state s_1 with process P_1' where

$$P_1' = [[[skip]^1]^2 \rightarrow [[sInv(MS)]^5\|[sInv(SS)]^3]^5]^5$$

By running the Algorithm 2 for PBS to get the response time of PBS, it will return the value 2, therefore state s_1 has the response time of 2 ms. After the calculating the response time, the $skip$ are removed from P_1', which result in process $P_1 = [[sInv(MS)]^5\|[sInv(SS)]^3]^5$ as shown in Figure 4. The calculation of other states is similar.

4.3 Discussion

If a system is verified that it does not satisfy the requirement that the response time is less than a ms in a state s, where $a \in \mathbb{R}_{\geq 0}$, it does not necessarily mean that such constraint will be violated in the state s during the execution. The response time is served as an estimated reference value. Furthermore, we do not take the response time, cost, and availability of internal operations into account. In reality, such information can be estimated using runtime monitoring method [12].

Table 3. Experiment Results

Services	Property	Result	#State	#Transition	Time(s)
CPS	(replyUser ∧ (responseTime>5))	invalid	21	29	0.0087
	□ responseTime≤5	valid	26	36	0.0089
	□ availability>0.6	valid	26	36	0.0083
LS	Reach (replyUser ∧ (responseTime>6))	invalid	106	241	0.0584
	□ responseTime≤6	valid	242	572	0.1866
TAS	Reach (replyUser ∧ (responseTime>3))	invalid	128	287	0.0631
	□ responseTime≤3	valid	264	622	0.0642
	Reach (replyUser ∧ (availability≤0.3))	invalid	128	287	0.0437

5   Evaluation

We evaluate our approach using three case studies. Each case study is a composite service represented as a BPEL process. The experiment data was obtained on a system using Intel Core I7 3520M CPU with 8GB RAM. The experimental results are summarized in Table 3.

5.1   Computer Purchasing Service (CPS)

As described in Section 2, CPS is used for allowing users to purchase a computer online using credit cards. The workflow of CPS is illustrated in Figure 1. The property $Reach$ $(replyUser \land (responseTime>5))$ is to verify whether the activity $reply\ user\ (ru)$ can be reached with response time more than 5 ms. The result is invalid as shown in Table 3, which implies that if the $reply\ user\ (ru)$ is reached, it will be always be less than 5 ms, which is the intended outcome we need. Properties □ $reponseTime\le5$ and □ $availability>0.6$ are LTL formulas, which are invariant properties denoted that the CPS's response time must always be less than two milliseconds and the CPS's availability is always larger than 50%. These two properties are both verified to be valid in the CPS system. The number of visited states, total transitions and time used for verification are listed in Table 3.

5.2   Loan Service (LS)

The goal of a Loan Service (LS) is to provide users for applying loans. The loan approval system has several component systems, Loan Record Service (RS), Loan Approval Service (LAS), Customer Details Service (CDS), Customer Loan History Service (CLHS), Customer Credit Card History Service (CCHS), Customer Employment Information Service (CES) and Customer Property Information Service (CPIS). Upon receiving the request from a customer, CDS will be invoked synchronously. If the requested load amount is less than $10000, CES is invoked and then RS is invoked to record the customer's loan information. After that, loan approval message will be replied to the customer. Otherwise, if the requested amount is not less than $10000, CLHS, CCHS, CES and CPIS are invoked concurrently to obtain more detailed information about the customer. Upon receiving all replies, LAS is invoked to determine whether to approve the load request of the customer or not. If the request is approved, RS is invoked synchronously and then loan approval message will be replied to the customer, otherwise, loan failure message will be replied to the customer. Two properties are verified for LS as listed in Table 3, we omit the discussion of the properties as they are similar to the properties of CPS.

5.3 Travel Agency Service (TAS)

Travel Agency Service (TAS) provides a service that helps users to arrange the flight, hotel, transport, etc., for a trip. Once the request is received from the user, Hotel Booking Service (HBS), Fight Booking Service (FBS), Local Transport Service (LoTS) and Local Agent Service (LAS) are triggered to search for available hotel, flight, local transportation and local travel agent concurrently that fulfill the user's requirements. If all four services have returned non-empty results, Record Booking Information Service (RBS) and Notify Agent Service (NAS) are invoked concurrently to store detailed booking information into the system and notify the agent about the customer's details. Finally, TAS replies the detailed booking information to the user. Otherwise, TAS replies booking failure result to the user. Three properties are verified for TAS as listed in Table 3. Properties $Reach\ (reply\ User \wedge (responseTime>3))$ and $\Box\ responseTime{\le}3$ are similar to the properties verified in CPS, therefore we omit discussion of these two properties here. Property $Reach\ (replyUser \wedge (availability{\le}0.3))$ is to verify whether $reply\ user\ (ru)$ can be reached with the availability less than 0.3. The result is invalid as shown in Table 3, which implies that if the $reply\ user\ (ru)$ is reached, the availability is always greater than 0.3, which is the intended result that we need.

The experiment shows that our approach can be used to verify the combined functional and non-functional property for real-world BPEL program efficiently.

6 Related Work

A number of approaches have been proposed to deal with requirements of web service composition. These work can be divided into two major directions. One direction is to transform WS-BPEL processes into intermediate formal models specified in some formal languages and then verify the functional behaviors of the service composition based on the formal models. Foster et al. [13] translate BPEL processes into finite state processes notation. Qian et al. [14] transform BPEL processes into timed automata, and then use Uppaal as the model checker to verify the functional properties of the TA model, such as reachability. In [9,15], the authors transform BPEL processes into Promela models and then use SPIN to verify the models. In [16], Yu et al. present a a lightweight specification language called PROPOLS to describe the temporal logic in a BPEL process. In [17], we translate processes into a new formal language proposed with formal operational semantics by themselves. Different from these approaches, our current approach verifies functional properties of BPEL processes based on its semantics, thus it does not need to be translated into any other formal languages since there are some disadvantages of using intermediate models as mentioned in Section 1. More important, our work combines verification of functional and non-functional requirements while works above only consider functional verification, which cannot verify functional and non-functional requirements at the same time.

Another direction has its focus on the non-functional aspect of BPEL processes. In [8], Koizumi and Koyama propose a performance model to estimate the processing execution time by integrating a Timed Petri Net model and statistical models. However, it only focuses on one type of non-functional requirements and does not consider the functional behaviors. In [7], Fung et al. propose a message tracking model to support QoS end-to-end management of BPEL processes. This work is based on the run-time data, which needs the deployment of the services, in addition, it does not consider the functional requirements of BPEL processes. Our approach verifies both functional and non-functional requirements at design time, which can detect errors at the early stage. In [18], Xiao et al. propose a framework to use the simulation technique to verify the non-functional requirements before the service deployment, which is similar to our work. While their work only focus on non-functional aspect, our work supports verification of combined functional and non-functional properties. In [19], we propose a fully automatic approach for synthesis the local time requirement based on the given global time requirement of Web service composition. Different from them, our work focuses on checking LTL constraint satisfaction. And to the best of our knowledge, our work is the first one to verify combined functional and non-functional properties.

7 Conclusion

In this paper, we have illustrated our approach to verify combined functional and non-functional requirements (i.e., availability, response time and cost) for web service composition. Furthermore, our experiments show that our approach can work on real-world BPEL programs efficiently. We plan to further improve and develop the technique presented in this paper. Firstly, we will consider various heuristics that could be used to reduce the number of states and transitions. Secondly, we will investigate applying state reduction techniques, such as partial order reduction [20], to improve the efficiency of our approach. Lastly, our work could be extended to other domains such as sensor networks.

References

1. Chinnici, R., Moreau, J.J., Ryman, A., Weerawarana, S.: Web services description language (WSDL) version 2.0, http://www.w3.org/TR/wsdl20/
2. Gudgin, M., Hadley, M., Mendelsohn, N., Moreau, J.J., Nielsen, H.F., Karmarkar, A., Lafon, Y.: Simple object access protocol (SOAP) version 1.2, http://www.w3.org/TR/soap12/
3. OASIS Web Service Business Process Execution Language (WSBPEL) Technical Committee: Web Services Business Process Execution Language Version 2.0 (2007), http://www.oasis-open.org/specs/#wsbpelv2.0
4. Yin, Z., Yuan, D., Zhou, Y., Pasupathy, S., Bairavasundaram, L.: How do fixes become bugs? In: ESEC/FSE 2011, pp. 26–36. ACM (2011)

5. Clarke, E.M., Grumberg, O., Peled, D.A.: Model Checking. MIT Press (2000)
6. Foster, H., Uchitel, S., Magee, J., Kramer, J.: WS-Engineer: A model-based approach to engineering web service compositions and choreography. In: Test and Analysis of Web Services, pp. 87–119 (2007)
7. Fung, C.K., Hung, P.C.K., Wang, G., Linger, R.C., Walton, G.H.: A study of service composition with qos management. In: ICWS 2005, pp. 717–724 (2005)
8. Koizumi, S., Koyama, K.: Workload-aware business process simulation with statistical service analysis and timed petri net. In: ICWS 2007, pp. 70–77. IEEE CS (2007)
9. Nakajima, S.: Lightweight formal analysis of web service flows. Progress in Informatics 2, 57–76 (2005)
10. Courcoubetis, C., Vardi, M., Wolper, P., Yannakakis, M.: Memory-efficient algorithms for the verification of temporal properties. Form. Methods Syst. Des. 1, 275–288 (1992)
11. Sun, J., Liu, Y., Dong, J.S., Pang, J.: Pat: Towards flexible verification under fairness. In: Bouajjani, A., Maler, O. (eds.) CAV 2009. LNCS, vol. 5643, pp. 709–714. Springer, Heidelberg (2009)
12. Moser, O., Rosenberg, F., Dustdar, S.: Non-intrusive monitoring and service adaptation for ws-bpel. In: WWW 2008, pp. 815–824. ACM (2008)
13. Foster, H., Uchitel, S., Magee, J., Kramer, J.: WS-Engineer: A model-based approach to engineering web service compositions and choreography. In: Baresi, L., Nitto, E.D. (eds.) Test and Analysis of Web Services, pp. 87–119. Springer (2007)
14. Qian, Y., Xu, Y., Wang, Z., Pu, G., Zhu, H., Cai, C.: Tool support for bpel verification in activebpel engine. In: ASWEC 2007, pp. 90–100 (2007)
15. Li, B., Zhou, Y., Pang, J.: Model-driven automatic generation of verified bpel code for web service composition. In: APSEC 2009, pp. 355–362. IEEE CS (2009)
16. Yu, J., Manh, T.P., Han, J., Jin, Y., Han, Y., Wang, J.: Pattern based property specification and verification for service composition. In: Aberer, K., Peng, Z., Rundensteiner, E.A., Zhang, Y., Li, X. (eds.) WISE 2006. LNCS, vol. 4255, pp. 156–168. Springer, Heidelberg (2006)
17. Sun, J., Liu, Y., Dong, J.S., Pu, G., Tan, T.H.: Model-based methods for linking web service choreography and orchestration. In: APSEC 2010, pp. 166–175. IEEE CS (2010)
18. Xiao, H., Chan, B., Zou, Y., Benayon, J.W., O'Farrell, B., Litani, E., Hawkins, J.: A framework for verifying sla compliance in composed services. In: ICWS 2008, pp. 457–464 (2008)
19. Tan, T.H., André, É., Sun, J., Liu, Y., Dong, J.S., Chen, M.: Dynamic synthesis of local time requirement for service composition. In: ICSE 2013, pp. 542–551 (2013)
20. Flanagan, C., Godefroid, P.: Dynamic partial-order reduction for model checking software. In: POPL 2005, pp. 110–121. ACM (2005)

vTRUST: A Formal Modeling and Verification Framework for Virtualization Systems

Jianan Hao[1], Yang Liu[1], Wentong Cai[1], Guangdong Bai[2], and Jun Sun[3]

[1] School of Computer Engineering, Nanyang Technological University
[2] NUS Graduate School for Integrative Sciences and Engineering
[3] ISTD, Singapore University of Technology and Design

Abstract. Virtualization is widely used for critical services like Cloud computing. It is desirable to formally verify virtualization systems. However, the complexity of the virtualization system makes the formal analysis a difficult task, e.g., sophisticated programs to manipulate low-level technologies, paged memory management, memory mapped I/O and trusted computing. In this paper, we propose a formal framework, vTRUST, to formally describe virtualization systems with a carefully designed abstraction. vTRUST includes a library to model configurable hardware components and technologies commonly used in virtualization. The system designer can thus verify virtualization systems on critical properties (e.g., confidentiality, verifiability, isolation and PCR consistency) with respect to certain adversary models. We demonstrate the effectiveness of vTRUST by automatically verifying a real-world Cloud implementation with critical bugs identified.

1 Introduction

Over the last few years, virtualization is widely used in many areas especially in Cloud computing. Enterprise users can save money on establishment and upgrading of fundamental computing resources by outsourcing their business logics on the virtualization server which provides instant-ready, pay-by-use and elastic computing services.

Technically, a virtualization server, especially Infrastructure-as-a-Service (IaaS), employs a middleware called hypervisor to multiplex limited hardware resources to multiple virtual machines (VMs). Each VM should provide an illusion of virtualized hardware whose configurations include processor count, memory size, storage space and communication capabilities. For a user, a typical virtualization service involves calculation of user-provided computation and feedback of the result. Therefore, it is critical for virtualization systems to guarantee critical properties such as secrecy of user's information and verifiability of computed results.

However, research [15] shows that virtualization systems are vulnerable due to a larger attack surface and immature implementations. Software bugs in critical components (e.g., hypervisor), improper usage of secure technique (e.g., Trusted Computing) and flawed security assumptions can all lead to vulnerabilities. To investigate whether vital properties of a virtualization system can be guaranteed, it is particularly necessary for the system to be formally verified before the deployment.

L. Groves and J. Sun (Eds.): ICFEM 2013, LNCS 8144, pp. 329–346, 2013.
© Springer-Verlag Berlin Heidelberg 2013

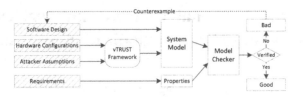

Fig. 1. Workflow

Unfortunately, virtualization systems are rarely analyzed by rigorous techniques like formal methods. So far, seL4 [8] is the only hypervisor that has been formally verified for functionalities at source code level using a theorem proving approach. However, the verification of seL4 on ARM platform took 20 person*year in total for complete proof based on Isabelle/HOL [10]. Since common hypervisors employed in Cloud systems are much bigger than seL4, it is arguably infeasible to verify them using a similar approach. Especially, because theorem proving is highly dependent on expert knowledge and manually created verification scripts can be error-prone. In this case, it is desirable to investigate an automatic approach to formally analyze virtualization systems.

In this paper, we propose a formal framework, namely vTRUST, to model and analyze virtualization systems using model checking tools with minimal manual effort. Fig. 1 presents the essential workflow to formally analyze the implementation of a virtualization system with the help of vTRUST. For a general virtualization system, it can be decomposed into 4 parts: software design, hardware configurations, attacker assumptions and service requirements are shown as slashed blocks for inputs. Based on software descriptions, the designer can implement executable programs on vTRUST architecture. Compared to real architecture (e.g., x86 and ARM), the vTRUST architecture focuses on the most critical (low-level) operations such as handling of virtualization traps, manipulation of memory protection and interaction with Trusted Computing, which are technically sophisticated and error-prone for software implementation. It is arguably safe to convert verified executable programs to native code on real architecture without the risk of introducing critical bugs. The designer can also model malicious programs according to various attacker assumptions. Based on hardware configurations and malicious programs, vTRUST framework can generate hardware and adversary models respectively. Additionally, critical properties will be specified in the system requirements. With the system model (including programs, hardware and adversary models) and the properties as inputs, a model checker can analyze the virtualization system. Especially, when a certain property is invalid, a counterexample will be given to direct implementation revision.

For page limitation, this paper only illustrates the most essential part of vTRUST. For more details, one may refer to [2] which includes full source code and testing results. The contributions of this paper can be summarized as follows.

- We propose a formal framework vTRUST, which is capable of modeling and analyzing virtualization systems with minimal manual efforts. It can cover common low-level details of virtualization systems and automatically explore design vulnerabilities. Moreover, the framework is extensible for more features.

- High-level properties of virtualization systems, e.g., confidentiality, verifiability, isolation and PCR consistency are formally specified. A verifier can test whether a property is satisfied with tolerance to a specific attacker model.
- As a case study, a Cloud implementation is modeled and analyzed by the vTRUST framework with PAT [1] as the model checker. A critical bug is found regarding unexpected relocation of hypervisor in a protected memory region, which is difficult to reveal manually.

Related Works. Formal verification of virtualization systems has been receiving more and more academic interest. One of the most famous works is the formal verification of seL4 [8], making it the only hypervisor verified at source code level so far. Although seL4 has only 8,700 and 600 lines of C and assembly code in ARM platform, the verification took 20 person*year to complete the proof on Isabelle/HOL, which makes the method infeasible to more complex systems. VCC [5] is another work to analyze the correctness of C programs by annotating the code with contracts in C preprocessor macros. Annotated programs are translated to logical formulas which will be passed to SMT solver Z3. Especially, Microsoft Hyper-V has been verified by VCC [9]. Other work focuses on verifying the integrity of hypervisor. Datta *et al.* [6] proposed a logic system to formally prove integrity of programs in the system using Trusted Computing. Vasudevan *et al.* [14] summarized the requirements for hypervisor based on hardware-assisted virtualization technology. Moreover, Soren Bleikertz *et al.* [4] proposed an automated verification approach for virtualized infrastructures.

2 Preliminary

2.1 CSP# Language

CSP# [12] is a modeling language which extends Hoare's CSP with new language features. CSP# integrates high-level modeling operators (e.g., parallel composition, choice, interrupt, channel communication, etc.) with shared variable and low-level procedural codes, for the purpose of efficient mechanical system verification. Part of the syntax of CSP# is given in the following, which will be used in the later content.

$$
\begin{array}{llll}
P ::= & [b]P & & \text{– state guard} \\
& | & e \to P & \text{– event prefixing} \\
& | & c?m \to P(m) \mid c!m \to P & \text{– channel input/output} \\
& | & P; Q & \text{– sequential composition} \\
& | & e\{program\} \to P & \text{– data operation prefixing} \\
& | & P \square Q & \text{– external choices} \\
& | & P \mid\mid\mid Q & \text{– interleaving} \\
& | & (\mid\mid\mid i : \{x..y\} \bullet P(i)) & \text{– indexed interleaving} \\
& | & P \triangle (e \to Q); & \text{– interrupt}
\end{array}
$$

where P and Q are processes, e is an event, b is a Boolean expression and c is a channel. In $e\{program\} \to P$, $program$ is executed atomically with the event e. Channel input and output events can be synchronous or asynchronous (with bounded channel buffer). $P \mid\mid\mid Q$ allows processes P and Q to execute independently except they communicate

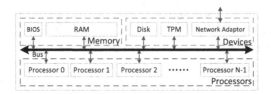

Fig. 2. Machine Model

with shared variables or synchronous channels. Especially, $(||| \ i : \{x..y\} \bullet P(i))$ is an indexed interleaving composition, which is equal to $P(x) \ ||| \ P(x+1) \ ||| \ ... \ ||| \ P(y)$ where x and y are integers (assuming $x \le y$). Similar syntax go for indexed external choices. $P \triangle (e \to Q)$ behaves as P until event e is engaged and then behaves as Q.

2.2 Hardware Technologies Related to Virtualization Systems

Virtualization systems rely on featured hardware technologies. First of all, processors should support classical virtualization, or trap-and-emulate virtualization [11], where the processor operates in dual modes, i.e., host and guest. Virtual Machine (VM) execution in the guest mode will be monitored for specific events. Upon an event, the execution in the guest mode will be suspended. A system software called hypervisor will take over to handle the event in the host mode. Especially, the guest program can actively invoke 'hypercall' for requesting services offered by the hypervisor. To provide memory resource among VMs, paged memory management are supported by Memory Management Unit. Memory-Mapped I/O is employed to access peripheral devices.

Virtualization systems can leverage on Trusted Computing for security enhancement. Trusted Computing is a technology aiming to enhance security of modern computers. Rather than confining what software can be carried out, Trusted Computing measures critical software stack, which is usually called Trusted Computing Base (TCB), as evidence. A secure chip, namely Trusted Platform Module (TPM) [13], must be installed to achieve Trusted Computing. TPM internally protects resources such as Platform Configuration Registers (PCRs), Endorsement Key (EK) and Storage Root Key (SRK). A PCR stores SHA-1 results from measuring memory data. Its value can be extended by inputting new data to it. Particularly, a method called Dynamic Root of Trust Measurement (DRTM) can be used to measure a piece of code as initial TCB with measurement result stored in PCR, and execute the code transactionally [3]. DRTM can only be performed by invoking 'late launch' instruction. The EK proves this TPM conforms to specification and SRK protects keys generated in the TPM. In addition, TPM can attest PCR value to a remote verifier. By comparing it to a known hash value of the software, one can realize what is running on the system.

2.3 Attacker Assumptions

For a virtualization system, attackers usually target the server where users' information is stored. In this work, we assume that attacks are performed by malicious software. The most important capability of the attacker is to construct malicious programs, and let the malicious programs be invoked on the server, which depends on the attacker's access

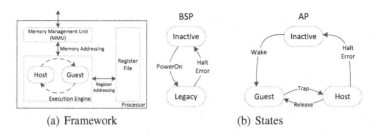

Fig. 3. Processor Model

right. Hence, we define type 1 attacker as the malicious virtualization user who can only interact with the server remotely. Therefore, the attacker will compromise uploaded computational program which will be executed on the server. We also define type 2 attacker as one who has physical access to the server. Such an attacker can overwrite programs stored on the server's harddisk.

3   vTRUST: A Formal Framework for Virtualization Systems

This section is devoted to the proposed framework vTRUST, which includes formal descriptions for hardware modeling, software modeling and adversary modeling. One may refer to [2] for the complete model.

3.1   Hardware Modeling

A virtualization system requires featured hardware for its functionalities. For example, Fig. 2 shows a typical hardware model, which consists of processors, memory and devices. An internal network will connect them for communication.

To efficiently model low-level details of these hardware components, we make necessary abstractions to facilitate automatic verification like model checking. However, the most critical behaviors of hardware features are preserved and kept similar to real hardware. We will explain each subsystem in the following paragraphs. Especially, we employ a uniform model for memory and device subsystems. Lastly, various models will be composed together as a complete system model.

Execution Model. Fig. 3(a) illustrates the internals of a processor. For processor i, it can be active or inactive, which is represented by Boolean state $active[i]$. When the processor is active, it can operate in different modes. Especially, the first active processor, or bootstrap processor (BSP), always works in the legacy mode where virtualization is disabled. Application processors (APs) can be woken up by invoking the instruction $WAKE$ in BSP or other active APs. When the AP is active, it operates in the guest mode initially and can be trapped into the host mode. After the hypervisor has done its job, it 'releases' the control back to the guest mode. The operational mode is modeled by state variable $mode[i]$ and transitions are illustrated by Fig. 3(b).

The multiprocessor subsystem can thus be composed by parallel composition as follows where $Proc(i)$ represents processor i. Process $Proc(i)$ can be activated by setting $active[i]$ to true and $mode[i]$ to legacy or guest for BSP or APs respectively. After event $wakeup.i$ is engaged, $LegacyOrGuest(i)$ models the execution in the legacy or guest mode as follows. The execution is essentially a loop of fetching and executing programs. The loop modeled by the $FELoop(i)$ can be interrupted when channel $prochalt[i]$ receives a message to halt current processor. In this case, $active[i]$ will be set to $false$ and the processor will wait for the next wake-up.

$Processors() = (||| \ i : \{0..(N-1)\} \bullet Proc(i));$
$Proc(i) = [active[i]]wakeup.i \rightarrow LegacyOrGuest(i);$
$LegacyOrGuest(i) = FELoop(i) \triangle (prochalt[i]?0\{active[i] = false; \} \rightarrow Proc(i));$

According to trap-and-emulate virtualization, the execution in the guest mode will be trapped into the host mode upon specific events such as access to privileged resource, executing illegal instructions or intentionally invoking hypercall. Process $Trap$ is employed to model the trap as follows.

$Trap(i, context) = g2h\{mode[i] = HOST; \ saveContext(context); \} \rightarrow Host(i);$
$Host(i) = FELoop(i) \triangle (release[i]?0\{mode[i] = GUEST; \} \rightarrow Skip);$

where parameter $context$ denotes the essential information (e.g., source, reason, affected instruction and operators, etc.) of the trap. Event $g2h$ models the transition from the guest mode to the host mode by changing operational mode and saving context. Process $Host(i)$ models the execution in the host mode. It is similar to $LegacyOrGuest(i)$ except that $FELoop(i)$ can be interrupted by receiving event of synchronous channel $release[i]$ which 'releases' the control back to the guest mode.

Specifically, every program in vTRUST is modeled as a CSP# process, e.g., $BIOS(i)$ or $Bootloader(i)$ where i indicates its execution environment on processor i. A program is a container of instructions and assigned with an identifier such as $Prog\_BIOS$ or $Prog\_Bootloader$. Processor i will fetch and execute a program each time repeatedly as modeled by $FELoop(i)$.

$FELoop(i) = fetch.i\{prog[i] = fetchProgram(pnp[i]); \ pnp[i] + +; \} \rightarrow Execute(i);$
$\qquad FELoop(i);$
$Execute(i) = [prog[i] == Prog\_BIOS]BIOS(i) \ \square$
$\qquad [prog[i] == Prog\_Bootloader]Bootloader(i) \ \square \ ...$

Event $fetch.i$ loads the current program from the memory address $pnp[i]$ which stands for the pointer to the next program. The $prog[i]$ will internally cache fetched programs during its execution. The pointer to the next program will be increased. After that, process $Execute(i)$ models the execution of program $prog[i]$ by dispatching according to program identifier.

Table 1. Primitive Instructions

Mnemonic	Legacy mode	Host mode	Guest mode
$MOVE\ dst,\ src$	$dst \leftarrow eval(src)$		
$JUMP\ adr$	$pnp \leftarrow eval(adr)$		
$WAKE\ hv,\ ptp,\ pnp$	Activate another processor. hv = hypervisor (physical address) ptp = paging table pointer (physical address) pnp = guest entry (logical address)		Trap
$HALT$	Inactivate current processor		Trap
$RELS$	Illegal	Release	Trap
$HYPC\ id$	Illegal	Illegal	Trap (Hypercall id)
$LL\ start,\ len$	Late launch	Illegal	Trap

Instruction Set. vTRUST defines only 7 primitive instructions whose semantics are summarized in Table 1. They are the only architectural interfaces defined to modify system states such as operational mode, register/memory values and device status. Each instruction is modeled as a CSP# process and its parameters are used to represent instruction operands. Note that an instruction may behave differently in different modes. For example, instruction $RELS$ can be modeled as follows[1].

$$RELS(i) = [mode[i] == LEGACY]Error(UNDEFINED\_INSTRUCTION) \ \square$$
$$[mode[i] == HOST]release[i]!0 \rightarrow Stop \ \square$$
$$[mode[i] == GUEST]Trap(i, INVOKE\_INSTR\_RELS)$$

Particularly, executing $RELS$ in legacy mode throws an error of undefined instruction. In the host mode, the instruction will terminate hypervisor's execution and release the control back to the guest program which triggers the trap. Lastly, when it is executed in the guest mode, it results in a trap with 'invoke $RELS$' as the context.

Primitive instructions used in every mode are $MOVE$ and $JUMP$. The former is used for data movement and the latter can intentionally modify the pointer to the next program. Note that function $eval(x)$ evaluates x based on the current execution environment and x stands for one of or a combination of register, memory and immediate number addressing modes. For example, $MOVE(Mem(0), Reg(x))$ copies data from register x to memory address 0. Moreover, the operand can also leverage CSP# syntax for arithmetic operations. For instance, $MOVE(Mem(0), Mem(0) + Mem(0))$ will double the value stored in $Mem(0)$.

As shown in Fig. 3(a), memory addressing is handled by MMU which is a featured component for virtualization systems to allocate memory resources among VMs. In the guest mode, every memory addressing will be processed by MMU for address translation and access right checking. The memory address referred to in the operand is called the logical address which is defined in the context of each processor; and the translated address is called the physical address which is globally indexed. Both logical and physical memory spaces are continuously grouped into pages as the granularity of memory management. The page size is configurable in vTRUST. A system structure called paging table describes how a logical address can be translated and what access rights are granted. Paging tables are stored in memory and a control register is employed to select

---

[1] In fact, CSP# does not allow a process to interrupt itself. The real implementation relies on another independent process as a proxy.

one of them as the active one in the guest mode. A paging table consists of a set of entries where entry $e(v, p, ac)$ indicates the vth page in logical memory space should be translated to the pth page in physical memory space. The ac stands for access control which describes the access rights granted for this page as a combination of $READ$, $WRITE$ and $EXECUTE$. However, MMU works differently in the legacy or host mode. The logical address is identically translated to the physical address and access right checking is omitted. This mechanism facilitates hypervisor to manage memory resources.

$$MOVE(i, dst, src) = iMOVE.i\{executeMOVE(i, dst, src)\} \rightarrow$$
$$if(lastState(i) == SUCCESS)\{/ * DoNothing * /$$
$$\}elseif(lastState(i) == FAILED)\{$$
$$if(mode[i] == LEGACY \parallel mode[i] == HOST)\{Error()\}$$
$$else\{Trap(i, Context(INSTR\_MOVE, dst, src))\}\}\}$$

MMU's behavior is modeled by data operations of each instruction. For example, above statements model the execution of instruction $MOVE$ in processor i. The program attached with event $iMOVE.i$ invokes function $executeMOVE$ to calculate state changes after execution of the instruction, which includes translation and access right checking in MMU. When it is successful, the updated state will be committed atomically at the occurrence of event $iMOVE.i$; otherwise, the state is unchanged and the processor will trigger an error or a trap according to current operational mode.

Additionally, $WAKE(hv, ptp, pnp)$ is the instruction to activate another application processor. Especially, the new activated processor will start execution in the guest mode where hv is the hypervisor entry, ptp is the paging table pointer and pnp is the logical memory address of the first guest program. On the contrary, $HALT$ is the instruction to inactivate the current processor.

Memory and Device Model. Unlike a processor that actively executes programs, memory is passive. Therefore, memory access is modeled as a part of data operations in instruction execution, e.g., in the function $executeMOVE$ for instruction $MOVE$. To access devices, Memory-Mapped I/O (MMIO) technology is employed. That is, from the view of a processor, when it performs memory addressing at particular physical memory address, the system bus can route the request to a specific device rather than memory. In other words, a physical address can be mapped to a memory unit or a functional port of a device; otherwise, it is reserved and thus illegal to be accessed.

As memory and devices work in a similar way by atomically responding to requests from the system bus, we can summarize their common behaviors using an unified base class in C#. Each type of device can thus be modeled as a derived class by implementing the interfaces such as configuration upon installation, response of reading from or writing to particular functional port, and initialization upon machine reset.

Currently, vTRUST provides 5 common devices, i.e., RAM, ROM, disk, network adapter and TPM as shown in Fig. 4. ROM (Fig. 4(a)) is the simplest device. It defines one readonly functional port. Reading on it retrieves internal content which represents the flashed data upon installation and will be persistent across power cycles. RAM

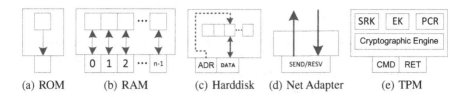

(a) ROM   (b) RAM   (c) Harddisk   (d) Net Adapter   (e) TPM

Fig. 4. Memory and Device Models

(Fig. 4(b)) is mostly used in the system. It defines n functional ports as memory units and each is linked to a corresponding internal data for reading and writing. Especially, initialization will zero all units to model its volatile property. Disk (Fig. 4(c)) provides permanent storage across power cycles. Different from memory, storage units in disk cannot be accessed directly. To visit a specific cell, one must write the offset of that cell to the selector port. After that, one can read/write the data port to access selected cell. Network adapter (Fig. 4(d)) offers capabilities to communicate with remote users. One can read from 'receive' port for retrieving data or write to 'send' port for transmitting data. Internally, they are modeled by receving/sending event of CSP# synchronous channel. Therefore, the execution of the instruction that involves receiving/sending will be blocked until connected a remote party is ready to send/receive data. TPM (Fig. 4(e)) plays a vital role in Trusted Computing. A port is defined to receive encapsulated command to the TPM; and the other port can be read to retrieve command result. Essential functionalities mentioned in Sec. 2.2 are modeled.

These 5 common devices are expected to cover popular virtualization hardware; if not, one may further model new devices by implementing additional subclasses.

3.2 Software Modeling

In the vTRUST framework, software is implemented as functional programs. Each program can be modeled as a CSP# process that mainly consists of primitive instructions. For example, a BIOS firmware program can be modeled by process $BIOS(i)$ where i represents the execution environment of processor i and its identifier will be $Prog\_BIOS$.

$$
\begin{aligned}
BIOS(i) &= DISKLOAD(i, Mem(1), 0);\ JUMP(i, 1); \\
DISKLOAD(i, dst, offset) &= MOVE(i, Mem(DISK\_SEL), offset); \\
&\quad MOVE(i, dst, Mem(DISK\_DATA));
\end{aligned}
$$

where $DISKLOAD$ defines a macro for loading a unit from harddisk to memory by calling two $MOVE$ instructions on selector and data ports of the harddisk respectively. $BIOS$ loads the first storage unit to $Mem(1)$ and transfers the control to it.

For a program that involves arithmetics and flow control, one can leverage CSP# syntax to achieve that. However, since the program executes in a single processor, syntax such as concurrency composition is not allowed.

3.3   Adversary Modeling

In vTRUST, an attack is performed by executing malicious software. First, malicious programs can be manually modeled as a vTRUST program. The program can additionally invoke $knowledge.add(x)$ to add a new entry x to the attacker's knowledge. Especially, a process $Eavesdrop$ is defined to add all accessible data (i.e., via memory and register addressing) to model eavesdropping. Furthermore, we use non-deterministic choice to enumerate all possible attack behaviors. In particular, vTRUST provides a library to model a piece of code that can execute arbitrary instructions.

$$
\begin{aligned}
ArbCode(i, n, opt) \quad &= Eavesdrop(); \\
&\quad if(n > 0)\{ArbInstruction(i, opt);\ ArbCode(i, n - 1, opt)\} \\
ArbInstruction(i, opt) &= Skip\ \Box \\
&\quad [opt.allowMOVE]ArbMOVE(i, opt.move)\ \Box \\
&\quad [opt.allowJUMP]ArbJUMP(i, opt.jump)\ \Box \\
&\quad [opt.allowLL]ArbLL(i, opt.ll)\ \Box\ ...
\end{aligned}
$$

Here, process $ArbCode(i, n, opt)$ models a piece of code that contains up to n instructions where each is modeled by process $ArbInstruction(i, opt)$. An eavesdropping behavior is inserted between every two arbitrary instructions. Internal choices are employed to model non-determinism including doing nothing ($Skip$) or executing a particular instruction with undetermined operands. Especially, opt describes options for constructing these instructions. The option contains Boolean switches for executing each instruction with constraints of the operands. For example, an instruction $JUMP(i, adr)$ with specific range as adr can be modeled as follows.

$$ArbJUMP(i, range) = (\Box\ adr : \{range_{min}..range_{max}\} \bullet JUMP(i, adr));$$

Constructing malicious code with non-determinism is powerful to discover vulnerabilities. However, due to large choices of instructions and their operands, modeling a malicious program tends to reach state explosion in model checking. As a tradeoff, a compromised program can be modeled as a revision to its original program. The designer may rely on his domain knowledge to insert pieces of malicious code to proper positions of the original program, or skip certain original instructions.

For type 1 attacker, only uploaded program can be compromised aiming to exploit bugs on server software. For type 2 attacker, he is able to compromise all software on server's harddisk including the bootloader and even the hypervisor.

3.4   Compose a Complete Model

To complete the system, models of hardware, software and adversary must be composed together. Before power on the server, its hardware must be configured, which can be modeled by $ConfigServer$ as follows.

$$
\begin{aligned}
ConfigServer() \; = \; & ConfigProcessors(4,4); \; InstallDev(0, ROM(Prog\_BIOS)); \\
& InstallDev(1, RAM(23)); \; InstallDev(24, Disk(Prog\_Bootloader)); \\
& InstallDev(28, TPM(AKey(ek), SKey(srk)); \\
& InstallDev(32, Net(chnout, chnin)); \\
OnlineServer() \; = \; & ResetAll(); \; (Processors() \; \triangle \; (sysreset?0 \rightarrow PowerOn())); \\
VirtSys() \quad\;\; = \; & ConfigServer(); \; (OnlineServer() \; ||| \; Users());
\end{aligned}
$$

where $ConfigProcessors(n, ps)$ plugs n processors with ps units as a memory page; $InstallDev(adr, dev)$ installs a device (memory is considered as a special device) dev on the system and maps its functional ports starting from physical memory address adr. Each device is initialized by a constructor in C#. $ROM(p)$ models ROM flashed by p as its content; $RAM(n)$ provides RAM with length of n; $Disk(x_0, x_1, ..., x_{n-1})$ models a harddisk whose storage units are initialized by array x; $TPM(ek, srk)$ configures a TPM chip with ek and srk as endorsement storage keys; and $Net(out, in)$ models a network adaptor binding its outbound and inbound ports to channels out and in.

Process $OnlineServer$ models server's running behaviors. $ResetAll$ resets all components. The server hardware will start to work as modeled by process $Processors$. The system can be interrupted only after reset, which is modeled by the synchronous channel $sysreset$. In this case, the server will be restarted by invoking $PowerOn$ again. The complete behaviors of the system can thus be modeled by process $VirtSys$ as a sequence of server configuration and interaction between online server and users.

4   Properties of Virtualization Systems

For a virtualization system, it is desirable to provide guarantees for its software implementation. This section discusses some important properties for virtualization systems.

Confidentiality. Confidentiality guarantees that the system can prevent user's program, data and computed result from disclosure. It is a general requirement for virtualization systems to convince their users that sensitive information outsourced to a server are safe. Confidentiality is vital because when it is unsatisfied, the user's information which may contain intellectual properties can be disclosed to an untitled entity, which leads to loss of commerce and reputation.

In vTRUST, an attacker's knowledge has been formally modeled by $knowledge$, which makes the specification straightforward. First, $NonConfidentiality$ defines the insecure state that the user's secret has been obtained by the attacker, which breaks the confidentiality requirement. In other words, $secret$ can be recovered from the attacker's $knowledge$ where $secret$ represents sensitive information which generally includes user-provided data, program and computational result. Therefore, the model checker can test the system's reachability to such insecure state, which is specified by $reaches$ syntax. If the result is valid, the model checker will generate an execution trace to break the confidentiality as a counterexample; otherwise, it indicates state $NonConfidentiality$ is unreachable, i.e., confidentiality is satisfied.

```
#define NonConfidentiality (knowledge.know(secret));
#assert VirtSys() reaches NonConfidentiality;
```

Verifiability. For the user who outsources his computation to a virtualization server, it is desirable to have a guarantee that the computational result is faithfully calculated from the input program and data. Verifiability defines a such property that users are capable of detecting if the result is forged. Similar to modeling confidentiality, we can model non-verifiability first and test its reachability, as shown below. The state of non-verifiability is reached when 'the user believes the result is good' but 'it is actually forged'. The definitions of two conditions are problem-specific.

```
#define NonVerifiability (BelieveGoodResult && ForgedResult);
#assert VirtSys() reaches NonVerifiability;
```

Isolation. For a cloud service with multiple users, it is desirable to guarantee the isolation among VMs. That is, any two VMs should not share same physical memory page unless it is expected. Especially, we specify 'strong isolation' and 'weak isolation' properties respectively. The former does not allow any overlapped mapping whereas the latter relaxes it by allowing shared memory page if $WRITE$ right is not granted.

Given any a processor i in the guest mode and another processor j in any mode, their active paging tables are denoted by pt_i and pt_j. The negative proposition of strong isolation can thus be defined as $\exists\, e_a \in pt_i, e_b \in pt_j \longrightarrow (e_a.p = e_b.p)$, where e_a and e_b refer to paging entries as mentioned in 3.1, and $e.p$ denotes its physical page number. Similarly, the negative proposition of weak isolation is defined as $\exists\, e_a \in pt_i, e_b \in pt_j \longrightarrow (e_a.p = e_b.p) \wedge (e_a.ac\& WRITE \neq 0)$. With the definitions of non-strong-isolation and non-weak-isolation, we model theses conditions in C# and test their reachability in the same way as confidentiality and verifiability.

PCR Consistency. For a system leveraging on Trusted Computing, when its PCR indicates a good TCB, the expected hypervisor should be always loaded for handling the traps, defined as PCR consistency. In other words, if a compromised hypervisor is activated to handle the traps but the PCR fails to reflect that the TCB is bad, PCR value is inconsistent with system status.

Suppose *goodpcr* is the condition to indicate whether the PCR is a good value and program *Hypervisor_Bad* refers to the malicious hypervisor that should never be executed in the host mode when the good PCR value is present. The inconsistent state can be modeled as follows.

```
#define InconsistentPCR (goodpcr && hv(Hypervisor_Bad));
#assert VirtSys() reaches InconsistentPCR;
```

where $hv(x)$ tests if program x is being executed in the host mode. Again, testing state reachability will verify the property.

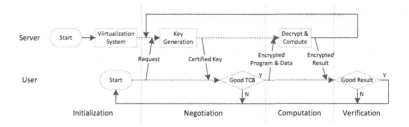

Fig. 5. Interactive Protocol

5   Case Study: Formal Analysis of Trusted Block as a Service

Trusted Block as a Service (TBaaS) [7] is a Cloud computing implementation. The system allows individual users to outsource their programs and data to the Cloud and retrieve computed results. We choose it as an example for its generality.

TBaaS involves interactions between a Cloud server and Cloud users. As shown in Fig. 5, the interactions can be divided into 4 stages: initialization, negotiation, computation and verification. In the initialization stage, the server is expected to setup a secure virtualization environment ready for providing services. In the negotiation stage, the user requests the service and a server will reply with evidence that the server system is securely built up. If the evidence is accepted, the user will enter the next stage; otherwise, the protocol aborts. The computation stage starts with uploading user's data and program to the server via an established secure channel. The server will create an isolated Trusted Block as a sandbox for the computation. The computed result and its integrity proof will be securely sent back to the user once the computation is done. In the verification stage, the user will verify the integrity of the result and finish the session.

Particularly, the initialization of the server involves considerable low-level operations with hardware. For example, it relies on bootloader to load the late launch entry (the first program after late launch) and the hypervisor into memory for DRTM. To minimize TCB, TBaaS moves potentially untrusted code such as network driver to the management VM. The isolation is achieved by paged memory management. As involved in DRTM, the late launch entry and the hypervisor must be bug-free.

5.1   System Modeling

In this section, we configure hardware and implement software from its design. Furthermore, we model malicious software according to attack assumptions.

Hardware Configuration. TBaaS server equips with 4 processors and groups 4 memory units as a page. First 24 physical memory units are allocated for ROM and RAM. Harddisk, TPM and network adaptor are installed in separate memory pages. The configuration is the same as mentioned in Sec. 3.4 except that harddisk stores programs *Prog_Bootloader*, *Prog_Driver*, *Prog_LLEntry* and *Prog_Hypervisor* in sequence.

Software Implementation. The server starts with the BIOS program which loads boot-loader and transfers the control to it.

```
#define PADR_LLENTRY 4;   #define PADR_HV 5;
Bootloader(i) =
    DISKLOAD(i, Mem(PADR_LLENTRY), 2);  //Mem(4) <= Prog(LLEntry)
    DISKLOAD(i, Mem(PADR_HV), 3);        //Mem(5) <= Prog(Hypervisor)
    LL(i, PADR_LLENTRY, 2);
```

Essentially, the bootloader loads late launch entry and hypervisor from harddisk to adjacent memory addresses defined by $PADR\_LLENTRY$ and $PADR\_HV$. Late launch is invoked with measurement of these memory units. If successful, late launch entry will take the control. Its task is to setup virtualization environment. Firstly, it prepares the paging table for the management VM (stored in $Mem(PADR\_MVMPT)$). The first page is mapped to the first physical page with all access rights for executing the driver program and accessing buffers; The second page is mapped to the functional port of the network adaptor (defined by $PADR\_NET$) with read/write access to allow the driver program to operate the adaptor. $PADR\_DRIVER$ and $LADR\_DRIVER$ respectively defines the driver's physical address and logical address based on newly prepared paging table. A $WAKE$ instruction is invoked to create the management VM by providing its hypervisor, paging table and entry point.

```
#define PADR_DRIVER 2;   #define LADR_DRIVER 2;
#define PADR_MVMPT 6;    #define PADR_NET 32;
LLEntry(i) =
    DISKLOAD(i, Mem(PADR_DRIVER), 1);      //Mem(2) <= Prog(Driver)
    MOVE(i, Mem(PADR_MVMPT), PageTable([0, RWX], [PADR_NET, RW]));
    WAKE(i, PADR_HV, PADR_MVMPT, LADR_DRIVER);  HALT(i);
```

The hypervisor is the most vital component in the system. TBaaS hypervisor only accepts two traps: the hypercall from the management VM for data arrival and the hypercall from a Trusted Block for the notification of completed computation. We summarize its structure in the following *pseudo-code* below due to space limitation.

```
Hypervisor(i) =
    if(hypercall from Management VM && FuncID == DATAARRIVAL){
        Response network message according to network protocol; RELS(i);
    }else if(hypercall from TB && FuncID == JOBDONE){
        Encapsulate the result of TB; Halt(i);
    }else{Error Handler}
```

The virtualization users interact with the server by network communication which is modeled by operating channels bound to the server's network adaptor. Especially, the computational program uploaded to the server must follow this template:

```
UserProg(i) = Read input data, calculate the result and store it to a specified location
              HYPC(i, JOBDONE);
```

Table 2. Model Checking Results

Attacker	Malicious Software			Properties	Results				
	Bootloader	Hypervisor	UserProg		Valid?	$\|S\|$	$\|T\|$	Time(s)	Mem(MB)
Type 1	-	-	5 instructions	NonConfidentiality	NO	762K	1182K	249	74
				NonVerifiability	NO	762K	1182K	247	93
				NonStrongIsolation	NO	762K	1182K	249	88
				NonWeakIsolation	NO	762K	1182K	248	123
				InconsistentPCR	NO	762K	1182K	253	143
Type 2	4 instructions	3 instructions	-	NonConfidentiality	YES	163K	251K	42	102
				NonVerifiability	YES	163K	251K	42	85
				NonStrongIsolation	YES	163K	251K	42	81
				NonWeakIsolation	YES	163K	251K	42	104
				InconsistentPCR	YES	163K	250K	42	106
Type 2 (Bug fixed)	4 instructions	3 instructions	-	NonConfidentiality	NO	2481K	6551K	705	104
				NonVerifiability	NO	2481K	6551K	713	95
				NonStrongIsolation	NO	2481K	6551K	713	141
				NonWeakIsolation	NO	2481K	6551K	710	109
				InconsistentPCR	NO	2481K	6551K	717	132

Malicious Software. For the type 1 attacker model, we assume one of the users, e.g., Alice, uploads a malicious program which can be modeled as follows.

$$UserProg\_Bad(i) = ArbCode(i, l, opt);$$

where l indicates how complex the malicious program will be constructed, and opt controls the options of modeled code. They should be adjusted according to time and space constraints in the verification, i.e., more capable attackers can have more ways to execute the code, but this leads to longer verification time.

Type 2 attacker can compromise any program on the harddisk. We model the malicious programs by inserting pieces of malicious code into the original programs at the proper positions. For example, compromised bootloader can be modeled by inserting malicious code before original late launch instruction. Compromised late launch entry, driver and hypervisor can be modeled similarly. To load these compromised programs, the original harddisk will be replaced by $Disk(Prog\_Bootloader\_Bad, Prog\_Driver, Prog\_LLEntry, Prog\_Hypervisor, Prog\_Driver\_Bad, Prog\_LLEntry\_Bad, Prog\_Hypervisor\_Bad)$.

5.2   Verification and Evaluation

The TBaaS system should satisfy the properties as mentioned in Sec. 4. Specifically, confidentiality is specified by defining the secret as good users' uploaded programs, data and computed results. For verifiability, we model user's judgement of the result's integrity as a variable $UserJudge$ which can be *undefined*, *good* and *forged*. The user should keep it as *undefined* before the verification stage where it will be updated to *good* or *forged* according to the interaction protocol. Therefore, condition $BelieveGoodResult$ in Sec. 4 can be defined as '$UserJudge == good$'. For the condition $ForgedResult$, it can be evaluated by comparing user-received result with the genuine result pre-computed by the designer. Strong isolation and weak isolation must be achieved to isolate user's information among TBs. As Trusted Computing is used in TBaaS, PCR consistency must be satisfied as well.

Based on the system model generated by vTRUST and specified properties, we analyze the system against certain adversary models. Table 2 summarizes the experimental results where the testbed is a workstation with Intel Xeon E3-1245 CPU and 8GB RAM. Depth-first search is used to verify the properties.

For type 1 attacker (Alice), uploaded program contains 5 arbitrary instructions (including macros such as $DISKLOAD$) with all options enabled. The result shows expected behavior that all properties are satisfied. For type 2 attacker, he compromises software on the server side: bootloader is compromised by adding 4 arbitrary instructions; a malicious hypervisor is modeled by introducing 2 arbitrary instructions before creating the Trusted Block and another arbitrary instruction before encryption of the computed result.

The experimental result shows that a critical bug is found to break all properties by compromising bootloader and hypervisor when type 2 attacker is present. Based on the counterexample generated by PAT, we reconstruct the malicious bootloader as follows.

```
Bootloader_Bad(i) =
    DISKLOAD(i, Mem(4), 2);    //Mem(4) <= Prog(LLEntry)
    DISKLOAD(i, Mem(5), 3);    //Mem(5) <= Prog(Hypervisor)
++ MOVE(i, Mem(1), Mem(4));    //Mem(1) <= Mem(4)
++ MOVE(i, Mem(2), Mem(5));    //Mem(2) <= Mem(5)
++ DISKLOAD(i, Mem(5), 6);     //Mem(5) <= Prog(Hypervisor_Bad)
++ LL(i, 1, 2);                //Late launch {Mem(1) | Mem(2)}
    LL(i, 4, 2);
```

The original code firstly loads good late launch entry and hypervisor to $Mem(4)$ and $Mem(5)$ where the malicious code relocates them to $Mem(1)$ and $Mem(2)$ and further overwrites $Mem(5)$ by the malicious hypervisor. Late launch with memory range $Mem(1)$ to $Mem(2)$ will be invoked. As a result, the same PCR value will be obtained as the original bootloader would, which makes Cloud user infeasible to distinguish the difference. In original late launch entry, instruction $WAKE$ assigns $Mem(5)$ as the hypervisor for the management VM, which grants the malicious hypervisor the right to execute in the host mode, making all properties unsatisfied. To amend it, the late launch entry must perform a sanity check of where it is being loaded at the very beginning. Verification shows that amended system can defend against type 2 attacker.

6   Discussion and Conclusion

The vTRUST framework is a tradeoff between details and efficiency. For complex virtualization systems, vTRUST models the most critical low-level features such as trap-and-emulate execution, paged memory management, Memory Mapped I/O and Trusted Computing. With these features, one can model complex software logic based on simplified instruction set which is the fundamental for automatic exploration of vulnerabilities. Abstraction techniques such as explicit definition of programs help to achieve the goal without losing capabilities of modeling high-level properties.

Specifically, CSP# allows to define user-customized data types and their determined behavior in C#, which facilitates vTRUST to model internal states and their transitions of hardware components. Most importantly, Object-Oriented Programming is utilized to model memory and devices for reusability. By implementing determined operations in C#, CSP# code can focus on non-determinism modeling and thereby improve readability. On the other side, we leverage CSP# syntax for flow-control and arithmetic operations and therefore avoid enlarging the instruction set.

The critical bug found by vTRUST is subtle. For the implementation regarding sophisticated technologies such as Trusted Computing and virtualization, it is common to overlook something in coding. For example, although the fact 'DRTM is irrelevant to memory location' can be derived by PCR extending operation, this issue is not highlighted in popular documents such as [3]. For a designer of virtualization systems, it is highly possible to overlook this deep-level information. Even worse, we argue similar bugs can hardly be revealed by traditional software testing or manual inspection. We remark that the properties that can be verified are not limited to the four types as shown in Sec. 4. Other functional properties like correctness can also be verified, which is mainly constrained by the model checker used.

In this paper, we proposed a formal framework vTRUST to analyze implementations of virtualization systems. Based on the vTRUST architecture, the system designer can implement software with low-level details as executable programs. The framework covers most common critical features in virtualization systems and thus can be used as a general modeling and analysis tool. Especially, we employed vTRUST to analyze a Cloud prototype, called TBaaS, and found a critical bug regarding a relocation issue which is arguably hard to discover by software testing or manual inspection. In the future, we will extend this work for more hardware features such as hardware interrupts and master devices. Hardware-based attacks will also be covered. Moreover, we will investigate optimization of modeling malicious code with more case studies.

Acknowledgement. We would like to thank project 'IDD11100102' from Singapore University of Technology and Design which supports this work.

References

1. Process Analysis Toolkit, http://www.comp.nus.edu.sg/
2. vTRUST Website, http://www.comp.nus.edu.sg/%7Epat/vtrust
3. AMD. Secure Virtual Machine Architecture Reference Manual
4. Bleikertz, S., Groß, T., Mödersheim, S.: Automated Verification of Virtualized Infrastructures. In: CCSW, pp. 47–58 (2011)
5. Cohen, E., Dahlweid, M., Hillebrand, M., Leinenbach, D., Moskal, M., Santen, T., Schulte, W., Tobies, S.: VCC: A Practical System for Verifying Concurrent C. In: Berghofer, S., Nipkow, T., Urban, C., Wenzel, M. (eds.) TPHOLs 2009. LNCS, vol. 5674, pp. 23–42. Springer, Heidelberg (2009)
6. Datta, A., Franklin, J., Garg, D., Kaynar, D.: A Logic of Secure Systems and its Application to Trusted Computing. In: SP, pp. 221–236 (2009)
7. Hao, J., Cai, W.: Trusted Block as a Service: Towards Sensitive Applications on the Cloud. In: TrustCom, pp. 73–82 (2011)
8. Klein, G., et al.: seL4: Formal Verification of an OS Kernel. In: SOSP, pp. 207–220 (2009)

9. Leinenbach, D., Santen, T.: Verifying the Microsoft Hyper-V Hypervisor with VCC. In: Cavalcanti, A., Dams, D.R. (eds.) FM 2009. LNCS, vol. 5850, pp. 806–809. Springer, Heidelberg (2009)
10. Nipkow, T., Paulson, L.C., Wenzel, M.T.: Isabelle/HOL. LNCS, vol. 2283. Springer, Heidelberg (2002)
11. Popek, G.J., Goldberg, R.P.: Formal Requirements for Virtualizable Third Generation Architectures. Communications of the ACM 17, 412–421 (1974)
12. Sun, J., Liu, Y., Dong, J.S., Chen, C.: Integrating Specification and Programs for System Modeling and Verification. In: TASE, pp. 127–135 (2009)
13. Trusted Computing Group. Trusted Platform Module Main Specification. Version 1.2, Revision 116 (2011)
14. Vasudevan, A., McCune, J.M., Qu, N., van Doorn, L., Perrig, A.: Requirements for an Integrity-protected Hypervisor on the x86 Hardware Virtualized Architecture. In: Acquisti, A., Smith, S.W., Sadeghi, A.-R. (eds.) TRUST 2010. LNCS, vol. 6101, pp. 141–165. Springer, Heidelberg (2010)
15. Williams, B., Cross, T.: Virtualization System Security. In: IBM (2010)

Formal Kinematic Analysis
of the Two-Link Planar Manipulator

Binyameen Farooq[1], Osman Hasan[2], and Sohail Iqbal[2]

[1] Research Center for Modeling and Simulation (RCMS)
[2] School of Electrical Engineering and Computer Science (SEECS),
National University of Sciences and Technology (NUST),
Islamabad, Pakistan
{binyameen.farooq,osman.hasan,sohail.iqbal}@seecs.nust.edu.pk

Abstract. Kinematic analysis is used for trajectory planning of robotic manipulators and is an integral step of their design. The main idea behind kinematic analysis is to study the motion of the robot based on the geometrical relationship of the robotic links and their joints. Given the continuous nature of kinematic analysis, traditional computer-based verification methods, such as simulation, numerical methods or model checking, fail to provide reliable results. This fact makes robotic designs error prone, which may lead to disastrous consequences given the safety-critical nature of robotic applications. Leveraging upon the high expressiveness of higher-order logic, we propose to use higher-order-logic theorem proving for conducting formal kinematic analysis. As a first step towards this direction, we utilize the geometry theory of HOL-Light to develop formal reasoning support for the kinematic analysis of a two-link planar manipulator, which forms the basis for many mechanical structures in robotics. To illustrate the usefulness of our foundational formalization, we present the formal kinematic analysis of a biped walking robot.

1 Introduction

Kinematic analysis [14] is the study of motion of a machine or mechanism without considering the forces that cause the motion. It mainly allows us to determine parameters like the position, displacement, rotation, speed, velocity and acceleration of a given mechanical structure and is thus used to design the geometrical dimensions and operational range of a mechanical structure according to the given specifications. The main idea behind kinematic analysis is to first identify the links (rigid bodies) and joints (allow rotation or sliding) of the given mechanical structure and then construct a corresponding kinematic (skeleton) diagram, which is a geometrical structure depicting the connectivity of links and joints. Finally, the kinematic diagrams are analyzed, using the principles of geometry, to determine the motion of any point of interest in the kinematic diagram.

Kinematic analysis allows us to extract useful information about the workspace, dexterity and precision of a given robotic design [26]. Thus, kinematic analysis is always performed during the conception phase of a robot to

L. Groves and J. Sun (Eds.): ICFEM 2013, LNCS 8144, pp. 347–362, 2013.

ascertain that the designed robot is appropriate to serve the given purpose [22]. For example, kinematic analysis has been used to judge the slope climbing capability of a biped robot [19] and the repairing the human aortic aneurysm capability of a minimal invasive surgical robot [7].

Given the safety-critical nature of many robotic applications, traditional techniques, like numerical methods or simulations, are not encouraged to be used for kinematic analysis [24]. Computer algebra systems, like Maple and Mathematica, offer complete packages (e.g. [25]) for kinematic analysis of mechanical systems. Despite being very efficient for computing mathematical solutions symbolically, these methods cannot be considered 100% reliable due to the involvement of unverified huge symbolic manipulation algorithms in their core. As an alternative, interval analysis has been used to find the *safe* kinematics for a minimum invasive surgical robot [11]. However sometimes, due to computational pessimism, the resulting interval becomes too large to provide any useful information. Moreover, interval analysis is not suitable to exhaustively check the initial hypothesis of the model properly and thus cannot be completely relied upon as well. Inaccuracies in kinematic analysis could lead to disastrous consequences, including a robot's breakdown [13], and thus investigating more reliable and sound kinematic analysis techniques is a dire need.

In the past couple of decades, formal methods have emerged as a successful verification technique for both hardware and software systems. The rigorous exercise of developing a mathematical model for the given system and analyzing this model using mathematical reasoning usually increases the chances for catching subtle but critical design errors that are often ignored by traditional techniques like paper-and-pencil based proofs or numerical methods. However, due to the continuous nature of the analysis and the involvement of analytical geometry, automatic state-based formal methods, like model checking, cannot be used to ascertain absolute correctness. On the other hand, leveraging upon the high expressiveness of higher-order logic, theorem proving can provide the ability to formally reason about the correctness of kinematic analysis. But to the best of our knowledge, the underlying principles of kinematic analysis have not been formalized in higher-order-logic so far and thus formal reasoning about the correctness of kinematic analysis is not a straightforward task.

As a first step towards using a higher-order-logic theorem prover for formally verifying the correctness of kinematic analysis, we present the formal reasoning support for a two-link planar manipulator [22], i.e., a simple yet the most commonly used mechanical structure in robotics. In particular, we present the formalization of forward and inverse kinematic analysis equations of a two-link planar manipulator by extending the recently developed analytical geometry theories available in HOL-Light [9]. The main advantage of these results is that they greatly minimize the user intervention for formal reasoning about kinematic analysis of many robots, mainly because any robot with multiple links and joints can be expressed in terms of a two-link planar manipulator. In order to demonstrate the practical effectiveness and utilization of the reported formalization, we utilize it to conduct the formal kinematic analysis of a biped robot [12,10], i.e., a two-legged mobile robot, in this paper.

The rest of the paper is organized as follows: Some related work about formal verification of mechanical systems and formalization of geometry theory is presented in Section 2. In Section 3, we provide a brief introduction about kinematic analysis of a two-link planar manipulator. The formalization of these foundations of kinematic analysis is provided in Section 4. We utilize this formalization to conduct the formal kinematic analysis of a biped robot in Section 5. Finally, Section 6 concludes the paper.

2   Related Work

The usage of formal methods in ascertaining the correctness of continuous and physical systems is increasingly being advocated these days [2]. In this context, formal verification of mechanical systems, particularly the ones used in automotive and robotic applications, have gained particular interest due to their safety-critical applications [8]. For example, formal verification of the movements of a Samsung Home-service Robot (SHR) is presented by analyzing its discrete control software using the Esterel model checker [6]. Similarly, an abstracted integer-valued behavior of the mobile outdoor robot RAVON is formally modeled in the synchronous language Quartz and is formally verified using the Averest model checker [17]. Moreover, in order to alleviate the problems associated with unintended acceleration due to faulty accelerator pedals, the electrical and mechanical components of Toyota's electronic throttle controller (ETC) have been formally modeled and verified based on the principles of timed automata and real-time logic [18]. Likewise, an abstraction approach for generating a discretized state-space of mechanical systems is reported in [21]. In all these model checking based verification efforts, the continuous dynamics of mechanical systems had to be discretized in order to be able to construct a corresponding automata-based model [20]. Such abstractions clearly compromise the accuracy of the analysis. These limitations can be overcome by using higher-order-logic theorem proving in the context of verifying mechanical systems. For example, the Isabelle theorem prover has been used to formally verify a collision-avoidance algorithm for service robots [23]. Real number and set theories have been utilized to formalize the contour of the robot as a convex polygon while obstacles are modeled as connected sets of points. This way, it has been formally verified that the moving robot is able to stop, upon detecting an obstacle, within the safety zone. The results have been verified without using any abstractions, which clearly indicates the usefulness of theorem proving in the context of verifying mechanical systems. With the same motivation, we plan to utilize higher-order-logic theorem proving for kinematic analysis in this paper, which, to the best of our knowledge, is a novelty.

The foremost requirement for conducting kinematic analysis in a higher-order-logic theorem prover is the ability to formally reason about geometry theory principles in a theorem prover. This capability is provided by a number of theorem provers. For example, a formal proof environment for Euclid's elements is presented in [1]. Some other recent developments include the axiomatic formalization of Euclidian plane geometry along with some interactive and automated reasoning support for geometrical properties in the Coq theorem prover[16], the formalization of the Cartesian-plane based geometry theory along with the proof that it can model the synthetic plane geometries in the Isabelle/HOL theorem prover [15], and the HOL-Light geometry theory formalized, based on n-dimensional real vector ($\mathtt{real^n}$), in the Euclidean space [9]. In this paper, we have chosen the HOL-Light theorem prover for developing the foundations of kinematic analysis. The main reasons behind this choice include the availability of all the topological and analytic foundations for vectors, which is expected to play a vital role in extending the reported formalization for analyzing other continuous aspects of mechanical systems, and our past familiarity with the HOL-Light.

3   Kinematic Analysis of Two-Link Planar Manipulator

A two-link manipulator [22], depicted in Figure 1, has two rotary degrees of freedom (DOF) in the same plane. In kinematic analysis of this system, we are mainly interested in the trajectory planning of the end-effector (tip) of the manipulator. In order to bring the end-effector from its initial Cartesian position to an arbitrary point in the Cartesian space, we need to find its relationships with the joint angles, i.e., θ_1 and θ_2. This can be done in two ways, i.e. forward or inverse kinematics.

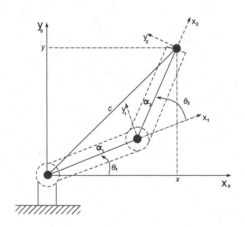

Fig. 1. Kinematic Diagram a Two-Link Planar Manipulator

3.1   Forward Kinematics

The forward kinematics is the problem of determining the Cartesian position of the end-effector of the manipulator in terms of the joint angles. This is not a straightforward task due to the presence of multiple coordinate frames, i.e.,

(x_0, y_0), (x_1, y_1) and (x_2, y_2). It is customary to resolve this issue by establishing a fixed coordinate system, usually referred to as the world or base frame, to which all objects, including the manipulator, can be referenced from. Mostly, this base coordinate frame is established at the origin of the manipulator. The Cartesian coordinates (x, y) of the end effector can now be expressed in this coordinate frame as [22]

$$x = \alpha_1 \cos \theta_1 + \alpha_2 \cos(\theta_1 + \theta_2) \tag{1}$$

$$y = \alpha_1 \sin \theta_1 + \alpha_2 \sin(\theta_1 + \theta_2) \tag{2}$$

where α_1 and α_2 are the lengths of the two links, respectively.

3.2   Inverse Kinematics

Inverse kinematics allows us to find the joint angles, θ_1 and θ_2, in terms of the position of the end-effector of the manipulator. The law of Cosines provides us with the following relationship for the angle θ_2

$$\cos \theta_2 = \frac{(x^2 + y^2 - \alpha_1^2 - \alpha_2^2)}{2\alpha_1\alpha_2} := D \tag{3}$$

If the desired Cartesian position coordinates (x, y) lie within the range of the manipulator's end-effector and the two links do not have to be fully extended to reach this point, then there are two different ways, i.e., elbow-up and elbow-down, in which the end-effector can reach the desired position, as shown in Figure 2. So, instead of obtaining θ_2 from the above equation, which does not distinguish between these two cases, we use the following relationships:

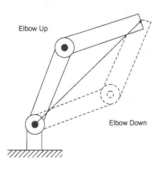

Fig. 2. Two solutions for Inverse Kinematics

$$\sin \theta_2 = \pm\sqrt{1 - D^2} \tag{4}$$

$$\theta_2 = \tan^{-1}\left(\frac{\pm\sqrt{1 - D^2}}{D}\right) \tag{5}$$

This way, both the elbow-up and elbow-down solutions can be obtained by choosing either the positive or the negative sign in Equation (5). Now θ_1 can be found in terms of θ_2 as follows:

$$\theta_1 = \tan^{-1}\left(\frac{y}{x}\right) - \tan^{-1}\left(\frac{\alpha_2 \sin\theta_2}{\alpha_1 + \alpha_2 \cos\theta_2}\right) \tag{6}$$

The main contribution of this paper is the formalization of the two-link planar manipulator in higher-order logic and the formal verification of the above mentioned equations in HOL-Light. The availability of this formalization will greatly minimize the human interaction required in formal reasoning about kinematic analysis of real-world robotic applications in HOL-Light.

4   Formalization of Kinematic Analysis

We formalized the two-link manipulator, depicted in Figure 1, in the Cartesian plane as the following higher-order-logic function in HOL-Light

Definition 1: *Two Link Manipulator*
⊢ ∀ A B. tl_manipulator A B = A + B

The function tl_manipulator accepts two vectors A and B of data type (real²), which represent the two links of the two-link manipulator, and returns their vectored sum, which is indeed the Cartesian position of the corresponding endeffector. By default, the common base frame of the two vectors is oriented at the origin. It is important to note that 2-dimensional vectors are used for the two links because of the planar nature of the mechanical system under consideration.

The two links of a general planar manipular with revolute joints can have both anticlockwise and clockwise rotations. In the context of the formal verification of the equations, presented in the previous section, it is very important to have a formal mechanism to distinguish between these two kinds of rotations. For this purpose, the following HOL-light predicate with data-type $(\text{real}^2 \rightarrow \text{real}^2 \rightarrow \text{real}^2 \rightarrow \text{bool})$ is used:

Definition 2: *Anticlockwise*
⊢ ∀ B A D. anticlockwise D (A,B) <=> 0 ≤ Im $\left(\frac{B-D}{A-D}\right)$

where Im represents the HOL-Light function that returns the imaginary part of a complex number or the y-component of a two-dimensional vector in the Cartesian plane. The predicate anticlockwise accepts three arbitrary points, A, B and D, in the Cartesian plane and returns *True* if the angle from DB to DA is considered in the anticlockwise direction.

A very interesting property, in the context of our verification, is the following addition relationship between three anticlockwise angles:

Theorem 1: *Anticlockwise Angle Addition*
⊢ ∀ A B C D. ~(collinear {D, A, B}) ∧ ~(C = D) ∧
        anticlockwise D (A,C) ∧
        anticlockwise D (C,B) ∧
        anticlockwise D (A,B) ⇒
        angle (A,D,B) = angle (A,D,C) + angle (C,D,B)

where A, B, C and D represent four points in the Cartesian plane. The predicate collinear accepts three points and returns *True* if all these three are collinear, i.e., they lie on a single straight line. Whereas, the function angle accepts three points (X,Y,Z) and returns the angle between the vectors XY and ZY.

Based on the fact that the main scope of the presented work is to build formal reasoning support for kinematic analysis in the plane geometry, we can work with a formal definition of a two dimensional angle. This choice simplifies our proofs considerably compared to the case if we had used the generic definition of an angle between n-dimensional vectors. The angle between two 2-dimensional vectors can be formally defined in terms of the angle between two n-dimensional vectors (angle) as follows:

Definition 3: *Two Dimensional Angle*
⊢ ∀ A B C. TDangle (A,B,C) =
      plus_minus (anticlockwise B (A,C)) * angle (A,B,C)

where the function plus_minus accepts a condition C and returns 1 if C is true and -1 otherwise.

Definition 4: *Plus-Minus*
⊢ ∀ plus_minus C = (if C then 1 else -1)

The the sign of the angle between two 2-dimensional vectors can be determined based on the angle of rotation between them.

4.1   Forward Kinematics

Now, we utilize the above mentioned definitions and theorem to formally verify the forward kinematic relationships, given in Equations (1) and (2). The verification of these equations is not very straightforward since all the possible scenarios for the link positions have to be considered for establishing a formal proof of the forward kinematic analysis. For example, both the links can be in the first quadrant of the Cartesian plane, as depicted in Figure 1, or one of them may lie in the first quadrant while the other one is in the third quadrant of the Cartesian plane. Our main motivation here is to verify generic theorems for kinematic analysis so that they can be used to reason about all possible scenarios.

We proceed in this direction by verifying two sub-theorems for the relationship, given in Equation (1). The first part deals with the situation when the first link lies in the upper half of the Cartesian plane while the second link and the end effector may lie any where in the Cartesian plane.

Theorem 2: *X-Component with the First Link in the Upper Half Plane*

```
⊢ ∀ A B. ~(A = vec 0) ∧ ~(B = vec 0) ∧
         anticlockwise (vec  0) (A,B) ∧
         anticlockwise (vec  0) (basis 1,A) ⇒
   (tl_manipulator A B)$1 =
     norm (A) * cos (vector_angle (basis 1) A) +
     norm (B) * cos (vector_angle A B + vector_angle (basis 1) A)
```

where A and B are the vectors representing the two links of the manipulator under consideration. The first two assumptions are used to avoid mathematical singularities. The third assumption ensures that the angle from the vector OB to OA, where O represents the origin (0,0) of the base frame, is taken in the anticlockwise direction, as the function vec converts 0 to its corresponding null vector. The fourth assumption, i.e., anticlockwise (vec 0) (basis 1,A), ensures that the vector A lies in the upper half of the Cartesian plane, i.e., in the first or second quadrant, since a point $P(x, y)$ in the Cartesian plane can be considered equivalent to the point in the complex-plane with x as its real part and y as its imaginary part. It is important to note that the allowable range of any angle in the geometry theory of Hol-Light is $[0, \pi]$. The conclusion of Theorem 2 represents Equation (1) in HOL-Light, since X$1 represents the first components of a two-dimensional vector X, the function norm accepts a vector and returns its corresponding norm or magnitude, the function vector_angle returns the angle between its two argument vectors and the function basis 1 returns a vector with magnitude 1 in the x direction only and thus the angle (vector_angle (basis 1) A) represents the angle of the vector A with the x-axis. The proof of Theorem 2 was done by splitting the main goal into eight subgoals, i.e., four corresponding to the cases where the first link is in the first quadrant and the end-effector is in one of the four quadrants one by one and the four corresponding to the case where the first link is in the second quadrant and the end-effector is in one of the four quadrants one by one. Some of these cases were verified based on contradiction while the rest were primarily verified based on Theorem 1 along with vector and geometry theoretic reasoning.

Now we consider the second case when the first link lies in the lower half of the Cartesian plane while the end effector may lie any where in the Cartesian plane. The corresponding HOL-Light theorem can be expressed as follows:

Theorem 3: *X-Component with the First Link in the Lower Half Plane*

```
⊢ ∀ A B. ~(A = vec 0) ∧ ~(B = vec 0) ∧
         anticlockwise (vec 0) (A,B) ∧
         ~(anticlockwise (vec 0) (basis 1,A)) ⇒
   (tl_manipulator A B)$1 =
     norm (A) * cos (vector_angle (basis 1) A) +
     norm (B) * cos (vector_angle A B - vector_angle (basis 1) A)
```

The only different assumption in this case is ~(anticlockwise (vec 0) (basis 1,A)), which ensures that the vector A lies in the lower half of the Cartesian plane, i.e., in the third or fourth quadrant. Now, Theorems 2 and 3 along with their counterparts with the assumption ~(anticlockwise (vec 0) (A,B)) can be utilized to verify the following theorem that covers all the possible cases for forward kinematic analysis of the x-component of the two-link manipulator (Equation 1)

Theorem 4: *X-Component of the Two-Link Manipulator*
```
⊢ ∀ A B. ~(A = vec 0) ∧ ~(B = vec 0) ⇒
    (tl_manipulator A B)$1 =
      norm (A) * cos (TDangle (basis 1,vec 0,A)) +
      norm (B) * cos (TDangle (A,vec 0,B) +
                      TDangle (basis 1,vec 0,A))
```

In a similar way, we also formally verified the forward kinematic equation for the y-component of the two-link manipulator (Equation 2) as follows:

Theorem 5: *Y-Component of the Two-Link Manipulator*
```
⊢ ∀ A B. ~(A = vec 0) ∧ ~(B = vec 0) ⇒
    (tl_manipulator A B)$2 =
      norm (A) * sin (TDangle (basis 1,vec 0,A)) +
      norm (B) * sin (TDangle (A,vec 0,B) +
                      TDangle (basis 1,vec 0,A))
```

A distinguishing characteristic of Theorems 4 and 5 is the presence of the function TDangle, which provides us with the exact information about the sign of the corresponding angle based on the placement of the two links in the Cartesian plane. This fact plays a very critical role in obtaining the right set of analysis assumptions, as will be seen in Section 5 of this paper.

4.2   Inverse Kinematics

In this subsection, we formally verify the expressions for joint angles in terms of the Cartesian position of the end-effector. The expression for the angle θ_2, which is the phase angle of the second link with respect to the reference frame of the first link of the two-link manipulator, as shown of Figure 1, can be verified in three main steps corresponding to Equations (3), (4) and (5). We verified the expression, given in Equation (3), as the following theorem,

Theorem 6: *Cos θ_2*
```
⊢ ∀ A B. ~(A = vec 0) ∧ ~(B = vec 0) ∧ ~(A + B = vec 0) ⇒
        cos (vector_angle A B) =
            ((((tl_manipulator A B)$1) pow 2) +
            (((tl_manipulator A B)$2) pow 2) - (norm (A) pow 2) -
                (norm (B) pow 2)) / (2 * norm (A) * norm (B))
```

where A and B are the vectors representing the two links of the manipulator under consideration. Besides the vectors A and B being non-null, their sum is also assumed to be non-null in this theorem. This assumption is used to make sure that we do not have the case where both the vectors are equal in magnitude but opposite in direction. Based on our formal definition of the two link manipulator, (tl_manilpulator A B)$1 represents the x-coordinate and (tl_manilpulator A B)$2 represents the y-coordinate of the end-effector. The function pow is used for real power in HOL-Light. The proof of the above theorem was primarily based on the Law of Cosines, which is available in the geometry theory of HOL-Light.

Similarly, the expression of Equation (4) can be verified as the following theorem:

Theorem 7: *Sin θ_2*
⊢ ∀ A   B. sin (vector_angle   A   B) =
         sqrt(1 - cos (vector_angle   A   B) pow 2)

where sqrt represents the HOL-Light function for square root. The proof of this theorem was also primarily based on some geometry theoretic reasoning and the existing theorems of the HOL-Light geometry theory were very helpful in this regard. Theorems 6 and 7 can now be used to verify our final results, i.e. Equation (5), as the following theorem.

Theorem 8: *θ_2*
⊢ ∀ A B. ~(A = vec   0) ∧ ~(B = vec   0) ∧ ~(A + B = vec 0) ⇒
         vector_angle   A   B =
          atn ((sqrt (1 - (cos (vector_angle A B) pow 2))) /
              cos   (vector_angle   A   B))

where atn represent the arc-tangent function in HOL-Light. The proof scripts for the definitions and theorems, presented in this section, is available at [3] and is composed of approximately 15,000 lines of code, which took about 700 man-hours of development time by a new HOL-Light user. The development time includes the time spent to learn the art of formal reasoning and to understand the definitions and theorems available in the multivariate and geometry theories of HOL-Light. We found the generic nature of the geometry theory, formalized in HOL-Light, very useful since most of the commonly used results can be found there and thus directly used. A significant portion of our proof script is composed of mapping between Cartesian to Polar coordinate system, which was required because of the referencing to the base frame for both links of the manipulator. These mappings had to be interactively done because of the different parameters and thus conditions involved. Moreover, in all the proofs we had to handle the placement of the links in each quadrant separately, which also required a considerable amount of human guidance.

The main benefit of the formalization, presented in this section, is that it can be built upon to model robotic structure and perform the kinematic analysis or formalize other kinematic analysis related foundations, which will in turn enhance the capabilities of the proposed formal kinematic analysis approach. To demonstrate the utilization and practical effectiveness of our results, we utilize them next to conduct the formal kinematic analysis of a biped robot.

5   Application: Biped Robot

A biped robot [12] can be simply defined as a two-legged walking robot. The biped robots usually exhibit human-like mobility and have found to be more efficient than the conventional wheeled robots for maneuvering fields with ladders, stairs, and uneven surfaces. The design and analysis of efficient biped robotic systems has attracted the attention of many researchers and it has been used as a classical case study for many domains in robotics, which is the main reason why we have also chosen to use it as an application to demonstrate the effectiveness of the proposed formal kinematic analysis approach.

The biped robot, depicted in Figure 3, consists of five links, namely the torso ($l3$), and the upper legs (thighs), i.e, $l2$ and $l4$, and the lower legs, i.e., $l1$ and $l5$. These links are connected via four rotating joints (two hip and two knee), which are considered to be friction free and each one is driven by an independent DC motor. The two hip joints can be considered as one joint as the effect of forces is ignored while conducting the kinematic analysis.

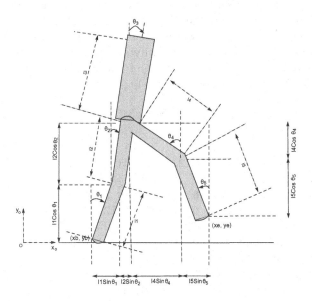

Fig. 3. Biped Robot [12]

The first step in the proposed formal kinematic analysis approach is to construct a formal model of the given system in higher-order logic. The definition of the two-link manipulator plays a vital role in this regard as it can be used to model most of the robot manipulators. The given biped robot can be formalized as a two-link planar manipulator where each link is itself a two-link planar manipulator, since both of the legs always move in the same plane:

Definition 5: *Biped Robot*

⊢ ∀ A B C D. biped A B C D =
       tl_manipulator (tl_manipulator A B) (tl_manipulator C D)

It is important to note that only four out of the five links are considered in the above definition. The reason being that these four links are the ones that can alter the dexterity and precision of the biped robot. Moreover, the point (x_b, y_b) of Figure 3 has been taken as the origin $(0,0)$ in our formalization.

The next step in the proposed kinematic analysis approach is to formalize the properties of interest as higher-order-logic proof goals. In the case of the biped robot, we are interested in verifying the forward kinematic equations:

$$x_e = x_b + l_1 \sin \theta_1 + l_2 \sin \theta_2 + l_4 \sin \theta_4 + l_5 \sin \theta_5 \tag{7}$$

$$y_e = y_b + l_1 \cos \theta_1 + l_2 \cos \theta_2 - l_4 \cos \theta_4 - l_5 \cos \theta_5 \tag{8}$$

corresponding to the x and y components of leg $l5$ of the biped robot, which have been verified using paper-and-pencil proof method in [12]. Besides formalizing these equations, we also need to mention the required assumptions in the proof goals but it is often the case that all the assumptions are not known upfront and we only add the obvious ones. However, the subgoals generated during the proof process provide very useful hints for identifying any missing assumptions, which may be added to the goal after confirmation from the mechanical designers. This way, we verified Equation (7) as the following theorem.

Theorem 9: *x-component of the Biped Robot*

⊢ ∀ 11 12 14 15.
~(11 = vec 0) ∧ ~(12 = vec 0) ∧ ~(14 = vec 0) ∧ ~(15 = vec 0) ∧
  anticlockwise (vec 0) (11,12) ∧ anticlockwise (vec 0) (15,14) ∧
        anticlockwise (vec 0) (basis 1,11) ∧
        anticlockwise (vec 0) (11,basis 2) ∧
        anticlockwise (vec 0) (basis 1,12) ∧
        anticlockwise (vec 0) (12,basis 2) ∧
        anticlockwise (vec 0) (basis 1,15) ∧
        anticlockwise (vec 0) (basis 2,15) ∧
        anticlockwise (vec 0) (basis 2,14) ∧
        ~ collinear {basis 1, vec 0, 15} ∧
        ~ collinear {basis 1, vec 0, 12} ∧
        ~ collinear {basis 2, vec 0, 14} ⇒
        (biped 11 12 14 15)$1 =
           norm (11) * sin (vector_angle (basis 2) 11) +
           norm (12) * sin (vector_angle (basis 2) 12) -
           norm (14) * sin (vector_angle (basis 2) 14) -
           norm (15) * sin (vector_angle (basis 2) 15)

where **basis 2** represents the y-axis of the Cartesian plane. The first four assumptions assure that all of the links must have non-zero lengths. The next two provide the angle measuring conventions between the links of each leg while the next eight assumptions provide the orientations of the angles, given in Figure 3, under which we are interested in analyzing the biped robot. For example, the assumptions `anticlockwise (vec 0) (basis 1,11)` and `anticlockwise (vec 0) (11,basis 2)` ensure that the angle θ_1 of leg $l1$ of the robot is considered in the clockwise direction from the x-axis of the base frame and in the anticlockwise direction with the y-axis of the base frame, or in other words that θ_1 lies in the first quadrant. All of the above mentioned assumptions are obvious and were used while defining the proof goal. While the next three, involving the function `collinear` are not so straightforward and thus were not known before the formal verification of the above theorem. These assumptions assure that the legs $l5$ and $l2$ cannot completely align with the x-axis of the base frame and the leg $l4$ cannot align with the y-axis of the base frame. These three assumptions were identified during the formal verification process of Theorem 9 in HOL-Light. These assumptions constitute an essential requirement for Equation (7) to hold and interestingly were not mentioned in the paper-and-pencil based proof of that equation given in [12]. The conclusion of Theorem 9 represents the statement of Equation (7) but instead of having all positive terms added together, as is the case in Equation (7), has the addition of two positive and two negative terms. Upon noticing this difference, we double checked our formalization and assumptions but everything was found to be consistent with the kinematic diagram of the biped robot, given in Figure (3), which was also the starting point of the paper-and-pencil proof method based kinematic analysis of the biped robot from where Equation (7) was verified [12]. Upon further investigation, we found Equation (7) to be erroneous. The problem may be an outcome of a human error during the paper-and-pencil based analysis or it may have occurred because of an incorrect swapping of the signs of the terms of Equations (7) and (8) in the original paper [12] as we also found a discrepancy in Equation (8), which has been correctly verified under the same assumptions as follows:

Theorem 10: *y-component of the Biped Robot*
⊢ ∀ 11 12 14 15.
~(11 = vec 0) ∧ ~(12 = vec 0) ∧ ~(14 = vec 0) ∧ ~(15 = vec 0) ∧
 anticlockwise (vec 0) (11,12) ∧ anticlockwise (vec 0) (15,14) ∧
   anticlockwise (vec 0) (basis 1,11) ∧
   anticlockwise (vec 0) (11,basis 2) ∧
   anticlockwise (vec 0) (basis 1,12) ∧
   anticlockwise (vec 0) (12,basis 2) ∧
   anticlockwise (vec 0) (basis 1,15) ∧
   anticlockwise (vec 0) (basis 2,15) ∧
   anticlockwise (vec 0) (basis 2,14) ∧
   ~ collinear {basis 1, vec 0, 15} ∧
   ~ collinear {basis 1, vec 0, 12} ∧
   ~ collinear {basis 2, vec 0, 14} ⇒
    (biped 11 12 14 15)$2 =
     norm (11) * cos (vector_angle (basis 2) 11) +

```
norm (12) * cos (vector_angle (basis 2) 12) +
norm (14) * cos (vector_angle (basis 2) 14) +
norm (15) * cos (vector_angle (basis 2) 15)
```

Nonetheless, the identification of the problem identifies the dire need of a sound analysis technique in the domain of kinematic analysis of robotic applications, which is quite cumbersome and thus prone to human errors if done using paper-and-pencil proof method because of the consideration of all the possible scenarios. The proofs of Theorems 9 and 10 were very straightforward and primarily based on Theorems 5 and 6 and the proof script consists of approximately 200 lines of code [3], which clearly indicates the usefulness of our work in the formal kinematic analysis of real-world applications.

It is important to note that, besides the identification of a bug in the paper-and-pencil based proof method of kinematic analysis of the biped robot, another distinguishing feature of the above theorems, when compared with the corresponding equations verified by paper-and-pencil proof methods [12], is the exhaustive set of assumptions that accompany them. Paper-and-pencil proof methods, simulation and numerical method based approach cannot ascertain the explicit availability of all of the required assumptions for the analysis even though failing to abide by any one of these assumptions may lead to erroneous system designs, which in turn even result in disastrous consequences in the case of safety-critical systems. On the other hand, given the intrinsic soundness of theorem proving, all the required assumptions are always guaranteed to be available along with the formally verified proofs.

6 Conclusion

This paper advocates the usage of higher-order-logic theorem proving for kinematic analysis, which is an essential design step for all robotic manipulators. Due to the high expressiveness of the underlying logic, we can formally model the geometrical relationships between the mechanical links and joints in their true form, i.e., without compromising on the precision of the model. Similarly, the inherent soundness of theorem proving guarantees correctness of analysis and ensures the availability of all pre-conditions of the analysis as assumptions of the formally verified theorems. To the best of our knowledge, these features are not shared by any other existing computer-based kinematic analysis technique and thus the proposed approach can be very useful for the kinematic analysis of safety-critical robots.

The main challenge in the proposed approach is the enormous amount of user intervention required due to the undecidable nature of the logic. We propose to overcome this limitation by formalizing kinematic analysis foundations and verifying their associated properties. As a first step towards this direction, this paper presents the formalization of forward and inverse kinematic analysis of a two-link planar manipulator, which can be built upon to model many practically used robotic manipulators. Based on this work, we are able to conduct the formal kinematic analysis of a biped robot in a very straightforward way. The formal analysis highlighted some of the key missing assumptions in the corresponding paper-and-pencil based analysis of the same problem [12], which clearly indicates the dire need of using sound methods for kinematic analysis and usefulness of the ideas presented in this paper.

This paper opens the doors towards a novel and promising usage of theorem proving. The formal kinematic analysis of many other safety-critical robots can be performed. A classical example would be the widely used Selective Compliant Assembly Robot Arm (SCARA) [4]. Formal reasoning support for other motion related parameters, such as displacement, rotation, speed, velocity and acceleration, may also be developed by using our results along with the topological and analytic foundations for vectors available in Hol-Light. By extending our coordinate frame from 2D to 3D, we are also working on the formal verification of the Denavit Hartenberg (DH) parameters [5], which are based on the convention of attaching the coordinate frame to spatial linkages. This verification will pave the way for conducting the formal kinematic analysis for a much wider range of robotic applications.

Acknowledgements. We would like to thank Dr. John Harrison from Intel Corporation for directing us to the definition of the function `anticlockwise` and the associated Theorem 1, which was widely used in our development.

References

1. Avigad, J., Dean, E., Mumma, J.: A Formal System for Euclid's Elements. Review of Symbolic Logic 2(4), 700–768 (2009)
2. Becker, B., Cardelli, L., Hermanns, H., Tahar, S.: Abstracts collection. In: Verification over Discrete-Continuous Boundaries. Dagstuhl Seminar Proceedings, vol. 10271. Schloss Dagstuhl - Leibniz-Zentrum fuer Informatik, Germany (2010)
3. Binyameen, M.: Formal Kinematic Analysis of the Two-Link Planar Manipulator using HOL-Light (2013), http://save.seecs.nust.edu.pk/students/binyameen/tlpm.html
4. Chivarov, N., Galabov, V.: Kinematics of Scara Robots. In: Problems of Engineering Cybernetics and Robotics, pp. 51–59 (2008)
5. Denavit, J., Hartenberg, R.S.: A Kinematic Notation for Lower-Pair Mechanisms based on Matrices. Trans. ASME Journal of Applied Mechanics 23, 215–221 (1955)
6. Esposito, J.M., Moonzoo, K.: Using Formal Modeling with an Automated Analysis Tool to Design and Parametrically Analyze a Multirobot Coordination Protocol: A Case Study. IEEE Transactions on Systems, Man and Cybernetics, Part A: Systems and Humans 37(3), 285–297 (2007)
7. Fryziel, L., Fried, G., Djouani, K., Iqbal, S., Amirat, Y.: A Kinematic Analysis for a Hybrid Continuum Active Catheter. In: Proceedings of the 7th France-Japon Congress 5th Europe-Asia Congress on Mechatronics (MECHATRONICS 2008), Le Grand Bornand, France (2008)
8. Haddadin, S., Albu-Schäffer, A., Hirzinger, G.: Requirements for Safe Robots: Measurements, Analysis and New Insights. International Journal of Robotics Research 28(11-12), 1507–1527 (2009)

9. Harrison, J.: The HOL Light Theory of Euclidean Space. Automated Reasoning 50(2), 173–190 (2013)
10. Hurmuzlu, Y., Ganot, F., Brogliato, B.: Modeling, Stability and Control of Biped Robots: general framework. Automatica 10 (2004)
11. Iqbal, S., Mohammed, S., Amirat, Y.: A Guaranteed Approach for Kinematic Analysis of Continuum Robot Based Catheter. In: Robotics and Biomimetics, pp. 1573–1578 (2009)
12. Lum, H.K., Zirbi, M., Soh, Y.C.: Planning and Control of a Biped Robot. International Journal of Engineering Science 37, 1319–1349 (1999)
13. Merlet, J.P.: A Formal Numerical Approach for Robust In-Workspace Singularity Detection. IEEE Transactions on Robotics 23, 393–402 (2007)
14. Myszka, D.: Machines and Mechanisms: Applied Kinematic Analysis, 4th edn. Prentice Hall (2011)
15. Petrovic, D., Maric, F.: Formalizing Analytic Geometries. In: Automated Deduction in Geometry (2012)
16. Pham, T.-M., Bertot, Y., Narboux, J.: A Coq-based Library for Interactive and Automated Theorem Proving in Plane Geometry. In: Murgante, B., Gervasi, O., Iglesias, A., Taniar, D., Apduhan, B.O. (eds.) ICCSA 2011, Part IV. LNCS, vol. 6785, pp. 368–383. Springer, Heidelberg (2011)
17. Proetzsch, M., Berns, K., Schuele, T., Schneider, K.: Formal Verification of Safety Behaviours of the Outdoor Robot RAVON. In: Informatics in Control, Automation and Robotics, pp. 157–164 (2007)
18. Ras, J., Cheng, A.M.K.: On Formal Verification of Toyota's Electronic Throttle Controller. In: Systems Conference, SysCon (2011)
19. Shores, B.E., Minor, M.A.: Design, Kinematic Analysis, and Quasi-steady Control of a Morphic Rolling Disk Biped Climbing Robot. In: Robotics and Automation, pp. 2721–2726 (2005)
20. Sloth, C.: Formal Verification of Continuous Systems. PhD thesis, Aalborg University (2013)
21. Sloth, C., Wisniewski, R.: Abstractions for Mechanical Systems. IFAC Workshop Series, pp. 96–101 (2012)
22. Spong, M.W., Hutchinson, S., Vidyasagar, M.: Robot Modeling and Control, 1st edn. Wiley (2005)
23. Walter, D., Täubig, H., Lüth, C.: Experiences in applying Formal Verification in Robotics. In: Schoitsch, E. (ed.) SAFECOMP 2010. LNCS, vol. 6351, pp. 347–360. Springer, Heidelberg (2010)
24. Wang, Y., Chirikjian, G.S.: Propagation of Errors in Hybrid Manipulators. In: International Conference on Robotics and Automation, pp. 1848–1853 (2006)
25. Wolfram Research. Mathematica Mechanical Systems: Kinematic and Dynamic Analysis in Mathematica, 3rd edn. (2005), http://www.wolfram.com
26. Yoshikawa, T.: Manipulability of Robotic Mechanisms. The International Journal of Robotics Research 4(2), 3–9 (1985)

Formal Modelling
of Resilient Data Storage in Cloud

Inna Pereverzeva[1,2], Linas Laibinis[1], Elena Troubitsyna[1],
Markus Holmberg[3], and Mikko Pöri[3]

[1] Åbo Akademi University, Turku, Finland
[2] Turku Centre for Computer Science, Turku, Finland
[3] F-Secure, Helsinki, Finland
{inna.pereverzeva,linas.laibinis,elena.troubitsyna}@abo.fi,
{ext-markus.holmberg,mikko.pori}@f-secure.com

Abstract. Reliable and highly performant handling of large data stores constitutes one of the major challenges of cloud computing. In this paper, we propose a formalisation of a cloud solution implemented by F-Secure – a provider of secure data storage services. The solution is based on massive replication and the write-ahead logging mechanism. To achieve high performance, the company has abandoned a transactional model. We formally derive a model of the proposed architectural solution and verify data integrity and consistency properties under possible failure scenarios. The proposed approach allows the designers to formally define and verify essential characteristics of architectures for handling large data stores.

Keywords: Formal modelling, Event-B, refinement, replication, data integrity, large data stores.

1 Introduction

Rapid development of digital technology puts a high demand on reliable handling and storage of large volumes of data. It is forecasted that worldwide consumer digital storage needs will grow from 329 exabytes in 2011 to 4.1 zettabytes in 2016 [3]. Often algorithms for data storage in cloud reuse the ones that have been proposed for databases. The transactional model adopted in databases guarantees ACID properties – Atomicity, Consistency, Isolation and Durability, and as such delivers high resilience guarantees. However, in a pursue of high performance, cloud data storages rarely rely on the transactional model and hence deliver weaker guarantees regarding data integrity. In this paper, we undertake a formal study of data integrity and consistency properties that can be guaranteed by several different architectures of cloud data stores.

Our work is motivated by a cloud solution developed by F-Secure – a provider of secure data storage services. To achieve a high degree of fault tolerance, the company has combined write-ahead logging (WAL) [7,10] – a widely used mechanism for database error recovery – and massive data replication. As such, this

L. Groves and J. Sun (Eds.): ICFEM 2013, LNCS 8144, pp. 363–379, 2013.
© Springer-Verlag Berlin Heidelberg 2013

combination gives very high resilience guarantees (usually in the form of eventual consistency). However, these guarantees are different in non-transactional settings typical for cloud. Moreover, data integrity and consistency properties vary in the synchronous, semi-synchronous and asynchronous architectures used for data replication. Therefore, it is useful to rigorously define and compare the properties that can be ensured by different solutions.

In this paper, we use the Event-B method and the associated Rodin platform to formally model write-ahead logging in replicated data stores. Event-B [1] is a formal framework that is particularly suitable for the development of distributed systems. System development starts from an abstract specification that is transformed into a detailed specification in a number of correctness-preserving refinement steps. In this paper, we separately model the synchronous, semi-synchronous and asynchronous replication architectures. Event-B and the Rodin platform [11] allow us to explicitly define the data integrity and consistency properties as model invariants and compare them in all three models. We believe that the proposed approach allows the designers to gain formally grounded insights on properties of cloud data stores and their resilience.

The paper is structured as follows: in Section 2 we give a brief overview of the Event-B formalism. In Section 3 we describe the WAL mechanism as well as the general architecture of a cloud data store. In Section 4 we present a formal development of the asynchronous replication model. In Section 5, we briefly (due to similarity with the asynchronous model) overview the models for the synchronous and semi-synchronous architectures and compare the data consistency properties of three replication modes. Finally, in Section 6 we overview the related work, discuss the obtained results and outline future work.

2   Modelling in Event-B

Event-B is a state-based formal approach that promotes the correct-by-construction development paradigm and formal verification by theorem proving. In Event-B, a system model is specified using the notion of an *abstract state machine* [1]. An abstract state machine encapsulates the model state, represented as a collection of variables, and defines operations on the state, i.e., it describes the dynamic behaviour of a modelled system. The variables are strongly typed by the constraining predicates that together with other important system properties are defined as model *invariants*. Usually, a machine has an accompanying component, called a *context*, which includes user-defined sets, constants and their properties given as a list of model axioms.

The dynamic behaviour of the system is defined by a collection of atomic *events*. Generally, an event has the following form:

$$e \ \widehat{=} \ \textbf{any} \ a \ \textbf{where} \ G_e \ \textbf{then} \ R_e \ \textbf{end},$$

where e is the event's name, a is the list of local variables, and (the event *guard*) G_e is a predicate over the model state. The body of an event is defined by a *multiple* (possibly nondeterministic) assignment to the system variables. In Event-B, this assignment is semantically defined as the next-state relation R_e.

The event guard defines the conditions under which the event is *enabled*, i.e., its body can be executed. If several events are enabled at the same time, any of them can be chosen for execution nondeterministically.

Event-B employs a top-down refinement-based approach to system development. A development starts from an abstract specification that nondeterministically models the most essential functional requirements. In a sequence of refinement steps we gradually reduce nondeterminism and introduce detailed design decisions. In particular, we can add new events, refine old events as well as replace abstract variables by their concrete counterparts, i.e., perform *data refinement*. In the latter case, we need to define *gluing invariants*, which define the relationship between the abstract and concrete variables. The proof of data refinement is often supported by supplying *witnesses* – the concrete values for the replaced abstract variables. Witnesses are specified in the event clause **with**.

The consistency of Event-B models, i.e., verification of model well-formedness, invariant preservation as well as correctness of refinement steps, is demonstrated by discharging the relevant proof obligations. The Rodin platform [11] provides an automated support for modelling and verification. In particular, it automatically generates the required proof obligations and attempts to discharge them.

Event-B adopts an event-based modelling style that facilitate a correct-by-construction development of a distributed system. Since cloud data storage is a large-scale distributed system, Event-B is a natural choice for its formal modelling and verification. In the next section, we give an overview of the general data storage architecture that we will formally develop in Event-B.

3   Resilient Cloud Data Storage

Essentially, a cloud data storage can be seen as a networked online data storage available for its clients as a cloud service. Data are stored in virtualised data stores (pools) usually hosted by third parties. Physically, the data stores may span across multiple distributed servers. Cloud data storage providers should ensure that their customers can safely and easily store their content and access it from their computers and mobile devices. Therefore, there is a clear demand to achieve both resilience and high performance in handling data.

Write-ahead logging (WAL) is a standard data base technique for ensuring data integrity. The main principle of WAL is to apply the requested changes to data files only after they have been logged, i.e., after the log has been stored in the persistent storage (disk). The WAL mechanism ensures fault-tolerance because, in case of a crash, the system would be able to recover using the log. Moreover, the WAL mechanism helps to optimise performance, since only the log file (rather than all the data changes) should be written to the permanent storage to guarantee that a transaction is (eventually) committed.

The WAL mechanism has been thoroughly studied under the reliable persistent storage assumption, i.e., if the disk containing the log never crashes. However, in the cloud implementing such a highly-reliable data store is rather unfeasible. Therefore, to ensure fault tolerance, F-Secure has proposed a solution that combines WAL with replication. The resulting system – distributed data store (DDS) – consists of a number of nodes distributed across different physical locations. One of the nodes, called *master*, is appointed to serve incoming data requests from DDS clients and report on success or failure of such requests. As a result, for instance, the client may receive an acknowledgment that the data have been successfully stored in the system. The remaining nodes, called *standby nodes*, contain replicas of the stored data.

Each request received by the master is translated into a number of reading and writing commands. These commands are first recorded in the *master log* and then applied to the stored data. After this, an acknowledgement is sent to the client. (In the non-replicated version of WAL widely used in the databases, an acknowledgement to the client is sent already after the request is written in the log). The standby nodes are constantly monitoring and streaming the master log records into their own logs, before applying them to their persistent data in the same way. Essentially, the standby nodes are continually trying to "catch up" with the master. If the master crashes, one of the standby nodes is appointed to be the master in its stead. At this point, the appointed standby effectively becomes the new master and starts serving all data requests.

DDS can implement different models (architectures) of logging. In the asynchronous model, the client request is acknowledged after the master node has performed the required modifications in its persistent storage. The second option – the cascade master-standby – is a semi-synchronous architecture. The client receives an acknowledgement after both the master and its warm standby (called upper standby) has performed the necessary actions. Finally, in the synchronous model, only after all replica nodes have written into their persistent storage, i.e., fully synchronised with the master node, the transaction can be committed. Obviously, such different logging models deliver different resilience guarantees.

In our formal modelling, we aim at formally defining and comparing data integrity and consistency properties that can be ensured by each architecture. In the next section, we present a development of the asynchronous architecture.

4   Modelling the Asynchronous Architecture

In the asynchronous model of replication, the standby nodes may stream the master log records only after the required changes have been committed and reported to the client. If the master crashes shortly after committing the required modifications, some changes will not be replicated thus leading to an inconsistent system state. In particular, this might happen because a standby node has not yet received (streamed) all the master log records when the master failed. To minimise such a data loss, the node that has the freshest (and hence the most complete) copy of the master log is chosen to become the next master. A graphical representation of the system architecture is shown in Fig.1.

Abstract Specification. The initial model – the machine Replication1_m0 abstractly describes the behaviour of the master node – receiving and processing of the received requests. The overall model structure is given on Fig.2.

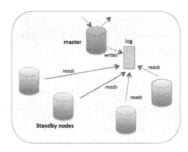

Fig. 1. Asynchronous model

The variable *comp*, *comp* ⊆ *COMP*, represents the dynamic set of active system nodes (data stores), where *COMP* is a set (type) of all available data stores. The variable *master*, such that *master* ∈ *comp*, represents the master node. The other variables *buffer*, *inprocess* and *processed* represent the received data requests at different stages of their processing by the master. They are modelled as disjoint sets of the abstract data type *REQUESTS*. In particular, the variable *buffer* stores the requests that have been received by the master and are waiting to be handled. The variable *inprocess* contains the requests that the master node is currently processing, while the variable *processed* keeps the requests that are completed and acknowledged to the client.

The event RequestIn specifies arriving of a new request to the master. Processing of the received requests and sending notifications to the client are modelled

---

Machine Replication1_m0
Variables *comp, master, buffer, inprocess, processed*
Invariants *comp* ⊆ *COMP* ∧ *master* ∈ *comp* ∧ *buffer* ⊆ *REQUESTS* ...
Events

RequestIn ≙   // arriving of a new request
  any *r*
  where *r* ∈ *REQUESTS* ∧ *r* ∉ *buffer* ∧ *r* ∉ *inprocess* ∧ *r* ∉ *processed*
  then   *buffer* := *buffer* ∪ {*r*}
  end

Process ...   // request processing

RequestOut ≙   // completion of a request
  any *r*
  where *r* ∈ *inprocess*
  then   *processed* := *processed* ∪ {*r*} ‖ *inprocess* := *inprocess* \ {*r*}
  end

ChangeMaster ≙   // changing the master
  any *new_master, n_buffer, n_inprocess, n_processed*
  where
       new_master ∈ *comp* ∧ *new_master* ≠ *master* ∧ *n_inprocess* ∩ *n_buffer* = ∅ ∧
       n_inprocess ∩ *n_processed* = ∅ ∧ *n_processed* ∩ *n_buffer* = ∅ ∧
       n_buffer ∪ *n_inprocess* ∪ *n_processed* ⊆ *buffer* ∪ *inprocess* ∪ *processed*
  then
       master := *new_master* ‖ *buffer* := *n_buffer* ‖ *inprocess* := *n_inprocess* ‖
       processed := *n_processed* ‖ *comp* := *comp* \ {*master*}
  end

CompActivation ...   // activation of a new system component
CompDeactivation ...   // deactivation of a system component

Fig. 2. Asynchronous model: the abstract model

by the events Process and RequestOut respectively. The events update the variables *buffer, inprocess* and *processed* to reflect the progress in request handling.

The event ChangeMaster models a crash of a master and selection of a new master. One of the remaining nodes is non-deterministically chosen to become a new master, while the old master is removed from the set of active nodes. Due to possible data loss, the requests being handled by the new master may be only a subset of those of the failed master. This is reflected by the guard condition:

$$n\_buffer \cup n\_inprocess \cup n\_processed \subseteq buffer \cup inprocess \cup processed,$$

where *n_buffer, n_inprocess*, and *n_processed* are the corresponding data structures of the new master.

Finally, the last two events, CompActivation and CompDeactivation, model a possibility to add new data storage nodes from the cloud and remove some currently active nodes from the system respectively. Only standby nodes can be activated and deactivated in this way.

First Refinement. In the first refinement step (defined by the machine Replication1_ref1), we extend the abstract model by explicitly representing the behaviour of the standby nodes.

To accomplish this, we lift the abstract variables *buffer, inprocess, processed* to become node-dependent functions. In Event-B, this is achieved by data refinement that replaces these variables with the new variables *comp_buffer, comp_inprocess* and *comp_processed*. The following gluing invariants are defined to to prove correctness of data refinement:

$$comp\_buffer \in comp \rightarrow \mathbb{P}(REQUESTS) \wedge comp\_buffer(master) = buffer \wedge$$

$$comp\_inprocess \in comp \rightarrow \mathbb{P}(REQUESTS) \wedge comp\_inprocess(master) = inprocess \wedge$$

$$comp\_processed \in comp \rightarrow \mathbb{P}(REQUESTS) \wedge comp\_processed(master) = processed.$$

The overview of the refined model is presented in the Fig. 3. The set of model events includes the refined versions of the abstract events (RequestInMst, ProcessMst, RequestOutMst, ChangeMaster, CompActivation, and CompDeactivation) as well as new events describing the behaviour of standby nodes.

We refine the event ChangeMaster to a deterministic procedure of choosing the node with the freshest log as a new master to the failed master. We formulate this condition as a new guard of the event ChangeMaster in the following way:

$$(\forall c \cdot c \in comp \wedge c \neq new\_master \wedge c \neq master \Rightarrow$$

$$comp\_buffer(c) \cup comp\_inprocess(c) \cup comp\_processed(c) \subseteq$$

$$comp\_buffer(new\_master) \cup comp\_inprocess(new\_master) \cup$$

$$comp\_processed(new\_master)). \quad (1)$$

The standby nodes are continuously streaming the master log. Essentially, this means that, as soon as the master node completes the request(s), i.e., performs the required modifications in its persistent storage, the standby nodes start copying the corresponding entries in the master log. This behaviour is modelled by the new event RequestInStb. Similarly as for the master node, the processing of requests and their completion by the standby nodes are respectively modelled by the events ProcessStb and RequestOutStb.

```
Machine Replication1_ref1 refines Replication1_m0
Variables comp, master, comp_buffer, comp_inprocess, comp_processed, failed, in_transit
Invariants ...
Events
RequestInMst refines RequestIn  ...            // arriving of a new request to the master
ProcessMst refines Process  ...                // request processing by the master
RequestOutMst refines RequestOut  ...          // completion of a request by the master
RequestInStb ≙  ...                            // reading the master by a standby
  any r
  where  c ∈ comp ∧ c ≠ master ∧ r ∈ comp_processed(master) ∧
         r ∉ comp_buffer(c) ∧ r ∉ comp_inprocess(c) ∧ r ∉ comp_processed(c)
         c ∉ failed ∧ master ∉ failed
  then   comp_buffer(c) := comp_buffer(c) ∪ {r}
  end
ProcessStb  ...                                // request processing by a standby
RequestOutStb  ...                             // completion of a request by a standby
ChangeMaster refines ChangeMaster ≙            // changing the master
  any new_master
  where  new_master ∈ comp ∧ new_master ≠ master ∧
         master ∈ failed ∧ new_master ∉ failed ∧
         (∀c·c ∈ comp ∧ c ≠ new_master ∧ c ≠ master ⇒
              comp_buffer(c) ∪ comp_inprocess(c) ∪ comp_processed(c) ⊆
                     comp_buffer(new_master) ∪ comp_inprocess(new_master) ∪
                     comp_processed(new_master))
  with   n_buffer = comp_buffer(new_master)
         n_inprocess = comp_inprocess(new_master)
         n_processed = comp_processed(new_master)
  then   master := new_master ‖ comp_buffer := {master} ◁ comp_buffer ‖
         comp_inprocess := {master} ◁ comp_inprocess ‖
         comp_processed := {master} ◁ comp_processed ‖
         comp := comp \ {master} ‖ failed := failed \ {master} ‖ in_transit := TRUE
  end
CompActivation ...      // activation of a new component into the system
CompDeactivation ...    // deactivation of a component from the system
CompFailure ...         // modelling a component failure
CompStbRecovery ...     // recovery of a standby
TransitionOver ...      // all the standby nodes have only the requests already processed by
the new master
```

Fig. 3. Asynchronous model: the first refinement

In our model, we assume that the nodes might become temporary unavailable (i.e., crush and recover). The new variable *failed*, $failed \subseteq comp$, is introduced to store such failed nodes. The new event CompFailure and CompStbRecovery model possible node crashes and recoveries correspondingly.

Now we are ready to formulate and prove some data consistency properties expressing the relationships between the requests handled by the master and those handled by the standby nodes. Since any standby node is continuously copying the master log, we can say that any standby node is logically "behind" the master node. Mathematically, this means that all the standby requests (no matter what stage of processing they are in) are subset of those of the master node. Moreover, all the requests that are now handled by a standby node should have been already completed by the master before. We can formulate these two properties as the following system invariants:

$$(\forall c·c \in comp \land c \neq master \Rightarrow$$
$$comp\_buffer(c) \cup comp\_inprocess(c) \cup comp\_processed(c) \subseteq$$
$$comp\_buffer(master) \cup comp\_inprocess(master) \cup comp\_processed(master)), \quad (2)$$

$$(\forall c \cdot c \in comp \land c \neq master \Rightarrow$$
$$comp\_buffer(c) \cup comp\_inprocess(c) \cup comp\_processed(c) \subseteq$$
$$comp\_processed(master)). \quad (3)$$

As it turns out, the last property cannot be proven as an (unconditional) invariant of the system. Indeed, it can be violated right after one of the standby nodes is appointed the new master. A short transitional period may be needed for the new master to "catch up" with some of the standby nodes that got ahead by handling the requests still not committed by the new master. It is easy to show termination of this transitional period, since all such standby nodes are blocked from reading any new requests from the master until the master catches up with them by processing its requests.

We can formally model this transitional stage by introducing the variable $in\_transit$, $in\_transit \in BOOL$. The variable obtains the value $TRUE$ when a new master is appointed, and reobtains the value $FALSE$ (in the new event TransitionOver) when all the remaining standby nodes have the requests already processed by the new master.

Then we can reformulate the property (3) as a system invariant and prove its preservation:

$$in\_transit = FALSE \Rightarrow (\forall c \cdot c \in comp \land c \neq master \Rightarrow$$
$$comp\_buffer \cup comp\_inprocess(c) \cup comp\_processed(c) \subseteq$$
$$comp\_processed(master)). \quad (4)$$

Second Refinement. In the previous refinement step we introduced the standby nodes and their interactions with the master. We also modelled how the received data requests are transferred through the different processing stages on the master and standby sides. The variables $buffer$, $inprocess$ and $processed$ were used to store incoming, processing and processed requests. The goal of our second refinement step is explicitly model the WAL mechanism and the resulting interdependencies between the master and standby logs.

Mathematically, any log can be represented as a sequence, i.e., as a function of the type

$$any\_log \in 1..k \rightarrow ELEMENTS,$$

where k is the index of the last written element.

In our case, we want to store in the node log all the requests – received, being processed, or completed. This can be represented as partitioning of the component log into three separate parts. To achieve that, we introduce three variables $index\_written$, $index\_inprocess$, and $index\_processed$:

$$index\_written \in comp \rightarrow NAT, \ index\_inprocess \in comp \rightarrow NAT,$$
$$index\_processed \in comp \rightarrow NAT,$$

such that

$$\forall c \cdot c \in comp \Rightarrow index\_inprocess(c) \leq index\_written(c),$$
$$\forall c \cdot c \in comp \Rightarrow index\_processed(c) \leq index\_inprocess(c).$$

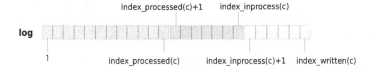

Fig. 4. The log partition

For any component c, $index\_written(c)$ defines the index of the last written log entry, $index\_inprocess(c)$ – the index of the last request being processed, and $index\_processed(c)$ – the index of the last completed request. Graphically, this can be represented as shown in Fig.4.

Then the logs of all the components can be defined as the following function:

$$log \in comp \rightarrow (NAT \nrightarrow REQUESTS),$$

such that

$$\forall c \in comp \cdot \mathbf{dom}(log(c)) \ = \ 1 .. index\_written(c),$$

where **dom** is the functional domain operator.

The function log is introduced to replace (data refine) the abstract variables $comp\_buffer$, $comp\_inprocess$, and $comp\_processed$. To prove correctness of such data refinement, the following gluing invariants are added:

$$\forall c \cdot c \in comp \Rightarrow log(c)[index\_inprocess(c) + 1 .. index\_written(c)] = comp\_buffer(c),$$

$$\forall c \cdot c \in comp \Rightarrow log(c)[index\_processed(c) + 1 .. index\_inprocess(c)] = comp\_inprocess(c),$$

$$\forall c \cdot c \in comp \Rightarrow log(c)[1 .. index\_processed(c)] = comp\_processed(c),$$

where $R[S]$ denotes relational image of R with respect to the given set S.

An introduction of the sequential representation of the component log allows us to refine some proven invariants as well as prove some new ones. For instance, the invariant property (4) now can be reformulated in terms of new variables:

$$in\_transit = FALSE \ \Rightarrow (\forall c \cdot c \in comp \wedge c \neq master \Rightarrow$$

$$log(c)[1 .. index\_written(c)] \subseteq log(master)[1 .. index\_processed(master)]). \quad (5)$$

The formulated data refinement also affects all the events where the abstract variables were used. For instance, the event RequestOutMst (see Fig. 5) now specifies completion of master request processing by recording this in the node log, i.e., by increasing $index\_processed(master)$.

We can refine the procedure of choosing a new master by reformulating the guard condition (1) of the event ChangeMaster as follows:

$$\forall c \cdot c \in comp \wedge c \neq master \wedge c \neq new\_master \Rightarrow$$

$$index\_written(c) \leq index\_written(new\_master). \quad (6)$$

Here we check that the new candidate for the master has the largest $index\_written$, i.e., the freshest log copy. The other events are refined in a similar way. The overview of the refined model is presented in Fig. 5.

```
Machine Replication1_ref2 refines Replication1_ref1
Variables comp, master, comp_buffer, comp_inprocess, comp_processed, failed, in_transit
Invariants...
Events
RequestInMst ≙ refines RequestInMst  ...        // arriving of a new request to the master
ProcessMst refines ProcessMst  ...              // request processing by the master
RequestOutMst ≙ refines RequestOutMst  ...      // completion of a request by the master
  when  index_processed(master) ≠ index_inprocess(master) ∧ master ∉ failed
  with   r = log(master)(index_processed(master) + 1)
  then   index_processed(master) := index_processed(master) + 1
  end
RequestInStb ≙ refines RequestInStb  ...        // reading the master by a standby
  any c
  where  c ∈ comp ∧ c ≠ master ∧ c ∉ failed ∧ master ∉ failed ∧
         index_written(c) < index_processed(master)
  with   r = log(master)(index_written(c) + 1)
  then   log(c) := log(c) ∪ {index_written(c) + 1 ↦ log(master)(index_written(c) + 1)} ||
         index_written(c) := index_written(c) + 1
  end
ProcessStb ≙ refines ProcessStb  ...            // request processing by a standby
RequestOutStb ≙ refines RequestOutStb  ...      // completion of a request by a standby
ChangeMaster ≙ refines ChangeMaster  ...        // changing the master
...
```

Fig. 5. Asynchronous model: the second refinement

Moreover, we can explicitly formulate and prove the log data integrity properties as model invariants:

$$\forall c, i \cdot c \in comp \wedge i \in 1 .. index\_written(c) \Rightarrow log(c)(i) = log(master)(i),$$

$$\forall c1, c2, i \cdot c1 \in comp \wedge c2 \in comp \wedge i \in 1 .. index\_written(c1) \wedge$$
$$i \in 1 .. index\_written(c2) \Rightarrow log(c1)(i) = log(c2)(i). \quad (7)$$

These properties state that the corresponding log elements of any two storage (master or standby) nodes are always the same. In other words, all logs are consistent with respect to the log records of the master node.

5   The Cascade Master-Standby and Synchronous Architectures

An alternative, semi-syncronous replication model is the *cascade master-standby*. Besides the *master* node that serves incoming data base requests, we single out another functional node – *upper standby*. The upper standby node starts streaming the master log as soon as the master records the requests in its log. Moreover, the master node waits until the upper standby reads its processed records and, only after that, commits the changes and reports to the client.

In its turn, the other standby nodes are constantly monitoring and streaming the upper standby log records into their own logs and applying them in the same way as described in Section 4. Essentially, the standby nodes are continually trying to catch up with the upper standby.

If the master node goes down, the upper standby node is automatically appointed to be the master in its stead. Moreover, the next candidate for the new upper standby node becomes the node that is closest (with respect to the copied log file) to the current upper standby.

Let us note that this proposed cascade replication mode allows to decrease the possibility of loss of the committed changes if the master node fails. Indeed, at that point, when the master node fails, the upper standby node had already recorded all the changes that were committed and reported to the client by master before. Therefore, such an architectural solution increases the system resilience. A possibility of data loss leading to an inconsistent system state is still present. However, for this to happen, the master node and the upper standby node should both fail in a very short time period. A graphical representation of the system architecture is shown on Fig.6.

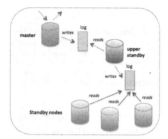

Fig. 6. Cascade system architecture

The formal development of the proposed replication model consists of an initial specification and its two refinements. The initial model abstractly describes the system behaviour focusing on the master and the upper standby nodes. The first refinement step introduces the remaining standby nodes and their interoperation with the upper standby, while the second refinement explicitly models the sequential logging mechanism and the interdependencies between the master, the upper standby and others standby logs. Let us note that the development is similar to that of the asynchronous model. Due to the lack of space we will only highlight the most significant differences between them.

Abstract Specification. In the initial model defined by the machine Replication2_m0 we focus on the master and upper standby components and their interoperation. The overall model structure is given on Fig. 7.

In addition to the master node, we single out one more node to serve as an upper standby node. We model this by introducing the variable $ups\_stanbdy$, such that $ups\_stanbdy \in comp$ and $ups\_standby \neq master$.

The variables m_buffer, $m\_inprocess$, $m\_processed$ represent the received requests at different stages of their processing by the master. Similarly, the variables ups_buffer, $ups\_inprocess$, $ups\_processed$ are introduced to model the respective data structures for the upper standby. The events RequestInMst,

```
Machine Replication2_m0
Variables comp, master, ups_standby, m_buffer, m_inprocess, m_processed, m_buffer, ...
Invariants comp ⊆ COMP ∧ master ∈ comp ∧ ups_standby ∈ comp...
Events ...

RequestInMst   ...                    // arriving of a new request to the master node
ProcessMst ...                        // request processing
RequestOutMst ≙                       // completion of a request by the master
  any r
  where r ∈ m_inprocess ∧ (r ∈ ups_buffer ∪ ups_inprocess ∪ ups_processed)
  then   m_processed := m_processed ∪ {r} ∥ m_inprocess := m_inprocess \ {r}   end
ProcessUps ...                        // request processing by the upper standby
ChangeMaster ≙                        // changing the master
  any new_ups_standby, n_buffer, n_inprocess, n_processed
  where
          new_ups_standby ∈ comp ∧ new_ups_standby ≠ ups_standby ∧
          new_ups_standby ≠ master ∧ ...
          (n_buffer ∪ n_inprocess ∪ n_processed ⊆
                                    ups_buffer ∪ ups_inprocess ∪ ups_processed)
  then
          master := ups_standby ∥ ups_standby := new_ups_standby ∥
          m_buffer := ups_buffer ∥ m_inprocess := ups_inprocess ∥
          m_processed := ups_processed ∥ comp := comp \ {master}...
  end
ChangeUpsStb ...                      // changing the upper standby node
CompActivation ...                    // activation of a new system component
CompDeactivation ...                  // deactivation of a system component
```

Fig. 7. Cascade architecture: abstract model

ProcessMst, RequestOutMst and RequestInUps, ProcessUps, RequestOutUps specify the corresponding request stages for the master and upper standby nodes.

The master node can not commit the changes until the upper standby reads them. We model this requirement by adding the following guard condition in the event RequestOutMst:

$$r \in ups\_buffer \cup ups\_inprocess \cup ups\_processed.$$

The process of changing of the master node by the upper standby is modelled by the event ChangeMaster. The event also specifies the selection procedure of a new upper standby. Due to possible data loss, the requests being handled by the new upper standby may be only a subset of those of the current upper standby:

$$n\_buffer \cup n\_inprocess \cup n\_processed \subseteq ups\_buffer \cup ups\_inprocess \cup ups\_processed.$$

Moreover, a similar event, ChangeUpsStb, models the selection of a new upper standby in the case when the current one fails.

First Refinement. In the first refinement step we extend the abstract model by explicitly introducing the behaviour of the remaining standby nodes. Similarly as for the asynchronous model, we data refine the abstract variables m_buffer, m_inprocess, m_processed and ups_buffer, ups_inprocess, ups_processed by the new functional variables comp_buffer, comp_inprocess and comp_processed.

In addition, a number of the new events are added to describe the behaviour of standby nodes, node failures and recovery (RequestInStb, ProcessStb, RequestOutStb, CompFailure, CompStbRecovery).

As for the asynchronous model, we can formulate and prove data consistency properties between the involved components. The property (2) (stating that a standby node is always behind the master in terms of handled requests) corresponds to two properties for the cascade replication mode: the first one stating this property between any standby and the upper standby, while the second one stating the same property between the upper standby and master nodes.

$$(\forall c \cdot c \in comp \wedge c \neq master \ \wedge c \neq ups\_standby \Rightarrow$$
$$comp\_buffer(c) \cup comp\_inprocess(c) \cup comp\_processed(c) \subseteq$$
$$comp\_buffer(ups\_standby) \cup comp\_inprocess(ups\_standby)$$
$$\cup comp\_processed(ups\_standby)), \quad (8)$$

$$comp\_buffer(ups\_standby) \cup$$
$$comp\_inprocess(ups\_standby) \cup comp\_processed(ups\_standby) \subseteq$$
$$comp\_buffer(master) \cup comp\_inprocess(master) \cup comp\_processed(master), \quad (9)$$

The property (4) for the asynchronous mode expresses the relationships between the processed requests of the master node and read requests of the standby nodes. This property again corresponds to two properties for the cascade mode: one between the upper standby and remaining standbys, and the other one between the master and upper standby nodes. In both cases, the properties may be violated for a short period (indicated by $in\_transit = TRUE$) right after a new upper standby node is chosen to replace a failed one:

$$in\_transit = FALSE \ \Rightarrow \ (\forall c \cdot c \in comp \wedge c \neq master \ \wedge c \neq ups\_standby \Rightarrow$$
$$(comp\_buffer(c) \ \cup comp\_inprocess(c) \cup comp\_processed(c)$$
$$\subseteq \ comp\_processed(ups\_standby)), \quad (10)$$

$$in\_transit = FALSE \ \Rightarrow \ (comp\_processed(master) \subseteq comp\_buffer(ups\_standby) \cup$$
$$comp\_inprocess(ups\_standby) \cup comp\_processed(ups\_standby)). \quad (11)$$

Note how the requirement that the master cannot commit a request before it is read by the upper standby reverses the inclusion relationship in the (11).

Second Refinement. The goal of our second refinement step is explicitly model the write-ahead logging mechanism and the resulting interdependencies between the master, upper standby and other standby logs.

We data refine the abstract variables $comp\_buffer$, $comp\_inprocess$, and $comp\_processed$ by the introduced function log. The following gluing invariants allow us to prove correctness of such a data refinement:

$$\forall c \cdot c \in comp \Rightarrow log(c)[index\_inprocess(c) + 1 \mathrel{..} index\_written(c)] = comp\_buffer(c),$$
$$\forall c \cdot c \in comp \Rightarrow log(c)[index\_processed(c) + 1 \mathrel{..} index\_inprocess(c)] = comp\_inprocess(c),$$
$$\forall c \cdot c \in comp \Rightarrow log(c)[1 \mathrel{..} index\_processed(c)] = comp\_processed(c).$$

Introducing the sequential representation of the component log allows us to reformulate some proven invariants as well as prove some new ones. For instance, the invariant properties (10) and (11) now can be reformulated in terms of the new variables as follows:

$$in\_transit = FALSE \Rightarrow$$
$$(\forall c \cdot c \in comp \land c \neq master \land c \neq ups\_standby \Rightarrow$$
$$log(c)[1 .. index\_written(c)] \subseteq$$
$$log(ups\_standby)[1 .. index\_processed(ups\_standby)]). \quad (12)$$

$$in\_transit = FALSE \Rightarrow log(master)[1 .. index\_processed(master)]$$
$$\subseteq log(ups\_standby)[1 .. index\_written(ups\_standby)]. \quad (13)$$

Finally, the log data integrity properties (in the exact form as in (7)) are formulated and proved for this replication mode as well.

Synchronous Architecture. The last development formalises the *synchronous replication architecture*, which can be considered as a combination of both asynchronous and cascade models. The essential differences of this model are following. The standby nodes start streaming the master log records as soon as master records the commands in its log. Moreover, the master node waits until *all the standby nodes* read processed records from its log and, only after that, commits the corresponding changes and reports to the client. If the master goes down, one of the standby nodes is appointed to be the master in its stead. Essentially, it is a generalisation of the cascade model where all the standby nodes play the role of upper standby.

This architecture allows to avoid a possibility of loss of the committed changes if the master fails. Indeed, at that point, all the standby nodes have already recorded all the changes that were committed and reported to the client by master. On the other hand, the necessity for the master to synchronise in such a way with all the standbys may negatively affect the performance of this model.

Developing the formal model of this architecture, we essentially repeat the refinement steps of the asynchronous model. In particular, the initial model is the same as the abstract model presented on Fig.2. In the first refinement step, in the RequestOutMst event modelling the commitment of the changes by master, we have to impose an additional restriction for this behaviour. Namely, the master node can not commit the changes until all the standby nodes have read them. We model this requirement by adding the following guard condition to the event:

$$\forall c \cdot c \in comp \land c \neq master \Rightarrow$$
$$r \in comp\_buffer(c) \cup comp\_inprocess(c) \cup comp\_processed(c),$$

where we check that the request r has already been recorded by all the standby nodes. Moreover, in the eventRequestInStb, we relax its guard by allowing to copy the master log as soon as the master records requests in its log.

Similarly as for the first two models, we formulate and prove log data consistency properties. Specifically, the property (2), stating that the standby nodes

are continuously trying to catch up with the master in terms of handled requests, can be proved for this architecture as well. Moreover, since the master
can not commit the changes until the all standbys have read the corresponding
log records, it means that all the requests committed by the master have been
previously read by all standbys. We can formulate this property as follows:

$$in\_transit = FALSE \Rightarrow (\forall c \cdot c \in comp \land c \neq master \Rightarrow$$
$$comp\_processed(master) \subseteq comp\_buffer(c) \cup comp\_inprocess(c) \cup$$
$$comp\_processed(c)). \quad (14)$$

Note that, once again, this property can be violated right after a new master is
appointed and thus a transitional period is needed. This property is very similar
to that of (11) (for the cascade architecture) and is inverse, with respect to the
inclusion relation, to that of (4) (for the asynchronous architecture).

As in the previous two developments, in the second refinement step we introduce component logs as sequences. In terms of the new variables, the (14)
property can be then reformulated as follows:

$$in\_transit = FALSE \Rightarrow (\forall c \cdot c \in comp \land c \neq master \Rightarrow$$
$$log(master)[1 .. index\_processed(master)] \subseteq log(c)[1 .. index\_written(c)]). \quad (15)$$

Finally, the log data integrity properties (7), stating that the corresponding
log elements of any two storage components are always the same, are proved for
this model as well. The full formal developments can be found in [9].

Proof Statistics To verify correctness of the presented formal developments,
we have discharged around 400 proof obligations for the first model, more than
750 proof obligations for the second model, and around 400 for the third model.
In total, around 90% of them have been proved automatically by the Rodin
platform and the rest have been proved manually in the Rodin interactive proving
environment. The proof statistics in terms of generated proof obligations for the
presented Event B developments is shown in the Table 1. The numbers represent
the total number of proof obligations and the percentage of manual effort for
each model in each refinement step. The whole development and proving effort
has taken around one person-month.

Table 1. The proof statistics

step	Asynchronous model			Cascade model			Synchronous model		
	Total	Manual	Manual %	Total	Manual	Manual %	Total	Manual	Manual %
m0	18	0	0	53	0	0	18	0	0
ref1	145	0	0	257	1	0.3	146	0	0
ref2	193	42	21.7	442	75	16.9	232	42	18.1
Overall	356	42	11.7	752	76	10.1	396	42	10.6

6   Conclusions and Related Work

In this paper, we formalised an industrial approach to implementing resilient cloud data storage. To ensure resilience, F-Secure combined the WAL mechanism with the log replication. We have formally expressed data integrity and consistency properties in three different replication architectures and explicitly identified situations that lead to data loss. These properties can inform industry practitioners on resilience guarantees inherent to each solution. The proposed modelling approach can facilitate early design exploration and evaluate benefits of different fault tolerance mechanisms in implementing resilience requirements.

The problem of data consistency in replicated data stores, in particular for the cloud, has been actively studied in both database and fault tolerance communities, e.g., see [2,8]. However, most of these approaches aim at proposing new protocols guaranteeing correctness of data replication. For instance, the work [8] presents a Dynamic Multi-Replica Provable Data Procession scheme. It is based on probabilistic encryption used to periodically verify the correctness and completeness of multiple data copies stored in the cloud. In our work we aim at modelling architectural aspects of data stores and verifying qualitative characteristics of data handling in the cloud.

Formal analysis of data base replication protocols has been proposed in [6]. The authors establish safety and liveness correctness criteria that need to be verified by a replication protocol. In contract, in our work we focus on ensuring data integrity and consistency properties based on the concrete write-ahead logging mechanism.

The WAL has been investigated in [4,5]. In those works the authors analyse the performance aspects of this technique. They distinguish four types of the delays that the WAL mechanism can impose on transaction handling and propose an approach to increase log scalability. In our work, we focus on verifying properties concerning data consistency and data loss under possible failure scenarios using the WAL mechanism.

In [12] the authors investigate data properties in the presence of server failures, however considering the full ACID properties. A formal modelling of fault-tolerant transactions for replicated database systems using Event-B has been also undertaken by D. Yadav et al. [13]. The work focuses on data atomic commitment of distributed transactions.

In our future work we are planning to analyse performance and other quantitative characteristics of different replication architectures. It particular, it would be interesting to integrate probabilistic verification to evaluate the trade-offs between performance and reliability.

References

1. Abrial, J.R.: Modeling in Event-B. Cambridge University Press (2010)
2. Barsoum, A.F., Hasan, M.A.: Integrity Verification of Multiple Data Copies over Untrusted Cloud Servers. In: CCGRID 2012, pp. 829–834. IEEE Computer Society (2012)

3. F-Secure,
   http://www.f-secure.com/en/web/operators_global/content-anywhere
4. Johnson, R., Pandis, I., Stoica, R., Athanassoulis, M., Ailamaki, A.: Aether: A Scalable Approach to Logging. In: VLDB Endowment, vol. 3, pp. 681–692 (2010)
5. Johnson, R., Pandis, I., Stoica, R., Athanassoulis, M., Ailamaki, A.: Scalability of Write-Ahead Logging on Multicore and Multisocket Hardware. The VLDB Journal 21(2), 239–263 (2012)
6. de Mendvil, J., Armendriz-Iigo, J.E., Garitagoitia, J.R., Muoz-Esco, F.D.: A Formal Analysis of Database Replication Protocols With SI Replicas and Crash Failures. The Journal of Supercomputing 50(2), 121–161 (2009)
7. Mohan, C., Haderle, D., Lindsay, B., Pirahesh, H., Schwarz, P.: Aries: A Transaction Recovery Method Supporting Fine-Granularity Locking and Partial Rollbacks Using Write-Ahead Logging. ACM Transactions on Database Systems 17, 94–162 (1992)
8. Mukundan, R., Madria, S., Linderman, M.: Replicated Data Integrity Verification in Cloud. IEEE Data Eng. Bull. 35, 55–64 (2012)
9. Pereverzeva, I., Laibinis, L., Troubitsyna, E., Holmberg, M., Pöri, M.: Formal Modelling of Resilient Data Storage in the Cloud. Tech. rep., Turku Centre for Computer Science (2013)
10. PostgreSQL: WAL,
    http://www.postgresql.org/docs/9.2/static/wal-intro.html
11. Rodin: Event-B Platform, http://www.event-b.org/
12. Wei, Z., Pierre, G., Chi, C.-H.: Scalable Transactions for Web Applications in the Cloud. In: Sips, H., Epema, D., Lin, H.-X. (eds.) Euro-Par 2009. LNCS, vol. 5704, pp. 442–453. Springer, Heidelberg (2009)
13. Yadav, D., Butler, M.: Rigorous Design of Fault-Tolerant Transactions for Replicated Database Systems Using Event-B. In: Butler, M., Jones, C.B., Romanovsky, A., Troubitsyna, E. (eds.) Fault-Tolerant Systems. LNCS, vol. 4157, pp. 343–363. Springer, Heidelberg (2006)

Linking Operational Semantics and Algebraic Semantics for Wireless Networks

Xiaofeng Wu and Huibiao Zhu*

Shanghai Key Laboratory of Trustworthy Computing,
Software Engineering Institute, East China Normal University, Shanghai, China
{xfwu,hbzhu}@sei.ecnu.edu.cn

Abstract. Wireless technology has achieved lots of applications in computer networks. To model and analyze wireless systems, a calculus called CWS and its operational semantics have been investigated. This paper considers the linking between the algebraic semantics and the operational semantics for this calculus. Our approach is to derive the operational semantics from the algebraic semantics. Firstly we present the algebraic semantics and introduce the concept of head normal form. Secondly we present the strategy of deriving the operational semantics from the algebraic semantics. Based on the strategy, an operational semantics is derived, which shows that the operational semantics is sound with respect to the algebraic semantics. Then the equivalence between the derivation strategy and the derived transition system is proved. This shows the completeness of the derived operational semantics. Finally, we investigate the mechanical approach to our linking method using the equational and rewriting logic system Maude. We mechanize the algebraic laws, the derivation strategy and the derived operational semantics.

1 Introduction

Wireless technology has achieved a wide range of applications in computer networks. To model and analyze wireless systems, various process calculi have been introduced, like CBS [12], CBS# [9], CMN [7], CMAN [2], CWS [6], etc. Some calculi employ special constructs to represent the topology and the behavior of network. With concepts like device location and transmission range, broadcast can be local, i.e., broadcasted messages can only be received by nodes within the transmission range. Most calculi treat broadcast as an atomic action to abstract away from collisions due to simultaneous transmissions from different sources. While interference is an essential aspect in CWS, which gives rise to complex situations on interactions in wireless systems. For CWS, the operational semantics has been developed including a reduction semantics and a labelled transition system. The main technical result of this approach is the equivalence between the two operational semantics [6].

In this paper, we consider the algebraic semantics for CWS as well as the consistency between its algebraic semantics and operational semantics. In order

---

* Corresponding author.

L. Groves and J. Sun (Eds.): ICFEM 2013, LNCS 8144, pp. 380–396, 2013.
© Springer-Verlag Berlin Heidelberg 2013

to prove the consistency, we explore the linking between the two semantics. The exploration can be achieved by deriving the operational semantics from the algebraic semantics. The linking theories between different semantic models (operational semantics, algebraic semantics and denotational semantics) [5,11,13] for a language provide the correct understanding for one semantics based on the viewpoint of another, which is advocated in Hoare and He's Unifying Theories of Programming [4].

To support the linking from the algebraic semantics to the operational semantics, we first introduce several typical types of guarded choices and a set of algebraic laws. They are used to construct the head normal form of networks. The derivation of the operational semantics from the algebraic semantics is based on the head normal form. Then we define the derivation strategy. Based on the strategy, a set of transition rules can be achieved by strict proof. This can be regarded as the soundness consideration of the operational semantics from the viewpoint of the algebraic semantics. Furthermore, we explore the equivalence between the derivation strategy and the derived transition system to show the completeness of the operational semantics from the viewpoint of the algebraic semantics. Besides the above theoretical approach, we also investigate the practical aspect of the linking. We mechanize the algebraic semantics, the head normal form, the derivation strategy and the derived operational semantics. The mechanized results indicate that the transition system of the derived operational semantics is the same as the one based on the derivation strategy.

The remainder of this paper is organized as follows. Section 2 recalls the core language of CWS. Section 3 investigates the algebraic semantics by introducing four types of guarded choices and a collection of parallel expansion laws. Section 4 defines the head normal form of networks based on the algebraic laws. Section 5 is devoted to the derivation of operational semantics from the algebraic semantics. The derivation strategy is defined and a set of transition rules is generated. Also, the equivalence between the derivation strategy and the derivation operational semantics is proved. Section 6 mechanizes our linking method. Section 7 concludes this paper.

2   Overview of CWS

The Calculus for Wireless Systems (abbreviated as CWS) has been introduced in [6]. This language contains categories of syntactic elements as follows.

$$P ::= \mathbf{out}\langle e\rangle.P \mid \langle v\rangle.P \mid \mathbf{in}(x).P \mid (x).P \mid \mathbf{0}$$

$$N ::= n[P]_{l,r}^c \mid N|N \mid \mathbf{0}$$

- $\mathbf{out}\langle e\rangle.P$ is a begin-transmission process willing to broadcast the value of e. It evolves to $\langle v\rangle.P$ when the broadcast is initiated, where $[\![e]\!] = v$.
- $\langle v\rangle.P$ is an end-transmission process. It indicates that the value v is currently broadcasting. It becomes P if the transmission is terminated.
- $\mathbf{in}(x).P$ is a begin-reception process willing to receive. It becomes $(x).P$ if it is activated by a transmission.

- $(x).P$ is an end-reception process. It is receiving and evolves to P if the transmission is terminated successfully or a collision happens due to another transmission. In the former case the received value is bound to x in process P. In the latter case a special value $\perp$ is bound to x denoted as $P\{\perp/x\}$ indicating failure of receiving caused by interference.
- **0** represents an inactive process, which cannot perform any actions.

The process part describes the behavior of a node. A transmission is modeled by two boundary events which introduces interference explicitly.

- $n[P]_{l,r}^c$ denotes a node owning a network address n, located at physical location l with dissemination radius r and using communication channel c. Within the node, process P executes sequentially.
- $N|N$ indicates that a network is composed of two subnetworks.
- **0** represents an empty network, defined as $n[\mathbf{0}]_{l,r}^c =_{df} \mathbf{0}$. For any network N, it satisfies $\mathbf{0}|N=N=N|\mathbf{0}$.

The network part indicates that a wireless system is modelled as a collection of nodes running in parallel. Each node is assumed to occupy a unique identifier and two nodes cannot share the same physical location. A distance function $d(\cdot,\cdot)$ is used [6,7] to return the distance between two locations.

Example 2.1. Let $N_1 =_{df} n_1[\mathbf{out}\langle e_1\rangle.P]_{l_1,r_1}^{c_1}$ and $N_2 =_{df} n_2[\mathbf{out}\langle e_2\rangle.Q]_{l_2,r_2}^{c_2}$ be two nodes. Assume that $d(l_1,l_2) \leqslant r_1$ and $d(l_2,l_1) > r_2$, then N_2 is in the transmission range of N_1, but not vice versa. □

According to the prefix of a process inside a node, all nodes can fall into four categories:

(1) transmitter, in the form $n[\mathbf{out}\langle e\rangle.P]_{l,r}^c$, is willing to start a transmission if its environment is not occupied by communication from other nodes.
(2) active transmitter, in the form $n[\langle v\rangle.P]_{l,r}^c$, is currently broadcasting.
(3) receiver, in the form $n[\mathbf{in}(x).P]_{l,r}^c$, is waiting for being activated.
(4) active receiver, in the form $n[(x).P]_{l,r}^c$, is currently receiving.

Node status of a node $n[P]_{l,r}^c$ is defined as a triple $s =_{df} (l,r,c)$, whose elements are the node's location, radius, and channel respectively.

Active transmitters T is a set of nodes (represented by their node status) which are currently transmitting in the network, i.e., (l,r,c) is an element of set T iff the node $n[P]_{l,r}^c$ is an active transmitter.

Active neighbours of a node $n[P]_{l,r}^c$ is a subset of active transmitters T, denoted as $T|(l,r,c)$. It contains the nodes which are currently transmitting and whose transmissions can be received by the node with status (l,r,c). Formally,

$$T|(l,r,c) =_{df} \{ (l',r',c') \mid (l',r',c') \in T \ \wedge \ d(l',l) \leqslant r' \ \wedge \ c' = c \}$$

Example 2.2. Let $N_1 =_{df} n_1[\mathbf{out}\langle e\rangle.P]_{l_1,r_1}^c$, $N_2 =_{df} n_2[\mathbf{out}\langle f\rangle.Q]_{l_2,r_2}^c$, $N_3 =_{df} n_3[\mathbf{in}(x).R]_{l_3,r_3}^c$ and $N_4 =_{df} n_4[\mathbf{in}(y).S]_{l_4,r_4}^c$ be four nodes. Assume that N_3 is in the transmission range of N_1 and N_2 (i.e., $d(l_1,l_3) \leqslant r_1$ and

$d(l_2, l_3) \leqslant r_2$), N_2 and N_4 are in the transmission range of N_1 and N_2 respectively (i.e., $d(l_1, l_2) \leqslant r_1$ and $d(l_2, l_4) \leqslant r_2$).

Then $Net = N_1|N_2|N_3|N_4$ is a network composed of four nodes using the same channel c. Initially, the active transmitters of this network is the empty set. So N_1 and N_2 can begin their own transmissions. We consider the transition initiated by N_2 with N_3 and N_4 activated. Before the termination of transmission from N_2, N_1 is free to start its transmission as it is out of the transmission range of N_2. Hence, interference occurs at N_3 but not at N_4 which is out of the transmission range of N_1. We present this transition as following.

$$n_1[\mathbf{out}\langle e\rangle.P]^c_{l_1,r_1} \mid n_2[\mathbf{out}\langle f\rangle.Q]^c_{l_2,r_2} \mid n_3[\mathbf{in}(x).R]^c_{l_3,r_3} \mid n_4[\mathbf{in}(y).S]^c_{l_4,r_4}$$
$$\longrightarrow n_1[\mathbf{out}\langle e\rangle.P]^c_{l_1,r_1} \mid n_2[\langle[\![f]\!]\rangle.Q]^c_{l_2,r_2} \mid n_3[(x).R]^c_{l_3,r_3} \mid n_4[(y).S]^c_{l_4,r_4}$$
$$\longrightarrow n_1[\langle[\![e]\!]\rangle.P]^c_{l_1,r_1} \mid n_2[\langle[\![f]\!]\rangle.Q]^c_{l_2,r_2} \mid n_3[R\{\bot/x\}]^c_{l_3,r_3} \mid n_4[(y).S]^c_{l_4,r_4}$$
$$\longrightarrow n_1[\langle[\![e]\!]\rangle.P]^c_{l_1,r_1} \mid n_2[Q]^c_{l_2,r_2} \mid n_3[R\{\bot/x\}]^c_{l_3,r_3} \mid n_4[S\{[\![f]\!]/y\}]^c_{l_4,r_4}$$

3 Algebraic Semantics

3.1 Guarded Choice

In order to linearize the parallel composition and to model the scheduling of interactions among nodes, we introduce a transmission tag t to record currently scheduled node, which is one of the following three forms.

(1) *none*, which indicates that no node is scheduled now.
(2) $\mathbf{out}\langle e\rangle@s$, which indicates that node s is scheduled to start its transmission.
(3) $\langle v\rangle@s$, which indicates that node s is scheduled to finish its transmission.

Now we introduce the concept of the guarded choice, which enriches the language to support the algebraic laws. The guarded choice is expressed in the form:

$$\{H_1 \to (N_1\langle T_1, t_1\rangle)\} \, [\!] \, ... \, [\!] \, \{H_n \to (N_n\langle T_n, t_n\rangle)\}$$

Each element $H \to (N\langle T, t\rangle)$ of the guarded choice is a guarded component, where

- H can be a guard in one of the following five forms: $\mathbf{out}\langle e\rangle@s$, $\langle v\rangle@s$, $\mathbf{in}(x)@s$, $(x)@s$, or $\mathbf{idle}$. The last form indicates that the network is waiting for actions performed by its environment. Other forms indicate the performance of the corresponding action by node s.
- $N\langle T, t\rangle$ reflects the network after H is fired. If H is performed or fired, the subsequent network is N and its network status is $\langle T, t\rangle$. T is all the transmitting nodes in network N and t is the scheduled node.

To represent a network in the form of the guarded choice, we introduce four typical types of guarded choices as following.

The first type of guarded choice is composed of a set of begin transmission components and a set of end transmission components, called transmission selection guarded choice.

(form-1) $[\![_{i \in I}\{\mathbf{out}\langle e_i\rangle @s_i \to (M_i\langle T_i, t_i\rangle)\} [\![[\![_{j \in J}\{\langle v_j\rangle @s_j \to (N_j\langle T_j, t_j\rangle)\}$

The second type of guarded choice is composed of a set of begin reception guard components. The guard can be fired if the receiver s_i can receive the transmission from the scheduled node.

(form-2) $[\![_{i \in I}\{\mathbf{in}(x_i)@s_i \to (M_i\langle T_i, t_i\rangle)\}$

The third type of guarded choice is composed of a set of end reception guard components. It can be fired by a transmitter or corresponding active transmitter. The former case causes interference as the receiver is currently communicating with another transmitter while in the latter case the reception terminates successfully.

(form-3) $[\![_{i \in I}\{(x_i)@s_i \to (M_i\langle T_i, t_i\rangle)\}$

The fourth type of guarded choice is the idle guarded choice. It is introduced to represent the situation that no action is allowed to perform, for instance, a transmitter exposed to other transmissions. If no action can be performed in the whole network, the idle guard is fired.

(form-4) $[\![_{i \in I}\{\mathbf{idle} \to (M_i\langle T_i, t_i\rangle)\}$

3.2   Algebraic Laws

In this section, we explore a collection of parallel expansion laws, which are used to derive the operational semantics.

In this work, we consider the algebraic laws for networks expressed in the form $(N\langle T, t\rangle) = (M\langle T, t\rangle)$, where N and M stand for networks, T stands for the set of active transmitters, and t stands for the transmission tag. It indicates that the behavior of network N and M are equivalent under the active transmitters set T and transmission tag t. We write $N =_{\langle T, t\rangle} M$ for $(N\langle T, t\rangle) = (M\langle T, t\rangle)$.

We define a function to reduce the number of parallel expansion laws by covering several cases at the same time. Let

$$\mathbf{par}(M, N, T, t) =_{df} \begin{cases} (N\langle T, t\rangle) & \text{if } M = \mathbf{0} \\ (M\langle T, t\rangle) & \text{if } N = \mathbf{0} \\ (M|N \ \langle T, t\rangle) & \text{otherwise} \end{cases}$$

Here we only consider half of the laws since the commutativity of parallel composition is considered, i.e., $N|M = M|N$. Our exploration for the algebraic laws is based on the four typical types of guarded choices.

We first consider the case that two parallel components are transmission selection guarded choices with a transmission tag *none*. The tag indicates that no node is scheduled. So any nodes from both parallel branches can be scheduled. In the result of parallel composition, the network status of the selected branch is applied to the **par** function. Law (par-1) reflects this case as below.

(par-1) Let $M =_{\langle T, none\rangle} [\![_{i \in I}\{\mathbf{out}\langle e_i\rangle @s_i \to (M_i\langle T_i, t_i\rangle)\} [\![[\![_{k \in K}\{\langle v_k\rangle @s_k \to (W_k\langle T_k, t_k\rangle)\}$

$\qquad N =_{\langle T, none\rangle} [\![_{j \in J}\{\mathbf{out}\langle e_j\rangle @s_j \to (N_j\langle T_j, t_j\rangle)\} [\![[\![_{o \in O}\{\langle v_o\rangle @s_o \to (V_o\langle T_o, t_o\rangle)\}$

$\quad$ Then $\quad M|N =_{\langle T, none\rangle} [\![_{i \in I}\{\mathbf{out}\langle e_i\rangle @s_i \to \mathbf{par}(M_i, N, T_i, t_i)\}$

$\qquad\qquad\qquad [\![[\![_{k \in K}\{\langle v_k\rangle @s_k \to \mathbf{par}(W_k, N, T_k, t_k)\}$

$$[] \ []_{j \in J} \{\mathbf{out}\langle e_j \rangle @ s_j \to \mathbf{par}(M, N_j, T_j, t_j)\}$$
$$[] \ []_{o \in O} \{\langle v_o \rangle @ s_o \to \mathbf{par}(M, V_o, T_o, t_o)\}$$

Next we explore the case that both parallel components are the second type of guarded choice with a tag $\mathbf{out}\langle e \rangle @ s$. This indicates that s is scheduled to begin a transmission and all nodes in both branches can be activated by the scheduled node shown as below.

(par-2) Let $M =_{\langle T, \mathbf{out}\langle e \rangle @ s \rangle} []_{i \in I} \{\mathbf{in}(x_i) @ s_i \to (M_i \langle T_i, t_i \rangle)\}$ and

$\qquad N =_{\langle T, \mathbf{out}\langle e \rangle @ s \rangle} []_{j \in J} \{\mathbf{in}(x_j) @ s_j \to (N_j \langle T_j, t_j \rangle)\}$

Then $\quad M|N =_{\langle T, \mathbf{out}\langle e \rangle @ s \rangle} []_{i \in I} \{\mathbf{in}(x_i) @ s_i \to \mathbf{par}(M_i, N, T_i, t_i)\}$

$\qquad\qquad\qquad [] \ []_{j \in J} \{\mathbf{in}(x_j) @ s_j \to \mathbf{par}(M, N_j, T_j, t_j)\}$

If both parallel components are the third type of guarded choice, the parallel result is related to the transmission tag. Cases are shown in law (par-3) and law (par-4) respectively. The tag $\langle v \rangle @ s$ represents that node s is scheduled to terminate its transmission of value v. Hence the corresponding active receivers of the scheduled node can receive the value v successfully. $M_i\{v/x_i\}$ represents that the value v is bound to the variable x_i.

(par-3) Let $M =_{\langle T, \langle v \rangle @ s \rangle} []_{i \in I} \{(x_i) @ s_i \to (M_i \langle T_i, t_i \rangle)\}$ and

$\qquad N =_{\langle T, \langle v \rangle @ s \rangle} []_{j \in J} \{(x_j) @ s_j \to (N_j \langle T_j, t_j \rangle)\}$

Then $\quad M|N =_{\langle T, \langle v \rangle @ s \rangle} []_{i \in I} \{(x_i) @ s_i \to \mathbf{par}(M_i\{v/x_i\}, N, T_i, t_i)\}$

$\qquad\qquad\qquad [] \ []_{j \in J} \{(x_j) @ s_j \to \mathbf{par}(M, N_j\{v/x_j\}, T_j, t_j)\}$

The tag $\mathbf{out}\langle e \rangle @ s$ indicates that node s is scheduled to start its transmission. Collisions occur for active receivers which are in the transmission range of the scheduled node. A special value is bound to the corresponding variable. Law (par-4) reflects this case as below.

(par-4) Let $M =_{\langle T, \mathbf{out}\langle e \rangle @ s \rangle} []_{i \in I} \{(x_i) @ s_i \to (M_i \langle T_i, t_i \rangle)\}$ and

$\qquad N =_{\langle T, \mathbf{out}\langle e \rangle @ s \rangle} []_{j \in J} \{(x_j) @ s_j \to (N_j \langle T_j, t_j \rangle)\}$

Then $\quad M|N =_{\langle T, \mathbf{out}\langle e \rangle @ s \rangle} []_{i \in I} \{(x_i) @ s_i \to \mathbf{par}(M_i\{\bot/x_i\}, N, T_i, t_i)\}$

$\qquad\qquad\qquad [] \ []_{j \in J} \{(x_j) @ s_j \to \mathbf{par}(M, N_j\{\bot/x_j\}, T_j, t_j)\}$

Law (par-5) shows that we deal with interference first when a node is scheduled to begin a transmission.

(par-5) Let $M =_{\langle T, \mathbf{out}\langle e \rangle @ s \rangle} []_{i \in I} \{\mathbf{in}(x_i) @ s_i \to (M_i \langle T_i, t_i \rangle)\}$ and

$\qquad N =_{\langle T, \mathbf{out}\langle e \rangle @ s \rangle} []_{j \in J} \{(x_j) @ s_j \to (N_j \langle T_j, t_j \rangle)\}$

Then $\quad M|N =_{\langle T, \mathbf{out}\langle e \rangle @ s \rangle} []_{j \in J} \{(x_j) @ s_j \to \mathbf{par}(M, N_j\{\bot/x_j\}, T_j, t_j)\}$

If one parallel component is an idle guarded choice while another parallel component is not an idle guarded choice, the parallel result follows the behaviour of the branch which is not in the **idle** form. This case is shown by law (par-6) as below, where the guard H_i is not in the form of **idle**.

(par-6) Let $M =_{\langle T, t \rangle} []_{i \in I} \{H_i \to (M_i \langle T_i, t_i \rangle)\}$ and

$\qquad N =_{\langle T, t \rangle} []_{j \in J} \{\mathbf{idle} \to (N_j \langle T_j, t_j \rangle)\}$

Then $\quad M|N =_{\langle T, t \rangle} []_{i \in I} \{H_i \to \mathbf{par}(M_i, N, T_i, t_i)\}$

If both parallel components are idle guarded choices, the parallel result is still an idle guarded choice. We apply the network status from the left branch to the function **par** in the result. This case is expressed as below.

(par-7) Let $M =_{\langle T,t \rangle} []_{i \in I} \{ \text{idle} \rightarrow (M_i \langle T_i, t_i \rangle) \}$ and

$$N =_{\langle T,t \rangle} []_{j \in J} \{ \text{idle} \rightarrow (N_j \langle T_j, t_j \rangle) \}$$

Then $M|N =_{\langle T,t \rangle} []_{i \in I} \{ \text{idle} \rightarrow \textbf{par}(M, N, T_i, t_i) \}$

4   Head Normal Form

In order to support the derivation of the operational semantics from the algebraic semantics, we introduce the head normal form. The head normal form is expressed in the form of one step forward based on four typical types of guarded choices. We use the notation $\mathcal{HF}(N \langle T, t \rangle)$ to stand for the head normal form of the network N with its corresponding network status $\langle T, t \rangle$.

The head normal form of a single node is directly defined according to the corresponding network status. For a network which composed of non-empty subnetworks, its head normal form can be calculated by using the parallel expansion laws.

We first consider the cases for a transmitter with a transmission tag *none*. If it is not exposed to other transmissions (ensured by $T|(l, r, c) = \emptyset$), its head normal form is defined as the first type of guarded choice. Meanwhile the network status of the subsequent network is updated shown as below.

(1-1) $\mathcal{HF}(n[\textbf{out}\langle e \rangle.P]^c_{l,r} \langle T, none \rangle)$

$=_{df} ([]\{ \textbf{out}\langle e \rangle @(l,r,c) \rightarrow (n[\langle v \rangle.P]^c_{l,r} \langle T \cup \{(l,r,c)\}, \textbf{out}\langle e \rangle @(l, r, c) \rangle) \} \langle T, none \rangle)$

$\qquad\qquad\qquad\qquad\qquad\qquad\qquad\qquad\qquad\qquad\qquad$ if $\quad T|(l, r, c) = \emptyset$

Otherwise, the transmitter is not allowed to perform any action. Hence the head normal form is defined as an idle guarded choice without updating the network status of the subsequent network shown as below.

(1-1') $\mathcal{HF}(n[\textbf{out}\langle e \rangle.P]^c_{l,r} \langle T, none \rangle)$

$=_{df} ([]\{ \text{idle} \rightarrow (n[\textbf{out}\langle e \rangle.P]^c_{l,r} \langle T, none \rangle) \} \langle T, none \rangle)$ if $\quad T|(l, r, c) \neq \emptyset$

When the transmission tag is not *none*, the head normal form is defined as an idle guarded choice with the tag reset to *none*.

(1-2) $\mathcal{HF}(n[\textbf{out}\langle e \rangle.P]^c_{l,r} \langle T, t \rangle)$

$=_{df} ([]\{ \text{idle} \rightarrow (n[\textbf{out}\langle e \rangle.P]^c_{l,r} \langle T, none \rangle) \} \langle T, t \rangle)$ if $t \neq none$

Next we present the head normal form for an active transmitter. If the transmission tag is *none*, the head normal form is expressed as the first type of guarded choice with the network status of the subsequent network updated.

(2-1) $\mathcal{HF}(n[\langle v \rangle.P]^c_{l,r} \langle T, none \rangle)$

$=_{df} ([]\{ \langle v \rangle @(l, r, c) \rightarrow (n[P]^c_{l,r} \langle T \backslash \{(l, r, c)\}, \langle v \rangle @(l, r, c) \rangle) \} \langle T, none \rangle)$

Otherwise, similar to definition (1-2), the head normal form is defined as an idle guarded choice.

(2-2) $\mathcal{HF}(n[\langle v \rangle.P]^c_{l,r} \langle T, t \rangle) =_{df} ([]\{ \text{idle} \rightarrow (n[\langle v \rangle.P]^c_{l,r} \langle T, none \rangle) \} \langle T, t \rangle)$ if $t \neq none$

Then we present the head normal form for a receiver. When the transmission tag is *none* or in the form of $\langle v \rangle @s$, the head normal form is expressed as an idle guarded choice shown as (3-1) and (3-2) respectively. Definition (3-1) indicates that the receiver is listening and waiting for a transmission from its environment. Definition (3-2) expresses the case that an end transmission action has no effort on a receiver.

(3-1) $\mathcal{HF}(n[\mathbf{in}(x).P]^c_{l,r}\langle T, none \rangle) =_{df} ([]\{\mathbf{idle} \rightarrow (n[\mathbf{in}(x).P]^c_{l,r}\langle T, none \rangle)\}\langle T, none \rangle)$

(3-2) $\mathcal{HF}(n[\mathbf{in}(x).P]^c_{l,r}\langle T, \langle v \rangle @s \rangle) =_{df} ([]\{\mathbf{idle} \rightarrow (n[\mathbf{in}(x).P]^c_{l,r}\langle T, none \rangle)\}\langle T, \langle v \rangle @s \rangle)$

When the tag is in the form $\mathbf{out}\langle e \rangle @s$, the head normal form is related to whether the receiver is in the transmission range of the scheduled node. If the receiver is not exposed to other transmissions and in the transmission range of the scheduled node s (ensured by $T|(l, r, c) = \{s\}$), the head normal form is expressed as the second type of guarded choice. Otherwise, it is an idle guarded choice. These cases are shown by (3-3) and (3-3′) respectively.

(3-3) $\mathcal{HF}(n[\mathbf{in}(x).P]^c_{l,r}\langle T, \mathbf{out}\langle e \rangle @s \rangle)$
$=_{df} ([]\{\mathbf{in}(x)@(l,r,c) \rightarrow (n[(x).P]^c_{l,r}\langle T, \mathbf{out}\langle e \rangle @s \rangle)\}\langle T, \mathbf{out}\langle e \rangle @s \rangle)$ if $T|(l, r, c) = \{s\}$

(3-3′) $\mathcal{HF}(n[\mathbf{in}(x).P]^c_{l,r}\langle T, \mathbf{out}\langle e \rangle @s \rangle)$
$=_{df} ([]\{\mathbf{idle} \rightarrow (n[\mathbf{in}(x).P]^c_{l,r}\langle T, none \rangle)\}\langle T, \mathbf{out}\langle e \rangle @s \rangle)$ if $T|(l, r, c) \neq \{s\}$

The head normal form of an active receiver involves more cases than other kinds of nodes because it is vulnerable to interference. When the tag is *none*, the head normal form is defined as an idle guarded choice. This indicates that the active receiver is receiving.

(4-1) $\mathcal{HF}(n[(x).P]^c_{l,r}\langle T, none \rangle) =_{df} ([]\{\mathbf{idle} \rightarrow (n[(x)P]^c_{l,r}\langle T, none \rangle)\}\langle T, none \rangle)$

When the transmission tag is not *none*, the head normal form is related to whether the active receiver is within the transmission range of the scheduled node. Definition (4-2) and (4-2′) show the cases with a transmission tag in the form $\mathbf{out}\langle e \rangle @s$, which indicates that a transmitter is scheduled to begin its transmission. If the active receiver is in the range of the scheduled node, the head normal form is expressed as the third type of guarded choice indicating the occurrence of a collision. Otherwise there is no effort on the receiver, the head normal form is an idle guarded choice.

(4-2) $\mathcal{HF}(n[(x).P]^c_{l,r}\langle T, \mathbf{out}\langle e \rangle @s \rangle)$
$=_{df} ([]\{(x)@(l,r,c) \rightarrow (n[P]^c_{l,r}\langle T, \mathbf{out}\langle e \rangle @s \rangle)\}\langle T, \mathbf{out}\langle e \rangle @s \rangle)$ if $\#T|(l, r, c) = 2$

(4-2′) $\mathcal{HF}(n[(x).P]^c_{l,r}\langle T, \mathbf{out}\langle e \rangle @s \rangle)$
$=_{df} ([]\{\mathbf{idle} \rightarrow (n[(x)P]^c_{l,r}\langle T, none \rangle)\}\langle T, \mathbf{out}\langle e \rangle @s \rangle)$ if $\#T|(l, r, c) \neq 2$

where $\#$ returns the number of elements of a finite set.

Definition (4-3) and (4-3′) show the cases with a tag in the form $\langle v \rangle @s$. If the active receiver is in the transmission range of node s, the head normal form is expressed as the third type of guarded choice indicating that it terminates the communication successfully. Otherwise the active receiver keeps receiving and its head normal form is an idle guarded choice.

(4-3) $\mathcal{HF}(n[(x).P]^c_{l,r}\langle T, \langle v\rangle @s\rangle)$

$\quad =_{df} (\mathbb{]}\{(x)@(l,r,c) \to (n[P]^c_{l,r}\langle T, \langle v\rangle @s\rangle)\}\langle T, \langle v\rangle @s\rangle)$ $\qquad$ if $\quad T|(l,r,c) = \emptyset$

(4-3') $\mathcal{HF}(n[(x).P]^c_{l,r}\langle T, \langle v\rangle @s\rangle)$

$\quad =_{df} (\mathbb{]}\{\mathbf{idle} \to (n[(x).P]^c_{l,r}\langle T, none\rangle)\}\langle T, \langle v\rangle @s\rangle)$ $\qquad$ if $\quad T|(l,r,c) \neq \emptyset$

(5) $\mathcal{HF}(M \mid N \langle T,t\rangle)$ can be defined as the result of applying the corresponding parallel expansion laws for $\mathcal{HF}(M\langle T,t\rangle) \mid \mathcal{HF}(N\langle T,t\rangle)$.

5 Deriving Operational Semantics from Algebraic Semantics

In this section we investigates the derivation of the operational semantics from the algebraic semantics, aiming for the consistency between the two semantics.

5.1 Derivation Strategy

The transitions are written in a special notation Structural Operational Semantics (SOS) [11], which are of the two types:

$$C \longrightarrow C' \quad \text{or} \quad C \xrightarrow[s]{\theta} C'$$

where C and C' are the configurations representing the states before and after an execution of a step. The first type is used to model the update of the network status. The second type models a θ transition performed by node s, where θ is in one of the following forms: $\mathbf{out}\langle e\rangle$, $\langle v\rangle$, $\mathbf{in}(x)$, v, and $\perp$.

The configuration can be expressed as $\langle N, \sigma, T, t\rangle$, where

(1) The first component N is a network defined according to the syntax of CWS.
(2) The second component σ is the state of all the variables. We assume that each node owns its local variables which are distinct from variables of others.
(3) The third component T is the set of active transmitters.
(4) The forth component t is the transmission tag.

Now we consider the derivation strategy for deriving the operational semantics from the algebraic semantics. For the network N with the network status $\langle T,t\rangle$, the derivation strategy is based on its head normal form $\mathcal{HF}(N\langle T,t\rangle)$.

Definition 5.1 Derivation Strategy

(1) If $\mathcal{HF}(N\langle T, none\rangle) = (\ \mathbb{]}_{i\in I}\{\mathbf{out}\langle e_i\rangle @s_i \to (M_i\langle T\cup\{s_i\}, \mathbf{out}\langle e_i\rangle @s_i\rangle)\}$

$\qquad\qquad\qquad\qquad \mathbb{]}\ \mathbb{]}_{j\in J}\{\langle v_j\rangle @s_j \to (N_j\langle T\setminus\{s_j\}, \langle v_j\rangle @s_j\rangle)\}\langle T, none\rangle)$

then $\qquad$ (1.a) $\langle N, \sigma, T, none\rangle \xrightarrow[s_i]{\mathbf{out}\langle e_i\rangle} \langle M_i, \sigma, T\cup\{s_i\}, \mathbf{out}\langle e_i\rangle @s_i\rangle$

$\qquad\qquad$ (1.b) $\langle N, \sigma, T, none\rangle \xrightarrow[s_j]{\langle v_j\rangle} \langle N_j, \sigma, T\setminus\{s_j\}, \langle v_j\rangle @s_j\rangle$

(2) If $\mathcal{HF}(N\langle T,t\rangle) = (\mathbb{]}_{i\in I}\{\mathbf{in}(x_i)@s_i \to (N_i\langle T,t\rangle)\}\langle T,t\rangle)$

then $\qquad \langle N, \sigma, T, t \rangle \xrightarrow[s_i]{\text{in}(x_i)} \langle N_i, \sigma, T, t \rangle$

(3) If $\mathcal{HF}(N\langle T, \langle v\rangle@s\rangle) = (\llbracket_{i \in I}\{(x_i)@s_i \rightarrow (N_i\langle T, \langle v\rangle@s\rangle))\}\langle T, \langle v\rangle@s\rangle)$

then $\qquad \langle N, \sigma, T, \langle v\rangle@s \rangle \xrightarrow[s_i]{v} \langle N_i, \sigma[v/x_i], T, \langle v\rangle@s \rangle$

(4) If $\mathcal{HF}(N\langle T, \mathbf{out}\langle e\rangle@s\rangle) = (\llbracket_{i \in I}\{(x_i)@s_i \rightarrow (N_i\langle T, \mathbf{out}\langle e\rangle@s\rangle))\}\langle T, \mathbf{out}\langle e\rangle@s\rangle)$

then $\qquad \langle N, \sigma, T, \mathbf{out}\langle e\rangle@s \rangle \xrightarrow[s_i]{\perp} \langle N_i, \sigma[\perp/x_i], T, \mathbf{out}\langle e\rangle@s \rangle$

(5) If $\mathcal{HF}(N\langle T, t\rangle) = (\llbracket_{i \in I}\{\mathbf{idle} \rightarrow (N\langle T, none\rangle))\}\langle T, t\rangle)$ and $t \neq none$

then $\qquad \langle N, \sigma, T, t \rangle \longrightarrow \langle N, \sigma, T, none \rangle$

If the head normal form of a network is expressed as a transmission selection guarded choice, then it can perform a transition of item (1.a) or a transition of item (1.b). If the head normal form is expressed as the second type of guarded choice, then the network can perform a transition shown as (2) above. If the head normal form of a network is expressed as the third type of guarded choice, the transition it can perform depends on the transmission tag. When the tag is in the form $\langle v\rangle@s$, the network can perform a transition shown as (3) above. The corresponding variable of the receiver is updated by the received value and other variables keep unchanged, denoted as $\sigma[v/x_i]$. When the tag is in the form $\mathbf{out}\langle e\rangle@s$, the network must perform a collision transition and a special value is bound to the corresponding variable shown as (4) above. If the head normal form is expressed as an idle guarded choice, then the network should perform an idle transition resetting the tag to $none$ in order to proceed the next scheduling.

5.2   Deriving Operational Semantics

In this section we derive the operational semantics according to the derivation strategy. This procedure shows the soundness of our operational semantics, i.e., all transition rules in the operational semantics can be generated from the algebraic semantics. The derived operational semantics is expressed as theorems to be proved. Theorem 5.1 to Theorem 5.4 are achieved directly from the definition of the head normal form and the derivation strategy. Theorem 5.5 explores the rules for parallel composition of networks.

Theorem 5.1

(1) $\langle n[\mathbf{out}\langle e\rangle.P]^c_{l,r}, \sigma, T, none \rangle \xrightarrow[(l,r,c)]{\mathbf{out}\langle e\rangle} \langle n[\langle v\rangle.P]^c_{l,r}, \sigma, T \cup \{(l,r,c)\}, \mathbf{out}\langle e\rangle@(l,r,c)\rangle$
$\qquad\qquad\qquad\qquad\qquad\qquad\qquad\qquad\qquad\qquad$ if $T|(l,r,c) = \emptyset$

(2) $\langle n[\mathbf{out}\langle e\rangle.P]^c_{l,r}, \sigma, T, t \rangle \longrightarrow \langle n[\mathbf{out}\langle e\rangle.P]^c_{l,r}, \sigma, T, none \rangle$ $\qquad\qquad$ if $t \neq none$

The above theorem illustrates the transition rules for a node willing to start a broadcast. The first rule shows that a transmitter can start its transmission if it is not exposed to other transmissions. The second rule indicates that the transmitter cannot be scheduled when another node is scheduled.

Theorem 5.2

(1) $\langle n[\langle v\rangle.P]^c_{l,r}, \sigma, T, none \rangle \xrightarrow[(l,r,c)]{\langle v\rangle} \langle n[P]^c_{l,r}, \sigma, T \setminus \{(l,r,c)\}, \langle v\rangle@(l,r,c)\rangle$

(2) $\langle n[\langle v\rangle.P]^c_{l,r},\sigma,T,t\rangle \longrightarrow \langle n[\langle v\rangle.P]^c_{l,r},\sigma,T,none\rangle$ \hfill if $t\neq none$

The above theorem illustrates the transition rules for an active transmitter. It can be scheduled to finish its transmission without any additional conditions if the transmission tag is *none*. Otherwise it performs an idle transition.

Theorem 5.3

(1) $\langle n[\mathbf{in}(x).P]^c_{l,r},\sigma,T,\mathbf{out}\langle e\rangle@s\rangle \xrightarrow[(l,r,c)]{\mathbf{in}(x)} \langle n[(x).P]^c_{l,r},\sigma,T,\mathbf{out}\langle e\rangle@s\rangle$, if $T|(l,r,c)=\{s\}$

(2) $\langle n[\mathbf{in}(x).P]^c_{l,r},\sigma,T,\mathbf{out}\langle e\rangle@s\rangle \longrightarrow \langle n[\mathbf{in}(x).P]^c_{l,r},\sigma,T,none\rangle$, if $T|(l,r,c)\neq\{s\}$

(3) $\langle n[\mathbf{in}(x).P]^c_{l,r},\sigma,T,\langle v\rangle@s\rangle \longrightarrow \langle n[\mathbf{in}(x).P]^c_{l,r},\sigma,T,none\rangle$

The above theorem illustrates the transition rules for a receiver. The receiver is activated if the scheduled node starts a transmission that can reach it and it is not exposed to other transmissions. Otherwise it keeps waiting for being activated and performs an idle transition.

Theorem 5.4

(1) $\langle n[(x).P]^c_{l,r},\sigma,T,\mathbf{out}\langle e\rangle@s\rangle \xrightarrow[(l,r,c)]{\perp} \langle n[P]^c_{l,r},\sigma[\perp/x],T,\mathbf{out}\langle e\rangle@s\rangle$, if $\#T|(l,r,c)=2$

(2) $\langle n[(x).P]^c_{l,r},\sigma,T,\mathbf{out}\langle e\rangle@s\rangle \longrightarrow \langle n[(x).P]^c_{l,r},\sigma,T,none\rangle$, \hfill if $\#T|(l,r,c)\neq2$

(3) $\langle n[(x).P]^c_{l,r},\sigma,T,\langle v\rangle@s\rangle \xrightarrow[(l,r,c)]{v} \langle n[P]^c_{l,r},\sigma[v/x],T,\langle v\rangle@s\rangle$, \hfill if $T|(l,r,c)=\emptyset$

(4) $\langle n[(x).P]^c_{l,r},\sigma,T,\langle v\rangle@s\rangle \longrightarrow \langle n[(x).P]^c_{l,r},\sigma,T,none\rangle$, \hfill if $T|(l,r,c)\neq\emptyset$

The above theorem illustrates the transition rules for an active receiver. When a node is scheduled to begin a transmission that can reach the active receiver, a collision occurs. The first rule expresses this case. If the corresponding active transmitter is scheduled, then the active receiver can terminate successfully.

Theorem 5.5

(1) If $\langle N,\sigma,T,t\rangle \xrightarrow[s]{\beta} \langle N',\sigma',T',t'\rangle$, then

$$\langle N|M,\sigma,T,t\rangle \xrightarrow[s]{\beta} \langle N'|M,\sigma',T',t'\rangle, \quad \langle M|N,\sigma,T,t\rangle \xrightarrow[s]{\beta} \langle M|N',\sigma',T',t'\rangle$$

where β is in one of the following forms: $\mathbf{out}\langle e\rangle$, $\langle v\rangle$, v, and $\perp$.

(2) If $\langle N,\sigma,T,t\rangle \xrightarrow[s]{\mathbf{in}(x)} \langle N',\sigma,T,t\rangle$ and $\langle M,\sigma,T,t\rangle \xrightarrow[s]{\perp}\!\!\!\!/\,$, then

$$\langle N|M,\sigma,T,t\rangle \xrightarrow[s]{\mathbf{in}} \langle N'|M,\sigma,T,t\rangle, \quad \langle M|N,\sigma,T,t\rangle \xrightarrow[s]{\mathbf{in}} \langle M|N',\sigma,T,t\rangle$$

where $\xrightarrow[s]{\perp}\!\!\!\!/\,$ represents that the network cannot perform a collision transition.

(3) If $\langle N,\sigma,T,t\rangle \longrightarrow \langle N,\sigma,T,t'\rangle$ and $\langle M,\sigma,T,t\rangle \longrightarrow \langle M,\sigma,T,t'\rangle$, then

$$\langle N|M,\sigma,T,t\rangle \longrightarrow \langle N|M,\sigma,T,t'\rangle, \quad \langle M|N,\sigma,T,t\rangle \longrightarrow \langle M|N,\sigma,T,t'\rangle$$

The above theorem illustrates the transition rules for the parallel composition of networks. The first rule considers all θ transitions except the begin reception transition. The second rule describes that a begin reception transition can be fired if no collision transition can be performed. The third rule indicates that an idle transition can be fired if all parallel components can perform an idle transition.

5.3   Equivalence of Derivation Strategy and Transition System

The collection of the transition rules derived from the derivation strategy in the previous subsection can be viewed as an operational semantics of CWS. The derivation approach shows the soundness of the operational semantics, but there remains another issue about the equivalence between the derivation strategy and the transition system, i.e., the set of transition rules derived from the derivation strategy should be the same as the set of transitions generated from the transition systems.

In order to prove the equivalence, we need to prove that the transition exists in the transition system if and only if it exists in the derivation strategy, which can be divided as the following two items:

(1) If the transition $\langle N, \sigma, T, t \rangle \xrightarrow{\alpha} \langle N', \sigma', T', t' \rangle$ exists in the transition system, then it also exists in the derivation strategy.

(2) If the transition $\langle N, \sigma, T, t \rangle \xrightarrow{\alpha} \langle N', \sigma', T', t' \rangle$ exists in the derivation strategy, then it also exists in the transition system.

Here "$\xrightarrow{\alpha}$" stands for the two types of transitions defined in section 5.1.

As our transition system is derived from the derivation strategy, the item (1) should be correct. So we consider item (2) as a theorem to be proved.

Theorem 5.6. If the transition $\langle N, \sigma, T, t \rangle \xrightarrow{\alpha} \langle N', \sigma', T', t' \rangle$ exists in the derivation strategy, then it also exists in the transition system.

Proof. First, we give the proof for a single node. Here we consider the proof for a transmitter and the proof of others are similar. We know that this node has two kinds of head normal form with different network status. Assume

$$\mathcal{HF}(N\langle T, t \rangle) = (\![\{\mathbf{out}\langle e \rangle @ (l, r, c) \rightarrow (n[\langle v \rangle.P]^c_{l,r}\langle T', \mathbf{out}@(l, r, c) \rangle)\}\langle T, t \rangle)$$

where t is in the form of *none*, $T' = T \cup \{(l, r, c)\}$ and $T|(l, r, c) = \emptyset$.

According to item (1) in Definition 5.1, N can perform the transition as below:

$$\langle n[\mathbf{out}\langle e \rangle.P]^c_{l,r}, \sigma, T, none \rangle \xrightarrow[(l,r,c)]{\mathbf{out}\langle e \rangle} \langle n[\langle v \rangle.P]^c_{l,r}, \sigma, T \cup \{(l, r, c)\}, \mathbf{out}\langle e \rangle @ (l, r, c) \rangle$$

This exists in the transition systems (i.e., rule (1) in Theorem 5.1). Assume

$$\mathcal{HF}(N\langle T, t \rangle) = (\![\{\mathbf{idle} \rightarrow (N\langle T, none \rangle)\}\langle T, t \rangle)$$

According to Definition 5.1(5) in derivation strategy, N can perform the transition as below:

$$\langle n[\mathbf{out}\langle e \rangle.P]^c_{l,r}, \sigma, T, t \rangle \longrightarrow \langle n[\mathbf{out}\langle e \rangle.P]^c_{l,r}, \sigma, T, none \rangle \quad \text{if } t \neq none$$

This transition is in accordance with the transition rule (2) in Theorem 5.1. So it also exists in the transition system.

Further, we give the proof for a network composed of two nonempty subnetworks. Here we consider the situation in which the head normal form of both subnetworks are in the first type of guarded choice, the proof of others are similar. Assume

$$\mathcal{HF}(N_1\langle T, t \rangle) = (\![_{i \in I}\{\mathbf{out}\langle e_i \rangle @ s_i \rightarrow (M_i\langle T_i, t_i \rangle)\} [\!] [\!]_{j \in J}\{\langle v_j \rangle @ s_j \rightarrow (W_j\langle T_j, t_j \rangle)\}\langle T, t \rangle)$$

$$\mathcal{HF}(N_2\langle T, t \rangle) = (\![_{k \in K}\{\mathbf{out}\langle e_k \rangle @ s_k \rightarrow (U_k\langle T_k, t_k \rangle)\} [\!] [\!]_{o \in O}\{\langle v_o \rangle @ s_o \rightarrow (V_o\langle T_o, t_o \rangle)\}\langle T, t \rangle)$$

According to the derivation strategy, N_1 can perform transitions as following:

$$\langle N_1, \sigma_{N_1}, T, t \rangle \xrightarrow[s_i]{\textbf{out}\langle e_i \rangle} \langle M_i, \sigma_{N_1}, T_i, t_i \rangle, \quad \langle N_1, \sigma_{N_1}, T, t \rangle \xrightarrow[s_j]{\langle v_j \rangle} \langle W_j, \sigma_{N_1}, T_j, t_j \rangle$$

N_2 can perform transitions as following:

$$\langle N_2, \sigma_{N_2}, T, t \rangle \xrightarrow[s_k]{\textbf{out}\langle e_k \rangle} \langle U_k, \sigma_{N_2}, T_k, t_k \rangle, \quad \langle N_2, \sigma_{N_2}, T, t \rangle \xrightarrow[s_o]{\langle v_o \rangle} \langle V_o, \sigma_{N_2}, T_o, t_o \rangle$$

The head normal form of $N_1 | N_2$ can be achieved by applying expansion law (par-1) and the result is shown as below.

$\mathcal{HF}(N_1 | N_2 \langle T, t \rangle)$

$= ([\!]_{i \in I} \{ \textbf{out}\langle e_i \rangle @ s_i \to (M_i | N_2 \langle T_i, t_i \rangle) \} [\!] \ [\!]_{j \in J} \{ \langle v_j \rangle @ s_j \to (W_j | N_2 \langle T_j, t_j \rangle) \} [\!]$

$[\!]_{k \in K} \{ \textbf{out}\langle e_k \rangle @ s_k \to (N_1 | U_k \langle T_k, t_k \rangle) \} [\!] \ [\!]_{o \in O} \{ \langle v_o \rangle @ s_o \to (N_1 | V_o \langle T_o, t_o \rangle) \} \langle T, t \rangle)$

According to the derivation strategy, $N_1 | N_2$ can perform transitions as below:

$$\langle N_1 | N_2, \sigma, T, t \rangle \xrightarrow[s_i]{\textbf{out}\langle e_i \rangle} \langle M_i | N_2, \sigma, T_i, t_i \rangle, \quad \langle N_1 | N_2, \sigma, T, t \rangle \xrightarrow[s_j]{\langle v_j \rangle} \langle W_j | N_2, \sigma, T_j, t_j \rangle$$

$$\langle N_1 | N_2, \sigma, T, t \rangle \xrightarrow[s_k]{\textbf{out}\langle e_k \rangle} \langle N_1 | U_k, \sigma, T_k, t_k \rangle, \quad \langle N_1 | N_2, \sigma, T, t \rangle \xrightarrow[s_o]{\langle v_o \rangle} \langle N_1 | V_o, \sigma, T_o, t_o \rangle$$

These transitions also exist in the transition system and can be directly proved by applying the first rule in Theorem 5.5. $\qquad \square$

6 Mechanical Approach to Linking Algebraic Semantics and Operational Semantics

In this section, we apply the mechanical method to link the algebraic semantics and the operational semantics for wireless systems by using the equational and rewriting logic system Maude [1].

6.1 Mechanizing Algebraic Semantics and Head Normal Form

To mechanize the algebraic semantics and the head normal form, we implement guarded components $\textbf{out}\langle e \rangle @ s$ as Guard1 and $\langle v \rangle @ s$ as Guard2 respectively in Maude. Similarly, $\textbf{in}(x) @ s$, $(x) @ s$ and $\textbf{idle}$ are implemented as Guard3, Guard4 and Guard5 respectively. Then different kinds of guarded components are implemented according to the type of guards. All the guarded components are declared as type GComponent. Below is the declarations of guarded components in Maude.

```
subsort GComp1 GComp2 GComp3 GComp4 GComp5 < GComponent .
subsort Guard1 Guard2 Guard3 Guard4 Guard5 < GuardPrefix .
op '(_<_,_>') : Network Act Tag -> GuardPostfix [ctor] .
op _->>_ : GuardPrefix GuardPostfix -> GComponent [ctor] .
op _->>_ : Guard1 GuardPostfix -> GComp1 [ctor] .
...
op _->>_ : Guard5 GuardPostfix -> GComp5 [ctor] .
```

Based on the five kinds of guarded components, we can define the guarded choice (i.e., GChoice) by implementing guarded component as its element.

```
subsort SelectGChoice < GChoice .
op {_} : GComponent -> GChoice [ctor] .
op {_} : GComp1 -> SelectGChoice [ctor] .
```

```
op {_} : GComp2 -> SelectGChoice [ctor] .
op _[]_ : SelectGChoice SelectGChoice -> SelectGChoice [ctor] .
```

In above definitions, `SelectGChoice` is the implementation of the first type of guarded choice, which is declared as a subsort of `GChoice`. It is composed of `GComp1` and `GComp2` separated by `[]`. Definitions of other types of guarded choices are similar.

The head normal form is declared as equations using the keyword `eq` (or `ceq` for conditional one) in Maude. We use `HF(N<T,t>)` to represent the head normal form $\mathcal{HF}(N\langle T, t \rangle)$ introduced in section 4.

```
eq HF(n[<v>.P](l,r,c)<T,none>) =
    ({<v>@(l,r,c)->>(n[P](l,r,c)<T\(l,r,c),<v>@(l,r,c)>)}<T,none>) .
ceq HF(n[<v>.P](l,r,c)<T,out<f>@s>) =
    ({idle->>(n[<v>.P](l,r,c)<T,none>)}<T,out<f>@s>) if t=/=none .
```

Above are the declarations of the head normal form of an active transmitter with different types of transmission tags. They are expressed in perfect accordance with the head normal form definition (2-1) and (2-2) respectively.

For parallel composition of networks, the head normal form is calculated by using parallel expansion laws according to the type of guarded choice of each parallel branch. Below is the case where the head normal form of both branches are of the first type of guarded choice.

```
ceq HF(M|N<T,t>) = (comp1(M-Select,N)[]comp2(N-Select,M)<T,t>)
    if (M-Select<T,t>) := HF(M<T,t>)/\(N-Select<T,t>) := HF(N<T,t>) .
```

The head normal form of M and N with network status `<T,t>` are expressed as `M-Select` and `N-Select` respectively. Both of them are transmission selection guarded choice. Hence, the head normal form is calculated by using parallel expansion law (par-1) as `comp1(M-Select,N)[]comp2(N-Select,M)`, where `comp1(M-Select,N)` indicates that node in M is scheduled.

Example 6.1. Let *Net* be the network in Example 2.2. The head normal of this network under the network status $\langle \emptyset, none \rangle$ is calculated in Maude by using the command **reduce** as below, which shows the two possible choices of its first transition step.

```
reduce in NORMAL-FORM :
(  {out<e>@(l1,r1,c)->>(n1[<[[e]]>.P](l1,r1,c)|n2[out<f>.Q](l2,r2,c)|
            n3[in(x).R](l3,r3,c)|n4[in(y).S](l4,r4,c)<(l1,r1,c),out<e>@(l1,r1,c)>)}
[]{out<f>@(l2,r2,c)->>(n1[out<e>.P](l1,r1,c)|n2[<[[f]]>.Q](l2,r2,c)|
            n3[in(x).R](l3,r3,c)|n4[in(y).S](l4,r4,c)<(l2,r2,c),out<f>@(l2,r2,c)>)}
    <empty,none> )
```

6.2 Mechanizing the Derivation of Operational Semantics from Algebraic Semantics

The derivation strategy is declared as rules by keyword `crl` (i.e., conditional rule). Each rule is defined as a transition of configurations based on the head normal form. We give the declaration of the item (1.a) in Definition 5.1 below.

```
crl [1.a]:.<N,env,T,none> => <Ni,env,T U s,out<e>@s>
```

```
if (hgc-sl<T,none>):=HF(N<T,none>)/\(hgc[]
{out<e>@s->>(Ni<T U s,out<e>@s>)}[]hgc'<T,none>):=(hgc-sl<T,none>) .
```

From the condition of this rule, we know that the head normal form of N under the network status `<T,none>` is `hgc-sl` and `hgc-sl` has a component `out<e>@s->>` `(Ni<T U s,out<e>@s>)`. Hence, the network can perform a transition reflecting that the transmitter s is scheduled to start a transmission and the active transmitters set is updated from T to T U s.

Example 6.2. We use the network *Net* in Example 2.2 to illustrate the effectiveness of our derivation strategy. Assume that the initial network status is `<empty,none>`. We use the command **search** to generate its transitions in Maude. And one of the transition paths is shown below.

```
< n1[out<e>.P](l1,r1,c)|n2[out<f>.Q](l2,r2,c)|n3[in(x).R](l3,r3,c)|n4[in(y).S](l4,r4,c),
  init,empty,none >
==> < n1[out<e>.P](l1,r1,c)|n2[<[[f]]>.Q](l2,r2,c)|n3[(x).R](l3,r3,c)|n4[(y).S](l4,r4,c),
  init,(l2,r2,c),none >
==> < n1[<[[e]]>.P](l1,r1,c)|n2[<[[f]]>.Q](l2,r2,c)|n3[R](l3,r3,c)|n4[(y).S](l4,r4,c),
  (x,interf),(l1,r1,c)U(l2,r2,c),none >
==> < n1[<[[e]]>.P](l1,r1,c)|n2[Q](l2,r2,c)|n3[R](l3,r3,c)|n4[S](l4,r4,c),
  (x,interf)u(y,[[f]]),(l1,r1,c),none >
```

Initially, the state of variables is set to the initial state `init`. According to the head normal of this network shown in Example 6.1, N_1 and N_2 can start their transmissions. After N_2 begins its transmission, a collision occurs in N_3 caused by N_1 and a special value `interf` (stands for $\perp$) is bound to x. When N_2 finishes its broadcast transmission, N_4 receives the value `[[f]]` successfully by updating the state of variable y to `[[f]]`.

6.3   Mechanizing the Derived Operational Semantics

This section is devoted to mechanize the derived operational semantics. The operational semantics is declared by rules or conditional rules. We can implement transition rules in Theorem 5.1 to Theorem 5.5 into Maude system directly. We use the first transition in Theorem 5.5 (with β in the form of **out**$\langle e \rangle$) to illustrate the mechanization as below. Others are similar.

```
crl[Theorem5.5-1.1]:.<M|N,env,T,none> => <M'|N,env,T',out<e>@s>
            if .<M,env,T,none> => <M',env,T',out<e>@s> .
crl[Theorem5.5-1.2]:.<M|N,env,T,none> => <M|N',env,T',out<e>@s>
            if .<N,env,T,none> => <N',env,T',out<e>@s> .
```

From the conditions of the two rules, we know that one parallel branch can perform a begin transmission transition. Hence, the two rules show that the whole network can also perform the begin transmission transition regardless of another branch.

Consider the network *Net* in Example 2.2 again. Its transitions can be generated in Maude by applying the transition rules of the derived operational semantics directly. The generated transitions are exactly the same as those generated by using derivation strategy in Example 6.2 in the previous subsection.

This result supports the claim of the equivalence between the derivation strategy and the derived transition system.

7   Conclusion

In this paper we have explored the linking theories between the algebraic semantics and the operational semantics of CWS. This approach starts from the algebraic laws. Our consideration is to derive the operational semantics from the algebraic semantics.

Our approach is new to a calculus of wireless systems. We first introduced the algebraic laws based on four typical forms of guarded choices and gave the parallel expansion laws. Then we defined the head normal form and presented the derivation strategy for deriving the operational semantics from the algebraic semantics. Finally an operational semantics was derived. This exploration shows the soundness of the operational semantics with respect to the algebraic semantics. Further, the equivalence between the derivation strategy and the derived operational semantics is investigated, which shows the completeness of the operational semantics from the viewpoint of the algebraic semantics. We also mechanized the linking between the algebraic semantics and the operational semantics. The mechanical results support that the derived operational semantics is the same as the derivation strategy.

For the future, we are continuing to explore the semantics and the unifying theories for wireless systems. The denotational semantics and the deduction method [3] for wireless systems are very challenging.

Acknowledgement. This work was partly supported by the Danish National Research Foundation and the National Natural Science Foundation of China (Grant No. 61061130541) for the Danish-Chinese Center for Cyber Physical Systems. And, it is also supported by National Basic Research Program of China (Grant No. 2011CB302904), National High Technology Research and Development Program of China (Grant Nos. 2011AA010101 and 2012AA011205), National Natural Science Foundation of China (Grant Nos. 61021004 and 91118008), Shanghai STCSM Project (No. 12511504205), and Shanghai Knowledge Service Platform Project (No. ZF1213).

References

1. Clavel, M., Durán, F., Eker, S., Lincoln, P., Martí-Oliet, N., Meseguer, J., Talcott, C.L.: The Maude 2.0 System. In: Nieuwenhuis, R. (ed.) RTA 2003. LNCS, vol. 2706, pp. 76–87. Springer, Heidelberg (2003)
2. Godskesen, J.C.: A Calculus for Mobile Ad Hoc Networks. In: Murphy, A.L., Vitek, J. (eds.) COORDINATION 2007. LNCS, vol. 4467, pp. 132–150. Springer, Heidelberg (2007)
3. Hoare, C.A.R.: Algebra of Concurrent Programming. In: Meeting 52 of WG 2.3 (2011)

4. Hoare, C.A.R., He, J.: Unifying Theories of Programming. Prentice Hall International Series in Computer Science (1998)
5. Hoare, C.A.R., Hayes, I.J., He, J., Morgan, C.C., Roscoe, A.W., Sanders, J.W., Sorenson, I.H., Spivey, J.M., Sufrin, B.A.: Laws of Programming. Commun. ACM 30(8), 672–686 (1987)
6. Lanese, I., Sangiorgi, D.: An Operational Semantics for a Calculus for Wireless Systems. Theor. Comput. Sci. 411(19), 1928–1948 (2010)
7. Merro, M.: An Observational Theory for Mobile Ad Hoc Networks (full version). Inf. Comput. 207(2), 194–208 (2009)
8. Mezzetti, N., Sangiorgi, D.: Towards a Calculus for Wireless Systems. Electr. Notes Theor. Comput. Sci. 158, 331–353 (2006)
9. Nanz, S., Hankin, C.: A Framework for Security Analysis of Mobile Wireless Network. Theor. Comput. Sci. 367(1-2), 203–227 (2006)
10. Ostrovsky, K., Prasad, K.V.S., Taha, W.: Towards a Primitive Higher Order Calculus of Broadcasting Systems. In: PPDP 2002, pp. 2–13 (2002)
11. Plotkin, G.: A Structural Approach to Operational Semantics. J. Log. Algebr. Program. 60-61, 17–139 (2004)
12. Prasad, K.V.S.: A Calculus of Broadcasting Systems. Sci. Comput. Program. 25(2-3), 285–327 (1995)
13. Scott, D., Strachey, C.: Toward a Mathematical Semantics for Computer Languages. Technical report PRG-6, Oxford University Computer Laboratory (1971)

Automated Specification Discovery
via User-Defined Predicates

Guanhua He[1], Shengchao Qin[1,2,*], Wei-Ngan Chin[3], and Florin Craciun[4]

[1] Teesside University
[2] Shenzhen University
shengchao.qin@gmail.com
[3] National University of Singapore
[4] Babes-Bolyai University

Abstract. Automated discovery of specifications for heap-manipulating programs is a challenging task due to the complexity of aliasing and mutability of data structures. This task is further complicated by an expressive domain that combines shape, numerical and bag information. In this paper, we propose a compositional analysis framework in the presence of user-defined predicates, which would derive the summary for each method in the expressive abstract domain, independently from its callers. We propose a novel abstraction method with a bi-abduction technique in the combined domain to discover pre-/post-conditions that could not be automatically inferred before. The analysis does not only prove the memory safety properties, but also finds relationships between pure and shape domains towards full functional correctness of programs. A prototype of the framework has been implemented and initial experiments have shown that our approach can discover interesting properties for non-trivial programs.

1 Introduction

In automated program analysis, certain kinds of program properties have been well explored over the last decades, such as numerical properties in linear abstraction domain, and shape properties for list-manipulating programs in separation domain. However, previous works have not yet automatically analysed program properties involving complex mixed domains, particularly for programs with sophisticated data structures and strong invariants involving both structural and pure (numerical and content) information. For example, it is still non-trivial to discover program properties, such as a list becoming sorted during the execution of a program, a binary search tree remaining balanced before and after the execution of a procedure, or the elements of a list remain unchanged after reversing the list. This difficulty is not only due to sharing and mutability of data structures under manipulation, but is also due to closely intertwined program properties, such as structural numerical information (length and height), symbolic contents of data structures (bag of values), and relational numerical information (sortedness and balancedness).

---

* Corresponding author.

L. Groves and J. Sun (Eds.): ICFEM 2013, LNCS 8144, pp. 397–414, 2013.

In addition to classical shape analyses (e.g. [4,14,24]), separation logic [22] has been applied to analyse shape properties in recent years [5,8,26]. These works can automatically infer method specifications in the shape domain. Some other works such as [17,18] also incorporate simple numerical information into the shape domain to allow automated synthesis of properties like data structure size information.

However, these previous analyses mainly deal with predesignated data structure properties with fixed numerical templates, such as pointer safety for lists and list length information. To overcome this limitation, we propose in this paper a compositional program analysis in a combined abstract domain with *shape*, *numerical* and *bag* information. Our analysis not only handles both functional correctness and memory safety together, but can also discover relationships between shape and pure (numerical and bag) domains. Unlike traditional approaches [18] which usually analyse the shape first before turning to pure properties, our approach analyses programs over both domains at the same time. This is very necessary as verifying functional correctness for certain programs may require us to consider both shape and pure information at the same time. Without pure information, a shape analysis may not be able to find useful program specifications (an example is the merge procedure discussed in [5]). Our approach can handle this kind of programs smoothly, and we will illustrate our method using the merge example in Section 2.

Our analysis is compositional. It analyses a program fragment without any given contextual information, and it analyses each method in a modular way independent of its callers. To generate the summary (pre-/post-conditions) for each method, our analysis adopts a new bi-abduction mechanism over the combined domain, which generalises the bi-abduction technique proposed by Calcagno et al. [5] to a more expressive abstract domain. In summary, this paper makes the following contributions:

- We have designed a compositional analysis to discover *full program specifications* (in the form of pre-/post-conditions involving shape, numerical and bag properties) with user-given data structure predicates.
- For such an analysis, we have designed a *bi-abductive abstract semantics* which incorporates a generalised bi-abduction procedure to facilitate specification discovery over the combined abstract domain.
- In addition to a normal abstraction function, we have also proposed a novel *abductive abstraction* function over the combined domain. This new abstraction function allows us to find stronger method specifications that are often necessary for the successful verification for higher level of functional correctness.
- We have built a prototype system and conducted some initial experiments, which help confirm the viability and precision of our solution in inferring non-trivial program specifications.

2   The Approach

In this section we give some preliminaries and illustrate our approach via an example.

2.1 Preliminaries

Separation Logic. Separation logic [22] extends Hoare logic to support reasoning about shared mutable data structures. It provides separation conjunction ($*$) to form formulae like $p_1 * p_2$ to assert that two heaps described by p_1 and p_2 are domain-disjoint.

User-defined Predicates. In our analysis, users are allowed to define inductive predicates in separation logic to specify both separation and pure properties of recursive data structures. For example, given a data structure data Node { int val; Node next; }, one can define a predicate for a list with its content as

$$\text{llB}(\text{root}, n, S) \equiv (\text{root}=\text{null} \wedge n=0 \wedge S=\emptyset) \vee$$
$$(\exists v, q, n_1, S_1 \cdot \text{root} \mapsto \text{Node}(v, q) * \text{llB}(q, n_1, S_1) \wedge n_1=n-1 \wedge S=S_1 \sqcup \{v\})$$

The parameter root for the predicate llB is the root pointer referring to the list. The length and content of the list are denoted resp. by n and the bag S, and $\sqcup$ indicates multiset (bag) union. If one wants to verify a sorting algorithm, they can specify a non-empty sorted list as follows:

$$\text{sllB}(\text{root}, mi, mx, S) \equiv (\text{root} \mapsto \text{Node}(mi, \text{null}) \wedge mi=mx \wedge S=\{mi\}) \vee$$
$$(\text{root} \mapsto \text{Node}(v, q) * \text{sllB}(q, m_1, mx, S_1) \wedge v=mi \wedge v \leq m_1 \wedge m_1 \leq mx \wedge S=S_1 \sqcup \{v\})$$

where it keeps track of the minimum (mi) and maximum (mx) values in the list as well as the bag of all values (S). Note that we use a shortened notation that unbound variables, such as q, v, m_1 and S_1, are implicitly existentially quantified.

Such predicates play an important role in our analysis as (i) they are used to help specify desired properties about data structures under manipulation, and (ii) they serve as a guide for our analysis to discover desired program specifications. To reduce the burden of supplying such predicates, we have defined a library of predicates covering popular data structures and variety of properties.

Entailment. In our work we make use of the separation logic prover SLEEK [7] to prove whether one formula Δ' in the combined abstract domain entails another one Δ: $\Delta' \vdash \Delta * R$. R is called the *frame* which is useful for our analysis. For instance, by entailment proof

$$\exists y \cdot x \mapsto \text{node}(vx, y) * \text{llB}(y, n, S) \vdash \text{llB}(x, m, S_1) * R$$

We can generate the frame R as $m=n+1 \wedge S_1=S \sqcup \{vx\}$.

Bi-Abduction. In an earlier work [5], a bi-abductive entailment is proposed for the *shape* domain: given two shape formulae G, H, the bi-abduction $G * [A] \rhd H * [F]$ infers the *anti-frame* A and the *frame* F along the entailment proof. An example taken from [5] is

$$x \mapsto \text{null} * z \mapsto \text{null} * [\underline{\text{list}(y)}] \rhd \text{list}(x) * \text{list}(y) * [\underline{z \mapsto \text{null}}]$$

where the $\text{list}(\cdot)$ predicate describes acyclic, null-terminated singly-linked lists. In the current work, we will generalise such bi-abductive reasoning to the combined domain (involving shape, user-defined predicates, numerical and bag information). A simple example of the generalised bi-abductive reasoning is

$$\exists y \cdot x \mapsto \text{node}(vx, y) * y \mapsto \text{node}(vy, \text{null}) * [\underline{A}] \rhd \text{sllB}(x, mi, mx, S) * [\underline{F}]$$

where $\underline{A} \equiv (vx \leq vy)$ and $\underline{F} \equiv (mi=vx \wedge mx=vy \wedge S=\{vx, vy\})$.

```
1   Node merge(Node x, Node y)      9        Node t = x.next;
2   {                              10        x.next = merge(t, y);
3     if (x == null) {             11        return x;
4       return y;                  12      } else {
5     } else if (y == null) {      13        Node t = y.next;
6       return x;                  14        y.next = merge(x, t);
7     } else                       15        return y;
8       if (x.val <= y.val) {      16  } }
```

Fig. 1. Merging two sorted lists

2.2 An Illustrative Example

We illustrate our analysis approach via the merge method (used in the merge-sort), which has been declared as an unverifiable example in [5], since their analysis does not keep track of data values stored in the list during their shape analysis. The method (Fig. 1) merges two sorted lists into one sorted list. Automated specification discovery for merge is tricky due to two facts: (1) only one input list is fully traversed; (2) both input lists are required to be sorted. For (1), if we apply the shape abduction [5], we can only discover two disjoint lists (for precondition) - one ending with null and one ending with an unknown pointer, which cannot guarantee the memory safety of the method. For (2), if an analysis cannot infer that the two input lists are sorted, it will not be able to discover that the output list is sorted, which will not be sufficient for one to verify the functional correctness of the enclosing merge-sort method. The two input lists being unsorted also causes the unknown pointer problem mentioned above. To overcome these difficulties, we propose a compositional analysis in a combined shape and pure domain, where program properties over the combined domain are processed at the same time during the analysis. Our analysis adopts a novel bi-abduction mechanism to help discover program preconditions in the combined domain.

For the merge example, the shape predicate selected for our analysis is $slsB$ which keeps track of the minimal (mi) and maximal (mx) values, bag of values (S) and tail pointer (p) of a sorted list segment.

$$slsB(root, mi, mx, S, p) \equiv (root \mapsto Node(mi, p) \land mi = mx \land S = \{mi\}) \lor$$
$$(root \mapsto Node(mi, q) * sllB(q, m_1, mx, S_1, p) \land mi \leq m_1 \land m_1 \leq mx \land S = S_1 \sqcup \{mi\})$$

Our analysis aims at finding a sound and precise specification (summary) of the method. Starting from an initial specification ($Pre_0 \equiv emp$, $Post_0 \equiv false$), our analysis iterates the method body by symbolic execution a number of times until a fixed point is reached for the pre-/post-condition pair. During the symbolic execution, we use a pair of states ($infP$, $Curr$) to keep track of the precondition that the analysis has discovered ($infP$) so far and the current state the execution has reached ($Curr$), respectively. If the current abstract state does not meet the precondition required by the current program command, we use an abductive inference mechanism (mentioned in the previous subsection) to synthesise a candidate precondition as the missing precondition.

For the merge example, the initial specification ($Pre_0 \equiv$ emp, $Post_0 \equiv$ false) allows the analysis to skip the branches with recursive calls to merge. The symbolic execution in the first fixpoint iteration starts from state (infP$\equiv$emp, Curr$\equiv$emp), since the analysis assumes no prior knowledge about the starting program state. To enter line 4, the condition x==null needs to be met by the current abstract state. We apply abduction and discover x=null which is then added to the precondition. Similarly, we have y=null from the second branch. After the first iteration, a summary is found as

$$(Pre_1 \equiv (\texttt{x=null} \lor \texttt{y=null}), Post_1 \equiv (\texttt{x=null} \land \texttt{res=y} \lor \texttt{y=null} \land \texttt{res=x})) \qquad (1)$$

where res denotes the return value. Using this new summary for recursive calls to merge, symbolically executing the method body again (but with an updated starting state (infP$\equiv Pre_1$, Curr$\equiv Pre_1$) yields the summary (Pre_2, $Post_2$):

$$(Pre_2 \equiv \texttt{x=null} \lor \texttt{y=null} \lor \texttt{x} \mapsto \texttt{Node}(xv_1, xp_1) * \texttt{y} \mapsto \texttt{Node}(yv_1, yp_1)$$
$$\land (xv_1 \leq yv_1 \land xp_1 = \texttt{null} \lor xv_1 > yv_1 \land yp_1 = \texttt{null}),$$
$$Post_2 \equiv \texttt{x=null} \land \texttt{res=y} \lor \texttt{y=null} \land \texttt{res=x} \lor \texttt{x} \mapsto \texttt{Node}(xv_1, xp_1) * \texttt{y} \mapsto \texttt{Node}(yv_1, yp_1)$$
$$\land (xv_1 \leq yv_1 \land \texttt{res=x} \land xp_1 = \texttt{y} \lor xv_1 > yv_1 \land \texttt{res=y} \land yp_1 = \texttt{x}))$$
$$\qquad (2)$$

After the third iteration of symbolic execution, we generate a precondition as:

$$\texttt{x=null} \lor \texttt{y=null} \lor \texttt{x} \mapsto \texttt{Node}(xv_1, xp_1) * \texttt{y} \mapsto \texttt{Node}(yv_1, yp_1)$$
$$\land (xv_1 \leq yv_1 \land xp_1 = \texttt{null} \lor xv_1 > yv_1 \land yp_1 = \texttt{null}) \qquad (3)$$

$$\lor \texttt{x} \mapsto \texttt{Node}(xv_1, xp_1) * xp_1 \mapsto \texttt{Node}(xv_2, xp_2) * \texttt{y} \mapsto \texttt{Node}(yv_1, yp_1)$$
$$\land (xv_1 \leq yv_1 \land (xv_2 \leq yv_1 \land xp_2 = \texttt{null} \lor xv_2 > yv_1 \land yp_1 = \texttt{null})) \qquad (4)$$

$$\lor \texttt{x} \mapsto \texttt{Node}(xv_1, xp_1) * \texttt{y} \mapsto \texttt{Node}(yv_1, yp_1) * yp_1 \mapsto \texttt{Node}(yv_2, yp_2)$$
$$\land (xv_1 > yv_1 \land (xv_1 \leq yv_2 \land xp_1 = \texttt{null} \lor xv_1 > yv_2 \land yp_2 = \texttt{null})) \qquad (5)$$

Branch (4) says that the program only touches the second node of x list (the list referred to by x) if $xv_1 \leq yv_1$. Furthermore, if $xv_2 \leq yv_1$, xp_2 should be null; otherwise yp_1 must be null to guarantee the termination of the method and memory safety. Branch (5) states a similar condition when touching the second node of y list. The information kept in this formula is very precise, but keeping such a level of details will not allow the analysis to scale up. According to the given predicate slsB, we could abstract the shape of the x list (and that of the y list) to be a sorted list segment. However, the formula itself does not contain sufficient information for us to carry out this abstraction, i.e. the sortedness information about the x list (and the y list) is missing. This missing information is the numerical relation between xv_1 and xv_2 in the x list (and that between yv_1 and yv_2 in the y list). In other words, we need to use abduction to discover $xv_1 \leq xv_2$ (resp. $yv_1 \leq yv_2$) during the abstraction from the shape of the x list (resp. the y list) to a sorted list segment in the branch (4) (resp. (5)), e.g. for the x list:

$$\texttt{x} \mapsto \texttt{Node}(xv_1, xp_1) * xp_1 \mapsto \texttt{Node}(xv_2, xp_2) * \boxed{[xv_1 \leq xv_2]} \rhd \texttt{slsB}(\texttt{x}, xv_1, xv_2, xS_1, xp_2) * R$$

The inspiration for this *abductive abstraction* comes from the definition of the predicate slsB. We use such predicates to help infer data structure properties that are anticipated from some program code. Note that a standard abstraction would only be able to obtain an abstraction of an ordinary list segment without any sortedness information.

By applying such an *abductive abstraction* against the predicate slsB and then joining the branches with the same shape, the precondition from two iterations becomes:

$$\texttt{x=null} \lor \texttt{y=null} \lor \texttt{slsB}(\texttt{x}, xmi_0, xmx_0, xS_0, xp_0) * \texttt{slsB}(\texttt{y}, ymi_0, ymx_0, yS_0, yp_0)$$
$$\land (xmx_0 \leq ymx_0 \land xp_0 = \texttt{null} \lor xmx_0 > ymx_0 \land yp_0 = \texttt{null})$$

Continuing the analysis, the fixed point of the program summary (Pre,Post) is reached:

$\mathtt{Pre} \equiv \mathtt{x=null} \lor \mathtt{y=null} \lor \mathtt{slsB}(\mathtt{x}, \mathtt{xmi_0}, \mathtt{xmx_0}, \mathtt{xS_0}, \mathtt{xp_0})*$
$\quad \mathtt{slsB}(\mathtt{y}, \mathtt{ymi_0}, \mathtt{ymx_0}, \mathtt{yS_0}, \mathtt{yp_0}) \land (\mathtt{xmx_0} {\leq} \mathtt{ymx_0} \land \mathtt{xp_0} {=} \mathtt{null} \lor \mathtt{xmx_0} {>} \mathtt{ymx_0} \land \mathtt{yp_0} {=} \mathtt{null}),$

$\mathtt{Post} \equiv \mathtt{x=null} \land \mathtt{res=y} \lor \mathtt{y=null} \land \mathtt{res=x} \lor \mathtt{slsB}(\mathtt{x}, \mathtt{xmi_1}, \mathtt{xmx_1}, \mathtt{xS_1}, \mathtt{xp_1})$
$\quad *\mathtt{slsB}(\mathtt{y}, \mathtt{ymi_1}, \mathtt{ymx_1}, \mathtt{yS_1}, \mathtt{yp_1}) \land \mathtt{xS_0} {\sqcup} \mathtt{yS_0} {=} \mathtt{xS_1} {\sqcup} \mathtt{yS_1} \land \mathtt{xmi_1} {=} \mathtt{xmi_0} \land \mathtt{ymi_1} {=} \mathtt{ymi_0} \land$
$\quad (\mathtt{xmi_0} {\leq} \mathtt{ymi_0} \land \mathtt{res=x} \land \mathtt{xp_1} {=} \mathtt{y} \land \mathtt{xmx_1} {\leq} \mathtt{ymi_1} \lor \mathtt{xmi_0} {>} \mathtt{ymi_0} \land \mathtt{res=y} \land \mathtt{yp_1} {=} \mathtt{x} \land \mathtt{ymx_1} {\leq} \mathtt{xmi_1}$

The essential steps to terminate the search for suitable preconditions are abstraction and widening. Both operators are tantamount to weakening a state, and they are over-approximations and are sound for the synthesis of postconditions. However, when such steps are applied to the synthesis of preconditions, it may make the precondition too weak for the program to establish the postcondition. So after the analysis, we shall use a forward analysis process to check the discovered summary (a similar process is also carried out in [5]).

From this example, we observe that the memory safety is not only related to the shape of data structures, but may also relate to data values stored in them. For the merge example, our analysis can find that one input list is traversed to its end, i.e. until null is reached, and the other input list is partially traversed till it reaches an element that is larger than the maximal value of the former list. As captured in the inferred precondition, the rest of the list will not be accessed by the program. Similarly, the inferred postcondition captures a fairly precise specification that represents the merged list using two list segments that either begins from x or from y, depending on which of the two input lists contains the smallest element.

3   Language and Abstract Domain

To simplify presentation, we employ a strongly-typed C-like imperative language in Fig. 2 to demonstrate our approach. A program *Prog* written in this language consists of declarations *tdecl*, which can be data type declarations *datat* (e.g. Node in Section 2), predicate definitions *spred* (e.g. 11B and slsB), as well as method declarations *meth*. The definitions for *spred* and *mspec* are given later in Fig. 3. We assume that methods come with no specifications (i.e. no *mspec** part), and our proposed analysis will discover them. Our language is expression-oriented, and thus the body of a method (e) is an expression formed by program constructors. Note that d and $d[v]$ represent respectively heap-insensitive and heap sensitive commands. k^τ is a constant of type τ. The language allows both call-by-value and call-by-reference method parameters, separated with a semicolon (;). These parameters allow each iterative loop to be directly converted to an equivalent tail-recursive method, where mutations on parameters are made visible to the caller via pass-by-reference. This technique of translating away iterative loops is standard and is helpful in further minimising our core language.

Our specification language (in Fig. 3) allows (user-defined) shape predicates *spred* to specify program properties in our combined domain. Note that such predicates are constructed with disjunctive constraints Φ. We require that the predicates be well-formed [7]. The first parameter of a predicate is the pointer referring to the data structures itself. A conjunctive abstract program state σ has mainly two parts: the heap

$$
\begin{array}{llll}
Prog & ::= tdecl^* \ meth^* & tdecl & ::= datat \mid spred \\
datat & ::= \texttt{data} \ c \ \{ field^* \} & field & ::= t \ v \qquad t ::= c \mid \tau \\
meth & ::= t \ mn \ ((t \ v)^*; (t \ v)^*) \ mspec^* \ \{e\} & & \tau ::= \texttt{int} \mid \texttt{bool} \mid \texttt{void} \\
e & ::= d \mid d[v] \mid v{:=}e \mid e_1; e_2 \mid t \ v; \ e \mid \texttt{if} \ (v) \ e_1 \ \texttt{else} \ e_2 \\
d & ::= \texttt{null} \mid k^\tau \mid v \mid \texttt{new} \ c(v^*) \mid mn(u^*; v^*) \\
d[v] & ::= v.f \mid v_1.f{:=}v_2 \mid \texttt{free}(v)
\end{array}
$$

Fig. 2. A Core (C-like) Imperative Language

(shape) part κ in the separation domain and the pure part π in convex polyhedra domain and bag (multi-set) domain, where π consists of γ, ϕ and φ as aliasing, numerical and multi-set information, respectively. $k^{\texttt{int}}$ is an integer constant. The square symbols like $\sqsubset$, $\sqsubseteq$, $\sqcup$ and $\sqcap$ are multi-set operators. The set of all σ formulae is denoted as SH (*symbolic heap*). During the symbolic execution, the abstract program state at each program point will be a disjunction of σ's, denoted by Δ. Its set is defined as $\mathcal{P}_{\text{SH}}$. An abstract state Δ can be normalised to the Φ form [7].

$$
\begin{array}{lll}
spred & ::= p(\texttt{root}, v^*) \equiv \Phi \qquad \Phi ::= \bigvee \sigma^* \qquad & \sigma ::= \exists v^* {\cdot} \kappa {\wedge} \pi \\
mspec & ::= requires \ \Phi_{pr} \ ensures \ \Phi_{po} \\
\Delta & ::= \Phi \mid \Delta_1 {\vee} \Delta_2 \mid \Delta {\wedge} \pi \mid \Delta_1 {*} \Delta_2 \mid \exists v {\cdot} \Delta \\
\kappa & ::= \texttt{emp} \mid v {\mapsto} c(v^*) \mid p(v^*) \mid \kappa_1 * \kappa_2 & \pi ::= \gamma \wedge \phi \\
\gamma & ::= v_1 {=} v_2 \mid v {=} \texttt{null} \mid v_1 {\neq} v_2 \mid v {\neq} \texttt{null} \mid \gamma_1 {\wedge} \gamma_2 \\
\phi & ::= \varphi \mid b \mid a \mid \phi_1 {\wedge} \phi_2 \mid \phi_1 {\vee} \phi_2 \mid \neg \phi \mid \exists v \cdot \phi \mid \forall v \cdot \phi \\
b & ::= \texttt{true} \mid \texttt{false} \mid v \mid b_1 {=} b_2 & a ::= s_1 {=} s_2 \mid s_1 {\leq} s_2 \\
s & ::= k^{\texttt{int}} \mid v \mid k^{\texttt{int}} {\times} s \mid s_1 {+} s_2 \mid -s \mid max(s_1, s_2) \mid min(s_1, s_2) \mid |B| \\
\varphi & ::= v {\in} B \mid B_1 {=} B_2 \mid B_1 {\sqsubset} B_2 \mid B_1 {\sqsubseteq} B_2 \mid \forall v {\in} B {\cdot} \phi \mid \exists v {\in} B {\cdot} \phi \\
B & ::= B_1 {\sqcup} B_2 \mid B_1 {\sqcap} B_2 \mid B_1 {-} B_2 \mid \emptyset \mid \{v\}
\end{array}
$$

Fig. 3. The Specification Language.

Using entailment [7], we define a partial order over these abstract states:

$$\Delta \preceq \Delta' =_{df} \Delta' \vdash \Delta * R$$

where R is the (computed) residue part. And we also have an induced lattice over these states as the base of fixpoint calculation for our analysis.

The memory model of our specification formulae can be found in [7]. In our analysis, variables include both program and logical variables.

4   Generalised Bi-abduction for the Combined Domain

We present a new bi-abduction procedure over the combined domain (which generalises the previous bi-abduction [5] over only the shape domain).

Given σ and σ_1, the bi-abduction procedure $\sigma * [\sigma'] \rhd \sigma_1 * \sigma_2$ (shown in Fig. 4) aims to find the anti-frame part σ' and the frame part σ_2 such that $\sigma * \sigma' \vdash \sigma_1 * \sigma_2$ where σ and σ_1 can be the current program state and the precondition of next instruction, respectively. Our abduction procedure can handle more than one predicates in the analysis, while the shape abduction [5] caters for only one specified shape predicate domain. Another advance is that we can infer numerical and bag properties together with the shape formulae as the anti-frame to improve the precision of the analysis.

$$\frac{\sigma \nvdash \sigma_1 * \mathbf{true} \quad \sigma_1 \vdash \sigma * \sigma' \quad \sigma * \sigma' \vdash \sigma_1 * \sigma_2}{\sigma * [\sigma'] \rhd \sigma_1 * \sigma_2} \text{ Residue}$$

$$\frac{\sigma \nvdash \sigma_1 * \mathbf{true} \quad \sigma_1 \nvdash \sigma * \mathbf{true} \quad \sigma_0 \in \mathrm{unroll}(\sigma) \quad \mathrm{data\_no}(\sigma_0) \leq \mathrm{data\_no}(\sigma_1)}{\begin{array}{c} \sigma_0 \vdash \sigma_1 * \sigma' \text{ or } \sigma_0 * [\sigma'_0] \rhd \sigma_1 * \sigma' \quad \sigma * \sigma' \vdash \sigma_1 * \sigma_2 \\ \hline \sigma * [\sigma'] \rhd \sigma_1 * \sigma_2 \end{array}} \text{ Unroll}$$

$$\frac{\sigma \nvdash \sigma_1 * \mathbf{true} \quad \sigma_1 \nvdash \sigma * \mathbf{true} \quad \sigma_1 * [\sigma'_1] \rhd \sigma * \sigma' \quad \sigma * \sigma' \vdash \sigma_1 * \sigma_2}{\sigma * [\sigma'] \rhd \sigma_1 * \sigma_2} \text{ Reverse}$$

$$\frac{\sigma \nvdash \sigma_1 * \mathbf{true} \quad \sigma_1 \nvdash \sigma * \mathbf{true} \quad \sigma * \sigma_1 \vdash \sigma_1 * \sigma_2}{\sigma * [\sigma_1] \rhd \sigma_1 * \sigma_2} \text{ Missing}$$

$$\frac{\sigma \nvdash \sigma_1 * \sigma'_1 * \mathbf{true} \quad \sigma_1 * \sigma'_1 \nvdash \sigma * \mathbf{true} \quad \sigma \vdash \sigma'_1 * \mathbf{true}}{\begin{array}{c} \sigma * [\sigma'] \rhd \sigma_1 * \sigma'_2 \quad \sigma * \sigma' \vdash \sigma_1 * \sigma'_1 * \sigma_2 \\ \hline \sigma * [\sigma'] \rhd (\sigma_1 * \sigma'_1) * \sigma_2 \end{array}} \text{ Remove}$$

Fig. 4. Bi-Abduction rules

The 1st rule Residue triggers when the LHS (σ) does not entail the RHS (σ_1) but the RHS entails the LHS with some formula (σ') as the residue. This rule is quite general and applies in many cases. For instance, if LHS is emp (σ), RHS is $x \mapsto \mathrm{Node}(xv, xp)(\sigma_1)$, the RHS can entail the LHS with residue $x \mapsto \mathrm{Node}(xv, xp)(\sigma')$. The abduction then checks whether σ plus the frame σ' implies $\sigma_1 * \sigma_2$ for some σ_2 (emp in this example), and returns $x \mapsto \mathrm{Node}(xv, xp)$ as the anti-frame.

The 2nd rule Unroll deals with the case where neither side entails the other, e.g. for $\mathrm{slsB}(x, xmi, xmx, xS, \mathrm{null})$ as LHS and $\exists p, u, v \cdot x \mapsto \mathrm{Node}(u, p) * p \mapsto \mathrm{Node}(v, \mathrm{null})$ as RHS. As the shape predicates in the antecedent σ are formed by disjunctions according to their definitions (like slsB), its certain disjunctive branches may imply σ_1. As the rule suggests, to accomplish abduction $\sigma * [\sigma'] \rhd \sigma_1 * \sigma_2$, we first unfold σ ($\sigma_0 \in \mathrm{unroll}(\sigma)$) and try entailment or further abduction with the results (σ_0) against σ_1. If it succeeds with a frame σ', then we confirm the abduction by ensuring $\sigma * \sigma' \vdash \sigma_1 * \sigma_2$. For the example above, the abduction returns $\exists u, v \cdot xS = \{u, v\}$ as the anti-frame σ' and discovers the nontrivial frame $u = xmi \wedge v = xmx \wedge u \leq v$ as σ_2. The function $\mathrm{data\_no}$ returns the number of data nodes in a state, e.g. it returns 1 for $x \mapsto \mathrm{Node}(v, p) * \mathrm{llB}(p, n, T)$. This syntactic check prevents unlimited number of times of unrolling from happening when the abduction procedure invokes this rule recursively. The unroll unfolds all shape predicates once in σ, normalises the result to a disjunctive form ($\bigvee_{i=1}^n \sigma_i$), and returns the result as a set of formulae ($\{\sigma_1, ..., \sigma_n\}$).

The 3rd rule Reverse handles the case where neither side entails the other, and the 2nd rule does not apply, e.g. $\exists p, u, v, q \cdot x \mapsto Node(u, p) * p \mapsto Node(v, q)$ as LHS and $\exists xS \cdot slsB(x, xmi, xmx, xS, xp)$ as RHS. In this case the antecedent cannot be unfolded as it contains only data nodes. As the rule suggests, it reverses two sides of the entailment and applies the second rule to uncover the constraints σ_1' and σ'. Then it checks that the LHS (σ), with σ' added, does entail the RHS (σ_1) before it returns σ'. For the example above, the anti-frame is inferred as $u \leq v$.

When an abduction procedure is conducted, the first three rules should be attempted exhaustively in the given order; if they do not succeed in finding a solution, then the rule Missing is invoked to add the consequence to the antecedent, provided that they are consistent. It is effective for situations like $x \mapsto Node(\_, \_) \nvdash y \mapsto Node(\_, \_)$, where we should add $y \mapsto node(\_, \_)$ to the LHS directly. In our analysis, we assume that different variables refer to different nodes unless aliasing is suggested in the program code. For example, the if-statement if $(x == y)\{c\}$ suggests that x and y are aliased in code c. Note that when the third rule is applied, the abduction procedure in the premise, namely $\sigma_1 * [\sigma_1'] \rhd \sigma * \sigma'$, is not allowed to apply the third rule again. This is to prevent an infinite number of applications of the third rule.

If the first four rules fail, the Remove rule then tries to find a part of consequent (σ_1') which is entailed by the antecedent. The abduction is then applied to the remaining part of the consequent (σ_1) to discover the anti-frame (σ'). For example, the bi-abduction question $11B(x, n, S) \wedge n > 2 * [\sigma'] \rhd x \mapsto Node(v_1, p_1) * y \mapsto Node(v_2, p_2) * \sigma_2$ needs this rule to remove $x \mapsto Node(v_1, p_1)$ from consequent before applying the Missing rule to find the anti-frame $\sigma' = y \mapsto Node(v_2, p_2)$.

Our earlier work [20] gives a restricted form of abduction focusing on discovering pure information with the assumption that either complete or partial shape information is available. Our bi-abduction algorithm presented here generalises it to cater for full specification discovery scenarios, whereby, we do not have the hints to guide the analysis anymore due to the absence of shape information in pre/post-conditions; but at the same time we can have more freedom as to what missing information to discover. One observation on abduction is that there can be many solutions of the anti-frame σ' for the entailment $\sigma * \sigma' \vdash \sigma_1 * \sigma_2$ to succeed. Therefore, we define "quality" of anti-frame solutions with the partial order $\preceq$ given in the previous section, i.e. the smaller (weaker) one is regarded as better. We prefer to find solutions that are (potentially locally) minimal with respect to $\preceq$ and consistent. However, such solutions are generally not easy to compute and could incur excess cost (with additional disjunction in the analysis). Therefore, our abductive inference is designed more from a practical perspective to discover anti-frames that should be suitable as preconditions for programs, and the partial order $\preceq$ sounds more like a guidance of the decision choices of our abduction implementation, rather than a guarantee to find the theoretically best solution.

5   Analysis Algorithm

Our proposed analysis algorithm is given in Fig. 5. It takes three input parameters: $\mathcal{T}$ as the set of method specifications that are already inferred, the procedure to be analysed $t\ mn\ ((t\ x)^*; (t\ y)^*)\ \{e\}$, and a pre-set upper bound n on the number of shared logical variables that we keep during the analysis.

As in a standard abstract interpretation framework, our analysiscarries out the fixed-point iteration until a fixed-point $(\mathsf{Pre}_i, \mathsf{Post}_i)$ (for some i) is reached. To infer the pre-conditions, our abstract semantics is equipped with bi-abduction over the combined domain. To allow the discovery of more precise preconditions, our abstraction procedure is also equipped with abduction, yielding the novel *abductive abstraction* (abs_a) for precondition discovery. The postcondition inference still employs the normal abstraction mechanism (abs).[1]

Fixpoint Computation in the Combined Domain
Input: $\mathcal{T}$, $t\ mn\ ((t\ x)^*; (t\ y)^*)\ \{e\}$, n
Local: $i := 0$; $\mathsf{Pre}_i := \mathsf{emp}$, $\mathsf{Post}_i := \mathsf{false}$;
1    $\mathcal{T}' := \mathcal{T} \cup \{t\ mn\ ((t\ x)^*; (t\ y)^*)\ requires\ \mathsf{Pre}_0\ ensures\ \mathsf{Post}_0\ \{e\}\}$;
2   **repeat**
3       $i := i + 1$;
4       $(\mathsf{Pre}_i, \mathsf{Post}_i) := [\![e]\!]_{\mathcal{T}'}^{\mathsf{A}}(\mathsf{Pre}_{i-1}, \mathsf{Pre}_{i-1})$;
5       $(\mathsf{Pre}_i, \mathsf{Post}_i) := (\mathsf{abs}_a{}^\dagger(\mathsf{Pre}_i), \mathsf{abs}^\dagger(\mathsf{Post}_i))$;
6       $(\mathsf{Pre}_i, \mathsf{Post}_i) := (\mathsf{join}^\dagger(\mathsf{Pre}_{i-1}, \mathsf{Pre}_i), \mathsf{join}^\dagger(\mathsf{Post}_{i-1}, \mathsf{Post}_i))$;
7       $(\mathsf{Pre}_i, \mathsf{Post}_i) := (\mathsf{widen}^\dagger(\mathsf{Pre}_{i-1}, \mathsf{Pre}_i), \mathsf{widen}^\dagger(\mathsf{Post}_{i-1}, \mathsf{Post}_i))$;
8   **if** $\mathsf{Pre}_i{=}\mathsf{false}$ **or** $\mathsf{Post}_i{=}\mathsf{false}$ **or** $\mathsf{cp\_no}(\mathsf{Pre}_i){>}n$ **or** $\mathsf{cp\_no}(\mathsf{Post}_i){>}n$
         then return fail end if
9       $\mathcal{T}' := \mathcal{T} \cup \{t\ mn\ ((t\ x)^*; (t\ y)^*)\ requires\ \mathsf{Pre}_i\ ensures\ \mathsf{Post}_i\ \{e\}\}$;
10   **until** $\mathcal{T}'$ does not change
11    $\mathsf{Post} = [\![e]\!]_{\mathcal{T}'}\mathsf{Pre}_i$;
12   **if** $\mathsf{Post} = \mathsf{false}$ **or** $\mathsf{Post} \nvdash \mathsf{Post}_i * \mathsf{true}$ **then return fail**
13   **else return** $\mathcal{T}'$
14   **end if**

Fig. 5. Main analysis algorithm

We first set the precondition as `emp` and postcondition as `false` which signifies that we know nothing about the method (line 1). Then for each iteration, a forward bi-abductive analysis is employed to compute a new pre-/post-condition (line 4) based on the current specification. The analysis performs abstraction on both pre-/post-conditions obtained to maintain the finiteness of the shape domain. The obtained results are joined with the results from the previous iteration (line 6), and a widening is conducted over both to ensure termination of the analysis (line 7). If the analysis cannot continue due to a program bug, or cannot keep the number of shared logical variables/cutpoints (counted by `cp_no`) within a specified bound (n), then a failure is reported (line 8). At the end of each iteration, the inferred summary is used to update the specification of mn (line 9), which will be used for recursive calls (if any) of mn in next iteration. Finally we judge whether a fixed-point is already reached (line 10). The last few lines (from line 11)

---

[1] The analysis uses lifted versions of these operations (indicated by †), which will be explained in more detail later.

ensure that inferred specifications are indeed sound using a standard abstract semantics (without abduction). Any unsound specifications will be ruled out.

Intuitively, the join† operator is applied over two abstract states, and tries to find a common shape as an abstraction for the separation part of both states. If such common shape is found, it performs convex hull and bag join for the pure parts. Otherwise it keeps a disjunction of the two states. The widen† is analogous to join†. The difference is that we expect the heap portion of the first state is subsumed by the second one, and then it applies the pure widening for the pure part. The formal definitions of join† and widen† and other details are left in our report [13] due to page limit.

Bi-Abductive Abstract Semantics. As shown in Fig. 5, our analysis employs two abstract semantics: a bi-abductive abstract semantics (i.e. the one equipped with abduction) (line 4), and an underlying abstract semantics (i.e. the one without abduction) (line 11). We first give the definition of the underlying semantics. Its type is defined as

$$[\![e]\!] \; : \; \mathsf{AllSpec} \to \mathcal{P}_{\mathsf{SH}} \to \mathcal{P}_{\mathsf{SH}}$$

where AllSpec contains procedure specifications. For some program e and its given precondition Δ, the semantics calculates the postcondition $[\![e]\!]_\mathcal{T}\Delta$, for a given set of method specifications $\mathcal{T}$.

The essential constituents of the underlying semantics are the basic transition functions from a conjunctive abstract state (σ) to a conjunctive or disjunctive abstract state (σ or Δ) below:

$$
\begin{aligned}
\mathsf{unfold}(x) &\; : \; \mathsf{SH} \to \mathcal{P}_{\mathsf{SH}[x]} & &\text{Unfolding} \\
\mathsf{exec}(d[x]) &\; : \; \mathsf{AllSpec} \to \mathsf{SH}[x] \to \mathcal{P}_{\mathsf{SH}} & &\text{Heap-sensitive execution} \\
\mathsf{exec}(d) &\; : \; \mathsf{AllSpec} \to \mathsf{SH} \to \mathcal{P}_{\mathsf{SH}} & &\text{Heap-insensitive execution}
\end{aligned}
$$

where $\mathsf{SH}[x]$ denotes the set of conjunctive abstract states in which each element has x exposed as the head of a data node ($x \mapsto c(v^*)$), and $\mathcal{P}_{\mathsf{SH}[x]}$ contains all the (disjunctive) abstract states, each of which is composed by such conjunctive states. Here $\mathsf{unfold}(x)$ rearranges the symbolic heap so that the cell referred to by x is exposed for access by heap sensitive commands $d[x]$ via the second transition function $\mathsf{exec}(d[x])$. The third function defined for other (heap insensitive) commands d does not require such exposure of x.

The unfolding function is defined by the following two rules:

$$
\frac{\sigma \vdash x \mapsto c(v^*) * \sigma'}{\mathsf{unfold}(x)\sigma \rightsquigarrow \sigma} \qquad
\frac{\sigma \vdash p(x, v^*) * \sigma' \quad p(\mathbf{root}, v^*) \equiv \Phi}{\mathsf{unfold}(x)\sigma \rightsquigarrow \sigma' * [x/\mathbf{root}, u^*/v^*]\Phi}
$$

The symbolic execution of heap-sensitive commands $d[x]$ (i.e. $x.f_i$, $x.f_i := w$, or $\mathtt{free}(x)$) assumes that the rearrangement $\mathsf{unfold}(x)$ has been done prior to execution:

$$
\frac{\sigma \vdash x \mapsto c(v_1, .., v_n) * \sigma'}{\mathsf{exec}(x.f_i)(\mathcal{T})\sigma \rightsquigarrow \sigma \wedge \mathbf{res} = v_i} \qquad
\frac{\sigma \vdash x \mapsto c(u^*) * \sigma'}{\mathsf{exec}(\mathtt{free}(x))(\mathcal{T})\sigma \rightsquigarrow \sigma'}
$$

$$
\frac{\sigma \vdash x \mapsto c(v_1, .., v_n) * \sigma'}{\mathsf{exec}(x.f_i := w)(\mathcal{T})\sigma \rightsquigarrow \sigma' * x \mapsto c(v_1, .., v_{i-1}, w, v_{i+1}, .., v_n)}
$$

The symbolic execution rules for heap-insensitive commands are as follows:

$$\mathsf{exec}(k)(\mathcal{T})\sigma =_{df} \sigma \wedge \mathbf{res}{=}k \qquad \frac{isdatat(c)}{\mathsf{exec}(\mathbf{new}\ c(v^*))(\mathcal{T})\sigma =_{df} \sigma * c(\mathbf{res}, v^*)}$$

$$\mathsf{exec}(x)(\mathcal{T})\sigma =_{df} \sigma \wedge \mathbf{res}{=}x$$

$$\frac{\begin{array}{c} t\ mn\ ((t_i\ u_i)_{i=1}^m; (t'_i\ v_i)_{i=1}^n)\ requires\ \Phi_{pr}\ ensures\ \Phi_{po} \in \mathcal{T} \\ \rho = [x'_i/u_i]_{i=1}^m \circ [y'_i/v_i]_{i=1}^n \quad \sigma \vdash \rho\Phi_{pr} * \sigma' \\ \rho_o = [r_i/v_i]_{i=1}^n \circ [x'_i/u_i]_{i=1}^m \circ [y'_i/v'_i]_{i=1}^n \quad \rho_l = [r_i/y'_i]_{i=1}^n \quad fresh\ logical\ r_i \end{array}}{\mathsf{exec}(mn(x_1,..,x_m;y_1,..,y_n))(\mathcal{T})\sigma \rightsquigarrow (\rho_l\sigma') * (\rho_o\Phi_{po})}$$

The first three rules deal with constant (k), variable (x) and data node creation ($\mathbf{new}\ c(v^*)$), respectively, while the last rule handles method invocation. The test *isdatat*(c) returns true iff c is a data node. In the last rule, the call site is ensured to meet the precondition of mn, as signified by $\sigma \vdash \rho\Phi_{pr} * \sigma'$. In this case, the execution succeeds and the post-state of the method call involves mn's postcondition as signified by $\rho_o\Phi_{po}$.

A lifting function † is defined to lift unfold's domain to $\mathcal{P}_{\mathsf{SH}}$:

$$\mathsf{unfold}^{\dagger}(x) \bigvee \sigma_i =_{df} \bigvee(\mathsf{unfold}(x)\sigma_i)$$

and this function is overloaded for exec to lift both its domain and range to $\mathcal{P}_{\mathsf{SH}}$:

$$\mathsf{exec}^{\dagger}(d)(\mathcal{T}) \bigvee \sigma_i =_{df} \bigvee(\mathsf{exec}(d)(\mathcal{T})\sigma_i)$$

Based on the transition functions above, we can define the abstract semantics for a program e as follows (where loops are already translated into tail-recursions):

$$\begin{array}{ll} [\![d[x]]\!]_{\mathcal{T}}\Delta & =_{df}\ \mathsf{exec}^{\dagger}(d[x])(\mathcal{T}) \circ \mathsf{unfold}^{\dagger}(x)\Delta \\ [\![d]\!]_{\mathcal{T}}\Delta & =_{df}\ \mathsf{exec}^{\dagger}(d)(\mathcal{T})\Delta \\ [\![e_1; e_2]\!]_{\mathcal{T}}\Delta & =_{df}\ [\![e_2]\!]_{\mathcal{T}} \circ [\![e_1]\!]_{\mathcal{T}}\Delta \\ [\![x := e]\!]_{\mathcal{T}}\Delta & =_{df}\ [x'/x, r'/\mathbf{res}]([\![e]\!]_{\mathcal{T}}\Delta) \wedge x{=}r'\ \ fresh\ logical\ x', r' \\ [\![\mathbf{if}\ (v)\ e_1\ \mathbf{else}\ e_2]\!]_{\mathcal{T}}\Delta & =_{df}\ ([\![e_1]\!]_{\mathcal{T}}(v\wedge\Delta)) \vee ([\![e_2]\!]_{\mathcal{T}}(\neg v\wedge\Delta)) \end{array}$$

We shall now present the definitions of our bi-abductive abstract semantics. Its type is

$$[\![e]\!]^A\ :\ \mathsf{AllSpec} \rightarrow (\mathcal{P}_{\mathsf{SH}} \times \mathcal{P}_{\mathsf{SH}}) \rightarrow (\mathcal{P}_{\mathsf{SH}} \times \mathcal{P}_{\mathsf{SH}})$$

It takes a piece of program code and a specification table, and maps a pair of (disjunctive) set of symbolic heaps to another such pair (where the first in the pair is the accumulated precondition and the second is the current state). It relies on the following two basic functions:

$$\begin{array}{ll} \mathsf{Unfold}(x)\ :\ (\mathsf{SH} \times \mathsf{SH}) \rightarrow (\mathcal{P}_{\mathsf{SH}} \times \mathcal{P}_{\mathsf{SH}}) \\ \mathsf{Exec}(ds)\ :\ \mathsf{AllSpec} \rightarrow (\mathsf{SH} \times \mathsf{SH}) \rightarrow (\mathcal{P}_{\mathsf{SH}} \times \mathcal{P}_{\mathsf{SH}}) \end{array}$$

The definitions of both functions are given below:

$\mathsf{Unfold}(x)(\sigma', \sigma) =_{df}$
   $\mathbf{if}\ (\sigma*[\sigma_m] \rhd x{\mapsto}c(y^*)*\mathbf{true}\ for\ fresh\ logical\ vars\ y^*) \wedge (\sigma'*\sigma_m \nvdash \mathbf{false})$
   $\mathbf{then}\ \mathbf{let}\ \Delta{=}\mathsf{unfold}(x)(\sigma*\sigma_m)\ \mathbf{in}\ (\sigma'*\sigma_m, \Delta)$
   $\mathbf{else}\ (\sigma', \mathbf{false})$

$\mathsf{Exec}(ds)(\mathcal{T})(\sigma', \sigma) =_{df}\ \mathbf{let}\ \Delta{=}\mathsf{exec}(ds)(\mathcal{T})\sigma\ \mathbf{in}\ (\sigma', \Delta)$
   $where\ ds\ is\ either\ d[x]\ or\ d,\ except\ for\ procedure\ call$

$$t\ mn\ ((t_i\ u_i)_{i=1}^{m};(t_i'\ v_i)_{i=1}^{n})\ requires\ \Phi_{pr}\ ensures\ \Phi_{po} \in \mathcal{T}$$
$$\rho = [x_i'/u_i]_{i=1}^{m} \circ [y_i'/v_i]_{i=1}^{n}\quad \sigma * [\sigma_1'] \rhd \rho\Phi_{pr} * \sigma_1 \quad \sigma'*\sigma_1' \nvdash false$$
$$\rho_o = [r_i/v_i]_{i=1}^{n} \circ [x_i'/u_i]_{i=1}^{m} \circ [y_i'/v_i]_{i=1}^{n}\quad \rho_l = [r_i/y_i']_{i=1}^{n}\quad fresh\ logical\ vars\ r_i$$
$$\overline{\mathsf{Exec}(mn(x_{1..m};y_{1..n}))(\mathcal{T})(\sigma',\sigma) =_{df} (\sigma' * \sigma_1', (\rho_o\Phi_{po})*(\rho_l\sigma_1))}$$

The Unfold function firstly tests (using bi-abduction) whether the node $x{\mapsto}c(y^*)$ is in σ, if not, abduction is applied to find the missing σ_m. If σ' and σ_m do not contradict, it unfolds $\sigma * \sigma_m$ to expose x (via the unfold function defined earlier in this section), and adds σ_m to precondition. Otherwise, it returns false for the current state.

The Exec function symbolically executes the command ds (via the exec function defined earlier in this section) and translates the current state σ to a disjunction of new states Δ. The special case is the method invocation, which may require bi-abduction to be applied for the current state. When the method mn is invoked, we take its current specification (Φ_{pr}, Φ_{po}) from $\mathcal{T}$, and substitute the formal parameters u_i and v_i by the current arguments x_i' and y_i' respectively. Note that prime notations x_i' and y_i' denote the current values of x_i and y_i in the current state σ. Then we apply bi-abduction from the current state σ to the precondition $\rho\Phi_{pr}$. If it succeeds, the discovered missing state σ_1' will be propagated back to the precondition σ' to help make the symbolic execution to succeed. The postcondition of mn, Φ_{po} is substituted by ρ_o in order to be added to the current state. Since the variables y_i are call-by-reference, we let r_i to be the intermediate variables, while the variables y_i' denote the latest values.

A lifting function † is defined to lift Unfold's and Exec's domains:

$$\mathsf{Unfold}^{\dagger}(x) \bigvee(\sigma_i',\sigma_i) \quad =_{df} \bigvee(\mathsf{Unfold}(x)(\sigma_i',\sigma_i))$$
$$\mathsf{Exec}^{\dagger}(ds)(\mathcal{T}) \bigvee(\sigma_i',\sigma_i) =_{df} \bigvee(\mathsf{Exec}(ds)(\mathcal{T})(\sigma_i',\sigma_i))$$

Based on the above functions, the bi-abductive abstract semantics is defined as follows:

$$[\![d[x]]\!]_{\mathcal{T}}^{A}(\Delta',\Delta) \quad\quad\quad =_{df} \mathsf{Exec}^{\dagger}(d[x])(\mathcal{T}) \circ \mathsf{Unfold}^{\dagger}(x)(\Delta',\Delta)$$
$$[\![d]\!]_{\mathcal{T}}^{A}(\Delta',\Delta) \quad\quad\quad =_{df} \mathsf{Exec}^{\dagger}(d)(\mathcal{T})(\Delta',\Delta)$$
$$[\![e_1;e_2]\!]_{\mathcal{T}}^{A}(\Delta',\Delta) \quad\quad =_{df} [\![e_2]\!]_{\mathcal{T}}^{A} \circ [\![e_1]\!]_{\mathcal{T}}^{A}(\Delta',\Delta)$$
$$[\![x := e]\!]_{\mathcal{T}}^{A}(\Delta',\Delta) \quad\quad =_{df} [x'/x,r'/\mathtt{res}]([\![e]\!]_{\mathcal{T}}^{A}(\Delta',\Delta \wedge x{=}r'))\quad fresh\ logical\ x',r'$$
$$[\![\mathtt{if}\ (v)\ e_1\ \mathtt{else}\ e_2]\!]_{\mathcal{T}}^{A}(\Delta',\Delta) =_{df} ([\![e_1]\!]_{\mathcal{T}}^{A}(\Delta',v{\wedge}\Delta)) \vee ([\![e_2]\!]_{\mathcal{T}}^{A}(\Delta',\neg v{\wedge}\Delta))$$

Abductive Abstraction. As we mentioned earlier in the $\mathtt{merge}$ example, to verify such programs may require very precise preconditions that a standard abstraction mechanism may fail to achieve. To cater for such a need, we design a novel *abductive abstraction* function $\mathsf{abs_a}$, which equips abstraction with an abductive reasoning capacity where necessary. In such scenarios, user-specified predicates can offer some guidance in the abstraction in order to discover extra data structure properties for precondition. The new abductive abstraction function is given as follows:

$$\mathsf{abs_a}(\sigma \wedge x_0{=}e) =_{df} \sigma[e/x_0]$$
$$\mathsf{abs_a}(\sigma \wedge e{=}x_0) =_{df} \sigma[e/x_0] \qquad \frac{x_0 \notin \mathsf{Reach}(\sigma)}{\mathsf{abs_a}(\mathrm{H}(c)(x_0,v^*) * \sigma) =_{df} \sigma * \mathtt{true}}$$

$$p_2(u_2^*) \equiv \Phi \qquad \mathrm{H}(c_1)(x, v_1^*) * \sigma_1 \vdash p_2(x, v_2^*) \wedge \pi_2$$
$$\frac{\mathrm{Reach}(p_2(x, v_2^*) \wedge \pi_2 * \sigma_3) \cap \{v_1^*\} = \emptyset}{\mathsf{abs_a}(\mathrm{H}(c_1)(x, v_1^*) * \sigma_1 * \sigma_3) =_{df} p_2(x, v_2^*) \wedge \pi_2 * \sigma_3}$$

$$p_2(u_2^*) \equiv \Phi \qquad \mathrm{H}(c_1)(x, v_1^*) * \sigma_1 \nvdash p_2(x, v_2^*) \wedge \pi_2$$
$$\frac{\mathrm{H}(c_1)(x, v_1^*) * \sigma_1 * [\sigma'] \rhd p_2(x, v_2^*) \wedge \pi_2 \qquad \mathrm{Reach}(p_2(x, v_2^*) \wedge \pi2 * \sigma_3) \cap \{v_1^*\} = \emptyset}{\mathsf{abs_a}(\mathrm{H}(c_1)(x, v_1^*) * \sigma_1 * \sigma_3) =_{df} p_2(x, v_2^*) \wedge \pi_2 * \sigma_3}$$

where $\mathrm{H}(c)(x, v^*)$ denotes $x \mapsto c(v^*)$ if c is a data node or $c(x, v^*)$ if c is a predicate. The function $\mathrm{Reach}(\sigma)$ returns all pointer variables which are reachable from free variables in the abstract state σ. The first two rules eliminate logical variables, and the third rule drops heap garbage that is unreachable from program variables. The fourth rule combines shape formulae and eliminate logical pointer variables which are not reachable from other program variables. The predicate p_2 is selected from the user-defined predicates environments and it is the target shape to be abstracted to.

The last rule applies when the state $\mathrm{H}(c_1)(x, v_1^*) * \sigma_1$ cannot be abstracted to the predicate p_2 using standard abstraction but can be abstracted to predicate p_2 with the help of abductive reasoning. When applying such an abstraction function during the precondition discovery, the extra information σ' discovered by abduction will be propagated back to the precondition to improve the precision.

The lifting function is applied for $\mathsf{abs_a}$ to lift both its domain and range to disjunctive abstract states $\mathcal{P}_{\mathsf{SH}}$: $\mathsf{abs_a}^\dagger \bigvee \sigma_i =_{df} \bigvee \mathsf{abs_a}(\sigma_i)$, allowing it to be used in the analysis.

The soundness and termination of our analysis are given in the technical report [13].

6   Experiments and Evaluation

We have implemented a prototype system and evaluated it over a number of heap-manipulating programs to test the viability and precision of our approach. Our experimental results were achieved with an Intel Core 2 Quad CPU 2.66GHz with 8GB RAM. We have also defined a library of predicates covering popular data structures and variety of properties. These properties can be grouped in the following categories: MS (*memory safety*): all memory accesses are safe, no dangling/null pointers dereferences; SC (*same content*): the content of the final data structure remains the same as that of the input data structure; IN (*insertion*): the input data is inserted into the final data structure; SO (*sorted*): data structures are sorted according to a criterion, eg. in case of a list each node's content is less than or equal to its successor's; BS (*binary search*): data structures are binary search trees; DL (*double-linked list*): data structures are double-linked lists; and AL (*AVL tree*): data structures are AVL trees. The predicates required as input by our tool can be selected from the library or can be supplied by users, according to the input program data structures and the properties of interest. Usually, the upper bound of cutpoints is set to be twice the number of input program variables to improve the precision. Some of our results are presented in Table 1.

In comparison to previous approaches, the first observation concerns the precision of our analysis. Since our tool uses a combined domain it can discover more expressive specifications to guarantee memory safety and functional correctness. For example in case of the take program which traverses the list down for a user-specified number n of

Table 1. Experimental Results. The column **LOC** is for the number of program lines; **Time** expresses our tool running time (in seconds); **Prop** denotes the inferred specification properties.

Prog.	LOC	Time	Prop	Prog.	LOC	Time	Prop
Singly Linked List				Doubly Linked List			
create	10	1.12	MS	create	15	1.47	MS/DL
delete	9	1.20	MS/SO	append	24	2.53	MS/DL/SC/SO
insert	9	1.16	MS/SO/IN	insert	22	2.32	MS/DL/IN/SO
traverse	9	1.35	MS/SO/SC	Binary Search Tree			
length	11	1.28	MS/SO/SC	create	18	2.58	MS/BS
append	11	1.47	MS/SO/SC	delete	48	4.76	MS/BS
take	12	1.28	MS/SO/SC	insert	22	3.57	MS/BS/IN
reverse	13	1.72	MS/SC	search	22	2.78	MS/BS/SC
filter	15	2.37	MS/SO	height	15	1.56	MS/BS/SC
Sorting algorithm				count	17	1.63	MS/BS/SC
insert_sort	32	2.72	MS/SC/SO	flatten	32	2.74	MS/BS/DL/SC/SO
merge_sort	78	4.18	MS/SC/SO	AVL Tree			
quick_sort	70	5.72	MS/SC/SO	insert	114	27.57	MS/BS/AL/IN
select_sort	45	3.16	MS/SC/SO	delete	239	34.42	MS/BS/AL

nodes, we can find that the input list length must be no less than n. However the previous tools based on shape domains (like Abductor [5]) can only discover a precondition that requires the input list to be non-empty which would not be sufficient to guarantee memory safety. Moreover more complex functional properties regarding the data structures content (like SO for `merge` program but in general for all sorting programs) can also not be discovered by the previous tools (like Abductor) based on a simple shape domain. There are other tools (like Xisa [6] or Thor [18]) that can work on a combined domain but require certain annotations to guide their analysis. Thor [18] requires shape information for each input parameter and Xisa [6] requires shape information for program variables used in loops. Since our shape domain includes tree data structures, our tool is able to discover complex functional specifications for binary search trees and AVL trees in contrast to the previous approaches. For example in case of the `flatten` program our tool is able to discover that the input data structure is a binary search tree while the output data structure is a sorted doubly linked list having the same data content (values stored inside the nodes) as that of the input.

The second observation regarding our experimental results is that the analysis may discover more than one correct specification for some programs. For example, given two predicates, ordinary linked list and sorted list, we can obtain two specifications for most of the sorting algorithms. When there are more than one user-supplied predicate definitions, the analysis can have multiple choices during the abstraction. Multiple specifications can be useful in program verification, e.g. the sorted version for the `append` method, where the two input lists and the output list are all sorted, is useful in the verification of `quick_sort`, while the sorted list version for the `insert` method is also useful to help verify the functional correctness of `insert_sort`.

7   Related Work and Conclusion

Dramatic advances have been made in synthesising specifications for heap-manipulating programs. The local shape analysis [8] infers loop invariants for list-processing programs, followed by the SpaceInvader/Abductor tool to infer full method specifications over the separation domain, so as to verify pointer safety for larger industrial codes [5,26]. The SLAyer tool [9] implements an inter-procedural analysis for programs with shape information. A combination of shape and bag abstraction is used in [25] to verify linearizability. Compared with them, our abstraction is more general since it is driven by predicates and is not restricted to linked lists. To deal with size information (such as number of nodes in lists/trees), Thor [18] transfers a heap-processing program to a numerical one, so that size properties can be obtained by further analysis. A similar approach [10] combines a set domain (for shape) with its cardinality domain (for corresponding numerical information) in a more general framework. Compared with these works, our approach can discover specifications with stronger invariants such as sortedness and bag-related properties, which have not been addressed in the previous works. The analyses [6,19,20] can all handle shape and numerical information over a combined domain, but require user given preconditions for the program whereas here we compute the whole specification at once. Recently, Rival and Chang [23] propose an inductive predicate to summarise call stacks along with heap structures in a context of a whole-program analysis. In contrast our analysis is modular.

There are also other approaches that can synthesise shape-related program invariants. The shape analysis framework TVLA [24] is based on three-valued logic. It is capable of handling complicated data structures and properties, such as sortedness. Guo et al. [11] report a global shape analysis that discovers inductive structural shape invariants from the code. Kuncak et al. [15] develop a role system to express and track referencing relationships among objects. Hackett and Rugina [12] can deal with AVL-trees but is customised to handle only tree-like structures with height property. Bouajjani et al. [2,3] propose a program analysis in an abstract domain with SL3 (Singly-Linked List Logic) and size, sortedness and multi-set properties. However, their heap domain is restricted to singly-linked list only, and their shape analysis is separated from numerical and mutli-set analyses. Compared with these works, separation logic based approaches benefit from the frame rule with support for local reasoning.

There are also approaches which unify reasoning over shape and data using either a combination of appropriate decision procedures inside Satisfiability-Modulo-Theories (SMT) solvers (e.g. [21,16]) or a combination of appropriate abstract interpreters inside a software model checker (e.g. [1]). Compared with our work, their heap domains are mainly restricted to linked lists.

Conclusion. We have reported a program analysis which automatically discovers program specifications over a combined separation and pure(numerical and bag) domain. The novel components of our analysis include an abductive abstract semantics and an abductive abstraction mechanism (for precondition discovery)in the combined domain. We have built a prototype system and the initial experimental results are encouraging.

Acknowledgement. This work was supported in part by EPSRC project EP/G042322.

References

1. Beyer, D., Henzinger, T.A., Théoduloz, G.: Configurable software verification: Concretizing the convergence of model checking and program analysis. In: Damm, W., Hermanns, H. (eds.) CAV 2007. LNCS, vol. 4590, pp. 504–518. Springer, Heidelberg (2007)
2. Bouajjani, A., Dragoi, C., Enea, C., Sighireanu, M.: On inter-procedural analysis of programs with lists and data. In: PLDI (2011)
3. Bouajjani, A., Drăgoi, C., Enea, C., Sighireanu, M.: Abstract domains for automated reasoning about list-manipulating programs with infinite data. In: Kuncak, V., Rybalchenko, A. (eds.) VMCAI 2012. LNCS, vol. 7148, pp. 1–22. Springer, Heidelberg (2012)
4. Bozga, M., Iosif, R., Lakhnech, Y.: Storeless semantics and alias logic. In: PEPM (2003)
5. Calcagno, C., Distefano, D., O'Hearn, P., Yang, H.: Compositional shape analysis by means of bi-abduction. J. ACM 58(6) (2011)
6. Chang, B.Y.E., Rival, X.: Relational inductive shape analysis. In: POPL (2008)
7. Chin, W.N., David, C., Nguyen, H.H., Qin, S.: Automated verification of shape, size and bag properties via user-defined predicates in separation logic. Sci. of Comp. Prog. 77 (2012)
8. Distefano, D., O'Hearn, P.W., Yang, H.: A local shape analysis based on separation logic. In: Hermanns, H., Palsberg, J. (eds.) TACAS 2006. LNCS, vol. 3920, pp. 287–302. Springer, Heidelberg (2006)
9. Gotsman, A., Berdine, J., Cook, B.: Interprocedural shape analysis with separated heap abstractions. In: Yi, K. (ed.) SAS 2006. LNCS, vol. 4134, pp. 240–260. Springer, Heidelberg (2006)
10. Gulwani, S., Lev-Ami, T., Sagiv, M.: A combination framework for tracking partition sizes. In: Shao, Z., Pierce, B.C. (eds.) POPL (2009)
11. Guo, B., Vachharajani, N., August, D.I.: Shape analysis with inductive recursion synthesis. In: PLDI (2007)
12. Hackett, B., Rugina, R.: Region-based shape analysis with tracked locations. In: POPL (2005)
13. He, G., Qin, S., Chin, W.N., Craciun, F.: Automated specification discovery in a combined abstract domain - reseach report (2012), http://pls.tees.ac.uk/~guan/fullspec/techreport.pdf
14. Jonkers, H.: Abstract storage structures. In: Algorithmic Languages (1981)
15. Kuncak, V., Lam, P., Rinard, M.C.: Role analysis. In: POPL (2002)
16. Lahiri, S.K., Qadeer, S.: Back to the future: revisiting precise program verification using smt solvers. In: POPL (2008)
17. Magill, S., Tsai, M.-H., Lee, P., Tsay, Y.-K.: Thor: A tool for reasoning about shape and arithmetic. In: Gupta, A., Malik, S. (eds.) CAV 2008. LNCS, vol. 5123, pp. 428–432. Springer, Heidelberg (2008)
18. Magill, S., Tsai, M.-H., Lee, P., Tsay, Y.-K.: Automatic numeric abstractions for heap-manipulating programs. In: POPL (2010)
19. Qin, S., He, G., Luo, C., Chin, W.N., Chen, X.: Loop invariant synthesis in a combined abstract domain. Journal of Symbolic Computation 50 (2013)
20. Qin, S., Luo, C., Chin, W.-N., He, G.: Automatically refining partial specifications for program verification. In: Butler, M., Schulte, W. (eds.) FM 2011. LNCS, vol. 6664, pp. 369–385. Springer, Heidelberg (2011)
21. Rakamarić, Z., Bruttomesso, R., Hu, A.J., Cimatti, A.: Verifying heap-manipulating programs in an smt framework. In: Namjoshi, K.S., Yoneda, T., Higashino, T., Okamura, Y. (eds.) ATVA 2007. LNCS, vol. 4762, pp. 237–252. Springer, Heidelberg (2007)
22. Reynolds, J.C.: Separation logic: A logic for shared mutable data structures. In: LICS (2002)
23. Rival, X., Chang, B.Y.E.: Calling context abstraction with shapes. In: POPL (2011)

24. Sagiv, M., Reps, T.W., Wilhelm, R.: Parametric shape analysis via 3-valued logic. ACM Trans. Program. Lang. Syst. 24(3) (2002)

25. Vafeiadis, V.: Shape-value abstraction for verifying linearizability. In: Jones, N.D., Müller-Olm, M. (eds.) VMCAI 2009. LNCS, vol. 5403, pp. 335–348. Springer, Heidelberg (2009)

26. Yang, H., Lee, O., Berdine, J., Calcagno, C., Cook, B., Distefano, D., O'Hearn, P.W.: Scalable shape analysis for systems code. In: Gupta, A., Malik, S. (eds.) CAV 2008. LNCS, vol. 5123, pp. 385–398. Springer, Heidelberg (2008)

Path-Sensitive Data Flow Analysis Simplified

Kirsten Winter[1], Chenyi Zhang[1], Ian J. Hayes[1], Nathan Keynes[2],
Cristina Cifuentes[3], and Lian Li[3]

[1] School of ITEE, University of Queensland, Australia
[2] Oracle Brisbane, Australia
[3] Oracle Labs, Brisbane, Australia

Abstract. Path-sensitive data flow analysis pairs classical data flow analysis with an analysis of feasibility of paths to improve precision. In this paper we propose a framework for path-sensitive backward data flow analysis that is enhanced with an abstraction of the predicate domain. The abstraction is based on a three-valued logic. It follows the strategy that path predicates are simplified if possible (without calling an external predicate solver) and every predicate that could not be reduced to a simple predicate is abstracted to the *unknown* value, for which the feasibility is undecided. The implementation of the framework scales well and delivers promising results.

1 Introduction

Data flow analysis (DFA) [Kil73, NNH99] is a static analysis technique for compiler optimisation and program verification that scales to large code bases. In classical DFA, efficiency is achieved by conservatively over-approximating the behaviour of a program, taking all possible paths into account. When the framework is applied on static program analysis, the result is not precise: firstly, it loses information at join points of the program when data flow values from different paths are merged, and secondly, it may report bugs that arise from infeasible paths. This can lead either to a large number of false positives (i.e., a tool reports non-existing bugs) if the analysis reports all bugs that might occur on some paths, or a large number of false negatives (i.e., bugs that are missed by the analysis) if the analysis reports a bug only if it is encountered on all paths. On large code bases a high rate of reported false positives obstructs the debugging process whereas generally, a high rate of false negatives renders the analysis ineffective.

In order to detect most existing bugs with a low false positive rate, several approaches have been proposed to make DFA *path-sensitive*. Path-sensitive DFA collects path information which indicates feasibility or infeasibility of a path, and only reports bugs from feasible paths. Path information is given through the flow predicates that determine the flow of control in a program. During the analysis the flow predicates are combined to larger predicates, the satisfiability of which is in general undecidable if all path information is taken into account. Hence, full path sensitivity is hard to scale.

L. Groves and J. Sun (Eds.): ICFEM 2013, LNCS 8144, pp. 415–430, 2013.

In this paper we propose a theoretical framework for a path-sensitive backward DFA which we enhance with an abstraction mechanism. The framework utilises Dijkstra's *weakest preconditions* and assertions added to the code to represent preconditions that are required for correctness. As such, assertions are a general means to indicate violations in the code and in our context they play the role of data flow facts. A feature of our approach is that path information and data flow facts are both encoded in the same predicate domain. Hence, they can be merged and the resulting predicate simplified. The abstraction is defined on the predicate domain to abstract from predicates that are too complex and to let the DFA procedure manipulate simple predicates only. We base this abstraction on a 3-valued logic which includes *unknown* as a third truth value. The abstraction maps each complex predicate onto a special predicate Δ, which is semantically *unknown* and hence can be either *true* or *false*.

The predicative backward DFA is implemented in the Parfait tool [CS08] which is a bug-checker built on top of LLVM [LA04]. We use the analysis to detect bugs such as memory leaks, use-after-free, double-free and free-of-non-allocated-pointer in sequential code. The results are encouraging and show that with the abstraction the analysis scales to code bases of over 6 million lines of code with a precision that delivers a false-positive rate of less than 5%.

The paper is organised as follows. Sections 2 and 3 recount the basic concepts of data flow analysis. The framework for a predicative backward DFA is introduced in Section 4 and its application is demonstrated in Section 5. Section 6 introduces our abstraction mechanism on the predicate domain and justifies the soundness for the approach. Section 7 reports on the experimental results when applying the implementation in the Parfait tool to the Solaris ON B20 source code. Section 8 discusses related work of path sensitive approaches in DFA. Section 9 concludes the paper.

2   Data Flow Graphs

We define a flowchart language that consists of states and a transition relation on states. The states and the transition relation are represented as a flow graph $G = (N, E, n_0, n_x)$ where N is a set of nodes, $E \subseteq N \times N$ a set of edges, $n_0 \in N$ a distinguished start node, and $n_x \in N$ a distinguished exit node. For an edge $e = (n, n') \in E$ we say n is the *source* of e, written as $src(e)$, and n' is the *destination* of e, written as $dst(e)$. A *path* π is a sequence of consecutive edges $e_1 e_2 \ldots$ satisfying $dst(e_i) = src(e_{i+1})$ for all i. The set of immediate predecessors of a node n is defined as $pred(n) = \{n' \mid (n', n) \in E\}$, and the set of immediate successors of a node n is $succ(n) = \{n' \mid (n, n') \in E\}$. A *program* is a tuple $Prog = (G, Var, effect)$, where G is the flow graph of the program, Var is the set of variables of the program, and edge labelling $effect : E \rightarrow \Phi$ where Φ is the set of statements (or their semantics) in the program. As usual, we define a program state as a mapping from variables to values.

For the analysis we enhance the program code with *assertions* (also called *assumptions* in the literature) which are specific to the analysis performed.

```
void example(char *file){
    int err = 0, fd;
    int *tmp = malloc(..);
    if(tmp == Null) {
        err = 1;
        goto cleanup;
    }
    close(fd);
    free(tmp);
cleanup:
    if(err != 0) {
        free(tmp);
    }
}
```

Fig. 1. An example program and its flow graph

They are added to the code at particular points which are also specific to the problem to be analysed. We consider assertions as a type of statement in the program. Hence, the set of statements Φ includes assignment statements, guards (or flow conditions), and assertions.

Example 1. In Figure 1 we give an example flow graph on the right where the edges are labelled with the effects that correspond to the C code on the left. □

3 Data Flow Analysis

The classical data flow analysis (DFA) framework for *forward* and *backward* directed analysis, is defined as a tuple $\mathcal{L} = (\mathcal{D}, \sqcup, \sqsubseteq, \top, \bot, \mathsf{T}_b, \mathsf{T}_f)$, where we have $(\mathcal{D}, \sqcup, \sqsubseteq, \top, \bot)$ a complete semi-lattice with $\top \in \mathcal{D}$ the top element and $\bot \in \mathcal{D}$ the bottom element, $\sqcup : \mathcal{D} \times \mathcal{D} \to \mathcal{D}$ a join operator, and $\sqsubseteq$ a partial order on $\mathcal{D}$ (with $x \sqsubseteq y$ iff $x \sqcup y = y$). Informally, $\mathcal{D}$ is a set of data flow values which abstractly represent the states of a program with respect to some specific characteristics. The set $\mathcal{D}$ together with an abstraction function α, which maps each concrete state onto an element in the abstract domain, constitutes the *abstract domain* (as defined in [CC77, RM07]). The function $\mathsf{T}_b : \Phi \to (\mathcal{D} \to \mathcal{D})$ is a *backward transfer function* that defines for each side effect the impact on the data flow values. Similarly, $\mathsf{T}_f : \Phi \to (\mathcal{D} \to \mathcal{D})$ is a *forward transfer function*.

Given a program *Prog* and a DFA framework $\mathcal{L}$, a data flow problem is to compute a mapping $D : N \to \mathcal{D}$ that assigns a data flow value to each node in the flow graph of *Prog* such that each node is labelled with the data flow value that is "achievable" at that point. To compute this mapping requires a fixpoint computation that is bound by the height of the semi-lattice in $\mathcal{L}$. For each node (simultaneously) the algorithm iteratively computes the following constraint: (1) in the forward analysis and (2) in the backward analysis.

$$D_{i+1}(n) = \left(\bigsqcup_{n' \in pred(n)} \mathrm{T}_f(\mathit{eff}(n', n))(D_i(n')) \right) \qquad (1)$$

$$D_{i+1}(n) = \left(\bigsqcup_{n' \in succ(n)} \mathrm{T}_b(\mathit{eff}(n, n'))(D_i(n')) \right) \qquad (2)$$

for any $i \geq 0$, where $D_0(n) = \bot$ for all $n \in N$. This leads to a sequence of values $D_0(n) \sqsubseteq D_1(n) \sqsubseteq \ldots$, which terminates when a fixpoint is reached. As can be seen, the forward analysis requires the information from all predecessor nodes $n \in pred(n)$ and uses the function T_f, whereas the backwards analysis builds on the information of the successor nodes, $n' \in succ(n)$, and uses T_b.

The interpretation of the semi-lattice and the join operator $\sqcup$ depend on the analysis problem and the chosen approach. In the context of this paper, we target a so called *may* analysis which collects information that may be true on some paths and computes an *over-approximation* of the behaviour. The join operator $\sqcup$ is interpreted as set union $\cup$, and $\sqsubseteq$ is the subset relation $\subseteq$.

Example 2. As an example we use the DFA approach to solve the problem of memory leak detection of the local pointer variable tmp in the program of Figure 1. (Note that there might be other violations in the code that might be analysed at a later stage, e.g., an attempted closing of a file pointed to by fd which has not been opened). In a path-insensitive DFA (without information about the control flow) a violating path through nodes $entry$-n_1-n_2-n_5-n_6-n_7-$exit$ will be reported as a potential memory leak. This path, however, is a false positive for two reasons: firstly, the path is infeasible due to the test on err, and secondly it also requires tmp to be Null (i.e., malloc to fail) in which case no memory is allocated and hence no leak has occurred. In this case, the information necessary to identify this report as a false positive is given through the flow condition $err = 0$ that is falsified by the preceding assignment $err := 1$.   □

4   Predicative Backward DFA

In a backward DFA, the function D provides a conservative over-approximation of the program's state (in terms of its achievable data flow values) at each node. To achieve a more precise result and to rule out infeasible paths we are aiming at a *path-sensitive* analysis that collects control flow information along the paths through the flow graph. This leads us to a *predicative* backward DFA, in which $\mathcal{D}$ becomes the domain of predicates *Pred* and $D : N \to Pred$. *Pred* is the set of predicates that capture the states from which there exists a *feasible* path (usually as a conservative over-approximation) along which the data flow value, we aim to calculate, is achievable. We refer to *Pred* as the *predicate domain*.

The predicative data flow framework instantiates the simple DFA framework by choosing a particular abstract domain $\mathcal{D}$, transfer function T_b (in the backward case) and join operator $\sqcup$. In the following we provide detailed definitions of these constituents.

Predicate Domain. We define the predicate domain *Pred* as a set of predicates over program variables. We write $var(p)$ to denote the variables in predicate p. The set of predicates forms a lattice in which $p \sqsubseteq q$ is defined in terms of entailment: the logical implication of predicates that holds for all states, written $(p \Rightarrow q)$. We let *true* be the top element of the lattice which is satisfied by all states, and *false* the bottom element, representing the empty set of states.

Transfer Function. The transfer function for the predicative backward DFA is given as the *predicate transformer* $\overline{wp} : \Phi \rightarrow (Pred \rightarrow Pred)$. We define this function based on the dual of Dijkstra's *weakest precondition* (wp) [Dij76, HFL01], namely $\overline{wp}(\mathit{eff})(p) = \neg wp(\mathit{eff})(\neg p)$. The dual of the weakest precondition, $\overline{wp}(\mathit{eff})(p)$, intuitively computes the set of pre-states from which there *exists* a possible execution of the statement *eff* such that p is satisfied after the statement. This leads us to the following rules:

$$
\begin{array}{lll}
\overline{wp}(\{A\})(p) & = & def(A) \Rightarrow \neg A \vee p \quad\quad \text{(assertion)} \\
\overline{wp}([\,g\,])(p) & = & def(g) \Rightarrow g \wedge p \quad\quad \text{(guard)} \\
\overline{wp}(v := E)(p) & = & def(E) \Rightarrow p[E/v] \quad\quad \text{(assignment)} \\
\overline{wp}(S; R)(p) & = & \overline{wp}(S)(\overline{wp}(R)(p)) \quad\quad \text{(sequential composition)} \\
\overline{wp}(S \sqcap R)(p) & = & \overline{wp}(S)(p) \vee \overline{wp}(R)(p) \quad \text{(non-deterministic choice)}
\end{array}
$$

where $p[E/v]$ denotes the predicate in which all free occurrences of variable v are replaced by expression E, $(S; R)$ denotes the sequential composition of statements S and R, and $(S \sqcap R)$ denotes the non-deterministic choice between the two statements. With $def(A)$, $def(g)$ and $def(E)$ we denote the requirement that A, g and E, respectively, must be well-defined. In the following we assume the well-definedness of assertions, variables and expressions, which is subject to another analysis. An assertion is a condition that must be satisfied at a node, in the sense that condition $\neg A \vee p$ is used to tag paths that lead to states that *violate* A. Note that this transfer function allows us to collect path information (when conjoining a path predicate with the guard) as well as information of potential violations of assertions (when disjoining the path predicate with the negation of the encountered assertion).

Join Operator. Since the predicate transformer $\overline{wp}.\mathit{eff}$ provides the computation along one path, one computes the disjunction of predicates at join points which effectively models the non-deterministic choice of paths. Thus, we establish a simultaneous solution by computing for all $n \in N$ the weakest precondition $D(n)$ that satisfies the following data flow constraint in which the join operator becomes disjunction.

$$
D_{i+1}(n) = \bigvee_{n' \in succ(n)} \overline{wp}(\mathit{eff}(n, n'))(D_i(n')).
$$

Initialisation. We start the analysis with the bottom element and initialise the labelling of each node with *false*, i.e., $D_0(n) = \mathit{false}$ for all $n \in N$. Hence, for all $n \in N$, the fixpoint algorithm computes a sequence of values which are ordered by entailment, i.e, $D_0(n) \Rightarrow D_1(n) \Rightarrow \ldots$ A fixpoint is reached if $D_{i+1}(n) = D_i(n)$, for some $i \geq 0$. Note that a fixpoint may not be reachable within finite number of iterations in the presence of loops given the infinite domain *Pred*, nevertheless, we construct a prototype for the algorithm that quickly converges under the abstraction and simplification rules introduced in Section 6. The iterative application of the transfer function during the algorithm will result in a predicate at each node which represents the set of states that lead to erroneous paths ending at a final state where not all assertions are satisfied.

5   Applying the Predicative Backward DFA

We are using the predicative backward DFA as introduced above in the context of the static analysis tool Parfait [CS08] in which a potential bug list is established prior to the analysis. Each of these potential bugs is analysed in turn to decide if it is a real bug or a false positive. For each run of the analysis we *instrument* the analysis for the particular bug in focus. Instrumentation refers to formulating and automatically adding assertions to the code, as well as abstracting the statements that are specific to the potential bug. We demonstrate this using our example.

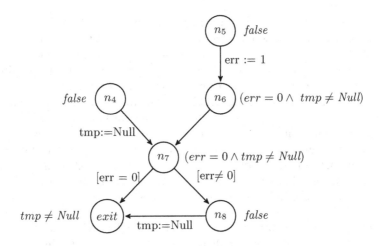

Fig. 2. Labelling the flow graph during memory-leak analysis

Example 3. We consider a potential memory leak in the code fragment introduced in Example 1 (see Figure 1). This example focuses on the pointer variable *tmp* which is allocated memory through the statement $tmp := malloc()$. To analyse this potential memory leak we assume that *malloc* has not failed (if it fails memory cannot leak). We abstract this statement by $tmp := NonNull$. Similarly, we abstract any occurrence of *free(tmp)* to $tmp := Null$ to capture deallocation. We replace the edge labelling in the flow graph in Figure 2 according to this abstraction.

The postcondition of this function is that the allocated memory has been freed at the end of the procedure. Using our abstraction, this is specified as $tmp = Null$. Since we want to find memory leaks, we label the exit node with the *inverse* of the postcondition specifying that memory has leaked, i.e., $tmp \neq Null$ (see Figure 2).

The predicative backward DFA labels each node n with a predicate $D(n)$ characterising the states at that node for which it is possible for a memory leak (i.e., a violation of the postcondition) to occur. A label of *false* at the entry node indicates that there are no paths leading to the exit where $tmp \neq Null$ is satisfied, and hence the code is free of memory leaks.

Initially, all nodes (except the exit node) are labelled with the predicate *false* and we start the analysis at the exit node. Applying $\overline{wp}$ along a backward traversal through the graph we label the nodes as indicated in Figure 2. At nodes n_4 and n_5 the analysis results in the predicate *false* which terminates the analysis (i.e., all nodes preceding n_4 and n_5 in Figure 1 are also labelled with *false*) as there are no more assertions added above those points. The result indicates that no memory leak is possible along any paths through the program.   □

Another type of bug to be investigated is *free-of-non-allocated-pointer*. This can indicate a path on which *double-free* occurs or an attempted *free* after the allocation has failed. In this case we need to consider all possible outcomes of the memory allocation and hence a different kind of abstraction is required than for memory leak detection. We demonstrate the analysis in the following example.

Example 4. For an analysis to detect all paths along which a *free-of-non-allocated-pointer* occurs, we abstract the assignment $tmp := malloc()$ by the non-deterministic choice between the successful and the unsuccessful allocation of memory to the pointer tmp, i.e., $(tmp := NonNull) \sqcap (tmp := Null)$. The call $free(tmp)$ is abstracted to $\{tmp \neq Null\}; tmp := Null$. We modify the edge labelling in the flow graph to incorporate the abstraction. The assertion to be added to the code requires that memory space must be allocated to tmp in order to have a correct call to the *free* operation. We replace $free(tmp)$ with an abstraction that includes the assertion $\{tmp \neq Null\}$ which must hold *before* the call to $free(tmp)$. The assertions can be found in the sequential composition labelling the edges (n_4, n_7) and $(n_8, exit)$ in Figure 3.

Initially, all nodes (including the exit node) are labelled with *false*. Applying $\overline{wp}$ along a backwards traversal of the program graph in Figure 3 leads to a labelling of nodes as shown: Every node is labelled with a predicate characterising the states from which there is a possible violation. The resulting *true* labelling of the *entry* node indicates that there exists a path along which the assertion is violated and a *free* has been called on a non-allocated pointer.

Generally, a labelling $D(entry) \neq false$ indicates that there is a path that that starts with a state satisfying $D(entry)$ and leads to the bug in question through the path $entry$-n_1-n_2-n_5-n_6-n_7-n_8-$exit$. In this particular case, we may further split the nondeterministic side effect of $malloc(..)$ into $(tmp := NonNull)$ and $(tmp := Null)$, and apply the two parts of the transfer function on the predicates separately. This gives $\overline{wp}((tmp := NonNull))((err \neq 0 \wedge tmp \neq Null) \vee tmp =$

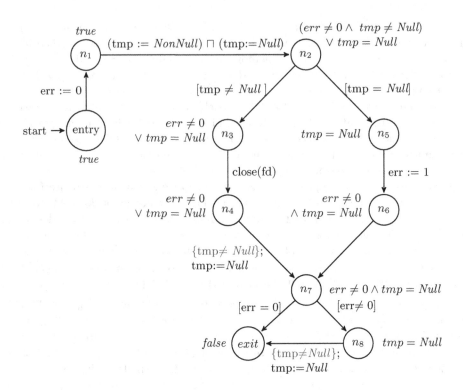

Fig. 3. Labelling the flow graph during the free-non-allocated-pointer analysis

Null) which is the predicate (*err* $\neq$ 0), and $\overline{wp}((tmp := Null))((err \neq 0 \wedge tmp \neq$ *Null*) $\vee$ *tmp* = *Null*) which is just *true*. As the predicate (*err* $\neq$ 0) is made *false* by the assignment edge (*entry*, n_1), this reveals that it is the failed *malloc(..)* that has caused the *free-of-non-allocated-pointer* bug.   □

As mentioned in Section 4, in the presence of loops, the iterative method may not converge to a fixpoint. In practice this can be handled by an abstraction that computes a less precise solution, which is introduced in the following section.

6   Simplifying the Predicate Expression

In practice the treatment of large predicates is costly in particular if an external predicate solver is invoked to simplify expressions. To avoid this complexity, we propose an abstraction that maps all predicates that cannot be easily simplified to a special predicate Δ representing *unknown*. Hence, the granularity of the abstraction is (inversely) related to the notion of simplification: the more predicates are simplified within our implementation, the less predicates will need to be abstracted.

As a first step we create an *embedding* of our 2-valued predicate domain *Pred* by defining a homomorphism h (i.e., h is injective and structure-preserving)

that maps predicates into a 3-valued predicate domain, $Pred^3$. Apart from 2-valued predicates, $Pred^3$ also contains the symbol Δ. As a second step we define an abstraction function α from the 3-valued predicate domain into an abstract domain $Pred^A$ which contains predicates that are simplified into a disjunctive form (see Definition 3 in Section 6.2) as well as Δ. The two steps are depicted in Figure 4.

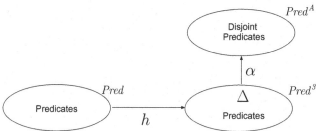

Fig. 4. Embedding and abstracting the predicate domain

Formulas over the embedding $Pred^3$ are captured by $\mathcal{L}^\Delta$, the *logic with unknown*, which is defined in Section 6.1. The definition of the abstraction α is given in Section 6.2.

6.1   The Logic with Unknown

Let P be the set of primitive predicates (e.g., relations representing flow conditions of a program). We define the syntax of the logic $\mathcal{L}^\Delta$ as follows:

$$\varphi := true \mid false \mid p \mid \Delta \mid \neg\phi \mid \varphi_1 \wedge \varphi_2 \mid \varphi_1 \vee \varphi_2$$

with $p \in P$ and Δ as the special symbol for *unknown*. We use the 3-valued semantic domain $\mathcal{D} = \mathbb{P}_1(\{tt, ff\})$ (the powerset of Booleans excluding the empty set[1]) and the interpretation $\phi : \mathcal{L}^\Delta \to \mathcal{D}$, such that $\phi(true) = \{tt\}$, $\phi(false) = \{ff\}$, $\phi(p) \in \{\{tt\}, \{ff\}\}$ for all $p \in P$, and $\phi(\Delta) = \{tt, ff\}$ (either tt or ff, we don't know).

Remark 1. $\mathcal{L}^\Delta$ may be regarded as a restricted form of Kleene's three-value logic, it is different, however, in the following aspects.

– We have Δ in the syntax in addition to the three-value semantic domain.
– Every *known* primitive predicate p is always assigned with a definite meaning, i.e., a singleton in $\mathcal{D}$. Only the special symbol Δ remains *unknown*.
– In Kleene's system there is no (nontrivial) tautology, but in our specialized logic $\mathcal{L}^\Delta$ we have valid formulas. For example $p \Rightarrow p$ is valid for any $p \in P$, simply because p cannot be unknown.

---

[1] The domain $\mathcal{D}' = \mathbb{P}(\{tt, ff\})$ includes the empty set $\{\}$ which would represent *contradiction*, the top element in Ginsberg's smallest non-trivial bilattice [Gin88].

Semantics. Let $\oplus$ be a binary Boolean operator and $\ominus$ an unary Boolean operator. We lift these operators into $\mathcal{D}$ using the notation $[\![\oplus]\!] : \mathcal{D} \times \mathcal{D} \to \mathcal{D}$ and $[\![\ominus]\!] : \mathcal{D} \to \mathcal{D}$, respectively. The semantics is defined as point-wise application of the corresponding Boolean operator on the elements in the Boolean set, i.e., $\phi(\varphi_1 \oplus \varphi_2) = \{[\![\oplus]\!](b_1, b_2) \mid b_1 \in \phi(\varphi_1) \wedge b_2 \in \phi(\varphi_2)\}$ (the set of values $b_1 \oplus b_2$ for any b_1 and b_2 that are possible interpretations of φ_1 and φ_2, respectively), and $\phi(\ominus(\varphi)) = \{[\![\ominus]\!](b) \mid b \in \phi(\varphi)\}$ (the set of values $\ominus b$ for any b that is a possible interpretation of φ). In particular, for any $d \in \mathcal{D}$, $\phi(\mathit{true} \wedge d) = \phi(d)$ and $\phi(\mathit{false} \wedge d) = \{\mathit{ff}\}$. On Δ the lifted operators are resolved as follows

$$
\begin{aligned}
\phi(\Delta \wedge \mathit{true}) &= \{\mathit{tt}, \mathit{ff}\}[\![\wedge]\!]\{\mathit{tt}\} &&= \{\mathit{tt} \wedge \mathit{tt}, \mathit{ff} \wedge \mathit{tt}\} &&= \{\mathit{tt}, \mathit{ff}\} &&= \phi(\Delta) \\
\phi(\Delta \wedge \mathit{false}) &= \{\mathit{tt}, \mathit{ff}\}[\![\wedge]\!]\{\mathit{ff}\} &&= \{\mathit{tt} \wedge \mathit{ff}, \mathit{ff} \wedge \mathit{ff}\} &&= \{\mathit{ff}\} &&= \phi(\mathit{false}) \\
\phi(\Delta \vee \mathit{true}) &= \{\mathit{tt}, \mathit{ff}\}[\![\vee]\!]\{\mathit{tt}\} &&= \{\mathit{tt} \vee \mathit{tt}, \mathit{ff} \vee \mathit{tt}\} &&= \{\mathit{tt}\} &&= \phi(\mathit{true}) \\
\phi(\Delta \vee \mathit{false}) &= \{\mathit{tt}, \mathit{ff}\}[\![\vee]\!]\{\mathit{ff}\} &&= \{\mathit{tt} \vee \mathit{ff}, \mathit{ff} \vee \mathit{ff}\} &&= \{\mathit{tt}, \mathit{ff}\} &&= \phi(\Delta) \\
\phi(\neg\Delta) &= [\![\neg]\!]\{\mathit{tt}, \mathit{ff}\} &&= \{\mathit{ff}, \mathit{tt}\} &&= \phi(\Delta)
\end{aligned}
$$

and similarly, $\phi(\Delta \wedge \Delta) = \phi(\Delta \vee \Delta) = \phi(\Delta)$. With the standard predicate logic rules $((c \wedge d) \Leftrightarrow c) \equiv (c \Rightarrow d)$ and $((c \vee d) \Leftrightarrow d) \equiv (c \Rightarrow d)$, we can conclude from the above that $\mathit{false} \Rightarrow \Delta$ and $\Delta \Rightarrow \mathit{true}$, hence $\mathit{false} \Rightarrow \Delta \Rightarrow \mathit{true}$.

Information Order. Predicates are partially ordered by implication. We have $\mathit{false} \Rightarrow p \Rightarrow \mathit{true}$ for all predicates p, including Δ. However, Δ is incomparable to any other predicate in P in this ordering. To relate results in the embedding domain (and later on the abstract domain) with results in the concrete domain, we introduce an *information order* which lies orthogonal to the partial order on truth values (see also [Gin88, SRW02]).

Definition 1 (Information Order). *The information order, $\leq_i$, is a relation over formulas in $\mathcal{L}^\Delta$ such that for any formulas $\varphi_1, \varphi_2 \in \mathcal{L}^\Delta$, $\varphi_1 \leq_i \varphi_2 \Leftrightarrow \phi(\varphi_1) \supseteq \phi(\varphi_2)$.*

Intuitively, Δ provides less information to an analysis than any definite formulas, and from this definition it follows that $\Delta \leq_i \varphi$ for any formula $\varphi \in \mathcal{L}^\Delta$. As can be shown, the information order $\leq_i$ is a partial order over $Pred^3$ and all the logical operators are monotone with respect to $\leq_i$. In particular, for any predicates p and q, we have $\Delta \leq_i (\Delta \vee p) \leq_i q \vee p$ and $\Delta \leq_i (\Delta \wedge p) \leq_i q \wedge p$.

Simplification. Simplification is crucial for an effective path-sensitive DFA as it allows one to collapse predicates that otherwise grow very complex, but it is computationally expensive. Formulas in $Pred^3$ can be simplified using the rules of standard predicate logic. In our implementation some simplifications are realised, namely those that do not require expensive reasoning power. In particular, we restrict the simplification to *base predicates*, which commonly occur in programs where simple flags are used to control the flow.

Definition 2 (Base Predicate). *A base predicate is either true or false or a term of the form "x op c" where "x" is a variable, "c" is a constant* *value, and "op" is a binary operator from the set* $\{=, \neq, <, \leq, >, \geq\}$ *(tests) or* $\{\&_{all}, \&_{any}, \overline{\&}_{all}, \overline{\&}_{any}\}$ *(bit-field tests).*

The set of base predicates, denoted by *BasePred*, is a subset of the set of flow conditions, i.e, *BasePred* $\subseteq P$. From the definition it follows that for all $p \in BasePred$ the variable set $var(p)$ refers to at most one variable. Bit-field tests are defined based on C's *bit-wise and* operator "&" as outlined in Figure 5, where k is a constant bit mask.

$$(x \ \&_{all} \ k) \equiv (x \ \& \ k) == k$$
$$(x \ \&_{any} \ k) \equiv (x \ \& \ k) \neq 0$$
$$(x \ \overline{\&}_{all} \ k) \equiv (x \ \& \ k) == 0$$
$$(x \ \overline{\&}_{any} \ k) \equiv (x \ \& \ k) \neq k$$

Fig. 5. Bit field tests

We denote the simplification of formulas with the operator $\lceil \cdot \rceil : \mathcal{L}^\Delta \to \mathcal{L}^\Delta$. For any formula $\varphi \in \mathcal{L}^\Delta$ we have $\llbracket \varphi \rrbracket = \llbracket \lceil \varphi \rceil \rrbracket$, i.e., the simplification preserves the semantics. In particular, $\lceil \varphi \wedge true \rceil = \lceil \varphi \rceil$, $\lceil \varphi \vee true \rceil = true$, $\lceil \varphi \wedge false \rceil = false$, $\lceil \varphi \vee false \rceil = \lceil \varphi \rceil$, $\lceil \varphi \wedge \varphi \rceil = \lceil \varphi \vee \varphi \rceil = \lceil \varphi \rceil$.

For any predicate $a \neq \Delta$ we simplify $\lceil a \vee \neg a \rceil$ to *true* and $\lceil a \wedge \neg a \rceil$ to *false*. We exploit associativity, idempotence, and absorption of the Boolean operators to simplify predicates, e.g., $\lceil a \vee (a \wedge b) \rceil = a$. Bit-field tests can be simplified following the above, when taking into account the facts that $(x \ \&_{all} \ k) \equiv \neg(x \ \overline{\&}_{any} \ k)$ and $(x \ \&_{any} \ k) \equiv \neg(x \ \overline{\&}_{all} \ k)$.

To enable further simplification, we represent the right hand side of any $p \in BasePred$ that is a test (rather than a bit-field test) as a vector of integer intervals. That is, the predicate $x = k$ is represented as $x \in \langle [k, k] \rangle$ (i.e., $k \leq x \leq k$), and $x < k$ as $x \in \langle [Min, k-1] \rangle$, where Min is the smallest representable integer in the machine. This allows us to compute the disjunction and the conjunction of base predicates with the same left hand side, if they are of the interval type, by applying interval union and intersection, respectively. That is, $(x \in S) \vee (x \in T)$ simplifies to $x \in (S \cup T)$, and $(x \in S) \wedge (x \in T)$ simplifies to $x \in (S \cap T)$, where the operators $\cup$ and $\cap$ are defined as merging and intersecting, respectively, of ordered sequences of intervals. The empty interval $\langle [\ ] \rangle$ is simplified to *false* and the maximal range $\langle [Min, Max] \rangle$ to *true*. Note, that any predicate whose right hand side is represented as an interval vector is considered a base predicate.

6.2   Abstraction

The intention of our abstraction scheme is to keep only simple predicates and map all other (complex) predicates onto Δ. By "simple" predicates we mean predicates in disjunctive normal form (DNF) that consist of clauses of base predicates and negated assertions only. We consider the negation of assertions since the transfer function $\overline{wp}$, when applied to an assertion A and postcondition p, constructs the disjunction of the *negated assertion* $\neg A$ and p (i.e., $\overline{wp}(\{A\})(p) = def(A) \Rightarrow \neg A \vee p$). Hence the negation of the assertion will appear in the abstract predicate domain. We call the predicates in the abstract predicate domain *disjoint predicates* and they are defined in terms of the set of base predicates, *BasePred*, and the set of negated assertions, *Assertion*.

Definition 3 (Disjoint Predicate). *The set of* disjoint predicates, *denoted as* DisjointPred, *comprises predicates of the form* $p = p_1 \vee \ldots \vee p_n$ *such that for all* $1 \leq i \leq n$, *either* $p_i \in BasePred \cup Assertion \cup \{\Delta\}$ *or* $p_i = b \wedge a$ *with* $b \in BasePred$ *and* $a \in Assertion$.

That is, the abstraction maintains base predicates as well as assertions which take the role of data flow facts. For a particular analysis *Assertion* is usually a singleton (e.g., in Example 3, $Assertion = \{tmp \neq Null\}$, and in Example 4, $Assertion = \{tmp = Null\}$). In that sense *Assertion* is a parameter to the predicative DFA framework that can be instrumented for a variety of analysis problems.

We define the abstract domain $Pred^A$ as the set of disjoint predicates and the unknown symbol (as shown in Figure 4). The simplification rules are applied to the formulas whenever possible immediately after the transfer function is applied and before abstraction is performed. We specialise the DFA computation as follows, where $D^A(n)$ represents the predicative data flow value at node n in the abstract domain.

$$D^A_{i+1}(n) = \alpha \left(\left\lceil \bigvee_{n' \in succ(n)} \lceil \overline{wp}(\mathit{eff}(n, n'))(D^A_i(n')) \rceil \right\rceil \right) \tag{3}$$

Since the result is computed as a value in $Pred^A$, the size of a disjoint predicate is linearly bounded by the number of variables in the program. This is because a predicate in $Pred^A$ can have at most $|N| + 1$ disjuncts (or clauses) each as a base predicate associated with a distinct program variable, or the unknown predicate Δ as defined in the abstraction α outlined below.

A number of specialised simplification rules are introduced for disjoint predicates. These more complex simplifications also preserve the semantics of the predicate. For example, for merging predicates from the *true* and *false* branches at an if-then-else node, we apply $\lceil (p \wedge (\varphi \vee \varphi_1)) \vee (\neg p \wedge (\varphi \vee \varphi_2)) \rceil = \varphi \vee \lceil (p \wedge \varphi_1) \vee (\neg p \wedge \varphi_2) \rceil$, i.e., we extract the common part out of the disjoint predicates from both branches before simplifying the conjunctions. The final result of simplification is a disjoint predicate in DNF, i.e., in the form of $\bigvee_{i \in I} \varphi_i$ such that each clause φ_i is a single base predicate or an assertion, or a conjunction of a base predicate and an assertion, or predicate Δ (see Definition 3). The abstraction function, $\alpha : Pred^3 \to Pred^A$, is defined as follows.

- $\alpha(\Delta) = \Delta$.
- For each $p \in BasePred \cup Assertion$, we have $\alpha(p) = p$ and $\alpha(\neg p) = \neg p$.
- If φ is a conjunction of the form $a \wedge \varphi'$ with assertion a, we have $\alpha(\varphi) = a \wedge \alpha(\varphi')$. (Note that a clause in a disjoint predicate cannot have more than one assertion as they can only be introduced via disjunction.)
- If φ is a conjunction of more than one base predicate, we have $\alpha(\varphi) = \Delta$. In particular, $\alpha(p \wedge q) = \Delta$ if $var(p) \neq var(q)$, since $p \wedge q$ cannot be simplified into a single base predicate. Similarly, if $var(p) = var(q)$ and $p \wedge q$ cannot be simplified into a single base predicate, the abstraction results in Δ.
- An abstract disjoint predicate is given as the disjunction of the abstracted clauses, i.e., $\alpha(\bigvee_{i \in I} \varphi_i) = \bigvee_{i \in I} \alpha(\varphi_i)$.

It is obvious from this definition that α is monotone with respect to the information order, i.e., $\phi(\alpha(p)) \leq_i \phi(p))$ for all predicates p. Moreover, in the presence of loops the DFA on the abstract domain will in most cases converge to a simple predicate or to Δ. If a base predicate does not converge, e.g., when it extends its range in each iteration, the analysis exits the loop with an approximation after a small number of iterations.

Example 5. Applying the outlined abstraction scheme to the flow graph in Example 4 (see Figure 3) does not change the labelling. Hence we modify the example slightly and change the flow conditions: We label the edge (n_2, n_3) with $[fd \neq -1]$ and the edge (n_2, n_5) with $[fd = -1]$. This yields a more complex predicate labelling node n_2, namely $D(n_2) = ((err \neq 0 \lor tmp = Null) \land fd \neq -1) \lor (tmp = Null \land fd = -1)$ which reduces to $(tmp = Null) \lor (err \neq 0 \land fd \neq -1)$. The abstraction simplifies this predicate to $D(n_3)^A = (tmp = Null) \lor \Delta$. (The labelling for nodes n_1 and *entry* remains unchanged, i.e., equals *true*.) The result indicates that if $(tmp = Null)$ then there exists a path from n_3 that does lead to a *free-of-non-allocated-pointer*. Otherwise, a *free-of-non-allocated-pointer* might occur along some path from n_3, we do not know.   □

From the abstraction we require that the results computed in the abstract domain $Pred^A$ coincide with the results that are computed in the original domain $Pred$, unless Δ is reported. If the analysis results in Δ, it is inconclusive and no statement can be made whether an assertion was violated or not. In that sense Δ comprises both possibilities, *true* and *false*, as its semantic value suggests, namely $\phi(\Delta) = \{tt, ff\}$. If the analysis results in the entry node being labelled with $p \lor \Delta$ it indicates that there is a bug along the paths where p holds, on all other paths, there might be a bug, we do not know. Following this observation, soundness can be stated on the basis of the information order.

Theorem 1 (Soundness). *The predicative DFA on the abstract domain $Pred^A$ is sound with respect to the information order $\leq_i$, i.e., for all nodes $n \in N$, we have $D^A(n) \leq_i D(n)$.*

The proof of this result follows straightforwardly from the monotonicity of the abstraction with respect to the information order and the fact that the simplification is semantic-preserving, i.e., $\lceil \varphi \rceil = \varphi$. We conclude that the final result $D^A(n)$ iteratively computed from Equation 3 is either a precise answer, or an *unknown*.

7   Experimental Results

The path-sensitive framework has been implemented in the static bug checking tool Parfait [CS08]. Parfait is currently used for the detection of memory leaks, use-after-free, double-free, free-of-non-allocated, and other bug-types. During the bug checking procedure, Parfait first populates a list of *potential bugs* generated by a path-insensitive DFA, and then applies the path-sensitive backwards DFA to verify whether the reported bugs in the list are real bugs (i.e., occurring along a feasible path). The form of disjoint predicates with simple disjuncts in the analysis is the key to scalability, which enables Parfait to spend a relatively short amount of time processing millions of lines of code. Nevertheless, this simple abstraction does not significantly impact the precision of the algorithm, as the abstract domain closely mirrors the way in which programmers typically manage control flow in practice, i.e., by setting up one or two constant flag variables that are later identified in the cleanup phase at the end of the program.

Parfait also supports inter-procedural analysis by summarising effects of the functions. We seed the process with predefined summaries for the common standard C library functions such as `malloc` and `free` and also generate function summaries for other functions. These are propagated bottom-up through the call graph. In the case of memory-leak analysis, function summaries would include information about allocation and de-allocation of pointer variables, stores into any pointer variables, and escapes of any pointer values (by storing into globally accessible memory or returning a pointer value). We then perform an intra-procedural data flow analysis over each function that contains a potential bug, making use of the summaries generated for each call site.

For each potential bug to be examined, the predicative DFA returns one of the four cases: a non-false value (definitely a bug), *false* (definitely not a bug), Δ (unknown), and $p \vee \Delta$ (definitely a bug along some paths). We observe, however, that if a potential bug is a false alarm (i.e., not reachable), then most of the time it is reported as *false*, thanks to the way in which most programmers handle control flow with simple constant flags. Therefore, in the current version we choose to report both the non-false and the Δ cases as (potential) bugs, which consequently enables the tool to report significantly more bugs, but also permits false positives at a tolerable low rate. The large-scale experiment data, which was manually evaluated, further justifies our decision.

The current (inter-procedural) version of Parfait has been run over 6 million lines of the Solaris ON B20 source code in X4270 server equipped with 2×3.3GHz Xeon X5680 CPUs and 144Gb RAM, running Solaris 11.1. Our experiment spreads eight threads in parallel and completes in 24 minutes, reporting 674 memory-leak bugs with a false positive rate of 4.6% (31/674).

8   Related Work

As one of the early works on path-sensitive data flow analysis Holley and Rosen [HR80] proposed a general approach to improve the precision by computing path feasibility under a given set of assertions on variable values, and construct a new problem that contains only qualified paths. Bodík et al. in [BGS97] developed a strategy to detect infeasible paths using the notion of *branch correlations* (i.e., the dependence of a branch predicate on a previous branch or program statement). The process is demand-driven: at branch b with predicate p a query about the satisfiability of p is raised which is propagated backwards in the flow graph until it is resolved along all paths. The resolution of the query is then passed forward to branch *b* that caused the query and the flow graph labelled accordingly. Fisher et al. [FJM05] base their analysis on a structure called a *predicated lattice* whose elements are mappings from predicates to dataflow values. In this framework dataflow values are only merged in the case when they are associated to the same predicate. Their analysis works in a forward fashion and hence requires a set of predicates P as input. If P is not sufficient to produce a precise result they iteratively refine P and add more predicates according to the false positives encountered (similar to lazy abstraction [HJMS02]). This process is repeated until the analysis provides a precise (or precise enough) solution.

Property simulation has been proposed by Das et al. [DLS02, HYD05, DDY06] and implemented in the ESP tool. The analysis is also performed in a forward fashion. The framework is based on an adjustable abstraction which represents symbolic states of the program. A property state machine specifies the property pattern to be checked and is exercised in parallel with the program code (through instrumentation of the program), where a simulation state represents path information. The tool applies a decision procedure to reason about feasibility of the paths.

Rival and Mauborgne [RM07] build a general framework for *trace partitioning* which allows for path sensitivity. The idea is to extend the general data flow analysis (following the abstract interpretation framework of [CC77]) with *tokens* which allow the partitioning of the state space, qualifying classes of states according to the history of execution. The set of tokens T is variable in the framework and can be set according to the analysed problem. If T is a singleton then the analysis coincides with the classical DFA.

All existing works in the literature for path sensitive program analysis separate the analysis on paths from the analysis on data, in a way that first explores the correlated predicates or properties to settle feasible path flows, and subsequently applies the analysis only on the feasible paths. Our work integrates data flow analysis with predicate analysis in a general weakest precondition framework. This allows us to merge and simplify paths predicates and data flow values (which are predicates here) during the analysis for better scalability.

9   Conclusion and Outlook to Future Work

This paper proposed a path-sensitive data flow analysis framework which combines path predicates with data flow values. The transfer function is based on Dijkstra's weakest precondition to reason about data flow values or violations via assertions. This approach supports the analysis of a large variety of bug patterns, such as locking-not-followed-by-unlocking and use-after-free, which can be simply described as a relationship between two distinct program points along a feasible path. We also introduced effective simplification and abstraction to facilitate the efficiency of the analysis. The work has been implemented in the static bug checker Parfait and the result scales to programs with millions of lines of code.

As further experiments, we are interested in refining the abstraction to include more complex predicates (e.g., allow for disjoint predicates with clauses with more than two conjuncts). This would enable us to relate the trade-off between efficiency and preciseness to the granularity of the abstraction.

In comparison to flow-sensitive forward analysis, predicative backward DFA has the advantage of being able to discover relevant predicates at an early stage (i.e., by selecting predicates that guard bug related assertions). However as many DFA problems can only be encoded in a forward analysis, it is of interest to explore forward DFA in the future, taking advantage of strongest postconditions and effective ways to extract predicates related to the problem.

References

[BGS97]   Bodík, R., Gupta, R., Soffa, M.L.: Refining data flow information using infeasible paths. In: Proc. of ESEC/FSE, pp. 361–377. ACM (1997)

[CC77]   Cousot, P., Cousot, R.: Abstract interpretation: a unified lattice model for static analysis of programs by construction or approximation of fixpoints. In: Proc. of POPL, pp. 238–252. ACM (1977)

[CS08]   Cifuentes, C., Scholz, B.: Parfait – designing a scalable bug checker. In: Proc. of the Static Analysis Workshop, pp. 4–11. ACM (2008)

[DDY06]   Dhurjati, D., Das, M., Yang, Y.: Path-sensitive dataflow analysis with iterative refinement. In: Yi, K. (ed.) SAS 2006. LNCS, vol. 4134, pp. 425–442. Springer, Heidelberg (2006)

[Dij76]   Dijkstra, E.W.: A Discipline of Programming. Prentice Hall (1976)

[DLS02]   Das, M., Lerner, S., Seigle, M.: ESP: Path-sensitive program verification in polynomial time. In: Proc. of PLDI, pp. 57–68. ACM (2002)

[FJM05]   Fisher, J., Jhala, R., Majumdar, R.: Joining dataflow with predicates. In: Proc. of ESEC/FSE, pp. 227–236. ACM (2005)

[Gin88]   Ginsberg, M.: Multivalued logics: A uniform approach to inference in artificial intelligence. Computational Intelligence 4, 265–316 (1988)

[HFL01]   Hayes, I.J., Fidge, C.J., Lermer, K.: Semantic characterisation of dead control-flow paths. IEE Proceedings—Software 148(6), 175–186 (2001)

[HJMS02]   Henzinger, T., Jhala, R., Majumdar, R., Sutre, G.: Lazy abstraction. In: Proc. of POPL, pp. 58–70. ACM (2002)

[HR80]   Holley, L.H., Rosen, B.K.: Qualified data flow problems. In: Proc. of POPL, pp. 68–82. ACM (1980)

[HYD05]   Hampapuram, H., Yang, Y., Das, M.: Symbolic path simulation in path-sensitive dataflow analysis. In: Proc. of PASTE, pp. 52–58. ACM (2005)

[Kil73]   Kildall, G.A.: A unified approach to global program optimization. In: Proc. of POPL, pp. 194–206. ACM (1973)

[LA04]   Lattner, C., Adve, V.: LLVM: A Compilation Framework for Lifelong Program Analysis & Transformation. In: Proc. of the International Symposium on Code Generation and Optimization (CGO 2004), pp. 75–86 (2004)

[NNH99]   Nielson, F., Nielson, H.R., Hankin, C.: Principles of program analysis. Springer (1999)

[RM07]   Rival, X., Mauborgne, L.: The trace partitioning abstract domain. In: ACM TOPLAS (August 29, 2007)

[SRW02]   Sagiv, S., Reps, T.W., Wilhelm, R.: Parametric shape analysis via 3-valued logic. In: ACM TOPLAS, vol. 24(3), pp. 217–298 (2002)

Reconstructing Paths for Reachable Code

Stephan Arlt, Zhiming Liu, and Martin Schäf

United Nations University, IIST,
Macau S.A.R., China
{arlt,lzm,schaef}@iist.unu.edu

Abstract. Infeasible code has proved to be an interesting target for static analysis. It allows modular and scalable analysis, and at the same time, can be implemented with a close-to-zero rate of false warnings. The challenge for an infeasible code detection algorithm is to find executions that cover all statements with feasible executions as fast as possible. The remaining statements are infeasible code. In this paper we propose a new encoding of programs into first-order logic formulas that allows us to query the non-existence of feasible executions of a program, and, to reconstruct a feasible path from counterexamples produced for this query. We use these paths to develop a path-cover algorithm based on blocking clauses. We evaluate our approach using several real-world applications and show that our new prover-friendly encoding yields a significant speed-up over existing approaches.

1 Introduction

Recently, static verification techniques are being used to prove the existence of *infeasible code* [16,13,4,21]. These techniques prove the existence of statements that do not occur on any feasible (complete) control-flow path in a program. Such statements could be unreachable code, a null-check of memory that has already been accessed, or a guaranteed violation of a run-time assertion. Infeasible code is an interesting target for static verification: proving the absence of feasible executions can be done on a code snippet in isolation without knowing its context, and the proof still holds if the context is extended, which allows scalable implementations at a close-to-zero false positives rate.

To detect infeasible code, one has to prove that any complete path containing a particular statement is infeasible. This is usually done by computing a first-order logic formula of (an over-approximation of) the weakest-liberal precondition of the set of paths containing this statement with respect to the empty post-state. Then a theorem prover is used to check if this formula is valid. If the proof succeeds, then there is no terminating execution along any of these paths.

To check if there is *any* infeasible code in a program, we have to repeat this check for every statement. Of course, this is very inefficient. Several optimizations are possible. E.g., the existence of a feasible complete control-flow path containing a particular statement immediately implies that all other statements

L. Groves and J. Sun (Eds.): ICFEM 2013, LNCS 8144, pp. 431–446, 2013.

on this path have a feasible execution as well. However, such optimizations require that counterexamples from the theorem prover can be mapped to feasible executions.

The problem we are addressing in this paper is the following: If we query the theorem prover with the weakest-liberal precondition formula of a code snippet, the counterexample we receive only states the existence of *at least one* feasible path through this snippet, it, in general, does not allow us to reconstruct any particular path. This is, because the query we sent to the theorem prover allows the prover to find a satisfying valuation that represents several program executions, but, as the program we encoded into the formula is deterministic, we cannot match this valuation to one execution in the input program. Hence, the formula has to be augmented to force the prover to find a valuation that can be mapped to exactly one deterministic execution.

In this paper, we propose a new encoding of code into logic formulas for infeasible code detection that allows us to identify a feasible path (actually, a path that we cannot prove infeasible) immediately from a counterexample of the theorem prover. Based on this encoding, we propose an algorithm to detect all statements for which the prover cannot find a feasible execution. We show how the new encoding can be used to develop much faster tools for infeasible code detection.

Related Work. The problem of reconstructing information about error traces from counterexamples in static verification was first discussed by Leino et al. [18]. They introduce so-called labels which are emitted by the theorem prover if a proof of correctness fails. These labels refer to particular assertions that could not be proved correct, and allow the reconstruction of an error trace. The motivation of this approach is essentially the same as ours, but their technique cannot be applied to infeasible code detection, as it only works for weakest precondition encodings with failing assertions. In the case of weakest liberal precondition, no label would be emitted by the prover.

There is a lot of related work on infeasible code detection. Under different names, infeasible code detection has been proposed in many papers. Probably the most significant work is the paper by Engler [10] which also forms the basis of the static analysis in Coverity's Prevent tool. In this work, infeasible code is called *contradicting believes* and detected using syntactic pattern matching. Findbugs [15] uses a similar pattern matching to identify a subset of infeasible code. In [8], infeasible code is called (sequential) semantic inconsistency or source-sink errors. They further detect non-sequential semantic inconsistencies which are not infeasible code. None of these approaches uses static verification based encodings of programs, so the problem and solution described in this paper do not apply there.

Different approaches have been presented that use weakest-liberal precondition encodings of programs for infeasible code detection. Janota et al. [16] present an approach to detect unreachable code in the presence of logic specifications. They only focus on the subset of infeasible code that is not forward reachable. To reduce the number of queries, they make use of the dominator relationship between statements in the control-flow graph to identify a minimal subset of statements that have to be checked. In [13] and [14], an approach to detect infeasible code is presented that uses auxiliary Boolean variables and the dominator and post-dominator relation on control-flow locations to minimize the number of theorem prover queries. In [4] and [2] the term infeasible code is introduced. There, we used auxiliary integer variables and an *effectual set* to define a query optimal algorithm to detect infeasible code. Another approach for infeasible code detection is presented in [21], which refers to it as *fatal code*.

All of the above approaches that detect infeasible code using static verification see the problem of finding infeasible code as a coverage problem of the control-flow graph. They try to find an optimal coverage strategy to find all feasible paths and use a theorem prover as an oracle for feasibility queries. They propose different strategies based on helper variables to send more informed queries to the prover and thus reduce the overall number of queries. In this paper, however, we believe that a theorem prover is too complex to be treated as a blackbox: we assume that helper variables that constraint the theorem prover may refrain the prover from building useful knowledge and thus make each query more expensive.

2   Examples

Infeasible code is an interesting target for static analysis. First of all, it can be detected without too much noise (i.e., false positives), and second, infeasible code is usually a good indicator for security vulnerabilities as it shows the existence of code that cannot be executed or fails inevitably. And, most importantly, infeasible code occurs in practice, and it is not rare, as shown in our experiments in Section 6. We motivate the usefulness of infeasible code detection using two instances of infeasible code in Fig. 1 that we found in the software used for the German eID[1]. Both examples are not necessarily bugs, but they show problems in the error model of the applications. In the first example, the `equals` procedure compares the `.bases` field of two objects, by first checking if the one on the left hand side is `null` and the other one is not. If so, it returns `false` otherwise it compares the size of the `bases`. Now, consider the case that `bases` and `other.bases` are `null`. In that case, the `else`-branch of the `if` statement in line 4 is executed. And, on any execution, where this `else`-branch is executed we cause a `NullPointer` exception in line 8. Hence, the `else`-branch of the conditional in line 4 is infeasible code (and a bug if we can find a test case that executes this code).

The second example is even more obvious: if i is bigger than (`len-1`), the procedure throws an exception at line 3. Hence, the return statement in line 7 can never be reached and thus is infeasible code. Even though, no error occurs, it makes a significant difference if a method returns normal or with an exception, thus we assume a conceptual flaw in the error model that we have yet to confirm with the developers.

---

[1] http://www.openecard.org/

```
1  // org.openecard.bouncycastle.crypto.params.
       NTRUSigningPrivateKeyParameters
2  public boolean equals(Object obj) {
3      if (bases == null) {
4          if (other.bases != null) {
5              return false;
6          }
7      }
8      if (bases.size() != other.bases.size()) {
9          return false;
10     }
11 }
```

```
1  // org.openecard.bouncycastle.pqc.math.linearalgebra.
       GF2Polynomial
2  public void xorBit(int i) throws RuntimeException {
3      if (i < 0 || i > (len - 1)) {
4          throw new RuntimeException();
5      }
6      if (i > (len - 1)) {
7          return;
8      }
9      value[i >>> 5] ^= bitMask[i & 0x1f];
10 }
```

Fig. 1. Two examples of infeasible code taken from the German eID software

In both cases, the infeasible code is not a bug, but it shows problems in the error model, as there is some error handling code, but still there are cases which are not handled or handled multiple times. Other examples can be found using our tool, Joogie [2]. Usually, infeasible code in large methods tends to be more interesting but is not suitable to be presented in a paper.

3   Preliminaries

Throughout this paper, we only consider programs written in the simple unstructured language given shown in Figure 2. The language can be seen as a simplified version of Boogie [19] which is sufficient for demonstration purposes. The language is simple but yet expressive enough to encode high-level languages such as Java. In our experiments in Section 6, we use the Joogie tool [2] to translate Java programs into this language.

We represent executions of statements in our language by pairs of states. A state s is a function that maps program variables to values of appropriate sort. We use $s(x)$ to denote the value of a variable x at the state s. We use the weakest precondition to describe the semantics of the statements in our language. Given a statement st, and two states s, s', we say that s followed by s' is an execution of st

$$Program ::= Block^*$$
$$Block ::= label:\ Stmt;^*\ \textbf{goto}\ label^*;$$
$$Stmt ::= VarId := Expr;\ |\ \textbf{assert}\ Expr;\ |$$
$$\textbf{assume}\ Expr;$$

Fig. 2. The syntax of our simple (unstructured) Language

if and only if $s \models wp(st, s')$. Furthermore, we use the weakest-liberal precondition to check if a statement has no execution at all: a statement has no execution if the formula $\models wlp(st, false)$ is valid (for brevity, we use the empty set of states and the Boolean $false$ interchangeably, which is not really clean but safes a lot of writing). That is, a statement has no execution if, for any pre-state s it's execution ends in $false$ (which is not possible), or does not terminate (see definition of wlp).

A path is a sequence of statements $\pi = st_0; \ldots; st_{n-1}$; connected by sequential composition, an execution of π is a sequence of states $s_0 \ldots s_n$ such that for any $0 \le i < n$, $s_i \models wp(st_i, s_{i+1})$, and in particular $s_0 \models wp(\pi, s_n)$. Hence, a path π has no execution, if $wlp(\pi, false)$ is valid. For brevity, we treat statements connected by sequential composition as sequences of statements and omit the semicolon if possible. We say a path is feasible if it has at least one execution and that it is infeasible otherwise.

st	$wlp(st, Q)$	$wp(st, Q)$
assume E	$E \implies Q$	$E \implies Q$
assert E	$E \implies Q$	$E \wedge Q$
$VarId := Expr$	$Q[Expr/VarId]$	$Q[Expr/VarId]$
$S; T$	$wlp(S, wlp(T, Q))$	$wp(S, wp(T, Q))$
$goto\ S_0 \ldots S_n$	$\bigwedge_{0 \le i \le n} wlp(S_i, Q)$	$\bigwedge_{0 \le i \le n} wlp(S_i, Q)$

Fig. 3. The weakest (liberal) precondition semantic of our language from Figure 2

We extend the computation of wp and wlp from paths to programs in the obvious way. We use the standard approach to compute a formula representation of the weakest-liberal precondition shown in Figure 3. For a more detailed description of this encoding which includes language features such as procedure, we refer to [7,11].

To show that a statement st has no execution within a program P, we simply have to show that each complete path π in P that contains st has no execution. Here, a complete path is a path of P that starts in a unique initial statement and ends in a unique final statement. Throughout the rest of the paper the term path always refers to a complete path unless stated different.

Definition 1. *Given a statement ⌀ in a program P. The statement ⌀ is infeasible in P if, for any complete path π in P that contains ⌀, the formula $wlp(\pi, false)$ is valid.*

Here, a program could be a real program, a procedure, or simply a set of related paths. For simplicity, we use the term program.

Computing a formula representation of the weakest-liberal precondition that can be understood by a theorem prover usually requires some sort of abstraction. In general, looping control-flow and the type system of high-level programming languages cannot be encoded into a first-order logic formula that can be solved by an automated theorem prover. Hence, abstraction is necessary. Such an abstraction may include elimination of looping control-flow, an approximation of finite programming language types by infinite logic types, etc. The details of such an abstraction are not in the scope of this paper and we refer to the related work for more details (e.g., [14,9]).

From here on, we assume that we have an abstraction $P^{\#} = abstract(P)$ that, for a given program P, provides us with an abstraction $P^{\#}$ of P that satisfies the following properties: a) we can compute a formula representation of $wlp(P^{\#}, false)$ that is decidable by the decision procedure of our choice, b) $P^{\#}$ has only finite paths (i.e., is loop-free), and c) $P^{\#}$ is a sound abstraction of P. That is, if we can prove that $P^{\#}$ has no execution (by showing that $wlp(P^{\#}, false)$ is valid), then P does not have an execution either. Formally, we define the soundness of the abstraction as follows:

Definition 2 (Sound abstraction). *Given a program P and an abstraction $P^{\#} = abstract(P)$. The program $P^{\#}$ is a sound abstraction of P, if there exists a mapping of paths in $P^{\#}$ to pahts in P such that each feasible path π can be mapped to a feasible path $\pi^{\#}$ in $P^{\#}$.*

We emphasize that this notion of soundness is different from soundness in verification, where the abstraction has to preserve the infeasible executions instead of the feasible ones. Implementations of such abstractions are, for example, presented in [4,14,21].

Given such an abstraction, we are able to check if a program P has a feasible execution by asking a theorem prover if there is a valuation s such that $s \not\models wlp(P^{\#}, false)$. Now, it would be nice if we could obtain a feasible execution of $P^{\#}$ from s. Unfortunately, and this is the main motivation of this paper, this is not possible. Our query checks for the non-existence of a feasible path in $P^{\#}$, a counterexample to this can be an arbitrary number of feasible paths. For the theorem prover, it may be sufficient to find values for a few program variables to satisfy $wlp(P^{\#}, false)$. All remaining variables are then assigned to arbitrary values. Hence, for the general case, s does not represent any particular feasible path. However, an efficient implementation that detects infeasible code needs this information to cover all feasible paths in $P^{\#}$ (because all statements that cannot be covered are infeasible in P). In the following we present a new encoding of wlp that allows us to extract exactly one execution and its corresponding control-flow path in $P^\#$ from a counterexample for $wlp(P^\#, false)$. Based on this encoding, we further propose an algorithm to detect all infeasible statements in the original program.

4   Encoding of the Weakest-Liberal Precondition

Computing the formula representation of the weakest (liberal) precondition of our abstract program $P^\#$ is straight forward and has been discussed in many previous articles (e.g., [3,17,11,12]). We avoid the exponential explosion of the formula's size that comes with branching, by introducing auxiliary variables, which we call *block variables*. Using these variables avoids copying the wlp of the successor blocks. For each block

$$Block_i ::= \ell_i : S_i; \textbf{goto } Succ_i$$

we introduce a variable b_i that represents the formula $\neg wlp(Block_i, \textsf{false})$, where $Block_i$ is the basic block at label ℓ_i. These variables can be defined as

$$WLP : \bigwedge_{0 \le i < n} b_i \implies \neg wlp\left(S_i, \bigwedge_{j \in Succ_i} \neg b_j\right)$$
$$\wedge\, b_n \implies \neg wlp(S_n, \textsf{false}).$$

Where B_n denotes a unique exit block of the program. We can now find an execution of our program $P^\#$ starting from its initial location ℓ_0 by asking the theorem prover of our choice to find a satisfying valuation for

$$WLP \wedge b_0$$

Note that, unlike in the previous section, we use the negated weakest-liberal precondition. That is, we say that $P^\#$ has an execution if there exists a state s such that $s \models wlp(P^\#, false)$. From a logic point of view, both ideas are the same, but for the theorem prover finding a satisfying valuation is usually easier.

Lemma 1. *There is a satisfying valuation s for the formula WLP with $s(b_i) =$ true if and only if there exists an execution for the program fragment starting at the block $Block_i$.*

Proof is given in [4]. A satisfying valuation s of $WLP \wedge b_0$ corresponds to the existence of an execution of the program fragment. Moreover if $s(b_i)$ is true, the same valuation also corresponds to an execution starting at the block $Block_i$. However, it does not mean that there is an execution that starts in the initial state, visits the block $Block_i$, and then terminates. This is because the formula does not encode that $Block_i$ is reachable from the initial state.

To overcome this problem one may use the strongest postcondition to compute the states for which $Block_i$ is reachable. This roughly doubles the formula. In our case there is a simpler check for reachability. Based on the auxiliary variables that we already introduced to encode the weakest-liberal precondition, we encode the forward reachability as follows: let Pre_i be the set of predecessors of $Block_i$, i.e., the set of all j such that the final **goto** instruction of $Block_j$ may jump to $Block_i$. Then we can encode that a block has to be also forward reachable on a satisfying assignment as follows:

$$VC : WLP \wedge b_0 \wedge \bigwedge_{1 \leq i \leq n} \left(b_i \implies \left(\bigvee_{j \in Pre_i} b_j \right) \right).$$

That is, like in the case of WLP, given a valuation s such that $s \models VC$, $s(b_0)$ is *true* if there exists a complete and feasible path. Further, by requiring that $s(b_i)$ can only be *true* if this also holds for at least one of its predecessors, $s(b_i)$ can only be *true* if it occurs on a complete and feasible path. Thus, we can reconstruct a feasible path through our program by collecting all statements in blocks whose block variables evaluate to *true*.

Theorem 1. *There is a valuation s that satisfies VC with $s(b_0) = true$ if and only if s gives rise to the execution of a complete path π. Moreover, the value of any block variable $s(b_i)$ is true if and only if there is an execution of a path π starting in s that visits block $Block_i$.*

Proof (Sketch). The proof trivially follows by induction: from Lemma 1, we already know that $s(b_0)$ is *true* if and only if there exists a complete feasible path through the program fragment. For b_1, however, the implication $b_1 \implies (\bigvee_{j \in Pre_i} b_j)$ requires that b_1 can only be *true* if there exists at least one predecessor that is also *true* (here, it can only be b_0). Further, by Lemma 1, b_1 can only be *true* if there is a feasible execution of the program starting in b_1. As our input programs are deterministic, we also know that there can only be one predecessor $block_j$ of a block $block_i$, such that $s(b_j) = true$. Hence, by induction it follows that for a valuation $s \models VC$, the valuation $s(b_i)$ is *true* if and only if b_i has a feasible prefix and suffix path and thus is on a feasible and complete path.

The encoding of VC is the main contribution of this paper: similar to WLP, it allows us to check for the non-existence of a feasible path in our program P. But, in addition to that, a counterexample of VC also provides us a feasible path in $P^\#$ as a witness. The major benefit of our encoding over existing approaches is that VC does not introduce additional variables (besides the ones introduced by WLP). In our experiments, we will show that this encoding allows significantly faster algorithms than existing approaches.

Now, to identify infeasible code in the original program P, we have to identify the subset of statements in $P^\#$ which do not occur on feasible paths. For that, in the following section, we show an algorithm to detect infeasible code using our new encoding by gradually excluding feasible paths from $P^\#$ until VC becomes unsatisfiable.

5   Covering Algorithm

With the encoding from the previous section, each time we obtain a valuation $s \models VC$ from the theorem prover of our choice, we can identify a feasible path in $P^{\#}$ by checking the valuation of each reachability variable b_i. Now, to find all statements that occur on feasible paths, we want to make sure that the next time we ask our prover for a satisfying assignment of VC it provides us with a s' that executes a different path. In the following, we propose an algorithm to achieve this by using *enabling clauses*, which force the prover to set at least one b_i to true, that has not been true before.

Enabling Clauses. Each time we query our prover, we want to further restrict our formula to those valuations that represent feasible paths of previously uncovered blocks. Therefore, we propose algorithm *EnblClause* in Algorithm 1 that uses *enabling clauses*. An enabling clause is the disjunction of all block variables that have not been assigned to true by previous satisfying valuation of the reachability verification condition.

Algorithm 1. *EnblClause*

Input: VC: A reachability verification condition,
　　　　$\mathcal{B} = \{b_0, \ldots, b_n\}$: The set of block variables
Output: $\mathcal{I}$: The set of block variables that do not have feasible executions.

```
 1 begin
 2 │   I ← B
 3 │   s ← checksat(VC)
 4 │   while s ≠ {} do
 5 │   │   φ ← false
 6 │   │   foreach bᵢ in I do
 7 │   │   │   if s(bᵢ) = true then
 8 │   │   │   │   I ← I \ {bᵢ}
 9 │   │   │   else
10 │   │   │   │   φ ← φ ∨ bᵢ
11 │   │   │   endif
12 │   │   endfch
13 │   │   s ← checksat(VC ∧ φ)
14 │   endw
15 │   return I
16 end
```

The algorithm takes as input a reachability verification condition VC, and the set of all block variables $\mathcal{B}$ used in this formula, and returns the set of block variables which cannot occur on any feasible complete path. The algorithm uses the prover checksat (lines 3,13) which takes a formula ϕ as input and returns a valuation $s \models \phi$ if ϕ is satisfiable or the empty set, otherwise. First, our algorithm sets the set of infeasible block variables $\mathcal{I}$ to the set of all block variables $\mathcal{B}$ (line 2). Then, it checks if there exists any satisfying valuation s for VC (line 3). If so, the algorithm removes all b_i from $\mathcal{I}$ which evaluate to true in s, as those occur on a feasible path (line 8). The block variables which do not evaluate to true in s are added to the enabling clause (line 10) to ensure that checksat will evaluate at least one of them to true in the next iteration. The algorithm terminates if all blocks have been visited once (and therefore, the enabling clause ϕ becomes $false$), or if there is no feasible execution passing the remaining blocks.

Theorem 2 (Correctness of $EnblClause$**).** *Given a (abstract) program P with reachability verification condition VC. Let $\mathcal{B}$ be the set of block variables used in VC. Algorithm EnblClause, started with the arguments VC and $\mathcal{B}$, terminates and returns a set of block variables $\mathcal{I}$ for which no feasible execution exists.*

Proof. In every iteration of the loop at least one variable of the set $\mathcal{I}$ will be removed. This is because the formula ϕ will only allow valuations such that for at least one $b_i \in \mathcal{I}$ the valuation $s(b_i)$ is true. Since $\mathcal{I}$ contains only finitely many variables the algorithm must terminate. If π is a feasible path visiting the block associated with the variable b_i, then there is a valuation s that satisfies VC with $s(b_i) = true$. Such a valuation must eventually be found, since $VC \wedge \phi$ is only unsatisfiable if $b_i \notin \mathcal{I}$.

Hence, $EnblClause$ is a sound and complete way to detect infeasible code for loop-free programs given a complete implementation of the decision procedure checksat. In practice, of course, infeasible code detection is not complete as the computation of a loop-free program requires abstraction and decision procedures are usually not complete.

What we have presented so far is an encoding of loop-free programs into formulas that allows us to reconstruct feasible executions of this (abstract) program from a satisfying valuation of the formula. Based on this, we have presented an algorithm to detect all blocks in a program that do not have feasible executions (in the original program). The question now is, if this approach allows the theorem prover to discover infeasible code more efficiently than existing approaches.

Optimization. To check if there is a feasible execution for each block, it is not necessary to include all block variables in the enabling clause. We follow the idea of [4] and compute an *effectual set* of blocks which is sufficient to find at least one feasible execution for each basic block. For that we proceed as follows: we define a relation $\preceq$ on basic blocks, such that $b_i \preceq b_j$ if every complete path that contains b_i also contains b_j. The relation $\preceq$ can be easily constructed as a combination of dominator and post-dominator relation. As $\preceq$ is reflexive and transitive, we can define an equivalence relation $\simeq$ as $\simeq = \preceq \cap \preceq^{-1}$. We denote by $[B]$ the equivalence class of blocks B under $\simeq$. The elements of $[B]$ blocks that only appear together on a path. The partial order $\preceq$ is extended from blocks to equivalence classes of blocks as expected: $[B] \preceq [B']$ if and only if $B \preceq B'$.

Under $\preceq$, an equivalence class $[B]$ which is minimal contains blocks that only occur on paths containing (all) elements of $[B]$. Hence, finding a feasible execution for each block is equivalent to finding one execution for one element of each minimal equivalence class (see [4] for a proof). In the following we call a set *effectual* if it contains exactly one element of each minimal equivalence class.

Hence, applying *EnblClause* to an effectual set of blocks gives us the set of all infeasible blocks in the effectual set. From there, we can look up the set of all infeasible blocks from the Hasse diagram that is given by $\preceq$ (e.g., [14]).

6   Experiments

The question we are trying to answer is *does the new encoding allow us to detect infeasible code faster than existing approaches?* For that, we compare four different approaches: our approach from *EnblClause* only applied to an effectual set of block variables (**ExtWlp**); *EnblClause* applied to all block variables (**EnablingClause**), an approach similar to ours that uses *blocking clauses* instead of enabling clauses presented in [5] (**BlockingClause**); and the algorithm from [4] that injects integer variables into the program and uses assertions of linear inequalities to implement a query optimal algorithm (**OptimalCover**).

Experimental Setup. We evaluate our approach on six open-source applications under test (AUTs): Open eCard, a software to support the German eID, the CASE tool ArgoUML, the mind-mapping tool FreeMind, the time-keeping software Rachota, the word processor TerpWord, and the software that we used to analyze these programs, Joogie [2]. Table 1 gives an overview of our AUTs, including lines of code, number of analyzed procedures, and detected infeasible statements.

Table 1. Results of applying Joogie to the test applications

Program	LOC	# checked methods	# found
Open eCard	456,220	15,654	26
ArgoUML	156,294	9,981	28
FreeMind	53,737	5,613	10
Joogie	11,401	973	0
Rachota	11,037	1,279	1
TerpWord	6,842	360	3

For comparison, we have implemented all four algorithms in Joogie[2]. Joogie provides the necessary abstraction of Java programs into loop-free programs that can be translated into logic formulas. Loops are abstracted by redirecting the back-edge of a loop to the loop exit and adding non-deterministic assignments to all variables modified inside the loop to the loop entry and exit.

Furthermore, Joogie injects run-time assertions for `null` de-reference, array-bound violations, and division by zero. Joogie applies the infeasible code detection to each procedure in isolation. I.e., it does not perform inter-procedural analysis. Calls to procedures are replaced by non-deterministic assignments to all variables that could be modified by the called function.

---

[2] http://www.joogie.org/

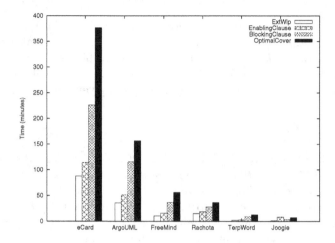

Fig. 4. Performance of the proposed encoding of the weakest liberal precondition compared to other approaches that detect infeasible code

We use the same abstraction for each experiment, and, since all four algorithms are complete for abstract programs, the detection rate is the same in each case. Thus, we only have to compare the computation time.

All experiments are run on a workstation with 3 GHz CPU, 8 GB RAM, and 640 GB HDD. To avoid bias by the employed theorem prover, we run our experiments with Princess [20] (which is the standard prover in Joogie), and Z3 [6]. Each procedure is analyzed for at most 30 seconds. If the algorithm is not able to analyze the whole procedure within this time, we kill the prover and start over with the next procedure. Only the time spent inside the prover is stopped to eliminate noise that may be introduced by our implementation.

Results. Figure 4 shows the computation time for each algorithm on our AUTs using the theorem prover Princess. The results show that our proposed encoding together with the algorithm from the previous section yields a significant performance improvement over existing techniques. Furthermore, it shows that applying *EnblClause* only to an effectual subset of block variables results in a relatively small but visible performance improvement.

For all experiments, *EnblClause* applied on an effectual set computed a total 137, 997 queries in 152.33 minutes. *EnblClause* applied on all block variables used 131, 632 queries and 206.20 minutes, with blocking clauses 250, 566 queries and 424.11 minutes, and the algorithm from [4] 132, 976 queries and 646.21 minutes. Here, the time refers to the computation time inside the Princess theorem prover, not counting the overhead in Joogie. To our surprise, applying *EnblClause* only to an effectual set rather than to all block variables results in an increase of theorem prover queries, but reduces the computation time. We assume that, when working on all block variables, it is easier for the theorem prover to cover multiple blocks in one query, but this can create enabling clauses which are very hard to solve.

Table 2. Average time (in milliseconds) per method for each program using Z3 and Princess

Program	ExtWlp		EnablingClause		BlockingClause		OptimalCover	
	Z3	Princess	Z3	Princess	Z3	Princess	Z3	Princess
Open eCard	**62**	**335**	**81**	**437**	247	866	376	1444
ArgoUML	**68**	**215**	**92**	**308**	371	697	382	941
FreeMind	**33**	**112**	**45**	**169**	216	390	244	601
Joogie	**30**	**154**	**49**	**142**	223	482	367	990
Rachota	**273**	**702**	**354**	**875**	773	1306	817	1710
TerpWord	**137**	**370**	**153**	**435**	896	1559	966	2115

Table 2 compares the average computation time per AUT for each query for the theorem prover Princess and Z3. We can see that the performance improvements we achieve with the new encoding are visible regardless of the prover.

Figure 5 shows how many procedures of a particular size can be analyzed within a certain time frame using Princess or Z3 with *EnblClause*. Here, a darker color indicates that more procedures, and a lighter color means less. We can see that, for both provers, the majority of analyzed procedures up to 350 Jimple units (which is roughly the number of instructions) can be handled within 5 seconds or less. Z3 always computes an answer for procedures with less than 250 units while princess occasionally timeouts.

In conclusion, our experiments show that the new encoding results in a significant speedup of infeasible code detection compared to existing approaches. Infeasible code detection can be applied to real programs and even with a time limit of a few seconds, a large portion of the procedures in our AUTs can be analyzed.

Threats to Validity. There are several threats to validity to be considered. First, the AUTs are selected more or less randomly and may be biased towards GUI-applications. Different results may occur for other classes of applications, however, due to the size of the applications, we expect this not to happen. Another threat to validity is that we selected stable versions of the source code from the public repositories. Infeasible code detection should target code in production, rather than well tested code. However, this requires a controlled setting which is not available to us at the moment.

For implementation reasons, we have to measure the computation time of Princess and Z3 at slightly different positions in the code. That is, the experiments cannot be used to compare the provers with each other. They only show that our approach yields performance improvements in both cases.

Some threat to validity arises from our restriction to Java programs. E.g., we cannot compare approaches that focus on C (e.g., [8,21]), which may have a different encoding of programs into logic that affects the performance of our algorithm. However, this is unlikely to happen, as our algorithm only uses logic variables that are handled by the DPLL solver, whereas the memory model usually affects the performance of the theory solver.

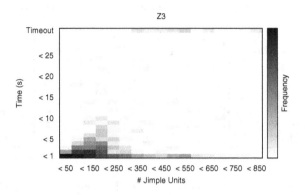

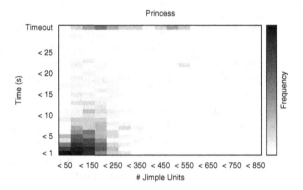

Fig. 5. Detailed comparison of the performance of configuration ExtWlp on all AUTs. The horizontal axis depicts the number Jimple Units (which is roughly LOC), the vertical axis depicts the analysis time of ExtWlp. The color of the individual boxes indicate the number of analyzed procedures.

7   Conclusion

We have presented a new encoding of weakest-liberal preconditions for infeasible code detection. This encoding allows us to reconstruct a feasible control-flow path (in the abstract program) from a counterexample of an unsatisfiability proof. With the ability to identify feasible control-flow paths, we were able to develop a simple algorithm to detect infeasible code. The algorithm is sound because the absence of feasible executions in the abstract program automatically implies the absence of feasible executions in the original program.

We have shown that our simple algorithm outperforms existing implementations for infeasible code detection. We assume that this is because we put less restriction on the theorem prover when searching for a feasible path, and, that our helper variables are pure logic variables that do not require handling by background theories. We believe that this encoding will allow us to develop specialized background theories for our theorem prover that consider the graph structure of the abstract program to avoid exploring irrelevant or redundant control-flow paths and thus can detect infeasible code even faster.

Our experiments indicate that our tool to detect infeasible code can be applied to real-world programs, and more important, that infeasible code exists even in well tested and stable programs. With that in mind, we are looking into other application domains for infeasible code detection such as compiler optimization, or worst-case execution time analysis.

Being able to obtain feasible executions (and control-flow paths) from the prover could also help to compute under-approximated summaries (e.g., [1]) that can be used for bounded, and inter-procedural infeasible code detection.

To summarize, we have presented a new encoding of wlp, and an algorithm for infeasible code detection based on this. We were able to show on real-world examples that this encoding detects infeasible code significantly faster than existing approaches and that, based on this encoding, several improvements to infeasible code detection are possible. Finally, we found a lot of infeasible code which we will report to the corresponding developers.

Acknowledgments. Our thanks go Philipp Rümmer for his suggestions on efficient encoding of programs, and the integration with Princess. Further, we would like to thank Jürgen Christ and Jochen Hoenicke for their valuable suggestions on the construction of prover friendly formulas, and their detailed comments on large parts of this paper. This work is in part supported by the grant PEARL (041/2007/A3) and COLAB of the Macao Science and Technology Development Fund.

References

1. Albarghouthi, A., Gurfinkel, A., Chechik, M.: Whale: An Interpolation-Based Algorithm for Inter-procedural Verification. In: Kuncak, V., Rybalchenko, A. (eds.) VMCAI 2012. LNCS, vol. 7148, pp. 39–55. Springer, Heidelberg (2012)
2. Arlt, S., Schäf, M.: Joogie: Infeasible Code Detection for Java. In: Madhusudan, P., Seshia, S.A. (eds.) CAV 2012. LNCS, vol. 7358, pp. 767–773. Springer, Heidelberg (2012)
3. Barnett, M., Leino, K.R.M.: Weakest-precondition of unstructured programs. SIGSOFT Softw. Eng. Notes 31, 82–87 (2005)
4. Bertolini, C., Schäf, M., Schweitzer, P.: Infeasible Code Detection. In: Joshi, R., Müller, P., Podelski, A. (eds.) VSTTE 2012. LNCS, vol. 7152, pp. 310–325. Springer, Heidelberg (2012)
5. Christ, J., Hoenicke, J., Schäf, M.: Towards Bounded Infeasible Code Detection. CoRR, abs/1205.6527 (2012)
6. de Moura, L., Bjørner, N.: Z3: An Efficient SMT Solver. In: Ramakrishnan, C.R., Rehof, J. (eds.) TACAS 2008. LNCS, vol. 4963, pp. 337–340. Springer, Heidelberg (2008)

7. Dijkstra, E.W.: A discipline of programming / Edsger W. Dijkstra. Prentice-Hall, Englewood Cliffs (1976)
8. Dillig, I., Dillig, T., Aiken, A.: Static error detection using semantic inconsistency inference. In: PLDI, pp. 435–445 (2007)
9. Donaldson, A.F., Haller, L., Kroening, D., Rümmer, P.: Software verification using k-induction. In: Yahav, E. (ed.) Static Analysis. LNCS, vol. 6887, pp. 351–368. Springer, Heidelberg (2011)
10. Engler, D., Chen, D.Y., Hallem, S., Chou, A., Chelf, B.: Bugs as deviant behavior: a general approach to inferring errors in systems code. In: SOSP, pp. 57–72 (2001)
11. Flanagan, C., Leino, K.R.M., Lillibridge, M., Nelson, G., Saxe, J.B., Stata, R.: Extended static checking for Java. SIGPLAN Not., 234–245 (2002)
12. Grigore, R., Charles, J., Fairmichael, F., Kiniry, J.: Strongest postcondition of unstructured programs. In: FTfJP, pp. 6:1–6:7 (2009)
13. Hoenicke, J., Leino, K.R.M., Podelski, A., Schäf, M., Wies, T.: It's Doomed; We Can Prove It. In: Cavalcanti, A., Dams, D.R. (eds.) FM 2009. LNCS, vol. 5850, pp. 338–353. Springer, Heidelberg (2009)
14. Hoenicke, J., Leino, K.R.M., Podelski, A., Schäf, M., Wies, T.: Doomed Program Points. Formal Methods in System Design (2010)
15. Hovemeyer, D., Pugh, W.: Finding bugs is easy. In: OOPSLA, pp. 132–136 (2004)
16. Janota, M., Grigore, R., Moskal, M.: Reachability analysis for annotated code. In: SAVCBS, pp. 23–30 (2007)
17. Leino, K.R.M.: Efficient weakest preconditions. Inf. Process. Lett., 281–288 (2005)
18. Leino, K.R.M., Millstein, T., Saxe, J.B.: Generating error traces from verification-condition counterexamples. Sci. Comput. Program, 209–226 (2005)
19. Leino, K.R.M., Rümmer, P.: A Polymorphic Intermediate Verification Language: Design and Logical Encoding. In: Esparza, J., Majumdar, R. (eds.) TACAS 2010. LNCS, vol. 6015, pp. 312–327. Springer, Heidelberg (2010)
20. Rümmer, P.: A Constraint Sequent Calculus for First-Order Logic with Linear Integer Arithmetic. In: Cervesato, I., Veith, H., Voronkov, A. (eds.) LPAR 2008. LNCS, vol. 5330, pp. 274–289. Springer, Heidelberg (2008)
21. Tomb, A., Flanagan, C.: Detecting inconsistencies via universal reachability analysis. In: ISSTA, pp. 287–297 (2012)

The Domain of Parametric Hypercubes
for Static Analysis of Computer Games Software

Giulia Costantini[1], Pietro Ferrara[2],
Giuseppe Maggiore[3], and Agostino Cortesi[1]

[1] Ca' Foscari University, Venice, Italy
{costantini,cortesi}@dsi.unive.it
[2] ETH Zurich, Switzerland
pietro.ferrara@inf.ethz.ch
[3] IGAD, NHTV University of Breda, The Netherlands
maggiore.g@nhtv.nl

Abstract. Computer Games Software deeply relies on physics simulations, which are particularly demanding to analyze because they manipulate a large amount of interleaving floating point variables. Therefore,
this application domain is an interesting workbench to stress the trade-off
between accuracy and efficiency of abstract domains for static analysis.

In this paper, we introduce Parametric Hypercubes, a novel disjunctive non-relational abstract domain. Its main features are: (i) it combines
the low computational cost of operations on (selected) multidimensional
intervals with the accuracy provided by lifting to a power-set disjunctive
domain, (ii) the compact representation of its elements allows to limit
the space complexity of the analysis, and (iii) the parametric nature of
the domain provides a way to tune the accuracy/efficiency of the analysis
by just setting the widths of the hypercubes sides.

The first experimental results on a representative Computer Games
case study outline both the efficiency and the precision of the proposal.

1   Introduction

Computer Games Software is a fast growing industry, with more than 200 million
units sold every year, and annual revenue of more than 10 billion dollars. According to the Entertainment Software Association (ESA), more than 25% of the
software played concerns sport, action, and strategy games, where physics simulations are the core of the product, and compile-time verification of behavioural
properties is particularly challenging for developers.

The difficulty arises because, usually, these programs feature (i) a `while` loop
which goes on endlessly, (ii) a complex state made up by multiple real-valued
variables, and (iii) strong dependencies among variables. Most of the times,
a simulation consists in the initialization of the state (i.e., the variables which
compose the simulated world) followed by an infinite `while` loop which computes
the numerical integration over time (i.e., the inductive step of the simulation).
Such a loop is executed until the game is stopped. In addition, the variables of

L. Groves and J. Sun (Eds.): ICFEM 2013, LNCS 8144, pp. 447–463, 2013.
© Springer-Verlag Berlin Heidelberg 2013

a physics simulation are real-valued, because they represent continuous values that map directly to physical aspects of the real world, like positions, velocities (speed plus direction), and accelerations. Finally, the variables of a simulation are strongly inter-related, because the simulation often makes decisions based on the values of particular variables. For example, the velocity of an object changes abruptly when there is a collision, which depends on the object position. Similarly, the position changes accordingly to the velocity, which in turn depends on the acceleration which may derive from the position (for a gravitational field) or from other parameters.

Interesting properties on physical programs are, for example, the insurance that a rocket reaches a stable orbit, or that a bouncing ball arrives at a certain destination. To prove such properties statically, we need to precisely track relationships between variables. However, traditional approaches to static analysis are not best suited to deal with these kind of properties. On the one hand, non-relational domains are usually too approximate. On the other hand, the computational cost of sophisticated relational domains like Polyhedra [11] or Parallelotopes [3] is too high, and their practical use becomes unfeasible.

In this paper, we introduce Parametric Hypercubes, a novel disjunctive non-relational abstract domain. Its main features are: (i) it combines the low computational cost of operations on (selected) multidimensional intervals with the accuracy provided by lifting to a power-set domain, (ii) the compact representation of its elements allows to limit the space complexity of the analysis, and (iii) the parametric nature of the domain provides a way to tune the trade-off between accuracy and efficiency of the analysis by just setting the widths of the hypercubes sides. The domain can be seen as the combination of a suite of well-known techniques for numerical abstract domain design, like disjunctive powerset, and conditional partitioning. The most interesting points of our work are: (i) the approach: the design of the domain has as starting point the features of the application domains, (ii) the self-adaptive parameterization: a recursive algorithm is applied to refine the initial set of parameters in order to improve the accuracy of the analysis without sacrificing the performance, and (iii) the novel notion of "offset" that allows to narrow the lack of precision due to the fixed width of intervals. The analysis has been implemented, and it shows promising results in terms both of efficiency and precision when applied to a representative case study of Computer Games Software.

The rest of the paper is structured as follows. Section 2 presents the language syntax, and Section 3 introduces the case study which we use to experiment with our approach. Sections 4 and 5 formally define the abstract domain and semantics, respectively. Section 6 contains the experimental results on the case study of Section 3. Section 7 presents the related work and Section 8 concludes.

2   Language Syntax

Let $\mathcal{V}$ be a finite set of variables, and $\mathcal{I}$ the set of all real-valued intervals. Figure 1 defines the language. We focus on programs dealing with mathematical computations over real-valued variables. Therefore, we consider expressions built

$$V \in \mathcal{V}, I \in \mathcal{I}, c \in \mathbb{R}$$
$$E := c|rand(I)|V|E < aop > E \text{ where } < aop > \in \{+, -, \times, \div\}$$
$$B := E < bop > E|B \text{ and } B|not \ B|B \text{ or } B \text{ where } < bop > \in \{\geq, >, \leq, <, \neq\}$$
$$P := V = E|\texttt{if}(B) \text{ then } P \text{ else } P|\texttt{while}(B) \ P|P; P$$

Fig. 1. Syntax

through the most common mathematical operators (sum, subtraction, multiplication, and division). An arithmetic expression can be a constant value ($c \in \mathbb{R}$), a non-deterministic value in an interval ($rand(I)$ where $I \in \mathcal{I}$), or a variable ($V \in \mathcal{V}$). We also consider boolean conditions built through the comparison of two arithmetic expressions. Boolean conditions can be combined as usual with logical operators (and, or, not). As for statements, we support the assignment of an expression to a variable, $if - then - else$, while loops, and concatenation. Even though this syntax is simple and limited, many physical simulations can be built through it [6], since their complexity lies mostly in their logic and not in the used constructs.

3   The Case Study of Bouncing Balls

Consider the program in Figure 2. It generates a bouncing ball that starts at the left side of the screen (even though the exact initial position is not fixed), and it has a random initial velocity. The horizontal direction of the ball is always towards the right of the screen, since $vx \geq 0$. Whenever the ball reaches the bottom of the screen, it bounces (i.e., its vertical velocity is inverted). When the ball reaches the right border of the screen, it disappears. We want to verify that T seconds after the generation of the ball, such ball has already exited from the screen (we call this *Property 1*).

The structure of this program respects the generic structure of a physics simulation, as explained in Section 1. The meanings of the variables are as follows. (px, py) represents the current position of the ball in the screen, and its initial values are generated randomly. (vx, vy) represents the current velocity of the

```
px = rand([0.0,  10.0]),  py = rand([0.0,  50.0])
vx = rand([0.0,  60.0]),  vy = rand([−30.0, −25.0])
dt = 0.05, g = −9.8, k = 0.8

while (true) do
    if ( py >= 0.0 ) then
        (px, py) = (px + vx ∗ dt, py + vy ∗ dt)
        (vx, vy) = (vx, vy + g ∗ dt)
    else
        (px, py) = (px + vx ∗ dt, 0.0)
        (vx, vy) = (vx, −vy) ∗ k
```

Fig. 2. Case study: bouncing-ball code

```
balls  = Set.empty
dt = 0.05,  creationInterval  = 3.0, timeFromLastCreation = 0.0
while (true) do
    foreach  ball  in  balls
        updateBall( ball )
    if (timeFromLastCreation >= creationInterval)
        generateNewBall()
        timeFromLastCreation = 0.0
    else
        timeFromLastCreation += dt
```

Fig. 3. Bouncing ball generation

ball, and its initial values are generated randomly as well. dt represents the time interval between iterations of the loop. This value is constant and known at compile time (dt = $1/20 = 0.05$ considering a simulation running at 20 frames per second). g represents the force of gravity (-9.8). k represents how much the impact with the ground decreases the velocity of the ball.

The while loop updates the ball position and velocity. To simulate the bouncing, we update the horizontal position according to the rule of uniform linear motion, while we force the vertical position to zero when the ball touches the ground and we invert the vertical velocity. In addition, we decrease both the horizontal and vertical velocity through the constant factor k, to consider the force which is lost in the impact with the ground.

Verifying Property 1 on this program has a significant practical interest, since it is a basic physics simulation which can be used in many contexts [12]. For instance, consider the program in Figure 3, where updateBall(b) moves the ball b (through the body of the while loop of Figure 2) and generateNewBall() creates a new ball (with the values of the initialization of Figure 2). It discreetly generates bouncing balls on the screen. The interval between the creation of two balls (creationInterval) is constant and known at compile time.

Proving *Property 1* on the program in Figure 2 means that a single ball will have exited the screen after T seconds. In addition, in the program of Figure 3, we generate one ball each creationInterval seconds. This means that, having verified *Property 1*, we can guarantee that *a maximum of* $\lceil \frac{T}{\texttt{creationInterval}} \rceil$ *balls will be on the screen at the same time*. Such information may be useful for performance reasons (crucial in a game), since each ball requires computations for its rendering and updating.

Non-disjunctive or non-relational static analyses are not properly suited to verify *Property 1*. Consider for example the Interval domain where every variable of the program is associated to a single interval. After a few iterations, when the vertical position possibly goes to zero, the analysis is not able to distinguish which branch of the $if - then - else$ to take anymore. In this case, the lub operator makes the vertical velocity interval quite wide, since it will contain both positive and negative values. After that, the precision gets completely lost, since the velocity variable affects the position and vice-versa. On the other hand, the accuracy that would be ensured by using existing disjunctive domains has a computational cost that makes this approach unfeasible for practical use.

4   The Parametric Hypercubes Domain

Intuitively, an abstract state of the Parametric Hypercubes domain ($\mathcal{H}$) tracks disjunctive information relying on floating-point intervals of fixed width. A state of $\mathcal{H}$ is made by a set of hypercubes of dimension |Vars|. Each hypercube has |Vars| sides, one for each variable, and each side contains an abstract non-relational value for the corresponding variable. Each hypercube represents a set of admissible combinations of values for all variables.

The name Hypercubes comes from the geometric interpretation of the elements of $\mathcal{H}$. The concrete state of a program with variables in Vars is an environment in Vars $\rightarrow \mathbb{R}$. This can be isomorphically represented by a tuple of values where each item of the tuple represents a program variable. Seen in this way, the concrete state corresponds, geometrically, to *a point* in the |Vars|-dimensional space. The hypercubes of our domain $\mathcal{H}$ are *volumes* in the same |Vars|-dimensional space.

4.1   Lattice Structure

An abstract state of $\mathcal{H}$ tracks a *set* of hypercubes, and each hypercube is represented by a tuple of abstract values. The dimension of these tuples is equal to the number of program variables. We abstract floating-point variables through intervals of real values. A set of hypercubes allows us to track disjunctive information, and this is useful when the values of a variable are clustered in different ranges. The performance of this domain, though, becomes a crucial point, because the number of possible hypercubes in the space is potentially exponential with respect to the number of partitions along each spatial axis.

First of all, the complexity is lightened by the use of a *fixed* width for each variable, by partitioning the possible intervals, and by the efficiency of set operators on tuples. Then, another performance booster is the use of a smart representation for intervals: in order to store the specific interval range we just use a single integer representing it. This is possible because each variable x_i is associated to an interval width (specific only for that variable), which we call w_i and which is a parameter of the analysis. Each width w_i represents the width of all the possible abstract intervals associated to x_i. More precisely, given a width w_i and an integer index m, the interval uniquely associated to the variable x_i is $[m \times w_i..(m + 1) \times w_i]$. Notice that the smaller the width associated to a variable, the more granular and precise the analysis on that variable (and the heavier computationally the analysis). In Section 5 we will show how to compute and adjust automatically the widths.

Example: Consider the case study of Section 3 and in particular the two variables px and py. Suppose that the widths associated to such variables are $w_1 = 10.0, w_2 = 25.0$. The hypercubes in this case are 2D-rectangles that can be represented on the Cartesian plane. Each side of a hypercube is identified by an integer index, and a 2D hypercube is then uniquely identified by a pair of integers. For instance, the hypercube $h_1 = (0, 1)$ represents px $\in [0.0..10.0]$

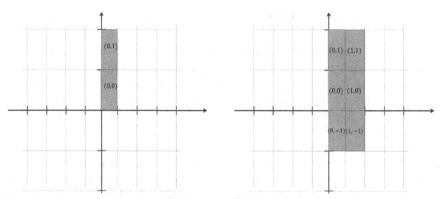

(a) The abstract state after the initialization of the variables px, py, when their
widths are, respectively, 10.0 and 25.0

(b) The abstract state of px, py after the
first iteration of the loop (widths are, respectively, 10.0 and 25.0)

Fig. 4. Cartesian plans

and py $\in$ [25.0..50.0], while the hypercube $h_2 = (0,0)$ associates px to [0.0..10.0]
and py to [0.0..25.0]. Figure 4a depicts the two hypercubes associated to the
initialization of the case study (i.e., h_1 and h_2). Instead, Figure 4b depicts the
six hypercubes obtained after executing the first iteration of the while loop.

We now formalize our abstract domain. Each abstract state is a set of hy-
percubes, where each hypercube is composed by |Vars| integer numbers. The
abstract domain is then defined by $\mathcal{H} = \wp(\mathbb{Z}^n)$ where $n = $ |Vars|. The definition
of lattice operators relies on set operators. Formally, $\langle \wp(\mathbb{Z}^n), \subseteq, \cup, \cap, \emptyset, \mathbb{Z}^n \rangle$.

4.2   Concretization Function

We denote by $\mathcal{A}$ the non-relational abstract domain on which our analysis is
parameterized, and by n the number of variables of the program. Let $\sigma \in \mathbb{R}^n$ be
a tuple and $\sigma_i \in \mathbb{R}$ be the i-th element of such tuple. Also, let $\gamma_{\mathcal{A}} : \mathcal{A} \to \wp(\mathbb{R})$
be the concretization function of abstract values of the non-relational abstract
domain $\mathcal{A}$, and $getAbsValue_v : \mathbb{N} \to \mathcal{A}$ be the function that, given an integer
index, returns the abstract value (in the domain $\mathcal{A}$) which corresponds to that
index inside the tuple v. Then, the function $\gamma_{\text{Val}} : \wp(\mathcal{A}^n) \to \wp(\mathbb{R}^n)$ concretizes
a set of hypercubes to a set of vectors of n floating point values. Formally,
$\gamma_{\text{Val}}(V) = \{\sigma : \exists v \in V : \forall i \in [1..n] : \sigma_i \in \gamma_{\mathcal{A}}(getAbsValue_v(i))\}$ where $V \in \wp(\mathcal{A}^n)$
is a set of hypercubes. Finally, based on γ_{Val}, we can define the function $\gamma_{\mathcal{H}}$, which
maps a subset V of $\wp(\mathcal{A}^n)$ into an environment. The function $\gamma_{\mathcal{H}} : \wp(\mathcal{A}^n) \to$
$\wp(\text{Vars} \to \mathbb{R})$ concretizes the hypercubes domain. Formally, $\gamma_{\mathcal{H}}(V) = \{[\mathbf{x} \mapsto$
$\sigma_{varIndex(\mathbf{x})} : \mathbf{x} \in \text{Vars}] : \sigma \in \gamma_{\text{Val}}(V)\}$. $\gamma_{\mathcal{H}}$ maps the vectors returned by γ_{Val} to
concrete environments relying on $varIndex : \text{Vars} \to \mathbb{N}$, that, given a variable,
returns its index in the tuples which compose the elements of $\mathcal{H}$.

4.3   Convergence of the Analysis

The number of hypercubes in an abstract state may increase indefinitely. In order to make the analysis convergent, we fix for each variable of the program a maximum integer index n_i such that n_i represents the interval $[n_i \times w_i.. + \infty]$. The same happens symmetrically for negative values. In this way, the set of indices of a given variable is finite, the resulting domain has finite height, and the analysis is convergent.

This approach may seem too rough since we establish the bounds of intervals before running the analysis. However, when analysing physics simulations the initialization of variables and the verified property may give hints on convenient bounds for the intervals. For instance, in the case study of Section 3 we want to check if a ball stays in the screen, that is, if px is greater than zero and less than a given value w representing the width of the screen. Since we are only interested in proving that, once a ball has exited the screen, it does not come back, we can abstract together all the values that are greater than w.

4.4   Offsets

A loss of precision may occur due to the fact that hypercubes proliferate too much, even using small widths. Consider, for example, the statement x = x + 0.01 (which is repeated at each iteration of the while loop) with 1.0 as the width associated to x. If [0.0..1.0] was the initial interval associated to x, the sequence of abstract states would be: $\{[0.0..1.0]\}$, $\{[0.0..1.0], [1.0..2.0]\}$, $\{[0.0..1.0], [1.0..2.0], [2.0..3.0]\}$ and so on. At each iteration we would add one interval.

In order to overcome these situations, we further improve the definition of our domain: in each hypercube, each variable v_i (associated to width w_i) is related to (other than an integer index i representing the fixed-width interval $[i \times w_i..(i+1) \times w_i]$) a specific offset (o_m, o_M) *inside* such interval. In this way, we use a sub-interval (of arbitrary width) inside the fixed-interval width, thereby restricting the possible values that the variable can assume. Both o_m and o_M must be smaller than w_i, greater than or equal to 0 and $o_m \leq o_M$. Then, if i and (o_m, o_M) are associated to v_i, this means that the possible values of v_i belong to the interval $[(i \times w_i) + o_m..(i \times w_i) + o_M]$.

An element of our abstract domain is then stored as a map from hypercubes to tuples of offsets. In this way, we keep the original definition of a hypercube adding a tuple of offsets (one for each variable) to each hypercube. Now an abstract state is defined by $M : \mathbb{Z}^{|Vars|} \rightarrow (\mathbb{R} \times \mathbb{R})^{|Vars|}$. The least upper bound $\sqcup$ is then defined by

$$\forall h \in dom(M) : M(h) = \begin{cases} M_1(h) & \text{if } h \in dom(M_1) \wedge h \notin dom(M_2) \\ M_2(h) & \text{if } h \in dom(M_2) \wedge h \notin dom(M_1) \\ merge(M_1(h), M_2(h)) & \text{otherwise} \end{cases}$$

where $dom(M) = dom(M_1) \cup dom(M_2)$, and $merge(o_1, o_2)$ creates a new tuple of offsets by merging the two tuples of offsets in input: for each pair of corresponding offsets (for example (m_1, M_1) and (m_2, M_2)), the new offset is the widest combination possible (i.e., $(\min(m_1, m_2)$ and $\max(M_1, M_2)))$. Note that this definition corresponds to the pointwise application of the least upper bound operator over intervals. The widening operator is extended in the same way: it applies the standard widening operators over intervals pointwisely to the elements of the vector representing the offsets.

5   Abstract Semantics

For the most part, the abstract semantics applies existing semantic operators of boxed Intervals [10]. In this section, we sketch how these operators are used to define the semantics on $\mathcal{H}$.

First of all, $\mathbb{I}$ defines the semantics of arithmetic expressions on a single hypercube by applying the well-known arithmetic operators on intervals.

We use the semantics $\mathbb{I}$ to define the abstract semantics $\mathbb{B}$ of Boolean comparisons. Given a hypercube and a Boolean comparison $E_1 < bop > E_2$ where $< bop > \in \{\geq, >, \leq, <, \neq\}$, $\mathbb{B}$ returns an *abstract value of the boolean domain* (namely, *true*, *false*, or $\top$) comparing the intervals obtained from E_1 and E_2 through $\mathbb{I}$. Therefore, given a Boolean condition and a set of hypercubes, we partition this set into the hypercubes for which (i) the condition surely holds, (ii) the condition surely does not hold, and (iii) the condition may or may not hold. In this way, we can discard all the hypercubes for which a given Boolean condition surely holds or does not hold. The semantics of the logical operators *not*, *and*, *or* is defined in the standard way.

$\mathbb{I}$ is used to define the semantics $\mathbb{S}$ of variable assignment as well. The standard semantics of $\mathtt{x} = \mathtt{exp}$ is to (i) obtain the interval representing the right part $(\mathbb{I}[\![\mathtt{x} = \mathtt{exp}, \sigma]\!] = [m..M])$, and (ii) assign it in the current state. This approach does not necessarily produce a single hypercube, since the interval to assign could have a greater width than the fixed width of the assigned variable (for example, the interval $[0..6]$ when $w = 5$). It could also happen that the resulting interval width is smaller than the fixed width, but the interval spans over more than one hypercube side, due to the fixed space partitioning (for example, the interval $[3..6]$ when $w = 5$, because the space is partitioned in $[0..5], [5..10]$, etc.). In these cases, we build up several hypercubes that cover the interval $[m..M]$. This can be formalized by $assign(h, V_i, [a..b]) = \{h[i \mapsto m] : [m \times w_i..(m+1) \times w_i] \cap [a..b] \neq \emptyset\}$, where h is a hypercube, V_i is the assigned variable, and $[a..b]$ is the interval we are assigning (which depends on the hypercube h, since we use its variables values to compute the result of the expression). We repeat this process for each hypercube h in the abstract state by using it as input for the computation of $assign$. In this way, we are able to over-approximate the assignment while also keeping the fixed widths of the intervals, which are very important for performance issues.

Offsets. Offsets allow us to recover some precision when computing the abstract semantics of assignment. In particular, as the expression semantics $\mathbb{I}$ returns intervals of arbitrary widths, we can use such exact results to update the offsets of the abstract state. Formally, the semantics of the assignment is defined as follows:

$$assign(h, V_i, [a..b]) = \{h[i \mapsto (m, o_m, o_M)] : [m \times w_i..(m + 1) \times w_i] \cap [a..b] \neq \emptyset\}$$

where h is a hypercube, V_i is the assigned variable, $[a..b]$ is the interval we are assigning and o_m, o_M are computed as:

$$o_m = \begin{cases} 0 & \text{if } a \leq (m \times w_i) \\ a - (m \times w_i) & \text{otherwise} \end{cases} \qquad o_M = \begin{cases} w_i & \text{if } b \geq ((m + 1) \times w_i) \\ b - (m \times w_i) & \text{otherwise} \end{cases}$$

Note that, when we extract from a hypercube the interval associated to a variable, we use the interval delimited by the offsets, so that abstract operations can be much more precise.

Consider the evaluation of statement x = x + 0.01 inside a while loop with 1.0 as width of x and [0..1] as initial value of x. After the first iteration, the abstract semantics computes [0.0..1.0] and [1.0..2.0] with offsets [0.01..1.0] and [1.0..1.01], respectively. In this way, at the following iteration we would obtain again the same two intervals with the offsets changed to [0.02..1.0] and [1.0..1.02]. This results is strictly more precise than the one obtained without offsets, and it is an essential feature of our abstract domain. For instance, in the case study of Figure 2 offsets will allow us to discover if a bouncing ball exits the screen after N iterations of the while loop.

5.1   Initialization of the Analysis

Before starting the analysis we have to determine the number of sides each hypercube will have. To do this, we must find all the variables ($Vars$) of the program which are not constants (i.e., assigned only once at the beginning of the program). We require the program to initialize all the variables at the beginning of the program. The initialization of the analysis is made in two steps. First, for each initialized variable, we compute its abstraction in the non-relational domain chosen to represent the single variables. The resulting set of abstract values could contain more than one element. Let us call $\alpha(V)$ the set of abstract values associated to the initialization of the variable $V \in Vars$. Then we compute the Cartesian product of all sets of abstracted values (one for each variable). The resulting set of tuples (where each tuple has the same cardinality as $Vars$) is the initial set of hypercubes of the analysis. Formally, $\mathcal{H} = \bigtimes_{V \in Vars} \alpha(V)$.

Consider the code of our case study in Figure 2. First of all, we must identify the variables which are not constants: dt, g, k are assigned only during the initialization, so we do not include them in $Vars$. The set of not-constant variables is then $Vars = \{V_1 = px, V_2 = py, V_3 = vx, V_4 = vy\}$, and so $|Vars| = 4$.

5.2   Tracking the Origins

During the analysis of a program we also track, for each hypercube of the current abstract state, the initial hypercubes (*origins*) from which it is derived. To store such information, we proceed as follows. Let H_i be the set of hypercubes obtained for the i-th statement of the program. The data structure of a hypercube h contains also an additional set of hypercubes, h^{or}, which are its origins and are always a subset of the initial set of hypercubes, i.e., $\forall h : h^{or} \subseteq H_0$. At the first iteration, each hypercube contains only itself in its origins set: $\forall h \in H_0 : h^{or} = \{h\}$. When we execute a statement of the program, each hypercube produces some new hypercubes: at this stage, the origins set is simply propagated. For example, if h generates h_1, h_2, then $h_1^{or} = h_2^{or} = h^{or}$. When merging all the newly produced hypercubes in a single set (the abstract state associated to the point of the program just after the executed statement), we also merge through set union the sets of origins of any repeated hypercube. For example, consider $H_i = \{h_a, h_b\}$ and let h_1, h_2 be the hypercubes produced by h_a executing statement i-th and h_2, h_3 be those produced by h_b. Then, $H_{i+1} = \{h_1, h_2, h_3\}$ and $h_1^{or} = h_a^{or}$, $h_2^{or} = h_a^{or} \cup h_b^{or}$ and $h_3^{or} = h_b^{or}$.

5.3   Width Choice

The choice of the interval widths influences both the precision and efficiency of the analysis. On the one hand, if we use smaller widths we certainly obtain more precision, but the analysis risks to be too slow. On the other hand, with bigger widths the analysis will be surely faster, but we could not be able to verify the desired property. To deal with this trade-off, we implemented a recursive algorithm which adjusts the widths automatically. We start with wide intervals (i.e., coarse precision, but fast results) and we run the analysis for the first time. At the end of the analysis, we check, for each hypercube of the *final* set, if it verifies the desired property. We then associate to each *origin* (i.e., initial hypercube) its final result by merging the results of its derived final hypercubes (we know this relationship because of the origins set stored in each hypercube): some origins will certainly verify the property (i.e., they produce only final hypercubes which satisfy the property), some will not, and some will not be able to give us a definite answer (because they produce both hypercubes which verify the property and hypercubes which do not verify it). We partition the starting hypercubes set with respect to this criterion (obtaining, respectively, the *yes* set, the *no* set and the *maybe* set), and then we run the analysis again with halved widths, but *only* on the origins which did not give a definite answer (the *maybe* set). This step is only performed until we reach a specific threshold, i.e., the *minimum width* allowed for the analysis. The smaller this threshold is, the more precise (but slower) the analysis becomes.

The analysis is then able to tell us which initial values of the variables bring us to verify the property (the union of all the *yes* sets encountered during the recursive algorithm) and which do not. Thanks to these results, the user can modify the initial values of the program, and run the analysis again, until the answer is that the property is verified *for all initial values*. In our case study, for example, we can adjust the possible initial positions and velocities until we are sure that the ball will exit the screen in a certain time frame.

The formalization of this recursive algorithm is presented in Algorithm 1.

Algorithm 1. The width adjusting recursive algorithm

> **function** ANALYSIS($currWidth, minWidth, startingHypercubes$)
>   **return** ($yes \cup yes', no \cup no', maybe'$)
>   **where**
>   ($yes, no, maybe$) = $hypercubesAnalysis(currWidth, startingHypercubes$)
>   **if** $currWidth/2.0 \geq minWidth$ **then**
>   ($yes', no', maybe'$) = $Analysis(currWidth/2.0, minWidth, maybe$)
>   **else**
>   ($yes', no', maybe'$) = ($Set.empty, Set.empty, maybe$)
>   **end if**
> **end function**

6 Experimental Results

In this section we present some experimental results on the case study presented in Section 3. We want to check if *Property 1* is verified on the program of Figure 2 and, in particular, we want to know which subset of starting values brings to verify it. We implemented our analysis in the F# language with Visual Studio 2012. We ran the analysis on an Intel Core i5 CPU 1.60 GHz with 4 GB of RAM, running Windows 8 and the F# runtime 4.0 under .NET 4.0.

We set the initial widths associated to all variables to 100.0 and the minimum width allowed to 5.0. As for *Property 1*, we set $T = 5$, i.e., we want to verify if the ball is surely out of the screen within 5 seconds from its generation. Since $dt = 0.05$, a simulation during 5 seconds corresponds to $5/0.05 = 100$ iterations of the while loop. To verify this property, we apply trace partitioning [19] to track one abstract state per loop iteration until the 100-th iteration (we do not need to track precise information after the 100th iteration). The position which corresponds to the exiting from the screen is 100.0: if after 100 iterations the position px is surely greater than 100.0, then *Property 1* is verified. The whole of these values (starting variables values and widths, minimum width allowed, number of iterations, position to reach) make up our *standard workbench data*. We will experiment to study how efficiency and precision change when modifying some parameters of the analysis.

For each test, the analysis returns three sets of starting hypercubes: the initial values of the variables which satisfy the property (*yes* set), which surely do not satisfy the property (*no* set), and which may or not satisfy the property (*maybe* set). To make the results more immediate and clearer, we computed for each *yes* and *no* set the corresponding volume covered in the space by their hypercubes. We also consider the *total* volume of the variable space, i.e., the volume covered by all possible values with which the program variables are initialized. In the case of the standard workbench data, the *total* volume is $10.0 \times 50.0 \times 60.0 \times 5.0 = 150000$. Dividing the sum of *yes* and *no* volumes by the *total* volume, we obtain the percentage of the cases for which the analysis gives a definite answer. We will call this percentage the precision of the analysis.

Table 1. Varying the minimum width allowed (MWA)

MWA	Time (sec.)	$yes + no$ volume	Precision
3	530	131934	88%
5	77	99219	66%
12	11	40625	27%
24	1	25000	17%
45	0.2	0	0%

Varying the Minimum Width Allowed. First of all, we run the analysis modifying the *minimum width allowed* (MWA) parameter and we reported the results of these tests in Table 1. We can clearly see the trade-off between performance and precision.

Finding Appropriate Starting Values. In Table 2 we reported the results of a series of successive tests obtained by changing the horizontal velocity of the ball (vx). In particular, we made up a series of tests simulating the behavior of a developer using our analysis to debug his code. Let us suppose that we wrongly inserted a starting interval of negative values (between -120 and 0) for the horizontal velocity. The first test (# 1) shows us that the program does not work correctly, since the *no* volume is 100%. Also, to give this answer, the analysis is very quick because a low MWA (45) suffices. After that, we try (test # 2) with very high positive velocities (between 60 and 120) and we obtain (also very quickly) a 100% of positive answer: we know for sure that with these velocities the program works correctly. Now it remains to verify what happens with velocities between 0 and 60, and we try this in test # 3, where we decrease the MWA because we need more precision (the results with greater MWA were presented by the previous Section). Some values of vx (i.e., ≥ 31.25) ensure that the property is verified, some other values (i.e., ≤ 12.5) ensure that the property is not verified, but the ones in between are uncertain. Tests # 4 and # 5 are just double checks. So we try with a smaller MWA (3) in test # 6 on the interval [15..30]: about a quarter of the starting values produces *yes* and another quarter produces *no*. The *no* derives from low values (smaller than 18) and we confirm this in test # 7. As for medium-high values, test # 6 shows that, with a velocity greater than 25, the answer is *almost* always *yes*. It is not always yes because, with this range of velocities, the values of other variables become important to verify the property. Test # 8, in fact, shows us that velocities within 25 and 30 produce an 82% of *yes*, but a 18% of *maybe* remains. Finally, in test # 9 we modify also other two variables (with values chosen looking at the results from test # 6 and # 8) and, with such values, the answers are 100% *yes*.

After these tests, the developer of the case study is sure that horizontal velocities below 18 will certainly not make the program work. On the other hand, values greater than 30 certainly make the program work. For values between 25 and 30, other variable values must be changed (px and py) to make the program work correctly. Making some other tests, we could also explore what happens with values between 18 and 25.

Table 2. Varying the horizontal velocity (vx)

Test	vx interval	MWA	Time (sec)	Answer	Comment
# 1	[-120 .. 0]	45	1	$no = 100\%$	With negative values the answer is always no.
# 2	[60 .. 120]	45	0.2	$yes = 100\%$	With very high positive values the answer is always yes.
# 3	[0 .. 60]	5	77	$yes = 45\%$ $no = 21\%$	Uncertainty. High values (≥ 31.25) imply yes, low values (≤ 12.5) imply no.
# 4	[0 .. 15]	24	0.5	$no = 100\%$	Double check on low values: answer always no.
# 5	[30 .. 60]	5	30	$yes = 100\%$	Double check on medium-high values: answer always yes.
# 6	[15 .. 30]	3	526	$yes = 27\%$ $no = 25\%$	Uncertainty. Low values (≤ 18) imply no, for high values (≥ 25) depends also on other variables.
# 7	[15 .. 18]	5	7	$no = 100\%$	Double check on medium-low values: answer always no.
# 8	[25 .. 30]	3	164	$yes = 82\%$ $maybe = 18\%$	Double check on medium-high values: answer almost always yes. In this case, also values of other variables influence the result.
# 9	[25 .. 30]	5	1	$yes = 100\%$	Modified also py ([40 .. 50]) and px ([5 .. 10]). Answer always yes.

Discussion. In this scenario, we ran the analysis by manually changing the initial values of program variables. Notice that this process could be automatized. This process can be highly interactive, since the tool could show to the user even partial results while it is automatically improving the precision by adopting narrower intervals on the *maybe* portion as described by Algorithm 1. In this way, the user could iterate the process until it finds suitable initial values.

The execution times obtained so far underline that the analysis is efficient enough to be the basis of practical tools. Moreover, the analysis could be parallelized by running in parallel the computation of the semantics for each initial hypercube: exploiting several cores or even running the analysis in the cloud, we could further improve the efficiency of the overall analysis.

7   Related Work

Various numerical domains have been studied in the literature, and they can be classified with respect to a number of different dimensions: finite (e.g., *Sign*) versus infinite (e.g., *Intervals*) height, relational (e.g., Octagons [20]) versus non-relational (e.g., *Intervals*), convex (e.g., Polyhedra [11]) versus possibly non-convex (e.g., donut-like domains [14]). Hypercubes track disjunctive information relying on Intervals. Similarly, the powerset operator [13] allows one to track disjunctive information, but the complexity of the analysis grows up exponentially. Instead, we designed a specific disjunctive domain that reduces the practical complexity of the analysis by adopting indexes and offsets.

Noticeable efforts have been put both to reduce the loss of precision due to the upper bound operation, and to accelerate the convergence of the Kleene iterative algorithm [16,23,22,4], but they do not track disjunctive information.

The trace partitioning technique designed by Mauborgne and Rival [19] provides automatic procedures to build suitable partitions of the traces yielding to a refinement that has great impact both on the accuracy and on the efficiency of the analysis. This approach tracks disjunctive information, and it works quite well when the single partitions are carefully designed by an expert user. Unluckily, given the high number of hypercubes tracked by our analysis, this approach is definitely too slow for the scenario we are targeting.

Our spatial representation and width adjustment resembles Howe et al.'s hierarchical quadtree data-structure [18]. However, this paper contains only a preliminary discussion of the quadtree domain, and as far as we know it has not been further developed nor applied. Moreover, their domain is targeted to analyse only machine integers and the width is the same in each spatial axis.

Our self-adaptive parametrization of the width shares some common concepts with the CounterExample Guided Abstraction Refinement (CEGAR) [8]. CEGAR begins checking with a coarse (imprecise) abstraction of the system and progressively refines it, based on spurious counterexamples seen in prior model checking runs. The process continues until either an abstraction proves the correctness of the system or a valid counterexample is generated.

Gurfinkel and Chaki [15] introduced the Boxes domain, a refinement of the Interval domain with finite disjunctions: an element of Boxes is a finite union of boxes. Each value of Boxes is a propositional formula over interval constraints and it is represented by the Linear Decision Diagrams data structure (LDDs). Note that the size of an LDD is exponential in the number of variables. We use a fixed width and a fixed partitioning on each hypercube dimension, while they do not employ constraints of this kind. In addition, Boxes uses a specific abstract transformer for each possible operation (for example, distinguishing $x = x + v$, $x = a \times x$, $x = a \times y$ and also making assumptions on the sign of constants) while our definitions are more generic. Finally, Boxes' implementation is based on the specific data structure of LDDs and cannot be extended to other base domains.

If on the one hand Parametric Hypercubes have been tailored to Computer Games Software applications, on the other hand some of their features may also be applied to other contexts. In particular, our definition of Computer Games Software applications (i.e., an infinite reactive loop, a complex state space with many real-valued variables, and strong dependencies among variables) exactly matches that of real-time synchronous control-command software (found in many industries such as aerospace and automotive industries). Hybrid systems and hybrid automata have been widely applied to verify this software. The formal analysis of large scale hybrid systems is known to be a very difficult process [2]. In general, existing approaches suffer from performance issues or limitations on the property to prove, on the shape of the program, etc. For instance, Bouissou et al. [7] deal with a simpler example than ours (a bouncing ball with only vertical motion) and in their benchmarks the variable space is quite limited: the velocity is a fixed constant, and the starting position varies only between 10 and 10.1. Instead, our Hypercubes can deal with velocities and positions bound inside any intervals of values. Also Bouissou's variable space [5] is more restricted than in our approach. In addition, this analysis returns an abstraction of the final state of the program, while we also give information about which starting values are responsible for the property verification and which not. Halbwachs et al. [17] present an application of the abstract interpretation by means of convex polyhedra to hybrid systems. This work is focused on a particular class of hybrid systems (*linear* ones), and it is able to represent only convex regions of the space, since it employs the convex hull approximation of a set of values. Alur et al. [1] present algorithms and tools for reachability analysis of hybrid systems by relying on predicate abstraction and polyhedra. However, this solution suffers from the exponential growth of abstract states and relies on expensive abstract domains. Finally, Ratschan and She [21] consider safety verification of non-linear hybrid systems, starting from a classical method that uses interval arithmetic to check whether trajectories can move over the boundaries in a rectangular grid. This approach is similar to ours in the data representation (boxes). However, they do not employ any concept of offset, their space partitioning is not fixed and the examples they experimented with cover a very limited variable space.

8   Conclusions and Future Work

In this paper we presented Parametric Hypercubes, a disjunctive non-relational abstract domain which can be used to analyse physics simulations. Experimental results on a representative case study show the precision of the approach. The performance of the analysis makes it feasible to apply it in practical settings.

Note that our approach offers plenty of venues in order to improve its results, thanks to its flexible and parametric nature. In particular, we could: (i) increase the precision by intersecting our hypercubes with arbitrary bounding volumes which restrict the relationships between variables in a more complex way than the offsets presented in Section 5; (ii) increase the performance of Algorithm 1 by halving the widths only on some axes, chosen through an analysis of the distribution of hypercubes in the *yes,no,maybe* sets; and (iii) study the derivative with respect to time of the iterations of the main loop in order to define temporal trends to refine the widening operator. In addition, our domain is modular w.r.t. the non-relational abstract domain adopted to represent the hypercube dimensions. By using other abstract domains it is possible to track relationships between variables which do not necessarily represent physical quantities.

Acknowledgments. This work was partially supported by the SNF project "Verification-Driven Inference of Contracts" and by the MIUR PRIN Project "Security Horizons".

References

1. Alur, R., Dang, T., Ivančić, F.: Reachability analysis of hybrid systems via predicate abstraction. In: Tomlin, C.J., Greenstreet, M.R. (eds.) HSCC 2002. LNCS, vol. 2289, pp. 35–48. Springer, Heidelberg (2002)

2. Alur, R., Henzinger, T.A., Lafferriere, G., Pappas, G.J.: Discrete abstractions of hybrid systems. Proceedings of the IEEE 88(7), 971–984 (2000)

3. Amato, G., Scozzari, F.: The abstract domain of parallelotopes. Electronic Notes Theoretical Computer Science 287, 17–28 (2012)

4. Bagnara, R., Hill, P.M., Zaffanella, E.: Widening operators for powerset domains. In: STTT, vol. 9(3-4), pp. 413–414 (2007)

5. Bouissou, O.: Proving the correctness of the implementation of a control-command algorithm. In: Palsberg, J., Su, Z. (eds.) SAS 2009. LNCS, vol. 5673, pp. 102–119. Springer, Heidelberg (2009)

6. Bouissou, O.: From control-command synchronous programs to hybrid automata. In: ADHS 2012 (June 2012)

7. Bouissou, O., Mimram, S., Chapoutot, A.: Hyson: Set-based simulation of hybrid systems. In: RSP 2012, pp. 79–85 (2012)

8. Clarke, E.M., Grumberg, O., Jha, S., Lu, Y., Veith, H.: Counterexample-guided abstraction refinement. In: Emerson, E.A., Sistla, A.P. (eds.) CAV 2000. LNCS, vol. 1855, pp. 154–169. Springer, Heidelberg (2000)

9. Costantini, G., Ferrara, P., Cortesi, A.: Linear approximation of continuous systems with trapezoid step functions. In: Jhala, R., Igarashi, A. (eds.) APLAS 2012. LNCS, vol. 7705, pp. 98–114. Springer, Heidelberg (2012)

10. Cousot, P.: The calculational design of a generic abstract interpreter. In: Calculational System Design. NATO ASI Series F. IOS Press, Amsterdam (1999)

11. Cousot, P., Halbwachs, N.: Automatic discovery of linear restraints among variables of a program. In: Proceedings of POPL 1978. ACM Press (1978)

12. Eberly, D.H.: Game Physics. Interactive 3D technology series. Elsevier Science (2010)

13. Filé, G., Ranzato, F.: The powerset operator on abstract interpretations. Theor. Comput. Sci. 222(1-2), 77–111 (1999)

14. Ghorbal, K., Ivančić, F., Balakrishnan, G., Maeda, N., Gupta, A.: Donut domains: Efficient non-convex domains for abstract interpretation. In: Kuncak, V., Rybalchenko, A. (eds.) VMCAI 2012. LNCS, vol. 7148, pp. 235–250. Springer, Heidelberg (2012)

15. Gurfinkel, A., Chaki, S.: Boxes: A symbolic abstract domain of boxes. In: Cousot, R., Martel, M. (eds.) SAS 2010. LNCS, vol. 6337, pp. 287–303. Springer, Heidelberg (2010)

16. Halbwachs, N., Merchat, D., Gonnord, L.: Some ways to reduce the space dimension in polyhedra computations. Formal Methods in System Design 29(1), 79–95 (2006)

17. Halbwachs, N., Raymond, P., Proy, Y.-E.: Verification of linear hybrid systems by means of convex approximations. In: LeCharlier, B. (ed.) SAS 1994. LNCS, vol. 864, pp. 223–237. Springer, Heidelberg (1994)

18. Howe, J.M., King, A., Lawrence-Jones, C.: Quadtrees as an abstract domain. Electronic Notes in Theoretical Computer Science 267(1), 89–100 (2010)

19. Mauborgne, L., Rival, X.: Trace partitioning in abstract interpretation based static analyzers. In: Sagiv, M. (ed.) ESOP 2005. LNCS, vol. 3444, pp. 5–20. Springer, Heidelberg (2005)

20. Miné, A.: The octagon abstract domain. In: Higher-Order and Symbolic Computation (2006)

21. Ratschan, S., She, Z.: Safety verification of hybrid systems by constraint propagation based abstraction refinement. In: Morari, M., Thiele, L. (eds.) HSCC 2005. LNCS, vol. 3414, pp. 573–589. Springer, Heidelberg (2005)

22. Sankaranarayanan, S., Ivančić, F., Shlyakhter, I., Gupta, A.: Static analysis in disjunctive numerical domains. In: Yi, K. (ed.) SAS 2006. LNCS, vol. 4134, pp. 3–17. Springer, Heidelberg (2006)

23. Seladji, Y., Bouissou, O.: Fixpoint computation in the polyhedra abstract domain using convex and numerical analysis tools. In: Giacobazzi, R., Berdine, J., Mastroeni, I. (eds.) VMCAI 2013. LNCS, vol. 7737, pp. 149–168. Springer, Heidelberg (2013)

Author Index